AF839552

CROSS-BORDER EU COMPETITION LAW ACTIONS

This book, written within the framework of a research project funded by the European Commission Civil Justice Programme, identifies the ways in which cross-border EU competition law actions can best be handled in Europe. Employing traditional library-based legal research methods as well as qualitative interviews with legal practitioners in Germany and England (countries sharing different legal traditions) and policy-makers in Brussels, the book considers how private EU competition law actions are functioning at the moment and how they could and should be developed. The study proposes solutions for some of the most pressing practical problems, and includes chapters by the following academics, legal practitioners and judges: Judge I Pelikánová (General Court of the EU); J Lawrence and A Morfey (Freshfields); P Lasok QC (Monckton Chambers); H Mercer QC (Essex Court Chambers); J Webber (Shearman & Sterling); T Reher (CMS Hasche Sigle, Germany); P Bos and J Möhlmann (BarentsKrans, the Netherlands); P Beaumont (Aberdeen); S Bariatti (Milan); G Howells (Manchester); D Fairgrieve (BIICL); J Fitchen (Aberdeen); A Andreangeli (Edinburgh); D Tzakas (Athens Bar, Greece); S Dnes (Sidley Austin, Brussels); F Becker and J Kammin (Kiel University, Germany); and M Danov (Brunel University).

Volume 4 in the series Hart Studies in Competition Law

Hart Studies in Competition Law

Volume 1: *Intellectual Property, Antitrust and Cumulative Innovation in the EU and the US*
Thorsten Käseberg

Volume 2: *State Aid and the European Economic Constitution*
Francesco de Cecco

Volume 3: *The Private Enforcement of Competition Law in Ireland*
David McFadden

Cross-Border
EU Competition Law Actions

Edited by

Mihail Danov
Florian Becker
and
Paul Beaumont

•HART•
PUBLISHING
OXFORD AND PORTLAND, OREGON
2013

Published in the United Kingdom by Hart Publishing Ltd
16C Worcester Place, Oxford, OX1 2JW
Telephone: +44 (0)1865 517530
Fax: +44 (0)1865 510710
E-mail: mail@hartpub.co.uk
Website: http://www.hartpub.co.uk

Published in North America (US and Canada) by
Hart Publishing
c/o International Specialized Book Services
920 NE 58th Avenue, Suite 300
Portland, OR 97213-3786
USA
Tel: +1 503 287 3093 or toll-free: (1) 800 944 6190
Fax: +1 503 280 8832
E-mail: orders@isbs.com
Website: http://www.isbs.com

© The editors and contributors severally, 2013

The editors and contributors have asserted their right under the Copyright, Designs and Patents Act 1988, to be identified as the authors of this work.

All rights reserved. No part of this publication may be reproduced, stored in a retrieval system, or transmitted, in any form or by any means, without the prior permission of Hart Publishing, or as expressly permitted by law or under the terms agreed with the appropriate reprographic rights organisation.
Enquiries concerning reproduction which may not be covered by the above should be addressed to Hart Publishing Ltd at the address above.

British Library Cataloguing in Publication Data
Data Available

ISBN: 978-1-84946-374-4

Typeset by Hope Services, Abingdon
Printed and bound in Great Britain by
Lightning Source UK Ltd

Contents

Part V Recognition and Enforcement of Foreign Judgments

List of Contributors

Arianna Andreangeli Lecturer in Competition Law, Edinburgh Law School, University of Edinburgh

Stefania Bariatti Professor of Private International Law, School of Law, University of Milan, Italy; Member of GEDIP-Groupe Européen de Droit International Privé

Paul Beaumont Professor of European Union and Private International Law and Director of the Centre for Private International Law of the University of Aberdeen

Florian Becker Chair of Public Law, Christian Albrechts Universität zu Kiel, Germany

Pierre Bos *Advocaat*, Member of The Hague Bar, Partner, BarentsKrans, the Netherlands

Mihail Danov Senior Lecturer in Law, School of Law, Brunel University

Stephen Dnes Associate, Sidley Austin LLP, Brussels, Belgium

Duncan Fairgrieve Senior Fellow in Comparative Law and Director of the Product Liability Forum, British Institute of International and Comparative Law

Jonathan Fitchen Lecturer in Law, School of Law, University of Aberdeen

Geraint Howells Professor of Commercial Law and Head of Law School, University of Manchester

Julian Kammin Research Assistant, Christian Albrechts Universität zu Kiel, Germany

Paul Lasok QC Barrister, Monckton Chambers, London

Jon Lawrence Partner, Freshfields Bruckhaus Deringer LLP, London

Hugh Mercer QC Barrister, Essex Court Chambers, London and Brussels

Anna Morfey Associate, Freshfields Bruckhaus Deringer LLP, London

Joost Möhlmann *Advocaat*, Member of The Hague Bar, Senior Associate, BarentsKrans, the Netherlands

Tim Reher Partner, CMS Hasche Sigle, Hamburg, Germany

Irena Pelikánová Judge, General Court of the European Union, Luxembourg

Dimitrios-Panagiotis L Tzakas Advocate (Dikigoros) Athens Bar, Greece

James Webber Counsel, Shearman & Sterling LLP, London

1

Introduction – Cross-Border EU Competition Law Actions

MIHAIL DANOV AND FLORIAN BECKER

I. BACKGROUND

Articles 101 and 102 (ex Arts 81 and 82 TEC) are the main competition law provisions contained in the Treaty on the Functioning of the European Union. Article 101 TFEU prohibits agreements between undertakings which prevent, restrict or distort competition within the Member States. Article 102 TFEU prohibits conduct which amounts to abusive behaviour by a dominant undertaking in a relevant market.

A centralised enforcement scheme was set up by Regulation 17/1962. Regulation 1/2003 replaced the centralised system with a directly applicable exception system, in which the competition authorities and Member States' courts have the power to apply and enforce Articles 101 and 102 TFEU. In *Courage v Crehan*,[1] the Court of Justice held that 'the practical effect of the prohibition laid down in article [101(1)] would be put at risk if it were not open to any individual to claim damages for loss caused to him by a contract or by conduct liable to restrict or distort competition.' In other words, private enforcement is intended to complement public enforcement, by allowing those who have suffered from a competition law infringement to bring a legal action before a court.[2] The aim of EU competition law enforcement policy is to deter infringements and provide redress to those who have suffered losses from them.[3]

Private parties are supposed to play an increasingly important role in aiding enforcement of Articles 101 and 102 TFEU by means of private actions for damages before national courts. The UK Government has very recently launched public consultations seeking to reform the UK regime for private actions in competition law.[4] The contemplated reform is meant to 'allow consumers and businesses to obtain compensation for losses they have

[1] C-453/99, *Courage v Crehan* [2001] ECR I-6297 [26].

[2] Commission Staff Working Paper, Annex to the Green Paper on damages actions for breach of the EC antitrust rules SEC(2005) 1732, paras 1–3.

[3] See more: WJ Wils, *Principles of European Antitrust Enforcement* (Oxford, Hart Publishing, 2005) 116–18; AP Komninos, *EC Private Antitrust Enforcement: Decentralised Application of EC Competition Law by National Courts* (Oxford, Hart Publishing, 2008) 7–8.

[4] Department for Business Innovation & Skills, *Private Actions in Competition Law: A Consultation on Options for Reform*,24April2012www.bis.gov.uk/assets/biscore/consumer-issues/docs/p/12-742-private-actions-in-competition-law-consultation.pdf . The BIS's proposed options for reform were discussed at a BIICL seminar, 'Rapid-Response Seminar: Private Actions in UK competition law: BIS's proposed options for reform', British Institute of International and Comparative Law, London, 9 May 2012.

suffered as a result of anticompetitive behaviour.'[5] However, the enforcement of EU competition law is peculiar in many respects, and has the following specific features which need to be carefully considered by the policy-makers in a cross-border context.

II. EU COMPETITION LAW INFRINGEMENTS: CROSS-BORDER IMPLICATIONS AND SPECIFIC ISSUES TO BE CONSIDERED

The majority of agreements and practices that could give rise to EU competition law concerns may involve legal entities from different countries and affect the markets, businesses and consumers in several countries. In other words, the majority of EU competition law infringements would have cross-border implications. Bearing this in mind, it should be recalled that:

> the standard economic rationale for making a cartel illegal is not that it charges too high a price or that it redistributes income from consumers to cartel members, but that it restricts output causing a deadweight or efficiency loss . . . a loss to consumers without an offsetting gain to producers. To prevent this loss one can penalize cartel members by an amount sufficient to deter them from organizing a cartel in the first instance.[6]

Given the cross-border implications of EU competition law actions, optimal sanctions will be imposed and infringements detected only if there is an adequate 'institutional structure of antitrust enforcement'[7] in Europe. Indeed, it is well established that 'the effective enforcement of a body of law requires effective sanctions for violators and an institutional structure that enables violations to be determined with reasonable accuracy and at reasonable cost'.[8] In this context, it would be essential to consider the specific features of the EU competition law enforcement system and its cross-border implications in the European context.

A. Public Enforcement and Private Antitrust Enforcement – Cross-Border Co-ordination

EU competition law provisions are enforced by national courts as well as by regulators across Europe. Articles 5 and 6 of Regulation 1/2003 state that the national competition authorities (NCAs) and national courts have the powers to apply Articles 101 and 102 TFEU in individual cases. Article 7 of Regulation 1/2003 goes further to state that 'where the Commission . . . finds that there is an infringement of Article [101 and/or 102 TFEU], it may by decision require the undertakings . . . concerned to bring such infringement to an end.' In other words, there would be multiple enforcers of EU competition law which may lead to parallel proceedings, and, as a result, there may be a risk of inconsistent findings of law and fact by the various enforcers. Articles 15 and 16 of Regulation 1/2003 are meant to guarantee uniform and consistent application of EU competition law in proceedings before

[5] ibid p 3.

[6] WM Landes, 'Optimal Sanctions for Antitrust Violations' (1983) 50 *University of Chicago Law Review* 652, 653.

[7] DA Crane, *The Institutional Structure of Antitrust Enforcement* (Oxford, OUP, 2011).

[8] RA Posner, *Antitrust Law*, 2nd edn (Chicago, University of Chicago Press, 2001) 266.

the Commission and in cross-border EU competition law before Member State courts. In particular, through Article 16 of Regulation 1/2003 the EU legislator has entrusted the proceedings before the European Commission with certain primacy over private proceedings before Member State courts because the Commission is a supranational organ.[9] Nonetheless, it has been submitted that EU competition law proceedings before NCAs have no primacy over private EU antitrust law proceedings before Member State courts, and that the two should be seen as independent.[10]

However, one recent analysis of the current institutional architecture of EU competition law enforcement has noted:

> public antitrust enforcement is the superior instrument to pursue the objectives of clarification and development of the law and of deterrence and punishment, whereas private actions for damages are superior for the pursuit of corrective justice through compensation, then the optimal antitrust enforcement would appear to be a system in which public antitrust enforcement aims at clarification and development of the law and at deterrence and punishment, while private actions for damages aim at compensation.[11]

Such a separate-task approach, which according to Wils[12] appears to be adopted in the White Paper for damages,[13] would give rise to several problems in a cross-border context in Europe. The Commission Work Programme 2012[14] has identified that interrelation between private enforcement and public enforcement is an important area where a legislative measure would be needed. The contemplated measure is described as follows:

> The objective of this legislative initiative would be to ensure effective damages actions before national courts for breaches of EU antitrust rules and to clarify the interrelation of such private actions with public enforcement by the Commission and the national competition authorities, notably as regards the protection of leniency programmes, in order to preserve the central role of public enforcement in the EU. The right of victims of antitrust infringements to such damages has already been established by the Court.[15]

The legislative initiative may be seen as an opportunity for the EU legislator to look at the 'separate-task approach' and its cross-border implications. There are several issues which might need to be carefully addressed.

First, problems are bound to arise with regard to public antitrust enforcement proceedings before an NCA located in one Member State, and parallel private proceedings related to the same breaches of Article 101 TFEU and/or Article 102 TFEU before a court in another Member State. Although the regulation provides for mechanisms to ensure that

[9] A Komninos, 'Relationship Between Public and Private Enforcement: *Quod Dei Deo, quod Caesaris Caesari*', 16th Annual EU Competition Law and Policy Workshop – Integrating Public and Private Enforcement of Competition Law: Implications for Courts and Agencies, Florence, 17–18 June 2011 http://ssrn.com/abstract=1870723 (a version of the latter paper will be published in P Lowe and M Marquis (eds), *European Competition Law Annual 2011: Integrating Public and Private Enforcement of Competition Law: Implications for Courts and Agencies* (Oxford, Hart Publishing, 2014) (forthcoming) 10.

[10] A Komninos, 'Effect of Commission Decisions on Private Antitrust Litigation: Setting the Story Straight' (2007) 44 *CML Rev* 1387, 1426; Komninos, above n 9. See also Case C-360/09 *Pfleiderer AG v Bundeskartellamt* [2011] 5 *CML Rev* 219, Opinion of AG Mazák [40].

[11] WPJ.Wils, 'The Relationship Between Public Antitrust Enforcement and Private Actions for Damages' (2009) 32 *World Competition* 3, 18 – accessible http://papers.ssrn.com/sol3/papers.cfm?abstract_id=1296458.

[12] ibid.

[13] Commission (EC), 'White Paper on Damages actions for the breach of the EC antitrust rules', COM (2008) 165.

[14] Commission Work Programme 2012 http://ec.europa.eu/atwork/pdf/cwp2012_annex_en.pdf .

[15] ibid p 3.

'competition authorities of the Member States shall apply the [EU] competition laws in close co-operation',[16] it does not deal with the problem of coherent and uniform application of EU competition law in proceedings before an NCA located in one Member State, and private EU antitrust law proceedings related to the same breaches of Article 101 TFEU and/or Article 102 TFEU before a court in another Member State.

Secondly, in the context of follow-on actions, the EU legislator seems to be considering the adoption of a rule to the effect that a Member State court cannot take decisions running counter to a final decision of an NCA finding an infringement of Articles 101 and 102 TFEU.[17] A recent comparative study appears to suggest that 'only in two countries (Germany and Sweden) are national courts bound by the decisions taken by a foreign NCA.'[18] Is a Member State court entitled to refuse the recognition of a decision taken by a foreign national competition authority that does not respect due process rules in its adoption?[19] Article 6(1) ECHR states that 'In the determination of his civil rights and obligations . . ., everyone is entitled to a fair and public hearing within a reasonable time by an independent and impartial tribunal established by law.' It is well established that Article 6(1) ECHR requires that, in the determination of civil rights and obligations, decisions taken by administrative authorities should be subject to a judicial body that has full jurisdiction.[20] Similar requirements would have to be satisfied with regard to decisions taken by NCAs.[21] While a national court would apply civil procedure rules that presuppose respect of due process, an NCA would apply administrative procedure rules that could potentially raise concerns as to the undertaking's right to a fair trial and hearing.[22] If the EU legislator provides for procedural safeguards to ensure that a national court's judgment given in one Member State would not take effect in another Member State unless the defendant's right to a fair trial and his rights of defence as guaranteed in Article 47 of the EU Charter on Fundamental Rights are adequately protected, then, by analogy, such safeguards should be in place for NCA decisions finding an infringement of Articles 101 and 102 TFEU.[23]

Thirdly, even if the regulator had respected the due process rules in the adoption of its decision, the two-task structure of institutional enforcement would create specific prob-

[16] Arts 11–14 of Council Regulation 1/2003. See further, S Brammer, *Co-operation Between National Competition Agencies in the Enforcement of EC Competition Law* (Oxford, Hart Publishing, 2009).

[17] White Paper (n 13) [2.3].

[18] P Buccirossi, M Carpagnano, L Ciari et al, *Collective Redress in Antitrust* www.europarl.europa.eu/document/activities/cont/201206/20120613ATT46782/20120613ATT46782EN.pdf, p 25.

[19] M Danov, 'EU Competition Law Enforcement: Is Brussels I suited to dealing with all the challenges?' (2012) 61 *ICLQ* 27.

[20] *Le Compte v Belgium* (1982) 4 EHRR 1. See also WPJ Wils, *Principles of European Antitrust Enforcement* (Oxford, Hart Publishing, 2005) 46–47; IS Forrester, 'Due Process in EC Competition Cases: A Distinguished Institution with Flawed Procedures' (2009) 34 *EL Rev* 817, 821.

[21] Wils (n 20) 47; Forrester (n 20) 821.

[22] Forrester (n 20); J Killick and P Berghe, 'This is Not the Time to Be Tinkering with Regulation 1/2003 – It is Time for Fundamental Reform – Europe Should Have Change We Can Believe in' (2010) *Competition Law Review* 259. The due process issue may receive renewed attention after the entry into force of the Lisbon Treaty. See Art 6(1) TEU. See also Art 6(1) ECHR and Art 47(2) of the Charter of Fundamental Rights of the European Union [2000] OJ C364/1. See further, J Kuhling, 'Fundamental Rights' in A von Bogdandy and J Bast (eds), *Principles of European Constitutional Law*, 2nd edn (Oxford, Hart Publishing, 2010) 479–514; P Craig, *The Lisbon Treaty: Law, Politics and Treaty Reform* (Oxford, OUP, 2010) 193–245. See also: R Nazzini, 'Administrative Enforcement: Judicial Review and Fundamental Rights in EU Competition Law: A comparative contextual-functionalist perspective' (2012) 49 *CML Rev* 971, 1005.

[23] Proposal for a Regulation on Jurisdiction and the Recognition and Enforcement of Judgments, COM(2010) 748 final [3.1.1].

lems when it comes to imposing personal liability for EU competition law infringements in a cross-border context. Articles 101 and 102 TFEU are meant to prevent anti-competitive 'activities of undertakings'.[24] Due to the two-task enforcement structure, the anti-competitive activities of a group of companies which is acting as one undertaking (or one economic entity/unit) for the purposes of EU competition law would be caught by Articles 101 and/or 102 TFEU. This may well be justified by the fact that an anti-competitive agreement may be implemented by groups of companies which may have set up subsidiaries across Europe. This was recently confirmed by the European Union Court of Justice in *Akzo Nobel.*[25] In the latter case, the court held:

> 55. . . . the concept of an undertaking, in the same context, must be understood as designating an economic unit even if in law that economic unit consists of several persons, natural or legal (Case C-217/05 *Confederación Española de Empresarios de Estaciones de Servicio* [2006] ECR I-11987, paragraph 40).
>
> 56. When such an economic entity infringes the competition rules, it falls, according to the principle of personal responsibility, to that entity to answer for that infringement (see, to that effect, Case C-49/92 P *Commission* v *Anic Partecipazioni* [1999] ECR I-4125, paragraph 145; Case C-279/98 P *Cascades* v *Commission* [2000] ECR I-9693, paragraph 78; and Case C-280/06 *ETI and Others* [2007] ECR I-10893, paragraph 39).
>
> 57. The infringement of Community competition law must be imputed unequivocally to a legal person on whom fines may be imposed and the statement of objections must be addressed to that person (see, to that effect, *Aalborg Portland and Others* v *Commission*, paragraph 60, and Joined Cases C-322/07 P, C-327/07 P and C-338/07 P *August Koehler and Others* v *Commission* [2009] ECR I-0000, paragraph 38).[26]

Following this line of reasoning, it seems clear that the liability for the EU competition law infringement must be imputed to a legal person who should be liable to damages which must be proved and assessed by the court in the course of private antitrust proceedings. The concept of undertaking used by the regulator when establishing an infringement, and the fact that most multinational businesses would involve not a single legal entity, but groups of companies, would suggest that there are specific problems which must be addressed with regard to private proceedings. Whilst 'a rebuttable presumption that the parent company does in fact exercise a decisive influence over the conduct of its subsidiary'[27] would allow the Commission to impose fines on the ultimate parent company, problems would be bound to arise in private proceedings, as it may be far from clear 'which legal entities within a corporate group are liable for an infringement of Article 101(1) TFEU and to what extent'.[28] Indeed, the following questions would be key in a cross-border context. Can a victim of an EU competition law infringement sue in England a local subsidiary that is not named in the Commission's decision? Will there be a binding finding that there is an infringement by a local subsidiary that is a part of a group of companies which was found to be one infringing undertaking within the meaning of Articles 101 and 102 TFEU? Would such an action be a stand-alone action or a follow-on action? These are

[24] Joined Cases C-204/00 P, C-205/00 P, C-211/00 P, C-213/00 P, C-217/00 P and C-219/00 P, *Aalborg Portland and Others v Commission* [2004] ECR I-123 [59].

[25] Case C-97/08 P, *Akzo Nobel v Commission of the European Communities* [2009] ECR I-8237 [54].

[26] ibid [55–57].

[27] ibid [60].

[28] *Cooper Tire & Rubber Company Europe Ltd & Others* [2010] EWCA Civ 864 [47].

not academic questions, but very practical ones, which have been subject to heated debate before the English courts.[29]

Fourthly, the two-task enforcement structure also suggests that the need for taking evidence by the foreign competition authority in support of private proceedings in England, for example, could arise because the regulator's decision establishing that a group of companies had committed an EU competition law infringement would not have dealt with such issues as, for example, whether an actual claimant had suffered damages, and what damages should be awarded in order for a plaintiff to be compensated. It has been recently stated by Lord Justice Jacob that:

> the party claiming damages is not a party to the proceedings before the regulator. Facts about causation and damages, which will normally include an investigation into whether and if so how the infringing conduct affected that particular party, are not necessarily a part of the regulator's inquiry.[30]

In other words, despite the fact that a party could be relying on an infringement decision taken by the European Commission or an NCA, evidence as to the causation and assessment of damages would need to be collected in a follow-on action. An important issue would be whether an English court could request evidence from a foreign regulator in support of private EU competition law proceedings in England.

B. The Principle of National Procedural Autonomy and Cross-Border EU Competition Law Damages Actions

It is well established that 'The principal argument for awarding damages to private enforcers is to create powerful enforcement incentives.'[31] The English court has held that the cause of action for EU competition law damages is a mixture of EU law and 'domestic' law.[32] It is well established that 'the claimant must prove not only that the relevant [EU competition law provision] has been broken [as a matter of EU law], but also that the breach in question has caused him a relevant loss'[33] under the domestic law.

The case law has made clear that much of the EU law is directly applicable and may also have 'direct effect'.[34] For example, the Court of Justice held that Articles 101(1) and 102 TFEU (ex Arts 81(1) and 82 TEC) produce direct effects in relations between individuals and create rights for individuals concerned, which the national courts must safeguard.[35] Regulation 1/2003 replaced the centralised system with a directly applicable exception system, in which the competition authorities and Member States' courts have the power to

[29] eg, *Roche Products Ltd, Roche Vitamine Europe AG (Switzerland), F Hoffmann-La Roche AG (Switzerland) v Provimi Ltd* [2003] EWHC 961 (Comm); *Cooper Tire* (n 28); *KME Yorkshire Ltd v Toshiba Carrier* [2012] EWCA Civ 1190; *Nokia Corporation v AU Optronics Corporation* [2012] EWHC 731 (Ch); *Emerson Electric Co v Morgan Crucible Company PLC and Ors* [2011] CAT 4.

[30] *Enron Coal Services Ltd (in liquidation) v English Welsh & Scottish Railway Ltd* [2011] EWCA Civ 2, [2011] UKCLR 303 [150].

[31] Landes (n 6) 675.

[32] *Provimi* (n 29) [25].

[33] *Devenish Nutrition Ltd v Sanofi-Aventis SA* [2007] EWHC 2394, [2008] 2 WLR 637, Ch [18], affd *Devenish Nutrition Ltd v Sanofi-Aventis SA* [2008] EWCA Civ 1086, [2009] 3 WLR 198, CA.

[34] See Case 26/62 *Van Gend en Loos v Nederlandse Administratie der Belastingen* [1963] ECR 1.

[35] Case 127/73 *BRT v SABAM* [1974] ECR 51 [16]; Case C-282/95 P *Guerin Automobiles v Commission* [1997] ECR I-1503 [39]; *Courage* (n 1) [23].

apply not only Articles 101(1) and 102, which had been deemed to have direct effect by virtue of the Court of Justice case law,[36] but also Article 101(3).[37] Articles 101 and 102 TFEU do not indicate how the defendant's liability is to be determined and how the assessment of antitrust damages suffered by businesses in a number of Member States is to be made by a court seised with a cross-border EU competition law action. The EU case law lays down the general principle of national procedural autonomy,[38] which can be summarised as follows:

> in the absence of Community rules on this subject, it is for the domestic legal system of each Member State to designate the courts having jurisdiction and to determine the procedural conditions governing actions at law intended to ensure the protection of the rights which citizens have from the direct effect of Community law, it being understood that such conditions cannot be less favourable than those relating to similar actions of a domestic nature.[39]

Therefore, even when, under the two-task enforcement structure, a regulator has detected and established an EU competition law infringement, the question whether a concrete claimant has suffered a loss, and, if so, whether the claimant would be entitled to recover the pleaded loss, is to be decided by the domestic legal order. In other words, under the current regime, the question of whether there is a breach of Articles 101 and 102 TFEU is to be determined as a matter of EU law, but Member States' domestic laws would be relevant to determine such issues as for example the standard of proof.[40] Furthermore, national legal orders should determine the limitation periods,[41] relevant rules for remoteness of damages,[42] the available remedies for breach of EU competition law (eg whether punitive (or exemplary) damages,[43] which may be subject to considerations of public policy,[44] would be available); and assessment of damages.[45] The fact that these questions have been left to be determined by the Member States' national orders indicates that the cross-border nature of most European competition law infringements, in which damages would often be suffered by businesses and consumers in a number of jurisdictions, could increase the uncertainty and fuel the litigation costs.[46] Different Member States may adopt different solutions with regard to appropriate measures of damages in an EU competition

[36] *BRT* (n 35) [14]–[16]; *Guerin Automobiles* (n 35) [39]; *Courage* (n 1) [23].

[37] See Recital 4 of Regulation 1/2003.

[38] Case 33/76 *Rewe-Zentralfinanz eG and Rewe-Zentral AG v Landwirtschaftskammer für das Saarland* [1976] ECR 1989 [5]. See also: Case C-261/95 *Palmisani* [1997] ECR I-4025 [27]; Joined Cases C-295/04–298/04 *Manfredi v Lloyd Adriatico Assicurazioni SpA* [2006] 5 CMLR 17. See also Case C-126/97 *Eco Swiss China Time Ltd v Benetton International NV* [1999] ECR I-3055 [43]–[48]. See more: F Becker, 'Application of Community law by Member States' Public Authorities: between autonomy and effectiveness' (2007) 44 *CML Rev* 1035.

[39] *Rewe-Zentralfinanz* (n 38) [5].

[40] See Recital 5 of Regulation 1/2003. See more: M. Danov, *Jurisdiction and Judgments in Relation to EU Competition Law Claims* (Oxford, Hart Publishing, 2010) ch 5.

[41] *Deutsche Bahn v Morgan Crucible Company* [2012] EWCA Civ 1055.

[42] *D'Almeida Araujo Lda v Frederick Becker & Co Ltd* [1953] 2 QB 329.

[43] Case Number: 1178/5/7/11, *2 Travel Group Plc (In Liquidation) v Cardiff City Transport Services Ltd* [2012] CAT 19. Compare: *Devenish* (HC) (n 33).

[44] Recital 32 of the Rome II Regulation. See also M Danov, 'Awarding Exemplary (or Punitive) Antitrust Damages in EC Competition Cases with an International Element – the Rome II Regulation and the Commission's White Paper on damages' (2008) 29 *ECL Rev* 430.

[45] Oxera and multi-jurisdictional team of lawyers led by Dr A Komninos, 'Quantifying Antitrust Damages: Towards Non-Binding Guidance for Courts – Study prepared for the European Commission'. See also: PR Beaumont and Z Tang, 'Classification of Delictual Damages – *Harding v Wealands* and the Rome II Regulation' (2008) 12 *Edinburgh Law Review* 131; KM Stanton, 'New Forms of the Tort of Breach of Statutory Duty' (2004) LQR 324, 338–39.

[46] See Ch 3.

law claim. In view of that, certain limits on that principle have been placed by the Court of Justice with regard to EU competition law claims,[47] so that when determining how the relevant issues will be determined by the various legal orders across Europe, the Member States must not make 'practically impossible or excessively difficult the exercise of rights conferred by [EU] law'.[48] Is there a tension between the principle of national procedural autonomy and effective enforcement of EU competition law, given the cross-border nature of most of these infringements?[49]

An interesting question for the Court of Justice may be whether the availability of a passing-on defence in a particular Member State would make it practically impossible or excessively difficult for a 'private enforcer' (eg a larger purchaser) to seek antitrust damages from a legal entity which was engaged in anti-competitive practices.[50] Difficulties are bound to arise because the domestic legal orders would not only indicate the relevant national rules for remoteness of damages,[51] but also the availability of any rules that could limit the defendant's liability. An important defence that may be raised in the latter context is the so-called 'passing-on defence'.[52] It has been submitted that, in competition cases, such a defence could be a significant substantive law barrier.[53] However, it is far from certain if its availability would make the exercise of rights conferred by EU competition law practically impossible or excessively difficult.

Does EU law make a distinction between a vested right and the right's enforcement?[54] In a different context, Van Gerven has submitted that:

> Procedural rules *sensu stricto* should be distinguished from *remedial rules* . . . The latter category covers, in my view, rules governing the conditions, and restrictions, under which individuals are enabled to bring and maintain actions before courts of law in order to safeguard their rights . . . whilst the former category refers to practical rules according to which the remedy is to be pursued in a court of law.[55]

However, the proposed definition may be difficult to apply in practice, as 'substance and procedure cannot be relegated to clear cut categories'[56] in cross-border EU competition law

[47] *Courage* (n 1).

[48] *Manfredi* (n 38) [62]. See also F Becker, 'Application of Community Law by Member States' Public Authorities: between autonomy and effectiveness' (2007) 44 *CML Rev* 1035.

[49] See Ch 3.

[50] cp: Case 199/82 *Amministrazione delle Finanze v San Giorgio* [1983] ECR 3595. In this case, Italian law made the repayment of national charges levied contrary to the requirements of EU law conditional upon the production of proof that those charges have not been passed on to other persons.

[51] cp: *D'Almeida Araujo Lda v Frederick Becker & Co Ltd* [1953] 2 QB 329.

[52] 'That defence is that the claimant had in fact not made any loss because they were able to pass on the loss to their own customers, the final consumers.' See D Sheehan, 'Competition law meets restitution for wrongs' (2009) 125 *LQR* 225.

[53] R Mulheron, 'Reform of collective redress in England and Wales: a perspective of need', research paper for submission to the Civil Council of England and Wales www.civiljusticecouncil.gov.uk/files/collective_redress.pdf. See also: D Beard, 'Damages in Competition Law Litigation' in T Ward and K Smith, *Competition Litigation in the UK* (London, Sweet & Maxwell, 2005) 257, 271–72; M Hellwig, 'Private Damage Claims and the Passing-On Defense in Horizontal Price-Fixing Cases – An Economist's Perspective' in J Basedow (ed), *Private Enforcement of EC Competition Law* (The Hague, Kluwer Law International, 2007) 121; *Devenish* (CA) (n 33) [99], [114 and 130].

[54] cp: CM Schmitthoff, *The English Conflict of Laws*, 3rd edn (London, Steven & Sons, 1954) 395. See also: A Scott, 'Substance and Procedure and Choice of Law in Torts' (2007) *Lloyd's Maritime and Commercial Law Quarterly* 44; M Illmer, 'Neutrality matters – Some Thoughts about the Rome Regulations and the so-called Dichotomy of Substance and Procedure in European Private International Law' (2009) *Civil Justice Quarterly* 237.

[55] W van Gerven, 'Of Rights, Remedies and Procedures' (2000) 37 *CML Rev* 501, 524.

[56] S Szaszy, 'The Basic Connecting Factor in International Cases in the Domain of Civil Procedure' (1966) 15 ICLQ 436, 455. See also D Waelbroeck, D Slater and G Even-Shoshan, *Study on the Conditions of Claims*

actions. Brealey and Hoskins,[57] by making reference to the case law, demonstrate that in so far as the issues are not dealt with by the EU legislator, domestic legal orders would determine how the rights derived by TFEU should be protected – national laws would apply to issues of procedure and evidence as well as to substantive[58] law issues.[59] Given the broad scope of the principle of national procedural autonomy, one might say that there may be a degree of variation in the enforcement of EU competition law unless the private international law framework is suited to dealing with the specific cross-border challenges arising in this context. The potential variations can be easily demonstrated by considering the various heads of damages that may be available in cross-border EU competition law cases. Although the Court of Justice has held that a person who is injured by anti-competitive practice or conduct, must be able to seek compensation for actual loss and loss of profit plus interest,[60] there could be different amounts of damages awarded by the different Member State courts because different countries may have different rules with regard to the availability of exemplary or punitive antitrust damages, for example.

On the one hand, it is generally accepted by the Court of Justice that it is possible for a Member State court to award exemplary or punitive damages.[61] In England, there are instances in which the plaintiff can recover not only the compensatory loss, which will put the injured party in the same position he would have been in had he not sustained the wrong,[62] but also exemplary damages.[63] The English Competition Appeal Tribunal very recently held that 'exemplary damages can in theory be awarded where there is an intentional breach of the law i.e. the defendant acts *knowing* that what he does constitutes an infringement of competition law and *intending* that infringement.'[64] In other words, a cross-border litigant may seek exemplary damages in England if the infringement of EU competition law was deliberate and carried out with full knowledge of the illegality of the actions leading to an important distortion of competition, which is of exclusive benefit to the infringers.[65] If *Devenish* is to be believed, punitive damages are also known in Cyprus and in Ireland.[66] On the other hand, punitive (or exemplary) damages are not only unknown in some Member States (eg France[67], Hungary[68] and Spain[69]), but may also be contrary to the public policy of the forum in some Member States (eg Germany[70] and Italy[71]).

for Damages in Case of Infringement of EC Competition Rules (Ashurst Report) http://ec.europa.eu/competition/antitrust/actionsdamages/comparative_report_clean_en.pdf, p 131.

[57] M Brealey and M Hoskins, *Remedies in EC Law*, 2nd edn (London, Sweet & Maxwell, 1998).

[58] eg heads of damages (including exemplary damages). See Joined Cases C-46/93 and C-48/93, *Brasserie du Pecheur and Factortame* [1996] ECR I-1029 [90].

[59] Brealey and Hoskins (n 57) 107–108.

[60] *Manfredi* (n 38) [26].

[61] ibid [93] and [99].

[62] *Livingston v Rawyards Coal Co* (1880) 5 App Cas 25, 39.

[63] *Rookes v Barnard* [1964] AC 1129; *Devenish* (HC) (n 33) [44] affd *Devenish* (CA) (n 33) [143]. See also V Wilcox, 'Punitive Damages in England' in H Koziol and V Wilcox (eds), *Punitive Damages: Common Law and Civil Law Perspectives* (Vienna/New York, Springer, 2009) 7.

[64] *Cardiff City Transport Services* (n 43) [485]. *Devenish* (HC) (n 33) [44].

[65] Joined Cases C-46/93 and C-48/93, *Brasserie du Pecheur and Factortame* [1996] ECR I-1029 [90].

[66] See also: *Ashurst Report* (n 56).

[67] JS Borghetti, 'Punitive Damages in France' in Koziol and Wilcox (n 63) 55.

[68] A Menyhard, 'Punitive Damages in Hungary' in Koziol and Wilcox (n 63) 87, 91.

[69] P del Olmo, 'Punitive Damages in Spain' in Koziol and Wilcox (n 63) 137.

[70] Punitive damages may be incompatible with fundamental principles of German law. See N Jansen and L Rademacher, 'Punitive Damages in Germany' in Koziol and Wilcox (n 63) 75, 76. See also *Devenish* (HC) (n 33) [33].

[71] AP Scarso, 'Punitive Damages in Italy' in Koziol and Wilcox (n 63) 103, 108.

Moreover, a recent study has presented the various methods and models which can be used in quantifying antitrust damages.[72] In the absence of unified practice throughout the EU, different Member States could employ different methodology. It seems that a private antitrust law claimant in Europe could be awarded a different amount of damages for the very same breach of Articles 101 and 102 TFEU, depending on whether, for example, the action is brought in England (where punitive antitrust damages are available[73]) or Germany (where they are not available). Furthermore, the variations would be amplified if one considers the various national rules which would be applied in the absence of EU legislation with regard to procedure (eg speed[74]), evidence (eg evidential presumptions[75]), costs.[76]

Would there really be a level of variation when it comes to the enforcement of competition law across Europe? If yes, would the level of variation with regard to the various procedural and substantive laws across Europe fuel uncertainty[77] and litigation costs in cross-border EU competition law actions? Would there be advantages in choosing to conduct a trial in one Member State rather than another? How would these affect litigants' tactics? Would different strategies be employed by consumers, SMEs and large purchasers, for example? Is a private antitrust claimant entitled to choose where to bring his EU competition law claim? Which court/s would have jurisdiction to hear and determine the claim? How mobile is an EU competition law claimant? How would parallel proceedings be avoided, if one class of claimants is less mobile than another class? What would be the applicable law/s? Will the rendered damages award be recognised across Europe? How about the preclusive effect of the settlements? Is the current private international framework suitable to deal with the challenges of private antitrust enforcement, and does it promote the effective enforcement of EU competition law across Europe?

C. The Important Role of Private International Law

Previous research has shown that, through enhanced private antitrust enforcement reform, private international law has gained a pivotal role in EU competition law disputes with an international element in Europe.[78] The important role of private international law in the context of competition law enforcement is further reiterated in a very recent book edited by Basedow, Francq and Idot.[79] The most important private international law rules that operate at EU level are the Brussels I regime (which covers the Brussels I Regulation and the Lugano Convention) and the Rome regime (which includes the Rome I Regulation and the Rome II Regulation). Although, there are some minor differences between them, the structure and the basic principles are common to all of those instruments.[80] The focus in

72 Oxera Study (n 45).

73 See also: *Manfredi* (n 38).

74 *Cooper Tire* (n 28) [54–55].

75 Case 199/82 *Amministrazione delle Finanze v San Giorgio* [1983] ECR 3595. See also: Brealey and Hoskins (n 57) 108.

76 C Hodges, M Tulibacka and S Vogenauer (eds), *The Costs and Funding of Civil Litigation* (Oxford, Hart Publishing, 2010).

77 *Ashurst Report* (n 56) 131.

78 Danov (n 40).

79 J Basedow, S Francq and L Idot (eds), *International Antitrust Litigation: Conflict of Laws and Coordination* (Oxford, Hart Publishing, 2012).

80 See more A Briggs and P Rees, *Civil Jurisdiction and Judgments*, 5th edn (London, Informa, 2009) 6–10; J Hill, *International Commercial Disputes in English Courts*, 3rd edn (Oxford, Hart Publishing, 2005) 6–7.

this book will be on the Brussels I Regulation,[81] since this is the fundamental instrument for determining jurisdiction in all proceedings brought on or after 1 March 2002. It is well established that the question whether a national court has jurisdiction to hear and determine an EU competition law dispute in the European context is to be determined by the relevant jurisdictional rules contained in the Brussels I Regulation. The importance of jurisdictional rules should not be questioned in view of the fact that the principle of national procedural autonomy[82] unequivocally suggests that it is for a national domestic system to decide what would be the set of procedural rules which would be employed. The importance of jurisdictional rules is also demonstrated by making reference to the most recent English case law which clearly shows that the issue of jurisdiction is subject to a heated debated before the courts.[83]

Moreover, given the fact that, as already noted, Member States' domestic laws would be relevant to determine such issues as for example the standard of proof, the limitation periods, relevant rules for remoteness of damages, the available remedies for breach of EU competition law, the available defences and assessment of damages, there is no doubt that it will be for the choice-of-law rules to determine which law would govern the issues in question.[84] Therefore, choice-of-law problems would arise particularly sharply in situations where the conduct causing anti-competitive harm within one Member State is agreed between a group of companies with the parent company in another Member State and affecting markets in a number of countries across Europe. Rome I and Rome II deal with choice of law with regard to contractual obligations (Rome I) and non-contractual obligations (Rome II). There is a high degree of harmonisation of choice of law rules relating to contractual and non-contractual obligations in Europe. The Rome I Regulation,[85] which replaced the Rome Convention for contracts concluded after 17 December 2009, applies, in situations involving conflict of laws, to contractual obligations in civil and commercial matters. The Rome II Regulation[86] lays down the law applicable to non-contractual obligations in civil and commercial matters and applies as from 11 January 2009.

Although it is justifiable to employ private international law when allocating jurisdiction and identifying the applicable law in cross-border private EU competition law actions brought against defendants who are not domiciled in a Member State, it might be questioned whether the EU should use the current EU private international law framework with regard to cross-border EU competition law actions brought in the European context. Should the EU use the current private international law in claims that are directly based on substantive EU competition law rules which are harmonised at EU level? It has been submitted that 'The purpose of [Brussels I, Rome I and Rome II] is clearly the unification of private international law, not the harmonisation of the substantive laws of the Member

[81] Art 65 of the EC Treaty was the legal basis for new private international law initiatives; see P Beaumont, 'European Court of Justice and Jurisdiction and Enforcement of Judgments in Civil and Commercial Matters' (1999) 48 *ICLQ* 223, 225. See now Art 81 TFEU.

[82] *Rewe-Zentralfinanz* (n 38).

[83] *Provimi* (n 29); *SanDisk Corporation v Koninklijke Philips Electronics and others* [2007] EWHC 332 (Ch), [2007] Bus LR 705; *Cooper Tire* (n 28); *Toshiba Carrier* (n 29); *Emerson Electric* (n 29). See more: Chs 3, 11 and 13.

[84] cp: CGJ Morse, 'Torts in Private International Law: a New Statutory Framework' (1996) 45 ICLQ 888, 895. See also: Danov (n 40) ch 5.

[85] Regulation (EC) 593/2008 of the European Parliament and of the Council of 17 June 2008 on the law applicable to contractual obligations (Rome I) [2008] OJ L177/6.

[86] Regulation (EC) 864/2007 of the European Parliament and of the Council of 11 July 2007 on the law applicable to non-contractual obligations (Rome II) [2007] OJ L199/40.

States, on which it may be more difficult to reach agreement.'[87] However, Articles 101 and 102 TFEU, forming part of each Member State's legal order, are not only harmonised, but also at the heart of an EU competition law claim, so that the use of private international law in cross-border private antitrust proceedings may be questioned. Should there be 'a degree of harmonisation of fundamental concepts of national civil law (both substantive and procedural)'?[88] Is it possible to achieve such a level of harmonisation? Should there rather be a private international law solution to address the specific features of cross-border EU competition law actions as well as the diversity across Europe?

D. The Role of the EU Courts – Diverse Europe: Different Legal Traditions and Heritages across Europe

The EU relies on the individual Member States' legal orders to enforce the EU competition law provisions and the rights of the individuals derived from the TFEU in this context. It has been submitted that there are 'three types of Community Court, not just two: the ECJ, the CFI, *and* national courts. . . . The rationale for inclusion of national courts in [the EU judicial system] is of course that they are enforcers of [EU] law in their own right.'[89] However, there may be a level of variation across Europe, as the 27 Member States share different legal traditions and legal heritages. The challenge for the EU competition law enforcement policy (similar to the challenge for the EU[90] itself) is the process of creation of a European enforcement regime 'which is based on the existing diversity of member states"'[91] legal orders.

Indeed, it is well established that today's European Union is integrating two major legal traditions – 'the "civil law" (an imperfect but received designation) and the "common law".'[92] In this context, Legrand makes reference to:

> sociological findings that the English 'feel definitely uncomfortable with systems of rigid rules,' that there is even to be found in England 'an emotional horror of formal rules,' and that the English 'pride themselves that many problems can be solved without formal rules.'[93] . . . And . . . sociological findings that the Germans 'have been programmed since their early childhood to feel comfortable in structured environments' and that they 'look for a structure in their organizations, institutions, and relationships which makes events clearly interpretable and predictable' to the point where 'even ineffective rules satisfy [the] people's emotional need for formal structure.'[94, 95]

[87] A Mills, *The Confluence of Public and Private International Law* (Cambridge, CUP, 2009) 185. See also Council of the European Union, 'The Hague Programme: strengthening freedom, security and justice in the European Union' http://ec.europa.eu/justice_home/doc_centre/doc/hague_programme_en.pdf 31.

[88] *Ashurst Report* (n 56) 131.

[89] P Craig, 'The Jurisdiction of the Community Courts Reconsidered' in G de Burca and JHH Weiler (eds), *The European Court of Justice* (Oxford, OUP, 2001) 177, 178. See also: J Komarek, 'Federal Elements in the Community Judicial System: Building Coherence in the Community Legal Order' (2005) 42 *CML Rev* 9, 10; J Komarek, 'In the court(s) we trust? On the need for hierarchy and differentiation in the preliminary ruling procedure' (2007) *EL Rev* 467, 468.

[90] J Shaw, 'Postnational Constitutionalism in the European Union' (1999) *Journal of European Public Policy* 579, 586.

[91] Shaw (n 90) 586.

[92] P Legrand, 'Against a European Civil Code' (1997) 62 *MLR* 44.

[93] G Hofstede, *Cultures and Organizations: Software of the Mind* (London, McGraw-Hill, 1991) 145, 121 and 121 cited in Legrand (n 92) 47. See also: G Hofstede, GJ Hofstede and M Minkov, *Cultures and Organisations: Software of the Mind: Intercultural Cooperation and its Importance for Survival*, 3rd edn (New York, McGraw-Hill, 2010) 304, 210 and 210, respectively.

[94] Hofstede (n 93) 121, 116 and 121, respectively. See also: Hofstede, Hofstede and Minkov (n 93) 197–98, 209, and 209, respectively.

[95] Legrand (n 92) 47.

The picture has become even more colourful since the 2004 and 2007 enlargements of the European Union, when 12 new Member States joined the Union. In spite of the mechanisms envisaged by Regulation 1/2003, the judges in some of the new Member States lack experience in dealing with complicated antitrust laws. The problems are rooted in the fact that antitrust laws in some of those countries were adopted only in the 1990s. Although those laws mirrored the western model, they ignored the specific features of the socialist heritage and lack the decades of experience in applying those laws.[96] Moreover, the Commission has outlined the risk that some of the new Member States may be unable to correctly apply EU law unless they achieve irreversible progress on their judicial reforms.[97] As a part of a specifically designated Cooperation and Verification Mechanism, the Commission reports every six months on the progress of Bulgaria and Romania with judicial reform and the fight against corruption. The last reports from July 2012 appear to suggest that further progress is required.[98] This may result in inconsistent enforcement of EU competition law across Europe.

One may object to such a deduction by saying that differences in procedural rules will hardly endanger the uniform application of EU competition law. It may be put forward that most of the actions are brought as follow-on actions, so that such actions in different jurisdictions will not endanger the consistent application of European competition law by the regulator. But, then the competition authorities would not have the resources to pursue all the infringements, so that inconsistent enforcement by some Member State courts could be a problem. Furthermore, the inconsistent enforcement might happen even in follow-on action as it is well established that 'the full effectiveness of Article [101/102 TFEU] would be put at risk if it were not open to any individual to claim damages for loss caused to him'[99] as a result of the infringement established by the regulator.

How should the EU legislator address the problem? The Court of Justice would be expected to have an important role to play in order to ensure uniform application and interpretation of EU competition law.[100] But, is the European legal system in its current format suited to dealing with the challenges? In a report dated January 2000, the Working Party has observed that if there is a significant increase in EU competition law cases before the European Courts in future, jurisdiction to rule on preliminary references in this area might be assigned to the General Court.[101] Is there a need for a reform of the institutional architecture of antitrust enforcement? How important is it for the EU legislator to act? What should be the way forward? There are some complex and difficult issues to be considered with regard to legislative reform. Is the current EU private international law framework suited to dealing with the challenges of private antitrust enforcement? Are there any specific issues arising with regard to cross-border EU competition law actions? Should

[96] T Varady, 'The Emergence of Competition Law in (Former) Socialist Countries' (1999) 47 *American Journal of Comparative Law* 229, 261.

[97] eg Commission (EC), 'Bulgaria's Progress on Accompanying Measures Following Accession' (Report) COM (2007) 377 final; Commission (EC), 'Romania's progress on accompanying measures following Accession' (Report) COM (2007) 378 final.

[98] See the Reports on Progress in Bulgaria and Romania http://ec.europa.eu/cvm/progress_reports_en.htm.

[99] *Courage* (n 1) [26].

[100] Adaptation of the provisions of Title IV of the Treaty establishing the European community relating to the jurisdiction of the Court of Justice with a view to ensuring more effective judicial protection ('Communication from the Commission') COM(2006) 346 final. See also: Information Note on references from national courts for a preliminary ruling OJ [2011] C160/1.

[101] 'Report by the Working Party on the Future of the European Communities' Court System' (Working Party for the European Commission, January 2000), 34–35 at http://ec.europa.eu/dgs/legal_service/pdf/due_en.pdf.

there be a harmonisation of substantive law with regard to EU competition law damages claims? Should there be harmonisation of procedural laws in this context? Should there be a regulatory competition? What should be the role of the European Courts?

On the one hand, the fact that there are 27 Member States with different legal, political and economic heritages may require a more direct and harmonised instrument that would guarantee uniform and coherent application of the EU competition law provisions. Indeed, it appears that 'the problems relating to the uniformity of interpretation of uniform law made by the courts of each State'[102] should be carefully considered in the European context. The report on the functioning of Regulation 1/2003 seems to suggest that the current mechanisms are not efficient in this respect,[103] indicating that the EU legislator may need to intervene. On the other hand, it is well established that any harmonised instrument 'pre-supposes a certain affinity between the legal systems amongst which unification is to be achieved. Otherwise, the provisions of the uniform laws run the risk of being substantially altered when they are adapted to the various internal legal systems.[104] How to strike the balance in Europe?

III. IMPORTANT AND RELEVANT RESEARCH STUDIES

The appropriate role for private competition law claims in Europe has been widely discussed in the literature.[105] Indeed, there are a number of research projects which have been conducted for the European Commission[106] and the European Parliament.[107] These studies provide some useful background information as to what are the conditions of claims for antitrust damages in the Member States, as well as to the evolution of such claims in Europe, and possible ways forward.

A. 'Ashurst Report'[108]

A comparative report on the conditions of claims for EU competition law damages was produced by Waelbroeck, Slater and Even-Shoshan from the law firm, Ashurst. The 2004 report was written on the basis of answers by national reporters from 25 Member States to questionnaires pre-prepared by the European Commission. The study was intended to compare the conditions of claims for damages in case of infringement of EU competition

[102] M Matteucci, 'The Methods of the Unification of Law' in UNIDROIT International Institute for the Unification of Private Law, *Unification of Law* Vol II (Rome, Editions 'UNIDROIT, 1957) 7.

[103] See Commission (EC), 'The functioning of Regulation 1/2003' (Report) COM (2009) 206 final.

[104] Matteucci (n 102) 87.

[105] Wils (n 3); Basedow (n 53); Komninos (n 3); M Brealey and N Green, *Competition Litigation: UK Practice and Procedure* (Oxford, OUP, 2010); K Gotts (ed), *The Private Competition Enforcement Review,* 3rd edn (Law Business Research, 2010); J Basedow, JP Terhechte and L Tichy (eds), *Private Enforcement of Competition Law* (Baden-Baden, Nomos, 2011).

[106] *Ashurst Report* (n 56). Report for the European Commission, Contract DG COMP/2006/A3/012, *Making Antitrust Damages Actions More Effective in the EU: Welfare Impact and Potential Scenarios* http://ec.europa.eu/competition/antitrust/actionsdamages/files_white_paper/impact_study.pdf; Basedow, Francq and Idot (n 79).

[107] *Collective Redress in Antitrust* (n 18).

[108] *Ashurst Report* (n 56).

rules, and identify the real obstacles to private EU competition actions in Europe.[109] Given that the comparative report was produced pursuant to a tender carried out by the Commission, one should wonder whether harmonisation of some of these rules was not considered by the EU legislator. Indeed, it is well established that 'a comparison of divergent rules is an indispensable preliminary to any proposals for the unification of private law.'[110] In this context, it should be noted that in their comparative report, the Ashurst Report clearly stated:

> The picture that emerges from the present study on damages actions for breach of competition law in the enlarged EU is one of astonishing diversity and total underdevelopment. As regards the latter point, the study has revealed only around 60[111] judged cases for damages actions (12 on the basis of EC law, around 32 on the basis of national law and 6 on both). Of these judgments 28 have so far resulted in an award being made (8 on the basis of EC competition law, 16 on national law and 4 on both).[112]

The report went on to specify seven key areas which had to be looked at carefully by the policy-makers in order for private competition litigation to be facilitated across Europe.[113] First, the access to courts, in terms of standing requirements as well as incentives to bringing collective redress proceedings, was considered to be an important issue. Secondly, the litigation risks, which were due to the uncertainty of the outcome in inherently complex competition law cases, were outlined. Thirdly, the issues regarding evidence and standard of proof were seen as important. Fourthly, the high litigation costs were noted as a possible obstacle to some competition law claims. In addition, some incentives, such as punitive damages, for example, and/or the use of the defendants' profits, were put forward as well. Sixthly, the issues of transparency and publicity were regarded as important by the authors. In particular, they thought that more information being made available to potential claimants could potentially promote private antitrust enforcement.[114] Finally, the authors of the report made the following submission:

> General uncertainty as to the limits imposed on national procedural autonomy and the fact that general national law may not in fact be compatible with those limits can create difficulties for national courts in how to apply the law, and thus uncertainties for parties as to how their claim will be handled. . . .
>
> One way to reduce these uncertainties and thus create greater legal certainty and facilitate private actions would be some degree of harmonisation of national procedural rules applicable to EC competition law-based damages actions. It should be noted that such a development would, however, constitute an inroad into the principle of national procedural autonomy and possibly also involve a degree of harmonisation of fundamental concepts of national civil law (both substantive and procedural).[115]

[109] ibid.

[110] HC Gutteridge, *Comparative Law,* 2nd edn (Cambridge, CUP, 1949) 174 quoted in Matteucci (n 102) 39.

[111] 'No official statistics are available on this issue. These figures have been compiled from the information gathered in the national reports. To this figure should be added a large number of parallel cases for small amounts brought in Italy by customers of members of an insurance cartel (probably around 50). There are, however, a number of ongoing questions in these cases which remain unresolved, especially regarding the legality of the procedure followed. These are described in full in the Italian report.' See *Ashurst Report* (n 56) 1.

[112] *Ashurst Report* (n 56) 1.

[113] ibid 9–13 and 118–32.

[114] ibid 12.

[115] ibid 131.

Is harmonisation possible? Or, is harmonisation desirable? Although these questions were beyond the scope of this informative and much needed comparative study, it is well established that 'one must make a clear distinction between the possibility and desirability of the unification.'[116]

B. 'Making Antitrust Damages Actions More Effective in the EU: Welfare Impact and Potential Scenarios'[117]

Following the Ashurst Report, in 2005 the Commission published a Green Paper on EU antitrust damages actions.[118] The paper identified some of the main obstacles preventing victims from bringing actions for damages in the Member States, and proposed a set of solutions to be considered. Subsequently, the Commission published a White Paper on antitrust damages which was intended to allow claimants to have access to redress mechanisms and get compensation for the harm they have suffered.[119] The study on *Making Antitrust Damages Actions More Effective in the EU: Welfare Impact and Potential Scenarios* was made in this context in order to support the impact assessment of the concrete policy measures proposed by the White Paper. In their 2007 Report for the European Commission,[120] the researchers noted that:

> analysis . . . suggests that things have not significantly improved since [the Ashurst Report was produced in 2004], although in a very narrow set of countries antitrust damages actions seem to be slowly becoming more frequent. As a matter of fact, 17 of the 27 Member States still have no trace of private antitrust damages actions, and also in other Member States private antitrust litigation seems very sparse and related to isolated streams of cases. In the EU27, public enforcement remains by far the most common remedy for antitrust infringement.[121]

In view of the limited data from Europe, the Report assessed the potential impact of more antitrust enforcement by relying predominantly on data from the US[122] where significantly more antitrust litigation has been traditionally witnessed.[123] The authors of the Report noted that an effective private antitrust enforcement regime in Europe potentially may result in increased corrective justice, enhanced deterrence, internal market benefits, competition law being brought closer to the citizen, and macroeconomic impacts.[124] The Report concludes:

> After providing an estimate of the potential impact of a more effective system of private antitrust enforcement in Europe, which we find to potentially lead to damage recoveries of €25.7 billion yearly, we compare alternative scenarios that could, although to different degrees, approximate this potential. . . . we found strong evidence in favour of action at EU level, as the use of soft law measures does not seem suitable to significantly increase the corrective justice and deterrence goals that are embedded in this policy initiative.[125]

[116] Gutteridge (n 110) 39.
[117] *Making Antitrust Damages Actions More Effective in the EU* (n 106).
[118] Green Paper on Damages Actions for Breach of the EC Antitrust Rules COM(2005) 672 final.
[119] White Paper on Damages Actions for Breach of the EC Antitrust Rules COM(2008) 165.
[120] *Making Antitrust Damages Actions More Effective in the EU* (n 106).
[121] ibid 28.
[122] ibid 10.
[123] See S Salop and L White, 'Private Antitrust Litigation: An Introduction and Framework' in L White (ed), *Private Antitrust Litigation, New Evidence, New Learning* (Cambridge MA, MIT Press, 1988).
[124] *Making Antitrust Damages Actions More Effective in the EU* (n 106) 10.
[125] ibid 26. See also ibid 36.

That said, the Report went on to state that there could be high harmonisation costs. In particular, these costs would be significant if the proposed measure runs counter to deeply rooted principles forming part of a Member State's legal order.[126] For example, multiple damages would be contrary to public policy in most Member States.[127] Similarly, exemplary damages as a legislative measure may not be adopted at EU level without significant harmonisation costs.[128] Some of the collective redress mechanisms, and, in particular, any opt-out rule may fuel the harmonisation costs.[129]

C. 'Collective Redress in Antitrust'[130]

The comparative study, which was funded by the European Parliament, was intended to analyse and develop the issues of collective redress in antitrust matters. In addition to engaging with the publicly available information on the national legislation, the data was gathered from the responses to a questionnaire submitted to scholars, practitioners, judges, national competition authorities and national consumer protection institutions in all Member States.[131] The 2012 Report, in line with the 2004 and 2007 Reports discussed above, demonstrated that the number of collective redress actions related to antitrust infringements is still very limited in Europe.[132]

As a matter of fact, 'To date collective actions resulting in damages awarded to the victims have been observed only in Austria and in the UK.'[133] Regarding the UK, it should be noted that the Report makes reference to the *JJB* case which settled. The latter case is far from being an example for effective redress for consumers, due to the small numbers of consumers receiving compensation.[134] The authors of the collective redress report thought that the fact that there is very little quantitative data 'also suggests that the implemented [collective redress] systems have not been very successful.'[135] In view of that, it was concluded that:

> the most effective legislative act for a sector-specific initiative in EU competition law would be a **regulation.** Since existing national collective redress systems have general scope and are not limited to competition law enforcement, the introduction of an *ad hoc* special mechanism by means of regulation would create a uniform effective EU procedural instrument to be added to existing national ones. On the contrary, a directive has to be implemented by national legislators. Problems of compatibility with existing national legislations and risk of the adoption of non-harmonised solutions across Member States might then arise.[136]

However, would such a harmonised mechanism be effective? Is it at all possible for the current European legal system to provide for its uniform and consistent application? Might

[126] ibid 48 and 173.
[127] ibid 196 and 225.
[128] ibid 236.
[129] ibid 311 and 316–17.
[130] *Collective Redress in Antitrust* (n 18).
[131] ibid 18.
[132] ibid 11 and 37.
[133] ibid 39.
[134] See more: Which?, 'JJB Sports: a case study in collective action' www.which.co.uk/documents/pdf/collective-redress-case-study-which-briefing-258401.pdf. See also Ch 18, below.
[135] *Collective Redress in Antitrust* (n 18) 40.
[136] ibid 88.

a new legislative instrument bring fresh uncertainty across Europe? It has been submitted that:

> to bring about genuine uniformity in a field such as procedural law you must not only have the same set of rules, but also common principles of interpretation and a common legal culture. And those necessary factors cannot be created as smoothly as common written rules; those factors have to develop over time and in connection with other legal rules and policy objectives to which they relate; as for procedural law that would mean e.g. a need to mature together with substantive law. If common procedural rules covering a large area are laid down too soon, they are bound to annoy judges and will be applied diversely and that they seem common in writing will only confuse parties affected.[137]

Might a private international law mechanism better accommodate the diverse legal traditions in Europe?

D. 'International Antitrust Litigation: Conflict of Laws and Coordination'[138]

The project, which was funded by the European Commission Civil Justice Programme, was intended to 'inquire into the functioning of and potential development of private international law techniques and instruments applicable for this specific kind of litigation.'[139] The book is comprehensive in its scope. It examines private international law rules on jurisdiction, applicable laws and on recognition and enforcement, as well as the regime for arbitration and issues with regard to collective redress antitrust proceedings. The complex and difficult issues on sharing evidence, and the interplay between administrative and judicial procedures, have been duly identified and examined as well. However, the question whether the current private international law could be used to promote regulatory competition across Europe along the lines suggested by the study on *Making Antitrust Damages Actions More Effective in the EU: Welfare Impact and Potential Scenarios*[140] was beyond the scope of the project led by Basedow, Francq and Idot. An important question therefore, which was not addressed, is this: might regulatory competition be promoted by a sophisticated private international law solution in the context of cross-border EU competition law actions?

Although the authors have identified some specific issues arising in the context of cross-border EU competition law actions, some of their interpretative proposals might not be effective in practice. For example, Costa, who clearly identifies some specific problems in applying Articles 5(1) and 5(3) Brussels I with regard to EU competition law claims brought by contracting parties, goes on to make some interpretative proposals for Articles 5(1) and 5(3) Brussels I. Costa, nonetheless, appears to be aware that, despite the interpretative proposals, some difficulties may well persist, but appears to be content that a plaintiff always has the option to resort to the general rule of Article 2.[141] Will an SME follow the defendant

[137] T Andersson, 'Approximation of procedural law in Europe' in M Storme (ed), *Procedural Laws in Europe* (Antwerp, Maklu, 2003) 55, 64–65.

[138] Basedow, Francq and Idot (n 79). See also: M Danov, Review of '*International Antitrust Litigation: Conflict of Laws and Coordination*, edited by Jurgen Basedow, Stephanie Francq and Laurence Idot, (Oxford, Hart Publishing, 2012)' (2013) 50 *CML Rev* 303–05.

[139] ibid 1.

[140] *Making Antitrust Damages Actions More Effective in the EU* (n 106) 555–56.

[141] Basedow, Francq and Idot (n 79) 29; see also: ibid 26.

to the Member State of his domicile? It is well established that a 'cross-border litigant may, as a practical matter, require two lawyers, one in his Home State to give preliminary advice, and one in the Host State to conduct the litigation.'[142] Will the high costs of cross-border competition litigation affect the litigiousness of SMEs?

Moreover, the role of Article 2 Brussels I should not be overstated in cross-border EU competition law cases because the concept of the 'undertaking' may often embrace a number of legal entities.[143] Will a claimant rather prefer to rely on Article 6(1) Brussels I and sue the local subsidiary with a view to secure jurisdiction against a non-UK domiciled parent company? The answer to this question is far from certain, because as noted by Wilderspin, English courts 'continue to require that, for the purposes of founding jurisdiction on the basis of Article 6(1), there must be a real issue between the claimant and the anchor defendant.'[144] Specific difficulties would arise in a case where an EU competition law claim is brought against the local subsidiary with a view to secure jurisdiction against a non-UK domiciled parent company. In such cases, the claimant would have to demonstrate that there is a real issue, which cannot be struck out, between him and the particular local subsidiary. This would be an extremely difficult and time-consuming task if the local subsidiary is not an addressee of the Commission decision.[145] This outcome is far from satisfactory, in view of the fact that the limited private antitrust litigation which happens at the moment is normally preceded by a decision of a regulator establishing a competition law infringement. One might well wonder whether a plaintiff could ever bring an EU competition law claim against the parent company of an English subsidiary in England under Article 5(5) of Brussels I. Might the concept of 'undertaking' be useful in this context? These issues do not appear to be addressed in the book.

Notwithstanding all this, the importance of the rules, which are meant to avoid parallel EU competition law proceedings, was duly acknowledged by Wilderspin and Rodger. Although Wilderspin states that 'no amendment' would be required with regard to Article 28 (as there is little evidence to support such an amendment) at the moment,[146] he himself has made a very interesting legislative proposal in the context of the same provision in Part I of the book. In particular, he thought that Article 28 Brussels I should be amended by:

1. the deletion of the words 'other than the court first seised' in paragraphs (1) and (2); and
2. the deletion of the concluding words (following the word 'together') in paragraph (3).[147]

This proposal for amendment is a very interesting one which ought to be carefully considered by the EU legislator. However, the new Proposal for a Regulation on Jurisdiction and the Recognition and Enforcement of Judgments (COM(2010) 748 final) contains no indication that the successor to Regulation 44/2001 would be amended by 'abandoning the rule that only the court second seised can stay its proceedings.'[148] Might another possibility for a reform be amending Regulation 1/2003 to address the problem of parallel EU competition law proceedings in order to avoid irreconcilable or inconsistent decisions in the European context? Indeed, Regulation 1/2003 does not deal with the problem of coherent

[142] See Green Paper from the Commission, *Legal Aid in Civil Matters: The Problems Confronting the Cross-border Litigant* COM(2000) 51 final p. 9.
[143] *Cooper Tire* (n 28) [47].
[144] Basedow, Francq and Idot (n 79) 47.
[145] *Toshiba Carrier* (n 29). See more: Ch 13.
[146] Basedow, Francq and Idot (n 79) 412.
[147] Ibid. Cp: ibid 412.
[148] ibid 59. Cp: ibid 412.

and uniform application of EU competition law in proceedings before an NCA located in one Member State and private EU antitrust law proceedings related to the same breaches of Article 101 TFEU and/or Article 102 TFEU before a court in another Member State. Problems are bound to arise in such cases. Is Brussels I applicable in the context of parallel EU competition law proceedings brought before an NCA located in one Member State and a court in another Member State? Although Basedow has noted in another context that: 'the White Paper proposal on the recognition of foreign NCA decisions should be extended in its scope and refined with regard to the preconditions of recognition',[149] the above EU competition law issues are not addressed specifically by the contributors.

IV. RESEARCH PROJECT – AIMS AND ACTIVITIES

Given the foregoing specific issues arising in the context of cross-border EU competition law actions, this research project, which was also funded by the European Commission Civil Justice Programme, aims to propose specific solutions. In particular, an important issue which researchers will consider is whether the European Union should use the current EU private international law framework with regard to cross-border EU competition law claims brought by private parties, or rather whether the EU legislator should set up a Special Regulation dealing with EU competition law proceedings arising in the European context. In this context, answers to the following key questions will be considered. (1) Should the current private international law framework be used to implement the post-2003 policy of the European Union favouring private enforcement of EU competition law? (2) Should the Brussels I Regulation have a special basis for jurisdiction in relation to EU competition law claims? Should there be a special Regulation dealing with private EU competition law actions? (3) Should there be the possibility of an appeal by private parties on a point of EU competition law before the General Court (ex-CFI)? The researchers will argue that the current private international law framework is not suited to dealing with the challenges of the private antitrust enforcement, and will go a step further to propose a private international law solution which will promote regulatory competition with regard to cross-border EU competition law actions in Europe.

As a part of their research, research teams undertook numerous activities which allowed them to take into account the opinions of other academics as well as legal practitioners and policy-makers. As the project aims to identify how cross-border EU competition law actions should be accommodated in Europe, qualitative interviews were conducted with legal practitioners in Germany and England (countries with different legal traditions) as well as with policy-makers in Brussels in order to consider their views on how private EU competition law actions are functioning at the moment and how they could and should be developed. In addition, there was a successful workshop held in Brunel University in November 2010 and a final Conference at the LSE in April 2012, where our preliminary findings were presented. Both events assembled legal practitioners and academics.

[149] ibid 397. See also: ibid 402 and 439.

V. BOOK – CONTENT AND STRUCTURE

As the study aims to propose solutions for some practical problems, in addition to our research findings, the book will include papers by the following leading legal practitioners and academics: Judge Irena Pelikánová (General Court of the EU); Jon Lawrence and Anna Morfey (Freshfields); Dr Paul Lasok QC (Monckton Chambers); Hugh Mercer QC (Essex Court Chambers); James Webber (Shearman & Sterling); Dr Tim Reher (CMS Hasche Sigle, Germany); Pierre Bos and J Möhlmann (BarentsKrans, the Netherlands); Professor Paul Beaumont (University Aberdeen); Professor Stefania Bariatti (University of Milan; Chiomenti Studio Legale, Italy); Professor Geraint Howells (University of Manchester); Dr Duncan Fairgrieve (British Institute of International and Comparative Law); Dr Jonathan Fitchen (University of Aberdeen); Dr Arianna Andreangeli (University of Edinburgh), Dr Dimitrios Tzakas (Athens Bar, Greece) and Stephen Dnes (Sidley Austin, Brussels).

In other words, in this book, we will present our research findings as well as the opinions of the contributors in the light of the specific issues arising in the context of cross-border EU competition law actions. The book will be divided into five Parts. Part I will provide summary of our research methodology and empirical research findings. The specific issues identified as a part of the empirical study and the previous research projects[150] will be explored in the subsequent parts by researchers as well as by contributors. Part II will look at the judicial activities of the General Court with regard to EU competition law cases as well as at the issue of the European Union competence to legislate in the context of cross-border EU competition law actions. The questions related to harmonisation and/or inter-jurisdictional regulatory competition will be discussed as well. Part III will discuss some specific procedural issues and their effect on litigants' strategies aiming to identify specific solutions in the context of cross-border EU competition law actions. The question as to how regulatory competition could be best promoted in the European context will be duly analysed as well. Part IV will examine the issue of the applicable law and the problems associated with defining it when antitrust damages are assessed in a cross-border context. Part V addresses issue related to procedural aspects of antitrust enforcement as well as questions regarding the recognition and enforcement of foreign judgments in relation to EU competition law actions. Finally, we will draw some conclusions on the basis of our research findings as well as the views expressed by the contributors. The possible answers to our research questions will be considered. The options which may be used to accommodate cross-border EU competition law actions will be briefly summarised.

[150] See above.

Part I

Research Methodology, Research Findings, Issues to be Addressed

2

Research Methodology

MIHAIL DANOV AND FLORIAN BECKER

I. INTRODUCTION

In Part I of the book we will present the results of our empirical study and identify the main problems which litigants face under the current institutional framework. The present chapter justifies the need for the empirical study and makes a summary of the research methodology. Chapter 3 will summarise the research findings from England and Wales in the hope of shedding some light on the litigation process, how it is functioning, and whether and how it might be reformed. Chapter 4 will briefly summarise the results of the empirical study conducted in Germany. In Chapter 5, the researchers will identify the issues which will need to be explored in the subsequent Parts of the Book, with a view to identifying workable solutions and promoting inter-jurisdictional regulatory competition in Europe.

II. THE NEED FOR EMPIRICAL RESEARCH

As already noted,[1] the comparative studies – revealed by the Ashurst Report[2] as well as by the Collective Antitrust Redress Report[3] – appear to be making a strong case that as yet, private antitrust litigation is in a nascent form in Europe. They also indicate that there is a level of variation on the conditions of claims (including individual and collective claims) for damages in the European Union. In view of that, the authors of the reports in question strongly suggest that harmonisation must be considered by the EU legislator.[4] That said, one should make a distinction between anti-competitive conduct, which is caught by Articles 101 and 102 TFEU 'when cartel agreements or abuses of a dominant position affect inter-State commerce',[5] and anti-competitive conduct which is covered by national competition laws 'when only intra-State commerce is affected'.[6] A case for further

[1] See Ch 1.

[2] D Waelbroeck, D Slater and G Even-Shoshan, *Study on the Conditions of Claims for Damages in Case of Infringement of EC Competition Rules (Ashurst Report)*, http://ec.europa.eu/competition/antitrust/actionsdamages/comparative_report_clean_en.pdf .

[3] P Buccirossi, M Carpagnano, L Ciari et al, *Collective Redress in Antitrust*, www.europarl.europa.eu/document/activities/cont/201206/20120613ATT46782/20120613ATT46782EN.pdf .

[4] *Ashurst Report* (n 2) 131; *Collective Redress in Antitrust* (n 3) 88.

[5] W van Gerven, 'Bringing (Private) Laws Closer to Each Other at the European Level' in F Cafaggi (ed), *The Institutional Framework of European Private Law* (Oxford, OUP, 2006) 37, 66.

[6] ibid 37, 66.

harmonisation might be made with regard to the former by pointing out that Articles 101 and 102 TFEU, forming part of each Member State's legal order, are already harmonised. If EU competition law provisions are at the heart of an EU competition law claim, then a harmonised instrument might be used to lay down the conditions of EU competition law damages actions across Europe. Indeed, the use of private international law in cross-border private antitrust proceedings may be questioned, as it may make the assessment of damages unduly complicated.

However, the diverse legal traditions and heritages of the countries forming the European Union[7] might suggest that the level of variation may remain unchanged after the adoption of such a harmonised regime in Europe because, as already noted, 'common principles of interpretation and a common legal culture' take some time to develop.[8] More importantly, a harmonised instrument without an appropriate institutional structure might bring fresh uncertainty across Europe. Furthermore, the study on *Making Antitrust Damages Actions More Effective in the EU,* unequivocally indicates that exemplary damages[9] as well as the various collective redress mechanisms (any opt-out rule, in particular)[10] that could be put into effect by legislative measures may result in significant harmonisation costs. It has been submitted by Kerber[11] that:

> collective decision-making implies large costs such as knowledge, rent-seeking problems, inefficiencies, or inflexibility, it might be that considerable costs through market failure must also be accepted before it is advisable to turn to centralization or mobility barriers.[12]

In other words, one might question the effectiveness of more centralisation in the area of private antitrust enforcement by devising another legislative instrument which is the result of a compromise reached at EU level. It is worth investigating whether a private international law solution might not be best suited to promoting regulatory competition across Europe. Such a regulatory competition with regard to cross-border damages claims may happen if claimants can choose directly between damages regimes of different jurisdictions and bring their claims there by benefiting from procedural and substantive laws of the jurisdiction where the claim is brought by relying on the law of the forum (*lex fori*).[13]

The possibility for regulatory competition in Europe with regard to EU competition law damages claims was first signalled by the authors of *Making Antitrust Damages Actions More Effective in the EU.* In particular, they noted that:

[7] The delay may be a problem in some countries (eg Italy – *Cooper Tire & Rubber Company Europe Ltd & Others* [2010] EWCA Civ 864 [54–55]). The lack of experience of the judiciary could be a problem in other countries (eg Bulgaria and Romania – see Commission (EC), 'Bulgaria's Progress on Accompanying Measures Following Accession' (Report) COM (2007) 377 final; Commission (EC), 'Romania's Progress on Accompanying Measures Following Accession' (Report) COM (2007) 378 final. See also: Reports on Progress in Bulgaria and Romania http://ec.europa.eu/cvm/progress_reports_en.htm.

[8] T Andersson, 'Approximation of procedural law in Europe' in M Storme (ed), *Procedural Laws in Europe* (Antwerp, Maklu, 2003) 55, 64–65.

[9] Report for the European Commission, Contract DG COMP/2006/A3/012, *Making Antitrust Damages Actions More Effective in the EU: Welfare Impact and Potential Scenarios* http://ec.europa.eu/competition/antitrust/actionsdamages/files_white_paper/impact_study.pdf, p 236.

[10] *Making Antitrust Damages Actions More Effective in the EU* (n 9) 311 and 316–17.

[11] W Kerber, 'Interjurisdictional competition within the European Union' (1999–2000) 23 *Fordham International Law Journal* S217.

[12] ibid S229.

[13] See Type (IV) regulatory competition via free choice of law, as described in W Kerber and O Budzinski, 'Towards a Differentiated Analysis of Competition of Competition Laws' (2003) *ZWeR – Journal of Competition Law* 411, 415.

> there would be reason[s] to believe that the 'race to the top' effect, which would lead to mutual learning and context-aware benchmarking between member states, is less likely to materialise than the 'race to the bottom' scenario, where states compete to entice firms to settle in their territory by signalling weak antitrust enforcement. At the same time, however, this effect may be mitigated as: (i) the application of antitrust damages rules would not depend on the place of the establishment of the defendant, but in principle on the *lex damni* (*i.e.* the 'law of the country where the market is, or is likely to be, affected'), as was recently stated by Article 6 of [Rome II]; (ii) in addition, the argument that firms may 'vote with their feet' may hold only at the margin, for firms wishing to enter a new market, whereas established undertakings are unlikely to move their headquarters only to follow less stringent competition rules.[14]

Although the authors of the report appear to be placing a significant importance on the applicable laws under Rome II, the jurisdictional rules might be even more important if someone wants to promote regulatory competition with regard to EU antitrust damages actions brought in the European context. Indeed, in the context of EU competition law damage actions, Khan has noted that '[t]he obstacles are mainly procedural'.[15] Are the procedural issues within the scope of Rome II? Article 1(3) clearly states that the Regulation does not apply to evidence and procedure. Such an approach appears to be in line with the principle of the English system of private international law that 'a person suing in this country must take the law as he finds it'.[16] In other words, the question 'whether certain evidence proves a certain fact . . . is to be determined by the law of the country where the question arises.'[17] The answer to this question in many cases would be pre-determined by establishing jurisdiction in the plaintiff's preferred forum.[18] The importance of the law of the forum could be further strengthened by making reference to Article 6(3)(b) of Rome II, which allows a private antitrust claimant to base his claim on *lex fori* in cases where the markets in several countries have been affected.[19]

Moreover, it should be noted that when one talks about EU competition law actions, it is not 'competition between competition laws'[20] (as suggested by the authors of the report *Making Antitrust Damages Actions More Effective in the EU*[21]), but, since Articles 101 and 102 TFEU enjoy direct effect in all the Member States, it is rather promoting competition between the different jurisdictions for laying down conditions for bringing such actions. Such conditions might include, for example, the various rules related to the pre-trial discovery and the availability of opt-out collective redress proceedings and/or exemplary/punitive damages as well as the speed of the legal proceedings and the experience of judges in the different jurisdictions.

Kerber and Budzinski have put forward that 'The working properties of regulatory competition seem to depend crucially on specific preconditions, the institutional framework

[14] *Making Antitrust Damages Actions More Effective in the EU* (n 9) 555–56.

[15] N Khan, 'Damages for Breaches of Competition Law' at the Conference on 'Remedies for Breach of EU Law Revisited' held at King's College London on 18 June 2010 http://ukael.org/past_events_24_1030208799.pdf.

[16] *De la Vega v Vianna* (1830) 1 B & Ad 284, 288 (Tenterden CJ). See also: E Spiro, 'Forum Regit Processum (Procedure is governed by the *lex fori*)' (1969) *ICLQ* 949, 952; JJ Fawcett and JM Carruthers, *Cheshire, North & Fawcett Private International Law,* 14th edn (Oxford, OUP, 2008) 75–76.

[17] *Bain v Whitehaven Rly Co* (1850) 3 HL Cas 1, 19. See also: *Cheshire, North & Fawcett* (n 16) 83.

[18] M Illmer, 'Neutrality matters some thoughts about the Rome Regulations and the so-called dichotomy of substance and procedure in European private international law' (2009) *Civil Justice Quarterly* 237, 242.

[19] See more: M Danov, *Jurisdiction and Judgments in Relation to EU Competition Law Claims* (Oxford, Hart Publishing, 2010).

[20] *Making Antitrust Damages Actions More Effective in the EU* (n 9) 611.

[21] ibid 611.

for regulatory competition, and the kind of legal rules and regulations itself.'[22] Whilst, the private international law framework (and its clarity) will certainly have an important role to play when it comes to selecting where to litigate (or even whether to litigate at all), the cross-border litigation costs may affect the mobility of the potential (or at least some of the potential) claimants. These costs/risks could be multiplied if the institutional framework is allowing for parallel proceedings with regard to the same infringement and/or if the regulator's decision establishing an infringement is not really useful in a subsequent follow-on damages claim. There are some important questions related to the tactics of the litigants with regard to cross-border EU competition law actions as the current regime appears to be shaping litigants' strategies. The answer to these questions might be useful in identifying the course of the potential reform.

As already noted,[23] the Ashurst study, which was conducted in 2004, appears to indicate that the private antitrust enforcement in Europe may be characterised by its 'astonishing diversity and total underdevelopment'.[24] An indication that this largely continues to be the situation with regard to class actions, at least, could be strengthened by making reference to the very recent report on *Collective Redress in Antitrust*.[25] However, since the Ashurst Report was completed eight years ago, the following questions need to be considered. Is there an enforcement gap at the moment? If yes, why is there an enforcement gap and who should close it? How strong is the case for the national legislator to act? How strong is the case for addressing the variation of the national regimes at EU level? What type of reform would best address the specific issues arising in the context of cross-border EU competition law actions? The answers to these questions could not be derived solely by analysing the case law, as both research studies clearly show that the quantitative data about the actual private enforcement is very limited at the moment. Indeed, part of the point, which is made by the studies so far, is that there are not many cases at the moment.[26] The researchers were particularly interested in whether there were procedural and substantive law advantages for a claimant to bring his EU competition law action in one Member State rather than another. The answer to this question was important, as it has been claimed that 'the age-old gap between the procedural families in Europe, especially the gap between the Civil Law and Common Law countries, has been reduced in size'.[27] But, do jurisdictional differences make a difference in an enlarged Europe?

Hence, it was necessary to turn to the views of legal practitioners and policy-makers. In this context, the researchers have undertaken a qualitative research project examining key questions concerning competition litigation with special reference to those cases with a cross-border element. Accordingly, as a part of their research, the researchers conducted qualitative interviews[28] with legal practitioners from Germany, England and Wales as well as with policy-makers from Brussels. Empirical data was required in order to identify the

[22] W Kerber and O Budzinski, 'Towards a Differentiated Analysis of Competition Laws' (2003) *ZWeR – Journal of Competition Law* 411, 413.

[23] See Ch 1.

[24] *Ashurst Report* (n 2) 1.

[25] *Collective Redress in Antitrust* (n 3).

[26] *cf.* the UK report delivered as a part of the Ashurst Study http://ec.europa.eu/competition/antitrust/actionsdamages/national_reports/united_kingdom_en.pdf.

[27] CH van Rhee, 'Introduction' in CH van Rhee (ed), *European Traditions in Civil Procedure* (Antwerp, Itersentia, 2005) 3, 22.

[28] HJ Rubin and IS Rubin, *Qualitative Interviewing: The Art of Hearing Data* (Thousand Oaks CA, SAGE Publications, 1995) 3–4.

important issues which appear to be affecting and shaping the litigants' tactics under the current regime. Once these issues were identified, then it would be possible to address head on the question if the current institutional framework is suited to deal with the challenges of private antitrust enforcement. If the current framework is not working well, then the empirical data might suggest which issues may need to be addressed by the legislator as a priority. An important hypothesis to be tested in this context is that an EU legislative reform must be undertaken, if the EU competition law provisions are to be enforced consistently across Europe.

III. RESEARCH METHODOLOGY

The researchers employed various research methods for testing the hypotheses. In addition to employing traditional library-based legal research methods (ie gathering information from the reported case law, governmental and non-governmental organisations' reports and academic publications), the researchers thought that it would be useful to have the opinions of policy-makers and legal practitioners, to consider their views on how private EU competition law actions are functioning at the moment and how they could and should be developed. The gathered data provided the researchers with the information which would be necessary for them to construe 'reality' and to do the study in a constructivist vein.[29]

Given that the study aims to identify how the cross-border EU competition law actions should be accommodated in Europe, the diverse legal and cultural traditions across Europe were taken account of.[30] As already noted, it is well established that today's European Union is integrating two major legal traditions – the civil law and the common law.[31] Bearing this in mind, it was felt that research, seeking to identify what the appropriate direction of possible reforms would be, should consider how EU competition law actions are functioning in countries representing the different legal traditions in Europe.

It is well established that any harmonisation of law should be preceded by comparative studies as, for example, the studies summarised in the Ashurst Report and Collective Redress in Antitrust Report. However, it has been noted that 'such comparison must be more than a pedestrian compilation of similarities and differences'.[32] Any such comparison must take account of the dynamics of the rules, and the way they shape the litigants tactics with regard to cross-border EU competition law actions. Such a comparison would be particularly important in determining whether substantive law rules require harmonisation at EU level or rather whether the private international law instruments, which are already

[29] NG Onuf, *The World of Our Making: Rules and Rule in Social Theory and International Relations* (South Carolina, University of South Carolina Press, 1989) 5; M Zehfuss, *Constructivism in International Relations: The Politics of Reality* (Cambridge, CUP, 2002) 2; NG Onuf, 'Constructivism: A User's Manual' in V Kubalkova, N Onuf and P Kowert (eds), *International Relations in a Constructed World* (Armonk, ME Sharpe, 1998) 58–59.

[30] R Wilson and W Dissanayake, 'Introduction: Tracking the Global/Local' in R Wilson (ed), *Global/Local: Cultural Production and the Transnational Imaginary* (Durham NC, Duke University Press, 1996); F Jameson and M Miyoshi, *The Cultures of Globalization* (Durham NC, Duke University Press, 1998).

[31] P Legrand, 'Against a European Civil Code' (1997) 62 *MLR* 44.

[32] HC Gutteridge, *Comparative Law,* 2nd edn (Cambridge, CUP, 1949) 174 quoted in M Matteucci, 'The Methods of the Unification of Law' in UNIDROIT International Institute for the Unification of Private Law, *Unification of Law* Vol II (Rome, Editions UNIDROIT, 1957) 39.

harmonised, require an amendment (or a number of amendments for that matter) in order to be suited for promoting inter-jurisdictional regulatory competition in the context of cross-border EU competition law actions.[33]

In order to consider how the EU competition law actions are functioning in two of the leading jurisdictions representing different legal traditions in Europe, qualitative interviews were conducted with legal practitioners in Germany and England, as well as with policy-makers in Brussels. The inclusion of the two categories (legal practitioners and policy-makers) can be justified as follows. First, the practising lawyers from Germany and England are well placed to answer questions regarding both consumer claims and claims by undertakings. Consumers and businesses normally need to use lawyers to litigate. The lawyers, being litigators, would know inter alia about the concerns of consumers and businesses. Given that the Georgetown project on private antitrust litigation appears to suggest that 'the vast majority of cases, possibly as many as 88 percent in [their] sample, settle before trial', it seems clear that the legal practitioners would have some useful insights as to how EU competition law litigation is functioning at the moment.[34] Indeed, legal practitioners were well placed to provide us with information about the four phases of litigation as identified by the academic literature. It is well established that:

> private litigation is part of a larger overall system consisting of four distinct phases: the business conduct of potential litigants, the suing decision of potential plaintiffs, the settlement offers of the litigants once a dispute has arisen, and the litigation strategies and expenditures of both parties if settlement cannot be reached.[35]

In particular, it was interesting to find out how the business conduct of potential litigants would affect potential plaintiffs' decision to sue. The other factors which would influence potential claimants' decision to sue were also of interest in the context of the policy objectives of our study. Additionally, legal practitioners were well placed to suggest why so many of the initiated EU competition law disputes settle as they have experience of settlement negotiations that are by their nature confidential and not reported. Finally, we wanted to take account of the litigation strategies used when a settlement cannot be reached.[36]

Secondly, the project examines possible proposals for the reform of the European Civil Justice system to accommodate the post-2003 policy of the EU favouring private law enforcement of EU competition law. The views of EU officials from Brussels are therefore very important; indeed, it has been submitted that the EU has competence to legislate,[37] and in view of the cross-border nature of EU competition law actions any legislative reform might be most effective at the EU level. In some regards, only EU-level reform may be

[33] *Making Antitrust Damages Actions More Effective in the EU* (n 9) 611.

[34] See S Salop and L White, 'Private Antitrust Litigation: An Introduction and Framework' in L White (ed), *Private Antitrust Litigation, New Evidence, New Learning* (Cambridge MA, MIT Press, 1988) 1, 23. See also: B Rodger, 'Private Enforcement of Competition Law, the Hidden Story: Competition Litigation Settlements in the United Kingdom, 2000–2005', (2008) 29 *European Competition Law Review* 96. See also: B Rodger, 'Competition Law Litigation in the UK Courts: A Study of all Cases 2005–2008: Part I', (2009) 2 GCLR 93; B Rodger, 'Competition Law Litigation in the UK Courts: A Study of all Cases 2005–2008: Part II', (2009) 3 GCLR 136.

[35] Salop and White (n 34) 16.

[36] ibid.

[37] F Rizzuto, 'Does the European Community have Legal Competence to Harmonise National Procedural Rules Governing Private Actions for Damages for Infringements of European Community Antitrust Rules', (2009) GCLR 29. Compare: From the Board, 'Two Steps Forward and One Step Back: Harmonizing the Unharmonizable', (2011) 38 *Legal Issues of Economic Integration* 207–11.

appropriate, again suggesting that the perspectives of policy makers and practitioners engaged at the EU level is most valuable.[38]

The researchers randomly[39] selected participants from each class (legal practitioners and policy-makers). The random selection was intended to ensure that the views of respondents were representative. Lawyers were randomly selected from the legal directories where they have featured on the basis of their experience in competition law. Although the legal directories are not themselves free of bias, they presented an opportunity to sample randomly which seemed preferable to other methods such as selection based on reputation, which might be prone to subjective bias. In the UK, the researchers approached both barristers and solicitors. There was of course a risk that the sample would over-represent defendants' interests, as most competition practice is heavily focused on defence, although this trend is certainly changing. To reduce this risk, a number of plaintiff-focused firms were also included in the sample. Additionally, there is also no reason in principle to assume that practising lawyers would not wish to see reform, as practice lost on the defence side might be made up for by claimant suits. Lawyers might reasonably be expected to be neutral between working for defendants or claimants, and the effect of reform on the overall amount of practice remains unclear.

Furthermore, as the study aims inter alia to look at the question if there is a need for a new Regulation to accommodate the cross-border EU competition law actions, the researchers invited leading legal practitioners and academics to present papers at a workshop as well as at a public conference. The importance to have different perspectives at the public conference discussing the possible solutions of the problems identified through our empirical study was extremely important. In this context, it should be noted that Mario Matteucci[40] in his capacity of Secretary General of the International Institute for the Unification of Private Law has strongly forewarned that:

> The failures experienced up to now are principally due to the fact that the promoters of unification have let the aspiration, undoubtedly generous but often utopian, towards universalism and towards the internationalisation of the law, get the better of the study of the concrete possibilities of realising such a unification.[41]

The researchers aimed to ensure that they will get the best from the study by taking into account a wide range of views on a specifically designated public conference on Cross-Border EU Competition Law Actions which was held in the London School of Economics on Friday 20 April 2012. Indeed, as already noted, other academics and legal practitioners (including a Judge from the General Court of the European Union and leading litigators from England, Germany and the Netherlands) presented papers, and have made written contributions to the book.

[38] See Art 81 TFEU. See also: P Beaumont and P McEleavy, *Private International Law, Anton* (Edinburgh, SULI/W Green, 2011) 16–17.

[39] WJ Goode and PK Hatt, *Methods in Social Research* (New York, McGraw-Hill, 1952) 214.

[40] Matteucci (n 32).

[41] ibid 39.

3

Cross-Border EU Competition Litigation: New Evidence from England and Wales

MIHAIL DANOV AND STEPHEN DNES*

I. INTRODUCTION

This chapter summarises the authors' findings from England and Wales in the hope of shedding some light on the litigation process, how it is functioning, and whether and how it might be reformed. To this end, the chapter will open with some preliminary remarks. Then, the authors will examine the issues of the legal certainty and consistent enforcement of EU competition law across Europe in order to indicate how these issues would affect litigants' strategies under the current system. In this context, the important role to be played by the European courts as well as the level of variation in the enforcement of EU competition law across Europe will be analysed. Then, the current litigation pattern in England and Wales will be carefully considered with a view to demonstrate that there is an enforcement gap at the moment. Finally, some tentative conclusions about the appropriate direction of reform will be put forward.

II. INTERVIEW PARTICIPANT SELECTION AND INTERVIEWS CONDUCTED BY THE UK-BASED RESEARCH TEAM

In the UK, the researchers wished to involve both barristers and solicitors. The sample of UK solicitors and barristers was drawn from the relevant sections of the *Legal 500*[1] and *Chambers and Partners*.[2] The sample from the European Commission was drawn from the relevant sections of the published personnel list. We included officials from the Legal Service within the European Commission as well as from both DG Competition[3] and

* The authors are grateful to the interview participants. The paper was presented at the 'Cross-border EU competition law actions' conference held at the London School of Economics on 20 April 2012. The authors are also very grateful to the conference participants, as well as to the participants in a workshop which took place at Brunel University on 12 November 2010. The usual disclaimer applies.

[1] *Legal 500*, editorial on London solicitors' EU and Competition practice at www.legal500.com/c/london/corporate-and-commercial/eu-and-competition.

[2] *Chambers and Partners*, list of London solicitors practising in competition/European law at www.chambersandpartners.com/UK/Editorial/38977.

[3] DG Comp personnel directory at http://ec.europa.eu/staffdir/plsql/gsys_www.branch?pLang=EN&pId=313&pDisplayAll=0.

Justice,[4] as the issues in the project concern both competition policy and cross-border civil justice. This resulted in a list of 338 people who were working as European Commission officials or legal practitioners in the area of EU and competition law, from which 192 individuals were randomly selected as potential participants. Safeguards were observed to ensure the best possible data quality and compliance with good research practices and ethical norms.[5]

Nineteen interviews involving 25 participants were conducted with legal practitioners in England and Wales from March to September 2011.[6] In addition, three interviews involving three participants were conducted with policy-makers in Brussels. The data so gathered was analysed with the qualitative research software, NVivo 9, to give an overall impression of competition litigation as it stands and its potential reform. The summary of the data will be presented below, after briefly considering the aims of competition law litigation.

III. PRELIMINARY REMARKS

The aim of competition law enforcement, stated very simply, is to deter infringements and provide redress to those who have suffered losses from them.[7] The primary means of enforcement in the EU has to date been through public enforcement, usually in the form of a fine after a complaint and investigation.[8] The investigations often involve the use of the European Commission's leniency policy, which is designed to provide incentives to whistleblowers by excusing them from some or all of the liability resulting from their conduct.[9] The aim of the EU legislator is 'to create an effective system of private enforcement by means of damages actions that complements, but does not replace or jeopardise, public enforcement.'[10]

The appropriate role for private competition law claims in Europe has been widely discussed in the literature.[11] The economic literature suggests that private enforcement may

[4] DG Justice personnel directory at http://ec.europa.eu/staffdir/plsql/gsys_www.branch?pLang=EN&pId=9151&pDisplayAll=0.

[5] Each potential participant was informed of the aims, methods, sources of funding and institutional affiliations of the researchers. Participants' informed consent was always sought before each interview; participants also signed a consent declaration. Participants were all over the age of 18 and engaged in a professional occupation, and were therefore in a position to decline a request for informed consent if they so wished. To ensure that participants could speak freely, they were also informed of the right to abstain from participation in the study or to withdraw consent to participate at any time without penalty. Every precaution was taken to respect and safeguard the privacy of each participant, and the confidentiality of each participant's information. All personal information was rendered anonymous as far as is possible and consistent with the needs of the study, and as early as possible in the data processing. Even though several participants were employed by large law firms, they could be expected to provide a fair account because of this anonymity, and their professionalism.

[6] Although some of the interviews involved more than one respondent, we decided that it would be only fair to count each interview as one case for data analysis purposes, although the separation of responses from different participants was always maintained.

[7] See more: WJ Wils, *Principles of European Antitrust Enforcement* (Oxford, Hart Publishing, 2005) 116–18; AP Komninos, *EC Private Antitrust Enforcement: Decentralised Application of EC Competition Law by National Courts* (Oxford, Hart Publishing, 2008) 7–8.

[8] Commission (EC), 'Report on Competition Policy 2010', COM (2011) 328, 14–18.

[9] Commission Notice on Immunity from Fines and Reduction of Fines in Cartel Cases, OJ 2006 C298/17.

[10] Commission (EC), 'White Paper on Damages actions for the breach of the EC antitrust rules', COM (2008) 165, section 1.2 final paragraph.

[11] Wils (n 7); J Basedow (ed), *Private Enforcement of EC Competition Law*, (Kluwer, 2007); Komninos (n 7); K Gotts (ed), *The Private Competition Enforcement Review*, 3rd edn (Law Business Research, 2010); J Basedow, JP Terhechte and L Tichy (eds), *Private Enforcement of Competition Law*, (Baden-Baden, Nomos, 2011).

further both pro- and anti-competitive aims, depending on the application, just as with public enforcement.[12] There have been persistent calls to encourage increased private litigation of competition law claims in Europe for some years,[13] although these have sometimes proved controversial[14] just as they have in discussions of similar reforms in other jurisdictions.[15] A major aim of modernisation implemented under Regulation 1/2003 was to encourage private claims, in part by replacing the centralised enforcement system, which was set up by Regulation 17,[16] with a directly applicable exception system. National Competition Authorities and Member States' courts were therefore given the power to apply not only Article 101(1) TFEU (ex Art 81(1) TEC) and Article 102 TFEU (ex Art 82 TEC), which had been deemed to have direct effect by virtue of the Court of Justice case law,[17] but also the exemption in Article 101(3) TFEU (ex Art 81(3) TEC), whose application had previously been reserved to the European Commission.[18]

Since 1 January 2004, Member States' courts have therefore been in a position to provide redress for competition law claims much more fully than before. Private enforcement seeks to complement public enforcement by allowing those who have suffered from a competition law infringement to bring a legal action before a court.[19] Thus a downstream supplier, consumer, or even a competitor might bring a claim to recover for losses suffered from the anti-competitive conduct[20] or to enjoin future anti-competitive conduct.[21] The UK Government has recently launched public consultations seeking to reform the UK regime for private actions in competition law.[22] The contemplated reform is meant to 'allow consumers and businesses to obtain compensation for losses they have suffered as a result of anticompetitive behaviour'.[23] The cross-border nature of most European competition law infringements, in which damages would often be suffered by businesses and consumers in a number of jurisdictions, could complicate the picture, however. It is well known that one of the underlying aims of the European Union, perhaps even the primary aim, has been the creation of an internal market in which the same terms of trade prevail throughout the

[12] This possibility is noted throughout economic analysis of antitrust enforcement. See W Landes, 'Optimal Sanctions for Antitrust Violations', (1983) 50 *University of Chicago Law Review* 652; W Baumol and J Ordover, 'Use of Antitrust to Subvert Competition', (1985) 28(2) *Journal of Law and Economics* 247; W Breit and K Elzinga, 'Private Antitrust Enforcement: The New Learning', (1985) 28(2) *Journal of Law and Economics* 405; F Easterbrook, 'Detrebling Antitrust Damages', (1985) 28(2) *Journal of Law and Economics* 445.

[13] Commission (EC), 'Modernisation of the Rules implementing Arts 85 and 86 of the EC Treaty' (White Paper) Programme 99/027.

[14] WJ Wils, 'Should Private Antitrust Enforcement be Encouraged in Europe' (2003) 26 *World Competition* 473 (arguing against private enforcement).

[15] K Roach and M Trebilcock, 'Private Enforcement of Competition Laws', (1996) *Osgoode Hall Law Journal* 461, 472.

[16] Council Regulation (EEC) 17 of 6 February 1962: first Regulation implementing Arts 81 and 82 of the Treaty OJ 1962 L13/204.

[17] Case 127/73 *BRT v SABAM* [1974] ECR 51 [14–16]; Case C-282/95 P *Guerin Automobiles v Commission* [1997] ECR I-1503 [39]; Case C-453/99 *Courage Ltd v Crehan* [2001] ECR I-6297 [23].

[18] See Recital 4 of Council Regulation (EC) No 1/2003 of 16 December 2002 on the implementation of the rules on competition laid down in Arts 81 and 82 of the Treaty OJ 2003 L1/1.

[19] Commission Staff Working Paper, Annex to the Green Paper on damages actions for breach of the EC antitrust rules SEC(2005) 1732 [1–3].

[20] *Courage* (n 17); Joined Cases C-295/04–C-298/04 *Manfredi v Lloyd Adriaticco* [2006] 5 CMLR 17.

[21] *Purple Parking Ltd and Meteor Parking Ltd v Heathrow Airport Ltd* [2011] EWHC 987 (Ch).

[22] Department for Business Innovation & Skills, *Private Actions in Competition Law: A Consultation on Options for Reform,* 24 April 2012 www.bis.gov.uk/assets/biscore/consumer-issues/docs/p/12-742-private-actions-in-competition-law-consultation.pdf. The BIS's proposed options for reform were discussed at a BIICL seminar, 'Rapid-Response Seminar: Private Actions in UK competition law: BIS's proposed options for reform', British Institute of International and Comparative Law, London, 9 May 2012.

[23] ibid p 3.

EU.[24] This is likely to have been a major factor in the increase in cross-border trade in European countries.[25] Despite being a testament to the success of the European Union at breaking down barriers to cross-border trade, this aspect of the internal market poses a challenge for competition litigation which increasingly must take on a cross-border element. In these cross-border cases, the current EU private international law framework should be used to allocate jurisdiction and identify the applicable national laws.[26] Given that the relevant private international law rules may not be suited to deal with the challenges of private antitrust enforcement,[27] the authors demonstrate that the level of national procedural autonomy and its tension with the effective enforcement of EU law will need to be looked at carefully by the EU legislator as the level of variation across Europe brings even more legal uncertainty,[28] which seemingly affects litigants strategies in particular deterring SMEs and consumers from bringing actions.

IV. LEGAL CERTAINTY AND CONSISTENT ENFORCEMENT OF EU COMPETITION LAW: SIGNIFICANT ISSUES UNDER THE CURRENT SYSTEM

Lack of legal certainty was first raised as an issue by the authors of the Ashurst Report.[29] Indeed, the cross-border nature of many competition law actions poses the question whether it would be possible to improve antitrust enforcement by increasingly relying on private parties to bring claims, while maintaining certainty and predictability in the rules to prevent the system becoming swamped with costs and delay. Another point of crucial importance in the EU system is whether this could occur without undermining the consistency of the rules and their enforcement in the different Member States.

As already noted, the main EU competition law Articles, Articles 101 and 102 of the Treaty on the Functioning of the European Union (hereafter TFEU), do not indicate how the defendant's liability is to be determined and how the assessment of antitrust damages is to be made by national courts. The Court of Justice has held that a person who is injured by anti-competitive practice or conduct must be able to seek compensation for actual loss and loss of profit plus interest.[30] It is well established that an EU competition law damages

[24] See Art 2 TEU; Art 3 TFEU.

[25] Exports as a percentage of gross domestic product increased in France from 14.65% in 1960 to 23.27% in 2009; in Germany, from 20.21% in 1960 to 40.83% in 2009; and in the Netherlands from 48.89% in 1960 to 69.22% in 2009. World Bank, *World Development Indicators* (Washington DC, World Bank, 2012). In the case of the UK, trade with the EU has increased from 35% of all trade in goods and services upon UK accession to the European Economic Area in 1973 to over half today, and the EU now accounts for 54% of foreign direct investment into the UK. See A MacDonald and C Bryan-Low, 'UK's Ambivalence on Europe,' *The Wall Street Journal Europe*, 10 January 2012, 6.

[26] See: Recitals 22 and 23 of the Rome II Regulation; M Monti, 'Competition Law Reform', speech made at the CBI Conference on Competition Law Reform, London, 12 June 2000 at http://ec.europa.eu/comm/competition/speeches/text/sp2000_008_en.html. See also: M Danov, *Jurisdiction and Judgments in Relation to EU Competition Law Claims* (Oxford, Hart Publishing, 2010); J Basedow, S Francq and L Idot (eds), *International Antitrust Litigation: Conflict of Laws and Coordination* (Oxford, Hart Publishing, 2012).

[27] M Danov, 'EU Competition Law Enforcement: Is Brussels I suited to dealing with all the challenges?' (2012) 61 ICLQ 27. See also: Ch 13.

[28] See also: D Waelbroeck, D Slater and G Even-Shoshan, *Study on the Conditions of Claims for Damages in Case of Infringement of EC Competition Rules (Ashurst Report)* http://ec.europa.eu/competition/antitrust/actionsdamages/comparative_report_clean_en.pdf, p 131.

[29] Ashurst Report (n 28) 10, 120 and 131.

[30] *Manfredi* (n 20) [26].

action is a mixture of EU law and Member States' laws. First, a claimant must show as a matter of EU law that there is a breach of Articles 101 and/or 102 TFEU. Secondly, it must be shown, as a matter of national law, that the defendant, by committing the particular EU competition law infringement, has caused damage to the claimant.[31] It has been submitted that 'The principle of national procedural autonomy means that in considering the issues of causation and quantum, it is appropriate first to apply the ordinary domestic rules applicable to claims of breach of statutory duty.'[32] The Member States' courts' procedural rules (eg standard of proof, disclosure rules) could have an important role to play in this context. Furthermore, depending on the applicable substantive laws, there could be different amounts of damages awarded as, for example, different countries may have different rules with regard to remoteness of damages, availability/non-availability of exemplary or punitive antitrust damages, and availability/non-availability of the pass-through defence.

A. Consistent Enforcement

Although the participants were not asked to specify the Member States which appear to be attracting more EU competition law actions, six participants volunteered that England and Wales, Germany and the Netherlands are amongst the leading jurisdictions at the moment. A further participant also mentioned England and Wales, Germany and the Netherlands as well as Spain. This appears to suggest that some Member States may be attracting more cross-border EU competition law actions than others, which is in line with the data available on the European Commission's website.[33]

In view of the cross-border nature of competition litigation, a fundamental question concerning our enquiry is whether there is any advantage to suing in one jurisdiction over another. Interview questions therefore raised the issue of jurisdictional selection, with regard to the risk of inconsistent application and enforcement. Twenty respondents thought that claimants could gain some procedural (and/or substantive law) advantages by bringing their claim in one jurisdiction rather than another.[34] However, two participants drew our attention to the fact that lawyers would normally be qualified in one jurisdiction only, and as a result they might have a bias towards their own jurisdiction. Nonetheless, on 17 occasions the disclosure rules were mentioned as a very important procedural aspect which could influence a claimant's decision where to bring an EU competition law action.[35] Only one participant was of the opinion that it would not matter where the claim is brought, and even there the participant in question appeared to think that a lawyer should take a client to the best forum to get the result for the claimant. The collected data[36] clearly indicate that there would be an advantage for a claimant to bring his claim in one country instead of another, so the cross-border aspects of competition law litigation would be an

[31] *Provimi v Aventis Animal Nutrition* [2003] EWHC 961 (Comm), [2003] ECC 29 [25].

[32] D Beard, 'Damages in Competition Law Litigation' in Ward and Smith, *Competition Litigation in the UK* (London, Sweet & Maxwell, 2005) 257, 270.

[33] See more: EUROPA – European Commission – Competition, 'National Judgments' http://ec.europa.eu/competition/elojade/antitrust/nationalcourts/. See also: S Peyer, 'Myths and Untold Stories – Private Antitrust Enforcement in Germany' (2010) http://papers.ssrn.com/sol3/papers.cfm?abstract_id=1672695&.

[34] See more below.

[35] See more below.

[36] See more below.

important factor to be taken into account by the policy-makers. There would be at least two important issues to be considered in this context. First, there would be cost implications[37] for claimants who wish to gain advantages by bringing their claim in another Member State. It is well established that a 'cross-border litigant may, as a practical matter, require two lawyers, one in his Home State to give preliminary advice, and one in the Host State to conduct the litigation.'[38] Thus, the cross-border litigation costs would be an important factor to be considered by consumers and SMEs who may prefer to sue in their home states[39] which seems to indicate that only large/sophisticated claimants could afford to be selective when deciding where to bring their claims.

Secondly, if claimants could gain advantages by bringing their claim in one jurisdiction rather than another, then it appears that jurisdictional differences would matter. In the European context, this would be a very important issue as jurisdictional differences might lead to inconsistent application of EU competition law. In view of that, the next question was whether these jurisdictional differences are leading to inconsistencies in the application of EU competition law. On 15 occasions, participants have submitted that there is a risk that the Member State courts apply EU competition law inconsistently at the moment. Two of them even thought that this is a fact of life. Six participants, however, thought that despite the fact there is some risk, such a risk could be managed through national appeals, and using the Commission's guidance and assistance. One of the latter group, nonetheless, was highly concerned at the possibility of widespread recognition of national competition authority (NCA) decisions, for fear that this would privilege consistency at the expense of quality and probity at the hands of some less-experienced regulators.

These concerns suggest that the increased private enforcement of European competition law suggests an increased role for the European Courts in dealing with preliminary references,[40] as well as appeals from public enforcement[41] which may accompany increased private claims.

B. The Role of the European Courts: Is There a Need for Reform?

The Court of Justice would therefore seem to have an important role to play in order to ensure uniform application and interpretation of EU competition law.[42] In a report dated January 2000, a European Commission Working Party observed that if in future there is a significant increase in EU competition law cases before the European Courts, jurisdiction to rule on preliminary references in this area might be assigned to the General Court.[43] In view of this, certain questions sought to take account of participants' views on how the

[37] See more below.

[38] Green Paper from the Commission, *Legal Aid in Civil Matters: The Problems Confronting the Cross-border Litigant* COM(2000) 51 final 9.

[39] See more: section V below.

[40] Art 267 TFEU.

[41] Arts 256 and 263 TFEU.

[42] Adaptation of the provisions of Title IV of the Treaty establishing the European community relating to the jurisdiction of the Court of Justice with a view to ensuring more effective judicial protection ('Communication from the Commission') COM(2006) 346 final. See also: Information Note on references from national courts for a preliminary ruling OJ 2009 C297/1.

[43] 'Report by the Working Party on the Future of the European Communities' Court System' (Working Party for the European Commission, January 2000), 34–35 at http://ec.europa.eu/dgs/legal_service/pdf/due_en.pdf.

current EU courts are currently functioning, and how the EU legal system could be improved to accommodate cross-border EU competition law actions. On nine occasions, participants thought that the current system is not wholly adequate. Four major shortcomings were put forward by the respondents.

First, delay was a major concern, as the participants thought that it takes far too long for the European Courts to deliver judgments. The authors think that this delay could lead to concern that the preliminary reference system might be abused by defendants to delay, possibly leading to an unfavourable settlement for claimants. Defendants might also cease the competitive abuse long before the case is remitted to a national court, rendering the case moot, but possibly undermining a complete remedy. The problem is compounded by the *periculum in mora* requirement for interim relief in the waiting period, which in some circumstances means that undertakings may face bankruptcy before interim relief is available.[44] This is especially problematic for competition law claims, because the structure of a market could be severely distorted by a competitive abuse without any single company nearing bankruptcy. For example, an inefficient competitor might be able to expand at the expense of a more efficient rival through anti-competitive means during the waiting period, but *ex post* relief may not be as effective as a carefully applied interim remedy. This presents a lacuna: although it is difficult to restrain inefficient abuses using interim measures, delay prevents effective redress even if the case reaches full trial.

Secondly, it was thought that sometimes the Court of Justice may avoid dealing with the most difficult issues. The authors think that it is doubtful that clear and consistent principles will emerge under the current system forbidding dissenting judgments. It would be naive to think that clear principles of competition enforcement and procedure will arise given the difference of opinion over the ambit of the substantive rules. Although any reform here would certainly be very controversial, and the current rules on unified judgments may serve other purposes, one consequence may be that relatively vague principles borne of compromise emerge from the cases.

Thirdly, on four occasions, the ability of some of the Members of the Court to deal with competition law issues was questioned. Each Member State is entitled to representation in the European judiciary. However, Member States vary dramatically in their experiences of competition law, especially the post-communist countries.[45] Many judges may therefore have limited exposure to competition law claims compared with, for example, the judges enforcing the federal competition laws in jurisdictions with more experience of competition law claims, whether in Europe or overseas.

Fourthly, even if the Court of Justice were to deal with the issues head-on, four participants thought that Member State courts might not be willing to refer to the Court of Justice. Nevertheless, on six occasions it was submitted that the current EU legal system is (probably) adequate. Another five participants had a mixed view on the adequacy of the current system. One of them thought that it was unsatisfactory that so few cases have reached the Court of Justice, but was of the opinion that preliminary references would be helpful and adequate to deal with some of the issues which were put forward in the Green and White Papers. Another three of them were unhappy with the delay, but one thought that preliminary references were

[44] See eg Joined Cases C-143/88 and C-92/89 *Zuckerfabrik Süderdithmarschen and Zuckerfabrik Soest* [1991] ECR I-415 [29].

[45] Although several Warsaw Pact countries did have a competition law on the books, it appears rarely to have been enforced. See T Varady, 'The Emergence of Competition Law in (Former) Socialist Countries,' (1999) 47(2) *American Journal of Comparative Law* 229.

a necessary and satisfactory solution in some cases, whilst the other two thought that the current system (despite the delay) allows Member States' legal orders to develop their own solutions in order best to accommodate cross-border EU competition law actions. Another participant noted that the preliminary reference system was not perfect because of its limited ability to review the correct application of law where significant questions of factual findings are involved, which is often the key question.

Participants were further asked whether a possibility for private parties to make an appeal on a point of EU competition law before any of the European Courts (eg the General Court) could solve the problem (or some of the problems). Eleven participants appeared to share the view that such a right of appeal 'would on the whole be to the detriment of effective and timely justice being done.' In particular, the increased delay which would result from such an appeal was a major argument raised, inter alia, by nine participants who were against private parties being allowed direct access to the European courts. The experience of the judges sitting in the Court was once again raised as another objection against such a right of appeal. The potential increase in the workload of the judges was another argument against the possible solution. One participant who was against it nonetheless went further to suggest that the possibility might be interesting if 'complete blue sky thinking' led to a competent and efficient separate new chamber, although this seemed unlikely.

Six other participants thought that it would probably be an attractive possibility. However, they raised some concerns which would need to be addressed. As noted, the competence of judges and their ability to deal with competition law issues was raised by five of them as an important issue to be addressed. Three participants went further to state that such a reform would require a special competition court or a special chamber.

Four other participants did not take a side, but shared very interesting views. One thought that this could go ahead only if there are no delays. Another one made the following observation:

> It's tricky. I mean the courts are already overloaded. Sure, instead of having once in a while a preliminary question if you have a more systematic and more frequent review, even though it does come at a certain cost as I said earlier, there's a certain virtue to have more of a federal court system, at least at the peak of it. I can see the charm of it, but whether it should be at number one spot of our priority list. Besides [it's] hardly sellable politically; that's probably for the next generation. Maybe.

Another participant noted that there would be some coherence to changing the 'judicial architecture' so that references go to the General Court as well as direct actions, but that making the change would add too much to the General Court's already heavy workload. Finally, another view was that the current system was only practically applicable to a case as a rare 'last possible option' when you are 'left with a series of judgments in the national courts which weren't to your liking . . . effectively putting an end to your claim.' In such a case, taking a point 'to the European courts' could 'breathe life back into the claim', but the participant thought that 'in most cases it's a tactic that wouldn't be used . . . too expensive, too time consuming, probably too uncertain as well.'

The authors share many of these views and think that there is a growing case that the growing demands on the European Courts implied by an increased role for private litigation might pose a problem if the Courts retain their current form. An illustrative example of the issue is the fairly recent, controversial judgment of the Court of Justice in *Pfleiderer*.[46]

[46] Case C-360/09 *Pfleiderer AG v Bundeskartellamt* [2011] 5 CMLR 219.

In this case the Court of Justice was asked to determine if someone who is adversely affected by a cartel may, for the purpose of bringing a damages claim, be given access to documents voluntarily submitted in that connection to an NCA by leniency applicants. The Court held that EU law must be interpreted as not precluding such a person from being granted access to such documents: 'It is, however, for the courts and tribunals of the Member States, on the basis of their national law, to determine the conditions under which such access must be permitted or refused by weighing the interests protected by European Union law.'[47] With respect, the difficult issues were not addressed head-on by the European judges, but instead the matter was referred back to the national courts. Although there is some appeal in leaving the matter to the EU legislator, as did the judges in *Pfleiderer*, this places a heavy responsibility on the legislator, which may face limitations of its own.

On the very next day, a similar issue to be addressed by the English High Court[48] involved a disclosure application in a follow-on damages action for an EU competition law infringement which was established by the Commission.[49] *Pfleiderer* appears to suggest that it is the national court which should conduct the weighing exercise referred to above, but Judge Roth nonetheless thought that it was necessary for the court to make an Article 15[50] request to the Commission. Although informal communication is encouraged under the Regulation, it is troubling that one of the most active and experienced jurisdictions for competition litigation appeared to have inadequate guidance under the European case law.

The Court of Justice's decision in *Pfleiderer*[51] and its subsequent application by the German court in *Pfleiderer*[52] and by the English court in *National Grid*[53] could therefore be seen as yet another indication of the possible deficiencies in the current European Courts' structure, suggesting that it may be ill-suited to ensure uniform application and interpretation of EU law, which may affect the consistent enforcement of EU competition law across Europe. There is a risk that increased private competition litigation in Europe might therefore lack adequate EU-level oversight. The result could be inconsistent enforcement of EU competition law across Europe, and increased uncertainty over the outcome of EU competition law cases, which appears to drive the very problems reforms have been supposed to address.

In this context, it should be noted that a high level of uncertainty surrounding competition law actions at the moment was noted on 15 occasions. According to participants, uncertainty may affect the willingness of the claimants to bring actions and deter SMEs and/or consumers from bringing actions as the uncertainty will increase the costs of competition litigation.[54] In particular, one participant has submitted:

> I've seen several cases where we've gone through some analysis of a potential claim and the clients have either given up or been apathetic because, yes, you might get half a million at the end of the day, but is it worth all the effort with all the uncertainty that you might lose or not [be] able to prove and so on and so forth?

[47] ibid [32].

[48] *National Grid Electricity Transmission PLC v ABB Ltd & Others* [2011] EWHC 1717 (Ch).

[49] Commission Decision of relating to a proceeding under Art 81 of the EC Treaty and Art 53 of the EEA Agreement Case Comp/F/38.899 – *Gas Insulated Switchgear* – C(2006)6762.

[50] Regulation 1/2003.

[51] *Pfleiderer* (n 46).

[52] In the *Pfleiderer* case, 'the German court ruled against disclosure of leniency documents'. The High Court referred to the judgment of the Amstgericht Bonn of 30 January 2012 in the *Pfleiderer* case. See *National Grid Electricity Transmission PLC v ABB Ltd & Others* [2012] EWHC 869 (Ch) [60].

[53] *National Grid* (n 52) [56 60].

[54] See more below.

Uncertainty may also allow defendants to prevent claims by employing delaying strategies.[55] The legal uncertainty which surrounds these actions in Europe taken together with the cross-border litigation risks might make the defendant more aggressive as he might escape liability even if he does not comply with EU competition law rules.[56]

On five occasions, participants went further to state that the current state of uncertainty might also drive settlement behaviour.[57] Furthermore, the fact that different Member States' legal orders may deal in different ways with such matters as disclosure, standard of proof, costs (eg the availability of contingency fees), the availability (or rather non-availability) of a pass-on defence, and the availability of punitive damages appears to suggest that there are some other important issues to be factored in by claimants when deciding whether and where to bring their EU competition law action. Such a deduction finds support in the literature which appears to suggest that these factors drive litigation and settlement patterns: the 'net expected values [of litigation] consist of four components: the benefit (or harm) of the business conduct at issue, the potential award, the costs of litigation, and the likelihood that the plaintiff prevails.'[58] It appears that claimants and defendants are engaged in nuanced weighing of these factors, which in turn affect the expected value of litigation, whether considered from the perspective of the welfare of an individual claimant, or the socially optimal level of litigation.

Therefore, it appears that there may be a case for legislative intervention in order to address the level of variation and the inherent uncertainty in the enforcement of EU competition law. Indeed, the principle of national procedural autonomy suggests that similar claims might be dealt with in different ways depending on the jurisdiction in which the claim is brought. Although the Member States' courts are under a duty to apply the same substantive rules, they may differ on crucial procedural points, which sometimes may determine the claim. Divergences on procedure, damages and costs all appear to play a leading role in competition litigation, and their relative importance may strengthen further the case for reform, as well as inform approaches to reform.

C. Procedure

The authors were particularly interested in whether there were procedural advantages for a claimant to conduct a trial in one Member State rather than another. On 20 occasions, it was submitted that a (sophisticated) claimant would normally consider Member States' procedural rules when deciding where to bring his EU competition law action. There was even the suggestion that procedural rules might be more significant than the amount of damages awarded in the choice of jurisdiction, with one participant submitting that 'the procedural rules . . . are much more important than the quantum of damages you will eventually get', 'because . . . getting something is better than getting nothing at all. And the procedural rules determine whether you get something at all, and when.' On that occasion, damages were referred to as a 'mere chimera number', compared with the 'paramount importance' of procedural rules.

[55] See more below.

[56] S Salop and L White, 'Private Antitrust Litigation: An Introduction and Framework', in L White (ed), *Private Antitrust Litigation, New Evidence, New Learning* (Cambridge MA, MIT Press, 1988) 1, 22.

[57] See more below.

[58] Salop and White (n 56) 18.

The most important aspects of procedure put forward by the participants could be summarised as follows. First, disclosure and discovery of evidence were considered to be very important considerations. As already noted,[59] on 17 occasions, the disclosure rules were mentioned as a very important procedural aspect which could influence a claimant's decision where to bring an EU competition law action. Disclosure would also benefit a defendant, especially if an action was brought in a jurisdiction where the pass-on defence is available. Secondly, the speed of the procedure (ie the time it takes for an award to be made, or for a claimant to force a settlement) was considered to be an important factor; this was submitted on 12 occasions. Thirdly, standing was mentioned as a possible problem on 10 occasions. However, it is only fair to note that, on five occasions, this was not regarded as the determinative problem. Nevertheless, five participants thought that standing could be an issue in cases involving consumer associations.

Seven participants submitted that the jurisdictional issue can be important: it seems that jurisdictional challenges could result in further delay and expenses.[60] Limitation periods also seemed important: seven participants outlined that limitation periods could be an important factor.[61] The experience of the judiciary was an important factor put forward by four participants, and three noted that the standard of proof is particularly important in many EU competition law damages cases. The multiplicity of courts was considered another important factor on two occasions. Finally, the method of proof, specifically whether there is scope to challenge a written report with oral questions, was also considered to be a relevant factor.

Overall, the prevailing view was clearly that the procedural rules are among the most important factors, if not the most important factor, to be considered by both claimants and defendants in an EU competition law action, and a wide range of procedural considerations dominated most responses. This can be explained by the fact that key procedural questions such as standard of proof and the availability of disclosure, which may be of fundamental importance to the success of a claim, vary depending on the Member State in which the claim is litigated. This may encourage strategic use of particular jurisdictions where rules are the most favourable to claimants, or even pre-emptive applications to jurisdictions where procedure most favours defendants. This could well result in the same competition law infringement being dealt with inconsistently depending on where the action is brought, even in the case of a pan-European cartel with claimants and cartelists scattered throughout the EU.[62]

[59] See above.

[60] *Provimi* (n 31); *SanDisk Corporation v Koninklijke Philips Electronics and others* [2007] EWHC 332 (Ch), [2007] Bus LR 705; *Cooper Tire & Rubber Company v Shell Chemicals UK Ltd* [2009] EWHC 2609 (Comm); *Cooper Tire & Rubber Company Europe Ltd & Others* [2010] EWCA Civ 864; *Toshiba Carrier UK Ltd and Other v KME Yorkshire Ltd & Others* [2011] EWHC 2665 (Ch); *Toshiba Carrier UK Ltd and Other v KME Yorkshire Ltd & Others* [2012] FWCA Civ 169; *Toshiba Carrier UK Ltd and Other v KME Yorkshire Ltd & Others* [2012] EWCA Civ 1190; *Ryanair Ltd v Esso Italiana Srl* – still pending before the Court of Appeal – Case Reference A3/2012/0471. See also: *Emerson Electric Co v Morgan Crucible Company PLC and Ors* [2011] CAT 4; *Emerson Electric Co v Morgan Crucible Company PLC and Ors* – still pending before the Court of Appeal – Case Reference C3/2011/1658.

[61] *Deutsche Bahn v Morgan Crucible Company* [2012] EWCA Civ 1055.

[62] *Provimi* (n 31); *Cooper Tire* (n 60).

D. Damages

Under the European case law, damages awards must not discriminate between European and domestic claims, and European claims must in some sense receive an effective remedy.[63] The level of award can vary substantially, however, the only guidance being that punitive damages *may* be available.[64] This could lead to different awards of damages for the same violation of European competition law if, for example, some jurisdictions reject punitive damages in private antitrust claims while others endorse them.[65]

The participants' views as to the importance of the level of damages which could be awarded in the various Member States were sought in order to find out whether the level of damages could affect forum selection. The participants' answers appear to indicate that the level of damages and their quantification is an important issue to be considered by a claimant in a cross-border EU competition law action. This is indeed submitted on 20 occasions, and is in line with literature suggesting that estimated damages are an important consideration at numerous points in the litigation pattern.[66]

A closer look at the data, however, indicates that there are two things that should be noted in this respect. First, as already noted, the potential damages which could be awarded would often be pre-determined by the procedure rules. Secondly, the availability of a pass-on defence was nonetheless highlighted by several respondents. The importance of knowing whether a pass-on defence was available was put forward on 13 occasions. One participant also flagged up the importance of the pass-on defence to the decisions of litigation funders over whether to fund litigation. The availability of a pass-on defence would therefore seem to enter into the choice of forum.

Inconsistency on this point would be a particular problem for EU competition law claims, because a single anti-competitive overcharge may ripple through a production chain, increasing prices of many products and affecting parties across the EU. Allowing each party to claim for the diffuse damage could therefore result in overcompensation, and might even compensate those who had managed to pass on the overcharge to their purchasers with no substantial loss.[67] It has been noted by the Commission in the White Paper that 'infringers should be allowed to invoke the possibility that the overcharge might have been passed on. Indeed, to deny this defence could result in **unjust enrichment** of purchasers who passed on the overcharge and in undue **multiple compensation** for the illegal overcharge by the defendant.'[68] On the other hand, if a windfall (or unjust enrichment) results from the pass-on defence not being available, it is hard to understand why the *infringer* is more deserving of this windfall than the direct purchaser who was buying the cartelised

[63] *Courage* (n 17) [26–29]; *Manfredi* (n 20) [72].

[64] *Manfredi* (n 20) [26].

[65] For example, the general rejection of punitive damages where a public fine has been imposed in *Devenish Nutrition Ltd v Sanofi-Aventis SA* [2007] EWHC 2394; [2008] 2 WLR 637 (Ch); Case Number: 1178/5/7/11, *2 Travel Group Plc (In Liquidation) v Cardiff City Transport Services Ltd* [2012] CAT 19.

[66] B Cornell, 'The Incentive to Sue: An Option-Pricing Approach', (1990) 19(1) *Journal of Legal Studies* 173.

[67] This is sometimes referred to as the 'Illinois Brick' problem after a major American case addressing it, *Illinois Brick Co v Illinois*, 431 US 720 (1977). The problem is especially severe in the increasingly prominent case of the 'hub-and-spoke' conspiracy, in which several levels in a distribution chain are involved with the communication required for a cartel. See O Odudu, 'Indirect Information Exchange: The Constituent Elements of Hub and Spoke Collusion', (2011) 7(2) *European Competition Journal* 205.

[68] White Paper (n 10) [2.6] (emphasis in original).

product.[69] The Commission itself has previously submitted that 'passing on does not necessarily result in the unjust enrichment of the claimant because it can equally result in a reduced volume of sales as the trader has to raise prices.'[70] In view of the foregoing, the availability of the pass-on defence appears to be a very political and practical question which seemingly requires some attention by the legislator. Substantive differences appear to be a key issue, not least because the EU courts have held such issues as for example the availability or non-availability of a pass-on defence to be down to national procedural autonomy when they are probably best described as substantive.

F. Costs

Interview questions attempted to explore the role of costs in the decision to bring a competition law case, and whether different cost rules play a role in forum selection.

On 12 occasions, it was submitted that competition law litigation is expensive. One participant went further to clarify that the primary factor is the evidentiary stage, where expensive discovery motions obtain evidence requiring further analysis by both lawyers and economists. More specifically, 11 participants thought that the high cost of the cross-border EU competition litigation could potentially deter some claimants from bringing EU competition law actions. Costs can be very high in all litigation,[71] but may be especially high in competition law claims[72] where defendant companies tend to employ very expensive law firms, and where economic experts are frequently employed at considerable expense. The cost of competition law litigation may be fuelled by the high level of uncertainty which appears to surround competition law actions.[73]

The problem is particularly acute for consumers or their representatives, who often lack the means to finance the risk presented by bringing a claim,[74] or for small and medium enterprises which may lack the resources to take on dominant players in 'bet-the-company' litigation.[75] The assertion that the weak or diffuse interests of such claimants are to be addressed by public enforcement may understate the political constraints faced by public enforcers,[76] which may dictate against the application of resources to smaller cases

[69] See M Rush, *The Defence of Passing On* (Oxford, Hart Publishing, 2006) 21. See more: O Odudu and G Virgo, 'Remedies for Breach of Statutory Duty', (2009) 68 *Cambridge Law Journal* 32 (discussing gain-based remedies).

[70] Commission Staff Working Paper, Annex to the Green Paper on Damages Actions for breach of the EC rules SEC(2005) 1732 para 169. The text is also cited in V Milutinovic, 'Private Enforcement: Upcoming Issues' in G Amato and C-D Ehlermann (eds), *EC Competition Law: A Critical Assessment* (Oxford, Hart Publishing, 2007) 725, 744.

[71] See C Hodges, M Tulibacka and S Vogenauer, 'The Oxford Study on Costs and Funding of Civil Litigation', in C Hodges, M Tulibacka and S Vogenauer (eds), *The Costs and Funding of Civil Litigation* (Oxford, Hart Publishing, 2010) 139. For example, repayment to a consumer of the €200 price paid for a product not delivered in the UK cost £105 in the study.

[72] Case No 1178/5/7/11, *2 Travel Group PLC (In Liquidation) v Cardiff City Transport Services Ltd* [2011] CAT 30, 14 October 2011 [17]. See also: *Yeheshkel Arkin v Borchard Lines and Others* [2005] EWCA Civ 655.

[73] See above.

[74] Third party funding from for-profit litigation funders may be available for these claimants: See J Peysner, 'England and Wales', in Hodges, Tulibacka and Vogenauer (eds) (n 71) 294.

[75] See discussion below of types of claimants.

[76] Commission Notice on the handling of complaints by the Commission under Arts 81 and 82 of the EC Treaty OJ 2004 C101/65 para 8. Statistical analysis suggests that the politicisation of competition enforcement is a serious problem and may lead to the overrepresentation of politically mobile parties such as large businesses. For a summary of the literature from an American perspective, see W Shughart and F McChesney, 'Public choice theory and antitrust policy', (2010) 142(3) *Public Choice* 385.

in regional markets where private litigation may have the greatest promise to assist consumers and SMEs.[77]

The respondents' position on costs was not entirely clear-cut, however. Two participants thought that even though costs play a role, they would not generally deter the big companies that appear to be bringing the actions at the moment. Three other participants noted that claimants who have strong claims would have ways to deal with the costs, as such claimants could enter into contingency fee agreements or refer to litigation funders, hedge funds, etc. On three other occasions, participants thought that cost risks and potential damages claims would be weighed. In terms of the consistency between cost rules, one respondent went so far as to suggest that cost rules could determine the choice of jurisdiction even between those jurisdictions where competition litigation is the most developed, citing Germany, the Netherlands and the UK. This suggests that inconsistencies in the cost rules are indeed distorting jurisdictional choices, even where the systems have had the most chance to develop.

On the one hand, it should be noted that the high level of uncertainty surrounding EU competition damages claims taken together with high costs may be seen to provide inadequate incentives to bring claims when it would be socially desirable.[78] Indeed, it should be noted that EU competition law damages actions are intended to 'produce beneficial effects in terms of **deterrence** of future infringements and greater compliance with EC antitrust rules'.[79] On the other hand, cost-shifting rules may discourage the bringing of weak claims, while the absence of cost-shifting may encourage them, although economic models of litigation suggest that the interplay between cost-shifting and substantive rules is complex.[80] Increased private enforcement without attention to the role of cost-shifting in sifting out abusive claims could potentially lead to weak or unsubstantiated claims being brought in jurisdictions without appropriate safeguards in the hope of favourable settlements, a well-known strategic abuse of litigation.[81] Once again, because of the pan-European nature of many of the infringements, unscrupulous claimants could pursue this tactic following cartel enforcement: after public or private enforcement begins in a 'leading light' jurisdiction where enforcement is common, such as Germany or the Netherlands, weak claims could begin to pour in in jurisdictions lacking the necessary control mechanisms in the hope of favourable settlement, based on the fact that the cartel affects consumers across the EU. This distinguishing feature makes the role of cost rules especially important if reform is to expand the role of private competition litigation without exporting nuisance litigation.

Therefore, it appears that despite the fact that the overwhelming view appears to be that the rules on procedure are the most important factor for a claimant to consider, the laws

[77] eg *JJ Burgess v OFT* [2005] CAT 25, concerning access to a single crematorium in Stevenage, Hertfordshire, England.

[78] S Shavel, 'The social versus the private incentives to bring suit in a costly legal system', (1982) 11 *Journal of Legal Studies* 333, 336. See also: JA Ordover, 'Costly Litigation in the Model of Single Activity Accidents' (1978) 7 *Journal of Legal Studies* 243.

[79] White Paper (n 10) [1.2]. Emphasis in original.

[80] See HSE Graville, 'The Efficiency Implications of Cost Shifting Rules', (1993) 13 *International Review of Law and Economics* 3; CF Beckner III and A Katz, 'The Incentive Effects of Litigation Fee Shifting When Legal Standards Are Uncertain', (1995) 15 *International Review of Law and Economics* 205.

[81] So-called 'nuisance' suits might be brought in some jurisdictions. See S Shavel, 'Suit, settlement and trial: A theoretical analysis under alternative methods for the allocation of legal cost' (1982) 11 *Journal of Legal Studies* 55, 72. See also: D Crane, *The Institutional Structure of Antitrust Enforcement* (Oxford, Oxford University Press, 2011) 58. See more: KG Elzinga and WC Wood, 'The Costs of the Legal System in Private Antitrust Enforcement' in White (n 56) 107, 134; EA Snyder and TE Kauper, 'Misuse of the Antitrust Laws: The Competitor Plaintiff' (1991) 90 *Michigan Law Review* 551.

on damages and costs also influence a claimant's choice of forum as well as their tactics. On the other hand, the high level of uncertainty surrounding EU competition damages claims taken together with high costs might affect the defendants' tactics.[82]

V. LEGAL UNCERTAINTY AND ITS EFFECT ON THE LITIGANTS' TACTICS

The above analysis appears to suggest that there is a high level of uncertainty[83] surrounding procedural points, especially concerning the level of national procedural autonomy and assessment of damages.[84] In view of that, it seems that the specific points concerning the tactics of claimants and defence would be key to determining whether there is a need for addressing the existing level of variation in the Member States' laws, and what the appropriate direction of possible reforms would be. In this context, it would be important to determine if there is a link between the high level of uncertainty and behaviour of the litigants by looking at their tactics.

A. Claimants' Tactics

As already indicated, seven participants submitted that the jurisdictional issue is particularly important, given that jurisdictional challenges can result in further delay and expenses.[85] Given the cross-border nature of many EU competition law actions, another tactical question upon which participants' views were sought was whether claimants would find it beneficial to sue in their home state. In providing their answers, many participants made a distinction between claims brought by consumers and SMEs, on the one hand, and claims brought by big companies, on the other hand. On some occasions, it was submitted that it would be beneficial especially for SMEs or consumers to sue in their home states (nine cases). The authors think that suing before the courts in their home state could be an important consideration for consumers and SMEs, especially if factored in together with the increased litigation costs and risks in a cross-border case, which could potentially increase the level of uncertainty.

Some participants, however, thought that although it would usually be beneficial for a claimant to sue in the home state, this would not always be the key factor as it would also depend on the home state in question (10 cases). Other participants went further to state that suing at home would not be greatly beneficial for a claimant as there are more important factors to be considered: indeed, the home turf factor seems to be less important for big or sophisticated claimants (10 cases).

Since many EU competition law cases, and cartels in particular, could potentially involve a number of defendants, the respondents' views were sought on whether it would be

[82] Beckner III and Katz (n 80) 207.

[83] JE Calfee and R Craswell, 'Some Effects of Uncertainty on Compliance with Legal Standards' (1984) 70 *Virginia Law Review* 965; R Craswell and JE Calfree, 'Deterrence and Uncertain Legal Standards' (1986) 2 *Journal of Law, Economics and Organisation* 279; AM Polinsky and S Shavell, 'Legal Error, Litigation and the Incentive to Obey the Law' (1989) 5 *Journal of Law, Economics and Organisation* 99.

[84] See also: Ashurst Report (n 28) 131.

[85] See above. See also: *Provimi* (n 31); *SanDisk* (n 60); *Cooper Tire* (n 60).

advantageous for a plaintiff to bring an EU competition law action against several defendants. On five occasions, it was submitted that it would be advantageous to bring multiple defendants actions. Such a tactic was justified by several factors. The most common factors that were put forward could be summarised as follows: (1) bringing the case in a jurisdiction which is more appropriate from the claimants' perspectives; (2) increasing the claimants' chances of getting a payout; (3) increasing the difficulties on the defence side of having to coordinate what they are doing procedurally; (4) accessing required information and/or documents through a disclosure order.

Nonetheless, the majority of the participants appear to prefer to go after one infringer initially, and then to go after another and, possibly, after that, to go after yet another. The latter approach has been favoured on 11 occasions. The main justifications that were put forward are as follows: (1) the defendant against whom the action was brought would normally bring in the other infringers; (2) the cost risk of suing one defendant is lower; (3) a settlement may be reached with the first, gaining compensation and possibly even useful evidence before moving on to the second defendant. The overwhelming majority of participants (including participants who would favour one approach over another) nevertheless say that the best approach would always have to be determined on a case-by-case basis by taking into account the factors enumerated above.

Therefore, it seems clear that the cost risks, which could be fuelled by the high level of uncertainty, would be an important factor to be considered in claims brought by consumers and SMEs who may be prone to economise on the costs.[86] The costs, however, would be less of an issue for large/sophisticated claimants who would rather gain some procedural (and/or substantive law) advantages by bringing their claim in one jurisdiction rather than another.

B. Defendants' Tactics

The defence strategy questions sought to take account of the respondents' opinions as to: (1) whether a defendant, who is threatened with an EU competition law action, would initiate a pre-emptive strike by bringing the case in a defendant-friendly jurisdiction before the claimant has the chance to bring it in a claimant-friendly one; (2) whether a defendant would employ any delaying strategies; (3) whether a more effective private enforcement system could undermine the leniency programme.

The majority of the participants have submitted that after the judgment in *Cooper Tire*, pre-emptive strikes would be a less attractive strategy for a defendant to employ. This was submitted on 15 occasions. Four participants observed that pre-emptive strikes would require a very specific case. Admittedly, pre-emptive strikes could be used in order for a defendant to have the case litigated where he wants it to be, this being submitted on five occasions. Another view, painting an interesting scenario, was that although it may seem 'very odd' 'to bring a declaration that you are not guilty of something,' one might 'try to influence the situation' using 'the threat of parallel actions in different member states.' It should however be noted that seven participants submitted that defendants threatened with a strong EU competition law case would rather try to settle.

[86] See more above. See also: Beckner III and Katz (n 80) 207.

On 15 occasions, it has been submitted that delaying would be quite a common strategy to be employed by a defendant in a cross-border EU competition law action. One respondent made the following candid submission:

> when [claimants] have filed their claim, make it as difficult as possible for them by picking a series of preliminary issues for interlocutory battles, so that will test the will of the claimant, spend their money, perhaps put them off and beat them down into some kind of settlement that they otherwise wouldn't have accepted.

Not all preliminary matters raised by the defence are abusive, however: five participants noted that preliminary matters are often raised simply because liability, and therefore damages, often hinge on a preliminary matter. Therefore, as already noted,[87] on the one hand, the high level of uncertainty may potentially deter claims brought by consumers and SMEs if they have no funding scheme in place. On the other hand, the high level of uncertainty may encourage large undertakings to bring such actions as a potential exposure to high costs for the defendants could drive their settlement behaviour. These tentative conclusions clearly indicate that the settlement as a tactical device should be carefully considered.

C. Settlements as a Tactical Device

As already noted, previous research has shown that a substantial number of the claims which were brought in the UK would eventually settle.[88] Indeed, it is established that parties would have strong incentives to settle, because a 'settlement avoids the costs and uncertainty associated with further litigation'.[89] In view of that, the authors thought that legal practitioners would be best placed to suggest why so many of the initiated EU competition law disputes settle. Participants divided when asked whether the high level of settlements reflected the weakness or strength of claims. Nonetheless, five participants thought that uncertainty, which would increase the litigation risks, could drive settlement behaviour in cross-border EU competition law cases. Five other participants were of the opinion that the high cost of competition litigation is the reason claimants settle. One participant thought that claimants 'take a view on what overcharge and pass through is, and try to avoid the costs of litigation and all the delays and all the rest of it, and quietly settle', 'the costs of litigation . . . often dictat[ing] that that is the appropriate approach'.

Different reasons may drive the settlement behaviour of the defendants. On four occasions, it was submitted that the defendants would normally want to 'put it behind them' and therefore enter into a settlement which indicates that a 'nuisance' factor may be taken into account in some suits. In other words, one might think that the high level of uncertainty may encourage large companies (eg large purchasers) to bring such claims in order to force a settlement, for example, with their suppliers (especially in follow-on cases where an infringement has been detected by the Commission or an NCA). Nonetheless,

[87] See above.

[88] B Rodger, 'Private Enforcement of Competition Law, The Hidden Story: Competition Litigation Settlements in the United Kingdom, 2000–2005', (2008) 29 *European Competition Law Review* 96. See also: B Rodger, 'Competition Law Litigation in the UK Courts: A Study of all Cases 2005–2008: Part I', (2009) 2 *Global Competititon Law Review* 93; B Rodger, 'Competition Law Litigation in the UK Courts: A Study of all Cases 2005–2008: Part II', (2009) 3 *Global Competititon Law Review* 136. See also: Salop and White (n 56) 23.

[89] Salop and White (n 56) 23.

four participants thought that the strength of the claim would be an important factor to be considered by the claimant, as a weak claim has no chance to settle. One participant noted that funding may sometimes be a factor which a defendant would consider before entering into a settlement which confirms once again that there may be a link between uncertainty, on the one hand, and costs and litigation risks, on the other.

This deduction finds support in the economic analysis of litigation, which appears to suggest that 'under the British system [of cost shifting], there will be a trial if and only if the plaintiff's estimate of the expected judgment exceeds at least the sum of their expected legal costs.'[90] Moreover, some claimants may be risk averse when faced with these costs.[91] Given the high cost of competition litigation,[92] which is fuelled by uncertainty, it should not therefore be surprising that so few cases proceed to trial. Taken cumulatively the costs, litigation risks and uncertainty may be the main reasons for claimants and defendants to settle. It has been submitted that 'the possibility of economising on litigation costs by settling can have adverse effects on the legal system when one or both parties use the threat of costly suit as a mechanism for inducing an adversary to submit to a costly settlement.'[93]

Widespread settlements do, however, pose an important question: there are many settlements, but one cannot say in isolation whether they are satisfactory.[94] A well-functioning settlement regime would provide cheap and speedy redress with an appropriate level of compensation. As things stand, there are very few indicators of whether the current state of settlements represents an efficient level of compensation, which might be an interesting area for future research. That said, it seems clear that the high costs, litigation risks and uncertainty taken cumulatively could be regarded as inadequate incentives for some claimants (consumers and SMEs) to bring EU competition law actions which would be socially desirable to provide compensation and to deter future infringements of EU antitrust rules. This raises the question whether there is an enforcement gap under the current system.

VI. LITIGATION PATTERN IN ENGLAND AND WALES: IS THERE AN ENFORCEMENT GAP?

The essential claim of those favouring more private litigation is that enforcement would improve with increased reliance on private parties to bring claims, whether as follow-on or stand-alone actions. In this context, it should be noted that private litigation across the world has certainly increased over recent decades. The most prominent jurisdiction to rely heavily on private enforcement is of course the United States, where private claimants are awarded treble damages and costs to represent the public interest in bringing their actions

[90] Shavel (n 81) 64.

[91] K Binmore, *Fun and Games: A Text on Game Theory* (Heath and Company, 1992) 193–94; A Farmer and P Pecorino, 'Pretrial Negotiations with Asymmetric Information on Risk Preferences,' (1994) 14 *International Review of Law and Economics* 273.

[92] *Cardiff City Transport* (n 72) [17]. See also: *Arkin* (n 80). See more, above.

[93] Salop and White (n 56) 27.

[94] For a summary of the law and economics literature, see R Cooter and D Rubinfeld, 'Economic Analysis of Legal Disputes and Their Resolution,' (1989) 27 *Journal of Economic Literature* 1067. The interplay of settlements and trials, especially regarding screening and information issues, suggests caution in analysing the efficient level of settlements.

as 'private attorneys general'.[95] Since procedural reforms in the 1970s, private antitrust cases have come to outnumber public enforcement in the United States by approximately a 10-to-one ratio.[96] In recent years, other jurisdictions have moved towards greater reliance on private litigation.[97]

The hybrid public and private nature of competition enforcement presents two important issues which need to be addressed in the context of the qualitative interviewing. First, it is worth considering whether claimants are actively bringing cross-border EU competition law actions in England and Wales. Secondly, respondents were asked whether a claimant would go first to the national competition authority and then proceed with a follow-on action before national courts or whether they would rather bring a stand-alone action before the courts. The answers to this question are particularly important in an EU context, as the current enforcement pattern of litigation in Europe appears to blend aspects of private and public enforcement, and this is especially noticeable in England and Wales.

A. Rise in Competition Litigation

The responses overwhelmingly suggest that competition litigation is picking up, and that follow-on actions outnumber stand-alone ones. In the vast majority of cases (18 out of 22), the participants are of the opinion that there are more EU competition law actions than there used to be; several participants went further to note that the number of actions may not disclose a significant number of settlements occurring as well. In this context, one participant noted that 'more of the litigation is getting to a trial, whereas previously the pattern was that the litigation came to an end fairly early on in the proceedings, usually because there was a settlement.' It was noted that the subject matter of the litigation has changed, with the same participant noting that the balance has shifted in favour of cartel litigation, and away from abuse of dominance litigation, in recent years. Another participant submitted that there had been a marked increase in litigation over the weeks immediately preceding the interview, although he/she stressed that this did not amount to the large increase in competition litigation predicted in some quarters. There was only one participant with the impression that competition litigation is not picking up. He felt that the availability of the pass-on defence, the high costs as well as the difficulties in proving the amount of damages and the non-availability of punitive damages would be significant hurdles which a claimant would face when bringing such an action before a national court.

[95] *Hawaii v Standard Oil Co of Cal* 405 US 251, 262 (1972). Section 4 of the Clayton Antitrust Act of 1914 provides 'threefold' damages with interest and a reasonable attorney's fee for 'any person . . . injured in his business or property' by an antitrust violation: 15 USCA §15(a). Section 16 further provides that 'any person, firm, corporation or association shall be entitled to sue for and have injunctive relief . . . against threatened loss or damage' resulting from such a violation: 15 USCA §26.

[96] The ratio dropped from 20:1 in the late 1970s to 10:1 in the mid-1980s. See Salop and White (n 56) 3–4. See also: Crane (n 81) 1.

[97] For example, private antitrust litigation in China has increased markedly in recent years and may now be more important than public enforcement in some contexts: See H Ha, J Hickin and G O'Brien, 'Civil Actions Under China's Anti-Monopoly Law – Five Major Cases, Five Major Lessons (Part II)' at www.mayerbrown.com/public_docs/ClientUpdate_CivilActions.pdf.

B. Competition Law Enforcement: NCA and/or Courts

Although the above data appears to suggest that competition litigation is picking up in England, a closer look at the collected data shows that the majority of the participants are of the view that the increase is only in respect of follow-on actions. In this context, it should be noted that the questions were broadly drafted and there were no questions which were asking the participants whether the increase is in respect of follow-on or standalone actions. Despite this, the participants clearly stated on 13 occasions that the follow-on actions are the ones picking up. One participant went further to state that: 'there are far fewer stand-alone actions than follow on damages actions now.' A similar opinion was expressed by four other participants. Although competition litigation has increased, in particular cartel litigation, this increase seems overwhelmingly to be in follow-on litigation.

Therefore, it seems clear that, in the present enforcement system, a regulator's decision would be at the heart of the follow on damages actions. This raises the question as to what is the prevalent strategy employed by victims of EU competition law infringements. The respondents were asked if such a person would launch a complaint with a competition authority or whether he would rather bring a private action and seek damages before national courts. Participants seemed to share the assumption that there is nothing wrong in principle with the public funding of private claims in this context, implicitly endorsing the English approach which blends public and private enforcement. In particular, it appears that the majority of the participants express the view that going to the competition authority first would be a normal strategy. This view has been expressed on 14 occasions.

However, institutional concerns reappeared about the role of National Competition Authorities, in particular the Office of Fair Trading. On the one hand, many noted that National Competition Authorities have access to public resources, making them attractive venues to the extent that a plaintiff need not meet the full costs of his action. It is also notable that the NCA is often well-placed to bring considerable pressure to bear following a complaint, not least for reputational reasons. On the other hand, the institutional limitations of NCAs surfaced several times. The most important downsides, which were put forward in this respect by many participants, can be summarised as follows. First, on 12 occasions, participants were concerned that a complaint may not be taken up. It is well established that 'public enforcers cannot investigate all complaints, but must set priorities in their treatment of cases.'[98] As a result, recent research has shown that the Office of Fair Trading has rendered only a few infringement decisions.[99] Secondly, the time which a competition authority would need to proceed with a complaint indicates that someone who needs a quick fix (or an injunction) would be better off to go to the courts. This observation has been put forward on 10 occasions. Thirdly, lack of control is another drawback of proceedings before national competition authorities where there is no real prospect for settlement. This was put forward as a factor in five cases. Fourthly, another drawback relates to the inability of a regulator to award damages or injunctive relief, which was seen as a problem by respondents on three occasions. Fifthly, some participants also alluded to political problems in terms of finding a sympathetic ear at the NCA. Finally, a few respon-

[98] Notice on the handling of complaints (n 76) [8]. See also: WJ Wils, 'Discretion and Prioritisation in Public Enforcement, in Particular EU Antitrust Enforcement' (2011) 34 *World Competition* 353.

[99] E Burrows and T Gilbert, 'OFT Competition Act Enforcement: Key Developments over the First Decade' (2010) *Competition Law Journal* 178, 179–82.

dents also noted the possibility that the involvement of administrative bodies such as NCAs may prevent robust precedents from developing as they might in courts.

In the context of private proceedings, one participant put forward the following observation:

> I think if there hadn't been a regulatory decision, it would be a big step to bring your own damages claim without relying on any kind of predetermined regulatory decision. I'm not sure that would be a particularly fruitful route.

Another participant neatly summarised the main factors, which may need to be considered when deciding whether to seise courts or NCAs, by submitting that 'there are a series of factors that a claimant needs to weigh in the balance, and they unquestionably include cost, control and remedy.' However, a closer analysis of data indicates that the choice is only available to big companies with deep pockets: this was indicated on eight occasions.[100]

It should be noted that the majority of the questions were framed in terms of EU competition law infringements, generally construed. Nevertheless, on five occasions, the participants appear to suggest that there might be different tactics depending on whether it is abuse of a dominant position case or a cartel. As a result, on four occasions participants have stated that the courts are the better place to go especially in abuse of dominant position cases. This can be further illustrated by the recent judgment of the High Court in *Purple Parking Ltd and Meteor Parking Ltd v Heathrow Airport Ltd*,[101] which addressed the use of injunctive relief in dominance cases. Despite a recent and prominent case, the responses appear to indicate that stand-alone actions before English courts would be preferable only when someone needs a quick fix (or an injunction). This has been put forward on 10 occasions during the course of the qualitative interviews.

The prospects of success under either path are still quite low, however, as one participant noted:

> Although competition authorities are usually in the best position to achieve results quickly, the only thing that you can rely on is that they're not going to do it. So for example if you are in real trouble, then there's nothing you can do because if you go to court with an application for an interim injunction and, for example, you are bringing proceedings against a dominant undertaking, there is a high possibility that you will get crushed to death, and if you go to a competition authority, you can guarantee that they will do nothing to help you.

Another participant also observed that claimants may face difficulties when bringing such actions before English courts:

> The courts have said these are very difficult actions, we should lean against those actions, we always require very, very full pleading at a stage when that pleading can't really be made. So the courts are attempting to lay down all sorts of hurdles in the way of getting those actions going here in the UK. Maybe not so much damages claims, but when you think of the Chancellor's judgment in *Emerald*.[102]

Indeed, the decision of the Court of Appeal in *Enron Coal Services Ltd (In Liquidation) v English Welsh & Scottish Ltd*[103] indicates that, even in a follow-on action, a claimant would face numerous evidential hurdles. As the Court noted, 'since a finding of infringement

[100] See below regarding claimant types.
[101] *Purple Parking* (n 21).
[102] *Emerald Supplies Ltd v British Airways Plc* [2009] EWHC 741 (Ch), [2010] EWCA Civ 1284.
[103] *Enron Coal Services Ltd (In Liquidation) v English Welsh & Scottish Ltd* [2011] EWCA Civ 2.

does not require proof that damage has in fact been caused to a rival undertaking, the fact that an infringement has been established does not show, as a necessary implication, that such damage has been caused.'[104] However, it may be far from efficient to have one set of proceedings before an NCA in order to establish a breach of competition law, and another set of proceedings before Member State courts in order for a claimant to prove that damage has been caused to him. Mechanisms allowing for some form of consolidation of the two sets of proceedings before national courts[105] might be desirable, as the outcome in the follow-on action would be highly dependent upon the evidence gathered in the course of the proceedings establishing the infringement.[106] Indeed, the interaction of the European Commission, NCAs and national courts presents problems which may need to be addressed by reforms increasing the role for private enforcement. At present, the interaction between the European Commission and NCAs is well defined in Regulation 1/2003, which provides for a balance of power based on oversight and soft-law guidance. The relative jurisdictions of an NCA located in one Member State and a court located in another Member State are not defined by the Regulation, however.

Some participants were concerned that an excessively claimant-friendly system would overcompensate through encouraging unmeritorious claims. In particular, some suggested that the class actions available to claimants under the federal antitrust laws of the United States led to overcompensation. Nonetheless, one regarded American-style litigation as a remote possibility in a system where the number of cases is so low to start with.[107] Therefore, the developments in the United States, where private antitrust cases have come to outnumber public enforcement by approximately a 10-to-one ratio, seem to be in a sharp contrast with the approach which is developing in Europe and England where the limited private litigation which occurs normally proceeds as a follow-on action based on a public enforcement action.[108] This could be a particular problem because public enforcement relies very heavily on leniency applications, and almost all litigation follows on from these decisions at present, but these applications could dry up in the wake of the uncertainty stemming from potential access to documents under *Pfleiderer*, as noted above.

The essential role of leniency applications in the initial detection of cartels suggests that an important issue which must be considered relates to the incentives created by the leniency programme, and the possible friction between the incentives created by leniency programmes and damages actions, as widely discussed at present.[109] The majority of the respondents share

[104] ibid [130].

[105] Compare: Department for Business Innovation & Skills, *A Competition Regime for Growth: A Consultation on Options for Reform*, 16 March 2011 www.bis.gov.uk/assets/biscore/consumer-issues/docs/c/11-758-competition-regime-for-growth-impact-assessment.pdf [241]–[243].

[106] *Pfleiderer* (n 46); *National Grid* (n 52). See also: Case 1077/5/7/07 *Emerson Electric Co v Mersen UK Portslade Ltd (sued as LE Carbon (Great Britain) Ltd)* [2011] CAT 4.

[107] Other distinguishing factors include the one-way nature of cost shifting in favour of claimants in federal American antitrust cases, as well as the possibility of treble damages in most cases: see above, n 36.

[108] eg *Provimi* (n 31). See also: Case No 1087/7/9/07 *The Consumer Association v JJB Sports PLC* [2009] CAT 2, 30 January 2009; *Emerald* (n 102); Case No 1088/5/7/07 *ME Burgess, JJ Burgess and SJ Burgess (trading as JJ Burgess & Sons) v W Austin & Sons (Stevenage) Ltd and Harwood Park Crematorium Ltd*, pending – registered 3 August 2008; *Cardiff City Transport* (n 65); *National Grid* (n 52); *Enron* (n 103); *Cooper Tire* (n 60).

[109] J Almunia, 'Policy Public Enforcement and Private Damages Actions in Antitrust' (European Parliament, ECON Committee Brussels, 22 September 2011) at http://europa.eu/rapid/pressReleasesAction.do?reference=SPEECH/11/598&format=PDF&aged=0&language=EN&guiLanguage=en. See also: JT Rosch, 'Does the EU Need a System of Private Competition Remedies to Supplement Public Law Enforcement?' (Remarks at the 2011 LIDC Congress, Christ Church, Oxford, England, 23 September 2011) 32, www.ftc.gov/speeches/rosch/110923privatecomp.pdf.

the view that leniency programmes create incentives for the infringing undertakings to submit leniency applications, this being submitted on 19 occasions. Only one participant thought that the various leniency programmes do not create incentives for infringing undertakings to submit leniency applications. Nevertheless, another respondent, who thought that although leniency programmes create incentives for the infringing undertakings to submit leniency applications, elaborated further, stating that one 'cannot assume that leniency applications are actually made by guilty undertakings. Some of them are not and may blame some undertakings.' It may be that some parties make strategic applications when not at fault themselves, or even where they do not believe there to be a cartel. If this allegation is true, the incentives to submit leniency applications would appear to be so strong that there is little prospect of private damages claims materially diminishing them. Far from civil damages undermining the incentives, parties appear to be willing to pretend to have breached competition law simply to make strategic use of the leniency programme, even though this exposes them to the risk of potential civil liability.

On only four occasions was it submitted that leniency applicants would not be deterred by the potential damages actions which could be brought against them. One participant drew attention to the so-called '*Masterfoods* problem',[110] whereby a leniency applicant can come to be disadvantaged. Normally a defendant to follow-on private damages claims can appeal the underlying Commission or NCA decision, which delays a follow-on claim based on it. However, if the party obtained leniency from the Commission or NCA, it may not have standing to bring an appeal against the enforcement proceeding and would not therefore benefit from the stay in the private damages case. The leniency applicant might therefore be liable for all the damages from the cartel under the principle of joint and several liability, including those of the parties named in the leniency application, until the appeal against the regulatory decision is concluded. This could well chill leniency applications.

One might think that leniency applicants could be further discouraged by the judgment of the Court of Justice in *Pfleiderer*.[111] As already mentioned, *Pfleiderer* held that EU law must be interpreted as not precluding victims of a cartel from being granted access to documents voluntarily submitted by leniency applicants to an NCA. In other words, claimants who bring follow-on damages claims might have access to such documents.[112] This has led some to suggest that this might cause 'the end of the EU cartel leniency programme'.[113] The judgment may yet bring home the disclosure problems previously confined to the amicus briefs the Commission frequently submitted to safeguard the leniency programme from permissive discovery in American litigation.[114]

Although the prevailing view, put forward on 16 occasions, was that leniency applicants would be deterred by the potential damages actions which could be brought against them, the majority of the participants went further, to state that the damage exposure is there anyway, and the leniency applicants would normally weigh it up. Only five participants observed that there is a chance that a more efficient damages system might undermine the leniency programme. In this context, one participant noted that although 'there is a possibility it will

[110] Case C-344/98 *Masterfoods v HB Ice Cream* [2000] ECR I-11369.

[111] *Pfleiderer* (n 46). See also: Case T-437/08 *CDC Hydrogene Peroxide Cartel Damages Claims v Commission* [2012] 4 *CML Rev* 12.

[112] I Vandenborre, 'The Confidentiality of EU Commission Cartel Records in Civil Litigation: The Ball is in the EU Court', (2011) 32 *ECLR* 116 (published between the AG's opinion in *Pfleiderer* (n 46), and the judgment of the Court).

[113] A Gieger, 'The end of the EU cartel leniency programme', (2011) 32 *ECLR* 535.

[114] See Vandenborre (n 112) 118.

undermine the leniency programme' to a degree, it was unlikely to 'destroy the programme . . . it will just mean that some cartels don't get reported that might otherwise be.' This suggests that the possible friction between leniency programmes and damages actions may be overstated to a degree.[115]

C. An Enforcement Gap?

A case for the existence of an enforcement gap could be made if one tries to identify the class of the parties bringing the actions at the moment. In view of that, the questions were drafted in order to identify the types of claimants who would sue in the courts and the types of claimants who would rather rely on competition authorities. The majority of our participants (14 out of 20 cases) seem to indicate that it is normally large companies that tend to bring EU competition law actions. A review of the reported cases would show that there appears to be only one claim which was brought on behalf of the consumers in the UK.[116] Few claims are brought by SMEs.[117] Several participants appear to indicate that there is an enforcement gap, as there is no redress for consumers and SMEs, who are not particularly active in bringing competition law actions at the moment.

It was not surprising that the overwhelming view, submitted on 17 occasions, was that consumers fare relatively badly under the current system. Only on one occasion was the view expressed that consumers fare acceptably under the current system. Another participant submitted that 'consumers rely on regulators to look after their rights', while litigation is 'far too expensive for an SME to get involved in'. This leaves the 'heavy lifting of damages claims' to 'bigger businesses' such as 'direct suppliers', for better or worse.

On five other occasions, it was stated that undertakings[118] generally (encompassing large businesses and SMEs) are more active than consumers. Only one person stated that consumers being gathered together by lawyers is working. Thirteen participants indicated that consumers do not have incentives to bring actions. Seven participants thought that an opt-out regime (representative or a hybrid 'opt-in' and 'opt-out' regime) could be used to encourage actions brought by consumers or on behalf of consumers.[119] Others thought that some innovative solutions could be considered. Three participants thought that ADR[120] (or administrative proceedings) could be the solution. However, four participants questioned whether consumers' claims should be incentivised at all.[121] In particular, one participant thought that 'there is a question about the utility of, or the proportionality of devoting a great deal of time and trouble to satisfy a very, very small concern'.

[115] Compare: *Private Actions in Competition Law: A Consultation on Options for Reform* (n 16) [7.1]–[7.11]. See also: *National Grid* (n 52) [56]–[60].

[116] *JJB Sports* (n 108).

[117] *Purple Parking* (n 21). See also: *Burgess* (n 108); *Cardiff City Transport* (n 65).

[118] eg *National Grid* (n 52); *Enron* (n 103); *Cooper Tire* (n 60); Case No 1077/5/7/07 *Emerson Electric* [2008] CAT 8, 28 April 2008; *Emerald* (n 102).

[119] *cf. Private Actions in Competition Law: A Consultation on Options for Reform* (n 16) [5.1]–[5.53].

[120] *cf.* ibid [6.1]–[6.46]. See also: C Hodges, 'European Competition Enforcement Policy: Integrating Restitution and Behaviour Control – An Integrated Enforcement Policy, Involving Public and Private Enforcement with ADR' (2011) 34 *World Competition* 383; C Hodges, 'Collective Redress in Europe: The New Model' (2010) 29 *Civil Justice Quarterly* 370; C Hodges, I Benohr and N Creutzfeldt-Banda, *Consumer ADR in Europe: Civil Justice System* (Oxford, Hart-CH Beck-Nomos, 2012).

[121] See J Davies and E Szyszczak, 'ADR: Effective Protection of Consumer Rights' (2010) 35 *EL Rev* 695.

However, the real concern is that the pattern which is developing in Europe and England in particular appears to indicate that the limited private litigation which occurs normally proceeds as a follow-on action based on a public enforcement action. As illustrated above, it may be far from efficient to have one set of proceedings before an NCA in order to establish a breach of competition law, and another set of proceedings before Member State courts in order for a claimant to prove that damage has been caused to him. Mechanisms allowing for some form of consolidation of the two sets of proceedings before national courts might be desirable to reconcile some of the conflicts identified between public and private enforcement in the current system, while retaining the desirable features of both systems of enforcement to the greatest possible extent. Courts seem well placed to mediate in the resolution of the tensions between private and public enforcement, provided that they receive clear guidance from the legislator and case law. The issue may stem from the fact that the modernisation programme of Regulation 1/2003 increased the role for national courts, but has in practice provided less guidance about how to exercise it than might be desirable from the perspective of consistency.

Furthermore, the current private litigation pattern might suggest that there could be an enforcement gap as public enforcers across Europe are unlikely to have the resources to investigate all the complaints they receive; private litigation might therefore provide extra resources to assist enforcement, which at present seems underdeveloped. Indeed, 'the fact that a complainant can secure the protection of his rights by an action before a national court'[122] may be factored in by the public enforcers when deciding if they would take a complaint or not. In other words, if the private enforcement system, which is in its nascent form in Europe, is not adequately reformed to safeguard the rights of individuals derived from Articles 101 and 102, then there would be an enforcement gap.[123] The most effective way to improve antitrust enforcement is likely to involve elements of both public and private enforcement, and it is difficult to argue that private litigation has no role to play.

VII. WAYS FORWARD – CONCLUDING REMARKS

Drawing the foregoing concerns together, the most significant problem appears to lie in the uncertainty facing claimants under the current system. The procedural points, especially concerning the level of national procedural autonomy and its tension with the effective enforcement of EU law, would need to be looked at carefully. Damages claims, in particular regarding the pass-on defence, should be addressed. The high level of uncertainty surrounding those issues leads to excessive expense, which is compounded by evidentiary problems and costs. Thus, if the EU legislator wishes to strengthen the incentives for private enforcement of EU competition law it may have to create an appropriate institutional enforcement structure to allow case law precedents to become more clearly established and developed, in turn encouraging more claims. This appears to raise some policy concerns surrounding the European Courts structure as it stands and the role of National Competition Authorities and their interaction with courts. These are important issues which seemingly require some attention by the policy-makers. This section will conclude

[122] Notice on the handling of complaints (n 76) [17].
[123] *cf.* ibid [18].

by addressing these institutional points in the context of the foregoing analysis, which affect the substance of a potential reform as well its format.

A. Alternative Dispute Resolution

An important concern when considering possible reforms is the nature of the most appropriate redress. The current administrative solutions appear at present to have failed. As already outlined, participants were concerned with the cost and delay of cumbersome administrative systems. Furthermore, regulators do not have the resources to investigate and prosecute all EU competition law infringements, but only a subset of infringements considered to do the most harm. Indeed, even if administrative resources were to increase, a system of prioritisation of cases would still seem to be inevitable. Proceedings before regulators also raise due process concerns which would be an important consideration following the entry into force of the Lisbon Treaty, and would need to be addressed before the expansion of administrative procedures.[124] With these concerns in mind, the prospect of an administrative system to collect and distribute compensation was received poorly by some. This contrasted with some participants who regarded an administrative system as the only viable approach to compensate end consumers, if that is taken to be a valid aim.

Nevertheless, the majority of the participants appear to indicate that ADR when used on a voluntary basis could be an appropriate and helpful mechanism to be used for settlement of some cross-border EU competition law actions and follow on actions in particular. This has been submitted on 19 occasions. Only one participant submitted that it is questionable whether ADR is appropriate in competition law cases which are not purely private disputes: 'one should bear in mind that competition law aims to safeguard the process of competition'.

On another occasion, although mediation was believed to be an appropriate mechanism, it was argued that 'arbitration . . . is a bad forum because you are not usually getting arbitrators who are competent judges anyway in the competition law and competition law in any event has a large public interest element to it which a court will always bear in mind but an arbitrator simply won't.' Two participants who thought that ADR could be useful went on to state that ADR as a mechanism would not allow for developing precedents which could promote certainty. On two other occasions, it was submitted it would be important to decide the stage of the dispute at which to adopt the mechanism. Three participants thought that ADR could be useful for resolving consumer claims; three other

[124] W Weiss, 'Human Rights and EU Antitrust Enforcement: News from Lisbon', (2011) 32 *ECLR* 186; I Forrester, 'A Challenge for Europe's Judges: The Review of Fines in Competition Cases' (2011) 36 *EL Rev* 185; R Nazzini, 'Administrative Enforcement: Judicial Review and Fundamental Rights in EU Competition Law: A Comparative Contextual-Functionalist Perspective' (2012) 49 *CML Rev* 971; HH Lidgard, 'Due Process in European Competition Procedure: A Fundamental Concept or a Mere Formality?' in P Cardonnel, A Rosas and N Wahl (eds), *Constitutionalising the EU Judicial System: Essays in Honour of Pernilla Lindh* (Oxford, Hart Publishing, 2012) 403; JR Calzado and G de Stefano, 'Rights of Defence in Cartel Proceedings: Some Ideas for Manageable Improvements' in P Cardonnel, A Rosas and N Wahl (eds), *Constitutionalising the EU Judicial System: Essays in Honour of Pernilla Lindh* (Oxford, Hart Publishing, 2012) 423. *cf.* A Arabadjiev, 'Unlimited Jurisdiction: What does it mean today? in P Cardonnel, A Rosas and N Wahl (eds), *Constitutionalising the EU Judicial System: Essays in Honour of Pernilla Lindh* (Oxford, Hart Publishing, 2012) 383. See also: Commission Notice on Best Practices for the Conduct of Proceedings Concerning Arts 101 and 102 TFEU, [2011] OJ C308/6; DG Competition's Antitrust Manual of Procedures, Internal DG Competition working documents on procedures for the application of Arts 101 and 102 TFEU, March 2012 http://ec.europa.eu/competition/antitrust/antitrust_manproc_3_2012_en.pdf.

participants thought that ADR would not be appropriate to consumer disputes. Another interesting opinion in this context was: 'You need a dispute before you can go to ADR, and consumer cases are not coming.' In addition, some believed that ADR would only work in the context of a workable judicial system.

There was a variation of opinions regarding which ADR mechanisms would be more appropriate. Nonetheless, it seems that mediation was favoured on 16 occasions. One participant, however, doubted that mediation would be all that useful in cartel damages actions where 'there's no dispute about what's gone on because it's written in the Commission decision'. This was seen to limit the incentive for defendants to mediate.

Determination of certain issues such as damages by an expert witness may be more promising, and was seen as an appropriate mechanism on four occasions (one participant thought that it could be used in the context of leniency applications; another that it could be useful with regard to claims brought on behalf of consumers). Three other participants were of the opinion that expert determination would not appeal to corporates and, as a result, might be a thorny issue.

However, one might wonder whether ADR is likely to develop before court actions themselves develop further from their very low base. In view of this, it appears that encouraging the competition law action is a pre-requisite for promoting ADR, which could be a good solution once the body of case law has been developed.

B. Encouraging EU Competition Law Damages Claims Further – Some Policy Concerns

One potential path for reform would be a new Regulation or Directive addressing some or all of the above concerns, but few participants saw much scope for this. In particular, they were concerned that new laws from Brussels would be unlikely to address the fundamental uncertainty that currently deters many claims, and might even enhance it. A solution including increased involvement of the European courts, which could provide for more certainty, was also rejected on the basis of concerns about increased delay. There was therefore little focus on whether a directive or regulation would be preferable. Very few participants considered soft law solutions to the issue. This leaves competition law enforcement in a difficult position, with widespread agreement that the system is malfunctioning but few suggestions of the direction reform could take.

The overwhelming majority of respondents instead favoured allowing the current system to evolve in its current form. As already submitted, the main reason articulated was that, although competition law actions have evolved from a low base, the number of actions is on the rise. Moreover, the concern that the number of cases in the current system is underdeveloped may be overstated: there have only been competition law actions for approximately 10 years in comparison with, for example, contract law actions which took 200 years to develop. (An interesting observation which was submitted on one occasion.) The majority of participants favoured modest reforms to the current system at the national level, allowing competition to develop between different jurisdictions. Although an increased number of claims might be seen, this compensation could come at a high price to the deeply embedded aim of cross-border consistency in European competition law. In this way, strong jurisdictions for bringing claims might emerge, but the question of their cross-border compatibility would remain largely unaddressed in the absence of case law or legislation to promote consistency: the substantive rules would continue to be dominated by procedural differences.

4

Cross-Border EU Competition Litigation: Qualitative Interviews from Germany

JULIAN KAMMIN AND FLORIAN BECKER

I. INTRODUCTION

In Germany, 11 interviews with 17 legal practitioners in the field of EU competition law were conducted between September 2011 and August 2012[1]. We decided to count each interview as one case for data analysis purposes, though some of the interviews involved two respondents. To enable us to compare the outcome with the data gathered by the UK team, we decided to structure the summary under the same headings.

II. LITIGATION PATTERN

The data was organised in order to help us identify how the litigation pattern has developed so far according to our participants. In the majority of cases (10 out of 11), the participants are of the opinion that competition litigation is picking up in Europe. It was stated that litigation is picking up 'in particular with a view to damage claims'. As a reason for this, one respondent mentioned 'the increasing number of cartel proceedings which are pending or have been made pending over the last years due to leniency applications on the European level and particularly in Germany'. Furthermore, the development was associated 'with the Green Book of the Commission which did not have any direct influence on the German legal system but motivated people to think about it a bit more'.

In this context, the 2005 reform of the Act against Restraints on Competition in Germany was also mentioned by interviewees as having 'added a new impetus to the whole subject'. Another opinion was that litigation was 'certainly picking up although you do not see that much of it because most of the processes are stuck in the settlement status'.

According to another interviewee, a 'broader development clearly started with the Ashurst study and the process of the Commission leading to the White Paper. Then there was a certain awareness of the potential of private enforcement of competition law.'

[1] The sample of German solicitors and barristers was drawn from the relevant sections of JUVE Handbuch, http://www.juve.de/handbuch/de/2011/fuehrendenamen/24250; this resulted in a sample of the 35 most respected solicitors and barristers in the area of competition law selected as potential participants. Safeguards were observed to ensure the best possible data quality and compliance with good research practices and ethical norms.

In five out of eleven cases, the participants observed that litigation is mostly picking up in follow-on cases. One interviewee assumed that 'there is no cartel case in Europe right now . . . where the lawyers do not have the follow-on action in the back of their minds'. It was further noted that 'in the big cases before courts, plaintiffs take the view that you can only have a good case in a follow-on situation'.

Nevertheless, it was stated that stand-alone actions can be observed in Article 102 TFEU cases: 'There is only a dominance case in the UK, but not in cartel cases.'

Only one participant disagreed regarding the increase of competition litigation, stating that 'the average number of newly initiated antitrust proceedings in the EU is relatively constant and has been very constant with the exception of the years 2004 and 2005, hence immediately following the entry into force of Regulation 1/2003.'Another interviewee who basically observed an increase of competition litigation admitted that there are still Member States where this development cannot be found.

III. TYPES OF CLAIMANTS

It was important for us to identify which type of plaintiffs normally initiate EU competition law actions (ie small and medium-sized undertakings, consumers, large companies, competitors). All interviewees stated 'there are more or less no consumers bringing actions or complaints to a National Competition Authority'. The majority of plaintiffs are small and medium-sized undertakings and competitors. It was submitted that there is a broad range of companies involved: 'Bigger ones are more or less obliged to pursue such claims, but the smaller ones also have a clear interest in pursuing those claims. Sometimes, organizations like the Cartel Damage Claims try to gather those claimants.'

A typical statement was:

> Mostly, undertakings or companies are initiating this kind of litigation. The private end-consumer does not benefit from this trend so far, not at all I would even say. This is true for both, initiating antitrust administrative proceedings by means of a complaint or by suing alleged cartelists. It is business driven and it is a business . . . not a consumer issue.

Another expert agreed with that, and reported that 'for an individual company it would be rare to start stand-alone litigations based on an alleged cartel infringement. It would probably bring a complaint to the Commission.'

IV. PLAINTIFFS' TACTICS

The answers to some questions were organised in order to identify what participants think is the best tactic for someone who believes he is a victim of an EU competition law infringement. The claimants' strategy questions sought to take account of the participants' opinions as to: whether claimants first address themselves to competition authorities and then proceed with a follow-on action before national courts, whether claimants find it beneficial to sue in their home state, whether claimants would go after all the infringing undertakings at the same time or rather consecutively, and whether plaintiffs consider cooperation with other victims of a cartel.

A. Competition Authority and/or Courts?

In eight out of eight cases, interviewees took the position that it is more advantageous to have an investigation by a competition authority before initiating a damages claim. It was assumed that 'starting a civil law proceeding without any clear decision by any competition authority is almost impossible.' This participant even stated he had never experienced a plaintiff in a stand-alone action.

A reason for this is the fact that 'in most cases you are not aware of competition law infringements unless a National Cartel Authority has already revealed the infringement, with the exception of the abuse of a dominant position which might be more obvious.' In this context one respondent said: 'It is still very difficult to do stand-alone actions. You would have to do the full investigation of the possible cartel. It may be easier if you look at an abuse of market dominance situation which is sometimes easier to discover and to prove.' Another interesting view is as follows: 'People are waiting for a decision by a competition authority. The difference is that the thought to bring damage actions arises very quickly whereas in the past you really had to trigger it or they even did not think about it. And that has really changed.'

Only one participant was not convinced that it is necessary to wait for a competition authority's decision, as 'you need to go to the court anyway'. But the same respondent later backtracked, and emphasised that he 'would certainly not advise a client to file a stand-alone lawsuit with respect to hard-core cartels', but instead would advise waiting for a potential decision of the Federal Cartel Office or the Commission.

Only one of the 11 interviewees had experienced stand-alone cases in the field of hard-core cartels.

B. Bringing an Action in the Home State?

Six out of seven interviewees (on four occasions no distinct answer was given) found it beneficial for plaintiffs to sue in their home state. One view was that: 'There is a certain inclination to do that. It is a cultural thing: you know the procedure, the lawyers, it is much more straightforward for them to anticipate what might be the outcome.' However, it was also assumed that it depends on the types of plaintiff: 'The big companies can afford a litigation process in nearly any jurisdiction even if it is not acquainted with the material or procedural aspects of this jurisdiction. But if you think of small and medium-sized undertakings, they probably feel more comfortable and familiar with their home jurisdiction. It is rather an emotional decision to stay at home.' On another occasion it was stated that language is still one of the major issues for choosing a court, from the perspective of a small or medium-sized undertaking: 'When we are talking about small and medium-sized undertakings I could really imagine that if it is . . . based in Germany for instance, they would never go to an English court in order to claim for damages.' Relating to this aspect, not only language but familiarity with the court system as well is seen as a soft factor.

Bringing the action in the home state is also relevant with regard to costs: 'If you stay at home, you usually save quite a bit of costs. If you talk about costs, you would say it is a home game which also helps you. Especially if you talk to clients who have their own legal department, the legal department will very often be more confident to stay in their own country. . . . At least Germans or other Europeans are a bit hesitant to go to the United Kingdom because of the enormous costs and the length of litigation sometimes.'

The disadvantages of the German court system were however emphasised on one occasion: 'Germany is not the most efficient court system. It is a very slow court system, a court system where you cannot use documents in electronic formats . . . We see other jurisdictions where especially judges take a more active role and that is why a lot of cases are brought in the UK and also in the Netherlands.'

Only one participant was not sure whether there is an inclination to sue in the home state, motivated by culture or language:

> I can see that it is maybe one soft factor but it is not the deciding factor as you can receive advice if you work with an international firm . . . Maybe you would take this factor into account but you would also take into account all the other factors which are maybe less soft but more compelling in terms of legal questions, procedural questions which help you to get to your goal.

C. Suing Several Defendants at the Same Time or Consecutively

Given the fact that many EU competition law cases, and cartels by definition, involve a number of defendants, the participants were asked whether it is advantageous for a plaintiff to sue several defendants at the same time or whether it is advisable to choose a single defendant at first.

In five out of 11 cases it was submitted that it is advantageous for various reasons to bring actions against multiple-defendants:

> It depends on the file and on the information I am able to gather from public sources and from the non-confidential version of the Commission's or the Federal Cartel Office's decisions. I think there is a clear tendency to sue all the defendants at the same time in order to do it most efficiently. If you only sue one of the defendants and this one was alleged to be a member of the cartel he will serve third party notices to the others anyway. It is my experience that plaintiffs try to sue all defendants at the same time in order to try to settle the case.

Besides the argument that it is more cost effective and that it facilitates to settle to sue more defendants at once, it was suggested that 'if [you] lose against one [you] may have the chance to win against others'.

However, the same expert mentioned disadvantages of suing three or four defendants at once. It is more work and complicates litigation, as 'you have so many parties and tons of submissions and annexes [and] all these third party interveners. This leads to a big mess [and] everybody has his own economic expert.' Another participant summed up: 'But at the end of the day you may not be able to avoid the complexity.'

Four interviewees held the opposite view and made clear that in their opinion suing one defendant is more advantageous. In particular, the presence of a leniency applicant can change the whole situation, as there are fewer problems in terms of proof. One respondent said: 'I think [the leniency applicant] is the easiest victim, I would leave it to the defendants to argue their compensation claims among themselves.'

Leniency indeed seems to be a significant issue relating to this question; thus, another statement was: 'If one defendant has filed for leniency, basically admitted the wrongdoing and maybe even accepted a settlement with the Commission or the Federal Cartel Office, then it is much easier to attack that party.' One respondent came to the same conclusion with another very interesting justification including the question of whether a court's decision is challenged:

> [T]here is a strong incentive to sue the immunity applicant because . . . in his case normally no appeal is pending as he has no interest in challenging the authority's decision. You have the faster final award whereas the others normally challenge the Commission's or the Federal Cartel Office's decision. This is one incentive and also the fact that the immunity applicant unequivocally admits the infringement.

One respondent stated that information provided by the leniency applicant cannot be used before courts: 'The leniency applicant goes to the Commission and speaks into a microphone and makes an oral application which is then transcribed by the Commission into a document which makes this document undiscoverable because it is produced by an authority and not by the cartel member.'

Another interesting view was:

> In many cases I recommend to do the opposite. I recommend just suing one defendant, for example the one who has admitted everything, who has a binding decision against him, no possibility to reject the cartel allegation or the defendant who was the main supplier for example. Otherwise the complexity of the litigation tends to be much higher. For example in the Cartel Damage Claims hydrogen peroxide case, there are so many parties involved that all the submissions and proceedings are proceeding very slowly . . . It is preferable in general to sue the weakest cartel member and [this] is the one who has admitted everything and has hardly any defence with regard to the substance of the cartel allegation and who was maybe the main supplier.

In two cases, the participants argued using cost-related considerations: 'You would not take the cost burden to go after the others which might take years of court proceedings just to get a decision stating that all the others have also infringed cartel law.' Another opinion was: 'I do not think that this is commercially very smart as long as you are not in risk of losing claims because they could be time-barred.'

Only two of the respondents were of the opinion that it does not make a significant difference in the end whether one or more cartelists are taken to court. This has been mainly substantiated with the third party notices:

> You can just claim against one of them but then very often the other co-cartelists will be brought into the proceeding by joining movements . . . and then you have all of them on the other side anyway. It is usually worthwhile for a claimant to try to keep the case simple as a general recommendation and therefore you can try to just bring your case against one defendant, but that is not really under your control at the end of the day.

In addition, it was assumed that there are sometimes also jurisdictional aspects to consider, like the question of whether it is possible to sue all the defendants in the same forum. The second expert supporting this point of view thought that it does not matter whether one or more defendants are sued due to the existence of third party notices: 'You pick one and they will bring others into play. Sometimes, if we represent a defendant it might be a psychological argument if you want to settle. Then they . . . pick the settling company and then you have to bring in all the others. In the end it does not really matter.'

D. Cooperation Between Plaintiffs

The prevailing view among the interviewees (nine out of 11) was that plaintiffs obviously consider cooperation with others in a similar situation. Various types of cooperation were mentioned,

> ranging from very low cooperation, for example to use the same economist . . . to have some synergies and maybe to share the cost of the joint economist, or really to bundle the claims legally by way of assignment like the Cartel Damages Claims model where they purchase the claims and then bring them together . . . And there are many types of cooperation in between, for example to share information, to retain the same lawyers.

Thus, according to the interviewees, it definitely makes sense to join forces, primarily to create synergies and reduce costs.

According to another interviewee, there is no cooperation other than the CDC-model: 'To be honest, we are not aware of any cooperation of claimants in that respect.'

The concept of Cartel Damage Claims is to create certain coordination by giving affected parties the opportunity to cede claims to them. This is identified as one of the most popular forms of cooperation. The main argument to cede claims instead of enforcing them on one's own is to facilitate litigation as such and the burden of proof in particular. In addition, the CDC model makes it possible 'to reach a conclusion based on a market-wide data basis. This is of course something a single claimant cannot provide.'

However, one respondent denied that CDC is a form of cooperation between plaintiffs, as only the organisation itself is in the position of the actual plaintiff: 'Cartel Damage Claims is a sort of cooperation between customers but not between plaintiffs because it is just one plaintiff who bundles all the claims.' This view was affirmed later: 'As CDC is the "owner" of the claims, there is no cooperation between the companies.'

Another participant further doubted the aforementioned advantages of cooperation: 'They cannot reduce costs because in Germany the costs are kept anyhow. It would only add more complexity. And the question is also what share you get in the end.'

On three out of 11 occasions it was stated that this issue is of increased importance for smaller undertakings as they fear the 'loser-pays rule': 'They are profiting from synergies in terms of cost-benefit calculation and this lowers the risks. This is quite beneficial and very attractive.'

One interviewee further submitted that smaller undertakings 'might have greater inclination to ask Cartel Damage Claims or similar organizations to bring the claims together in order to have a higher volume and also more potential for settlements.' This observation was agreed upon by another participant. There is a certain inclination to cooperate 'if you have consumers or . . . small and medium-sized undertakings which simply do not have the funds to hire economists, for instance.'

One attendee's argument was that plaintiffs already cooperate to collect information: 'You have this evidentiary problem and you have a better basis also for an economic study if you join forces. That is quite an obvious reason. In consumer actions you have the problem that the individual damage is often too small, there is an organization necessary. I do not know a case where a single consumer brought a claim.' According to the interviewee, the main reason why claims are bundled is to facilitate the proof of damage: 'You will not be able to show it by yourself; you need data from other customers.' Only on two occasions did the participants argue that cooperation between plaintiffs is not advisable. These interviewees favoured being the first to negotiate with the defendants: 'Sometimes it is good to have a quick mover advantage, to be the first one to reach a settlement or to bring a case. You do not want to wait and you do not want to have internal discussions on how to take the case further – tactical decisions.'

V. PROCEDURE – KEY ASPECT

The answers to some questions were organised in order to take account of the participants' views as to the importance of procedural rules in the context of forum selection in cross-border claims. Relating to the question whether it matters in which Member State of the European Union a cross-border competition law action is brought, national procedural rules were regarded as a decisive aspect in the majority of cases (ten out of 11). One respondent stated: 'Procedure is definitely among the most important aspects.'

The most relevant aspects of procedure that were put forward by the participants can be summarised as follows.

A. Disclosure

Disclosure and discovery were mentioned as very important aspects for claimants to consider as they entail advantages as well as disadvantages from a plaintiff's point of view. Access to evidence is a clear reason for all interviewees to choose Anglo-American jurisdictions, especially the United Kingdom: 'One of the main topics is how do you get access to evidence and obviously there is a difference between the continental system and the Anglo-American system. The United Kingdom with its procedural rules is the more attractive system.' Another participant stated: 'the more access to the file and the more disclosure you get, the easier will it be for a plaintiff to go to court.' One interesting opinion shows the ambivalence of disclosure and discovery and that there are not only positive implications: 'Discovery is something which is very interesting in theory but in practice it is a big part in the high costs we are seeing in United Kingdom litigation and therefore it is really a two-edged sword. It is only worth to go if you have a very big or complicated case.'

B. Standard of Proof

Standard of proof was mentioned as a decisive aspect as well:

> The [standard] of proof is another very important issue, also concerning the amount of damages. We have seen in the past that there are investigations going on, big claimants who asked several lawyers in several Member States to give their opinion on the advantages and maybe also on the disadvantages of their proper jurisdiction system. In the end the choice is made for a claim in the United Kingdom or Germany.

Another interesting view was that a low standard of proof can even be a replacement of equal value for the non-existence of disclosure: 'It is also very important to what extent there are other plaintiff-friendly instruments like presumptions and a low [standard] of proof. This can be an excellent substitute for a lack of disclosure.'

C. Statute of Limitation

The statute of limitation was emphasised in only one case as 'very important because we have widely different statutes of limitation periods in different countries'.

D. Speed of Proceedings

The speed of proceedings was considered on three occasions as another important aspect, as this is 'very hard to predict'.

E. Experience of Courts

The experience of the national courts was considered by four of the participants: '[T]here are still Member States with virtually no tradition in private enforcement of competition law. It can happen that you sue in front of a court with absolutely no antitrust experience. This can be a real nightmare.' Another participant underlined the importance of this aspect and found the appropriate term 'procedural experience': 'Procedural experience of the courts and other plaintiff-friendly instruments are of great importance.' This matter was further depicted by saying that the cement case was pending for five years at the District Court Düsseldorf which was overwhelmed by the complexity of the case.

The number of judges and their professional level should be considered as well: 'One problematic point is that you have in the Kammer für Handelssachen one professional judge. We have formulated a proposal to amend this situation, maybe to have three professional judges or a concentration in a chamber on the state level to one court.'

F. Service of Documents

Finally, the service of documents was mentioned as being a crucial factor: 'If you have to provide all the attachments in paper form – we are talking about huge files – and if you have to provide a copy of each submission to each [party], then this is a huge task for the court.'

G. Concluding Remarks – Procedural Aspects

One respondent finally summarised the decisive issues:

> The legal issues are interest, statutes of limitation, discovery, costs and fees, the role of experts, it is about how you can appeal decisions, whether the court can progress the case . . . and it is the

> way the local judge looks at the European Court of Justice. It is a long list. Usually, you have situations where twenty factors point one way and twenty-five point the other way.

VI. DAMAGES

The answers to some questions were organised in order to take account of the participants' views as to the importance of the level of damages that could be awarded in the various Member States and how this affects forum selection. Our data shows that the amount of damage and its quantification is an aspect to be considered by a claimant when choosing a jurisdiction: 'With regard to the binding effect it is not so much about facts anymore. The cartel is clearly investigated by the cartel authority . . . The focus in future will be on quantum – whether you are able to show . . . quantum – it is also about the various methods [of calculation] which the Commission has put into the draft guideline paper.' Another interviewee drew the same conclusion: 'If I was a plaintiff and I had full access to all of this, I still do not know what my damage would be.' Hence, it can be summarised that calculation and quantification of damages is a major aspect for choosing to pursue damages in a particular forum.

Accordingly, the participants were asked whether the passing-on defence can help to avoid double counting of the same damages. On three occasions, the respondents held that this is a very difficult question to answer; one of them even said that '[this] is a very disappointing issue because there is no ideal solution.' This participant further stated that: 'It is really a test of what we want. Do we want another deterrence tool? Then we certainly should abolish the passing-on defence and should only have the direct purchasers to sue. Or is it really about compensation? That is a different approach. That is classical civil law and what I was taught at university and what I still think is correct but I am afraid the trend goes into more deterrence and effective enforcement, whatever this means.'

Another interesting opinion is that

> the institution of the passing-on defence itself does not help or hinder double counting. The problem is rather that it is not harmonized among the Member States. The double counting problem occurs where one jurisdiction provides or applies the passing-on defence and another jurisdiction does not. It might come to a double counting of the partial amount of an indirect purchaser. It is not a matter of passing-on . . . or not, it is rather a question of harmonising the application of this.

Finally, it was stated that this matter can be a decisive factor when making a decision about the forum: '[W]e will maybe see competition between different jurisdictions and maybe this leads to some forum shopping. It is one of the main turning points in this kind of litigation, depending on the scheme adopted in the Member States. It could become a very crucial factor in determining where you go.'

This view was also expressed in another case: 'The experience shows that clients really take a lot of time in investigating on the advantages and disadvantages of several jurisdictional forums in Europe.'

According to another respondent, a higher interest rate can also be a decisive factor: 'Some Member States foresee a higher interest rate or the calculation of interest is based on compound interest and that can have a very significant effect in long lasting cartels.'

VII. COSTS

Account was also taken of participants' views as to how the high costs could affect the dynamics of cross-border EU competition litigation. All participants stated that costs are an important issue to bear in mind when deciding where to bring a cross-border competition law claim as a cost-benefit analysis is the basic principle which shows whether an action is economically attractive.

One respondent maintained that costs are primarily to be considered by plaintiffs. One reason for this is that defendants use delaying strategies. It is 'a very popular defendant strategy to slow down the whole process and hope that the other . . . side is running out of money and cannot afford any further delay . . . This really increases the willingness for a settlement.'

On three occasions, the costs of economic experts were mentioned explicitly: '[E]conomists play a big role in these cases. If you have a very good economic story, then we would be able to move a client forward to taking the action or either finding a complaint or getting a good settlement ahead of a complaint.' Another respondent agreed that: '[T]he economists come in and they also need to be briefed, that is a very, very time consuming business.'

However, only one respondent said that costs deter plaintiffs from bringing a competition law claim: 'You clearly have to make an assessment whether the amount which you have to invest is justified by the amount which is most likely to come out.' Another participant assumed that 'it depends on how big your claim is, on what the economists tell you about whether your case is robust. It depends on the legal budget companies have'. For example, 'a German small or medium-sized undertaking will really be deterred by going to an English lawyer, in a different system and a not really assessable outcome.'

Referring to the high costs for access to courts in the United Kingdom, one participant said that a settlement is driven by the costs of litigation. On two occasions, the participants compared the costs of the United Kingdom and the German system: 'In the United Kingdom, the costs are tremendous and also the cost reimbursement.' In addition, 'you have to pay your lawyer which . . . is much more costly than here in Germany.'

One interviewee summed up that 'one reason why end-consumers are virtually unable to bring such claims is really the costs.'

VIII. DEFENDANTS' TACTICS

The answers to some questions were organised in order to identify what participants think is the best tactic for someone who has allegedly infringed EU competition law provisions. The defendants' strategy questions sought to take account of the interviewees' opinion as to: whether a defendant, who is threatened with an EU competition law action, would initiate a pre-emptive strike, whether defendants employ any delaying strategies, and whether a more effective private enforcement system could undermine the leniency programmes.

A. Pre-emptive Strikes

In seven out of 11 cases, the respondents held the view that pre-emptive strikes such as the 'Italian or Belgian torpedo' are not a real option. One argument that was put forward was that defendants cannot be sure whether a pre-emptive strike is really efficient: '[Y]ou basically have to sue every potential claimant in this jurisdiction with respect to all of these claims. And usually this will not work, you do not get all of them and that means that you will be subject of an action which will be brought by one of the other plaintiffs.' In addition, it is necessary 'to have a potential Italian or Belgian plaintiff which is not often the case and the question is whether it is really possible to bring such a pre-emptive strike in Italy also with regard to all other cartelists.'

One participant thought that this tactic had no relevance at all, and stated:

> I believe that the Italian torpedo has been dead for 20 years. There is no one who seriously considers that and advises the client to do it. We will certainly not do that. I tested the torpedo 25 years ago myself in a case for compensation of a commercial agent where it made sense but a cartel case has all kinds of political ramifications, so you would not start that easily.

As a reason for this, the following disadvantages were put forward: 'You are the one who makes it public and the one who has to pay for it. And you are the one who has to make the case.' And 'as a cartel member you even run the risk to create the jurisdiction by bringing the torpedo because we could immediately bring a claim in that specific jurisdiction like Belgium or Italy or another slow jurisdiction like Germany.'

These observations were agreed upon by two respondents saying that the Italian torpedo is a rather theoretical issue having no relevance in cross-border competition litigation.

Only on three occasions did lawyers express that a more active approach was the best tactic for defendants: 'I would advise a defendant to take a very active approach and not to wait for the action to be brought by the plaintiff.' One respondent said that: 'Normally, one would wait until claimants come to see what their case is, how good it is and what they are asking for. But of course, this Italian or Belgium torpedo also plays a role.'

The following was described as an example: 'If the defendant has cooperated with the authority, I would not recommend using such an aggressive counter strategy. I would rather recommend entering into settlement discussions with key customers earlier in order to avoid litigation.'

B. Delaying Strategies in Cross-Border EU Competition Law Actions

The interviewees were asked whether it is possible for a defendant to employ any delaying strategies. In only five out of 11 occasions was it clearly stated that delaying is a strategy which can be employed by a defendant in a cross-border EU competition law action, as witnesses will not be available for ever, and claims can become time-barred.

One respondent said: 'Time is always in the interest of the defendant, gaining time is important. . . . There is an incentive to delay the proceedings as time is of the essence. Certain witnesses will walk away, certain employees will not be available for statements any more.' In addition, another participant pointed out that 'time is really of the essence, not only because of the statute of limitation, also because it is difficult to gather the evidence.'

One interviewee stated that delaying strategies are usually a successful tool: 'Due to the uncertainty and the lack of judgments, it is an easy tactic to prolong the procedure, and of course defendants are typically trying to make the cases longer and more complicated and expensive.'

Entering into settlement negotiations was put forward as an example for a delaying strategy: 'This will not change the statute of limitation for the pending case, but you may delay the overall proceeding.' Another respondent stated that it is possible to 'delay the whole process for one or two years only with formal challenges.'

However, one interviewee stated the opposite opinion stating that defendants cannot deter plaintiffs from bringing the action. He claimed that 'as a defendant you cannot really delay things. If somebody wants to bring a claim and watches his statute of limitations, the claim will be brought before the statutes run. And there is not much you can do about it. If you negotiate about settlements in between, then of course you have the extension of the statutes automatically, so that does not help you in terms of hoping for the best or hoping that people will not bring a lawsuit. And there are not really other ways of delaying.'

C. Leniency Programmes and Damage Claims

The interviewees were asked whether the current leniency policy creates incentives for infringing undertakings to submit an application, and whether prospective leniency applicants could be deterred by potential damage claims. In addition, the interviewers further asked whether encouraging private damage claims and strengthening leniency programmes are two approaches excluding each other or whether a more efficient system of private enforcement could undermine the leniency programmes.

On three occasions it was clearly stated that leniency policy creates incentives for cartelists to cooperate with the authorities: 'Absolutely, the leniency policy is a very strong incentive to apply for leniency and to disclose the misconduct voluntarily.' Another opinion was: 'In the view of a leniency applicant it is for sure that if you do not apply for leniency, you will be imposed with fines by the cartel authority. This is the risk you can avoid by applying for leniency and private enforcement may follow, but this is not for sure.' Another argument which was put forward was that: 'you save on a fine – if you are confident that what you can offer to the authority is juicy and interesting enough.'

On five occasions, the respondents stated that defendants still apply for leniency, though they bear in mind that there can be a follow-on action: '[L]eniency is still a very attractive option despite the fact that in a number of Member States, in particular in the United Kingdom or in Germany, you have efficient systems of follow-on actions.'

One interviewee's view was that 'the fact that you have an increasing number of damage claims has not resulted in a cooling off and a reduction of the number of leniency applications.'

Furthermore, the participants assumed that the answer to the question strongly depends on whether the Commission or a National Competition Authority is in charge: 'I think that depends on what happened and how "hard core" the violation was. It also depends on what you think on how the damage can be calculated . . . and also on whether the European Commission or the Cartel Office will be in charge of the case.'

Especially the level of fines can be decisive: 'To a certain extent the fines are now in a region which might go beyond the exposure that you may have from follow-on actions.' One respondent even said that 'damages are not yet a reason not to go for leniency.'

Nevertheless, on three occasions it was argued that the risk of damage claims has a very high significance when advising a client:

> In the times when the courts were only dealing with the claims from the United States, the rule of thumb was that each dollar you pay as a fine will also make you pay two dollars in terms of civil compensation and procedural costs. By now we are not quite there, but you could easily invent scenarios where the cost of the civil follow-up litigation including the damages to be paid could be quite high in proportion to any fines you would be saving from the leniency application.

Another interesting view was that: 'There are many lawyers and I am among them who argue that you should be very careful with applying for leniency if the market in question is likely to trigger follow-on claims.' This opinion was shared in another interview: '[M]any companies nowadays tend to be reluctant to apply for immunity.'

Five out of 11 interviewees were of the opinion that encouraging private actions for damages and leniency at the same time, while not impossible, is difficult as they contradict each other: these participants thought that the promotion of private enforcement of EU competition law holds a serious danger for the consistency of the leniency concept:

> De lege lata they are not excluding each other but at least there are clearly contradicting goals. If you want to have more leniency cases, you should take care of the private enforcement side, you should think of special advantages for leniency applicants when it comes to damage claims. Otherwise you should not be surprised if companies are unwilling to disclose their wrongdoing.

One participant was 'concerned that public enforcement will suffer. Look at the number of cases. The Commission and the Federal Cartel Office heavily rely on leniency applications. The Federal Cartel Office had 76 cases in 2009 and 2010 and significantly more than half of these cases are based on leniency applications. If this tool goes away, you will not see that many cases anymore.'

Another interviewee took this up: 'It is very right that a very effective private enforcement system would threaten the thought of leniency programmes because it is very easy to go for the leniency applicant first.'

There were interesting insights as to whether the two concepts can be combined. Four interviewees suggested introducing a civil law immunity for the leniency applicant: 'But both concepts can comply with each other if you privilege the leniency applicant in follow-on actions, like the United States did where plaintiffs cannot demand punitive damages from leniency applicants.' One participant proposed to at least limit the liability, as he was convinced that there is a 'need to think about a privilege for the immunity applicant, for example that he is not liable for damages at all or only for a limited amount – you offer some protection and an incentive to still go in.' The third interviewee favouring civil immunity was also convinced that the United States' system is a role model: 'The idea behind the leniency programme is cooperation versus financial benefit. And the same should apply on the civil side. If a leniency applicant fully cooperates with private plaintiffs, this leniency applicant should have a financial benefit. To me, the United States model is a very good thing.'

Another proposal was depicted:

> [W]hat we propose is a solution where the leniency applicant is free vis-à-vis the first claimant and can only be sued after the other cartel members have been sued unsuccessfully. There is also

> the possibility to limit the exposure of the leniency applicant in context of this contribution claims. If the leniency applicant is being sued, he can get the full contribution from the other cartel members.

Two participants disagreed, as such an approach would not be in line with the underlying structure of legal systems in Europe: 'The Americans have an easy fix. They just say that there are not any treble damages for the "first in" which is a sixty per cent discount, but this cannot be the fix here.' Thus, immunity against civil law claims 'would not fit into our civil law. That would make sense from an antitrust point of view but I doubt that we will change our basic principles of civil law.' It was further stated that: 'If you file a leniency application, you really save a lot of money. If you also provide immunity in a civil law perspective, the balance would probably not fit to the overall system.'

Another interesting view was this:

> If your aim is to stop cartels then you have to answer the question whether it is better to encourage leniency or . . . to enforce private actions because there is an inherent conflict of interests between the two tools. You cannot have it both. In my view it is much more efficient to offer leniency also to those who come in second or third and not be too picky about it and at the same time impose high fines if people are caught without cooperation. That is much more effective than encouraging private actions. I do not believe that private actions are really a good tool in our system because it is expensive and burdensome and takes time. It is not really beneficial for the individual and it overloads courts which are already overloaded and will not be upgraded in terms of staff and resources to deal with all these cases.

IX. CONSISTENT APPLICATION AND ENFORCEMENT OF EU COMPETITION LAW ACROSS EUROPE

The answers to some questions were organised in order to identify whether the participants feel that there is a risk of inconsistent application of EU competition law provisions and/or inconsistent enforcement of EU competition law. In eight out of 11 cases, the respondents stated that there is a risk of misapplication of EU competition law within the 27 Member States of the EU. It was assumed that there are obviously different levels of expertise: 'But that is the name of the game. Since law is directly applicable we have to live with that and this is why we have the reference mechanism.' Another participant thought that there are discrepancies in application of law between competition authorities and courts. According to this opinion, the lack of knowledge of the substantive EU competition law 'combined with a lack of procedural guarantees is a very dangerous mixture, especially in Eastern Europe'. According to a similar view, 'there is a certain risk, in particular when it comes to damage assessment, damage estimation or other aspects of a typical cartel case'.

However, it was also suggested that the danger of misapplication is not limited to the new Member States. While one respondent said that 'some courts in some new Member States might have a different approach to some competition law issues because they are not used to applying this', he referred to the fact that this can also happen in Germany where there were some questionable decisions in the lower courts. One participant even assumed that

> there is a serious non-application of competition rules in a lot of countries . . . I have rarely seen any cases in Greece, very few cases in Poland, the Czech Republic and all these countries which are

> effectively applying on a decent standard all these rules, but still you do not see the Commission dawn raiding in a similar frequency in those countries. My assumption is that there are not less cases to be found in those countries, it is just an obvious discrepancy between the diligence with which the Commission focuses on certain countries.

Another interviewee shared his opinion that this is not a competition law issue, but a general problem which is inherent in a European Union with 27 Member States:

> I think this is not a competition related question, it is a very important question with regard maybe to all harmonising acts around the European Union. On the other hand, it is simply a matter of life . . . And clearly in Riga you would have different experience in comparison with the High Court in London but that is simply a fact of life.

Furthermore, this interviewee stated that a diverse application of competition law can lead to an abuse of procedural rules in cross-border competition law cases. Nevertheless, it was hinted at the fact that the Commission is dedicating a lot of resources to the training of judges: 'That is a very good programme and it is also very efficient.'

Only one respondent refused to accept that there is a problem of misapplication of EU competition law: 'I do not think we have seen any outrageous decisions from Bulgarian or Romanian authorities or courts applying European law. I am not aware of anything like this.'

X. EUROPEAN JUDICIARY

The answers to some questions were organised in order to identify whether the participants feel that the current European court system is adequate to deal with the challenges of the private antitrust enforcement. At this point, the participants were asked whether there is a need for a Court of Appeal at EU level to ensure a uniform interpretation of EU competition law. In all cases, this suggestion was rejected:

> Leaving aside the question whether the Member States would be willing to accept such a mechanism, there is indeed no need for that. If national courts have certain doubts, they can and do make use of the right to refer cases to the Court of Justice and most cases and most decisions from [it] are very balanced and very good ones.

One respondent even feared 'a disastrous drawback for effective legal protection'. This has been reasoned by the fact that even today, decisions in EU competition law might take years if European courts are involved.

XI. SETTLEMENTS

Also, account was taken of the participants' views as to why so many EU competition law cases settle.

On three occasions, the respondents claimed that first of all psychological aspects influence the parties' decisions. The parties want to solve these legal problems as they consume time and affect their work: '[P]eople who are responsible or have filed an immunity application really want to get rid of it.'

On another occasions it was stated that 'settlements are generally attractive for both sides: The victim typically wants to have compensation for the suffered damage quickly. For the plaintiff it can be interesting because he gets the risks out of the books.'

In addition, the experts are aware of several reasons to settle, especially from a plaintiff's point of view. He has a very strong interest to settle because of the costs, the length of the dispute, the complexity of litigation and the problems with the quantification of damages. However, four out of 11 interviewees saw the main reason for defendants to enter into settlement negotiations in the on-going business relationships: 'The defendants have a very strong incentive to settle because they do not want to harm the customer relationship.' Another participant claimed: 'If you are in an on-going business relationship, they will very often be even eager to settle, they may even try to sweeten a settlement for themselves by entering into future business relationships.'

However, in the context of settlements, two dissenting opinions can be identified. One participant said that only a few cases in Europe settle due to legal uncertainty: 'The reason is that there are so many open questions and that there is no real incentive at the moment for the defendants to settle.' Another view against settlement was:

> Nevertheless, parties do not really like to settle because if you enter into the first settlement, even if you agree upon very strictly confidential issues, you could trigger an avalanche. From a defendant's point of view, I would try to avoid settlements since there are still some general legal arguments against overflowing damage claims. And the issue is of course, if you start entering into faithful settlement discussions, time limits will be stopped anyway.

Thus, entering into settlement negotiations 'is a much more severe disadvantage than going to court trying to delay the process.'

XII. ALTERNATIVE METHODS FOR DISPUTE RESOLUTION

It was also interesting to identify whether the participants feel that Alternative Methods for Dispute Resolution can be an appropriate mechanism to be used for the settlement of cross-border EU competition law claims. Five interviewees held the view that the Alternative Methods for Dispute Resolution, and especially mediation, are not a promising mechanism to be used for settlements. One participant stated: 'If you talk to the Commission, they are not so keen that arbitration is pushed. It is too secret and confidential.' Another view was: 'All in all, I do not expect too much from mediation.'

Another attendee underlined the advantages of settlements without any external participants like lawyers or mediators: 'I have always preferred the direct settlement. In many cases I recommended to leave out the lawyers.' The reason for this was as follows: 'Sometimes it makes things much easier as lawyers tend to be interested in a long mediation and settlement process.' Furthermore, this participant concluded that there is also a risk for the mediator: '[T]he mediator has always the difficulty that he has to take a decision, he has to make a precise proposal and . . . will hardly be able to find a real compromise.'

Nevertheless, the same respondent admitted it is an 'exciting idea . . . to ask the cartelist to agree on a joint economist . . . to investigate and find out whether there is a cartel damage. He should then make a suggestion how to settle these claims. This is very much like a mediation process, but it is at a very early stage.'

XIII. CONSUMERS

Account was also taken of the participants' views as to how the consumers fare under the current system and whether new remedies for claims brought by consumers (opt-in or opt-out regime, class actions) might change the situation. In the majority of the cases (nine out of 10) the participants submitted that consumers do not take an active part under the current system. One respondent even stated that 'consumers are really the losers in the current system . . . Unfortunately, under the legal framework consumers are practically not able to bring any damage claims successfully.'

The following reasons for the insignificant role of consumers and consumer organisations were put forward by two interviewees: 'Firstly, the individual harm is too low to afford a lawyer and to enter into the risk of a lawsuit and secondly, many consumers do not have sufficient documentation.' The negligible amount of damage and the consequence that consumers do not see the sense in pursuing it was given as the main reason for their inactivity in two other cases. And there is a problem of data protection when considering proving low-value damages with a sort of 'payback-/bonuscard system'.

Only on one occasion was the view expressed that at least very significant consumers play a role under the current competition law system: 'If you look at the big industrial customers they will usually bring damage claims themselves and they have been exposed to similar claims in the United States and here and know the game.' But this respondent also thought that small consumers rarely claim for damages, for the reasons suggested by the other experts: 'I have seen very few cases in which a small consumer brought a lawsuit to ask for damages and I doubt that he will take the procedural risks and is sophisticated enough to do it.'

Concerning the question of whether new remedies for claims brought by consumers like an opt-in or opt-out regime or class actions might change the situation, the participants had diverse views.

The majority of interviewees were not convinced by the idea that consumer organisations can change the game for the benefit of harmed consumers. One respondent referred to the idea of consumer groups or organisations representing a great number of consumers stating that such a solution gives rise to problems when it comes to the distribution of any compensation awarded. The costs for administration can equalise the advantages of such an action: '[T]he bureaucratic efforts might be extremely high and demanding so that the effect at the end is not positive.' Referring to consumer organisations, one interviewee was concerned that 'it is not the consumers who would benefit, [but] the associations'. Another interviewee came up with an interesting question:

> How will you distribute the money? There are so many difficult questions and if it is for 15€ per person, I do not see a political need to do that. I know Manfredi speaks a different language to some extent but it is a question of the amount you suffer. If you personally suffer a loss of 15€, you would not go to court irrespective of what the source of that loss is, a cartel or anything else. On the other hand, if the losses are significantly higher, we need a better tool in order to enable consumers to recover these amounts of money. But in my view, these cases are quite rare.

Concerning an opt-in regime, one interviewee proposed 'a mechanism which makes it easy and has low barriers to entry for end-consumers, e.g. web based agreements, where you click on "Yes, I agree" and you do not need to do anything further.' According to this respondent, the opt-in model is much closer to European legal traditions.

In this context, one participant took another approach, stating that consumers (just like every other market participant who is harmed by cartels) appreciate if cartels in general are stopped from infringing law, no matter how.

Only one of the participants was of the view that an opt-out regime would be the most efficient way, although 'there is a clear risk that this could be abused. So you have to balance advantages . . . and disadvantages. It is very difficult.' However, another interviewee took a more sceptical view: 'We have to avoid the excesses of the United States system and therefore we have to be cautious when introducing such things . . . For example, opt-out would be too daring – for me the United States system is rotten because it serves to finance the plaintiffs' bar.' This scepticism was shared by another respondent:

> I think the downsides are enormous. I do not think that it will bring additional justice to the individual whereas I see that it could really interfere with the well working system and I am very sceptical especially if you look at opt-out approaches. They are so foreign to most of the European legal systems and I think that they will be very hard to control. We have seen negative effects in the United States at least for someone with a civil law background, a European lawyer . . . It is Pandora's Box.

One interviewee offered a possible solution:

> What would certainly help from the end-consumer's perspective is to allow some sort of class action where all the small damages are combined to a very significant damage. Then such class action would be a very powerful tool and threat to the cartelist but that would be really going the American way which has certain downsides. It is a real dilemma. Before something like class actions is introduced, it should be investigated in detail to what extent cartel damages are really passed on to end consumers because I am pretty sure that in many cartel cases the harm is absorbed somewhere in between the cartelist and the end consumer . . . I think that the possibility for customer and consumer associations to bring damage claims will not work in the current German legal framework because the outcome of the financial damages will not directly go to the associations or to the end consumers but to the state.

Another possibility to solve this problem is to make sure that the fines imposed by the authorities are used to compensate consumers: 'One question could be whether the competition authority can claim on top of the fine a certain amount which would be dedicated to some public purpose . . . I think about funds which take a certain function for this particular consumer group but it cannot be the passing on of minimal amounts to individual consumers.'

XIV. WAYS FORWARD

One of the most interesting and most important observations is that none of the interviewees wanted to see fundamental changes to the current system. Drawing the foregoing concerns together, the most significant problems appear to be that (1) consumers do not play a role in cross-border competition law, (2) national procedural rules differ significantly, (3) there are high costs of litigating (especially in the United Kingdom), and (4) that damage claims and leniency programmes are in conflict with each other.

One participant asserted that changing procedural rules in order to simplify the conditions of actions is not a considerable solution: 'We cannot change our entire system of who can claim what just for private antitrust damage claims.'

Nevertheless, this interviewee conceded that 'there are maybe rules on evidence and on the burden of proof which could be adapted to make it easier for the courts and for both parties actually to deal with the question of quantum.' Also according to another respondent's expertise, a change of the legal scene, especially when it comes to full and unrestricted discovery, did not appear to be a solution.

The introduction of specific rules for competition law actions rather than using general civil law provisions was considered to be impossible: 'At the moment it is just an open question how you apply the traditional system to these kinds of cases . . . I would not go for specific rules but let a few years elapse in order to have the right answer to all these questions.'

However, the calculation of damages will probably remain the main challenge, apart from the jurisdictional issues: 'One of the main issues will remain: how you calculate the damages.' This opinion was expressed on another occasion as well: 'This is an issue which is very important in the whole area of private damages claims – the economic expertise must be very high.' Thereafter, it would be 'beneficial for everyone who is involved in the system to take a step back from the idea of precisely calculating damages even when making use of economic experts.'

It was stated on two occasions that the divergence between leniency and private enforcement is the decisive point when thinking about improving the current system. This was one interesting view:

> I think the crucial issue is how to harmonise the two conflicting goals of a high number of leniency applications with a high level of private enforcement. This is the huge challenge at EU level. It has not been solved yet and my impression is that we are much more away from a solution than maybe two or five years ago because now the trend is towards increasing private enforcement, collective redress and class actions. The question of how to protect the leniency is not really addressed with the same intensity because it is so difficult for the European Union, as it requires a change of national civil law.

Concerning the fact that private enforcement depends on effective leniency programmes, it was further analysed that there are already ramifications: 'We can already see the results of these conflicting goals which means that the number of leniency applications of good quality is decreasing at EU level and this is certainly not because there are less cartels.'

5

Concluding Remarks on Promoting Regulatory Competition: Issues to be Addressed

MIHAIL DANOV AND FLORIAN BECKER

I. ENFORCEMENT GAP

Is there an enforcement gap in Europe? Although the comparative studies – revealed by both the Ashurst Report[1] and the Collective Antitrust Redress Report[2] – appear to show strongly that private antitrust litigation is underdeveloped in Europe, the respondents from England and Germany overwhelmingly suggested that competition litigation is picking up.[3] In particular, in the vast majority of responses, they were of the opinion that there are more EU competition law actions than there used to be. Several participants noted that there may be a significant number of settlements occurring as well.[4] However, the current enforcement pattern, in which the limited private litigation is heavily dependent on a competition authority's decision establishing an infringement, inevitably leaves an enforcement gap as the public enforcers across Europe are unlikely to have the resources to investigate all the complaints they receive. This was clearly deduced from the data, which suggest unequivocally that the increase is only in respect of follow-on actions. Is this the case across Europe?

The collected data appear to suggest that there is a degree of variation when it comes to the enforcement of EU competition law in Europe. Judging from the interview responses, it appears that Germany, England, the Netherlands and possibly Spain are attracting more cross-border EU competition law actions than other countries. However, this also brings into question how effectively and consistently EU competition law provisions are enforced across Europe. The deduction that there is a level of variation when it comes to the enforcement of competition law across Europe could find further support in the recent quantitative data gathered by the authors of the Collective Redress in Antitrust study.[5] In particular, it has been submitted that:

[1] D Waelbroeck, D Slater and G Even-Shoshan, *Study on the Conditions of Claims for Damages in case of Infringement of EC Competition Rules (Ashurst Report)* http://ec.europa.eu/competition/antitrust/actionsdamages/comparative_report_clean_en.pdf.

[2] P Buccirossi, M Carpagnano, L Ciari et al, *Collective Redress in Antitrust* www.europarl.europa.eu/document/activities/cont/201206/20120613ATT46782/20120613ATT46782EN.pdf.

[3] See more: Ch 3.

[4] See more: Ch 3.

[5] *Collective Redress in Antitrust* (n 2).

> collective actions on antitrust have been brought only in six countries (Austria, France, Germany, Italy, Spain and UK), but in none of them were there more than five of these actions over the last five years . . . Moreover, only in Austria, Spain, France and the UK some collective actions have been admitted by courts and have reached the trial stage. To date collective actions resulting in damages awarded to the victims have been observed only in Austria and in the UK.[6]

Hence, it seems clear that there is an enforcement gap in some Member States which may be attracting less EU competition law actions, and, as a result, there may be less redress in those countries for the victims of such infringements. Furthermore, the fact that only a few consumers and SMEs are bringing actions in Germany and England at the moment reinforces the case that that there is an enforcement gap at the moment. On 24 occasions, it was stated that undertakings[7] generally (encompassing large businesses and SMEs) are more active than consumers. In view of the foregoing, it was not surprising that the overwhelming view, submitted on 17 occasions in England and Belgium (and Brussels in particular), and nine occasions in Germany, was that consumers fare relatively badly under the current system. Only on two occasions (one respondent from England, and one respondent from Germany) was the view expressed that consumers fare acceptably under the current system. How to close the enforcement gap and provide redress for consumers and SMEs?[8]

Given the fact that most EU competition law infringements would be imputed to groups of companies actively operating in a number of Member States, it would be important to note that any proposed solutions must take account of the fact that businesses and consumers would be affected in a number of jurisdictions.

II. IMPORTANT ASPECTS SHAPING LITIGANTS' STRATEGIES IN A CROSS-BORDER CONTEXT

Before discussing possible solutions, it would be important to demonstrate how the current private antitrust enforcement architecture appears to be shaping litigants' tactics. There are four aspects which are seemingly important in this context: (a) the two-step adjudication competition enforcement process; (b) the various procedural rules; (c) cross-border litigation costs/risks; and (d) levels of damages. These aspects need to be carefully considered in the course of any reform which is intended to promote more private antitrust litigation.

[6] ibid 39. Regarding the UK, it should be noted that the authors are referring to the *JJB* case which settled, and is far from being an example for effective redress for consumers due to the small numbers of consumers receiving compensation. See more: Which?, 'JJB Sports: a case study in collective action' www.which.co.uk/documents/pdf/collective-redress-case-study-which-briefing-258401.pdf.

[7] eg *Enron Coal Services Ltd (In Liquidation) v English Welsh* & *Scottish Ltd* [2011] EWCA Civ 2; *Roche Products Ltd, Roche Vitamine Europe AG (Switzerland), F Hoffmann-La Roche AG (Switzerland) v Provimi Ltd* [2003] EWHC 961 (Comm); *Cooper Tire & Rubber Company Europe Ltd & Others* [2010] EWCA Civ 864; *Toshiba Carrier UK Ltd and Other v KME Yorkshire Ltd & Others* [2012] EWCA Civ 1190; Case No 1077/5/7/07 *Emerson Electric* [2008] CAT 8, 28 April 2008.

[8] See the solution considered by the Department for Business Innovation & Skills, *Private Actions in Competition Law: A Consultation on Options for Reform,* 24 April 2012 www.bis.gov.uk/assets/biscore/consumer-issues/docs/p/12-742-private-actions-in-competition-law-consultation.pdf.

A. Private Litigation Dependant on Public Enforcement: Effect on Litigants' Tactics

A separate-task approach, in which arguably a regulator is better placed to detect and establish an infringement and, subsequently, a court is better placed to award damages,[9] affects claimants' tactics in a number of ways. First, the private litigation which occurs normally proceeds as a follow-on action based on a public enforcement action. The majority of our respondents thought that going to the competition authority first would be a normal strategy, rather than bringing a private action and seeking damages before national courts.

Secondly, defendants appeared to be employing a number of delaying strategies, raising preliminary issues in the course of private antitrust proceedings. Indeed, there would be a level of legal uncertainty as well as evidential hurdles, due to the two-step adjudication. For example, damages must be proved; a decision establishing an infringement on its own would not normally suffice,[10] as liability must be imputed to a particular legal entity, and this might be far from certain, as it is far from certain what the liability would be for a local subsidiary of a group of companies that was found to be an infringing undertaking within the meaning of Articles 101 and 102 TFEU.[11] Indeed, the concept of undertaking used by the regulator when establishing an infringement, and the fact that most multinational businesses would involve not a single legal entity, but groups of companies, would suggest that there are specific problems which must be addressed with regard to private proceedings. As already noted,[12] it may be far from efficient to have one set of proceedings before a national competition authority (NCA) in order to establish a breach of competition law, and another set of proceedings before Member State courts in order for a claimant to prove that damage has been caused to him.

The case for procedural inefficiencies of the current two-step adjudication (ie before the regulator, and before the courts) under the current enforcement regime may be further strengthened by putting forward that a reference to the Court of Justice may also be required which could potentially result in a further delay.[13] The view that a final decision may be significantly delayed if the European courts are involved was shared by a significant number of respondents. In view of that, one should wonder if, when it comes to cross-border EU competition litigation, 'the interlocking system of jurisdiction of the [EU] courts and the national courts serves to ensure the "rule of law", of which effective judicial protection and judicial review are intrinsic components.'[14]

[9] WPJ Wils, 'The Relationship Between Public Antitrust Enforcement and Private Actions for Damages' (2009) 32 *World Competition* 3, 18 – accessible at http://papers.ssrn.com/sol3/papers.cfm?abstract_id=1296458 .

[10] *Enron* (n 7).

[11] eg *Provimi* (n 7); *Cooper Tire* (n 7); *Toshiba Carrier* (n 7); *Emerson Electric Co v Morgan Crucible Company Plc and Ors* [2011] CAT 4; *Emerson Electric Co v Morgan Crucible Company Plc and Ors* – still pending before the Court of Appeal – Case Reference C3/2011/1658; *Nokia Corporation v AU Optronics Corporation* [2012] EWHC 731 (Ch).

[12] See Ch 3.

[13] eg Case C-453/99 *Courage Ltd v Crehan* [2001] ECR I-6297; Joined Cases C-295/04–C-298/04 *Manfredi v Lloyd Adriaticco* [2006] 5 CMLR 17; Case C-360/09 *Pfleiderer AG v Bundeskartellamt* [2011] 5 CMLR 219.

[14] K Lenaerts, 'The rule of law and the coherence of the judicial system of the European Union' (2007) 44 *CML Rev* 1625, 1626.

B. Procedure – A Key Factor in the Choice of Jurisdiction in Private Actions

The level of variation which was found to exist across Europe with regard to the enforcement of EU competition law may be explained by the fact that, as already noted,[15] the 27 Member States share different legal traditions and legal heritages. Some of the new Member State courts may have less experience in applying EU competition law, and bad private antitrust enforcement appears to be the result in those countries.

The gathered data clearly show that the procedural differences between the states shape the strategies of the claimants (in particular of the sophisticated claimants with deep pockets). Therefore, an overwhelming majority of respondents from Germany and England thought that claimants could gain some procedural (and/or substantive law) advantages by bringing their claim in one jurisdiction rather than another.[16] There was even the suggestion that procedural rules might be more important than the amount of damages awarded in the choice of jurisdiction.

The most important procedural aspects can be summarised as disclosure, speed of proceedings, and standard of proof. In particular, on 17 occasions in England and on 11 occasions in Germany, the disclosure rules were mentioned as a very important procedural aspect which could influence a claimant's decision where to bring an EU competition law action. The speed of the procedure (ie the time it takes for an award to be made, or for a claimant to force a settlement) was considered to be an important factor; this was submitted on 15 occasions (12 occasions in England and three occasions in Germany). Thirdly, the standard of proof was mentioned as a decisive factor in Germany and as an important factor by one participant in England as well.

Can the claimants be selective by bringing their claims where procedural rules are most appropriate? The high costs, which could be fuelled by the high level of uncertainty surrounding the cross-border EU competition law claims,[17] would be an important factor to be considered in claims brought by consumers and SMEs who may be prone to economise on the costs by bringing claims in their home states.[18] Six out of 11 interviewees from Germany thought that it would be beneficial for plaintiffs to sue in their home state. Many participants from England made a clear distinction between claims brought by consumers and SMEs, on the one hand, and claims brought by big companies, on the other hand. On nine occasions in England, it was submitted that it would be beneficial especially for SMEs or consumers to sue in their home states.[19]

C. Costs and Damages – Other Important Factors in the Choice of Jurisdiction

Costs may be especially high in competition law claims.[20] On the one hand, the high level of litigation costs, which could be fuelled by the high level of uncertainty with regard to

[15] See Ch 1.

[16] See more: Ch 3.

[17] Ch 3.

[18] See also: CF Beckner III and A Katz, 'The Incentive Effects of Litigation Fee Shifting When Legal Standards Are Uncertain', (1995) 15 *International Review of Law and Economics* 205, 207.

[19] Ch 3.

[20] Case No 1178/5/7/11, *2 Travel Group PLC (In Liquidation) v Cardiff City Transport Services Ltd* [2011] CAT 30, 14 October 2011 [17]. See also: *Yeheshkel Arkin v Borchard Lines and Others* [2005] EWCA Civ 655.

cross-border EU competition law claims,[21] can be a significant deterrent for claims brought by consumers and SMEs. They may not be able to afford to bring a claim if there is no funding scheme in place. The litigation costs could be further increased if the defendants employ delaying strategies which appear to be possible in the current state of uncertainty with regard to cross-border EU competition law actions.[22] On the other hand, one might think that the high level of uncertainty may encourage large companies (eg large purchasers) to bring such claims in order to force a settlement, for example, with their suppliers (especially in follow-on cases where an infringement has been detected by the Commission or an NCA), provided that their suppliers are risk-averse.[23]

Due to the high cross-border litigation costs, only large companies appear to be bringing cross-border EU competition law actions. Thus, the choice for consumers and SMEs under the current system might be suing at home or not suing at all, as litigation costs are another important factor which shapes claimants' tactics in a cross-border context. There is hardly any redress for consumers, who have no incentive to bring damages actions under the current system. Indeed, one could question even the consumers' interests in seeing the regulator impose fines in the region of hundreds of millions. 'First the customer suffers from the infringement and then suffers from the company trying to allocate the cost of the fine a second time.'[24]

The high litigation costs may be offset against the high level of damages which may be suffered as a result of EU competition law infringements, if there are effective redress mechanisms. The majority of the respondents noted that litigants will make a cost-benefit analysis before deciding whether and where to initiate a cross-border competition law claim. Although data from England appears to suggest that damages would be dominated by procedure, which would pre-determine what would be awarded, and when,[25] the majority of respondents from England and Germany clearly stated that availability of a passing-on defence would be an important consideration in a cross-border context.

Should these issues be dealt with at EU level? Should they be dealt with at national level, given the importance of procedure? How to close the enforcement gap? Should there be harmonisation/centralisation or should there be more diversity (decentralisation and inter-jurisdictional regulatory competition)?

III. CLOSING THE ENFORCEMENT GAP: WHO SHOULD ADDRESS IT? HOW?

There seems to be a strong case that the current institutional enforcement architecture, in which a regulator is regarded as being better placed to detect and establish an infringement and, subsequently, a court is better placed to award damages,[26] appears to generate a level

[21] Ch 3.

[22] eg jurisdictional challenges – *Provimi* (n 7); *Toshiba Carrier* (n 7); *Nokia* (n 9); leniency documents: Case C-360/09 *Pfleiderer* (n 13); *National Grid Electricity Transmission PLC v ABB Ltd & Others* [2012] EWHC 869 (Ch).

[23] Ch 3.

[24] HH Lidgard, 'Due Process in European Competition Procedure: A Fundamental Concept or a Mere Formality?' in P Cardonnel, A Rosas and N Wahl (eds), *Constitutionalising the EU Judicial System: Essays in Honour of Pernilla Lindh* (Oxford, Hart Publishing, 2012) 403, 421.

[25] See more: Ch 3.

[26] Wils (n 9) 18.

of uncertainty. Moreover, it is not only that such an institutional enforcement architecture is inefficient in so far as we witness two sets of proceedings with regard to the same infringement, but also it is questionable 'whether or not the entire process is fair'.[27] Whilst a national court would apply civil procedure rules that presuppose respect of due process, an NCA would apply administrative procedure rules that could potentially raise concerns as to the undertaking's right to a fair trial and hearing.[28] Nazzini has very recently argued that 'the current EU competition enforcement regime, which is characterised by an administrative decision-maker with no guarantees of independence and impartiality and deferential judicial review, is unconstitutional.'[29] Lidgard went on to state that 'a radical solution would be to deprive the Commission of any decision-making power and require that infringements are dealt with by an impartial tribunal'.[30] It may be the case that it is about time to realise that a regulator should not be regarded as being better placed to detect and establish an infringement, and encourage another set of proceeding with a view to award damages. Mechanisms allowing for some form of consolidation of the two sets of proceedings before national courts[31] might be desirable, as the outcome in the follow-on action would be highly dependent upon the evidence gathered as well as on the binding findings in the course of the proceedings establishing the infringement.[32] Thus, these issues might need to be carefully considered at EU level.

The other issue which requires attention is the level of variation regarding conditions for bringing EU competition law damages actions,[33] which potentially results in a level of variation with regard to private antitrust enforcement across Europe. The data clearly show that there may be advantages for claimants by suing in one jurisdiction rather than another, and, as a result, there would possibly be disadvantages for claimants bringing such actions in some jurisdictions. Should these issues be addressed at EU level? The EU legislator has adopted a special Regulation 1/2003 which is meant to ensure that Articles 101 and 102 TFEU are applied effectively and uniformly across Europe,[34] but does not address allocation of jurisdiction and assessment of damages, for example. It has been noted that the EU legislator may derive competence to harmonise procedural rules from Articles 81 and 114 TFEU.[35] Rizzuto went on to submit that:

[27] Lidgard (n 24) 421.

[28] IS Forrester, 'Due Process in EC Competition Cases: A Distinguished Institution with Flawed Procedures' (2009) 34 EL Rev 817; J Killick and P Berghe, 'This is Not the Time to Be Tinkering with Regulation 1/2003 – It is Time for Fundamental Reform – Europe Should Have Change We Can Believe in' (2010) *Competition Law Review* 259. The due process issue appears to be receiving renewed attention after the entry into force of the Lisbon Treaty. See Art 6(1) TEU. See also Art 6(1) ECHR and Art 47(2) of the Charter of Fundamental Rights of the European Union [2000] OJ C364/1. See further, J Kuhling, 'Fundamental Rights' in A von Bogdandy and J Bast (eds), *Principles of European Constitutional Law*, 2nd edn (Oxford, Hart Publishing, 2010) 479–514; P Craig, *The Lisbon Treaty: Law, Politics and Treaty Reform* (Oxford, OUP, 2010) 193–245.

[29] R Nazzini, 'Administrative enforcement: judicial review and fundamental rights in EU competition law: A comparative contextual-functionalist perspective' (2012) 49 *CML Rev* 971, 1005.

[30] Lidgard (n 24) 421.

[31] *cf.* Department for Business Innovation & Skills, *A Competition Regime for Growth: A Consultation on Options for Reform*, 16 March 2011 www.bis.gov.uk/assets/biscore/consumer-issues/docs/c/11-758-competition-regime-for-growth-impact-assessment.pdf paras 241–43.

[32] *Pfleiderer* (n 13); *National Grid* (n 22). See also: *Emerson* (n 11). See also: Ch 3.

[33] Ashurst Report (n 1).

[34] See Recitals 1–8 of Council Regulation No 1/2003 on the implementation of the rules on competition laid down in Articles 101 and 102 TFEU.

[35] From the Board, 'Two Steps Forward and One Step Back: Harmonizing The Unharmonizable', (2011) 38 *Legal Issues of Economic Integration* 207, 210.

> the [EU] has been conferred competence in the Treaty to bring forward legislative measures harmonising national procedural rules, or to enact autonomous [EU] rules designed to establish a uniform legal framework governing civil liability procedural rules to be applied by national courts for infringement of [EU] competition law, regardless of national procedural rules governing civil liability actions for breaches of national competition law or other [tortious] acts.[36]

Nonetheless, one should wonder, in light of the above data, whether harmonisation will bring more certainty or uncertainty. The German Government and *Bundeskartellamt* 'cannot discern any convincing reason for special private law and civil procedure rules for enforcing antitrust law . . . Damages actions . . . are largely enforced on the basis of general provisions that are in many ways fundamentally different in the various Member States.'[37]

A. Regulation at EU Level or Regulation at National Level: Harmonisation vs Diversity

The question whether there should be more harmonisation/centralisation[38] or diversity/decentralisation with regard to private antitrust law enforcement in Europe has been the subject of heated academic debate in Europe. One would have thought that the matter should by now be settled, in view of the fact that the White Paper on Modernisation of the Rules Implementing Articles 101 and 102 TFEU was intended inter alia to promote decentralised enforcement of EU competition law.[39] Indeed, the fact that the cause of action for EU competition law damages is a mixture of EU law and Member States' laws may be justified by the 'political and legal reality' in the Union.[40] The latter aims to strike a balance between the requirement of consistent enforcement of EU competition law across Europe, on the one hand, and the Member States' competence in matters of procedure broadly defined to cover the issues of causation and remedies.[41] Therefore, one should ask if harmonisation is really needed with regard to cross-border EU competition law actions.

Different commentators share conflicting views when answering this question. Van Gerven[42] has noted:

> [Harmonisation] is particularly needed in the field of competition law, now that Council Regulation No. 1/2003 . . . has given the national courts (and national competition authorities) full competence to apply Articles [101 and 102 TFEU] . . . in order to allow the national courts to perform this task adequately, they need uniform rules on remedies, not only with regard to claims

[36] F Rizzuto, 'Does the European Community have Legal Competence to Harmonise National Procedural Rules Governing Private Actions for Damages for Infringements of European Community Antitrust Rules?', (2009) *Global Competition Litigation Review* 29, 47.

[37] Comments of the Federal Ministry of Economics and Technology, the Federal Ministry of Justice, the Federal Ministry of Food, Agriculture and Consumer Protection and the Bundeskartellamt on the EU Commission's White Paper on 'Damages actions for breach of the EC antitrust rules' (courtesy translation) http://ec.europa.eu/competition/antitrust/actionsdamages/white_paper_comments/bund_en.pdf 3. See also: J Kortmann and C Swaak, 'The EC White Paper on Antitrust Damage Actions: Why the Member States are (right to be) less than Enthusiastic' (2009) *ECLR* 340.

[38] The choice between decentralisation and centralisation/harmonisation has been discussed by W Kerber, 'Interjurisdictional Competition within the European Union' (1999–2000) 23 *Fordham International Law Journal* S217, S228.

[39] White Paper on Modernisation of the Rules Implementing Articles 85 and 86 of the EC Treaty, Commission Programme No 99/027 [58]–[61].

[40] W van Gerven, 'Of Rights, Remedies and Procedures' (2000) *CML Rev* 501, 521.

[41] van Gerven (n 40) 521.

[42] W van Gerven, 'Harmonisation of Private Law: Do we need it?' (2004) 41 *CML Rev* 505.

> in compensation but also with regard to claims in nullity, restitution, interim relief and, possibly, collective claims on the part of consumers. That can only be done, in an orderly way by means of an additional [EU] regulation, ensuring that judicial remedies are made available which are similar, if not identical, substantively and procedurally, throughout the [EU], to allow plaintiffs to protect [EU] rights which have been impaired as a result of anti-competitive behaviour.[43]

Similarly, Dougan noted that 'it is readily apparent that inadequate national remedies and procedural rules can frustrate the effective application of [EU] law within each Member State.'[44] Following this line of thinking, it has been noted by Betlem that 'an individual should be entitled to damages for breach of [EU] competition law as a matter of [EU] law not national law.'[45] In other words, some form of a harmonisation may be justified by the need to avoid the anomaly allowing the different Member State courts to award different amount of damages with regard to the very same type of breach of the very same EU competition law provision. Therefore, the authors of the Ashurst Report and of the Report on Collective Redress in Antitrust appear to believe that harmonisation is needed with regard to claims based on EU competition law.

However, Weatherill has argued that 'in a geographically and functionally expanded European Union the establishment of common rules is not only increasingly difficult to achieve, it is also increasingly undesirable as a suppression of competitive and cultural diversity.'[46] A level of variation with regard to EU competition law damage actions brought in the EU context may be justified by the primary responsibility of individual Member States to decide on the relevant procedural rules and remedies available.[47] Accordingly, Marcos and Sanchez[48] have argued that:

> the diversity of Tort laws and Civil Procedure regulations generated in the field of private antitrust enforcement are only apparent as they constitute variations that arise naturally from the differences in national legal rules themselves. There is nothing wrong with that and the Commission should refrain from further actions directly aimed at ending such diversity. Besides, differences in tort legal rules may reflect different legal cultures and traditions, which are the result of a complex and valuable process of norms production adapted to national peculiarities and problems.[49]

Bearing these academic discussions in mind, it should be noted that the overwhelming majority of respondents from England[50] and Germany[51] favoured allowing the current system to evolve in its current form. As already noted,[52] the majority of respondents from England favoured modest reforms to the current system at the national level, allowing competition to develop between different jurisdictions. Few participants saw much scope

[43] ibid 524.

[44] M Dougan, *National Remedies Before the Court of Justice* (Oxford, Hart Publishing, 2004) 65.

[45] G Betlem, 'Torts, a European *Ius Commune* and the private enforcement of Community law' (2005) 64 *Cambridge Law Journal* 126, 142. See also: C Kremer, 'Liability for breach of European Community Law: An analysis of the new remedy in the light of English and German law' (2003) *Yearbook of European Law* 203, 211.

[46] S Weatherill, 'Why harmonise?' in T Tridimas and P Nebbia (eds), *European Union Law for the Twenty-First Century: Rethinking the New Legal Order* Vol 2 (Oxford, Hart Publishing, 2004) 11.

[47] van Gerven (n 40).

[48] F Marcos and AS Graells, 'Damages for Breach of the EC Antitrust Rules: Harmonising Tort Law through the back door (2008) InDret 1-18, www.indret.com/code/getPdf.php?id=1088&pdf=518_en.pdf .

[49] ibid 14. See also: F Cafaggi, 'Introduction' in F Cafaggi (ed), *The Institutional Framework of European Private Law* (Oxford, OUP, 2006) 1, 1–2.

[50] See more: Ch 3.

[51] See more: Ch 4.

[52] See more: Ch 3.

for a new Regulation or Directive. Respondents from England were concerned that new laws from Brussels would be unlikely to address the fundamental uncertainty that currently deters many claims, and might even enhance it, as they might bring fresh uncertainty.[53] Similarly, one of the most interesting and most important observations from the qualitative interviews from Germany is that none of the interviewees wants to see fundamental changes to the current system. Therefore a significant majority of our respondents appear to be against a reform at EU level and in favour of a system of regulatory competition between procedural and substantive regimes. The respondents appear to favour inter-jurisdictional regulatory competition in the area of EU antitrust law dispute resolution between the various Member States to attract claimants and produce efficient enforcement results.

As already noted, promoting inter-jurisdictional regulatory competition was indeed one of the possibilities for reform examined by the authors of the report on *Making Antitrust Damages Actions More Effective in the EU*.[54] Unfortunately, they examined this hypothesis under the 'no policy change' scenario.[55] As a result, the question of whether the current institutional framework is suited to promoting regulatory competition remained unaddressed. Indeed, a reform at EU level may be needed if the current institutional framework does not provide for a regulatory competition to materialise with regard to cross-border EU competition law actions. The institutional framework would be crucial in view of the diverse nature of the European Union following the 2004, 2007 and 2013 enlargements. The need for a policy change has been signalled by Cafaggi, who has stated:

> The design of the institutional framework of [European Private Law[56]] is relevant to strategic choices concerning what and how to integrate. It is, however, also important to organize the differences in the legal systems of Member States. The enlargement process has meant that higher levels of flexibility are needed in order to pursue the goals of creating an integrated market and a cohesive policy. The need to respect national legal identities means that new mechanisms for coordination between the European institutions, and between them and the institutions of Member States, are required.[57]

When it comes to cross-border EU competition law actions, the private international law framework would be crucial if Articles 101 and 102 TFEU were to be enforced consistently across the EU. The data indicate that if competition between the different jurisdictions for laying down conditions for bringing such actions were to be promoted in Europe, then the private international law framework would be key. In particular, collected data from England and Germany suggest that the jurisdictional rules would be crucial in this context as they would allow the claimants the possibility to engage in a strategic behaviour. It appears that, under the current framework, the choice of forum would be a major decision to be taken in a cross-border context. However, does the current private international law framework provide for regulatory competition? Might the EU legislator promote regulatory competition through it?

[53] See more: Ch 3.

[54] Report for the European Commission, Contract DG COMP/2006/A3/012, *Making Antitrust Damages Actions More Effective in the EU: Welfare Impact and Potential Scenarios* http://ec.europa.eu/competition/antitrust/actionsdamages/files_white_paper/impact_study.pdf.

[55] ibid 555.

[56] 'The "private law" nature of the obligations breached in the case of Articles [101 and 102 TFEU]' is well established. See W van Gerven, 'Bringing (private) laws closer to each other at the European level' in F Cafaggi (ed), *The Institutional Framework of European Private Law* (Oxford, OUP, 2006) 37, 56.

[57] F Cafaggi, 'Introduction' in F Cafaggi (ed), *The Institutional Framework of European Private Law* (Oxford, OUP, 2006) 1, 32–33.

B. Reforms at National Level and Regulatory Competition Promoted at EU Level

Given the importance of procedural rules, which dominate substantive issues at the moment, the best way forward may for those issues to be addressed at national level, as the EU legislator's intervention in these matters may bring fresh uncertainty. In particular, the national legislator may be best placed to 'devise an institutional architecture of competition law enforcement [at national level] which encourages the claims, where there is really harm to the market and the process of competition, and creates safeguards against claims where companies might be using the system for a variety of purposes not necessarily beneficial to the market and the process of competition.'[58] The procedural rules and the experience of the Member States' judiciary to deal with complex EU competition law cases would be key. In this context, it was recently observed that:

> the courts and judges of the EU Member States play an important role not only at the purely national level, but also as part of the Union judicial system. The EU is a highly *decentralised* system, implying that EU legal norms are in most cases applied and implemented by the authorities, including the courts, of the Member States rather than by the Union institutions which have enacted those norms.[59]

Therefore, national legislators may be actively encouraged to legislate in the area. It should be noted that the UK Government has already launched public consultations seeking to reform the UK regime for private actions in competition law.[60] The contemplated reform is meant to 'allow consumers and businesses to obtain compensation for losses they have suffered as a result of anticompetitive behaviour',[61] which would address the current enforcement gap at national level. To this end, the UK Government is consulting on proposals to: (1) establish the Competition Appeal Tribunal (CAT) as a major venue for competition actions in the UK; (2) introduce an opt-out collective actions regime for competition law; (3) promote Alternative Dispute Resolution; and (4) ensure private actions complement the public enforcement regime.[62] Similarly, the most significant problems, highlighted by the respondents from Germany, to be addressed by the national legislators, appear to be that (1) consumers do not play a role in cross-border competition law actions, (2) national procedural rules differ significantly, (3) there are high costs of litigating (especially in the United Kingdom), and (4) damage claims and leniency programmes are in conflict with each other.

Given the diverse nature of the European Union, it seems that inter-jurisdictional regulatory competition in the area of EU antitrust law dispute resolution may be best employed by the EU legislator as a new mode of governance which might produce efficient enforcement results in the area. Such a 'perspective would damn harmonisation itself as anti-competitive'.[63] Weatherill went on to state that:

[58] M Danov and S Dnes, 'Private Actions in Competition Law: A Consultation on Options for Reform. Response Form' submitted to the UK Government, Department for Business, Innovation and Skills on 24 July 2012.

[59] A Rosas, 'The National Judge as EU Judge: Opinion 1/09' in Cardonnel, Rosas and Wahl (n 24) 105.

[60] Department for Business Innovation & Skills, *Private Actions in Competition Law: A Consultation on Options for Reform*,24April2012www.bis.gov.uk/assets/biscore/consumer-issues/docs/p/12-742-private-actions-in-competition-law-consultation.pdf. The BIS's proposed options for reform were discussed at a BIICL seminar, 'Rapid-Response Seminar: Private Actions in UK competition law: BIS's proposed options for reform', British Institute of International and Comparative Law, London, 9 May 2012.

[61] ibid 3.

[62] ibid 5–6.

[63] Weatherill (n 46) 14.

> Why should there not be regulatory variation among Member States, with the market populated by consumers of regulation, *inter alia* commercial firms dictating which approach is 'best' by selecting the jurisdiction judged most hospitable, and using that as a base to supply the wider market? This, one might argue, is not State laws causing a distortion of competition – it *is* competition.[64]

Potential claimants may promote a form of regulatory competition by bring their EU competition law claims in the jurisdiction which, they think, is most appropriate. Accordingly, through regulatory competition strong jurisdictions for bringing cross-border EU competition law actions might emerge. An increased number of claims might be seen in some Member States. But, what if there are market failures driven by externalities or lack of mobility (or even low mobility) of market participants?[65] Externalities could be one cause for market failure when it comes to inter-jurisdictional regulatory competition in the area of EU antitrust law dispute resolution in the European context. It is well established that:

> Weak enforcement of antitrust rules . . . in one nation may have a negative impact on the profits of foreign based producers whose products are thereby squeezed out of the market. To the extent that these spillover effects are not based on market-clearing effects, but rather driven by strategic behaviour, suboptimal results must be antiticipated. To avoid welfare losses and market distortions, such externalities must be corrected through some form of interjurisdictional collective action.[66]

The EU legislator may be better placed than a national legislator to devise an adequate institutional framework (which should include suitably drafted jurisdictional rules) to promote regulatory competition (and avoid the problem of market failure).[67] Whilst a reform at national level must address the procedural and substantive aspects necessary to provide remedies for breach of Articles 101 and 102 TFEU, the cross-border nature of most European competition law infringements, in which damages would often be suffered by businesses and consumers in a number of jurisdictions, indicates that a legislative intervention by the EU may be required as well. In other words, although the harmonisation (ie more regulation at EU level) may limit the inter-jurisdictional regulatory competition, regulation at EU level may be justified if the current private international framework is not suited to promote regulatory competition.

In particular, private international law rules addressing the specific issues arising in the context of cross-border EU competition law action would be of crucial importance when designing an adequate institutional framework that is promoting regulatory competition and solving the problems which may be associated with lack of mobility (or low mobility) for some of the claimants across Europe. Article 81 TFEU leaves no doubt that the EU has competence in all private international law matters with a cross-border element, even when such legislative measures are not necessary for the proper functioning of the internal market.[68] Thus, EU intervention may be required, as the cross-border implications would

[64] ibid 14.

[65] DC Esty and D Geradin, 'Regulatory Co-operation' in DC Esty and D Geradin (eds), *Regulatory Competition and Economic Integration* (Oxford, OUP, 2001) 30, 32–40.

[66] Esty and Geradin (n 65) 34.

[67] Kerber (n 38) S228.

[68] P Beaumont and P McEleavy, *Private International Law, Anton* (Edinburgh, SULI/W Green, 2011) 16–17. See also: P Craig, *The Lisbon Treaty: Law, Politics and Treaty Reform* (Oxford, OUP, 2010) 343.

make any national legislation less than effective in the EU context.[69] What are the important issues to be addressed in this context?

IV. Important Issues To Be Considered

As already noted, the collected data show that consumers and SMEs may be prone to economise on the costs by bringing claims in their home states. Since evidently there is a lack of mobility of consumers and SMEs who have suffered damages as a result of an EU competition law infringement, it is a relatively safe prediction that the inter-jurisdictional regulatory competition market might fail to address the current enforcement gap. As a result, the inter-jurisdictional regulatory competition would lead to economic externalities – giving rise to welfare losses and market distortions[70] across Europe – unless the EU legislator provides a new architecture for EU competition law enforcement which would allow for Articles 101 and 102 TFEU to be consistently enforced. Furthermore, the lack of mobility of the SMEs and consumers, who appear to prefer to bring their EU competition law claims in their home states, constitutes strong evidence that parallel proceedings would be bound to arise in the European context. In order words, the EU competition law claims in respect of the same breach of the same antitrust provision could be brought before the courts in different Member States.

That said, it seems that jurisdictional rules which address the specific problems arising in the context of cross-border EU competition law actions would be crucial in this context. Indeed, suitably drafted jurisdictional rules may be employed by the EU legislator to 'channel the competition processes among jurisdictions toward a better fulfilment of individual preferences'[71] by allowing them to choose where to bring their claim. A major challenge that the EU legislator would face in this context is how to avoid the problem of parallel EU competition law proceedings[72] and ensure that a well-placed forum will hear and determine an EU competition law claim. Indeed, the EU legislature must address the problem of the application of EU competition law in proceedings before an NCA located in one Member State and private EU antitrust law proceedings related to the same breaches of Article 101 and/or Article 102 TFEU before a court in another Member State.[73]

A new institutional architecture could uphold the independence of Member State courts[74] in relation to NCAs, safeguarding the defendant's right to a fair trial and hearing.[75]

[69] HM Watt, 'Integration and Diversity: The Conflict of Laws as a Regulatory Tool' in F Cafaggi (ed), *The Institutional Framework of European Private Law* (Oxford, OUP, 2006) 107.

[70] Esty and Geradin (n 65) 34.

[71] Kerber (n 38) S229.

[72] See S Brammer, *Co-operation between National Competition Agencies in the Enforcement of EC Competition Law* (Oxford, Hart Publishing, 2009) 25.

[73] Ch 13. See more: M Danov, 'EU Competition Law Enforcement: Is Brussels I suited to dealing with all the challenges?' (2012) 61 *ICLQ* 27.

[74] Opinion 1/09 of the Court (Full Court), *Opinion delivered pursuant to Article 218(11) TFEU – Draft agreement – Creation of a unified patent litigation system – European and Community Patents Court – Compatibility of the draft agreement with the Treaties*, 8 March 2011 [66]. See also: Rosas (n 59) 118–19.

[75] Lidgard (n 24); JR Calzado and G de Stefano, 'Rights of Defence in Cartel Proceedings: Some Ideas for Manageable Improvements' in Cardonnel, Rosas and Wahl (n 24) 423. *cf.* A Arabadjiev, 'Unlimited Jurisdiction: What does it mean today?' In Cardonnel, Rosas and Wahl (n 24) 383. See also: Commission Notice on Best Practices for the Conduct of Proceedings Concerning Articles 101 and 102 TFEU, [2011] OJ C308/6; DG Competition's Antitrust Manual of Procedures, Internal DG Competition working documents on procedures for the application of Articles 101 and 102 TFEU, March 2012 http://ec.europa.eu/competition/antitrust/antitrust_manproc_3_2012_en.pdf.

This would be particularly important in view of the recent case law which leaves no doubt that 'it is for the national courts and tribunals and for the Court of Justice to ensure the full application of European Union law in all Member States and to ensure judicial protection of an individual's rights under that law'.[76] Hence, it is beyond doubt that any new institutional framework, which is meant to promote regulatory competition with regard to cross-border EU competition law actions, should also consider the role of the European judiciary. Hess has very recently stated that:

> it is high time for specialists in the area to reflect and discuss the role and the function of the European law of civil procedure and the architecture of the European judiciary . . . The role, function and objective of national procedural systems in the European Union must be discussed; additional issues relate to the proper role of national courts and procedures in a more and more harmonized European Judicial Area and their coordination by European law.[77]

Indeed, the fact that EU competition law provisions are to be applied by the European Commission and 27 national competition authorities, as well as by 27 Member State courts (28 Member States as from 2013), appears to suggest that an institutional framework that provides for the consistent enforcement of Articles 101 and 102 TFEU, which form part of each Member State's legal order and are so important for Europe to return to growth, should be at the top of the agenda.

The possible ways forward and the various potential solutions will be discussed head-on in Parts II, III and IV of this book.

[76] Opinion 1/09 (n 74) [68]. See also: Case C-432/05 *Unibet* [2007] ECR I-2271 [38]. See also: Rosas (n 74) 118–19.

[77] B Hess, 'The Brussels I Regulation: Recent case law of the Court of Justice and the Commission's proposed recast' (2012) 49 *CML Rev* 1075, 1112.

Part II

Cross-Border EU Competition Law Actions and the European Courts: Is there a Need for Reform at EU Level?

6

Introduction: Centralisation (Harmonisation) or Decentralisation (Inter-Jurisdictional Regulatory Competition)?

MIHAIL DANOV AND FLORIAN BECKER

I. INTRODUCTION

Devising an appropriate institutional framework that provides for the consistent enforcement of Articles 101 and 102 TFEU presupposes a review of the specific characteristics of the European juridical system. Indeed, any reform which is meant to promote further harmonisation or inter-jurisdiction regulatory competition should consider the role of the European judiciary, and its ability to coherently interpret and apply any proposed harmonised instrument.

It was noted earlier that a significant majority of the interview respondents appeared to be against more harmonisation at EU level and in favour of a system of regulatory competition between procedural and substantive law regimes.[1] The possibility for different Member States' laws to apply to matters of procedure and substance in claims, based on the very same directly applicable Treaty provisions, may lead to a situation where some Member States' courts are enforcing EU competition law more efficiently than others. Professors Weatherill and Beaumont have noted that '[a] situation where the application of [European Union] law varies significantly from member state to member state would be a denial of the rule of law and would make the [Union] untenable. However, the European Court's attempt to accommodate differences in national procedural law means that some variations will occur.'[2] The fact that a claimant may gain some procedural (and/or substantive law) advantages by bringing his claim in one jurisdiction rather than another[3] suggests that there is a level of variation when it comes to the enforcement of EU competition law in Europe.[4] This impression is strengthened by the Report on the functioning on Regulation 1/2003, which states that 'stakeholders have pointed to what they perceive as uneven enforcement of the E[U] competition rules by national courts.'[5] How strong is the case for addressing the variation of the various national regimes at EU level?

[1] See above Chs 3, 4 and 5.

[2] S Weatherill and P Beaumont, *EU Law: The Essential Guide to the Legal Workings of the European Union* (London, Penguin, 1999) 453.

[3] See more: Chs 3 and 5.

[4] See more: Ch 5.

[5] See Commission (EC), 'The Functioning of Regulation 1/2003' (Report) COM (2009) 206 final [34].

II. HARMONISATION OR REGULATORY COMPETITION: ISSUES TO BE CONSIDERED

As already noted, the collected data appear to suggest that procedural rules might be dominating the amount of damages awarded when litigants are deciding where to bring their EU competition law damages actions.[6] In other words, it seems that the question whether EU competition law is ultimately enforced before Member State courts would largely depend on the relevant procedural laws applicable in the enlarging and heterogeneous Union. Therefore, procedural rules would have an important role to play if EU competition law is to be effectively enforced in Europe. It has been recently noted that:

> Substantive law relies on procedure to effectuate the substantive mandate. Substantive law without any procedure at all would be a 'vain and hollow thing'.[7] Although some substantive laws may be merely aspirational or symbolic [. . .] it is surely true that generally speaking '[t]he best laws in the world are meaningless unless they can be meaningfully enforced.'[8],[9]

In other words, what we witness in Europe in the context of EU competition law damages actions clearly reaffirms that 'the progressive unification of substantive law [may well be] counteracted by the wide divergence in procedure.'[10] The deduction that it is the procedural rules which need to be addressed could be strengthened by a comparative research conducted by Hodges,[11] who has observed:

> It is well understood that there are major divergences between the civil procedure rules of European Member States and the efficiency of their operation. States which have recently undertaken significant reform of their rules of civil procedure, to try to introduce speed, efficiency, and lower and more proportionate transactional costs, include Spain, Germany, the United Kingdom, the Netherlands and Denmark. Sweden and Switzerland are reviewing their rules. Procedures are very slow in some states, such as Italy and Greece, where there is considerable scope for reducing complexity, cost and delay.[12]

As already noted,[13] the Union has become even more diverse, following the 2004 and 2007 Enlargements when 12 new Member States became part of it. In view of that, the White Paper on damages actions was intended to improve the legal conditions for victims of EU competition law infringements to exercise their right under the Treaty.[14] The following aspects were considered: standing – indirect purchasers and collective redress; access to evidence – disclosure *inter partes*; binding effect of decisions by national competition authorities; fault requirement; damages; passing-on overcharges; limitation periods; costs

[6] Chs 3, 4 and 5.

[7] EH Ailes, 'Substance and Procedure in the Conflict of Laws', 39 (1941) *Michigan Law Review* 392, 404 (referring to a right without a remedy), quoted by TO Main, 'The Procedural Foundation of Substantive Law' 87 (2009–2010) *Washington University Law Review* 801, 822.

[8] JR Sternlight, 'Dispute Resolution and the Quest for Justice', 14 (2008) *Dispute Resolution Magazine* 12 quoted by Main (n 7), 822.

[9] Main (n 7), 822.

[10] AF Lowenfeld, 'Introduction: The Elements of Procedure: Are They Separately Portable' 45 (1997) *American Journal of Comparative Law* 649, 651.

[11] C Hodges, 'Europeanization of Civil Justice: Trends and Issues' (2007) *Civil Justice Quarterly* 96.

[12] ibid 109.

[13] Ch 1.

[14] Commission (EC), 'White Paper on Damages actions for the Breach of the EC Antitrust Rules', COM (2008) 165 [1.2].

of damages actions; interaction between leniency programmes and actions for damages.[15] The White Paper goes on to state that:

> The **current ineffectiveness of antitrust damages actions** is best addressed by a combination of measures at both Community and national levels, in order to achieve effective minimum protection of the victims' right to damages under Articles 81 and 82 in every Member State and a more level playing field and greater legal certainty across the EU.[16]

However, it stops short of saying how the balance should be struck, and what measures would be considered at EU level. On the one hand, 'In the absence of centrally drafted uniform rules, free movement enables regulatory competition between legal orders.'[17] Given the importance of procedural rules,[18] which dominate substantive issues at the moment, one would have thought that the best way forward might be for the Union to encourage Member States to legislate in the area.[19] Thus, claimants can show their preferences by bringing their claim in one jurisdiction instead of another promoting competition between legal orders, and fostering the learning process across Europe.[20]

On the other hand, it is a relatively reliable prediction that the inter-jurisdictional regulatory competition market would fail to address the current enforcement gap since, due to the high cross-border litigation costs and lack of information as to the various rules across Europe, there is no mobility of the consumers and SMEs, who have suffered damages as a result of an EU competition law infringement.[21] Indeed, given the diverse nature of the enlarging European Union, one can say that harmonisation of Member State laws would provide for more certainty and predictability as to what an antitrust claimant would be entitled to recover in cross-border EU competition law actions.

Hence, one should consider if harmonisation of the Member States' substantive/procedure laws would be appropriate in this context. Is it possible to achieve harmonisation of procedural rules in this context? It has been submitted that:

> In the area of procedural law, given the strong connections between procedure and the social, political, and economic mores of a country and the consequent great differences in procedural laws between countries, harmonization has proved difficult with only a few limited regional examples such as the EU Council Regulation on Jurisdiction and Judgments.[22]

Should the Union build upon its success with the Brussels I Regulation, to design an instrument on jurisdiction and judgments in relation to EU competition law claims? Or

[15] ibid. See also: Hodges (n 11).

[16] White Paper (n 14) [1.1].

[17] J Snell, *Goods and Services in EC Law. A Study of the Relationship between the Freedoms* (Oxford, OUP, 2002) 37.

[18] Chs 3 and 4.

[19] Department for Business Innovation & Skills, *Private Actions in Competition Law: A Consultation on Options for Reform*, 24 April 2012 www.bis.gov.uk/assets/biscore/consumer-issues/docs/p/12-742-private-actions-in-competition-law-consultation.pdf. The BIS's proposed options for reform were discussed at a BIICL seminar, 'Rapid-Response Seminar: Private Actions in UK competition law: BIS's proposed options for reform', British Institute of International and Comparative Law, London, 9 May 2012.

[20] From the Board, 'Two Steps Forward and One Step Back: Harmonizing the Unharmonizable', (2011) 38 *Legal Issues of Economic Integration* 207, 211.

[21] DC Esty and D Geradin, 'Regulatory Co-operation' in DC Esty and D Geradin (eds), *Regulatory Competition and Economic Integration* (Oxford, OUP, 2001) 30, 34.

[22] R Garnett, *Substance and Procedure in Private International Law* (Oxford, OUP, 2012) 67–68. See also: The American Law Institute, *UNIDROIT Principles of Transnational Civil Procedure* (2004) www.unidroit.org/english/principles/civilprocedure/ali-unidroitprinciples-e.pdf.

should the Union try to achieve harmonisation with regard to substantive and procedural rules applicable by the various Member State courts in Europe?

III. THE ROLE OF THE EUROPEAN COURTS

Particularly difficult issues which would arise with regard to the latter scenario are to do with the diverse nature of the enlarged Union. In particular, the judges in the Member States, which share different legal traditions and heritages, may struggle to apply uniform procedural and substantive laws, which would result in a high level of uncertainty and delay across Europe.[23] Indeed, it is well established that enforcement of the rights derived from EU law 'would require citizens to petition national courts, direct access to the Union courts being exceptionally available'.[24] Given the number of national courts and their different legal traditions and heritages, there is a risk of inconsistent enforcement of EU competition law across Europe which could result in increased uncertainty over the outcome of EU competition law cases in different Member States.

Can there be uniform application of any harmonised instrument 'without a single scheme of jurisdiction',[25] with regard to private EU competition law actions brought in the European context? Although the preliminary reference procedure has an important role in shaping EU competition law, it does not give private parties direct access (but only indirect access) to the Court of Justice of the European Union.[26] Moreover, it is well established that 'the ECJ is not hierarchically superior to Member States' Supreme Courts. It cannot quash or annul their judgments. It can answer questions for a preliminary ruling, but the final say in applying the answers received belongs to the national court.'[27]

Harmonisation of procedural and/or substantive laws regarding EU competition law damages actions could not lead to consistent enforcement of Articles 101 and 102 TFEU across Europe unless there are mechanisms to ensure that such harmonised laws would be applied uniformly and coherently.[28] Under the current system, 'the national court, in collaboration with the Court of Justice, fulfils a duty entrusted to them both of ensuring that in the interpretation and application of the Treaties the law is observed.'[29] In view of this, as already noted in Chapter 3, certain questions sought to take account of participants' views on how the current EU courts are currently functioning, and how the EU legal system could be improved to accommodate cross-border EU competition law actions.

[23] T Andersson, 'Approximation of Procedural Law in Europe', in M Storme (ed), *Procedural Laws in Europe* (Antwerp, Maklu, 2003) 55, 64–65.

[24] C Timmermans, 'Multilevel Judicial Co-operation', in P Cardonnel, A Rosas and N Wahl (eds), *Constitutionalising the EU Judicial System: Essays in Honour of Pernilla Lindh* (Oxford, Hart Publishing, 2012) 14, 22.

[25] P Eleftheriadis, 'Federalism and Jurisdiction', in E Cloots, G de Baere and S Sottiaux (eds), *Federalism in the European Union* (Oxford, Hart Publishing, 2012) 45, 54.

[26] M Jaeger, 'Private Parties' Access to the Courts of Regional Economic Integration Organisations: A Comparative Analysis' in Cardonnel, Rosas and Wahl (n 24) 25, 35.

[27] Timmermans (n 24).

[28] See Ch 1.

[29] Opinion 1/09 of the Court (Full Court), *Opinion Delivered Pursuant to Article 218(11) TFEU – Draft agreement – Creation of a unified patent litigation system – European and Community Patents Court – Compatibility of the draft agreement with the Treaties*, 8 March 2011 [69]. See more: A Rosas, 'The National Judge as EU judge: Opinion 1/09' in Cardonnel, Rosas and Wahl (n 24) 105.

The concerns as to the consistent enforcement of EU competition law across Europe appeared in the responses put forward by the qualitative interviewees from Germany. In particular, one respondent felt that there are discrepancies in the application of law between competition authorities and courts, suggesting that the lack of knowledge of the substantive EU competition law provisions 'combined with a lack of procedural guarantees is a very dangerous mixture, especially in Eastern Europe'.[30] Another respondent from Germany went on to suggest that 'there is a serious non-application of competition rules in a lot of countries.'[31] The latter view was shared by another participant from Germany, who thought that inconsistent application of EU competition law across Europe can lead to an abuse of procedural rules in cross-border competition law cases. Is the harmonisation of procedural and/or substantive laws regarding EU competition law damages a solution? What should be the role of the European courts?

As already noted, although some respondents felt that the current EU legal system is (probably) adequate, several major shortcomings were put forward by the respondents from England.[32] First, delay was a major concern, as the participants thought that it takes far too long for the European Courts to deliver judgments. Secondly, it was thought that sometimes the Court of Justice may avoid dealing with the most difficult issues. Thirdly, even if the Court of Justice were to deal with the issues head-on, some respondents thought that Member State courts might not be willing to refer to the Court of Justice.

Participants were further asked whether a possibility for private parties to make an appeal on a point of EU competition law before any of the European Courts (e.g. the General Court) could solve the problem (or some of the problems). Although this idea for a fundamental change to the current system was not well received by the overwhelming majority of respondents,[33] one might wonder whether a single system of jurisdiction, in which the General Court of the European Union hears appeals in respect of judgments of national courts in relation to EU competition law claims, could work. If such a system would not work, then one should consider how inter-jurisdictional regulatory competition in the area of EU antitrust law dispute resolution may be best exploited by the EU legislator as a new mode of governance which might produce efficient enforcement results.

IV. THE STRUCTURE OF THIS PART

In view of the foregoing, Part II of this book is intended to look at the judicial activities of the General Court with regard to EU competition law cases as well as at options for reform. It opens with Judge Irena Pelikánová's analysis of the current judicial activities of the General Court in EU competition law cases. Then, Andreangeli addresses the question of whether the General Court could become a forum for appeals against judgments given by national courts in EU antitrust disputes. In this context, it is argued that a less 'radical', but perhaps no less effective, proposal lies in conferring on the General Court the power to

[30] See Ch 4.
[31] See Ch 4.
[32] See Ch 3.
[33] See Chs 3, 4 and 5. See also: the European Parliament, Draft Report on amending the Protocol on the Statute of the Court of Justice of the European Union and Annex I thereto (02074/2011 – C7-0090/2011 – 2011/0901A(COD), A7-0185/2012) – A7-0185/2012.

hear preliminary references in cases involving Articles 101 and 102 of the TFEU.[34] Finally, some conclusions will be drawn as to how the system could develop by taking into account the specific juridical characteristics, as well as the litigants' strategies.

[34] However, the General Court has more work at present than the Court of Justice, and therefore it is not an opportune time to reduce the workload of the latter while increasing the workload of the former, see the 2011 Annual Report of the Court of Justice of the European Union, http://curia.europa.eu/jcms/jcms/Jo2_7000/.

7

The General Court and its Role in EU Competition Law Cases

IRENA PELIKÁNOVÁ*

This contribution will address two very distinct but broad questions which are very closely linked. First, I will discuss actions for damages in competition cases from the point of view of the judge within the General Court. Secondly, I will draw attention to wider questions concerning the current situation at the General Court and explore possible, or perhaps even impossible, solutions.

I

We can observe the development of the system of European jurisdictions since 1989 with the creation of the Court of First Instance, after 2009 called the General Court, alongside the Court of Justice (created in 1952), and in 2005 the setting up of the first specialised jurisdiction – the Civil Service Tribunal. With the coming of each new jurisdiction, we have seen progressive changes in their functioning. Today, the General Court has evolved into more of an administrative court, but this does not present a complete picture. It also has competence in the law of torts, albeit very limited (Art 268 TFEU) and decides private law cases (arbitration clauses). Thus, the General Court has to decide both private and public law cases.

The procedure in EU competition law cases is essentially a public liability procedure. Every undertaking which takes part in an infringement acts illegally. In general, as far as a continental European lawyer is concerned, when somebody is harmed by the illegal behaviour of another person, he can demand compensation. Illegal behaviour may be in the form of competition infringement. More precisely, every national law foresees different conditions for successfully arriving at a judgment. A lawyer from the European continent speaks about public and private law; an English lawyer does not. For the European continent, competition law is public; tort law is mostly private.

European competition law sets down rules about both competition infringement and administrative procedure. A sanctioned undertaking can introduce an action against the European Commission's decision to the General Court, but cannot apply for compensation before this jurisdiction unless the damage was caused by a European institution,

* The article expresses the personal opinion of the author, not the official position of the General Court.

because the Treaty does not give this competence to the General Court. In competition cases it is mostly the competitor who is harmed, although this could be a consumer or a client.

The possibility of giving the General Court a new competence in preliminary rulings concerning actions for damages in competition cases has been examined. Theoretically it is possible, but I have no doubt that the Court of Justice would be very hostile to such a proposal. On the other hand, it is a very modest proposal.

I would like to propose another solution – to attribute the competence to decide appeals against national judges' decisions to the General Court. I suggest giving the General Court competence to decide, as a court of first instance, in actions for damages in competition cases decided by the European Commission.

First of all, it would be necessary to add this competence to the Treaty.

Secondly, following this, it would be necessary to ask the question 'What is substantive law?' European legislation could set down some rules. Unifying rules would be a real help to applicants. Appeals to the Court of Justice would assure the consistency of jurisprudence without needing to assign competence in the preliminary ruling to the General Court.

I personally think that this solution would be more useful than a new regulation on international private law. I must, unfortunately, admit that in this case the Member States will show signs of hostility to this proposal, as is their habit whenever new unification of laws is proposed.

We have many examples which bear this out. The common frame of reference of European contract law is only one silent failure. Nowadays we have a proposal for a Sales Act; the rest of this mammoth task has silently disappeared. In order to reassure you that my proposal is not without grounds, it would be apt to recall both the existence of and need for the Principles of European Tort Law proposal (PETL), in which liability questions have already been addressed.

If we observe US antitrust law, the question of compensation is part of the competition procedure, and I do not know why it cannot also be an integral part of the leniency procedure of the European Commission. The problem of access to a competition file would disappear, the problem of the competence of the General Court also. Furthermore, we could easily accept more closely following the US model and leave to the European Commission solely the inquiry, with the duty to introduce a criminal or civil action before the Court. The system would better fulfil the requirements of the ECHR. The introduction of personal liability for directors could significantly increase the efficiency of European competition law.

One might say these are pipe dreams, and unfortunately one would be right. Nevertheless, we must start somewhere and we should also ask why it is so difficult to decide on some pragmatic solutions when many specialists agree about what is lacking. There is a more general problem of European democracy.

I would like, as an aside, to remark that the problem of wider competences in described liability questions is not unique, while competition law brings others. The question of solidarity of fines is not very well understood and it also clashes with the absence of a European civil code. More recently we have read in the press: 'German Supreme Court will review a dispute between Arques and SKW, the parent and its former subsidiary, over liability for a fine imposed by the European Commission in a calcium carbide cartel. Arques believes SKW responsible for the cartel conduct and is seeking 6.8 million euros from it.'[1] So, a

[1] Information from Mlex 30 March 2012.

national judge intervenes in a European Commission decision about an administrative liability. The Munich court's judgment said that joint liability is justified. At the same time, the Commission's decision is under appeal at the EU courts. This parallelism is extremely dubious; nevertheless, it is certain that the question of competition infringement responsibility raises larger and more complicated questions. Recent news shows some tendency on the part of a national judge to accept wider competence. On the other hand a French decision about a similar question (2009, Tribunal de commerce de Grenoble) states that this is not within the competence of a national judge.

The German court (U 3283/11 *Kart*) decided on an application which invoked liability in damages. It said that German law was applicable because it was the applicant's will and reclassified the case as being not about liability, but about adjustment of joint and several obligations between several debtors, in spite of the origin of the obligation in the Commission's administrative decision. According to the German court, the BGB is also applicable to administrative duties, despite the EU regulation being applicable in this case. We are now waiting to see what the reaction of the German Supreme Court will be.[2]

II

It is necessary to explain the current situation at the General Court which directly affects competition procedure.

The report of the working group from 2000 is outdated, despite some elements which are still valid. However, we must take into consideration the 12 years of evolution and experience which have elapsed since then. For example, I personally think that the idea of advocates general could be very useful. On the other hand I do not agree with the idea of specialisation in some chambers inside the General Court.

More precisely, without formal specialisation, both our jurisdictions (the Court of Justice and the General Court) spontaneously and flexibly tend to do this from time to time. The unpredictable evolution of flux in a case does not lend itself to rigid organisation imposed from outside. All of the actions on a big cartel will be allocated to one reporting judge only, in the normal course of events. If we receive a large number of applications concerning, say, the freezing of funds, we tend to attribute them to the experienced judges already working on similar cases. The principle of good administration demands such action.

In 2000 the General Court had only 15 judges. Now we have 27, and about 700 new cases a year are lodged. The General Court proposed the creation of a special trade mark jurisdiction, which is permissible under the treaty. It is understandable that some filtration of cases is necessary, but we must select only the 'mass' cases – very numerous and at the same time simple cases. The group of cases must be stable in evolution. Every reasonable lawyer must recognise that it is not the most efficient system if both kinds of cases – easy 'mass' and complex competition cases – are treated by the same jurisdiction, the same judges. It is

[2] See more: German specialist literature – E Bueren, 'Einer für alle, alle für einen? Gesamtschuldnerische Bußgeldhaftung im europäischen Kartellrecht: Grundlage, Ausgestaltung und Konsequenzen' (2011) *Zeitschrift für Wettbewerbsrecht*, 185–311. See also S Thomas, 'Guilty of a Fault that one has not Commited. The Limits of the Group-Based Sanction Policy Carried out by the Commission and the European Courts in EU-Antitrust Law' (2012) 3 *Journal of European Competition Law and Practice* 1–18.

very difficult to create inside of one jurisdiction a special 'mass' cases chamber, in which judges of equal standing will treat only trade mark cases, while others will treat only complex cases.

A hierarchical structure of jurisdictional institutions is completely natural and present in every state. Why not in the EU? The Court of Justice has rejected the General Court's proposal on this matter. Both the public and politicians must finally understand that European Courts are real jurisdictions, and need to be treated accordingly.

The Court of Justice has opted for another solution for the General Court – to add 12 new judges. At first glance, everybody who is not very well informed about every detail of the functioning of the General Court will find the proposal attractive. Nevertheless, I am firmly convinced that this solution will bring a significant deterioration in the level of quality of our work, because it necessarily brings about a rotation of judges. This problem was totally ignored in the proposal. However, a calculation is simple: if the Court does not propose a second judge for every Member State, the decision of policy-makers will be to accept some rotation. Every rotation has consequences – mandates without the possibility of renewal. Actually, it is only the possibility of renewal which allows the General Court to face up to the inherent instability entailed in the six-year mandate of judges.

Although everybody at the national level recognises the need for judges to have a mandate for life, at the General Court we have only a six-year mandate, but we now risk adding a further rotation! Already, we have many very difficult problems when a judge retires or leaves for another reason, because this disrupts the flow of work. The length of experience of sitting judges will decrease considerably if this proposal is accepted.

What was a big surprise, was to see in 2011 that the British House of Lords recommended an increase in the General Court's judiciary: 'It must surely be possible for the Council to agree to appoint the necessary number, less than 27, which the Court should recommend at this stage. We suggest one third might be a reasonable number on a rotating basis.' I simply do not know how to explain how the high representation of the country with the greatest stability of judges cannot see what the consequences of their recommendation will be on the stability of the General Court and the quality of judgments.

After some discussion when the General Court tried to alert politicians and lawyers to the great risk concerning the General Court's performance, the noise quietened down, and the proposal continues on its way. The only question currently under discussion is the problem of nomination in relation to the Member States. The question of stability is being completely ignored.

One basic idea has been forgotten in all this; our main goal must always be a competent, skilled judge who will treat the most difficult cases efficiently and quickly. Any additional rotation excludes this.

Another important question was also forgotten or hidden – that of cost. The creation of a new jurisdiction is much cheaper than the addition of 12 new judges. A judge on the Civil Service Tribunal, which could be the model for a new trade mark court, has only one legal assistant and one secretary; a judge on the General Court has three legal assistants and two secretaries. The Civil Service Tribunal has only seven judges. This simple comparison of 72 and 21 persons speaks for itself. The procedure for nominating judges could be (unfortunately it is not) less political than for the General Court. It is most unfortunate that the nomination of judges falls within the political arena.

The treaty on the Functioning of the European Union contains a new Article 255 regarding the famous '255 Committee'. The idea was praiseworthy. It expresses the principle that the judicial profession must be liberated from the influence of politicians. It is only a first step, but it gives hope that in the future, the idea of a judge's real independence will be accepted too. The General Court is very happy with this development – this new mechanism allows the real competence of every candidate to be evaluated.[3]

However, another consequence must also be recognised. When the Committee rejects a candidate, the Member State is obliged to propose a new candidate, and this takes time. The General Court is currently waiting for two members to be replaced. The partial renewal of half of the General Court at the same time creates further difficulties. The same can be said for the Court of Justice.

In summary, the addition of 12 new judges would destabilise the General Court, would decrease the length of experience of judges and would significantly increase the cost of the jurisdiction.

Nevertheless, the proposal hiding the Court of Justice's aversion to giving the General Court competence in appeals and preliminary rulings was written without taking into consideration the opinion of the General Court itself. But the Treaty has created room for this possibility, the Civil Service Tribunal works well and we have another category of cases easily separable – trade mark cases; that is why the General Court proposed the creation of a new jurisdiction, the trade marks jurisdiction (or intellectual property tribunal). This proposal could be a part of the future architecture of the EU judiciary.

As we are concerned with competition cases, it is necessary to emphasise that these cases are difficult and complex, and it is essential to have a stable court with experienced, skilled judges. Every good lawyer knows that a big cartel calls for a judge working in at least their second mandate. How is it possible that the House of Lords' committee is able to propose the introduction of further rotation to the General Court and at the same time stress the importance of competition cases?

Nevertheless, the lack of vision as to the future architecture of the EU judiciary adapted to the current stage of European integration is the most important problem. If we imagine that in the future the backlog will only increase and the number of CJEU members remains stable, the idea of removing direct actions to the General Court is the only reasonable solution. The General Court could have competence for appeals in direct action cases, while at first instance they could be partly attributed to the specialised courts such as the Civil Service Tribunal or a Trade Mark Tribunal. In the near future we might need a specialised public procurement tribunal or another for competition cases. I am convinced that the time has come to address these very general questions.

[3] See Vesterdorf, B: 'La nomination des juges de la Cour de justice de l'Union européenne', *Cahiers de droit européen*, 2011, 3, s 601.

8

Private Antitrust Claims as a 'Special Case': Can the General Court be Envisaged as the Appellate Court vis-à-vis Decisions of National Courts?

ARIANNA ANDREANGELI*

I. INTRODUCTION

The Court of First Instance (now termed in the TEU as the General Court) was originally envisaged as a means to alleviate the case-load of the European Court of Justice (referred to in the TEU as the Court of Justice of the EU) in areas that were perceived as particularly 'labour-intensive'. It was therefore not surprising that at its inception the General Court would be empowered to deal with appeals in respect to staff and competition cases. Since then its role has evolved from a near 'specialised' court to a 'general forum' for actions lodged by non-privileged applicants as well as for appeals against the decision of the EU Civil Service Tribunal, established in 2005 in accordance with Article 225a of the 'old' Treaties. In addition, the Court retains 'potential' jurisdiction to deal with preliminary references in areas not yet identified by the Council of Ministers. The Treaty on the Functioning of the EU also confirms the possibility of creating additional 'specialised courts' in areas identified by the Statute.

This chapter seeks to analyse the implications of the proposal to confer on the General Court jurisdiction to hear appeals against decisions of the domestic courts dealing with private antitrust enforcement claims. First, it will consider the question of whether the need to uphold the consistency and uniformity of EU competition law, especially on account of the increasing importance of domestic courts in the application of these rules, resulting from the Modernisation Regulation, justifies the introduction of a 'specialised' jurisdiction in this area: for this purpose, the paper will consider the 2006 Report of the House of Lords Select Committee on the proposal for an 'EU Competition Court'.[1]

* The author would like to thank the participants at the workshop held at Brunel University on 12 November 2010, and the colleagues gathered at the conference held at the London School of Economics on 20 April 2012, for their comments and feedback on earlier drafts of this chapter.

[1] House of Lords Select Committee on the European Union, *XV Report: An EU Competition Court*, session 2006/07, www.publications.parliament.uk/pa/ld200607/ldselect/ldeucom/75/7504.htm#a1 (hereinafter referred to as the *XV Report*).

Thereafter, the chapter will examine the question of whether granting an 'appellate' jurisdiction to the General Court against domestic judgments is compatible with the existing principles governing the judicial architecture of the EU, with respect to both the jurisdiction enjoyed by the Luxembourg Courts and the relationship existing between them and the domestic courts. The chapter will argue that the Founding Treaties have always identified the Court of Justice as the 'key interlocutor' with the domestic courts, and have shaped this 'dialogue' in the form of the preliminary reference procedure, now enshrined in Article 267 of the TFEU. It will be submitted that conferring on the General Court powers of appeal against domestic judgments would not be compatible with the principle of cooperation between the Union and the national courts, in as much as it would result in changing that relationship into one of 'hierarchical subordination'.

The chapter will also consider the extent to which this 'appellate' jurisdiction can be justified, having regard to the rules governing the powers of the General Court itself: it will be argued that the General Court enjoys powers of review that are limited as to both the grounds of appeal that can be alleged in individual actions, and the nature of the decision that it can adopt should an appeal be successful, and therefore that it cannot 'remake' the impugned decision. As a result, it will be submitted that conferring on the Court powers of 'appeal', as envisaged by the proposal, would be difficult to reconcile with the nature of the jurisdiction envisaged by the Founding Treaties and confirmed by the TFEU itself.

Thereafter, this contribution will consider whether less radical proposals could be formulated in order to meet these concerns. It will be queried whether the General Court could be entrusted with the power to hear preliminary references, as envisaged by Article 256(3) TFEU, on the ground that this option may give rise to less serious concerns for maintaining the 'cooperative' nature of the relationship existing between the EU Courts and the domestic judiciaries and would not, in particular, require an amendment to the Treaty. However, it will also be illustrated that a similar change may be unlikely to be supported by several stakeholders, including the same Court of Justice, out of a concern for avoiding the 'multiplication' of layers of judicial control and thereby jeopardising the attainment of the very goals of efficiency and finality that these reforms purport to achieve. For these reasons, another option will be explored, ie the possibility of allowing the General Court to hear 'follow-on' damages actions brought by the victims of infringements that have been detected and sanctioned by the EU Commission.

This contribution will conclude that conferring on the General Court the power to hear appeals lodged against decisions of the domestic courts would not, at least in principle, be inconsistent with the genesis of the Court itself, or indeed with the need to secure speed and legal certainty in the resolution of private competition claims. However, this proposal raises a number of important questions and could especially lead to significant difficulties of a constitutional and institutional nature that cannot be resolved without resorting to an amendment of the Treaty and, perhaps most importantly, would require the endorsement of the EU courts themselves. For these reasons it will be suggested that greater consideration should be given to recent developments taking place in a number of Member States, which seem to indicate a willingness on the part of domestic authorities to take a more active role in shaping and implementing the private competition enforcement agenda: in this context, it will be queried whether encouraging courts to act as 'Union courts', and therefore to apply the EU competition rules to individual cases of their own initiative (if necessary by seeking advice from the Court of Justice), could be a preferable option for securing goals of speed, efficiency and finality in the adjudication of these claims.

II. CONSISTENCY IN THE INTERPRETATION OF THE EU COMPETITION RULES IN THE 'MODERNISED' ENFORCEMENT REGIME: LOOKING FOR A 'GUARDIAN' . . .

A. The impact of the Modernisation Regulation for the Jurisdiction of the National Courts and the Quest for Consistency: Summary Remarks

Due to the limited remit of this contribution, it is not possible to address in any detail the array of issues arising from the implementation of the 'Modernisation package' in the field of EU competition enforcement. Suffice to say that Council Regulation No 1/2003 sought to 'decentralise' the application of the Treaty antitrust rules, especially by abolishing the monopoly hitherto enjoyed by the Commission in applying the 'exemption clause' contained in Article 101(3), and thereby to encourage national courts to engage in their application to individual cases. This was not, however, a 'new move': as long ago as 1993 the Commission had issued a Notice on cooperation with national courts, seeking to boost the domestic judiciaries' involvement in competition decision-making.[2] According to the Commission, domestic courts would be empowered to apply both Articles 101(1), 101(2) and 102 in individual cases and to grant to the individuals or firms adversely affected by anti-competitive behaviour the redress available under domestic law.[3] Furthermore, if doubts arose as to the interpretation of these rules, the national court would retain the power to make a preliminary reference to the Court of Justice, in its capacity as 'guardian of the Treaty'.[4]

Thus, the shared nature of the jurisdiction enjoyed by the Commission and the domestic courts and the involvement of individuals as 'quasi-attorney general' in antitrust matters[5] was recognised as a means to ensuring the effectiveness of the Treaty competition rules.[6] Nonetheless, the lack at the time of a clear legal basis for a cause of action open to individuals wishing to seek redress for damages suffered arising from anti-competitive conduct constituted a clear obstacle to the emergence of a solid mechanism for the private enforcement of the competition rules, especially through actions for damages, in Europe.[7] It was not until the *Crehan* preliminary ruling that this cause of action was recognised,[8] although it is also clear that this decision did not bring about any 'surge' in individual lawsuits being lodged before the national courts.[9] In any event, it is not doubted that the concerns for the unity and consistency of the interpretation of the EU competition rules remain at the forefront of the debate leading to the enactment of the current Implementing Regulation.[10]

[2] [1993] OJ C39/6. For commentary, see eg J Shaw, 'Competition Complainants: A Comprehensive System of Remedies?' (1993) 18 *EL Rev* 427, esp 440–41.

[3] Commission Notice (n 2) [14]–[16].

[4] ibid. See also Shaw (n 2) 441.

[5] See eg A Andreangeli, 'From Complainant To "Private Attorney General"', in M Dougan and S Currie (eds), *Fifty Years of European Treaties* (Oxford, Hart Publishing, 2009) 234–35.

[6] See esp Case T-24/90 *Automec v Commission* [1992] ECR II-2223, esp [90]–[96].

[7] See C Jones, *Private Enforcement of Antitrust Law in the UK, the EU and the US* (Oxford, OUP, 1999) 77–78.

[8] Case C-453/99 *Courage v Crehan* [2001] ECR I-6297.

[9] See 'Study on the Conditions of Claims for Damages in Case of Infringement of the EC Competition Rules', prepared by D Waelbroeck, D Slater and G Even-Shoshan, 31 August 2004, available at: http://ec.europa.eu/comm/competition/antitrust/actionsdamages/comparative_report_clean_en.pdf (hereinafter referred to as 'the Ashurst Report'), Comparative Report, para 1.

[10] See inter alia C-D Ehlermann and I Atanasiu, 'The Modernization of EC Antitrust Law: The Consequences for the Role and Functions of the EC Courts' (2002) 23(2) *ECLR* 72, esp 76 ff; also Commission, White Paper on the Modernisation of the rules implementing Articles 81 and 82 EC Treaty, COM 909/0101/final, esp sections 36–38, 99–103.

Regulation No 1/2003 addresses this issue differently in respect to decisions adopted by the domestic courts as opposed to those of the NCAs. While the Commission can assert its role of 'leader' in the context of the European Competition Network, albeit in a spirit of mutual cooperation and in accordance with a principle of shared jurisdiction,[11] it has had to tread very carefully in dealing with the domestic judiciaries. Concerns for respecting the independence of national courts[12] as well as for preserving the integrity of their relationship with the ultimate 'guardian of the Treaty', ie the Court of Justice, prompted the introduction in the Modernisation Regulation of 'soft' forms of cooperation with the domestic judges. These take the shape of *amici curiae* briefs, which the Commission can submit before domestic courts in accordance with the requirements of national law, and of requests of information and assistance which could be made by national judges to DG Competition in respect of individual cases.[13]

It is also clear from Article 15 of Council Regulation No 1/2003 that unless a 'true' conflict between a decision adopted by the Commission and a judgment contemplated by a domestic court can be envisaged, national courts are not bound by any decision or statement made by the Commission,[14] and in any case, if they have serious doubts as to the way in which the competition rules should be interpreted in individual cases, can petition the Court of Justice via Article 267 TFEU.[15] In light of the foregoing, it is argued that the relationship of 'cooperation'[16] (albeit within the limits established in, inter alia, *Foto Frost* and *CILFIT*)[17] existing between the domestic courts and the Court of Justice, enforced via the preliminary reference procedure, taken together with the 'softer' cooperation options vis-à-vis the Commission, were regarded as an 'optimal' solution for the purpose of balancing the legal certainty in the application of the Treaty competition rules against the respect for the constitutional principle of the independence of the judiciary.[18]

This solution, however, has a serious practical drawback, ie the delays arising from the backlog faced by the Court of Justice in dealing with preliminary references: admittedly, this problem is not peculiar to competition law and has prompted a considerable amount of 'soul-searching', particularly in the run-up to the Treaty of Nice.[19] Proposals for the

[11] See eg A Komninos, 'Modernisation and Decentralisation: Retrospective and Prospective', in G Amato and C-D Ehlermann (eds), *EC Competition Law: A Critical Assessment* (Oxford, Hart Publishing, 2009) 629, 661–65; also, more recently, Case T-340/04 *France Telecom v Commission* [2007] ECR II-573 [79]–[80]; for commentary, inter alia, F Rizzuto, 'Parallel Competence and the Power of the EC Commission under Regulation No 1/2003 according to the Court of First Instance' (2008) 29(5) *ECLR* 286, 288–91.

[12] See inter alia Case C-344/09 *Masterfoods Ltd v HB Ice Cream Ltd* [2000] ECR I-11369 [47]; for commentary, inter alia, Komninos (n 11) 668–71.

[13] Council Regulation No 1/2003, Preamble, recital 21; Arts 15–16; see also Commission White Paper on Modernisation (n 10) [99]–[101] and [107]; for commentary, inter alia, K Lenaerts and D Gerard, 'Modernisation of the EC Competition Law Enforcement: Judges on the Frontline', (2004) 27 *World Competition* 313, 332–33; also A Andreangeli, 'The Enforcement of Article 81 EC Treaty before National Courts after the House of Lords' decision in *Crehan v Inntrepreneur Pub Co*', (2007) 32(2) *EL Rev* 260, 265–66.

[14] Case C-344/98 *Masterfoods Ltd v HB Ice Cream Ltd* [2000] ECR I-11369 [47]–[48]; also *Inntrepreneur Pub Co CPC v Crehan* [2006] UKHL 38, HL (Lord Bingham) [4]–[6].

[15] See eg Case C-234/89 *Delimitis v Henninger Brau* [1991] ECR I-935 [47]–[48], [53].

[16] Inter alia, Case 283/81 *CILFIT and another v Ministero della Sanita* [1982] ECR 3415 [7]–[8].

[17] Case 314/85 *Foto Frost v Hauptzollamt Lubeck Ost* [1987] ECR 4199 [13]–[14]; Case 283/81 *CILFIT and another v Ministero della Sanita* [1982] ECR 3415 [16]–[21].

[18] See Case C-344/98 *Masterfoods* (n 14) (AG Cosmas) [16]; also Lenaerts and Gerard (n 13) 334–35. More recently, see M Gustaffson, 'Some Legal Implications Facing the Realisation of the Commission White Paper on Modernisation of EC Antitrust Procedure and the Role of National Courts in a Post-White Paper Era' (2000) 27 *Legal Issues of European Economic Integration* 159, 174.

[19] See eg Friends of the Presidency group, report on amendments to be made to the Treaties with regard to the Court of Justice and the Court of First Instance, 31 May 2000, CONFER4747/00; also Report by the Working Party

introduction of a 'European certiorari', of a mechanism designed to oblige the national court to propose solutions to the questions they posed to the Court and for a modification of the rule enshrined in *CILFIT,* were floated as possible answers to this problem.[20] Among the solutions implemented in the text of the Treaty and confirmed after the Treaty of Lisbon was the possibility to confer to the General Court the jurisdiction to hear preliminary references in specific areas of EU law and it is perhaps not surprising that one of the areas identified as being well-suited for this purpose was competition law.[21]

According to the Report of the Working Party on the future of the EC Court system, compiled in the run-up to the Nice Inter-Governmental Conference, the impact of the decentralisation of the enforcement of the competition rules, which was being discussed at the time, would have resulted in both an increase in the number of references made to the Court of Justice by national courts and in more numerous direct actions being lodged against the Commission's infringement decisions as the Commission became more proactive in uncovering and sanctioning anti-competitive behaviour.[22] For this reason, a number of commentators called not only for the creation of a 'specialised competition panel', but also for the conferral to the General Court of the power to hear preliminary references in this field.[23] It was argued that, if the General Court was to discharge its functions consistently with the unity and the consistency of EU law, the two types of jurisdiction should go 'hand in hand'.[24]

Against this background, it is legitimate to ask whether the General Court could effectively act as a 'legitimate' interlocutor for the domestic courts.[25] This question is particularly relevant in light of the proposal that this chapter seeks to examine, ie whether it would be feasible, having regard to the structure and the principles underlying the EU judiciary, to confer 'appellate jurisdiction' to the General Court against domestic courts' decisions. Could the General Court be endowed of this type of jurisdiction without going against the overall judicial architecture created by the Treaties? And would its power be seen as 'legitimate' by the national courts themselves, forever accustomed to dealing with the Court of Justice itself via the preliminary reference procedure? These questions will be addressed in the following sections.

B. The (Old) Court of First Instance from Specialised Judge to 'General Court': Evolutionary Trends and Implications

The previous section provided a brief outline of some of the implications of the Modernisation Regulation. This section will attempt to provide a snapshot of the evolution of the CFI/General Court with a view to considering whether it can emerge as an effective and legitimate interlocutor for domestic judges in individual private antitrust claims.

on the future of the EC's court system, January 2000; for commentary, see inter alia L Heffernan, 'The Treaty of Nice: Arming the Courts to Defend a European Bill of Rights?', (2009) 65(2) *Law and Contemporary Problems* 189, esp 199 ff.

[20] See eg Friends of the Presidency Report (n 19) 21; for commentary, inter alia, A Johnston, 'Judicial reform and the Treaty of Nice', (2001) 38(3) *CML Rev* 499, 520–21.

[21] Report by the Working party on the future of the EC's court system (n 19) 33–37. See also Heffernan (n 19) 211–14.

[22] Report by the Working party on the future of the EC's court system (n 19) 34.

[23] See eg Johnston (n 20) 513–14.

[24] ibid 514; also Heffernan (n 19) 214.

[25] See eg Heffernan (n 19) 212–13 and 217–18; also Johnston (n 20) 519–20.

It is well known that the Court of First Instance was instituted in 1989 as an 'appendage' to the Court of Justice, designed to assist it in dealing with its increasing case law:[26] initially the CFI's jurisdiction was limited to cases that were perceived as being relatively fact-intensive, such as staff lawsuits.[27]

However, its jurisdiction has since evolved to cover all direct actions lodged by non-privileged applicants. In particular, the Treaty of Nice envisaged an ever more central and incisive role for the General Court, by conferring upon it potential jurisdiction to hear preliminary references in specific areas and to hear appeals against decisions adopted by 'specialised panels' or, to use the terminology of the Lisbon Treaty, 'specialised courts', albeit subject to ad hoc mechanisms of 'preview' and 'review' on the part of the Court of Justice in exceptional cases, to preserve the unity and consistency of EU law.[28] Although to date only one such specialised court has been created, namely the EU Civil Service Tribunal, it is undoubted that the Treaty drafters saw them as an indispensable factor to assist the General Court in discharging its function of general forum for first instance direct actions.[29]

In light of the above, it is submitted that today the General Court occupies a pivotal position in the EU judiciary: however, its role has evolved in a rather different direction as compared to the one that had been initially envisaged, having become a general forum for almost all direct actions. Furthermore, although the Treaty of Nice had conferred on the Court 'potential jurisdiction' to deal with preliminary rulings in ad hoc areas, no further action was taken in this sense.

Against this background, it could be argued that while its performance in dealing with competition appeals against the Commission decisions is fully established, the General Court does not enjoy a direct relationship with the domestic courts. Although, as was aptly put by Johnston, it is difficult to imagine the domestic judiciaries 'disrespecting' the General Court,[30] should the latter be empowered to hear preliminary references, it is equally clear that the Court of Justice remains the 'principal interlocutor' vis-à-vis the national courts.[31] This state of affairs was also confirmed by Article 15 of Council Regulation No 1/2003 which, in accordance with, inter alia, the *Masterfoods* judgment, expressly safeguards the domestic judges' power to make references under the new Article 267 TFEU.[32]

In light of the above, it is submitted that both the Treaty reforms and the enactment of Council Regulation No 1/2003 reiterated the status quo concerning both the structure of the EU judiciary and its relationship with the domestic courts: whereas the General Court would remain responsible for hearing appeals brought against the Commission competition decisions, the cooperation existing between the Court of Justice and the domestic judiciaries, fashioned around the preliminary reference procedure,[33] has been forcefully

[26] See eg B Vesterdorf, 'The Community Court System Ten Years from Now and Beyond: Challenges and Possibilities', (2003) 32(3) *EL Rev* 303, 306; see also Friends of the Presidency report (n 19) 23 ff.

[27] Friends of the Presidency report (n 19) 33–34.

[28] Inter alia, Heffernan (n 19) 204–205; see also ibid 209–11.

[29] Report by the Working party on the future of the EC's court system (n 19) 29–30; also Heffernan (n 19) 217.

[30] Johnston (n 20) 520.

[31] See eg Case 13/68 *Salgoil v Italian Ministry for Foreign Trade* [1968] ECR 453, esp 459–60; for commentary, inter alia, D O'Keefe, 'Is the Spirit of Article 177 under Attack? Preliminary references and admissibility', (1998) 23(6) *EL Rev* 509, 516–18; also B Vesterdorf, 'Judicial Review in EC Competition Law', (2005) 1(2) *Competition Policy International* 13, 27; L Lovdahl-Gormsen, 'A Judicial Panel for European Competition cases: why the House of Lords was right', (2009) 5 *Journal of Business Law* 494, 505–506.

[32] Case C-344/98, *Masterfoods Ltd v HB Ice Cream Ltd* [2000] ECR I-11369 [47]–[48]; also *Inntrepreneur Pub Co CPC v Crehan* [2006] UKHL 38, HL (Lord Bingham) [4]–[6].

[33] Inter alia, O'Keefe (n 31) 520–21.

confirmed as the main avenue through which to continue this dialogue.[34] Although national courts may seek assistance from the Commission in relation to individual cases, it is clear that Council Regulation No 1/2003 confirms their established direct connection with the Court of Justice.[35]

This is not, however, to suggest that alternative solutions may not be proposed. As was pointed out in section IIA, the preliminary reference procedure has put great strain on the Court of Justice's docket and has often resulted in lengthy proceedings; although the situation has improved in recent years, it was suggested that this may be a factor which is potentially incompatible with the need to secure an 'effective judicial remedy' to individual claimants.[36] Although the enactment of the Modernisation Regulation has not resulted in a surge of cases concerning private antitrust enforcement cases, maintaining the unity and consistency of EU competition law constitutes a pressing concern.[37] On this point, it should be emphasised that, the lack of uniform rules governing these actions across the Union was regarded by the Commission itself, as well as by many commentators, as a factor jeopardising their effectiveness in protecting individuals or firms affected by anti-competitive behaviour.[38]

Consequently, it is apparent that there are clear policy reasons, based on concern for securing legal certainty and for respecting the principle of effectiveness in this area, for the adoption of EU measures providing appropriate mechanisms to assist the national courts in the application of the Treaty antitrust rules in individual cases.[39] Enacting specific measures would be appropriate because it would uphold the importance of the Treaty competition rules as norms of 'public policy' and in particular would seek to 'give individuals a "clear picture of their basic rights"' in this area.[40] It would also lay down a set of common standards applicable across the EU with a view to creating a 'common playing field' for those aggrieved by the consequences of anti-competitive behaviour.[41] Taking action in this area would also be compatible with the principle of subsidiarity, given the significant diversity of the level of protection against the consequences of anti-competitive behaviour still characterising the laws of the Member States and the resulting risk of jeopardising the overall competitiveness of the EU business environment.[42]

However, uncertainties remain as to the form that this action should take in the area of judicial control over competition decisions adopted by domestic courts and as to what implications any such reform is likely to have for the overall structure of the Union judiciary and for the EU's institutional structure at large. Should a 'specialised competition court' be created and endowed with the power to hear appeals against all decisions involving the application of the Treaty competition rules, adopted by both the Commission and

[34] See Commission Staff Working Paper accompanying the White Paper on Damages Actions for breach of the EC antitrust rules, COM (2008) 165 final, para 141. For commentary, inter alia, Ehlermann and Atanasiu (n 10) 78–79.

[35] See Commission White Paper (n 10) 5–6.

[36] See most recently J Komarek, 'In the Court(s) We Trust: On the Need for Hierarchy and Differentiation in the Preliminary Ruling Procedure', (2007) 32(4) *EL Rev* 467, 468–69; see also 486–87.

[37] See Commission White Paper (n 10) 2; see also Commission Staff Working Paper (n 34) [76], [82].

[38] Commission White Paper (n 10) 2; see also p 8. For commentary, inter alia, J Kortmann and C Swaak, 'The EC White Paper on antitrust damages actions: why the Member States are right to be (less than) enthusiastic', (2009) 30(7) *ECLR* 340, 347–48.

[39] Commission White Paper (n 10) 8; also, Commission Staff Working Paper (n 34) [67]; see also [280].

[40] ibid [313–15]; see also Andreangeli (n 13) 250–51.

[41] Commission Staff Working Paper (n 34) [320].

[42] See eg Commission Impact assessment document accompanying the Commission White Paper on damages actions for breach of the EC competition rules, COM(168) final [165]; see also Case C-453/99 *Courage v Crehan* [2001] ECR I-6297 [28]–[29].

the national courts? Or should this power remain with the General Court in its role of 'general' judge? And if one decided to make way for the creation of such 'appellate' jurisdiction, would that option be compatible with the principles guiding the judicial framework created by the Treaties, especially in respect to the relationship with national courts? Perhaps most importantly, could a similar proposal attract sufficient consensus on the part not just of the EU institutions but also of the Member States, given the centrality of competition law vis-à-vis the whole EU legal system? These questions will be examined in the following sections.

III. THE GENERAL COURT AS A 'COMPETITION COURT': FROM THE 2006 HOUSE OF LORDS' REPORT TO PROPOSING THE CONFERRAL ON IT OF APPELLATE JURISDICTION AGAINST DOMESTIC JUDGMENTS

A. Creating a 'Specialised' Competition Jurisdiction: Challenges and Implications

Section IIB briefly considered the development of the General Court since its inception in 1989. It was emphasised that the Court, despite having been originally envisaged as a 'specialist' forum, designed to relieve the Court of Justice of a large part of the burden arising from 'labour-intensive' cases, has evolved to become a 'general' court, competent for hearing all direct actions with the exception of those reserved to the Court of Justice by the Statute or the Treaty. This trend has, however, presented a number of challenges: in respect to actions for annulment lodged against competition decisions, commentators and stakeholders argued that the length of these proceedings could jeopardise the applicants' right to an effective remedy, especially in merger cases.[43]

This argument prompted the Confederation of British Industry (CBI) to ask for an inquiry by the House of Lords Select Committee on the EU on the possibility of establishing an EU Competition Court. It was argued that although the 'fast-track procedure' has been used successfully in a number of cases, it was suggested that the General Court alone, given its docket, could not guarantee 'speed and finality' in dealing with these appeals.[44] Consequently, it was wondered whether a 'specialist court' could be established to hear these appeals, in accordance with Article 257 of the TFEU. [45] During the inquiry, however, several commentators suggested that, to ensure internal coherence in the interpretation of the EU competition rules, the remit of the panel should also be extended to the review of

[43] See inter alia House of Lords' Select Committee on the European Union, *XXXII Report: the review of the EC Merger Regulation*, sess 2001/2002 [241]. For commentary, see, eg J Temple Lang, 'Two Important Merger Regulation Judgments: the implication of *Schneider/Legrand* and *Tetra Laval/Sidel*', (2003) 28(2) *EL Rev* 259, 267–68.

[44] House of Lords' Select Committee on the European Union, *XV Report: An EU competition court*, session 2006/07, www.publications.parliament.uk/pa/ld200607/ldselect/ldeucom/75/7504.htm#a1 (hereinafter referred to as the *XV Report*), [1]–[2], [5] and [14].

[45] See Council Decision of 2 November 2004 establishing a European Civil Service Tribunal (2004/752/EC, Euratom), [2004] OJ L333/7. For commentary, B Vesterdorf, 'The Community Court System Ten Years from Now and Beyond: Challenges and Possibilities', (2003) 28(3) *EL Rev* 303, 313; also, specifically in respect to the CBI proposal, see eg A Andreangeli, 'Toward an EU Competition Court: "Article 6 proofing" antitrust proceedings before the Commission?', (2007) 30(6) *World Competition* 595.

Articles 101 and 102 TFEU decisions lodged by non-privileged applicants[46] and potentially to hearing preliminary references in this field.[47]

It is submitted that whilst being mainly prompted by the need to ensure the 'speedy appellate process' in all competition matters, with the exception of state aids, the 'specialised panel' envisaged by the CBI was destined to become the primary forum for the scrutiny of the Commission decisions. However, the House of Lords Select Committee questioned the extent to which its creation could have been reconciled with the judicial and institutional architecture of the Union as well as representing an appropriate response to the concerns raised in the inquiry.[48] A number of witnesses suggested that the new panel would have resulted in a more complex framework for the judicial scrutiny of the Commission decisions.[49]

It was also argued that the General Court itself had been established as a 'competition court' and, even taking into account the pressure stemming from having become a 'general' first instance court, had been able to discharge that function thoroughly.[50] Consequently, it was doubted that a specialised court could have been an appropriate option, even taking into account the 'special' features of competition litigation.[51] It was suggested that there would have been considerable difficulties in identifying 'pure' competition cases to be assigned to the specialised court, not only due to the often complex nature of the facts, but also because this exercise could undermine the central role of competition law and policy within the structure of the Treaties.[52] In this respect, commentators acknowledged that the Court of Justice retained a degree of control over the appeal decisions of the General Court vis-à-vis the specialised court's judgments; nonetheless, they doubted that this 'limited review' mechanism would have ensured coherence in the interpretation of EU law and, more generally, would have been consistent with the role of the Court as 'Guardian of the Treaties'.[53]

However, perhaps the most powerful argument against the establishment of such a specialised court was based on its actual ability to relieve the General Court of a significant part of its workload:[54] between 2000 and 2005, only 42 appeals were brought against competition decisions, of which about 15% were merger cases.[55] More recent figures confirm the previous trends. For instance, in 2009 the General Court completed 31 competition cases against a total of 439 cases; these figures may usefully be compared with the case law

[46] See eg CBI brief, 'The Need for an EU Competition Court', 15 June 2006. Also Vesterdorf (n 45) 311–12.

[47] See eg H Rasmussen, 'Remedying the Crumbling EC judicial system', (2000) 37(6) *CML Rev* 1071, 1083–84 and 1098–1101; see also Report by the Working party on the future of the EC's court system (n 19) 29–31.

[48] *XV Report* [16] and [38].

[49] Written evidence submitted by the International Bar Association to the House of Lords' Select Committee, Subcommittee E, www.parliament.uk/documents/upload/InternationalBarAssociation.DOC 3–4; see also written evidence submitted by the Office of Fair Trading, www.parliament.uk/documents/upload/OFT.doc 5–6.

[50] Written evidence submitted by Sir David Edward to the House of Lords Select Committee on the EU, Subcommittee E 7–8; also written evidence submitted by the Office of Fair Trading (n 49) 4. See also *XV Report* [79].

[51] See eg Minutes of Evidence given to the House of Lords' Select Committee on the EU, Subcommittee E by Sir Christopher Bellamy 44–45; also *XV Report* [118].

[52] ibid; see also Lovdahl-Gormsen (n 31) 505; Andreangeli (n 48) 598–99.

[53] See eg written evidence submitted by the Office of Fair Trading (n 49) 5–6; for commentary, Vesterdorf (n 45) 312.

[54] House of Lords Select Committee of the European Union, Subcommittee E, hearing of 22 November 2006, Minutes of Evidence, p l 6.

[55] See Annual Report of the Court of First Instance (2005), www.curia.europa.eu/en/instit/presentationfr/rapport/stat/st05tr.pdf 5.

in the field of intellectual property, which constitutes by far the 'bulk' of the General Court's activity, with 169 closed files.[56]

These trends seem to have remained unaltered in 2010 and 2011: according to the 2011 Report on the activity of the General Court respectively 79 and 39 new cases were launched in the field of competition law.[57] These figures may be contrasted against, respectively, 207 and 219 new proceedings instituted in the area of intellectual property law.[58] Thus, competition filings made about 15% of the 636 new cases lodged with the General Court in 2010, and in 2011 this percentage decreased to close to 8% of the total 722 new actions brought before the same court.[59] By contrast, intellectual property remained a prominent portion of the General Court's workload, making around 40% of the total new filings in both years.[60]

Similar figures characterise the 'split' between competition and intellectual property completed proceedings: in 2010, 38 competition cases were closed, compared with 180 intellectual property actions. In 2011, a bumper year, 100 competition actions were completed, higher than in the past few years, but still significantly lower than the 240 closed in the field of intellectual property.[61] This difference appears even more marked if these figures are seen against the background of the total number of proceedings closed in each year: in 2010 the General Court terminated a total of 527 cases, of which competition actions represented less than 10% and IP cases numbered almost a third. In 2011, although the number of Article 101 and 102 TFEU decisions rose significantly, it was still in the region of 14%, whereas IP decisions represented, once again, a third of the Court's decisions.[62]

The foregoing commentary shows that having a separate jurisdiction presents a number of significant problems: first of all, it may risk insulating a key area of EU law from the overall legal system centred upon the Founding Treaties. In addition, it was illustrated that due to the make-up of the workload of the General Court, instituting a specialised panel and thereby committing resources to this end, that may be used 'across the board' to deal with the whole array of appeals, may not be sustainable. On the contrary, the summary analysis of the General Court's activity has indicated that it is not competition appeals, but rather the review of patents, trade marks and copyright decisions that generate the most significant portion of the Court's case load. Consequently, it is suggested that the Member States' move toward the negotiation of a new 'EU Patent Convention' that is going to include the creation of a 'Patent Court' for the Union and the EEA is not entirely surprising. It is argued that this move can be read as evidence of a concern for efficient decision-making in these cases and for lightening the load pending before the EU judiciary, an issue which does not, however, seem to arise in relation to competition actions.[63]

These views seem to have been largely confirmed by a recent Report published by the House of Lords' Select Committee on the EU, concerning more specifically the issues aris-

[56] See Annual Report of the General Court (2009), http://curia.europa.eu/jcms/upload/docs/application/pdf/2010–05/ra09_stat_tribunal_final_en.pdf 165 ff; see especially p 170. For commentary, inter alia, Lovdahl-Gormsen (n 31) 499–500.

[57] See Annual Report on the Activity of the General Court (2011), http://curia.europa.eu/jcms/upload/docs/application/pdf/2012–03/ra2011_stat_tribunal_provisoire_en.pdf 4.

[58] ibid.

[59] ibid 6.

[60] ibid.

[61] ibid. 9.

[62] ibid. For commentary, see generally 'Commentary of the Max Planck Institute on the drafting of the new EU Patent Convention' (2009) *International Review of Intellectual Property and Competition Law* 817, 835–36.

[63] See inter alia, mutatis mutandis, T Lock, 'Taking National Courts More Seriously? A comment on Opinion 1/09', (2011) 36(6) *EL Rev* 576, 578.

ing from the creeping workload of the EU Courts.[64] The Select Committee emphasised that creating a specialised tribunal to deal with EU staff cases had not posed significant difficulties due to the nature of the rules involved and especially to their close connection with the EU's 'internal organisation'.[65] By contrast the 'proliferation' of sector-specific jurisdictions in other areas was regarded as giving rise to concerns in view of their potential impact on the inner consistency of EU law as a whole and on the integrity of the Court of Justice's own jurisdiction.[66] It was added that creating these specialist tribunals would also have serious implications for the EU Courts' own resources: according to the Select Committee, their presence would not significantly lessen the General Court's own docket.[67] Consequently, it was argued that whatever efficiencies could be gained from the existence of a 'competition tribunal' would not have been counterbalanced by the drawbacks, in terms of resources, arising from its institution.[68] Thus it was suggested that other measures should be considered, such as, inter alia, increasing the number of judges and adopting practices designed to facilitate their rotation across chambers, to secure the availability of specific expertise when required.[69]

In light of the above, it is suggested that serious doubts remain as to whether a 'specialised court' for Articles 101 and 102 TFEU proceedings can be justified, both from a policy standpoint and due to its resources' implications. [70] However, it cannot be excluded outright that some of that 'specialism', characterising the General Court at its inception, could be 'given back' to it in a different form.

A suggestion that was often made, and which was reiterated more recently in the House of Lords Select Committee on the EU's 2011 Report on the workload of the EU Court of Justice, concerned the introduction of 'specialised chambers' in the General Court.[71] As is well known, Article 12(1) of the General Court's Rules of Procedure allows the Court to 'lay down criteria by which cases are to be allocated to each of its chambers': these criteria can be based, inter alia, on the subject matter of individual appeals.[72] Consequently, it was suggested that competition cases should be heard by a specialised chamber within the general Court to ensure 'expertise' and 'continuity' in the adjudication of these cases.[73] This proposal was initially welcomed in some quarters: it was suggested that competition law had reached a sufficiently 'mature' stage in its development as to constitute a relatively unitary, albeit still integral, aspect of EU law and could therefore be feasibly and efficiently applied by the same group of judges to maintain its inner consistency.[74]

However, other scholars and stakeholders were rather critical of this suggestion: they pointed out that routinely the General Court already tended to concentrate, thanks to its informal organisational practice arrangements, competition cases in certain chambers; it

[64] House of Lords Select Committee on the EU, *XIV Report*, session 2010–11 (hereinafter referred to as *XIV Report*), available at: www.publications.parliament.uk/pa/ld201011/ldselect/ldeucom/128/128.pdf.

[65] ibid [129].

[66] ibid [135].

[67] ibid.

[68] ibid; see also, inter alia, mutatis mutandis, Lovdahl Gormsen (n 31) 500.

[69] ibid [136].

[70] See eg written evidence given by the European Commission, www.parliament.uk/documents/upload/Commission%2DLS%20draft%20Final.doc 3–4; also *XV Report* [192]–[194].

[71] See *XIV Report*, esp [118]–[121].

[72] See inter alia Ehlermann and Atanasiu (n 10) 79–80; also A Arnull, 'The Community Judicature and the 1995 IGC', 20 (6) *EL Rev* 599, 605–606.

[73] See eg Vesterdorf (n 45) 322–23; also M Harker et al, 'Judicial Scrutiny of Merger Decisions in the UK, the EU and the US', (2011) 60(1) *ICLQ* 93, 103.

[74] See eg Vesterdorf (n 45) 322; see also *XIV Report* [121]; also *XV Report* [56].

also sought to ensure that at least one judge would be an expert in dealing with these questions.[75] Thus, it was argued that entrenching these arrangements and thereby instituting officially specialised chambers would not significantly contribute to the swift adjudication of competition appeals and could even jeopardise the Court's efficiency by making case allocation excessively rigid.[76]

Similar concerns were raised by one of the members of the General Court: Judge Irena Pelikanova, speaking at a recent conference, expressed the view that 12 years since the Treaty of Nice have seen the Court itself responding effectively and appropriately to the challenges posed by the technical and fact-intensive nature of antitrust and merger appeals, by adopting a range of practices designed to provide sufficient expertise on the bench for each of these cases.[77] Therefore she doubted that institutionalising these arrangements would bear significant benefits for the Court's workload and suggested that adopting this option could result in dampening the efficiency of its adjudication.[78] More generally, she suggested that any reform impacting on the normal rotation of judges across chambers and on the way cases were assigned to each of them should be treated with caution to avoid taking away limited resources from the functioning of an already stretched General Court.[79]

In light of the above, it may be argued that the creation of specialised chambers could have some merit, at least in principle, in terms of 'expertise' and of 'continuity' on the bench, especially in complex cases. At the same time, it is clear that just as with specialised tribunals, any such positive outcome cannot counterbalance totally the potentially negative drawbacks that effectively taking away three if not five judges from the 'mainstream' Court could have on the already burdened resources available to the latter. It was also queried whether, since the General Court itself already exercises 'expert' adjudication thanks to its practical arrangements, it may be necessary to formalise these practices, by way of instituting these chambers. However, this conclusion should not be read as precluding outright the possibility for the General Court to develop more fully into a 'competition court', albeit in a different context, namely against the background of the decentralised framework for the application of Articles 101 and 102 TFEU.[80]

As the statistics show, the major source of workload for the Court of Justice comes from the preliminary reference procedure:[81] although the implementation of the 'Modernisation' reforms has not resulted in the expected 'surge' in references, envisaged by the EU legislature,[82] it may be wondered whether the General Court could become a more direct interlocutor for the domestic courts in this area. It was anticipated that the General Court, as a result of the amendments introduced at the Nice IGC, already enjoys potential jurisdiction to hear preliminary references, in areas identified by the Council of Ministers,

[75] See eg *XV Report* [56]; also *XIV Report* [101]–[102].

[76] See eg H Gilliams, 'Modernisation: from Policy to Practice', (2003) 28(4) *EL Rev* 451, 473–74; also Lovdahl-Gormsen (n 31) 497.

[77] Judge Irena Pelikanova, address given at the conference: 'Cross border EU competition law action', held at the London School of Economics, New Academic building, on 20 April 2012. See also Ch 7.

[78] ibid; see also, mutatis mutandis, *XIV Report* [109] and [120].

[79] See eg evidence given by Prof A Arnull to the House of Lords' Select Committee on the EU with a view to preparing the *XIV Report*, available at: www.parliament.uk/documents/lords-committees/eu-sub-com-e/CourtofJustice/CJEUoeawe.pdf 4; see also oral evidence, ibid 7–8.

[80] See eg, mutatis mutandis, S Peyer, 'Myths and Untold Stories – Private Antitrust Enforcement in Germany', CCP Working Paper 10–12, www.uea.ac.uk/polopoly_fs/1.170085!ccp10–12.pdf, esp 14–17.

[81] See eg 2011 Annual report of the EU Court of Justice – Statistics concerning the judicial activity, http://curia.europa.eu/jcms/upload/docs/application/pdf/2012–06/ra2011_statistiques_cour_en.pdf, esp 95–97.

[82] Inter alia, *XV Report*, paras 187–88; also eg Lovdahl-Gormsen (n 31) 506.

although this power has not been exercised yet. However, could the General Court also be envisaged as 'going a step beyond' the preliminary jurisdiction, and thereby become an appellate court vis-à-vis domestic decisions? The implications of these two options will be examined in greater detail below.

B. The General Court as an 'Appellate Court': What Does this Mean for the EU Judicial Architecture and for the Treaty as a Whole?

Section IIIA briefly considered the implications of creating a specialised jurisdiction within the structure of the General Court, either as a specialised tribunal or as a 'competition chamber'. It was argued that this proposal, despite being potentially appealing, would not be sustainable in terms of resources, or indeed consistent with the need to maintain the unity of EU law as a whole, given the centrality of the competition rules within the Treaties themselves. This section will consider the extent to which the role of the General Court in itself could be developed to accommodate the concerns for the speed and the finality of competition adjudication and will concentrate on examining the possibility of conferring on the Court the jurisdiction to hear appeals lodged against domestic judgments involving the application of Articles 101 and 102 TFEU.

It was anticipated that the General Court was primarily envisaged as a specialist court, responsible for the scrutiny of labour intensive cases such as competition appeals. Thus, it could be argued that its 'genesis' would in some way legitimise its role of 'specialised' forum in these matters. However, it is equally apparent that the scope of its jurisdiction remains confined to the limits of Article 263 TFEU, according to which it could only review the acts of the EU institutions and, perhaps most importantly, would only enjoy powers of scrutiny strictly defined by the Treaty in respect to both the intensity of this control and the grounds for appeal. On this point, it is emphasised that, according to the EU Courts, this limited type of review found its justification in the need to preserve the 'inter-institutional balance' established by the Treaty and especially the division of powers between the Union judiciary and the broadly 'executive' function fulfilled by the European Commission.[83]

When the 'complex economic assessment' of facts and their analysis in light of the competition rules is at issue, the powers of scrutiny should be confined to 'verifying whether the relevant procedural rules have been complied with, whether the statement of the reasons for the decision is adequate, whether the facts have been accurately stated and whether there has been any manifest error of appraisal or a misuse of powers'. [84] It is acknowledged that these judicial statements referred to the judicial scrutiny of competition decisions adopted by the Commission. However, it is argued that since they expressly define and justify the width of the powers of review enjoyed by the General Court, they are a relevant benchmark for considering whether to confer on the Court an appellate jurisdiction over domestic judgments.

It is submitted that adopting this option would have a number of wide-ranging consequences for the framework established by the Treaty. From a general standpoint, it is argued that subjecting domestic judgments to the review of the General Court would radically change the relationship between national courts and the Luxembourg courts from an

[83] Joined Cases T-68, 77–78/89 *Società Italiana Vetro SpA and Others v Commission* [1992] ECR II-1403 [319]–[320].

[84] Case 42/84 *Remia v Commission* [1985] ECR 2585 [26].

'egalitarian' interplay to a more hierarchical one. It could also result in an at least a partial shift of the 'centre of gravity' in the implementation of competition policy via individual decision making from the Commission to the General Court itself.[85] Consequently, it is suggested that a similar change could only be brought about by Treaty amendment.[86]

With regard to the nature of the powers that the Court would enjoy, a parallel may be drawn with the possibility to confer a 'jurisdiction on the merits' to it vis-à-vis a Commission decision, which was also discussed in the course of the debate leading to the House of Lords Select Committee on the EU's Report on the EU Competition Court. A number of witnesses regarded it as being relatively attractive, in as much as it would have led to definitive findings 'once and for all' over the case at hand.[87] However, the Select Committee itself recognised that creating such a pervasive type of jurisdiction would be very difficult to reconcile with the Treaties' own 'choice' as regards the way in which to distribute powers across the Union. It was argued that allowing it to conduct such a wide-ranging scrutiny of competition decisions could encourage the Court to exercise an 'over-intrusive review' of the facts and the evidence at the basis of individual decisions, going far beyond the scope of judicial scrutiny exercised by the Court of Justice itself.[88] It was added that this type of review would lead to the General Court's progressive empowerment in respect of the implementation of competition policy goals, a task that falls within the competence of the European Commission.[89] Thus, it was submitted that although the Commission itself would not be likely to 'stand idly by', conferring appeal-type review powers to the Court could endanger the overall institutional balance of the Union.[90]

It is acknowledged that these concerns were raised in respect to the issue of whether it would be compatible with the Founding Treaties to confer 'on the merits' jurisdiction to a specialised court vis-à-vis Commission infringement decisions, a question which is undoubtedly different from the one that is being examined in this contribution. However, it is argued that creating an appellate jurisdiction against domestic judgments and entrusting it with the General Court may give rise to equally pressing problems. Thus, having regard to their nature and intensity, it is submitted that powers of review proposed for the General Court appear radically different from those enjoyed by the EU courts in respect to decisions of the institutions, powers that are those akin to a 'review' jurisdiction, save for the specific case of financial penalties, according to Article 262 TFEU.[91] This type of jurisdiction would also be almost impossible to reconcile with the way in which domestic and EU courts have 'traditionally' been engaging in a dialogue, namely via the preliminary rulings procedure.[92]

As was anticipated above, the use of preliminary references fostered a relationship between national and Union judges inspired by reciprocal cooperation and by respect for

[85] See eg Lovdahl-Gormsen (n 31) 509–10.

[86] Inter alia, Andreangeli (n 48) 612 ff.

[87] See eg Minutes of Evidence given before the House of Lords Select Committee on the EU, Subcommittee E in the course of the 2006 inquiry by Sir Christopher Bellamy 43; Minutes of Evidence given by Sir David Edward 60–61.

[88] *XV Report* [76]; see also evidence submitted by the Office of Fair Trading 151 of the Report.

[89] *XV Report* [78]–[79]; see also evidence submitted by Philip Lowe (European Commission) to the House of Lords Select Committee on the EU, Sub-Committee E 74–75 of the Report.

[90] *XV Report* [79]; see eg evidence given by Bo Vesterdorf 99.

[91] See eg evidence given by Bo Vesterdorf 99; also, inter alia, A Andreangeli, 'Toward an EU competition court: "Article 6 proofing" antitrust proceedings before the Commission?' (2007) 30(6) *World Competition* 595, 603–604.

[92] Inter alia, Komarek (n 36) 476; also M Rosenfeld, 'Comparing Constitutional Review by the European Court of Justice and the US Supreme Court', (2006) 4(4) *International Journal of Constitutional Law* 618, 627.

judicial independence.[93] Against this background, it seems difficult to imagine how the 'hierarchical relationship' traditionally associated with appeals could be made to 'fit' within the principles guiding the dialogue between national and EU Courts established by the Treaty via the preliminary reference procedure.[94] Consequently, it is argued that conferring powers of appellate jurisdiction to the General Court in competition matters, while in principle not impossible, would bring about very significant changes in the institutional framework envisaged by the Treaty. It is suggested that it would transform the nature of the interaction existing between the Commission and the Court itself, by de facto involving the latter more closely in competition decision-making. Perhaps most importantly, however, it would have considerable consequences for the judicial framework established by the Treaties since it would result in wider powers enjoyed by the General Court (albeit in a limited area) vis-à-vis those currently assigned to the Court of Justice itself.[95]

It is added that, from a more general point of view, creating this right of appeal would entail yet another transfer of sovereignty, in this case concerning judicial powers, from the Member States to the Union. It is submitted that this proposal, if implemented, would deprive the domestic appellate courts of the corresponding powers to review the impugned judgment since 'final jurisdiction' over that judgment would be conferred to the EU Courts.[96] It follows from the foregoing analysis that arguing in favour of conferring appellate jurisdiction to the General Court in competition matters raises a further question which is of a political nature, namely whether consensus on the part of the Member States to a Treaty amendment allowing for this transfer would be forthcoming.

In the course of the House of Lords' EU Select Committee inquiry on an EU Competition Court, a similar question, arising in relation to the possibility to make way for a jurisdiction 'on the merits' in competition cases, was met with considerable scepticism, which was very eloquently voiced by Bo Vesterdorf. He took the view that a similar change in the Treaties would be possible only

> if Member States were willing to accept that the institutional balance, which has been set up carefully under the Treaty, allowing the Commission as a quasi-administrative political body to take those decisions, that specific power should be taken away and given to judges . . . But that is not of actuality because it cannot be done, and I fail to see Member States accepting that as a change.[97]

It is uncontested that the issues pending before the Select Committee were of a different nature. However, bearing in mind the doubts concerning the feasibility of a similar jurisdiction, expressed in the previous section, and their perceived unwillingness to carry out any more reforms of the EU judiciary beyond the relatively piecemeal ones adopted in the Nice IGC,[98] it could be doubted that the Member States could easily be convinced to embrace such a significant change.[99] It is suggested that introducing the proposed reform would also be very difficult to reconcile with the choice made by the EU legislature in the Modernisation

[93] See inter alia Case 13/61 *Bosch v de Geus* [1962] ECR 45; for commentary, see eg K Lenaerts, 'Interlocking legal orders in the European Union and comparative law' (2003) 52(4) *ICLQ* 873 at 881; also, mutatis mutandis, Gustaffson (n 18) 174.

[94] See inter alia J Rinze, 'The Role of the European Court of Justice as a Federal Constitutional Court', (1993) *Public Law* 426, 431.

[95] See, inter alia, Andreangeli (n 48) 608–609.

[96] See eg, mutatis mutandis, Lenaerts and Gerard (n 13) 334.

[97] Minutes of Evidence given before the House of Lords' Select Committee on the EU, Subcommittee E by Judge Bo Vesterdorf, 99.

[98] See inter alia Heffernan (n 19), esp 196–97; also Johnston (n 20) 515–17.

[99] *XV Report*, paras 192–94.

Regulation. As was illustrated in section II, Council Regulation No 1/2003 sought to reconcile the competing needs of securing consistency in the application of Articles 101 and 102 TFEU and of safeguarding the independence of the judiciary by establishing a mechanism of 'soft' cooperation between the Commission and the domestic judges.[100] Perhaps most importantly, it appears that the Regulation, by reiterating the function of preliminary references in the relationship between the domestic courts and the Court of Justice, sought to uphold the 'egalitarian' cooperation existing between the national and EU judiciaries rather than to look for an alternative to the status quo.[101]

In this specific respect, it should be emphasised that strong doubts as to the possibility to derogate from the structure of the judiciary provided by the Founding Treaty have been recently voiced by the Court of Justice itself. In its Opinion concerning the compatibility of a draft agreement designed, inter alia, to institute a special 'Patent Court',[102] the Court reiterated its commitment to maintaining the institutional setting originally established in the Treaty.[103] It took the view that any alteration of that framework, including the creation of an international court or panel empowered to apply EU law should remain compatible with and therefore respect the integrity of the Court of Justice's own powers.[104]

The Court of Justice recognised that the Patent Court would be external to the EU legal system and would enjoy jurisdiction limited to the area of patents and intellectual property law: however, it held that its establishment would have far-reaching effects on the powers enjoyed by the EU judiciary as well as for those conferred to the domestic courts as 'Union courts', thereby resulting in a significant change of the institutional balance within the judicial architecture of the Union.[105]

The Opinion explained that the creation of a 'EU and Community Patent Court' would, on the one hand, result in the national courts being divested of their authority in deciding private disputes arising in these areas and, on the other hand, prejudice the corresponding power of the Court of Justice to assist these courts by means of preliminary rulings which the domestic courts would no longer be able to seek.[106] It was added that since the Draft Agreement envisaged that the Patent Court would be empowered to make preliminary references to Luxembourg, as part of its exclusive jurisdiction, it would have radically altered the egalitarian relationship of trust linking the Court of Justice itself to the national courts, by introducing an external actor in the EU overarching judicial framework.[107]

On that basis the Court of Justice took the view that the Draft Agreement, to the extent that it provided for an international court, external to the Union judiciary and endowed with exclusive jurisdiction to apply EU Law as well as the Patent Convention and to ask for preliminary rulings in the course of individual proceedings, was incompatible with the TFEU. In the Court's view the 'transfer of jurisdiction' from the domestic courts to the Patent Court and the consequences it entailed for the Luxembourg Court's own jurisdiction under Article 267, affected the 'essential character' of the judicial structure

[100] See eg Lenaerts and Gerard (n 13) 332.

[101] See, inter alia, C Hodges, 'Competition Enforcement, Regulation and Civil Justice: What is the Case?' (2006) 43 *CML Rev* 1381, 1399.

[102] Opinion 1/09, Re: Draft Agreement – Creation of a unified patent litigation system – European and Community Patents Court, 8 March 2011, nyr (hereinafter referred to as EU Patents Court Opinion).

[103] ibid [64]–[65].

[104] ibid [77].

[105] ibid [77]–[79].

[106] ibid [82]; see also [84]. For commentary, see inter alia Lock, above 63, 582.

[107] ibid [84]–[85].

enshrined in the Treaty and indispensable to preserve the uniform application of EU law.[108]

It is acknowledged that the Draft Agreement for the institution of a 'European Patent Court' was significantly different from the proposed instruments seeking to create a 'EU Competition Court': it is emphasised that whereas the former envisaged the establishment of an international court, external to the EU overall institutional architecture, the 'EU Competition Court' would have been established as a specialised court attached to the General Court. However, one cannot fail to notice how the Court of Justice, out of a concern for preserving its own function as 'Guardian of the Treaty' and thereby defending the unity and the consistency of EU law, remained openly sceptical at the possibility of relinquishing its jurisdiction in favour of a separate judicial body, albeit in respect of a discrete area of the *acquis*.

Although the limited remit of this contribution does not allow for a consideration of these issues, it is noteworthy that a broadly similar attitude seems to have influenced also the Court of Justice's posture in the discussions concerning the drafting of the agreement for the accession of the EU to the European Convention on Human Rights. As is well known, the TFEU created an express legal basis for the Union to become a party to the Convention. In the course of the negotiations that have followed, the need to preserve the unity and the consistency of EU law, albeit subject to the observance of the obligations stemming from the ECHR, came prominently to the fore. One of the major issues in this area was how the Court of Justice of the EU could continue to fulfil its functions when allegations were made as to the infringement of the Convention resulting from the implementation of EU law, either directly or through the action of the authorities of the Member States.[109] To respond to the general concerns, for safeguarding the unity of Union Law, the draft accession agreement envisaged the possibility for the EU to appear as 'co-respondent' with the Members States in all cases brought against the latter in which it was alleged that there had been an infringement of the Convention owing to the fulfilment on the part of national authorities of EU law obligations. [110] Similarly, Member States could stand in the same capacity alongside the Union in the course of all proceedings concerning prima facie allegations 'calling into question the compatibility with the Convention' of a rule of primary Union law.[111]

This solution was generally, albeit cautiously, welcomed as 'a way to avoid gaps in participation, accountability and enforceability in the Convention system'[112] whenever the conformity of EU law with fundamental rights' guarantees was at stake.[113] In addition, and to deal with the more specific concern for protecting the integrity of the Court of Justice's jurisdiction, it was envisaged at a joint meeting between the Presidents of the Luxembourg Court and the European Court of Human Rights that an 'internal procedure' be put in place in order to secure the involvement of the EU Court of Justice in all cases in which the

[108] ibid [89]. For commentary, see eg Lock (n 63) 583–84.

[109] See eg Lock, 'Walking on a Tightrope: the draft ECHR accession agreement and the autonomy of the EU legal order', (2011) 48 *CML Rev* 1025, 1038–39; see also Lock, 'EU Accession to the ECHR: implications for judicial review in Strasbourg', (2010) 35(6) *EL Rev* 777, 780–81.

[110] Draft Accession Agreement, CDDH-UE (2011), see [9] and [37]; for commentary see Lock (2011) (n 109) 1039–40.

[111] See Art 3(3) Draft Accession Agreement (n 110).

[112] Draft Accession Agreement (n 110), Explanatory Memorandum [33].

[113] See Lock(2011) (n 109) 1039–40.

Union appeared as co-respondent.[114] Under this special procedure the Court of Justice would be granted the opportunity to 'review the compatibility with the Convention rights ... of the provision of EU law which has triggered the participation of the EU' to the litigation.[115] As a result, the ECJ would be allowed to rule, in accordance with what is envisaged as being an 'accelerated procedure',[116] over the issue and, if possible, to 'solve the matter internally', thus protecting the unity of EU law, before the Strasbourg Court decides on the merits of the case.[117]

In addition, Article 3(5) of the Draft Accession Agreement provides for the involvement of the ECJ in proceedings before the European Court of Human Rights in all cases concerning possible challenges of the validity of EU in light of the ECHR which the Court of Justice of the EU has not had the possibility of assessing.[118] Although several authors have raised concerns that it may not always be easy to identify when exactly this requirement would be fulfilled – except in completely 'novel' questions of law for the ECJ – Article 3(5) should be regarded as another tool to secure the autonomy and the unity of EU law.[119] More generally, and while it is clear that many of these questions will be dealt with in the course of the negotiations, it is argued that the debate surrounding the accession of the Union to the ECHR, just as the discussions arising from the possibility of an 'EU Patent Court' has shown a clear concern for maintaining the integrity and autonomy of the jurisdiction of the Court of Justice of the EU.

It may be wondered whether, perhaps out of a concern for upholding the strength of the existing powers enjoyed by the EU judiciary as a whole, another proposal might be made, ie conferring to the General Court, which is already the primary forum for all the actions for annulment lodged by non-privileged applicants, including those against competition decisions issued by the Commission, the power to hear follow on actions for damages brought by the victims of infringements that the Commission itself had detected and sanctioned. Judge Irena Pelikanova, from the General Court, argued that this option would be far less 'controversial' than either conferring on the Court the power to hear appeals against domestic judgments or indeed, as will be explored in the following section, than transferring to it the power to decide on competition referrals.[120] She pointed out that the General Court already enjoyed jurisdiction in respect to tort claims lodged against the EU; consequently, in her view this proposal would not amount to the creation of a 'brand new' type of jurisdiction and could have also been justified, more broadly, by the Union's exclusive jurisdiction in the field of competition according to Article 103(2)(d) TFEU.[121]

It is acknowledged that 'concentrating' on the EU judiciary not only powers of review of the legality of infringement decisions adopted by the Commission, but also the jurisdiction

[114] See Explanatory Memorandum (n 112) [57]–[58]; see also Joint Communication of the Presidents of the Court of Justice and of the European Court of Human Rights, http://curia.europa.eu/jcms/upload/docs/application/pdf/2011–02/cedh_cjue_english.pdf 2.

[115] Explanatory Memorandum (n 112) [58].

[116] ibid [59].

[117] ibid [58]; for commentary see eg Lock et al, 'EU Accession to the European Convention on Human Rights: a legal assessment of the Draft Accession Agreement of 14 October 2011', Foundation Robert Schumann Policy Paper – European issues, n 218, 7 November 2011 5–6.

[118] See Explanatory Memorandum (n 112) [61].

[119] See Lock et al (n 117) 14–16.

[120] Judge Irena Pelikanova, address given at the conference: 'Cross border EU competition law action', held at the London School of Economics, New Academic building, on 20 April 2012. See Ch 7.

[121] ibid.

to hear damages claims arising from unlawful practices that have been dealt with at Union level, may be rather attractive, especially because it could effectively safeguard the unity and consistency of the interpretation of the EU competition rules in both contexts.[122] However, it is respectfully submitted that this proposal would still require an amendment to the Founding Treaties: it is clear that recognising similar powers to the General Court, just as was illustrated in respect to the proposed creation of an appellate jurisdiction against domestic decisions, would result in a significant inroad in the powers enjoyed by the domestic judiciaries. It is in fact clear that national courts would, as a result of this option being adopted, be deprived of the jurisdiction to hear these tort claims, a power which stems from the direct effect enjoyed by Articles 101 and 102 TFEU. Consequently, it may be doubted that the consensus of the Member States, just as had been shown for other proposals affecting the Union's judicial architecture, would be forthcoming.[123]

On this point, it is well known that a debate is taking place in a number of European jurisdictions, including the UK, in respect to the options for reform of the existing competition framework, in order to make it more effective and, perhaps more relevantly, better equipped to deal with the demands for the restoration of harm suffered by society and its members as a result of unlawful practices.[124] It may be suggested that these discussions and proposals provide evidence of the resolve shown by many Member States to boost the tools for the redress of competition harm, especially when it affects large groups of victims.[125]

The UK Government is among the 'proactive' actors in this debate, having launched a consultation on the topic of how to encourage members of large groups to access the mechanisms of relief of the collective losses caused by anti-competitive practices: the document published in March 2012 focused the discussion on how to empower victims to seek relief of their injuries via a number of tools, both judicial and non-judicial, and envisaged a central role for alternative dispute resolution, which can involve also the competition agencies, whereas the courts would be a 'last resort'.[126]

In addition, it is well known that competition litigation rates have also grown in other Member States, such as Germany, where recent studies found an average increase in the take up of new cases ranging between 150 and 250 lawsuits per year in the period from 2005 and 2007 alone[127] and therefore questioned the original findings that private enforcement of the antitrust rules remained uniformly 'underdeveloped' across the Union.[128] Although the limited remit of this contribution does not allow for an in-depth assessment of these proposals, or indeed of the trends characterising the domestic adjudication in this area, it could be suggested that the German litigation data and the British evidence of debate might be seen as proof of the willingness of the Member States to take greater 'ownership' of the reform agenda in this area, especially due to the potentially

[122] ibid; see also inter alia Temple Lang (n 43) 271–72.

[123] See eg Vesterdorf (n 45) 320–21.

[124] See eg Dept of Business, Innovation and Skills Consultation document, 'Private actions in competition law', www.bis.gov.uk/assets/biscore/consumer-issues/docs/p/12-742-private-actions-in-competition-law-consultation.pdf (hereinafter referred to as BIS consultation document), esp 3–5.

[125] See inter alia C Hodges, 'The Reform of Class and Representative Actions in European Legal Systems' (Oxford, Hart Publishing, 2008) 149 ff.

[126] BIS Consultation document 3–6.

[127] See eg S Peyer, 'Private Antitrust Litigation in Germany between 2005 and 2007: empirical evidence' (2012) 8(2) *Journal of Competition Law and Economics*, esp 338–40.

[128] ibid 359; see also S Peyer, 'Cartel Members Only – Revisiting Private Antitrust Policy in Europe' (2011) 60(3) *ICLQ* 627, 647–48.

wide-ranging impact that any change in the civil procedure rules could have on national autonomy.[129]

Against this background, it is open to doubt whether concentrating into the hands of the General Court the jurisdiction to hear follow-on actions for damages, albeit based on existing Commission infringement decisions, would represent an 'appealing' option for the Member States. Instead, it could legitimately be queried whether the emphasis could shift toward empowering domestic courts to act as 'Union courts', and therefore take a more active role in adjudicating competition cases.[130] It is submitted that national judges are now able to tackle these cases competently and can also rely on both the 'informal' advice of the Commission and on the established preliminary reference procedure channels to seek assistance from the Court of Justice. Consequently, it could be argued that the proposal to confer on the General Court either the power to hear appeals against domestic decisions or the jurisdiction to decide on follow-on EU competition damages claims would not be easy to accommodate within the Union's institutional architecture as well as with the principles informing the Union judicial structure and would therefore require a change in the Founding Treaties.[131]

As the foregoing analysis has illustrated, while the objectives of clarity and consistency in the interpretation of the competition rules cannot be downplayed, it is questionable whether any of the proposals discussed so far would be likely to find support among the Member States, due to the impact they are likely to have on the way in which the EU judiciary functions. Nevertheless, as the current debate in the Member States shows, it could be more realistic to envisage the domestic courts as taking centre stage in private competition adjudication. It is therefore clear that the preliminary reference procedure is going to emerge, once again, as the key 'channel of communication' between the national courts and the EU legal system. The next section will therefore consider the question of whether the 'potential jurisdiction' conferred on the General Court by the Treaty of Nice could be used as a means to ensure the unity and consistency of EU competition law and the effective protection of the rights of individual claimants while at the same time remaining compatible with the Treaty's own institutional structure.

C. The General Court as the 'New Counterpart' of Domestic Courts via the Preliminary Reference Procedure: Less Pain, (More or Less) Same Gain?

Section IIIB above considered a few of the possible implications arising from widening the jurisdiction of the General Court in respect to direct actions, to include the power to either hear appeals against domestic competition judgments or to decide on follow on damages lawsuits based on existing Commission infringement decisions. It was argued that, whilst potentially beneficial for the legal certainty and the finality of litigation in this area, altering the scope of the jurisdiction exercised by the Court would have a considerable impact on the EU judicial and institutional structure and, given the scepticism surrounding the likeli-

[129] See also, mutatis mutandis, M Carpagnano, 'Private Enforcement of Competition Law Arrives in Italy: analysis of the judgment of the European Court of Justice in joined Cases C-295–289/04 *Manfredi*' (2006) 3(1) *Comp L Rev* 47, esp 69–72.

[130] See eg *XIV Report* [111].

[131] See eg *XV Report* [56]–[57].

hood of gathering sufficient consensus among the Member States, would not be achievable in practice.

This section will consider whether conferring on the General Court the power to hear preliminary rulings arising from competition law disputes would go some way toward addressing effectively the same concerns for the expeditiousness of these proceedings and the legal certainty in the interpretation of the Treaty antitrust rules. It was illustrated in section II that among the changes introduced at the Nice IGC was the conferral on the General Court of 'potential jurisdiction' to hear preliminary references in areas to be determined by the Statute of the Court. This change was welcomed as recognition of the importance of the role of the General Court as well as a means to 'ease' the workload of the Court of Justice.[132] It was suggested that due to its experience and record, the General Court could effectively become a new 'partner' for the national courts.[133]

Adopting a similar solution would also have a number of advantages for the Court of Justice itself: it was argued earlier that one of the drawbacks of the success of the procedure provided in Article 267 TFEU was the heavy workload affecting the Court.[134] Furthermore, this option appears to be far less controversial than conferring on the General Court a new appellate jurisdiction vis-à-vis national judgments since it would find its legal basis already in the Treaty. Consequently, it is suggested that, at least in principle, assigning to the General Court the power to deal with these questions would relieve the Court of Justice of at least some of the cases pending before it and, coupled with a 'fast track'-type procedure, akin to that adopted already in respect to, for instance, merger appeals, would secure finality, expeditiousness and consequently legal certainty in antitrust disputes.[135]

It is however undeniable that the General Court is itself under significant strain as a result of the workload deriving from direct actions (especially in the area of intellectual property). As a result, it may be suggested that this option would remain consistent with upholding its already solid reputation as a 'competition court' and could also be built on the already strong relation of trust between the Court of Justice and the domestic courts that has progressively developed thanks to the procedure enshrined in Article 267 TFEU.[136] Nonetheless, it should be emphasised that its practical implementation could run into difficulties due to the existing case-load of the General Court itself, which, if the proposed change were to be introduced, would inevitably increase. Consequently, it is argued that although the move toward Member States taking 'greater ownership' (inter alia by seeking to encourage their own judiciaries to apply the competition rules to individual cases) of the competition private enforcement agenda, anticipated in the previous section seems in many ways inevitable, a closer look as to how to resolve the practical questions arising from its impact on the EU judiciary remains central to the debate.

Crucially many of these issues, which had been raised after the 2000 Nice IGC, have since been left open. At that time, commentators suggested that it would be difficult in practice to identify 'purely competition cases' since national courts can (and often do) raise questions

[132] Inter alia, Heffernan (n 19) 204–205.

[133] ibid 209–11.

[134] Inter alia, T Tridimas and G Gari, 'Winners and Losers in Luxembourg: a statistical analysis of judicial review before the European Court of Justice and the Court of First Instance (2001–2005)', (2010) 35(2) *EL Rev* 131, 133–34.

[135] See eg, mutatis mutandis, Lovdahl-Gormsen (n 31) 496–97.

[136] See, inter alia, B Vesterdorf, 'A Constitutional Court for the EU?' (2006) 4(4) *International Journal of Constitutional Law* 607, 611–12.

spanning a number of areas within EU law.[137] Furthermore, and just as it had been argued in relation to the proposal for an EU competition court, transferring jurisdiction to the General Court in this area might create a risk for competition law to be 'insulated' from Union law and would thereby lose its central role within the system of the Treaty.[138]

Further concerns were raised in respect to the 'preview' and 'review' mechanisms envisaged by the Treaty and allowing, respectively, the General Court to 'transfer' a reference back to the Court of Justice if it raises questions 'affecting the unity and consistency of Union law' and the first Advocate General to refer a General Court's ruling to the Court for appeal, should there be a serious risk for the unity and consistency of EU law. However, it is undeniable that these mechanisms would limit at least in part the risk of 'anomalous' rulings and thereby protect the overall coherence of EU law.[139]

It was suggested that these mechanisms would result in adding a further 'layer' of jurisdiction, as 'problematic' references could potentially undermine the ability of the General Court's new preliminary jurisdiction to secure speed, finality and certainty in competition disputes.[140] Consequently, it was argued that, given the length characterising domestic judicial proceedings in several Member States,[141] and even taking into account the possibility of having references made to the General Court potentially 'fast-tracked', litigants would be exposed to the risk of having to wait a considerable amount of time before a resolution of the dispute is reached in 'controversial' cases.[142]

Many of these concerns were recently reiterated by the House of Lords Select Committee on the EU: in its 2011 Report the Committee pointed out that 'sharing' the preliminary references' jurisdiction between the two EU Courts, despite being in principle beneficial, had a number of practical drawbacks, such as the difficulties potentially arising from identifying any filtering criteria to allocate cases to each of the courts, and the danger of overloading an already stretched General Court.[143] However, the most significant criticism against this proposal is of a more fundamental nature, and concerns the question of whether the Court of Justice itself would be willing to lose control (albeit only partially) over one of its key powers to shape the interpretation and application of EU law.[144] Speaking at a recent conference, Judge Irena Pelikanova of the General Court went as far as to suggest that the proposal to transfer the power to hear competition preliminary references to the General Court would be even more 'radical' than any other option tabled thus far and affecting the EU Courts' judicial powers.[145] She pointed out that since it had taken the Court of Justice a significant number of years and considerable effort to build a reciprocal relationship of goodwill and cooperation with the domestic courts, this proposal would be likely to be regarded sceptically, if not altogether resisted.[146]

[137] See eg Heffernan (n 19) 212–13.

[138] See, inter alia, *XV Report* [79].

[139] Art 256 TFEU; see inter alia Johnston (n 20) 508.

[140] See eg Johnston (n 20) 509; see also, mutatis mutandis, Report by the Working Party on the Future of the EC's Court System (n 19) 33–34.

[141] See, inter alia, *Inntrepreneur Pub Co CPC and others v Crehan* [2006] UKHL 38. For commentary, see eg Andreangeli (n 13).

[142] See eg Heffernan (n 19) 210–11. Cf Johnston (n 20) 508–509.

[143] *XIV Report* [102], [104].

[144] See eg, mutatis mutandis, Opinion 1/09 (n 102) [82]–[83]; cf, inter alia, A Komninos, 'Article 234 and National Competition Authorities in the Era of Decentralisation', (2004) 29(1) *EL Rev* 106, 112–13.

[145] Judge Irena Pelikanova, address given at the conference: 'Cross border EU competition law action', held at the London School of Economics, New Academic building, on 20 April 2012. See Ch 7.

[146] ibid; also see *XIV Report* [106].

It is suggested that these views appear to be justified in light of the reluctance shown by the Court of Justice in its Opinion 1/09 on an EU Patent Court to allow for any curtailment of its powers as ultimate 'Guardian' of the interpretation of Union law.[147] It could be argued that the Court's attitude could have been motivated, at least in part, by the circumstance that the proposed court would have been external to the Union's judicial framework. However, it is undeniable that the Court was also concerned with maintaining the effectiveness and the integrity of its relationship with the domestic courts.[148] Thus, it may be suggested that any support on its part for the handing (albeit partial) of its Article 267 TFEU powers to the General Court would be rather unlikely to be forthcoming.[149] It should also be remembered that even if the General Court was allowed to hear these references, the Court of Justice would, upon advice of an Advocate General, still remain the ultimate judge of the question of whether the unity and consistency of EU law could be affected by the General Court's rulings that address 'controversial' or 'novel' questions.[150]

Against this background, it may legitimately be doubted whether this proposal could lessen the workload of the Court of Justice and thereby, given the efficiencies stemming from it, find additional support.[151] On this point, it is especially open to doubt whether, even if these cases were fast-tracked, the General Court could decide them within a short time frame, due to the nature of the subject matter and to its existing docket.[152] In addition, it is undeniable that transferring to the General Court the power to decide on preliminary references concerning competition law would entail isolating a key area of Union law from the whole legal system.[153] In the light of the foregoing, it is argued that the difficulties arising from devising 'filtering criteria' for case allocation, and especially from identifying 'pure' competition cases, would not be counterbalanced by any 'efficiency gains' potentially arising from taking these cases 'away' from the Court of Justice's docket and transferring them to the General Court's records.[154]

It is therefore concluded that moving to a shared Article 267 TFEU jurisdiction for competition cases, while potentially appealing, could actually create more problems than it can resolve. Although it is uncontested that the preliminary reference procedure will remain a key tool to protect the consistency of EU competition law, especially in a framework characterised by greater participation of the domestic courts, it is not clear whether reforming the EU judicial structure, as opposed to, for instance, encouraging the domestic courts to act as 'EU courts' could be the way forward to guaranteeing speed and legal certainty in private competition claims' adjudication.

[147] Opinion 1/09 (n 102) [82].
[148] *XIV Report* [105].
[149] ibid; see also [108].
[150] See Art 256(3) TFEU, see also *XIV Report* [106]–[107].
[151] *XIV Report* [101].
[152] ibid; see also [104].
[153] ibid [102]–[103].
[154] ibid; see also [106].

IV. LEGAL CERTAINTY, UNITY AND FINALITY IN COMPETITION LAWSUITS: COULD THE GENERAL COURT BECOME A 'SURROGATE' COURT OF JUSTICE? TENTATIVE CONCLUSIONS

The previous sections considered the question of whether the General Court could become a forum for appeals against judgments given by national courts in EU antitrust disputes. It was argued that concerns for the finality, the legal certainty and the consistency in the interpretation of the Treaty competition rules could, at least in principle, provide a powerful justification for the introduction of this 'special' jurisdiction. However, the examination of its implications revealed that this option would have far-reaching consequences which would be very difficult to reconcile with both the institutional structure of the Union[155] and the nature of the relationship existing between the domestic courts and the EU judiciary.[156]

It was added that such a 'special' appellate jurisdiction would constitute a radical departure from both the nature of the interplay existing between the EU Courts and the Commission in the field of competition enforcement and the eminently 'egalitarian' rapport existing between the EU Courts and the national judges, fashioned around the preliminary reference procedure.[157] On this point, it was suggested, in light of the Court of Justice's Opinion on the EU Patents Court and of the experience offered by the negotiations for the accession of the Union to the European Convention on Human Rights, that any alteration of this 'special relationship' is likely to be met with considerable resistance by the EU judiciary as well as with concern by several other institutional actors, such as Member States themselves.[158] It was emphasised, more generally, that due to the central role of the EU Courts in securing the unity and consistency of Union law, any proposal for reform affecting the Treaty's judicial architecture should be treated with great caution.[159]

Against this background, it was argued that creating a specialised jurisdiction in this area would risk undermining the unity and consistency of EU law as a whole, in as much as it would lead to the competition rules, which enjoy a central position in the Treaty framework, being 'insulated from the latter'.[160] It was also doubted that creating this 'special jurisdiction' would be sustainable, having regard to the necessary resources and to the number of cases potentially pending before the domestic courts every year.[161]

Consequently, this chapter has suggested adopting a prima facie less 'radical' yet still effective solution, especially for maintaining the consistency of the EU competition rules and of, at least potentially, ensuring speed in decision-making – namely conferring to the General Court the jurisdiction to hear preliminary references made by domestic courts

[155] See eg *XV Report* [192]–[194]; also Minutes of Evidence given to the House of Lords' Select Committee on the EU, Subcommittee E, by Bo Vesterdorf 99.

[156] See inter alia Case 13/68 *Salgoil v Italian Ministry for Foreign Trade* [1968] ECR 453, esp 459–60; for commentary, inter alia, O'Keefe (n 31) 516–18; also B Vesterdorf, 'Judicial Review in EC Competition Law' (2005) 1(2) *Competition Policy International* 13, 27; Lovdahl-Gormsen (n 31) 505–506.

[157] See eg Case 13/61 *Bosch v de Geus* [1962] ECR 89 [6] (AG Lagrange); also Case 6/64 *Costa v ENEL* [1964] ECR 1194 [7]; for commentary, most recently, Komarek (n 36) 476.

[158] Opinion 1/09 (n 102) [83], [89].

[159] See inter alia Lock et al (n 117) 16–17.

[160] *XV Report* [79]; see also, inter alia, Lovdahl-Gormsen (n 31) 505.

[161] See eg written evidence given by the European Commission, www.parliament.uk/documents/upload/Commission%2DLS%20draft%20Final.doc 3–4; also *XV Report* [77]–[78].

under Article 267 TFEU in cases involving Articles 101 and 102 of the Treaty. It was argued that this option would ensure legal certainty and coherence in the interpretation of these provisions as well as protecting their 'cohesion' vis-à-vis the Treaty as a whole;[162] it would also be far less controversial than establishing a novel 'appellate' jurisdiction for the General Court, since this latter jurisdiction is already provided for, albeit only provisionally, by Article 256 TFEU. Going down this road would also be more consistent with the manner in which domestic judges and the Luxembourg courts have engaged in a 'dialogue' since the inception of the Community/Union.[163]

However, even if this option were to be pursued with the necessary support of the Council of Ministers of the European Union, its outcome would not be immune from criticism. It was argued that any reform affecting the scope and the function of the preliminary reference procedure could not be implemented without adversely affecting a carefully crafted relationship, ie the one existing between the domestic judiciaries and the EU Court of Justice.[164] It was also emphasised that the Court of Justice itself has clearly resisted any attempt to reform the preliminary reference procedure, thus casting doubt on the viability of any such proposal.[165] Transferring the jurisdiction to hear preliminary rulings in the area of competition law to the General Court would also have considerable practical drawbacks, in as much as it would be unlikely to relieve the workload of any of the Union courts.[166]

In the light of the foregoing analysis it can be concluded that ensuring coherence, speed and finality in the litigation of competition claims is clearly a concern for the overall competition enforcement structure. However, it is unclear whether reforming important features of the EU judicial architecture may be an appropriate and proportionate response to these issues, especially bearing in mind the institutional and resource-related implications of any proposed changes. It is also questionable whether due to the resistance shown by the Court of Justice any proposal could stand the chance of securing the necessary support. It is recognised that the landscape in which competition adjudication takes place has undergone significant changes and that Member States especially appear to have taken greater responsibility in seeking to provide relief for the victims of restrictive practices infringing Articles 101 and 102 TFEU. Nonetheless, it is doubted that introducing reforms at EU level for the purpose of dealing in a fair, efficient and timely manner with these disputes may be the optimal response. It is therefore hoped that the domestic authorities will be drawn more closely in the implementation of the agenda for private competition enforcement in the Union, by laying down the 'right conditions' for the domestic courts to be able to act as 'Union courts', by relying, whenever necessary, on the assistance of the EU Court of Justice.

[162] See, inter alia, B Vesterdorf, 'A Constitutional Court for the EU?' (2006) 4(4) *International Journal of Constitutional Law* 607, 611–12.

[163] See inter alia Case C-7/97 *Oscar Bronner GmbH & Co KG v Mediaprint Zeitungs-und Zeitschriftenverlag GmbH & Co KG and others* [1998] ECR I-7791 [17]. For commentary, see eg, mutatis mutandis, J Temple Lang, 'The Duties of Cooperation of National Courts under Community Constitutional Law' (1997) 22(1) *EL Rev* 3, 6–7.

[164] See *XIV Report* [103].

[165] See eg Opinion 1/09 (n 102) [83], [89].

[166] Inter alia, Johnston (n 20) 508–509.

9

Conclusion: Cross-Border Aspects of EU Competition Law and Litigants' Strategies

MIHAIL DANOV AND FLORIAN BECKER

The possibility of different Member States' laws applying to matters of procedure and substance in claims, based on the very same directly applicable Treaty provisions, may lead to a situation where some Member States' courts enforce EU competition law more efficiently than others. Harmonisation at EU level may be an obvious solution. However, the above analysis shows that, even if one makes a case for harmonisation of substantive and procedural laws in Europe, the current European juridical structure would not be capable of promoting uniform application of any harmonised instrument. This may increase the workload of the European Courts and the General Court in particular. In this regard it has recently been submitted that:

> For several years now, the number of cases disposed of by the General Court has been lower than the number of new cases, so that the number of pending cases is rising constantly. Between 1 January and 12 October 2011, 572 cases were brought and 549 were disposed of. As at 12 October 2011, 1 323 cases were pending. In comparison, between 1 January and 12 October 2010, 514 cases were brought and 401 were disposed of. As at 12 October 2010, 1 304 cases were pending . . .
>
> The Court of Justice therefore considers that an increase in the number of Judges by at least 12, bringing the number of General Court Judges to 39, is necessary.[1]

Is there a case for even more drastic reform in revising the judicial architecture in order to better accommodate the EU competition law cases in the European context? Although Andreangeli demonstrates that ensuring coherence, speed and finality in EU competition litigation is a concern for the overall EU competition law enforcement structure which might justify legislative intervention at EU level,[2] it seems clear that it is not feasible to have a 'single scheme of jurisdiction'[3] with regard to private EU competition law actions. Andreangeli further argues that allowing private parties to make an appeal on a point of EU competition law before the European courts would fly in the face of the current institutional architecture of the Union, and, as a result, would be a radical departure from the current model which could undermine the unity and consistency of EU law as a whole. The way forward – she believes – is to give the General Court jurisdiction to hear preliminary

[1] Explanatory Statement from the Report on the draft regulation of the European Parliament and of the Council amending the Protocol on the Statute of the Court of Justice of the European Union and Annex I thereto (02074/2011 – C7-0090/2011 – 2011/0901A(COD)).

[2] See Ch 8.

[3] P Eleftheriadis, 'Federalism and Jurisdiction', in E Cloots, G de Baere and S Sottiaux (eds), *Federalism in the European Union* (Oxford, Hart Publishing, 2012) 45, 54.

references made by domestic courts under Article 267 TFEU in cases involving Articles 101 and 102 of the Treaty. In addition one may rely on the national legislators as well as on the Member State courts to promote EU competition law enforcement,[4] which appears to suggest that an efficient private international law mechanism may be desirable in the European context.

Judge Pelikánová proposes a very original solution, which might potentially result in a single jurisdiction over EU competition law damages actions. In particular, her proposal is to confer on 'the General Court competence to decide, as a court of first instance, in actions for damages in competition cases decided by the European Commission.'[5] This new competence would allow the General Court to hear and determine all follow-on actions preceded by a decision of the European Commission. Such a development would certainly address the problem of parallel proceedings arising in the European context. It would also allow for the European judiciary to develop a body of case law, resulting in further unification of the law in the area. As a part of her proposal, Judge Pelikánová also addresses the problems which are related to the two-task structure of EU competition law enforcement by suggesting that the legislator should 'leave to the European Commission solely the inquiry, with the duty to introduce a criminal or civil action before the Court. The system would better fulfil the requirements of the ECHR'. However, she herself acknowledges the difficult political reality in the Union, and admits that amending the Treaty to add a new competence of the General Court to hear damages actions will not be received well by the Member States.

Nonetheless, Judge Pelikánová goes further to demonstrate how inefficient the current juridical architecture is, as well as to question the effect of an increase of the number of judges. There are indeed persuasive arguments that an increase in the number of judges may adversely affect the quality and standards of work because it would bring about a rotation of judges. Although Judge Pelikánová appears to consider that a new regulation on private international law is a second-best solution,[6] the political reality in the Union and the inefficient European legal system clearly suggest that a new mode of governance which might produce efficient enforcement results in the area may be based on an effective private international law instrument which promotes regulatory competition across Europe.

The use of a private international law instrument may be further justified by the diverse nature of Europe. Mills has noted that 'Private international law is thus conceived as embodying a principle of "tolerance of difference", not in a paternalistic or permissive sense, but in the sense of respect between equals.'[7] However, one may question the ability of a private international law instrument to address all the problems, and the two-task enforcement structure of EU competition law in particular. As already noted,[8] the real concern is that the pattern which is developing in Europe and England in particular appears to indicate that the limited private litigation which occurs normally proceeds as a follow-on action based on a public enforcement action. In view of that, one may argue that '[t]he current ineffectiveness of antitrust damages actions'[9] is best addressed by an amendment of

[4] See Ch 8.

[5] See Ch 7.

[6] See Ch 7.

[7] A Mills, *The Confluence of Public and Private International Law: Justice, Pluralism and Subsidiarity in the International Constitutional Ordering of Private Law* (Cambridge, CUP, 2009) 14.

[8] See Chs 3 and 5.

[9] Commission (EC), 'White Paper on Damages actions for the breach of the EC antitrust rules', COM (2008) 165 [1.1].

Regulation 1/2003 with a view to addressing the specific issues of jurisdiction and judgments in relation to EU competition law claims as well as the issues due to the ineffective two-step adjudication in which arguably a regulator is better placed to detect and establish an infringement and, subsequently, a court is better placed to award damages[10] (referred to in this book as the 'two-task structure of EU competition law enforcement'). In the course of such a reform, private international law techniques may be used to promote regulatory competition. Is the current private international law framework not suited to deal with the challenges of the private antitrust enforcement? What are the specific problems which need to be addressed by the legislator?

Before analysing the current private international law framework and the way it is affecting potential litigants' strategies at the moment, it should be noted that the most important private international law rules that operate at EU level are the Brussels I regime (which covers the Brussels I Regulation and the Lugano Convention) and the Rome regime (which includes the Rome I Regulation and the Rome II Regulation). Whereas Brussels I is concerned with allocation of jurisdiction and the recognition and enforcement of judgments in civil and commercial matters, Rome I and Rome II deal with choice of law with regard to contractual obligations (Rome I) and non-contractual obligations (Rome II). Given that the EU legislator has clearly stated that 'the non-contractual obligations arising out of restrictions of competition in [Rome II] should cover infringements of both national and [EU] competition law',[11] only Rome II is addressed in this book.

I. SCOPE OF BRUSSELS I

The Brussels I regime covers the original Brussels Convention (as amended throughout the years), the Lugano Convention (signed between the states of the EEC and members of the EFTA) and the Brussels I Regulation.[12] Although, there are some minor differences between them, the structure and the basic principles are common to all of those instruments.[13] The focus here will be on the Brussels I Regulation,[14] since this is the fundamental instrument for determining jurisdiction in all proceedings brought on or after 1 March 2002. It is well settled that where a claim that has an international element relates to a 'civil and commercial matter', the court has jurisdiction to entertain a claim *in personam* solely in accordance

[10] WPJ Wils, 'The Relationship Between Public Antitrust Enforcement and Private Actions for Damages' (2009) 32 *World Competition* 3, 18 – accessible http://papers.ssrn.com/sol3/papers.cfm?abstract_id=1296458. See also: Ch 1, section IIA; Ch 5, section IIA.

[11] See recital 22 of the Rome II Regulation. See also A Dickinson, *The Rome II Regulation: The Law Applicable to Non-contractual Obligations* (Oxford, OUP, 2008) 270–71.

[12] Council Regulation (EC) 44/2001 of 22 December 2000 on jurisdiction and the recognition and the enforcement of judgments in civil and commercial matters [2001] OJ L12/1. The Brussels I Regulation, which entered into force on 1 March 2002, is in practice the successor of the Brussels Convention (Civil Jurisdiction and Judgments Act 1982 sch 1). (See more PR Beaumont, 'The Brussels Convention becomes a Regulation: implications for legal basis, external competence, and contract jurisdiction' in James J Fawcett (ed) *Reform and Development of Private International Law* (Oxford, OUP, 2002). It should be mentioned that Denmark is not subject to the Brussels Regulation, but has entered into an agreement with the EC that applies the same rules as the Brussels Regulation.

[13] See more A Briggs and P Rees, *Civil Jurisdiction and Judgments*, 5th edn (London, Informa, 2009) 6–10.

[14] Art 81 TFEU (ex-Art 65 of the EC Treaty) is the legal basis for new private international law initiatives; see P Beaumont, 'European Court of Justice and Jurisdiction and enforcement of judgments in civil and commercial matters' (1999) 48 *ICLQ* 223, 225.

with the Brussels I Regulation, if the dispute falls within its scope.[15] Are EU competition law claims within the scope of Brussels I? It is well established that an EU competition law claim brought before a Member State court is properly regarded as a 'civil and commercial matter' for the purposes of the Brussels I Regulation.

However, difficulties as to the scope of Brussels I are bound to arise because, despite the fact that Articles 101 and 102 TFEU regulate relationships between private undertakings, EU competition law provisions may often be enforced by NCAs in the public interest. Article 1 of the Brussels I Regulation, however, states that '[the Regulation] shall not extend, in particular, to . . . administrative matters'. It has been argued that if an EU competition law claim brought before national courts in order to establish an Article 101/102 infringement is regarded as a 'civil and commercial matter' for the purposes of Brussels I,[16] then there is no reason to suggest that the matter would be regarded differently only because the proceedings were brought before an NCA that is an administrative body.[17] But, is it really so? Does Brussels I adequately allocate jurisdiction in EU competition law cases?

II. EVIDENCE REGULATION[18]

The issue of taking evidence by a foreign NCA in support of private proceedings in England could be very important in many cross-border EU competition law actions. For example, it would be bound to arise in a follow-on EU competition law action brought before an English court. This would be particularly so if the decision of a Member State competition authority that establishes an infringement of Articles 101 and 102 TFEU were regarded as being within the scope of Brussels I.[19] The need for taking evidence by the foreign competition authority in support of private proceedings in England could arise because the NCA decision establishing that a foreign undertaking had committed an EU competition law infringement would not have dealt with such issues as, for example, whether an actual claimant had suffered damages, and what damages should be awarded in order for a plaintiff to be compensated.

In other words, despite the fact that a party could be relying on an infringement decision taken by an NCA, evidence as to the causation and assessment of damages would need to be collected in a follow-on action. This raises the question of whether an English court could request evidence from the foreign competition authority in support of private proceedings in England by relying on the Evidence Regulation, Article 1 of which states that:

> This Regulation shall apply in civil or commercial matters where the court of a Member State, in accordance with the provisions of the law of the State, requests: (a) the competent court of another Member State to take evidence; or (b) to take evidence directly in another Member State.

[15] Art 1 of Brussels Regulation. See more: L Collins and others (eds) *Dicey, Morris and Collins on the Conflict of Laws*, 14th edn (London, Sweet & Maxwell, 2006) 311–12.

[16] M Danov, *Jurisdiction and Judgments in Relation to EU Competition Law Claims* (Oxford, Hart Publishing, 2012) 12–14.

[17] M Danov, 'EU Competition Law Enforcement: Is Brussels I suited to dealing with all the challenges?' (2012) 61 *ICLQ* 27.

[18] Council Regulation (EC) No 1206/2001 of 28 May 2001 on cooperation between the courts of the member states in the taking of evidence in civil or commercial matters [2001] OJ L174/1 (Evidence Regulation).

[19] Danov (n 17). See also Commission (EC), *Damages Actions for Breach of the EC Antitrust Rules* (White Paper) COM(2008) 165 final [2.3].

Is an NCA to be regarded as a 'competent court' for the purposes of the Evidence Regulation? It has been submitted that it can be argued that requests to foreign competition authorities for taking evidence in support of private proceedings in England could be made under the Evidence Regulation. But is this deduction correct? Are there any specific issues arising in view of the two-task structure of EU competition law enforcement?

III. ROME II – THE APPLICABLE LAWS[20]

There is a high degree of harmonisation of choice of law rules relating to contractual and non-contractual obligations in Europe. The Rome II Regulation[21] lays down the law applicable to non-contractual obligations in civil and commercial matters and applies as from 11 January 2009. The Regulation deals with choice of law with regard to tort, unjust enrichment, *negotiorum gestio* and *culpa in contrahendo.*

The general rule is that the law applicable to a non-contractual obligation arising out of a tort/delict shall be the law of the country in which the damage occurs, irrespective of the country in which the event giving rise to the damage occurred and irrespective of the country or countries in which the indirect consequences of that event occur.[22] Article 6(3), the special rule designated to deal with non-contractual obligations arising out of restrictions of competition, is the most important choice-of-law rule in tort in the context of this book. According to Article 6(3)(a) of Rome II, the law applicable to non-contractual obligations arising out of restrictions of competition should be the law of the country where the market is, or is likely to be, affected. In cases where the market is, or is likely to be, affected in more than one country, Article 6(3)(b) allows the claimant in certain circumstances to choose to base his or her entire claim on the law of the seised court, the *lex fori.* How easy is it to apply Rome II with regard to EU competition law infringements which would affect business and consumers in variety of Member States, which may result in variety of applicable laws with regard to the assessment of damages?

Therefore, an analysis of the specific problems arising under the current private international law framework should be undertaken in order to identify the solutions which should be considered at EU level.

[20] See more: A Dickinson (n 11); R Plender and M Wilderspin, *The European Private International Law of Obligations,* 3rd edn (London, Sweet & Maxwell, 2009) 435–781.

[21] Regulation (EC) 864/2007 of the European Parliament and of the Council of 11 July 2007 on the law applicable to non-contractual obligations (Rome II) [2007] OJ L199/40.

[22] Art 4 of the Rome II Regulation.

Part III

EU Competition Law Actions: Jurisdiction and Some Practical/Procedural Issues Arising in a Cross-Border Context

10

Introduction: The Enforcement Pattern Shaping Litigants' Strategies

MIHAIL DANOV AND FLORIAN BECKER

I. INTRODUCTION

It has been demonstrated that an appropriate institutional framework should take account of the specific characteristics of the European juridical system. Part III goes a step further and demonstrates that litigants' strategies, which are shaped by the specific features of EU competition law infringements and the current enforcement regime,[1] are indicative as to which issues need to be considered by the policy-makers, as well as to how the issues in question should be reformed with a view to closing the current enforcement gap in Europe. In this context, some concrete proposals for reform will be made.

An analysis of the qualitative interview data and the reported/pending cases clearly identify the three main issues to be addressed. First, as already noted,[2] the current enforcement pattern, in which the limited private litigation is heavily dependent on a regulator's decision establishing an infringement, inevitably leaves an enforcement gap as the public enforcers across Europe are unlikely to have the resources to investigate all the complaints they receive. This deduction can find further support in an article by Burrows and Gilbert,[3] in which they reviewed the OFT infringement decisions over the first 10 years of the Competition Act 1998's operation, and made the following observation:

> the OFT has argued that by imposing very large fines in high profile industries and publicising the results widely, competition law is now a high priority in the UK board room. However, this does not deal fully with the 'enforcement gap' that has arisen from a lack of infringement decisions. In particular, an impression has been created that small cases in low priority sectors are unlikely to be pursued (in marked contrast to the European Commission's (the Commission) 'zero tolerance' policy for cartels). Similarly . . . it is seriously open to debate whether post-modernisation, Art 102 TFEU and/or Chapter II of the Act is being enforced in the UK in a meaningful manner at all, a situation that is compounded by the fact that there have only been two Chapter II infringement decisions produced by other authorities in the regulated industries in the decade.[4]

[1] See Ch 5.

[2] See Ch 5.

[3] E Burrows and T Gilbert, 'OFT Competition Act Enforcement: Key developments over the first decade' (2010) *Competition Law Journal* 178.

[4] ibid 182.

Moreover, the two-task structure of EU competition law enforcement, as explained in Chapter 1, could create specific problems when it comes to gathering evidence with a view to imposing personal liability for EU competition law infringements in follow-on damages actions before Member State courts. Indeed, the litigants' strategies in *Pfleiderer*[5] and its subsequent application by the German court in *Pfleiderer*[6] and by the English court in *National Grid*[7] could therefore be seen as yet another indication that the issue of evidence and the interrelation between public and private enforcement may be really important in Europe.

Secondly, due to the principle of national procedural autonomy,[8] Member States' laws would play an important role, as the question whether a concrete claimant has suffered a loss as a result of an EU competition law infringement, and, if so, whether the claimant would be entitled to recover the pleaded loss, is to be decided by the domestic legal order.[9] The fact that these questions have been left to be determined by the Member States' national orders indicates that there would be procedural advantages for a claimant to conduct a trial in one Member State rather than another. This reaffirms the importance of jurisdiction rules in view of the 'traditional and universal principle of procedural law that commands the application of *lex fori* (the law of forum) to all of the proceedings associated with any legal action in court.'[10] In other words, it would be extremely important for any proposed mechanism, intended to close the enforcement gap, to consider the issues of jurisdiction along with all of the proceedings associated with EU competition law actions.

II. JURISDICTION AND PROCEDURE: PROCEDURAL RULES SHAPE LITIGANTS' TACTICS IN A CROSS-BORDER CONTEXT

As noted elsewhere,[11] the question 'whether certain evidence proves a certain fact . . . is to be determined by the law of the country where the question arises.'[12] The answer to this question in many cases would be pre-determined by establishing jurisdiction in the plaintiff's preferred forum.[13] Although Regulation 1/2003 stipulates that the burden of proving an infringement of Articles 101(1) and 102 TFEU rests on the party or the authority alleging the infringement,[14] it does not set the standard of proof.[15] In fact, recital 5 of the Regulation states that:

[5] Case C-360/09 *Pfleiderer AG v Bundeskartellamt* [2011] 5 CMLR 219.

[6] In the *Pfleiderer* case, 'the German court ruled against disclosure of leniency documents'. The High Court referred to the judgment of the Amstgericht Bonn of 30 January 2012 in the *Pfleiderer* case. Cited in *National Grid Electricity Transmission PLC v ABB Ltd & Others* [2012] EWHC 869 (Ch) [60].

[7] See *National Grid* (n 6) [56]–[60].

[8] See more: Ch 5.

[9] Ch 1.

[10] J Dolinger and C Tiburcio, 'The Forum Law Rule in International Litigation – which procedural law governs proceedings to be performed in foreign jurisdictions: *Lex Fori* or *Lex Diligentiae*? (1998) 33 *Texas International Law Journal* 425, 427. See more: R Garnett, *Substance and Procedure in Private International Law* (Oxford, OUP, 2012) 5–10.

[11] M Danov, *Jurisdiction and Judgments in Relation to EU Competition Law Claims* (Oxford, Hart Publishing, 2012) ch 5.

[12] *Bain v Whitehaven Rly Co* (1850) 3 HL Cas 1, 19. See also: JJ Fawcett and JM Carruthers, *Cheshire, North & Fawcett Private International*, 14th edn *Law* (Oxford, OUP, 2008) 83.

[13] M Illmer, 'Neutrality Matters Some Thoughts About the Rome Regulations and the So-Called Dichotomy of Substance and Procedure in European Private International Law' (2009) *Civil Justice Quarterly* 237, 242.

[14] See Art 2 of Regulation 1/2003.

[15] J Faull and A Nikpay, *The EC Law of Competition*, 2nd edn (Oxford, OUP, 2007) 95.

> this Regulation affects neither national rules on the standard of proof nor obligations of competition authorities and courts of the Member States to ascertain the relevant facts of a case, provided that such rules and obligations are compatible with general principles of [EU] law.

This text could be interpreted as leaving the domestic legal system of each Member State to determine what the 'required legal standard' of proof is.[16] In other words, the standard of proof is to be determined by the law of the court where proceedings have been brought.[17] Given the importance of the law of procedure, it seems to us that any regime, which is intended to promote regulatory competition, would fail to address the current enforcement gap unless the specific jurisdictional issues are carefully considered with regard to cross-border EU competition law actions. There are specific issues which need to be addressed, as the problems are bound to arise in view of the fact that EU antitrust infringements, by definition, affect businesses and consumers in a number of Member States (ie the antitrust damage may occur in several jurisdictions). The importance of the rules, which are intended to avoid parallel EU competition law proceedings, could not be questioned. The need for such rules can be further strengthened by the analysis of jurisdictional rules and their application in EU competition law cases which appear to indicate that, on some occasions, it would be very difficult for claimants to centralise litigation.[18]

Moreover, the analysis of Mr Justice Teare in *Cooper Tire*[19] appears to suggest that in many EU competition law cases, the place where the event giving rise to the damage occurred may be very difficult indeed to determine. Given that, in the European context, there could be numerous differences in the procedural laws, a claimant may be entitled to subscribe to them by choosing to conduct a trial in one Member State rather than another. Since the procedural rules will be very important in an EU competition law damages action,[20] we will also examine, if there is a need for a jurisdiction rule which allows a claimant to centralise litigation against a group of the same companies before the courts at his preferred jurisdiction. In other words, one way to promote regulatory competition in Europe is by allowing a private antitrust claimant to choose where to bring his EU competition law claim. For example, these could include such matters as: disclosure; standard of proof; speed of proceedings; experience of judges; and an opt-out collective redress regime. Litigants' strategies are informative in devising an effective regime for jurisdiction which avoids parallel proceedings.

Part III also demonstrates that should the legislator/s wish to design an effective enforcement system, there are three important issues which need to be carefully considered. First, as already noted, there would be multiple victims in several Member States. Secondly, the multiple victims may have suffered different levels of damages, and, as a result, they may have different interests in so far as those affected by an EU competition law infringement may be up or down in the chain of distribution (ie passing on or absorbing the inflated price, for example). Thirdly, consumers would be reluctant to bring such actions due to the negligible amount of damages suffered by them in comparison with the high litigation costs. Indeed, the data indicate there is a lack of mobility for consumers, who may prefer to sue in their

[16] Faull and Nikpay (n 15) 95.

[17] Arts 1(3) and 22(1) of Rome II. See more: Danov (n 11) ch 5.

[18] *Cooper Tire & Rubber Company Europe Ltd & Others* [2010] EWCA Civ 864; *Toshiba Carrier UK Ltd and Other v KME Yorkshire Ltd & Others* [2012] EWCA Civ 1190; *Nokia Corporation v AU Optronics Corporation* [2012] EWHC 731 (Ch).

[19] *Cooper Tire & Rubber Company v Shell Chemicals UK Ltd* [2009] EWHC 2609 (Comm) [65].

[20] See Chs 2, 3, 4 and 5.

home jurisdictions, and there is a high level of mobility of large purchasers, who may be more selective in deciding where to bring their claims.[21] The lack of redress for consumers[22] and the level of variation, when it comes to EU competition law enforcement in the various Member States,[23] appear to indicate that an appropriately designed collective redress system, which incorporates an opt-out regime,[24] may be needed to close the enforcement gap and provide redress for consumers. In this context, one should investigate if the low mobility of consumers across Europe could justify an opt-out regime, which is implemented by a particular Member State, to operate for consumers from across Europe.

Bringing an EU competition law claim in one Member State rather than another may be a legitimate strategy with regard to anti-competitive practices, which are implemented in a number of Member States, and should not be regarded as 'forum shopping', which the EU legislator seeks to avoid.[25] However, since there is no European definition of 'forum shopping' for the purposes of Brussels I,[26] some commentators do appear to regard such strategic behaviour as 'forum shopping'.[27] In particular, Krauskopf and Tkacikova have very recently noted:

> Divergences in national procedural and substantive laws enable and increase the likelihood of claimants forum shopping or so-called 'litigation tourism'.
>
> (a) There are various factors that influence and induce shopping among various national fora. Accordingly, the claimants (lawyers) engage in developing strategies that take the case to the 'magic jurisdiction' that promises the most favourable outcome for their private claims leaving the claimant with the full jackpot . . . of this 'game'.
>
> (b) [T]he strategic selection of favourable venues from among a plural menu of alternatives, is a logical, important and underexplored consequence of the situation' where private parties are also likely to use the antitrust laws strategically to their private advantage, which in turn might tend to undermine the rule of law.[28]

Similarly, in their observations in respect of decentralised enforcement of EU competition law, seven Member States feared that the decentralisation could lead to forum shopping.[29] Furthermore, the risk of forum shopping has been raised by industry and lawyers as one of their main concerns.[30] The attitude towards forum shopping has generally been disapproving.[31]

[21] See Chs 3, 4 and 5.

[22] See Chs 3, 4 and 5. See also: P Buccirossi, M Carpagnano, L Ciari and others, *Collective Redress in Antitrust*, www.europarl.europa.eu/document/activities/cont/201206/20120613ATT46782/20120613ATT46782EN.pdf .

[23] See Chs 3, 4 and 5. See also: D Waelbroeck, D Slater and G Even-Shoshan, *Study on the Conditions of Claims for Damages in Case of Infringement of EC Competition Rules (Ashurst Report)* http://ec.europa.eu/competition/antitrust/actionsdamages/comparative_report_clean_en.pdf.

[24] See more on the advantages of an opt-out regime in R Mulheron, 'The case for opt-out class actions for European Member States: A legal and empirical analysis' (2008-2009) 15 *Columbia Journal of European Law* 409.

[25] Case C-539 *Roche Nederland BV and Others v Frederick Primus and Milton Goldenberg* [2006] ECR I-6535 [38]. *cf.* the Opinion of AG [99]. See also: M Wilderspin, 'Jurisdiction issues: Brussels I Regulation Articles 6(1), 23, 27 and 28 in Antitrust Litigation' in J Basedow, S Francq and L Idot (eds), *International Antitrust Litigation: Conflict of Laws and Coordination* (Oxford, Hart Publishing, 2012) 41, 46.

[26] Wilderspin (n 25) 46.

[27] PL Krauskopf and A Tkacikova 'Competition Law Violations and Private Enforcement: Forum Shopping Strategies' (2011) *Global Competition Litigation Review* 26.

[28] ibid 30.

[29] DG COMP White Paper on the Reform of Regulation 17 Summary of the observations February 29, 2000, http://europa.eu.int/comm/competition/antitrust/others/wp_on_modernisation/summary_observations.html, 16.

[30] ibid.

[31] See more AG Slater, 'Forum Non Conveniens: A View from the Shop Floor' (1988) 104 LQR 554, 561–62. See also M Monti, 'Competition Law Reform', speech made at the CBI Conference on Competition Law Reform London, June 12 http://ec.europa.eu/comm/competition/speeches/text/sp2000_008_en.html.

Nevertheless, 'forum shopping' describes the scenario of 'a plaintiff by-passing his natural forum and bringing his action in some alien forum which would give him relief or benefits which would not be available to him in his natural forum.'[32] Given the EU policies which are intended to encourage private antitrust enforcement (and provided that they aim to promote regulatory competition with regard to the directly applicable EU competition law provisions which enjoy direct effect), one should differentiate between a plaintiff in an EU competition law claim, who takes legitimate advantage of the applicable procedural laws in a particular Member State and one that is 'condemned' as a forum shopper.[33]

III. THE STRUCTURE OF THIS PART

Part III critically discusses the issue of allocating jurisdiction, along with some selected aspects in EU competition law actions, and the specific difficulties concerning EU competition law claims brought by consumers, or on behalf of consumers. Jon Lawrence and Anna Morfey consider the various tactical manoeuvres that could be undertaken by defendants to defeat an EU competition law action or delay a decision. Jurisdiction challenges and time limits for bringing claims as well as costs' implications and dynamics between co-defendants are examined in this context, amongst other important issues. Dr Tim Reher writes about his experience with bringing EU competition law actions on behalf of multiple claimants in a German context. This is followed by a discussion of the specific jurisdictional challenges with regard to EU competition law action with a view to proposing specific solutions to be considered in the European context. Next, the issue of staying civil damages litigation pending appeals in the European Courts is considered by Pierre Bos and Jon Möhlmann. After that, Dr Paul Lasok QC considers what a procedural matter is, as well as some important procedural issues with regard to stand-alone actions and follow-on outing the important role of the regulator in the latter context. His analysis is followed by some practical observations on *Pfleiderer* by James Webber. Then, the cross-border issues regarding jurisdiction and choice of law are examined. Finally, on the basis of the distinctive features of cross-border EU competition law actions, a proposal for an effective collective redress mechanism is made.

[32] *Boys v Chaplin* [1971] AC 356, 401 (Lord Pearson); J Fawcett, 'Forum Shopping Some Questions Answered' (1984) 35 *Northern Ireland Law Quarterly* 141.

[33] *cf* J Harris, 'Forum Shopping in International Libel' (2000) 116 *LQR* 562. See also *Berezovsky v Michaels* [2000] 1 WLR 1004, HL. See more: Danov (n 11) ch 5.

11

Tactical Manoeuvres in UK Cartel Damages Litigation

JON LAWRENCE AND ANNA MORFEY

As the Government deliberates the future of competition litigation in the UK, potential claimants (both consumers and businesses) stand at a crossroads. For 10 years, direct purchaser claims have been brought based on European Commission decisions and those of national competition regulators. None of the claims to date has come to trial. None of the claims has resulted in an award of damages.[1]

To an extent, this lack of development provides a firm basis for change, if there is a political will to stimulate an increase in compensation claims. On the other hand, the bare statistics mask a recent substantial increase in the volume of litigation, the development of a sophisticated claimant bar capable of bringing substantial claims in multiple European jurisdictions, and the increasingly frequent settlement of claims with substantial compensation payments being made.

This short chapter summarises the authors' perception of the dynamics at play, and some of the tactics and strategies that have been adopted over recent years, particularly by the defendants to claims that have been brought. It addresses in turn the issues of jurisdiction, limitation, the jurisdiction of the UK's Competition Appeal Tribunal (CAT), overcharge and pass-on, and costs, all of which are proving to be battlegrounds between claimants and defendants in cartel damages litigation. It also addresses the impact of joint and several liability on the approach taken by defendants.

I. JURISDICTION

Many claimants favour bringing their claims in the UK, for a variety of reasons, including benefiting from the extensive disclosure requirements available in English litigation, the 'loser-pays' costs rule, the availability of a modestly sized but developing claimant bar, and the increasing legal certainty around several issues as a result of previous cases having clarified various procedural and substantive issues from which new claimants can benefit.

[1] The CAT's only judgment awarding damages in a competition follow-on action, *2 Travel Group Plc (in liquidation) v Cardiff City Transport Services Ltd* [2012] CAT 19, concerned an abuse under c II Competition Act 1998/ Art 102 of the Treaty on the Functioning of the European Union.

Where a (potential) defendant is domiciled in an EU Member State, jurisdiction is determined by Regulation 44/2001 (the Brussels Regulation).[2] The general rule is set out in Article 2(1) of the Brussels Regulation – namely that a defendant should be sued in the Member State in which he is domiciled. Alternatives to this, which may be particularly relevant to cartel damages claims, include Article 5(1) (which relates to contract claims and provides for a defendant to be sued in the Member State where the obligation in question was or ought to have been performed) and Article 5(3) (which relates to claims in tort and provides for a defendant to be sued in the Member State where the harmful event occurred or may occur). Article 6(1) is also a key provision for purposes of competition litigation: it provides that, for claims against a number of defendants, claimants can bring a claim against all the defendants in a Member State where any one of them is domiciled, provided the claims are so closely connected that it is expedient to hear and determine them together, in order to avoid the risk of irreconcilable judgments resulting from separate proceedings.

The upshot of these jurisdiction rules is that claimants seeking to establish jurisdiction in the English courts can sue a UK-domiciled defendant (under Article 2) in order to 'anchor' the proceedings in England and Wales, and then bring the remainder of the defendants into the claim on the basis of Article 6. This has been relied upon recently, for example, in two claims brought against members of the Electrical and Mechanical Carbon and Graphite Products cartel.[3] Morgan Crucible (a UK company) was an addressee of the Commission's decision and the 'anchor defendant'; other (European) companies, including SGL Carbon, Le Carbone Lorraine (now Mersen) and Schunk, were also addressees and brought into the litigation on the basis of Article 6.

Going a step further, claimants have also sued UK-domiciled *subsidiaries* of addressees of Commission decisions (where none of the addressees themselves were domiciled in the UK), relying on the subsidiary as the anchor defendant in order to bring claims against other members of the cartel. This has been resisted by defendants in a number of contexts.

In the leading case of *Provimi*,[4] which arose out of the Commission's 2001 decision in the Vitamins cartel, a claim was brought in England by a German claimant against four companies in the Roche group, including the Swiss parent company and three subsidiaries which were English, Swiss and German. Of these, only the parent company was an addressee of the Commission's infringement decision. Jurisdiction was argued as a preliminary issue. The court held that the claimant had an arguable claim that the English subsidiary had 'implemented' the cartel by selling vitamins at the cartel prices, even if the subsidiary had no knowledge of the cartel itself. This judgment opened the door to litigation being brought in England against a number of defendants on the basis of an English anchor defendant which was merely a subsidiary of one of the addressees of a Commission decision, in circumstances where the subsidiary neither played a direct role in the cartel nor had knowledge of it.

The claimant tactic of relying on an English subsidiary to establish jurisdiction in England appears to have been cemented in the *Cooper Tire* litigation.[5] The claim was brought by a

[2] Council Regulation (EC) No 44/2001 of 22 December 2000 on jurisdiction and the recognition and enforcement of judgments in civil and commercial matters OJ [2001] L12/1.

[3] *Emerson Electric Co and Others v Morgan Crucible Company Plc and Others* and *Deutsche Bahn AG and Others v Morgan Crucible Company Plc and Others* – pending.

[4] *Provimi v Aventis* [2003] EWHC 961.

[5] *Cooper Tire & Rubber Company & Others v Shell Chemicals UK Ltd & Others* [2009] EWHC 2609 (Comm); *Cooper Tire & Rubber Company Europe Ltd & Others* [2010] EWCA Civ 864.

number of tyre manufacturers following the Commission's decision in the Synthetic Rubber cartel. The claim covered purchases from defendants across Europe, on the basis that English subsidiaries of some (but not all) of the cartelists had implemented the cartel in the UK by selling products at cartel prices. The defendants sought to have the claim struck out on grounds of jurisdiction, a move that was denied by the Court of Appeal.[6] In the Court's view, although the English subsidiaries were not addressees of the Commission's decision, the pleadings were sufficiently widely drafted to encompass the possibility that they had knowledge of, or were party to, the cartel. The result is that English courts have jurisdiction to hear Europe-wide cartel damages claims where the pleadings allege that an English-domiciled subsidiary of a cartelist implemented the cartel and either had knowledge of, or was party to, the anti-competitive conduct.

More recent attempts by defendants to challenge this approach (including by non-European defendants) have thus far been unsuccessful, notably in the recent Court of Appeal judgment in *Toshiba Carrier*[7] and in the first-instance *Nokia* judgment[8] (currently on appeal).

Scope remains for a number of further challenges to claims brought in England against European or world-wide cartels, which rely on UK-domiciled subsidiaries to anchor the claim in the jurisdiction. The *Nokia* litigation, for example, raises issues including how much detail of the English subsidiary's knowledge or implementation of the cartel must be pleaded in order to anchor the claim in the jurisdiction. A number of the (non-UK) defendants in that case argued that the claim as pleaded against the two anchor defendants was defective, and should be struck out, as a result of which the claims against the non-UK defendants should be struck out for lack of jurisdiction. The first-instance judge disagreed, however, finding that the claim (at least, as amended) was sufficiently pleaded.[9]

Nokia also demonstrates the scope for arguments to be run by defendants as to the sufficiency (or otherwise) of the claimant's pleadings. In that case, the non-UK defendants raised these arguments as a means to striking out the claim on jurisdiction grounds. But UK-domiciled defendants have also sought to strike out the claim against them simply on grounds that the claim is insufficiently pleaded, irrespective of any subsequent arguments: an application by the UK anchor defendant in a claim against members of the Industrial Bags cartel raised these very points.[10]

Further scope also remains for jurisdiction arguments to be developed concerning the application of Articles 5(1) and 5(3) of the Brussels Regulation. Conscious that defendants are not afraid to seek to strike out claims on jurisdiction grounds (in particular if limitation periods may have expired), claimants are increasingly arguing in their pleadings that the *effects* of the cartel were felt in the UK, in an effort to establish jurisdiction under Article 5(3) should the anchor defendant argument fail.[11] This is, in particular, argued by English claimants, although claimants domiciled in other countries who, for example, made purchases through an agent or subsidiary in the UK, have also sought to rely on it.

[6] *Cooper Tire & Rubber Company Europe Ltd & Others v Dow Deutschland Inc and Others* [2010] EWCA Civ 864.

[7] *KME Yorkshire Ltd & Others v Toshiba Carrier Ltd & Others* [2012] EWCA Civ 1190.

[8] *Nokia Corp v AU Optronics Corp* [2012] EWHC 731 (Ch). See in particular the reference at para 50 to the ECJ's judgment in Case C-196/99 P *Siderurgica Aristrain Madrid SL v European Commission* [2003] ECR I-11005.

[9] ibid at paras 51 et seq.

[10] *Bord na Móna Horticulture Ltd and Another v British Polythene Industries Plc and Others* [2012] UKHC 3346 (Comm).

[11] Although Art 5(3) will only enable claimants to recover damages suffered within the jurisdiction: see Case C-68/93 *Shevill v Presse Alliance SA* [1995] ECR I-415.

For a cartel largely operating in or affecting continental Europe, for example, Article 5(3) might be invoked by a cartelist bringing an action for a negative declaration in a continental European country where damage was allegedly done by the cartel in order to prevent a victim of the cartel from being able to bring an action against that cartelist in the English courts due to the lis pendens provision in Brussels I. Similarly, in circumstances where contracts between a victim and an alleged cartelist contain a jurisdiction clause conferring exclusive jurisdiction on all disputes between them to an EU country other than the UK, the alleged cartelist might argue that any claim for damages by the victim of the cartel should be heard in the jurisdiction specified in that clause. These arguments remain untested in the courts, and are ripe for future litigation.

II. TIME LIMITS FOR BRINGING CLAIMS

Defence tactics regarding limitation have also been used in order to strike out damages claims. Here, a division exists between claims brought in the High Court and those brought in the CAT. Different time limits apply to each, and the arguments raised and defence tactics employed are different.

The limitation period for proceedings in the High Court is six years from the date on which the cause of action accrues. In claims involving concealment (generally accepted to include secret cartels), the cause of action is deemed to have accrued when the claimant discovered or ought to have discovered it. Many claims are brought in the High Court up to six years after the date on which the Commission's infringement decision was published on its website and announced by the Commission (usually in a press release of the same date). Some claims, opting for a more cautious interpretation, appear to be brought calculating six years from the date on which the Commission's investigation, or the sending of the statement of objections, were announced (usually in the form of a press release on the Commission's website). But this approach remains largely untested in the courts.[12] Where the cartel has been brought to the Commission's attention by a whistleblower, for example, that company may refer to its potential liability in a stock exchange or other regulatory filing, which arguably starts time running for purposes of the six-year limitation period. Behind the scenes, settlements will often be reduced to reflect a number of uncertainties in a claim should it proceed to trial, limitation being one.

In the CAT, on the other hand, in a number of cases defendants have sought to strike out claims on the basis of the period that prescribes the CAT's jurisdiction. In the CAT, time for bringing a claim begins to run from the date on which the infringement decision becomes final, and runs for a period of two years from that date. The CAT can grant permission to bring a claim 'early', ie before the date on which the infringement decision becomes final, but cannot extend the time period beyond the two years provided for in section 47A of the Competition Act 1998.[13]

A number of claims brought in the CAT have been struck out – or their commencement has been postponed – on limitation grounds. First, in the *Emerson I* litigation (brought against a number of European addressees of the Commission's decision in the Electrical

[12] But see *Arkin v Borchard Lines* [2000] EuLR (Comm) (Coleman J).

[13] *BCL Old Co v BASF* [2010] EWCA Civ 1258 and *BCL Old Co v BASF* [2012] UKSC 45.

and Mechanical Carbon and Graphite cartel) the CAT held that, where a claim is to be brought against a number of defendants of which one has not appealed against the Commission's decision (and the other defendants have), time does not start to run for purposes of the two-year time period against *any* of the defendants until the Luxembourg appeals are all disposed of;[14] in *Emerson II* the claimants were, however, given permission to bring the claim 'early' against the (UK-domiciled) immunity applicant;[15] although in *Emerson III* the claimants were refused permission to bring the claim 'early' against the other defendants who were appealing against the infringement decision.[16]

The *BCL* litigation[17] took this a step further. The (proposed) defendants were addressees of the Commission's infringement decision in the Vitamins cartel, which they appealed to the General Court. The appeals were dismissed by the General Court, but further appeals were lodged at the European Court of Justice (ECJ). Those further appeals related to the level of the fine, not to the substantive infringement finding. The claimants waited until the defendants' appeals had been finally determined by the ECJ, and then sought to bring a follow-on claim in the CAT. The defendants argued, however, that the claim was brought out of time as it was filed more than two years after the General Court's judgment – which related to the *infringement* decision – had become final. This argument was accepted by the Court of Appeal:[18] the claimants were out of time to bring their case. *BCL* clarifies, therefore, that the two-year period for bringing claims in the CAT is calculated according to when the *infringement* decision becomes final (not when the decision, insofar as it relates solely to the level of the fine imposed, becomes final).

The *Deutsche Bahn* litigation has sought to take this even further.[19] The claimant, European railway companies, brought a claim against a number of European addressees of the Electrical and Mechanical Carbon and Graphite Products cartel. The UK anchor defendant had not appealed against the decision, but the other defendants had. The General Court handed down its judgments in those defendants' appeals in October 2008. Some of the defendants then appealed again to the ECJ on issues relating to the calculation of the fine only. The ECJ handed down its judgments in November 2009. Consistent with *BCL*, the claimants filed their claim in December 2010, just inside the two-year window calculated from the date on which the General Court's judgment became final. The UK-domiciled immunity applicant, who had not appealed against the Commission's decision, argued that the claim *as against it* was brought out of time, since the infringement decision, insofar as it concerned that company, had become final in 2004 (and so the limitation window closed in 2006). Although successful at first instance,[20] this argument was rejected on appeal.[21] The Court of Appeal's judgment, therefore, means that a single limitation period applies to claims brought in the CAT against a number of defendants, and that limitation period is calculated from the date on which the infringement decision against the (proposed) defendants becomes final. Permission has been sought to appeal to the Supreme Court.

The time period applicable to CAT proceedings is an area that, as the cases above indicate, has in recent years been a hotbed of litigation, strike-out applications and appeals. In

[14] *Emerson Electric Co and Others v Morgan Crucible Company Plc and Others* [2007] CAT 28.
[15] *Emerson Electric Co and Others v Morgan Crucible Company Plc and Others* [2007] CAT 30.
[16] *Emerson Electric Co and Others v Morgan Crucible Company Plc and Others* [2008] CAT 8.
[17] *BCL Old Co v BASF* [2009] EWCA Civ 434.
[18] *BCL Old Co v BASF* [2009] EWCA Civ 434.
[19] *Deutsche Bahn AG and Others v Morgan Crucible Company Plc and Others* [2011] CAT 16.
[20] ibid.
[21] *Deutsche Bahn AG and Others v Morgan Crucible Company Plc and Others* [2012] EWCA Civ 1055.

large part, this is a result of the wording of the relevant provisions of the Enterprise Act 2002 that set out the limitation period, which leaves ample scope for clarification. As these issues are resolved, the avenues open to defendants to challenge claims on limitation grounds will, of course, diminish. The limitation period applicable to cartel damages claims brought in the High Court remains relatively untested; however, few strike-out applications have been brought on the basis that the claim was brought out of time. But that is not to say that defendants cannot or do not use limitation as a defence tactic. On the contrary, claims brought in circumstances where there are good arguments to be made that the limitation has expired may often settle quietly and for nuisance value, which could be to a defendant's advantage, given the costs of a strike-out hearing to achieve the same end. Unless a defendant considers further claims are likely, in which case a judgment declaring the limitation period to have expired could be to its advantage, settlement could be a favourable option.

III. ADDITIONAL CONSIDERATIONS APPLICABLE TO PROCEEDINGS IN THE CAT

Further considerations apply where claimants elect to proceed with their claim in the CAT. The CAT was established under the Enterprise Act 2002 to hear, among other things, 'follow-on' damages claims – ie those following a decision of the national competition regulators or the Commission.[22] The CAT does not have jurisdiction to hear 'stand-alone' damages claims. Claimants bringing a damages claim in the CAT are therefore limited to claiming in respect only of damages flowing from the infringement found in the regulator's decision.[23] A key consideration for defendants to claims in the CAT is therefore whether the claim goes outside the scope of the decision; to the extent it does, there is scope to have the claim (or that part of it) struck out.

Such an approach was successful in the recent CAT judgment in the *Emerson Electric* proceedings, referred to above. The claimant companies sought to claim against, amongst others, the UK subsidiary (Mersen UK) of a French company, the French parent company being the addressee of the Commission's infringement decision. Mersen UK argued that, since it was not an addressee of the Commission decision, the claim against it was not a 'follow-on' claim, and could not therefore be brought in the CAT. The CAT agreed[24] – a judgment against which the claimants are appealing.

IV. OVERCHARGE AND PASS-ON

Claims in which the initial hurdles of jurisdiction and limitation are (or are likely to be) met, still present a number of opportunities for defendants in relation to the alleged damage suffered by the claimant. Overcharge and pass-on are two key elements.

[22] Enterprise Act 2002 (2002 c 40).
[23] *English Welsh and Scottish Railway Ltd v Enron Coal Services Ltd* [2009] EWCA Civ 647.
[24] *Emerson Electric Co and Others v Morgan Crucible Company Plc and Others* [2011] CAT 19.

A. Overcharge

In English litigation, it is for the claimant to prove its loss. The overcharge resulting from the cartel behaviour must, therefore, be established by the claimant. Disclosure is often the claimant's best route to showing overcharge: in theory, it gives the claimant the opportunity to compare its own purchase records with the defendant's sales records (and thereby fill in any gaps in its own data) and to seek documents relating to the defendant's costs and pricing methodology in the cartel period.

A study by the economic consultancy firm Oxera conducted for the Commission in 2009 (the Oxera report)[25] is frequently cited by claimants as a basis for claiming that a cartel caused a 20 per cent uplift in price. In the absence of any concrete basis for calculating the overcharge, claimants might be forgiven for clinging to such figures in their pleadings. In practice, however, since they are required to prove their loss, the 20 per cent figure is of little (if any) assistance – and, indeed, Oxera themselves have recently criticised the claimants' reliance on this figure alone as the basis for quantifying their losses.[26]

The calculation of overcharge is a key issue in cartel damages litigation, and defence tactics vary. In some cases, each party might involve expert economists in order to review the available data and calculate the overcharge as best they can. In other cases, the evidence might make clear a relatively narrow range as to what the overcharge was or was likely to have been, in which case the focus for defendants might shift to pass-on (discussed below). In the absence of any judgments awarding damages in cartel claims, defendants are continuing to assess overcharge as best they can on the basis of the data available to them. The amounts are frequently reduced further to take account of pass-on, and to reflect other uncertainties in the litigation (such as, for example, questionable limitation or jurisdiction issues, or uncertainties regarding the scope of the products or geographic areas covered by the cartel).

B. Pass-on

Claimants who are not end-users are also faced with the proposition that any overcharge they have paid has been passed on down the supply chain, meaning that their damages claim is significantly reduced or even eliminated. For obvious reasons, pass-on tends to be raised by defendants rather than claimants – although it is unclear whether the burden of proof would fall on the claimant to show that the overcharge *has not* been passed on (which would be consistent with the burden of proving their losses overall), or whether pass-on is to be proved by the defendant. Whoever bears the burden of proof, the judgment of the ECJ in *Manfredi*,[27] which appears to hold that full compensation must be available to all those who suffer losses as a result of infringements of the Treaty's competition rules, and therefore that damages claims by indirect purchasers should be permitted, indicates that, logically, pass-on should be available as a defence.

[25] 'Quantifying Antitrust Damages: Towards Non-Binding Guidance For Courts', a study prepared for the European Commission by Oxera (December 2009).

[26] 'Response To The Consultation On Private Actions In Competition Law', prepared by Oxera for the Department for Business, Innovation & Skills (July 2012).

[27] Case C-295/04 *Manfredi v Lloyd Adriatico* [2006] ECR I-6619.

Defence tactics regarding pass-on will also vary from case to case. Direct-purchaser claimants, who sell on to others down the supply chain, may pass on much of any overcharge they pay; end-user customers, on the other hand, cannot be argued to have passed on any loss. The amount passed-on will depend on a number of factors, including the industry in which the claimant operates and the buyer power of the claimant's customers. In an efficient supply chain, however, economic theory dictates that all costs will be passed on, albeit often over a period of time.

V. COSTS

English litigation is expensive compared to litigation in most continental European jurisdictions: parties involved in a complex case going all the way to trial may well incur costs of several million pounds each. In the High Court, the general rule is that costs follow the event, ie the losing party pays the costs of the successful party, although the Court ultimately retains discretion as to costs. There is no such general rule in the CAT, although it is thought that the same principle would usually be applied. In practice, however, even with a costs order in its favour, the winning party is unlikely to recover much more than two-thirds of its total expenditure.

The claimant bar in England has adapted quickly to the risks associated with competition litigation. A variety of mechanisms are used to minimise the claimant's cost risk while exposing the defendants to the claimant's costs, in order to bring them to the table to discuss settlement. In particular, the use of after-the-event (ATE) insurance and conditional fee arrangements (CFAs) (which provide for a no-win-no-fee payment model, but with an uplift of up to 100 per cent if the claim is successful) enable claims to be brought with no or very limited cost risk to the claimant.

Defendants have responded to these costs-shifting tactics in a number of ways. Undoubtedly, they incentivise defendants to discuss settlement of the claim early on, in order to minimise costs exposure. But settlement of the underlying claim need not necessarily include settlement of the costs: where these are considered excessive – for example, if the ATE insurance premium is too high, or the CFA uplift too great – defendants may prefer to chance their hand at a costs assessment and take the matter before a costs judge. There are no judgments in the area of cartel litigation costs to date, so it is unclear what level of insurance premium and CFA uplift will be considered reasonable and proportionate, and this is likely to differ from case to case in any event. However, insofar as CFA uplifts are concerned, recent judgments in other commercial cases indicate that an uplift approaching 100 per cent is unlikely to be accepted except in extreme circumstances.[28] Arguably this should be much less where liability has been established by a Commission decision.

Reforms of the High Court costs rules, which come into effect in April 2013, will prevent recovery of ATE insurance premiums from the unsuccessful party in High Court litigation, and will prevent the court from requiring the payment by one party of all or part of a success fee payable by another party under a CFA.[29] The reforms will also introduce contingency fees

[28] See eg *Yao Essai Motto & Ors v (1) Trafigura Ltd (2) Trafigura Beheer BV* [2011] EWCA Civ 1150.

[29] Legal Aid, Sentencing and Punishment of Offenders Act 2012 (2012 c 10), Pt II, ss 46 and 44.

(which provide for legal fees to be paid as a proportion of the damages recovered). These reforms will change the dynamic between claimants and defendants: in principle, claimants seeking to insure against adverse costs will ultimately pay the costs of the insurance premium themselves; and the introduction of contingency fees added to the non-recoverability of CFA success fees may relieve some of the costs pressure that claimants seek to put on defendants. The Government's consultation on reform of competition damages litigation indicates, however, that an exception may be made in order to permit CFAs success fees to continue to be recoverable in competition cases.[30] The costs dynamic and its impact on competition damages claims is therefore an area likely to develop further in coming years.

VI. DYNAMIC AMONG CO-DEFENDANTS

Although the point has not been formally determined by the courts, it is generally understood that in cases before both the CAT and the High Court, liability is likely to be joint and several in respect of defendants to cartel damages claims. Parties who find themselves as co-defendants in such litigation therefore have a range of issues to consider.

On one hand, it is in their collective interests to cooperate in order to defend the claim as robustly as possible, in particular in relation to consistency of legal arguments (such as jurisdiction or limitation points), overcharge and pass-on. The possibility of sharing costs (e.g. for economic experts) also favours a cooperative approach, where appropriate. On the other hand, co-defendants' interests may diverge in relation to various issues. The most obvious is how to apportion any damages: defendants making few or no sales to the claimant may seek a pro-rata apportionment, whereas those with significant sales may argue that damages should be divided equally. Other points of disagreement could include issues relating to disclosure, with defendants having made immunity or leniency applications possibly seeking to prevent their co-defendants from disclosing this material to the claimant; or on defence strategy, with some defendants possibly wanting to settle early on (and potentially offer cooperation to the claimant as part of the settlement) while others may wish to fight the claim.

Whether it is in any one defendant's interests to cooperate with its co-defendants will depend on the facts of each individual case, and that defendant's specific circumstances, such as its role within the cartel and its volume of sales to, or relationship with, the claimant.

'Contribution proceedings' add a further dynamic to the relationship between defendants. Defendants to a cartel damages claim may themselves sue other cartelists for a contribution to any damages they are ultimately ordered to pay. Contribution proceedings can be brought while the original claim is ongoing and up to two years after the date of a judgment awarding damages. The dynamic between the claimants and defendants in such proceedings (who are essentially co-cartelists) will again depend on the case.

In a follow-on claim, where both the claimant in the contribution proceedings and the defendants in the proceedings have all been found to have participated in the cartel, they may cooperate in a similar way to co-defendants – although ultimately the parties may be

[30] 'Private Actions in Competition Law: A consultation on options for reform' by the Department for Business Innovation and Skills (April 2012). See questions 17 and 18.

in different positions as regards their costs' exposure. Thus, for example, it might be in the defendant's interest to support the contribution claimant in an application to strike out the underlying claim against it, if to do so would eliminate the contribution claim. In a stand-alone claim, contribution proceedings may be less cooperative, given the increased incentive for the defendant in those proceedings to deny participation in anti-competitive conduct.

VII. CONCLUSION

Cartel damages litigation has increased significantly in the UK over the past 10 years. As more claims are brought, both claimants and defendants are developing tactics to deal with the various difficulties they face in adapting the English litigation system – in either the High Court or the CAT – to the specific circumstances of competition litigation. Although none of the claims has yet come to trial, and so no damages awards have been made, a number of judgments in interlocutory proceedings have clarified and are continuing to clarify the law applicable to these claims – including the limitation periods applicable in the CAT, various questions of jurisdiction, and issues of disclosure specific to cartel claims. Moreover, the reform of High Court costs and funding rules coming into force next year, and the reforms recently proposed by the Government to the broader competition litigation sphere including the CAT, will change the landscape further. Claimants and defendants will need to adapt their litigation tactics in the light of these changes.

12

Specific Issues in Cross-Border EU Competition Law Actions Brought by Multiple Claimants in a German Context

TIM REHER*

I. INTRODUCTION

In the absence of harmonised rules on the practice of antitrust litigation, the European Member States maintain a diversified set of domestic procedural and substantive rules governing such litigation. The purpose of this chapter is to report on the experiences gained with competition law actions brought by multiple claimants in a German context. The main focus will be on damages actions, as they have the greatest practical relevance.

Nowadays, we have a lively environment for damages claims in Germany. This is a complete change from the legal situation that existed up to about 2005, before the Seventh Amendment to the German Act against Restraints of Competition ('GWB'). Until then, successful claims for damages used to be virtually impossible. Today, hardly any fining decision imposed by the European Commission or the Federal Cartel Office ('FCO') goes by without follow-on damages actions. However, cross-border claims brought by multiple claimants remain the exception.

II. KEY ISSUE: 'FORUM SHOPPING'

One of the key issues in cross-border EU competition law actions is the choice between different national fora. 'Forum shopping', the practice of attempting to get a case heard in the jurisdiction thought most likely to provide a decision favourable to the party doing the shopping, is a reality in Europe.

The alternative fora for cross-border EU competition law actions are determined based on Council Regulation (EC) No 44/2001 ('Brussels I Regulation')[1]. Pursuant to Article 2(1) Brussels I Regulation, a national court has jurisdiction in antitrust matters if the defendant is domiciled in its jurisdiction. In addition, the jurisdiction in tort claims can rest with the

* This chapter is a recollection of a presentation held at the Cross-Border EU Competition Law Actions Conference, 20 April 2012, London.

[1] Council Regulation (EC) No. 44/2001 of 22 December 2000 on jurisdiction and the recognition and enforcement of judgments in civil and commercial matters.

courts of the Member State in which the cartel infringement occurred or may occur, according to Article 5(3) Brussels I Regulation. The place of the harmful event is interpreted twofold as the place of damages and the place of illicit behaviour. Furthermore, pursuant to Article 6(1) Brussels I Regulation, the litigation against all defendants may be concentrated in the courts for the place where one defendant is domiciled. A strategic advantages of this so-called 'anchor' mechanism is the possibility to choose a claimant-friendly forum.

As the aforementioned provisions show, most cross-border follow-on damages claims entail a variety of applicable fora. Relevant aspects for the choice of the most favourable forum are: (1) the mechanisms for aggregation of individual claims and collective actions; (2) the applicable procedural law; and (3) the applicable substantive law. In the following, an assessment of the German judicial system will give some insight as to how German law deals with these three issues, setting out the advantages and disadvantages for claimants.

III. THE GERMAN FORUM: ADMISSIBILITY OF COLLECTIVE ACTIONS

The German civil procedure law does not provide for specific rules on collective proceedings (eg class actions) in competition law matters. However, there are several mechanisms allowing the aggregation of individual claims for damages. First of all, although of minor practical importance, the accumulation of individual claims in the form of joint hearings is admissible. Secondly, section 34a GWB sets out a collective remedy for certain associations. And thirdly there is the practically important way to bundle individual damages' claims by way of assignment (the so-called 'assignment model').

A. Collective Remedy in section 34a GWB

Under section 34a GWB, associations for the promotion of commercial or independent professional interests are entitled to require cartelists to remit the economic benefits they have obtained to the federal budget. This provision was intended to remedy the lack of private litigation in cases of small and dispersed individual damages. However, the provision has proved to be irrelevant in practice, due to the lack of incentive. Filing a collective remedy entails high cost risks (legal and court fees, economic advisors), which are not countervailed by any financial incentives. The statutory reimbursement scheme is not sufficient for such complex cases. Even though there are plans to extend the scope of section 34a GWB to consumer protection associations in the Eighth Amendment to the GWB, the provision will likely remain practically irrelevant, due to the continued lack of financial incentives.

However, for reasons of consumer protection, both the Federal and a State Cartel Office have established a fallback solution for cases of dispersed and small individual damages, in the cases *Stadtwerke Uelzen*[2] and *Berliner Wasserbetriebe*.[3] In both cases the competition

[2] For the background of the case see Federal Supreme Court, Judgment of 10 December 2008 – KVR 2/08.

[3] Federal Cartel Office, Decision of 5 June 2012, press release (in German), www.bundeskartellamt.de/wDeutsch/aktuelles/presse/2012_06_05.php.

authorities initiated proceedings against public utility companies on suspicion of abuse of dominance. It was found that the companies were violating the GWB by charging their customers excessive prices. As the collective remedy in section 34a GWB is practically irrelevant, the authorities compensated the large group of affected customers by means of a decision. Based on section 32(2) GWB, they directly ordered a refund to the customers of the amounts excessively paid as part of the fining decision. Hereby, the competition authorities applied their powers rather extensively, as the purpose of the regulation is to bring to an end the respective infringement rather than to remedy the damages caused. However, the decision in *Stadtwerke Uelzen* was at least confirmed by the Federal Supreme Court in an obiter dictum in 2008,[4] and the draft of the Eighth Amendment to the GWB contains a new provision explicitly entitling the competition authorities to make such 'pay-back' orders.

Nonetheless, it remains to be seen whether this approach, developed for cases of abuse of dominance, will be applied in antitrust proceedings as well.

B. Assignment Model

The admissibility of the assignment model has been confirmed for the first time in the *German Cement* case.[5] In 2005, the Brussels-based company Cartel Damage Claims ('CDC') acquired the damage claims of 29 construction companies by way of purchase and assignment, and filed a 100 million euro lawsuit against six members of the cement cartel before the Regional Court of Düsseldorf. CDC runs a model whereby it acquires the claims of purchasers, runs the case and then returns a percentage of the winnings back to the purchasers.

So far, the proceedings primarily revolved around the question of admissibility. In 2008, the Court of Appeal in Düsseldorf deemed the claim to be admissible. Cartel-related claims may be sold and assigned to a third party and enforced by the third party at its expense and risk. However, standing is to be denied if a third party tries to enforce claims in the name of individual victims of an antitrust infringement.[6]

The decision was confirmed by the Federal Supreme Court in 2009, allowing proceedings on the substance to advance.[7] Today, after six years of litigation, the case is still pending.

As the assignment of the cartel-related claims is a prerequisite for the admissibility of the subsequent action, the assignment model is only feasible in certain cases. First of all, the individuals suffering damages have to be identifiable. Furthermore, the number of individual claims must be small enough to allow assignment, i.e. the assignment must be manageable. And finally, the aggregated amount of individual claims has to be big enough to create a sufficient financial incentive.

Therefore the assignment model is not feasible in cases of dispersed and small individual damages. Further negative aspects are high financial risks (legal and court fees, etc) and the long duration of proceedings.

[4] Federal Supreme Court, Judgment of 10 December 2008 – KVR 2/08.
[5] Court of Appeal Düsseldorf, Judgment of 14 May 2008 – IV-U (Kart) 14/07.
[6] ibid.
[7] Federal Supreme Court, Decision of 7 April 2009 – KZR 42/08.

C. Case Example: Hydrogen Peroxide

A current case example of a cross-border EU competition law action in a German context making use of the assignment model and the 'anchor' mechanism is *Hydrogen Peroxide.*

After the claim in the *German Cement* case was deemed to be admissible, the Brussels-based CDC lodged a claim against several members of a bleaching cartel (Akzo Nobel, Solvay, Kemira, Arkema France, FMC Foret and Degussa), seeking to recoup over 600 million euros in damages. Again, CDC acquired the damage claims of individual hydrogen peroxide customers by way of purchase and assignment.

Based on the 'anchor' mechanism in Article 6(1) Brussels I Regulation, the claim was filed at the Regional Court of Dortmund. However, after settlement with Degussa (the only German-domiciled cartel member), the company anchoring the litigation in Germany is no longer involved in the case. Hence, it is questionable whether the Dortmund court has jurisdiction in the claim against the other non-German companies, ie whether the joint infringement of antitrust law is sufficient to bring the claim to Germany. The Regional Court of Dortmund is understood to have referred the question of jurisdiction to the Court of Justice of the European Union.

IV. THE GERMAN FORUM: ANALYSIS OF PROCEDURAL LAW

With respect to follow-on damages claims the most important procedural characteristics of the German forum are:

A. Claimant-Friendly Aspects

- Predominantly claimant-favourable court decisions.
- Decisions of antitrust authorities are legally binding for follow-on damages claims.
- Lower standard of proof, which entitles judges to estimate the amount of damages on the basis of certain facts pursuant to section 287 ZPO.[8] The objective of this regulation is to compensate the claimant for potential difficulties in obtaining sufficient evidence. However, the claimant must provide the basis for the estimation, ie facts that allow conclusions on the price which would have existed under regular market conditions (hypothetical market price).
- Joint and several liabilities of the cartelists. Each cartelist is liable for the whole cartel damage caused.

[8] German Code of Civil Procedure.

B. Claimant-Adverse Aspects

- No deviation from 'the loser pays'.
- Access to documentation and evidence is limited. In contrast to most common law jurisdictions, German law does not provide for discovery proceedings.

V. THE GERMAN FORUM: APPLICABLE SUBSTANTIVE LAW

Since 11 January 2009, the applicable substantive law in cross-border EU competition law actions has been determined pursuant to Article 6(3) of the Council Regulation (EC) No 864/2007 ('Rome II Regulation').[9] Hereafter, the claimant may choose to base his claim on the law of the court seized, provided that the market in the respective Member State is directly and substantially affected by the restriction of competition.

Prior to the Rome II Regulation, the applicable substantive law was determined by national rules. Pursuant to section 130(2) GWB, German substantive law is applicable if the German market is affected by the restriction of competition. As there are as yet no authoritative judgments on its scope in cross-border follow-on damages claims, it remains to be decided whether section 130(2) GWB requires an effect on the German market for every single purchase of cartelised products, or whether an effect of the cartel as a whole on the German market is sufficient. Due to reasons of procedural efficiency, the principle of effectiveness set out in *Courage*[10] and the underlying notion of Article 6(3) of the Rome II Regulation the second option is preferable. If the specific conditions in section 130(2) GWB are not met, the German provisions regarding international private law apply. With respect to tort law, the general provision of Article 40 of the Einführungsgesetz zum Bürgerlichen Gesetzbuch (EGBGB) provides that the law of the state in which the infringement occurred or the law of the state in which the damage arose is applicable.

VI. THE GERMAN FORUM: ANALYSIS OF THE GERMAN SUBSTANTIVE LAW

With respect to follow-on damages claims the most important substantive characteristics of the German forum are:

A. Claimant-Friendly Aspects

- Three-year limitation period, beginning at the end of the year in which the claimant obtains knowledge of the circumstances giving rise to the damages claim, or would have obtained such knowledge in case of gross negligence; the limitation period is stayed for the duration of any proceedings conducted by the Federal Cartel Office, the European Commission or a competition authority of any Member State.

[9] Council Regulation (EC) No 864/2007 of 11 July 2007 on the law applicable to non-contractual obligations.
[10] Case C-453/99, *Courage Ltd v Bernard Crehan* [2001] ECR I-6297.

- Claimant-favourable approach in the calculation of damages, as courts are entitled to estimate the damages pursuant to section 287 ZPO provided the claimant puts forward a suitable basis for such estimation.
- Joint and several liabilities of the cartelists.
- Right to interest.

B. Claimant Adverse Aspect: Passing-On Defence

- In June 2011,[11] the Federal Supreme Court approved the passing-on defence, finally clarifying this much-disputed area of law. Essentially, cartel members are free to argue that the claimant has not suffered any damages because he passed on the cartel overcharge to its own customers (ie indirect purchasers). In this case only the indirect purchasers can claim damages.

In general, the burden of proof for 'passing on' rests upon the cartel members. However, under certain circumstances the burden of proof may shift to the claimant seeking redress. The Federal Supreme Court laid down some guidelines as to the specific prerequisites for such shift. In particular, the claimant may be obliged to show that he did not pass any damages if the defendant has no knowledge of the relevant facts and the shift of burden of proof is necessary and reasonable. However, a strict standard must be applied, as the cartelist shall not be unduly exonerated.

For example, a shift of the burden of proof is not necessary if the cartelist can request the customers of the claimant to join the proceedings as an additional party. However, this is not feasible if the individual customers are unknown, or the group of customers is unreasonably extensive.

Furthermore, depending on the facts of the case, the proof of a passing-on may be especially burdensome in cases where the cartelised products have been refined by the claimant and subsequently sold. However, this does not necessarily mean that the burden of proof is shifted to the claimant. Even in these cases a careful consideration of all relevant facts is necessary. The greater the possibility of a 'passing-on', the more a shift of the burden of proof to the claimant (at least to some extent) is likely.

Due to the fact that there is as yet no additional case law on the passing-on defence, and considering that German law provides only limited access to documentation (no discovery), the question of burden of proof seems likely to be one of the main points of dispute in future litigation.

VII. CONCLUSION

Overall, Germany provides an attractive forum for claimants to commence antitrust proceedings. The procedural as well as the substantive laws governing cross-border EU damages actions may be described as predominantly claimant-friendly. The most important aspects are:

[11] Federal Supreme Court, Judgment of 28 June 2011 – KZR 75/10.

- possibility to aggregate individual claims via the assignment model;
- joint and several liability of the cartelists;
- limitation period of three years;
- lower standard of proof, which allows courts to estimate the amount of damages.

13

Jurisdiction in Cross-Border EU Competition Law Cases: Some Specific Issues Requiring Specific Solutions

MIHAIL DANOV

I. INTRODUCTION

The architects of the decentralisation reform have largely ignored the question of how the EU policy encouraging private antitrust enforcement can be implemented under the current EU private international law framework.[1] It has been submitted that the importance of clear jurisdiction rules for effective private antitrust enforcement would be particularly important.[2]

However, there are no specific provisions to allocate jurisdiction in relation to EU competition law claims, and the question whether a national court has jurisdiction to deal with Articles 101 and 102 TFEU is to be determined by the Brussels I Regulation.[3] This is a problem, as there are specific issues which would arise with regard to cross-border antitrust actions, and, as a result, the most recent English case law clearly shows that the issue of jurisdiction could be a subject of heated debates before the courts.[4] Furthermore, given that the collected data clearly shows that consumers and SMEs may prefer to sue in their home states,[5] parallel and related antitrust court proceedings would be bound to occur in the European context.

[1] *cf* E de Smijter, C Stropp and D Woods (DG Comp, unit A-1), 'Green Paper on Damages Actions For Breach of the EC Antitrust Rules' (2006) *Competition Policy Newsletter* 1, 3. See also: M Monti, 'Competition Law Reform', Speech made at the CBI Conference on Competition Law Reform, London, 12 June 2000, http://ec.europa.eu/comm/competition/speeches/text/sp2000_008_en.html.

[2] See the respondents to the Green Paper, eg Freshfields' Response [54] and Linklaters' Response [12.2] http://ec.europa.eu/competition/antitrust/actionsdamages/green_paper_comments.html.

[3] M Danov, *Jurisdiction and Judgments in relation to EU Competition Law Claims* (Oxford, Hart Publishing, 2010) chs 1–4.

[4] See Ch 11. See also: *Roche Products Ltd, Roche Vitamine Europe AG (Switzerland), F Hoffmann-La Roche AG (Switzerland) v Provimi Ltd* [2003] EWHC 961 (Comm); *SanDisk Corp v Koninklijke Philips Electronics and others* [2007] EWHC 332 (Ch), [2007] Bus LR 705; *Cooper Tire & Rubber Company v Shell Chemicals UK Ltd* [2009] EWHC 2609 (Comm); *Cooper Tire & Rubber Company Europe Ltd & Others* [2010] EWCA Civ 864; *Toshiba Carrier UK Ltd and Other v KME Yorkshire Ltd & Others* [2011] EWHC 2665 (Ch); *Toshiba Carrier UK Ltd and Other v KME Yorkshire Ltd & Others* [2012] EWCA Civ 169; *Ryanair Ltd v Esso Italiana Srl* – still pending before the Court of Appeal – Case Reference A3/2012/0471. See also: *Emerson Electric Co v Morgan Crucible Company Plc and Ors* [2011] CAT 4; *Emerson Electric Co v Morgan Crucible Company Plc and Ors* – still pending before the Court of Appeal – Case Reference C3/2011/1658.

[5] See Chs 3 and 4.

In addition, the cross-border EU competition law cases are rather peculiar commercial cases, which may involve competition authorities as well as national courts.[6] The collected data not only show that going to the competition authority first would be a normal strategy, but also appear to indicate that competition authorities would have inherent limitations in dealing with EU competition law infringements.[7] This suggests that the issues of jurisdiction with regard to cross-border EU competition law infringements, which could cause damage to businesses and consumers in a number of Member States, need to be carefully considered by the EU legislator. Legislative intervention is indeed required, in view of the fact that Regulation 1/2003 does not deal with the problem of coherent and uniform application of EU competition law in proceedings before an NCA located in one Member State and private EU antitrust law proceedings related to the same breaches of the same provision before a court in another Member State.[8] It is further questionable whether the Brussels I Regulation can be relied upon to avoid the problem of parallel proceedings which are bound to arise in view of the various bodies responsible for the enforcement of Articles 101 and 102 TFEU.[9]

This chapter will analyse the application of the jurisdiction rules of Brussels I with a view to identify the specific problems arising in the context of cross-border EU competition law actions. The analysis will demonstrate that the current regime is not suited to dealing with the specific issues characterising cross-border EU competition law actions. In this context, answers to the question of how the current regime might be reformed will be considered. To this end, the chapter will open with a review of the case law, in order to identify the specific jurisdictional problems with regard to cross-border EU competition law actions. Articles 27 and 28 Brussels I will then be carefully considered with a view to demonstrating that they are not suited to dealing with the specific issues surrounding cross-border EU competition law actions. Finally, some tentative proposals and solutions, which must be considered by the EU legislator, will be outlined.

II. ALLOCATING JURISDICTION IN CROSS-BORDER EU COMPETITION LAW CASES

Article 1 of Brussels I states that the 'Regulation shall apply in civil and commercial matters whatever the nature of the court or tribunal'.[10] It is beyond doubt that an EU competition law claim brought before a Member State court is properly regarded as a 'civil and commercial matter' for the purposes of the Brussels I Regulation.[11] This was recently confirmed

[6] Arts 5 and 6 of Regulation 1/2003 state that the National Competition Authorities (NCAs) and national courts have the powers to apply Arts 101 and 102 TFEU in individual cases.

[7] Ch 3.

[8] M Danov, "EU Competition Law Enforcement: Is Brussels I suited to dealing with all the challenges?" (2012) 61 *ICLQ* 27.

[9] See S Brammer, *Co-operation between National Competition Agencies in the Enforcement of EC Competition Law* (Oxford, Hart Publishing, 2009) 25. See also Danov (n 8).

[10] Case 29/76 *LTU v Eurocontrol* [1976] ECR 1541 [5]. See also L Collins and others (eds), *Dicey, Morris and Collins on the Conflict of Laws*, 14th edn (London, Sweet & Maxwell, 2006) 314.

[11] See *SanDisk* (n 4); *Provimi* (n 4). See also: Commission Notice on the Co-operation between the Commission and the Courts of the EU Member States in the Application of Articles 81 and 82 [2004] OJ C101/04, 3; Commission (EC), *Damages Actions for Breach of EC Antitrust Rules* (Green Paper) COM(2005) 672 final, para 2.8; Office of Fair Trading, 'Response to the European Commission's Green Paper, *Damages Actions for Breach of the EC Antitrust Rules*' May 2006 OFT 844 www.oft.gov.uk/shared_oft/reports/oft_response_to_consultations/oft844.pdf; R di Brozolo, 'Antitrust Claims: Why Exclude Them from The Hague Jurisdiction and Judgment Convention', (2004) 25 ECLR 780, 783.

by the English High Court.[12] In particular, in the context of a recent cross-border antitrust damages claim, the Chancellor of the High Court held:

> With the immaterial exceptions specified in Article 1(1) and (2) [Brussels I] applies in civil and commercial matters whatever the nature of the Court or Tribunal. Article 2 lays down the general rule that persons domiciled in a Member State shall, whatever their nationality, be sued in the courts of that Member State. Article 3 enables a person domiciled in a Member State to be sued in the courts of another Member State only in accordance with the provisions of specified sections of that Regulation. The two provisions relevant to those applications are laid down in section 2 in Articles 5 and 6.[13]

In other words, the fact that there is no special rule to allocate jurisdiction with regard to cross-border EU competition law actions indicates that these cases should be treated the same as other civil and commercial cases.

A. Article 2 and its Application in Cross-Border EU Competition Law Cases

Article 2 of Brussels I can apply in cross-border EU competition law claims, so each person or legal entity that is infringing Articles 101 and 102 TFEU may be sued in the courts of the Member State where it is domiciled. Article 2 can be used to consolidate in one Member State a number of claims arising out of infringements of EU competition rules that are committed in different States. For example, a plaintiff can sue in England an English-domiciled defendant following his anti-competitive conduct in Germany, France and Italy. That is based on the assumption that it is the same legal entity responsible for each infringement.[14] In such cases, it would be advantageous for the plaintiff to bring his entire claim before the courts of the defendant's domicile under Article 2[15] as the jurisdiction under this provision is international and not restricted to the local harm.[16] It has been submitted that 'it is important to bear in mind the optional nature of the special heads of jurisdiction of Article 5 . . . the plaintiff has always the option to resort to the general rule of Article 2.'[17] In this context, it should be noted that, by relying on Article 2, the claimant would avoid unnecessary and lengthy jurisdictional challenges which could be an important factor in cross-border EU competition cases.[18] This might explain why the cut-flower importers, Emerald, sued the air freight service providers, British Airways, in England for global infringements of EU competition law (of course the procedural rules in England might

[12] *Toshiba Carrier* [2011] (n 1) [7].

[13] 'The added wording is the same as that in what was Article 22, but is now Article 28(3) of the Regulation. Those Articles deal with staying "related actions". The new words also reflect the rationale for Article 6(1), as interpreted by the Court of Justice in Case 189/97 *Kalfelis v Schroder* [1988] ECR 5565 [31].' See fn 92 in *Provimi* (n 4) [41]. See also Case C-539/03 *Roche Netherland BV and Others v Primus, Goldenberg* [2006] ECR I-6535, Court of Justice, First Chamber [22].

[14] See more: Danov (n 3).

[15] C Withers, 'Jurisdiction and Applicable Law in Antitrust Tort Claims' (2002) *Journal of Business Law* 250, 262.

[16] *SanDisk* (n 4). See also: Danov (n 3).

[17] BV Costa, 'How to Apply Articles 5(1) and 5(3) Brussels I Regulation to Private Enforcement of Competition Law: A Coherent Approach' in J Basedow, S Francq and L Idot (eds), *International Antitrust Litigation: Conflict of Laws and Coordination* (Oxford, Hart Publishing, 2012) 17, 29.

[18] See Ch 3.

have been another important factor for the claimants).[19] However, there are several specific issues, which would need to be considered by the claimants before relying on Article 2 Brussels I to bring their claim for cross-border antitrust law infringements.

First, the EU competition law concept of the 'undertaking' 'can embrace a number of legal entities, as long as they act as a single economic unit, and no legal entity acts independently for any relevant purpose.'[20] Given that it may be far from clear 'which legal entities within a corporate group are liable for an infringement of Article 101(1) TFEU and to what extent',[21] a claimant may prefer to initiate a claim against multiple defendants under Article 6(1) Brussels I instead. This would be particularly the case in stand-alone actions against a subsidiary forming part of a corporate group which consists of numerous subsidiaries, all of which form a single infringing 'undertaking' as well as in a follow-on action against a defendant, who, despite being a part of an infringing undertaking, is not named in the operative part of the Commission infringement decision (ie *dispositif*).[22] The latter issue was considered by the CAT in *Emerson*. In this case, the claimants brought a cross-border EU competition law action against Carbone GB and several other defendants including Carbone SA. The claim was preceded by a decision of the European Commission establishing a single and continuous infringement of Article 101(1) TFEU.[23] As a result, the Commission imposed fines on a number of legal entities, including Carbone SA. However, Carbone GB was not mentioned at all in the operative part of the Commission decision, which raised the question whether the finding that the parent company, Carbone SA, has infringed EU competition law is binding for the subsidiary, Carbone GB, so that it can be imputed with liability.[24] These issues, which may have implications for many cross-border competition law infringements, appear to indicate that it would be very common for a claimant to sue two or more defendants, domiciled in different states. If, as is natural, the plaintiff wishes to sue all the defendants together in a single action in one Member State, resort will have to be made to Article 6(1) Brussels I[25] rather than Article 2 Brussels I.

Secondly, another major disadvantage stems from the fact that if a claimant wishes to sue under Article 2, then he will have to follow the defendant to the Member State of his domicile. It is well established that a 'cross-border litigant may, as a practical matter, require two lawyers, one in his Home State to give preliminary advice, and one in the Host State to conduct the litigation.'[26] This would fuel the costs of competition litigation which could be a disincentive for claims brought by SMEs, for example. Moreover, the on-going litigation in *Emerson v Carbone* before the English Court of Appeal appears to suggest that even big multinational companies would aim to avoid bringing their damages claim in France (the Member State in which Carbone is domiciled). Therefore, the special jurisdic-

[19] The case raised a different issue, however. In particular, it was questioned whether the claimants and those whom they purport to represent have the 'same interest'. See *Emerald Supplies & Another v British Airways* [2009] EWHC 741 (Ch); *Emerald Supplies & Southern Glass House Produce v British Airways* [2010] EWCA Civ 1284.

[20] *Provimi* (n 4) [30]. See *Cooper Tire* [2010] (n 4) [47].

[21] See the reference request by Mr Rabinowitz in *Cooper Tire* [2010] (n 4) [47].

[22] See *Emerson* [2011] (n 4) [38].

[23] Case No C.38.359, *Electrical and Mechanical Carbon and Graphite Products* (2004) OJ L125/45. See also: *Emerson* [2011] (n 4) [47].

[24] See the transcript of the hearing before the CAT, pp 2–3 and 41.

[25] Danov (n 3). See also: M Wilderspin, 'Jurisdiction Issues: Brussels I Regulation Articles 6(1), 23, 27 and 28 in Antitrust Litigation' in Basedow, Francq and Idot (n 17), 41, 57.

[26] Green Paper from the Commission, *Legal Aid in Civil Matters: The Problems Confronting the Cross-border Litigant* COM(2000) 51 final, p 9.

tion rules contained in Articles 5 and 6 of Brussels I would appear to have an important role to play in cross-border EU competition law cases,[27] and if these are not suited to allocating jurisdiction, then legislative reform needs to be considered.

B. Articles 5(1) and 5(3) and their Application in Cross-Border EU Competition Law Cases

It is well established that an action for nullity of a contract under EU competition law falls within Article 5(1) of Brussels I,[28] which states that: '[a] person domiciled in a Member State may, in another Member State, be sued . . . in matters relating to a contract, in the courts for the place of performance of the obligation in question.' Although an agreement that infringes EU competition law is void and gives rise to no legal obligation,[29] it has been suggested that the court at the place of performance of the contractual obligation that allegedly distorts competition should have jurisdiction to determine whether a contract is in conflict with EU competition law.[30] However, analysis of the current case law suggests that a claim for EU competition law damages is not covered by Article 5(1) of Brussels I.[31]

The court which has jurisdiction under Article 5(1) to hear and determine if a contract is in conflict with EU competition law may not be able to rule on a claim for EU competition law damages unless the very same court has jurisdiction under Article 5(3) as well.[32] This is because a claim for EU competition law damages is tortious in nature, [33] and it is Article 5(3), which confers special jurisdiction 'in matters relating to tort, delict or quasi-delict on the courts for the place where the harmful event occurred or may occur'. The House of Lords has interpreted the ruling in the *Kalfelis* case as defining claims under Article 5(1) and (3) of Brussels I to be mutually exclusive.[34] The matter has to be characterised as either one relating to a tort, or as one relating to a contract, but not both.[35] It has been proposed for Article 5(1) to apply not only to nullity actions, 'but also to actions for damages claimed by one of the parties to the contract against their co-contractor in the event that the latter bears significant responsibility for the distortion of competition. This configuration is particularly likely to come up in relation to those distribution contracts in which the liability can be exclusively or mainly attributed to the supplier.'[36] Although this proposal might address some of the problems identified under the current framework,[37] some problems would still

[27] eg *Cooper Tire* [2010] (n 4).

[28] See more: Danov (n 3). See also Costa (n 17), 23.

[29] See Art 101(2) TFEU; Case 48/72 *Haecht v Wilkin-Janssen* [1973] ECR 77 [25]–[27]. See also *Gibbs Mew v Gemmell* [1998] EuLR 588, CA.

[30] *cf Boss Group v Boss France* [1996] 4 All ER 970, CA 975. See more: Danov (n 3).

[31] Danov (n 3).

[32] Danov (n 3).

[33] See recital 22 of the Rome II Regulation. See also: Dickinson, *The Rome II Regulation* (Oxford, OUP, 2008) 270–71; *Camera Care v Victor Hasselbland* [1986] ECC 373, CA [25]–[27]; *Application des Gaz v Falks Veritas* [1974] Ch 381, CA; *Garden Cottage Foods v Milk Marketing Board* [1984] AC 130, HL.

[34] See *Agnew v Länsförsäkringsbolagens* [2000] UKHL 7; [2001] 1 AC 223, HL and *Kalfelis* (n 13).

[35] J Fawcett and JM Carruthers (eds), *Cheshire, North & Fawcett Private International Law,* 14th edn (Oxford, OUP, 2008) 251; A Briggs and P Rees, *Civil Jurisdiction and Judgments,* 5th edn (London, Informa, 2009) 253–56.

[36] Costa (n 17), 24. See also C Castronovo, 'Private Law Remedies for Antitrust Violations – a point of view from Italy' in J Basedow, *Private Enforcement of EC Competition Law* (The Hague, Kluwer Law International, 2008) 107, 117.

[37] Danov (n 3).

arise in cases where the supplier was not aware of anti-competitive conduct, which could be an issue with regard to many EU competition law infringements.[38]

Moreover, it has been held by the Court of Justice that the expression 'matters relating to tort', 'covers all actions which seek to establish the liability of a defendant and which are not related to a "contract" within the meaning of Article 5(1).'[39] It is well established that a claim for a breach of EU competition law falls within the tort head of the Brussels I Regulation.[40] That has been accepted without discussion by the English courts in *Provimi*,[41] *Cooper Tire*[42] and *SanDisk*.[43] Under Article 5(3) of Brussels I, the court at the place where the harmful event occurred is an appropriate forum for deciding a tortious claim. This is so on grounds of proximity, the efficacious conduct of proceedings and ease of taking evidence.[44]

But, how will the expression 'place where the harmful event occurred' be defined with regard to cross-border EU competition law claims? The place of the harmful event has been interpreted by the Court of Justice to encompass both the place of the event giving rise to the damage and the place where the damage occurred.[45] In a recent EU competition law case, the English High Court held that 'The jurisdiction based upon the place of the harmful event will be international, while the jurisdiction based upon the relevant harm will be restricted to England and Wales.'[46] In other words, the courts in a Member State where damage was felt would only have jurisdiction for the damage that occurred in that state, and they would not have jurisdiction to award damages to the claimant for the damage he had suffered in other Member States. As a result, there is no doubt that it would be advantageous for the plaintiff to bring his entire claim before the courts of the place of the event giving rise to the damage. However, the analysis of Mr Justice Teare in *Cooper Tire* appears to suggest that in many EU competition law cases, the place where the event giving rise to the damage occurred may be very difficult indeed to determine. In particular, in this case the Judge held:

> In the present case the act complained of is a 'complex single and continuous infringement' of Article 81 of the Treaty by agreeing price targets, sharing customers by non-aggression agreements and exchanging sensitive commercial information relating to prices, competitors and customers. The meetings which gave rise to it took place in a number of locations including Milan, Vienna, Amsterdam, Brussels, Richmond-on-Thames, Frankfurt, Grosse Leder, and Prague. The cartel was ended at a meeting in London. I consider that this is a case where it is, at the very least, difficult to say where the event which gave rise to the damage occurred. It was suggested that the cartel was set in motion in England over the period 28–30 August 1995 and that that is sufficient

[38] See *Toshiba Carrier* [2012] (n 4) [20].

[39] *Kalfelis* (n 13), 5585. See also Case C-51/97 *Réunion Européenne v Spliethoff's Bevrachtingskantoor* [1998] ECR I-6511.

[40] J Fitchen, 'Allocating Jurisdiction in Private Competition Law Claims within the EU' (2006) 13 *Maastricht Journal of European and Comparative Law* 381; Withers (n 15), 260; JJ Fawcett and P Torremans, *Intellectual Property in Private International Law*, 2nd edn (Oxford, OUP, 2011) 501–505;

[41] *Provimi* (n 4).

[42] *Cooper Tire* [2009] (n 4).

[43] *SanDisk* (n 4).

[44] See to that effect: Case C-21/76 *Handelskwekerij Bier v Mines de Potasse D'Alsace* [1976] ECR 1735 [11] and [17]; Case C-220/88 *Dumez France and Tracoba v Hessische Landesbank (Helaba)* [1990] ECR I-49 [17]; Case C-68/93 *Shevill v Presse Alliance* [1995] ECR 415 [19]; Case C-364/93 *Marinari v Lloyds Bank* [1995] ECR I-2719 [10]; Case C-167/00 *Verein fur Konsumenteninformation v Karl Heinz Henkel* [2002] ECR I-8111 [46]. See more: Danov (n 3).

[45] *Bier* (n 44).

[46] *SanDisk* (n 4) [25]. See also: *Shevill* (n 44).

> to show that the place where the harmful event occurred was in England; see *Sandisk Corporation v Koninklijke Philips Electronics NV* [2007] EWHC 332 (Ch) at paragraphs 25 and 41. I have, I confess, a sense of unease, in concluding, in the context of a Europe-wide cartel orchestrated at meetings in several countries, that the place where the harmful event occurred is England because that is where the first meeting took place. That seems to me to be unrealistic. In truth the harmful events occurred in several countries. In these circumstances I consider that the Claimants can only rely on the place where the damage occurred. It is common ground that some damage occurred in England because some BR and ESBR was sold here. However, it is also common ground that if jurisdiction is established on that basis it is only established in respect of the damage which occurred in England. That is, I understand, a very small part of the whole.[47]

The foregoing problems would not arise if EU competition law cases were not treated like defamation cases and the *Shevill* case were not followed in Articles 101 and 102 TFEU cases. The *Shevill* case could be easily distinguished as the basis for an action for defamatory damages is English 'domestic' law, whereas an action for EU antitrust damages is based on EU law, and the scope of application of Articles 101 and 102 TFEU is not limited to the territory of a single Member State. A broader interpretation of Article 5(3) may be justified by 'The requirement that there must be an effect on trade "between Member States" [which] implies that there must be an impact on cross-border economic activity involving at least two Member States.'[48] It has been submitted that 'Protecting the defendant from broad jurisdictional obligations appears particularly misplaced in those instances where an infringement of competition law has already been found by a competent competition authority.'[49]

However, *Cooper Tire* leaves no doubt that an antitrust claimant would lose the advantage of bringing his claim before the courts at his home state (being the place where the damage occurred) where he could sue for the local damage only. Moreover, given that cross-border EU competition law infringements would by definition cause damage to businesses and consumers in a number of Member States, the narrow interpretation of Article 5(3) indicates that parallel and related proceedings may be brought by the different victims across Europe, which could potentially result in irreconcilable judgments. This would be a rather unfortunate result, especially in the light of the Commission's objective to encourage private EU competition law claims. It has been demonstrated that Articles 5(1) and (3) of Brussels I will not work adequately. One should say, nonetheless, that the EU competition law concept of 'undertaking' could suggest that Article 6(1) of the Brussels I Regulation could be used to remedy that result and centralise litigation in antitrust cases where competition law claims are brought against multiple defendants.[50]

[47] *Cooper Tire* [2010] (n 4) [65].

[48] Guidelines on the effect on trade concept contained in Articles 81 and 82 of the EC Treaty [2004] OJ C101/81 [21].

[49] J Basedow, 'International Cartels and the Place of Acting under Article 5(3) of the Brussels I Regulation' in Basedow, Francq and Idot (n 17) 31, 35.

[50] Danov (n 3).

C. Article 6(1) and Article 5(5) and their Application in Cross-Border EU Competition Law Cases

Article 6(1) of Brussels I, which is specifically designed for multi-defendant cases, states:

> a person domiciled in a Member State may also be sued[,] where he is one of a number of defendants, in the courts for the place where any one of them is domiciled, provided the claims are so closely connected that it is expedient to hear and determine them together to avoid the risk of irreconcilable judgments resulting from separate proceedings.

Its rationale is to centralise litigation against all defendants in one Member State and avoid the risk of (potentially) irreconcilable judgments if the different actions were brought in different Member States. Clearly, Article 6(1) of Brussels I contains no requirement to the effect that the actions relating to the various defendants must have the same basis, so that Article 6(1) applies in situations which involve contractual and non-contractual liability.[51] Article 6(1) will be particularly relevant for a plaintiff who wishes to pursue an EU competition law claim against two or more defendants. For example, if one of those companies is domiciled in England and another one is a French-domiciled company, then the plaintiff would be able to proceed against both companies in either England or France. Given the fact that multi-defendant litigation is quite common in EU competition law claims, Article 6(1) of Brussels I could be a relevant basis of jurisdiction. According to Wilderspin:

> there can be little doubt that, for a claimant who envisages bringing actions against several defendants in a single forum, which will often be the case in actions arising from competition law infringements, in particular cartels, Article 6(1) is among the most important provisions of the Regulation.[52]

To rely on Article 6(1), a plaintiff has to establish a 'good arguable case' that the English court has jurisdiction, and that the requirements of Article 6(1) Brussels I have been satisfied.[53] To this end, it must be shown that 'there is a real issue between the Claimants and one of the Anchor Defendants, that is, an issue which cannot be struck out.'[54] Under the Civil Procedure Rules, rule 3.4[55] the court may strike out a statement of case – 'striking out means the court ordering written material to be deleted so that it can be no longer relied upon'.[56] In this context, it has been submitted that:

> The most common grounds for applying for strike out are those set out in CPR, rule 3.4(2)(a): that the statement of case discloses no reasonable grounds for bringing/defending the claim. Statements of case that are suitable for striking out on this ground include those which raise an unwinnable case whose continuance would waste resources,[57] and claims that are not valid as a matter of law.[58] Statements of case are not generally struck out where jurisprudence is developing,[59] or where they

[51] Case C-98/06 *Freeport v Arnoldsson* [2007] ECR I-8319 [38]. See also Opinion of AG Mengozzi [45].
[52] Wilderspin (n 25) 52.
[53] *Cooper Tire* [2009] (n 4) [36]. See also *Provimi* (n 4) [46]–[49].
[54] *Cooper Tire* [2009] (n 4) [37]. See also: *FKI Engineering v Dewind Holdings* [2007] EWHC (Comm) [32].
[55] CPR Pt 3, The Court Case Management Powers, www.justice.gov.uk/courts/procedure-rules/civil/rules/part03.
[56] See CPR Glossary, www.justice.gov.uk/courts/procedure-rules/civil/glossary.
[57] *Harris v Bolt Burdon* [2000] CP Rep 70.
[58] *Price Meats Ltd v Barclays Bank plc* [2000] 2 All ER (Comm) 346.
[59] *Barrett v Enfield BC* [2001] 2 AC 550.

> raise serious issues that can only be determined by hearing oral evidence.[60] Strike out is not usually granted unless the court is satisfied that the claim or defence is 'bound to fail'.[61, 62]

Nonetheless, strike-out applications appear to be quite common in cases where the anchor defendants are subsidiaries forming part of a corporate group which has infringed Articles 101 and 102 TFEU. The case law shows that there may be some complex issues to be addressed by the courts at the jurisdiction stage in the context of Article 6(1). There are particularly difficult questions to be addressed in EU competition law cases due to the concept of 'undertaking' which, as already noted, may encompass a corporate group with numerous subsidiaries in order to take account of the pan-European nature of the business nowadays. Can a claim be struck out if the subsidiary was not mentioned by name in the Commission decision? Is there an infringement by a subsidiary when it implements an agreement entered into by its parent and other 'undertakings' within the meaning of Article 101 TFEU? Should the claim be struck out if the claimant cannot establish that the subsidiary knew that there was a cartel agreement (and what was going on in the cartel)? The issues were first addressed in *Provimi*, where Mr Justice Aikens held:

> If, as I have held, it is arguable that all companies within an '*undertaking*' who '*implemented*' the cartel are infringers of Article [101 TFEU], then their action in '*implementing*' the cartel could cause the loss that the claimants allege. On this analysis, each infringing entity is a tortfeasor. I do not think it matters whether they are to be regarded as joint or several tortfeasors for the purpose of the causation argument. Each entity would have contributed to a situation where it took part in the cartel, upheld the cartel prices and so (arguably) caused loss.[63]

Accordingly, in the *Provimi* case, the High Court concluded that there was a 'real issue' as between the German company and the two English companies. Based on that, it was concluded by the Court that antitrust claims by the German company were not artificial or advanced solely so that the company could take advantage of Article 6(1) of Brussels I and bring proceedings in England against a non-UK domiciled company.

In *Cooper Tire*, the English court was asked once more to address the issue whether a claimant has a claim, which cannot be struck out, against non-addressees, who are subsidiaries, of certain addressees of a Commission infringement decision. Mr Justice Teare held:

> An undertaking in European competition law is an economic unit. That unit is engaged in an economic activity. The prohibition in Article [101] is on agreements by such undertakings or economic units but Article [101] is infringed not only by making an agreement contrary to Article [101] but also by the implementation of such agreements. An undertaking may act by or through those legal entities which constitute the undertaking. Whilst the infringement of Article [101] is that of the undertaking, liability for the resulting fine or damages must be attached to a legal person. Where a subsidiary is personally involved in the infringement by implementing the offending agreement there is no need to enquire into whether or not the subsidiary is involved by having decisive influence over another legal entity. Since the legal entity which makes the offending agreement plainly has knowledge of it, a rational consequence of the concept of an undertaking as a single economic entity, made up of its constituent legal entities, is that the undertaking has knowledge of the offending agreement. There is therefore no need, before attaching liability to a legal entity which is part of that undertaking and has implemented the offending agreement, to

[60] *Bridgeman v McAlpine-Brown* [2000] LTL 19 Jan 2000.

[61] *Hughes v Colin Richards* [2004] EWCA Civ 266, [2004] PNLR 35. See, eg *Parkes v Esso Petroleum* [1999] 1 CMLR 455 (Sir Richard Scott VC).

[62] M Brealey and N Green, *Competition Litigation: UK Practice and Procedure* (Oxford, OUP, 2010) 157.

[63] *Provimi* (n 4) [40].

allege and prove that that legal entity had knowledge of the offending agreement. It is sufficient that the undertaking had such knowledge.[64]

The High Court, therefore, concluded that it had jurisdiction over the Dow defendants, pursuant to Article 6(1) of Brussels I.[65] The issue, however, was reopened before the Court of Appeal. Lord Justice Longmore took the opportunity to revisit the *Provimi* point by holding:

45. As to the *Provimi* point, we can readily agree that, as Aikens J said, it is 'arguable'. We would, however, add that it is also arguable the other way. Although one can see that a parent company should be liable for what its subsidiary has done on the basis that a parent company is presumed to be able to exercise (and actually exercise) decisive influence over a subsidiary, it is by no means obvious even in an Article 81 context that a subsidiary should be liable for what its parent does, let alone for what another subsidiary does. Nor does the *Provimi* point sit comfortably with the apparent practice of the Commission, when it exercises its power to fine, to single out those who are primarily responsible or their parent companies rather than to impose a fine on all the entities of the relevant undertaking. If, moreover, liability can extend to any subsidiary company which is part of an undertaking, would such liability accrue to a subsidiary which did not deal in rubber at all, but another product entirely? These and other difficulties have been ventilated by Mr Nicholas Khan in the 2003 volume of *European Lawyer* page 16 and Mr Brian Kennelly in the May 2010 issue of the *CPI Anti-Trust Journal.*

46. If it had been necessary to address the *Provimi* point, we would have been inclined to say that it would be necessary to make a reference to the ECJ before coming to a conclusion on jurisdiction. It would be possible to say that, because a claimant only has to show that he has a case against an anchor defendant which cannot be struck out, the fact that the *Provimi* point is arguable should not deter the English court from assuming jurisdiction. But that would mean that the *Provimi* point could never be decided in a jurisdiction (and possibly, therefore, in any other) context. That would not be a satisfactory state of affairs.[66]

Nevertheless, neither was the application struck out nor was a reference made to the Court of the Justice, as there was a valid claim that the defendants were knowingly involved in the infringement of Article 101 TFEU.[67]

The uncertainties were exploited by the defendants in *Toshiba Carrier and others v KME Yorkshire and others*[68] as the issue reappeared before the High Court. In this case, the claimants sought damages against the defendants, who were involved in a complex of anti-competitive agreements and concerted practices consisting of price-fixing and market-sharing in the industrial tubes sector. The infringement was detected and established by a decision of the European Commission which preceded the damages actions. Those named as undertakings and as legal entities in the Commission decision included KM Europa Metal AG, Trefimetaux SA and Europa Metalli SpA (ie companies in the KME group), Wieland-Werke AG (a company in the Wieland-Werke group) and Outokumpu Oyj (a company in the Outokumpu group). None of the named companies was domiciled in England. The claimants, however, decided to bring their actions in England against UK-domiciled anchor defendants, KME Yorkshire (a company in the KME group) as well as against Nemco and WW (UK) (companies in the Wieland-Werke group). It has been

[64] *Cooper Tire* [2009] (n 4) [50].
[65] *Cooper Tire* [2009] (n 4) [64].
[66] ibid [45]–[46].
[67] ibid [39]. See also: *Nokia Corporation v AU Optronics Corporation* [2012] EWHC 731 (Ch) [68].
[68] *Toshiba Carrier* [2011] (n 4).

argued that 'the claims [against the UK-defendants] have only been brought against them in order to secure jurisdiction in relation to the non-domiciled defendants',[69] which included the following companies: KM Europa Metal AG, Trefimetaux SA, Europa Metalli SpA, Wieland-Werke AG and Outokumpu Oyj.[70]

In the course of counsel's submissions, the High Court was asked to consider whether it was satisfied that the decisions of Aikens J in *Provimi* and Teare J in *Cooper Tire* were plainly wrong, and whether there should be a preliminary reference to the Court of Justice.[71] The Chancellor of the High Court held:

> 42. I am required to follow a decision of a judge of co-ordinate jurisdiction unless I am convinced that it is wrong. The decisions of Aikens and Teare JJ are, in this court, those of judges of co-ordinate jurisdiction. Whatever view I might have taken uninstructed by the views of the Court of Appeal in *Cooper Tire* it is clear from what that Court said in paragraph 45 of its judgment quoted in paragraph 30 above that I cannot conclude that the decisions of Aikens and Teare JJ are plainly wrong.
>
> 43. I have, of course, noted and carefully considered what the Court of Appeal there said about making a reference to the Court of the European Union. In my view it would not be appropriate to make a reference at this stage. First, the point will not arise unless and until the allegation of knowledge is not established at the trial. Second, it is usually better to withhold a reference until the facts have been found lest the Court of the European Union be troubled by points which are academic and therefore not necessary for the decision of the national court.[72]

The Chancellor of the High Court went on to state that claimants are entitled to rely on Article 6(1) and establish jurisdiction against the non-UK domiciled defendants. The defendants appealed. In the course of an application for a permission to appeal against the decision of the Chancellor, Lord Justice Kitchin made the following observation:

> [I]t is not at all clear to me that the decision of this court in *Cooper Tire* establishes that, in a case such as the present, where anchor defendants domiciled in the UK are said to be party to the cartel, it is never necessary to include particulars of knowledge until after disclosure. *Cooper Tire* was, as Mr Beard QC, appearing on behalf of the KME defendants, has emphasised this morning, a case concerned only with a strike-out application. I of course accept that in some cases the circumstances may be such that it is sufficient simply to allege that anchor defendants domiciled in the UK were parties to or aware of anti-competitive conduct. However, I do not accept that that is necessarily so in all cases. For example, if it appears that the allegations against anchor defendants are based on nothing more than mere speculation, then I think it at least arguable that the claim should not be allowed to proceed merely on the basis that something might turn up on disclosure.

The application for permission to appeal was granted. After hearing the appeal, the Court of Appeal held that there was a seriously arguable stand-alone claim against KME UK for infringement of Article 101 TFEU.[73] The stand-alone claim was that the defendant, KME UK, participated in, and implemented, the cartel arrangements with knowledge of the cartel agreement. In other words, it was accepted by the litigants that the claimants 'must prove KME UK's knowledge of the cartel agreement and practices'.[74] Although the

[69] *Toshiba Carrier* [2012] (n 4) [42].
[70] *Toshiba Carrier* [2011] (n 4) [16]–[17].
[71] ibid [39].
[72] ibid [43].
[73] *KME Yorkshire Ltd v Toshiba Carrier* [2012] EWCA Civ 1190 [29]–[32].
[74] *Toshiba Carrier* (n 73) [37].

claim had been preceded by a decision of the European Commission establishing an infringement by the KME group of companies, the claimant had to change its claim from a follow-on one to a stand-alone claim, in view of the fact that the defendant, a company from the KME group, was not named in the Commission decision as an infringing legal entity.[75]

Given that the respondents had made a stand-alone claim, the Court stated that the *Provimi* point did not arise in the present case. However, Lord Justice Etherton went on to briefly express his view on the issue,[76] and held:

> 38. The jurisprudence on this aspect is, in my view, plain and settled. Article 101 is concerned with agreements, decisions and concerted practices by and between undertakings. An undertaking for this purpose is any entity engaged in economic activity, regardless of its legal status and the way in which it is financed. Furthermore, in this context the concept of an undertaking includes an economic unit which may consist of more than one legal or natural person, such as a group of companies. Where, for example, a company does not decide independently on its own conduct on the market, but in all material respects carries out the instructions given to it by its parent company, having regard to the economic, organisational and legal links between them, the unlawful conduct of the subsidiary will be imputed to the parent company. In such a situation, in the language of EU jurisprudence, the parent exercises a 'decisive influence' over its subsidiary. The subsidiary is not absolved from its own personal responsibility, but its parent company is liable because in that situation they form a single economic entity for the purposes of Article 101. In EU jurisprudence, the (rebuttable) presumption is that a parent company exercises a decisive influence over the market conduct of a wholly owned subsidiary and that they therefore constitute a single undertaking within Article 101: Case C-97/08P *Akzo Nobel NV & Os v Commission* [2009] ECR 1–8247 (Advocate General Kokott at paras. 39–44, ECJ paras. 54–61 and 77); T-25/06 *Alliance One International Inc v Commission* 9 September 2011 (paras 80–85); Case T-43/02 *Jungbunzlauer AG v Commission* [2006] ECR II-3435 (para. 129).
>
> 39. By contrast, the mere fact that the share capital of two commercial companies is held by the same person or the same family is insufficient in itself to establish that those two companies are an economic unit with the result that, for the purposes of Article 101, the actions of one company can be attributed to the other. That was expressly held to be the position in Case C-196/99 P *Siderurgica Aristrain Madrid SL v Commission* [2003] ECR I-11005 at paragraph 99: see also Case T-358/06 *Wegenbouwmaatschappij J Heijmans BV v Commission* 4 July 2008 (Second Chamber) at paragraph 30. The views expressed by Aikens J in *Provimi* predated the judgment of the ECJ in *Siderurgica Aristrain Madrid* and were overtaken by it.[77]

Has the ECJ decision in *Aristrain* overtaken *Provimi*? The question was addressed head on by the High Court judgment in *Nokia Corporation v AU Optronics Corporation*,[78] which was concerned with another EU competition law claim against multiple defendants. In this case, Nokia brought an EU competition law claim against multiple defendants involving several distinct groups of companies. Nokia alleged that the defendants have been involved in anti-competitive practices contravening Article 101 TFEU. The defendants' conduct had allegedly inflated the prices for mobile telephone liquid crystal displays ('LCDs'). Most of the defendants were domiciled outside England and the rest of the United Kingdom. However, D12, a company from the Samsung group of companies, and D22, a company from the Hitachi group of companies, were companies registered and domiciled in

[75] ibid [22]. See also: *Toshiba Carrier* [2011] (n 4).
[76] *Toshiba Carrier* (n 73) [37].
[77] *Toshiba Carrier* (n 73) [38]–[39].
[78] *Nokia* (n 67).

England, and they were thus the 'anchor defendants' within the meaning of Article 6(1) of Brussels I.[79]

The defendants' conduct was investigated by the regulators, the US Department of Justice as well as the European Commission in Europe.[80] The Commission issued a Decision[81] finding of infringement of Article 101 in relation to the manufacture and supply of large LCDs, of 12-inch size and larger, but it did not address the question of possible infringements of Article 101 in respect of small LCDs for mobile telephones. Although Nokia could not benefit from the European Commission decision, civil legal proceedings in the United States resulted in some disclosure to Nokia of documents bearing on Nokia's claims.[82] The Samsung and Hitachi defendants brought strike-out applications. In this context, it was submitted by the defendants that 'the courts in *Provimi*, *Cooper Tire* and *Toshiba Carrier* had proceeded without reference to a relevant judgment of the ECJ, Case C-196/99 P *Siderurgica Aristrain Madrid SL v European Commission* [2003] ECR I-11005 ('*Aristrain*'), which showed that their analysis was wrong, to the *acte clair* standard.' Mr Justice Sales held:

> In my judgment, the position is very far indeed from being *acte clair* in favour of the defendants, so that it can be said with confidence that EU law does not found a damages claim against a company which is part of an undertaking which has participated in an unlawful cartel which has violated Article 101 and has in fact implemented arrangements worked out in breach of Article 101 by the cartel (e.g. by selling goods at prices inflated because of the effects of the cartel), albeit without itself having knowledge of the cartel. *Aristrain* does not establish that to be the case.[83]

The High Court went on to distinguish *Aristrain*.[84] First, in *Aristrain*, a fine was imposed only on one sister company for anti-competitive conduct, which was adopted by Aristrain and its sister company. However, there was no evidence that the former company 'had the power to direct the conduct of [its sister company] to the point of depriving it of any real independence in determining its own course of action.'[85] Secondly, the High Court made a distinction between liability for administrative fines, on the one hand, and liability for damages, on the other hand.[86] Different issues of policy and legal principle appear to be at stake when determining civil or administrative liability.[87] In a situation where the claim is for harm caused to a particular claimant, the court should consider the interests of the claimant, who has suffered loss as a result of the infringement, as well as 'the elements of an undertaking which has participated in a violation of Article 101 which has given rise to such losses.'[88] The judge stated:

> In my view, it is well arguable that as a matter of EU law a civil law damages claim can be maintained by a person who has suffered loss as a result of paying inflated prices by reason of cartel

[79] *Nokia* (n 67) [12].
[80] *Nokia* (n 67) [17].
[81] Case COMP/39.309 – LCD – Liquid Crystal Displays – notified under document C(2010) 8761 final http://ec.europa.eu/competition/antitrust/cases/dec_docs/39309/39309_3580_3.pdf.
[82] *Nokia* (n 67) [19].
[83] ibid [80].
[84] Case C-196/99 P *Siderurgica Aristrain Madrid SL v European Commission* [2003] ECR I-11005.
[85] *Aristrain* (n 84) [97].
[86] A similar distinction is made by S Thomas, 'Guilty of a Fault that one has not Committed. The Limits of the Group-Based Sanction Policy Carried out by the Commission and the European Courts in EU-Antitrust Law' (2012) 3 *Journal of European Competition Law and Practice* 1, 18.
[87] *Aristrain* (n 84) [81].
[88] *Nokia* (n 67) [81].

> arrangements in breach of Article 101 against a member of a participating undertaking which implemented the arrangements, albeit without knowledge of the cartel – at least where there is some significant element of influence or control by a member of the undertaking which does have knowledge of the cartel over the activities of the implementing member of the undertaking (control within the relevant undertakings is pleaded in this case).[89]

Although the strike out application was dismissed by Mr Justice Sales, at the moment of writing, the case is pending before the Court of Appeal.[90] Hence, Article 6(1) appears to be raising difficult and complex issues in cross-border EU competition law claims. The above examples clearly demonstrate that uncertainties may result in a significant delay which may result in higher costs for claimants. Indeed, the heated debates in *Provimi*, *Cooper Tire*, *Toshiba Carrier* and *Nokia* suggest that jurisdictional challenges may be used to 'wear down the will of the claimants or at least their financial resources.'[91] Therefore, the difficulties, which affect the litigants' strategies at present,[92] may be explained by the claimants' desire to sue the defendant in one jurisdiction rather than another.[93]

Problems could be exacerbated by the inefficiencies of the two-task enforcement structure.[94] In this context, it should be noted that proceedings were first commenced by Nokia in November 2009 in light of the ongoing Commission investigation. As a result, the court proceedings were stayed pursuant to Article 16(1) of Regulation 1/2003.[95] The Commission did not release the Decision into the public domain until 13 October 2011, when Nokia realised that it could not benefit from the findings of the Commission. Even when an infringement has been established by the regulator, the two-task enforcement structure may give rise to specific jurisdictional challenges, and delay the settlement of the dispute. As already noted, a claimant is often relying on a European Commission decision establishing an EU competition law infringement to show that a group (or groups) of companies has infringed Articles 101 and/or 102 TFEU.[96] A Commission decision allows a claimant to make a good arguable case that there is a real issue, which cannot be struck out, between him and the group of companies. In order for a claimant to centralise litigation in his preferred jurisdiction pursuant to Article 6(1) of Brussels I, his claim must be brought (and the real issue established) against a particular legal person domiciled in the UK. If such a claim is brought against the local subsidiary with a view to securing jurisdiction against a non-UK domiciled parent company, then the defendant would certainly argue that 'the infringement of [EU] competition law must be imputed unequivocally to a legal person.'[97] In other words, the claimant must demonstrate that there is a real issue, which cannot be struck out, between him and the particular local subsidiary. This would be an extremely difficult and time-consuming task if the local subsidiary is not an addressee of the Commission's decision. This outcome is far from satisfactory in view of the fact that private antitrust litigation is normally preceded by a decision of a regulator establishing a competition law infringement. Indeed, it may be even more difficult for a

[89] ibid [82].

[90] *Nokia Corporation v AU Optronics Corporation* – still pending before the Court of Appeal, Case Reference A3/2012/0853.

[91] Ch 22.

[92] Chs 3 and 11.

[93] See Pt I.

[94] See Chs 1 and 5.

[95] *Nokia* (n 67) [82].

[96] Case C-97/08 P *Akzo Nobel v Commission of the European Communities* [2009] ECR I-8237 [55].

[97] *Akzo Nobel* (n 96) [57].

claimant, who brings a stand-alone action, to establish a real issue, which cannot be struck out.

In view of the foregoing, one wonders if Article 5(5) of Brussels may not be used to resolve some of the problems. According to Article 5(5), 'a person domiciled in a Member State may, in another Member State, be sued as regards a dispute arising out of the operations of a branch, agency or other establishment, in the courts for the place in which the branch, agency or other establishment is situated.'[98] Article 5(5) allows, for example, an action to be brought in England against a French manufacturing company (a member of an international cartel) which markets a product (at an inflated price, in breach of EU competition law) in England through its English branch. The branch office cannot be sued as a defendant, since it is not a separate legal entity. The French manufacturing company, however, can be sued in England by virtue of Article 5(5) of Brussels I, provided that the dispute arises out of the operations of the branch.[99] If the branch markets a product at an inflated price in breach of EU competition law in England, this requirement will be satisfied. Practice, however, shows that in most competition cases the market would be penetrated through setting up a subsidiary. In a recent case before the Competition Appeal Tribunal, it has been submitted:

> the Commission's practice is not always to specify in the operative part all the legal entities which form the 'undertaking' which has been found to infringe. Where, for example, there is a corporate group with numerous subsidiaries, all of whom form a single infringing undertaking, he stated that the Commission's practice has been to specify the ultimate parent company or 'Topco', rather than listing in the operative part of the decision each and every subsidiary involved in the unlawful conduct. [Mr Jon Turner QC] submitted that where this occurs the legal person named in the operative part of the decision as the 'undertaking' will be a representative, and the finding of infringement is not limited to that entity.[100]

But, can a plaintiff bring an EU competition law claim against the parent company of an English subsidiary in England under Article 5(5) of Brussels I? Although the subsidiary may be covered by Article 5(5) in cases where it acts as if it were a branch,[101] the Court of Justice has held that the grantee of an exclusive sales concession who is subject neither to the control nor to the direction of the grantor cannot be regarded as being within the head of Article 5(5) of Brussels I.[102] This is justified by the fact that the subsidiary is a separate legal entity and lacks the authority to act on behalf of the parent company.[103] The doctrine of 'undertaking' for the purposes of Articles 101 and 102 TFEU is different from the concepts of 'persons' establishing jurisdiction under Brussels I.[104] It has been submitted that the '[subsidiary] normally acts for itself and not for the parent company, and will thus be outside the scope of Art 5(5)'.[105]

[98] See Case 14/76 *De Bloos v Bouyer* [1976] ECR 1497; Case C-139/80 *Blanckaert and Willems v Trost* [1981] ECR 819; Case C-218/86 *Sar Schotte GmbH v Parfums Rothschild SARL* [1987] ECR 4905; Case C-439/93 *Lloyd's Register of Shipping v Soc Campenon Bernard* [1995] ECR I-961. See *Cheshire, North and Fawcett* (n 35), 258–61.

[99] Case 33/78 *Somafer v Saar-Ferngas* [1978] ECR 2183.

[100] *Emerson* [2011] (n 4) [18].

[101] *Sar Schotte* (n 74).

[102] *De Bloos* (n 74) [23]. See also the opinion of AG Reischl in *De Bloos* (n 98) 1519.

[103] ibid 1519 (AG Reischel).

[104] Compare Cases 6 and 7/73 *Istituto Chemioterapico Italiano SpA and Commercial Solvents Corp v Commission of the European Communities* [1974] ECR 223, 263 (AG Warner).

[105] J Fawcett, 'A New Approach to Jurisdiction over Companies in Private International Law' (1988) 37 ICLQ 645, 659. See also: WA Allwood, 'Art 5(5): Meaning of 'Branch, Agency or Other Establishment' (1988) 13 *EL Rev* 213; *Blanckaert* (n 98); *Sar Schotte* (n 98) [15].

Therefore, normally, the fact that a subsidiary has a separate legal personality would probably exclude it from the scope of this provision. Indeed, the question whether the corporate veil should be lifted may give rise to a considerable debate before English courts.[106] Such an outcome would fly in the face of economic reality and ignore the fact that a group of companies could engage in anti-competitive conduct by setting up subsidiaries across Europe. Since it is very difficult to invoke Article 6(1) and sue the local subsidiary with a view to secure jurisdiction against a non-UK domiciled parent company, one would have thought that if subsidiaries are regarded as not covered by Art 5(5) of Brussels I, then, in some cases, it would be impossible or impractical to bring a claim against a non-UK domiciled parent company in England, even if this was an appropriate forum to deal with the dispute. Are there strong arguments suggesting that the corporate veil should be lifted so as to make a parent company liable for the infringement of EU competition law implemented in England by its English subsidiary?

As already noted, it is well established that if a subsidiary has no real freedom to determine its course of action, it is to be regarded as forming one economic unit with its parent company under the competition rules.[107] The European Union Court of Justice has recently held:

> In the specific case where a parent company has a 100% shareholding in a subsidiary which has infringed the Community competition rules, first, the parent company can exercise a decisive influence over the conduct of the subsidiary (see, to that effect, *Imperial Chemical Industries v Commission*, paragraphs 136 and 137) and, second, there is a rebuttable presumption that the parent company does in fact exercise a decisive influence over the conduct of its subsidiary (see, to that effect, *AEG-Telefunken v Commission*, paragraph 50, and *Stora*, paragraph 29).[108]

Following this line of reasoning, it can be inferred that the claimant in such cases can use Article 5(5) of Brussels I to subject to that jurisdiction a parent company, provided that the EU competition law claim has arisen out of the operation of the subsidiary. In such a case, some conduct by the subsidiary would be required. It seems to me that the implementation of the cartel agreement, on behalf of the parent, would satisfy the second requirement (ie the dispute will 'arise out of the operations of the branch'). If this analysis is correct, then there might well be cases where Article 5(5) of Brussels I could be a useful provision in EU competition law claims, arising out of the operation of exclusive distributors and subsidiaries as well.

Thus, for the purposes of an EU competition law claim, a legally independent undertaking may be regarded as an establishment under Article 5(5) of Brussels I because of its economic dependence. Accordingly, the English court may have jurisdiction in an antitrust claim against the parent company of a subsidiary firm established in England as long as the subsidiary is part of the same group of companies, and 'engaged in the same economic undertaking'.[109] This would be of great relevance in cases where a subsidiary implements a cartel agreement that is entered into by its parent and the parent's competitors. The need

[106] *Adams v Cape Industries* [1990] ChD 433, CA.

[107] Case 48/69 *ICI v Commission* [1972] ECR 619 [134]; Case 66/86 *Ahmed Saeed Flurgreisen v Zentrale zur Bekampfung unlauteren Wettbewerbs* [1989] ECR 803 [35]. Case 15/74 *Centrafarm v Sterling Drug* [1974] ECR 1183 [41]; Case C-73/95 *Viho v Commission* [1996] ECR I-5457. See also: *Provimi* (n 4) [31]. See more: J Faull and A Nikpay, *The EC Law of Competition*, 2nd edn (Oxford, OUP, 2007) 206–208. Compare *The Albazero* [1977] AC 774, HL, 807 (Roskill LJ); *Adams* (n 106) 532 (Slade LJ).

[108] *Akzo Nobel* (n 96) [60].

[109] *Toshiba Carrier* [2011] (n 4) [49].

to bring an antitrust claim also against the parent company may arise, because the subsidiary may not have many assets.

Nevertheless, even if the court is prepared to accept a wider interpretation of Article 5(5) with regard to cross-border EU competition law actions, there would be difficulties in such cases as well. First, a claimant may not be able to sue more than one group of companies at a time. Although this may well be a valid strategy in some cases,[110] this may result in parallel and related proceedings with regard to the same EU competition law infringement. Secondly, Article 6(3)(b) of Rome II seems to suggest that a private antitrust law claimant suing pursuant to Article 5(5) of Brussels I will face difficulties when it comes to the assessment of damages.[111] This would be especially so in cases where the market is affected in a number of Member States and the plaintiff wants to plead, for example, exemplary damages before English courts.[112]

Article 5(5) should be an important basis for jurisdiction if EU competition law litigation is to pick up in Europe. Article 6(1) not only creates the problems identified above but also it may not be relied upon by consumers (if their claims are brought under section 4 of Chapter II in the Brussels I Regulation). This conclusion can be deduced by analogy from the recent ruling in *Glaxosmithkline*.[113] The reading of the Court of Justice judgment, together with Article 15 of Brussels I, indicates that Article 6(1) (unlike Article 4 and Article 5(5)) will not be applicable to claims brought by consumers.

D. Section 4 of Chapter II of Brussels I and its Application to Cross-Border EU Competition Law Actions

Section 4 will be applicable where the defendant seller is domiciled, or deemed to be domiciled, in a Member State[114] and the other party to the contract (the consumer) is acting outside his trade or profession. It has been submitted that a Member State court would have jurisdiction over tortious claims for antitrust damages suffered by a consumer as a result of being subject to a contract that is in conflict with EU competition laws if brought together with a claim for invalidity of a consumer contract.[115] Nevertheless, it should be noted that one might argue that section 4 of the Brussels I Regulation would be relevant with regard to claims arising out of contract, but would not cover a closely related tortious claim. Such a deduction could be based on the fact that Article 15 is similar to Article 5(1) as both are using the expression 'matters relating to contract', so that the *Kalfelis* ruling should be applicable by analogy. Accordingly, the expression 'matters relating to contract' within the meaning of Article 15 of the Brussels I Regulation could be interpreted as not covering a situation in which there was no freely assumed reciprocal obligation by the parties.[116] It has been submitted by Advocate General Darmon in *Shearson* that 'the Court's interpretation of "matters relating to contract" in Article 5 should be taken into account

[110] Ch 3.
[111] See more: Danov (n 3).
[112] Case No 1178/5/7/11, *2 Travel Group Plc (In liquidation) v Cardiff City Transport Services Ltd* [2012] CAT 19.
[113] Case C-462/06 *Laboratoires Glaxosmithkline* [2008] ECR I-3965 (Court of Justice, First Chamber).
[114] Art 15 of the Brussels I Regulation.
[115] See more: Danov (n 3).
[116] Compare: Case C-96/00 *Gabriel v Schlanck & Schick* [2002] ECR I-6367 [49]; Case C-334/00 *Fonderie Officine Meccaniche Tacconi v Heinrich Wagner Sinto Maschinenfabrik* [2002] ECR I-7357 [23].

for interpreting the similar provision of Article 1[5].'[117] However, if Article 5(1) and Article 15 are only 'similar', then the question is: can they be distinguished in some cases?

The better view would be to distinguish Article 5(1) and Article 15, and accept a broader interpretation of the latter. In *Engler*, the Court of Justice has clearly made a distinction between Article 5(1) and Article 15.[118] In this case, it was explicitly stated that Article 15 constitutes a *lex specialis* in relation to Article 5(1) in so far as the latter provision relates specifically to contracts concluded by a consumer, but does not extend to cover a situation where no contract has been concluded.[119] Following this line of reasoning, it seems that once a contract by a consumer has been concluded, then Article 15 would be applicable with regard to all claims arising out of the contract. The difficulties that would be encountered with regard to contracts falling within Article 5(1)[120] would not arise in relation to EU competition law actions arising out of consumer contracts.[121]

Consequently, if a broader interpretation is adopted, Article 16 would be the basis for jurisdiction with regard to consumer claims based on contract and tort. Article 16 entitles a claimant to bring proceedings related to a consumer contract either in the place of his domicile or in the courts of the place of the seller or supplier's domicile. In other words, an English court would have jurisdiction over an EU competition law action brought under Article 16.[122] In such cases, there would be a contractual dispute about how the principle of severance of illegal provisions from otherwise lawful agreements is to affect the consumers' contract[123] and a tortious dispute regarding the issues of causation and assessment of antitrust damages.[124] Thus, Article 16 would have an important role in a substantial number of antitrust proceedings brought by consumers. The possibility for consumers to rely on special jurisdictional rules in such cases may be further justified by the Commission's initiative[125] to pave the way for private antitrust enforcement in Europe, which would be socially efficient.[126] As already outlined, in such cases the consumers may be unwilling to bear the expenses and uncertainties of a suit at the court of the defendant's domicile, where they could think that they would be treated unfavourably by a national court which could be tempted to promote 'national champions'. However, as already noted, this provision would not be an option in respect of cross-border actions brought against multi-defendants. Thus, parallel antitrust proceedings would be bound to arise in the European context.

[117] Case C-89/91 *Shearson Lehman Hutton* [1993] ECR I-139 [87] of the opinion of AG Darmon.

[118] Case C-27/02 *Petra Engler v Janus Versand GmbH* [2005] ECR I-481.

[119] *Engler* (n 118) [31], [32], [40], [44] and [49]. See also: Case C-180/06 *Ilsinger v Martin Dreschers (acting as administrator in the insolvency of Schlank & Schick GmbH* [2009] ECR I-3961 [52] and [53].

[120] See J Harris, 'Product Liability and the Conflict of Laws' in CJ Miller and RS Goldberg, *Product Liability*, 2nd edn (Oxford, OUP, 2004) 777, 792–95, 801–802.

[121] See more: M Danov, 'The Brussels I Regulation: Cross-Border Collective Redress Proceedings and Judgments' (2010) 6 *Journal of Private International Law* 359; Danov (n 3).

[122] See more: Danov (n 121); Danov (n 3).

[123] Compare: R Whish, *Competition Law* (Oxford, OUP, 2008) 313.

[124] See more Danov (n 3) chs 2, 3 and 5.

[125] See Council Regulation 1/2003 and White Paper on Damages actions for breach of the EC antitrust rules COM(2008) 165 final.

[126] See more regarding the theoretical framework which would favour rules facilitating collective redress actions in WN Landes and RA Posner, 'The Private Enforcement of Law' (1975) 33 *Journal of Legal Studies* 1, 33. See also KW Dam, 'Class Actions: Efficiency, Compensation, Deterrence, and Conflict of Interest' (1975) 4 *Journal of Legal Studies* 47.

III. AVOIDING PARALLEL EU COMPETITION LAW PROCEEDINGS IN EUROPE

As already noted,[127] the decentralisation reform means that there can be multiple enforcers of Articles 101 and 102 TFEU.[128] The importance of the rules, which are meant to avoid parallel EU competition law proceedings, could not be questioned in view of the fact that EU antitrust infringement, by definition, would affect businesses and consumers in a number of Member States. The need for such rules can be further strengthened by the analysis of jurisdictional rules and their application in EU competition law cases, which appear to indicate that, on some occasions, it would be very difficult for claimants to centralise litigation. As a result, the claimants (SMEs and consumers in particular) may prefer to sue for the local damage before the courts at their home state.

There is little doubt that one of the major challenges that Member State courts (as well as policy-makers) face in this context is how to avoid the problem of parallel EU competition law proceedings[129] and ensure that a well-placed court will hear and determine an EU competition law claim. Indeed, there are some specific issues which would arise in cross-border EU competition law actions. First, court proceedings may be initiated by claimants against various members of the same group/s of companies (representing one or more infringing undertakings) in different Member States.

Secondly, parallel EU competition law proceedings may arise before an NCA located in one Member State and private EU antitrust law proceedings related to the same breaches of Article 101 TFEU and/or Article 102 TFEU before a court in another Member State.[130] Articles 5 and 6 of the Regulation state that the National Competition Authorities (NCAs) and national courts have the powers to apply Articles 101 and 102 TFEU in individual cases. On the one hand, it is well established that an NCA may have the power to apply Articles 101 and 102 TFEU in cases where the markets in several Member States have been affected.[131] On the other hand, a Member State court may have jurisdiction to hear and determine a claim regarding an EU competition law infringement that has affected the markets in several countries, as well as having jurisdiction to award damages in such cases.[132] Regulation 1/2003 does not deal with the problem of parallel proceedings before an NCA located in one Member State and private EU antitrust law proceedings in another.[133] Is Brussels I applicable at all in this context?

[127] See Ch 1.

[128] Commission (EC), 'Modernisation of the Rules implementing Articles 85 and 86 of the EC Treaty' (White Paper) Programme 99/027 [101].

[129] See Brammer (n 9) 25.

[130] Danov (n 8).

[131] See Art 5 of Council Regulation 1/2003; Commission Notice on Cooperation within the Network of Competition Authorities [2004] OJ C101/43 [5]. Parallel actions by two or three NCAs may be appropriate in some cases. In such a scenario, the authorities dealing with the case may decide to designate one of them as a lead authority and to delegate some tasks to that designated lead authority. See ibid paras 12–13. See also Brammer (n 9) 159.

[132] See *Provimi* (n 4).

[133] Arts 15 and 16 of Regulation 1/2003 are meant to guarantee uniform and consistent application of EU competition law in proceedings before the Commission and in cross-border EU competition law claims before Member State courts.

A. Articles 27 and 28 Brussels I: Scope of their Application[134]

Under Brussels I there are circumstances in which, although a national court has jurisdiction, it is provided that proceedings must be stayed or jurisdiction must be declined. Articles 27 and 28 of Brussels I are 'intended to prevent parallel proceedings before the courts of different [Member States] and to avoid conflicts between decisions which might result therefrom.'[135] Article 27(1) of Brussels I states that:

> Where proceedings involving the same cause of action and between the same parties are brought in the courts of different Member States, any court other than the court first seised shall of its own motion stay its proceedings until such time as the jurisdiction of the court first seised is established . . .

This provision is intended to deal with the problem of *lis pendens*.[136] This is concerned with the situation where proceedings involving the same cause of action and between the same parties are brought in the courts of different Member States. Sub-section (1) states that the court second seised must stay its proceedings. Sub-section (2) provides that where the jurisdiction of the court first seised is established, 'any court other than the court first seized shall decline jurisdiction in favour of that court.' The Court of Justice held that the court second seised with the dispute is not entitled to examine the jurisdiction of the court first seised, even if the court first seised has not decided the question of its jurisdiction within a reasonable time.[137]

Article 28 of Brussels I states that 'where related actions are pending in the courts of different Member States, any court other than the court first seised may stay its proceedings', and it is designed to deal with those situations that do not fall within the strict confines of Article 27 of the Regulation. Article 28(2) goes further and gives an additional discretion to the court. Based on that provision, the court may decide to decline jurisdiction, as opposed to merely staying its proceedings if the court first seised has jurisdiction over the actions in question and its law permits the consolidation thereof. It should be clearly noted, however, that this is not a *forum conveniens* discretion: '[T]he question: "which court would be the more convenient or the more appropriate?" does not arise'.[138] A stay should be granted, in order to avoid irreconcilable judgments. Indeed, Articles 27 and 28 always give priority to the court first seised.[139]

Does Brussels I (and Articles 27 and 28 Brussels I) apply in the context of EU competition law proceedings before an NCA that seeks to establish an infringement of Article 101 and/or Article 102 TFEU?[140] It should be noted that the provision of Article 1 of Brussels I is somewhat widely drafted, and there are strong arguments suggesting that proceedings seeking to establish an EU competition law infringement before an NCA that is an admin-

[134] See more: Danov (n 8).

[135] *Gubisch Maschinen-fabrik v Palumbo* [1987] ECR 4861 [8].

[136] Latin for 'a pending lawsuit'. See also C McLachlan, 'Lis Pendens', in *International Litigation* (Leiden/Boston, Martinus Nijhoff Publishers, 2009).

[137] Case C-116/02 *Erich Gasser v MISAT* [2003] ECR I-14693 [42] and [54]. See for criticism of this ruling, TC Hartley, 'The European Union and the Systematic Dismantling of the Common Law of Conflict of Laws' (2005) 54 *ICLQ* 813, 820–21.

[138] *The 'Linda'* [1988] 1 Lloyd's Rep 175, QBD (Admlty) 179 (Sheen J).

[139] P Herzog, 'Brussels or Lugano, Should you race to the Courthouse or race for a judgement?' (1995) 43 *American Journal of Comparative Law* 379, 381–84.

[140] Danov (n 8).

istrative public authority are to be regarded as falling within the scope of Brussels I. It has been submitted that Brussels I 'also applies to civil or commercial matters brought before administrative tribunals'.[141] The Jenard[142] and Schlosser[143] reports seem to suggest that the question as to which set of procedural rules (ie administrative or civil) is applied does not arise when determining the scope of Brussels I. Neither set is relevant if the action is between a public authority and a person governed by private law.[144] A broader interpretation of the scope of Brussels I has already been adopted by the Court of Justice[145] in the context of Article 1 of the Regulation. Therefore, in order to determine whether proceedings before an NCA are to be regarded as falling within the scope of Brussels I an important factor would be whether the designated authority, having 'judicial characteristics',[146] is exercising judicial functions in a 'civil and commercial matter'.[147] In this context, it should be noted that, despite the fact that Articles 101 and 102 TFEU are meant to protect important public interests by maintaining the process of competition, it is well established that 'these provisions regulate the behaviour of private undertakings'.[148] If an EU competition law claim brought before national courts in order to establish an Article 101/102 infringement is regarded as a 'civil and commercial matter' for the purposes of Brussels I,[149] then there is no reason to suggest that the matter would be regarded differently only because the proceedings were brought before an NCA that is an administrative body.

In other words, for the purposes of Brussels I, the question would not be whether the action is pending before a court (or whether the action is pending before an administrative body), but rather what is the subject matter of the proceedings and whether the proceedings relate to civil and commercial matters. Therefore, Article 1 of Brussels I read together with the Jenard and Schlosser Reports leaves no doubt that the context in which the proceedings before an NCA are brought would be more important than the constitutional status of the public authority before which the proceedings are brought. Following this line of reasoning it can be argued that proceedings before NCAs should be regarded as within the scope of Brussels I as long as an NCA is exercising judicial functions in civil and commercial matters.

The test would not be satisfied and an NCA decision, or part of one, imposing fines on an undertaking that has infringed Articles 101 and 102 TFEU, would not be within the scope of Brussels I. This would be so because in those proceedings an NCA could not be regarded as exercising judicial functions in civil and commercial matters. Nevertheless, the test would be satisfied and the proceedings would be within the scope of Brussels I if an NCA seeks to determine whether an undertaking (or undertakings) committed an infringement of Articles 101 and 102 TFEU. Similarly, a decision (or part of a decision) of an NCA that establishes an infringement of Articles 101 and 102 TFEU should be within the scope of Brussels I. Such an interpretation would be consistent with the fact that the EU legislator

[141] Jenard Report OJ [1979] C59/1, 9; Schlosser Report OJ [1979] C59/71 [23].
[142] Jenard Report (n 141) 9.
[143] Schlosser Report (n 141) [23].
[144] *Eurocontrol* (n 10) [4].
[145] ibid.
[146] Case C-53/03 *Synetairismos Farmakopion Aitolias & Akarnanis (Syfait) v GlaxoSmithKline* [2005] ECR I–4609, Opinion of AG Jacobs [45].
[147] *cf Eurocontrol* (n 10[4].
[148] A Albors-Llorens, 'Consumer Law, Competition Law and the Europeanization of Private Law' in F Cafaggi (ed), *The Institutional Framework of European Private Law* (Oxford, OUP, 2006) 244, 260.
[149] See Danov (n 8).

seems to consider the adoption of a rule to the effect that a Member State court cannot take decisions running counter to a final decision of an NCA finding an infringement of Articles 101 and 102 TFEU.[150]

However, one might object to the deduction that an NCA final decision, or part of one, establishing an infringement of Articles 101 and 102 TFEU should be within the scope of Brussels I by pointing out that the right to a fair trial of an allegedly infringing undertaking might be undermined in the course of proceedings before NCAs. In particular, Article 6(1) ECHR states that 'In the determination of his civil rights and obligations . . . everyone is entitled to a fair and public hearing within a reasonable time by an independent and impartial tribunal established by law.' It is well established that Article 6(1) ECHR requires that, in the determination of civil rights and obligations, decisions taken by administrative authorities should be subject to a judicial body that has full jurisdiction.[151] Similar requirements would have to be satisfied with regard to decisions taken by NCAs.[152] These requirements seem to suggest that the recognition of an NCA decision (or part of a decision) would potentially have to overcome a public policy defence that could be based on the breach of the undertaking's right to fair trial and hearing in administrative proceedings.[153] This might be particularly difficult in cases where such decisions were taken by NCAs that are administrative bodies, combining the functions of a party to competition law proceedings and a judge.[154] In other words, the fact that Article 34(1) and (2) of Brussels I would allow for a national court to refuse the recognition of a decision taken by an NCA that does not respect due process rules in its adoption[155] may be seen as just another argument suggesting that an NCA final decision (or part of one) establishing an infringement of Articles 101 and 102 TFEU should be within the scope of Brussels I.

A broader interpretation of Brussels I would further uphold the independence of national courts, safeguarding the defendant's right to a fair trial. This would be particularly important in view of the White Paper's proposal for the adoption of a rule to the effect that a Member State court cannot take decisions running counter to a final decision of an NCA finding an infringement of Articles 101 and 102 TFEU. However, it is far from certain if such a broad interpretation would be adopted by the courts. Given the importance of the matter legislative intervention is recommended. Before making any proposals, nonetheless, it would be useful to see how Articles 27 and 28 would work with regard to cross-border EU competition law actions.

[150] White Paper (n 125) [2.3].

[151] *Le Compte v Belgium* (1982) 4 EHRR 1. See also WPJ Wils, *Principles of European Antitrust Enforcement* (Oxford, Hart Publishing, 2005) 46–47; IS Forrester, 'Due Process in EC Competition Cases: A Distinguished Institution with Flawed Procedures' (2009) 34 *EL Rev* 817, 821; R Nazzini, 'Administrative Enforcement: Judicial Review and Fundamental Rights in EU Competition Law: A comparative contextual-functionalist perspective' (2012) 49 *CML Rev* 971, 1005.

[152] Wils (n 151) 47; Forrester (n 151) 821.

[153] Art 34(1) and (2) of Brussels I. See more: Danov (n 8).

[154] Wils (n 151) 88.

[155] See Case C-7/98 *Krombach v Bamberski* [2000] ECR I–1395. See also J Fawcett, 'The Impact of Article 6(1) of the ECHR on Private International Law' (2007) 56 *ICLQ* 1; P Beaumont and E Johnston, 'Can *Exequatur* Be Abolished in Brussels I Whilst Retaining a Public Policy Defence?' (2010) 6 *Journal of Private International Law* 249.

B. Article 27 and its Application in Cross-Border EU Competition Law Actions

The effect of Article 27 of Brussels I is that any court other than the court first seised must, depending on the circumstances, either stay its proceedings or decline jurisdiction. One condition that could cause particular problems in connection with antitrust claims is to do with the requirement that 'proceedings [are] to be brought before the *courts* of different Member States'. It should be noted that the Court of Justice has held that Article 27 of Brussels I requires the parallel proceedings to involve three elements: the proceedings must have the same subject-matter (or the same object), as well as the same cause of action and the same parties.[156] In view of that it seems that the phrase 'same cause of action' in Article 27 should be regarded as a European concept which is not to be interpreted according to the criteria of national law.[157]

The provision was recently invoked in *Cooper Tire*. In this case, there were two sets of proceedings, involving not one claimant and one defendant, but several groups of companies on each side. The parallel EU competition law actions were preceded by a Commission decision[158] which established an infringement of EU competition law. Enichem commenced court proceedings in Italy against 28 defendants – tyre manufacturers – companies in the Pirelli, Michelin, Continental, Goodyear, Bridgestone and Cooper groups.[159] Enichem claimed that the cartel had no effect on the price of Butadiene Rubber ('BR') and Emulsion Styrene Butadiene Rubber (ESBR), and, as a result, the defendants suffered no damages. The parallel court proceedings in England were commenced a few months later by 26 companies of the same group of tyre manufacturers against 23 defendants, all of which were producers and sellers of BR and ESBR. The claimants sought damages from the producers and sellers in question for EU competition law infringements.

The facts of the case clearly illustrate the complex and specific issues which arise in the context of parallel cross-border EU competition law proceedings. In particular, the 'same parties' requirement would give rise to specific difficulties in EU competition law cases that could involve different companies from the different groups of companies liable for the EU competition law infringement which could be regarded as joint tortfeasors. In this context, Mr Justice Teare observed:

> The Claimants in the English proceedings are in essence the same as the defendants in the Italian proceedings. There was no dispute that they could be regarded as the same parties. The difficulty arose with the Claimants in the Italian proceedings, Enichem, and the Defendants in the English proceedings, all the producers of BR and ESBR save Enichem. Debate was joined on the issue whether they were the same parties.[160]

After carefully considering the degree of identity between the parties, and their interests, the judge held that Enichem and the defendants in England were not the same parties. Thus, the application for a mandatory stay under Article 27 of Brussels I was rejected. *Cooper Tire* clearly demonstrates that the 'same parties' requirement would be difficult to

[156] *Gubisch* (n 135) [14].

[157] Briggs and Rees (n 35) 314; *Cheshire, North & Fawcett* (n 35) 305. See also: *Royal & Sun Alliance Insurance v MK Digital FZE (Cyprus)* [2005] EWHC 1408 (Comm) ILPr 51, QBD (Comm) [66]; (reversed without reference to this point) [2006] EWCA Civ 629; [2006] 2 Lloyd's Rep 110, CA.

[158] Case COMP/F/38.638 – *Butadiene Rubber and Emulsion Styrene Butadiene Rubber.*

[159] *Cooper Tire* [2009] (n 4, [68].

[160] *Cooper Tire* [2009] (n 4, [69].

satisfy in most competition scenarios.[161] For example, proceedings in England against a local subsidiary of a German manufacturing company would not affect proceedings in France against the local subsidiary of the same German manufacturing company. Similarly, proceedings in France as to the validity of an anti-competitive agreement between a company and its French distributor would have little effect on the proceedings against its German distributor in Germany on a virtually identical contract which is arguably in conflict with EU competition law. There is little doubt that German proceedings would not be stayed. Moreover, 'a judgment in France as to the validity of the agreement with one's French distributor will not have effect when suing its German distributor in Germany on a virtually identical contract.'[162]

Nor would the 'same parties' requirement of Article 27 of Brussels I be satisfied in a case where there were court proceedings for enforcement of an allegedly anti-competitive contract in England, and administrative proceedings before the French competition authority, which were pending in respect of the same infringement resulting from the implementation by a dominant undertaking of the same allegedly illegal contract in France and England. The clamant, who might even have lodged the complaint before the French Competition Authority, would not be a party to the administrative proceedings in France, which would be conducted between the foreign NCA and the dominant undertaking.[163]

Thus, the question is: can parallel EU competition law proceedings be avoided by relying on Article 28?

C. Article 28 and its Application in Cross-Border EU Competition Law Actions

As already mentioned, Article 28 of Brussels I is designed to deal with those situations, which do not fall within the strict confines of Article 27 of Brussels I. In other words, if antitrust actions are not identical within the meaning of Article 27, but related, then Article 28 may be applied. The latter provision contains no requirement about the same cause of action or same parties in the two proceedings. The objective of Article 28 is to improve coordination of the exercise of judicial functions within the EU and to avoid conflicting and contradictory decisions,[164] thus facilitating the proper administration of justice in the EU.[165] In the context of cross-border EU competition law actions, Article 28 Brussels I could be an important provision which may be relied upon to promote the coherent and uniform application of Articles 101 and 102 TFEU. To this end, the court should determine two issues: are the antitrust actions related; and if so, whether to exercise its discretionary power?

Both issues were recently addressed by the court in *Cooper Tire* in which an application for a stay was put forward by the Dow and Bayer defendants. In this case, the court clearly

[161] Danov (n 3).

[162] V Korah, *An Introductory Guide to EC Competition Law and Practice,* 9th edn (Oxford, Hart Publishing, 2007) 221. See also: J Bourgeois and C Humpe, 'The Commission's Draft "New Regulation 17"' (2002) 23 *ECLR* 43, 46–47; Brammer (n 9) 27.

[163] See *Enron Coal Services Ltd (in liquidation) v English Welsh & Scottish Railway Ltd* [2011] EWCA Civ 2, [2011] UKCLR 303 [150].

[164] Case C-406/92 *Tatry* [1994] ECR I-5439 [32], [52]; see also [28] (AG Tesauro).

[165] *Sarrio v Kuwait Investment Authority* [1999] 1 AC 32, HL, 39 (Lord Saville). See also: A Briggs, 'Private International Law' (1997) *British Yearbook of International Law* 331, 339–42; J Harris, 'Related Actions and the Brussels Convention' (1998) *Lloyd's Maritime and Commercial Law Quarterly* 145.

established that a claim, brought by a cartel member in Italy for a declaration that no damage was caused by the cartel, and a claim for EU competition damages in England against some cartel members, 'cover the same ground . . . save that the Italian court is not asked to assess the quantum of damage suffered by each purchaser of BR and ESBR.'[166] In view of that, the court held that 'the extent of relatedness and the risk of inconsistent decisions is substantial'[167] since the English and Italian courts were considering broadly the same question.[168] Having affirmatively replied to the first question as to EU competition law actions being related, the judge went on to consider whether the court should exercise its discretion. Although some defendants had submitted to the jurisdiction of the English courts and made no application for a stay, Mr Justice Teare accepted that the English court was entitled to stay the proceedings in accordance with the objectives of Articles 27 and 28 Brussels I. However, he stated:

> 111. It seems to me that a particularly good reason would be required to justify a stay in such circumstances [i.e. some defendants submitted to the jurisdiction and made no application for a stay] and the Defendants in question would surely be entitled to be heard on the question. I do not consider that there is such a reason in circumstances where the Italian Court has dismissed the proceedings before it and accordingly (a) the prospect of a decision on the merits in Italy is contingent upon a successful appeal in Italy and (b) the English Court will ultimately have to exercise its own jurisdiction.
>
> 112. The stage reached in England is that the proceedings have been commenced and Particulars of Claim have been served. In Italy, the proceedings have been commenced but have been dismissed at first instance on jurisdictional and other grounds without consideration of the merits. The decision at first instance is now under appeal. If the appeal succeeds the Italian Court of Appeal will determine the merits.
>
> 114. . . . It is agreed that a decision on the merits in Italy is not likely until September 2013–2014 . . .[169]

The reading of the decision clearly show that the stage which the proceedings had reached, as well as the potential delay of the Italian courts, were significant factors that were taken into account by the judge in exercising his discretion.[170] Was the judge wrong to factor in the time necessary for the Italian court to render a decision in Italy? Lord Justice Longmore, sitting in the Court of Appeal, held the delay might indeed be an important factor to be taken account by the court when exercising its discretionary power pursuant to Article28 Brussels I. In particular, the judge stated:

> 54. The only substantive argument of Mr Rabinowitz which needs to be addressed is his submission that the judge was wrong to take into account the time when a decision was likely to be reached, in considering the stage which the proceedings had reached at the time of the application to the English court. He submitted that the judge was impliedly criticising the Italian court system by saying that it was unlikely a decision would be reached until September 2012. (In fact we now know that the next hearing in the appeal on the outright dismissal of the claim will not occur until January 2014).

[166] *Cooper Tire* [2009] (n 4) [81].
[167] ibid [106].
[168] ibid [106].
[169] ibid [111], [112] and [114].
[170] ibid [117]–[118].

> 55. But there is no such implied criticism. The fact that it may take different periods of time for similar proceedings to come to a conclusion in different jurisdictions, for whatever reasons, is not a criticism; it is merely a fact of life to which a judge cannot be expected to close his eyes.[171]

Indeed, by taking account of the delay factor when exercising his discretion, the judge successfully defeated the 'forum shopping' activities which Enichem was possibly engaging in. It is well established that a plaintiff who intends to delay settlement of a future substantive antitrust law dispute may deliberately commence pre-emptive proceedings before a court that is not appropriately placed to deal with an EU competition law case.[172] This was noted by some of the commentators, who submitted that:

> The discretionary nature of [Article 28] limits the risk of proceedings being delayed by torpedoes, as the courts second seised of related (but not identical) actions can always choose to proceed with those actions.[173]

Does this really solve the problem? Although under the current framework the court can choose not to stay its proceeding by exercising its discretionary power to proceed with the action, this is not an entirely satisfactory solution. The claimants in the English proceedings would remain defendants in the Italian proceedings. As a result, the litigants would incur even higher litigation costs with regard to the two sets of proceedings, which might be a disincentive for companies to bring such actions. The risk of irreconcilable judgments would remain. As a result, complex issues may arise at the recognition and enforcement stage[174] – the question '[w]hether joint tortfeasors have a sufficient privity of interest that might lead to the application of *res judicata* is not the subject of clear authority.'[175] Under the current regime, however, the Italian court could not stay its proceedings. A better solution would have been achieved if any court (no matter whether first seised or second seised) were entitled to stay its proceedings or decline jurisdiction should there be a more appropriate forum.[176]

The case for a reform with regard to cross-border EU competition law actions may be further strengthened by pointing out that particular difficulties could arise in cases where competition law proceedings were brought before a foreign NCA and private proceedings with respect to the same infringement were brought before an English court.[177] Even if NCAs (being bodies exercising judicial functions in civil and commercial matters) were regarded as 'courts' within the meaning of Article 28 of Brussels I, the question would remain whether NCAs should exercise their discretion to stay their proceedings or indeed decline jurisdiction. In some cases, such discretion could well be exercised as long as the allegedly anti-competitive practice had affected the competition within the market where the court seised was located, which would make such a court well placed to hear and determine an EU competition law claim. This can be justified by two main arguments.

[171] ibid [54]–[55].

[172] *Gasser* (n 137) (Opinion of AG Philip Leger) [68]. *cf Cooper Tire* [2010] (n 4). See also Hartley (n 112); P de Vareilles-Sommieres (ed), *Forum Shopping in the European Judicial Area* (Oxford, Hart Publishing, 2007); Danov (n 3).

[173] C Slothers, M Gardner and S Hinchliffe, 'Forum Shopping and "Italian Torpedoes" in Competition Litigation in the English Courts' (2011) *Global Competition Litigation Review* 67, 69.

[174] See Pt V of this book.

[175] *Cooper Tire* [2009] (n 4) [80].

[176] Danov (n 3). See also Wilderspin (n 25) 59.

[177] Danov (n 8).

First, a judicial decision presupposes respect for the right to a fair trial and a fair hearing, something that is far from guaranteed in respect of decisions taken by NCAs, which are administrative bodies combining the function of a party to competition law proceedings and a judge. If decisions of such NCAs are considered to be compatible with Article 6(1) ECHR only if subject to full review by a judicial body, then it can be argued that the right to fair trial would only be guaranteed if the court had actually reviewed the decision.[178] Following this line of reasoning, one could go a step further and say that an NCA should normally exercise its discretion and stay its proceedings in favour of the court seised with the related EU competition law dispute because the court would be able to guarantee adversarial proceedings. This deduction can be further strengthened by noting that the independence of NCAs can be questioned.[179]

Secondly, the submission that an NCA should normally exercise its discretion and stay its proceedings in favour of the court seised with the related EU competition law dispute can be further justified by pointing out that national courts would be able to establish that there was an infringement of Articles 101 and 102 TFEU, as well as being entitled to award damages[180] that would rectify the harm caused by the breach of EU competition law.[181] In other words, the fact that '[p]rivate actions ensure compensation for those harmed by anti-competitive conduct'[182] may be seen by NCAs as an important factor in favour of staying their proceedings or declining jurisdiction. Therefore, in many cases, the national courts may be better suited than the Member States' NCAs to establish an infringement of EU competition law. The possibility for an NCA to stay its proceedings would raise the question of whether the foreign NCA in question could be relied upon to take evidence in support of private proceedings in England.[183] This would be an important issue, which indicates that if the Commission wishes to create mechanisms to improve the legal conditions for EU antitrust claimants to get full compensation for suffered damages[184] as well as to promote the right to defence of allegedly infringing undertakings further, then it might consider setting up a Notice on the cooperation between NCAs and Member State courts.[185] Such a Notice might clearly outline that an NCA can carry out any inspection or other fact-finding measure under its national law on the request of a court of another Member State. This would be an important legislative development, which would have significant implications for cases in which an NCA decides to stay its proceedings in favour of a court seised with a related EU competition law dispute.

[178] Wils (n 151), 89. See more: Forrester (n 151); Nazzini (n 151).

[179] Wils (n 151) 90. See Arts 11(4) and (6). *cf.* Art 15 of Regulation 1/2003; Art 6(1) TEU. See also: Art 6(1) ECHR and Art 47(2) of the Charter of Fundamental Rights of the European Union [2000] OJ C364/1. See also Nazzini (n 151) 1005.

[180] Commission Staff Working Paper, *Annex to the Green Paper, Damages Actions for Breach of the EC Antitrust Rules* SEC(2005) 1732, para 8.

[181] J Basedow (ed), *Private Enforcement of EC Competition Law* (Kluwer, 2007) 1–2; A Komninos, *EC Private Antitrust Enforcement: Decentralised Application of EC Competition Law by National Courts* (Oxford, Hart Publishing, 2008) 7–8.

[182] Komninos (n 181) 8.

[183] *cf.* Council Regulation (EC) No 1206/2001 of 28 May 2001 on cooperation between the courts of the member states in the taking of evidence in civil or commercial matters [2001] OJ L174/1 (Evidence Regulation). See Danov (n 8).

[184] White Paper (n 125) [1.2].

[185] Danov (n 8).

In other cases, however, the various leniency programmes adopted by the Member States' competition authorities[186] may be seen as a strong factor suggesting that, in some cases, an NCA may decide not to stay their proceedings (or decline jurisdiction). Indeed, it could be argued that in some cases the competition authorities' leniency programmes would provide stronger incentives for infringing undertakings to cooperate in order for a breach of EU competition law to be established, so that an English court might decide to stay its proceedings and await the decision of a foreign NCA that might be better placed to deal with the case. Accordingly, there may well be cases in which the NCAs would be better suited than the national courts to establish an infringement of EU competition law.

Further difficulties would arise if a Member State court is given a discretionary power to stay their proceedings in favour of a foreign NCA that could be more appropriate or better placed to determine whether there was an infringement of EU competition law, as this would raise the question of the recognition and enforcement of a foreign NCA decision in England. The White Paper on modernisation seems to indicate that an NCA decision is enforceable only within the territory on which the authority in question operates.[187] The issue of the recognition and enforcement of decisions taken by NCAs is left out of Regulation 1/2003.[188] Nevertheless, there are strong arguments suggesting that a foreign NCA decision could be recognised by the OFT or another NCA if a request were made by the Member State that adopted the decision.[189] But would they be recognised by the courts in the context of cross-border private antitrust proceedings? Can NCA decisions be recognised and enforced under Brussels I? Are decisions of NCAs within the scope of the Brussels I Regulation?[190] All these specific competition law issues seemingly require specific attention by the EU legislator.

IV. WAYS FORWARD: PROPOSED SOLUTIONS TO THE IDENTIFIED SPECIFIC PROBLEMS

Given the fact that in the new Proposal for a Regulation on Jurisdiction and the Recognition and Enforcement of Judgments[191] there is no indication that special rules for parallel EU competition law proceedings in the successor to Regulation 44/2001 are on anyone's agenda, another possibility for reform might be amending Regulation 1/2003 to address the issues of jurisdiction in cross-border EU competition law cases as well as the problem of parallel EU competition law proceedings in order to avoid irreconcilable or inconsistent decisions in the European context. Although it would be difficult to elaborate a special

[186] See U Boge, 'Leniency Programs and the Private Enforcement of European Competition Law' in Basedow (n 156) 217, 218.

[187] White Paper (n 128) [60]. See Komninos (n 181) 77; Brammer (n 9) 426–36.

[188] It has been submitted that 'Article 10 EC [now Art 4(3) TEU], while not requiring Member States to automatically and mutually recognise the legal force of all decisions which are adopted to implement Article 81 or 82 EC [now Arts 101 and 102 TFEU], can certainly be construed in such a way as to impose a duty on Member States to recognise the validity of foreign NCA decisions on a case-by-case basis. This means that recognition would take place only when a request is made by the Member State which adopted the decision and only by the NCA of the Member State to which the request is submitted' (Brammer (n 9) 428–29). Even if this interpretation were correct, the effect of such recognition would be somewhat limited, as the foreign NCA would only be recognised by the local NCA being part of the same ECN. See more: Danov (n 8).

[189] ibid.

[190] See more: Danov (n 8).

[191] COM(2010) 748 final.

basis for jurisdiction which requires a substantial connection between the breach of Articles 101 and 102 TFEU and effects of the anti-competitive agreement or conduct within the territory of the Member State where the action is brought and in respect of which the EU antitrust law claim is brought,[192] there is a need for a jurisdiction rule which allows a claimant to centralise litigation against a group of the same companies before the courts at his preferred jurisdiction. Where, for example, there is a corporate group with numerous subsidiaries (all of whom form a single infringing undertaking), then it should be open for a claimant by establishing jurisdiction against one of the subsidiaries to centralise litigation against the whole group of companies as well as against the other group/s of companies who were party to the same anti-competitive agreement. This could be justified by the fact that EU competition law infringements would often directly and substantially affect the markets in several countries and/or regions.

In order to allow the parties to avoid parallel EU competition law proceedings, and centralise litigation before the court that is clearly appropriate to deal with the case, avoiding the problem of irreconcilable or inconsistent judgments, Regulation 1/2003 should go a step further and allow the court (or NCA) first seised to stay their proceedings, in cases where the agreement or practice has no substantial direct effects (whether actual or foreseeable) on competition within the Member State and where another court is better placed to deal with the case.[193] Such an approach would be better suited to deal with the difficulties that could arise in parallel court proceedings as well as with the problems arising in proceedings before an NCA located in one Member State and private proceedings related to the same infringement of Article 101 and/or Article 102 before another Member State court.[194] Although such a rule could work well in theory, the proposed solution in practice may bring even more uncertainty unless the architecture of the European judiciary is reconsidered by the EU legislator.

Indeed, a discretionary power without devising an appropriate institutional architecture would bring fresh uncertainty. This would be particularly so in cross-border EU competition law actions. The difficulties and the multiplicity of fora that will have a connection with the dispute and the alleged EU competition law infringement can be best illustrated by referring to the opinion of Mr Justice Teare in *Cooper Tire*:

> As to the 'proximity' of the English and Italian courts to the case it can be said that there is a significant connection with Italy because Enichem, an alleged key player in the cartel, is domiciled in Italy whilst the connections with England are slight. However, the connections with Italy are not such as to place the centre of gravity of the case in Italy. The cartelists were variously domiciled in Germany, the Netherlands, Italy, the Czech Republic, Switzerland and Poland. None was domiciled in England, though there were three subsidiaries in England and Enichem has two factories in England. The purchasers of BR and ESBR were companies in the Pirelli, Michelin, Continental, Goodyear, Bridgestone and Cooper groups who are registered in several countries including England, Italy, Germany, France, Belgium, Slovakia, the Czech Republic, Sweden, Portugal, Spain, Greece, Hungary and Poland. The meetings at which the cartel was agreed took place in Milan, Vienna, Amsterdam, Brussels, Richmond-on-Thames, Frankfurt, Grosse Leder, and Prague. The cartel was ended at a meeting in London. The tort alleged by the Claimants and as found by the Commission was, as submitted by the Claimants, a Europe-wide tort which crossed

[192] Danov (n 3).

[193] *cf* the European approach in respect of allocation of cases between the NCAs. See the Commission Commission Notice on Cooperation within the Network of Competition Authorities [2004] OJ C101/43 [8]. See further Danov (n 3) 281–83.

[194] Basedow (n 181) 1–2; Komninos (n 181) 7–8. See more: Danov (n 8).

> borders and was linked to numerous jurisdictions. I do not consider that 'proximity' with Italy is a significant factor in this case.[195]

Thus, it may be difficult to identify an appropriate court in Europe unless there are clear and objective criteria as to how the discretion could be best exercised. The specific issues arising with regard to EU competition law actions in the European context may need to be addressed by the EU legislator in a revised version of Regulation 1/2003.

The institutional architecture, however, is not a competition specific concern, and needs to be examined in a wider cross-border context in Europe.[196] Such a wider institutional reform might need to consider the role of the EU courts. The need for such a reform, which is now imminent, was first signalled by a Report by the Working Party on the Future of the European Communities' Court System.[197] The report clearly stated that 'the Working Party considers that preliminary questions concerning judicial cooperation should be withdrawn from the Court of Justice and assigned to a Community court with members drawn from specialist private international lawyers.'[198] Similarly, Hill has submitted that: 'The suggestion that, within the ECJ, there should be established a specialist chamber (of PIL experts) to deal with references under the Brussels I Regulation (and other PIL instruments) has been knocking around for well over 30 years. Such reform is seriously overdue.'[199] The current institutional architecture might need to be reviewed in order to address the issue of the uniform interpretation and application of the private international mechanisms across Europe.

[195] *Cooper Tire* [2009] (n 4) [115].

[196] See B Hess, 'The Brussels I Regulation: Recent case law of the Court of Justice and the Commission's proposed recast' (2012) 49 *CML Rev* 1075, 1112.

[197] 'Report by the Working Party on the Future of the European Communities' Court System' (Working Party for the European Commission, January 2000), 34–35, http://ec.europa.eu/dgs/legal_service/pdf/due_en.pdf.

[198] ibid 33.

[199] J Hill, 'Comments on the Review of the Brussels I Regulation', http://conflictoflaws.net/2009/brussels-i-review-jonathan-hill/.

14

Mastering *Masterfoods*: Food For Thought On Staying Civil Damages Litigation Pending Appeals Before The European Courts

PIERRE VF BOS AND JOOST A MÖHLMANN*

I. STARTER: DO NATIONAL COURTS HAVE AN EUROPEAN DILEMMA?

Nowadays national courts may be faced in follow-on damages litigation with the question of whether or not to continue the case pending an appeal of the European Commission's decision. There would be a risk that the material significance of a European Commission's decision in such damages litigation would be reduced to zero, should a stay be ordered. This applies too to a subsequent judgment by the General Court if an appeal is made to the European Court of Justice. It is submitted that staying damages litigation pending an appeal to the European Courts is incompatible with European Union law, and denies the significance and binding force of a decision of the European Commission or a judgment of the General Court. Also, it is submitted that a staying order is incompatible with the requirements for due process according to national procedural law. Should a national court stay a damages litigation decision until the decision of the European Commission, or a ruling given on it by a European Court has become final and binding, that national court postpones the adjudication of that case for several years. As a result, the interests of plaintiffs in the conclusion of the proceedings within a reasonable time would be seriously harmed. This may constitute, possibly unintentionally, a strong and discouraging message to parties injured by cartels that they have a very long process in civil proceedings before compensation for their damages can be granted. It creates unjustifiable exceptionally favourable treatment for the cartel members which – unlike defendants sued before a national court for unlawful conduct – have been provided a windfall of not having to account for themselves before a civil court for years as long as a legal remedy is available against the European Commission or General Court's decision. This is aggravated by the fact that over those years the claims of many parties injured by the members of the cartel at hand may actually become time-barred. This chapter's objective is to explore whether national courts have a dilemma, in that they should temporarily halt civil damages litigation pending an appeal before a European Court. It is submitted that they should not have such a dilemma and in most, if not all circumstances, deny a motion to stay.

* All opinions are personal and may not be attributed to current or future clients.

II. ENTREE: *MASTERFOODS* AND ITS LIMITED MEANING

In its judgment of 14 December 2000 (Case C-344/98 *Masterfoods*[1]), the European Court of Justice held that a national court is prevented under European Union law from taking a decision that contradicts a not yet irrevocable decision of the European Commission in a competition matter. *Masterfoods* requires loyalty from national authorities as regards competition policy pursued by the European Commission. It is submitted that only in the case where the national court doubts the validity of the decision – and for that reason would want to decide contrary to it, which however is not permitted in view of its loyalty obligation – does *Masterfoods* allow a national court to suspend its decision in order to see whether the decision will be upheld by the General Court or the European Court of Justice. Such doubt can by definition only develop, if a national court has actually been able to examine the decision at hand and has heard a debate on the European Commission decision between the litigants. Should a decision not have been published due to lack of agreement between the interested parties (ie the addressees of the cartel) and the European Commission (ie the Hearing Officer), then the court should not entertain a request to stay. This not only follows from the fact that a stay is only regarded as legitimate for a national court which disagrees with the European Commission, but is not allowed to articulate this in a ruling of its own. It also follows from the fact that a national court which does not have such doubts about the validity of the decision can just continue with the proceedings and decide the case in accordance with the European Commission's decision, even though there is an appeal pending against the Commission's decision. The European Court of Justice in *Masterfoods* considered that:

> 47 . . . On the other hand it [ie the European Commission] has exclusive competence to apply Articles 85(1) and 86 of the [EC] Treaty with the national courts . . . The latter provisions produce direct effects in relations between individuals and create direct rights in respect of the individuals concerned which the national courts must safeguard . . . They [ie *the national courts] thus continue to have jurisdiction* to apply the provisions of Articles 85(1) and 86 of the Treaty even after the Commission has initiated proceedings in application of Articles 2, 3 or 6 of Regulation No 17 . . .
>
> 52 It is even more important that when national courts rule on agreements or practices which are already the subject of a decision by the Commission, they cannot take decisions *running counter* to that of the Commission . . .
>
> 53 The fact that the president of the Court of First Instance suspended the application of Decision 98/531 until the Court of First Instance has given judgment terminating the proceedings before it is irrelevant. *Acts of the Community institutions are in principle presumed to be lawful until such time as they are annulled or withdrawn.*[2]

In his opinion[3] preceding the *Masterfoods* judgment, Advocate-General Cosmas also confirmed that a pending European appeal procedure against a decision does not prevent a national court from giving a judgment in accordance with this decision, before the decision in appeal is reviewed as to its validity. The national court is not required to stay its decision until it has been established in European proceedings that the decision retains its validity:

[1] Case C-344/98 *Masterfoods v HB Ice Cream* [2000] ECR I-11369
[2] ibid [47], [52] and [53] (emphasis added).
[3] ibid, Opinion of Advocate-General Cosmas, dated 16 May 2000.

Having stated that the [Irish] Supreme Court based on the interpretation of the Court of Justice with regard to the second and third questions referred for a preliminary ruling, considers that the decision of the High Court, in view of the facts it was to examine, was not legally correct because of a wrong interpretation and/or application of Articles 85(1) and 86 of the Treaty. In that case the decision in the first instance shall be annulled and have no further legal consequences. The conflict between this decision and the decision of the Commission shall then no longer exist.

If the principal action pending before the Supreme Court ends with the finding that the decision in the first instance is defective and with annulment of the final order in dispute in favour of HB, *the referring court can in my view resolve the case without having to know whether or not decision 98/531 is valid* and without running the risk that he is giving a ruling that contravenes the decision of the European Commission.[4]

A decision of the European Commission therefore has material significance in civil litigation, and its binding force must be respected by the national court. Apart from the case in which the court doubts the validity of the decision and must therefore stay its decision, *Masterfoods* makes it clear that the decision must simply be applied in civil proceedings and (notwithstanding an appeal brought against it) may form the basis for a decision by the national court. By staying its case pending a European appeal, a court however reduces to zero the material relevance of the decision of the European Commission for these proceedings. The European Court of Justice allows national courts (even the highest national courts) to decide the case in accordance with a Commission decision – notwithstanding an appeal brought against it. A court staying its proceedings would reduce the effect of a European Commission decision by departing from the *Masterfoods* criteria, and would act in contravention of the loyalty demanded of it. The most recent, authoritative analysis of the *Masterfoods* doctrine was given on 26 June 2012 by Advocate-General Cruz-Villalon, in a case on the elevator cartel.[5] This case focused on two questions referred for a preliminary ruling, ie whether the European Commission may represent the European Union in law, and whether the fact that as a civil party to the proceedings it can draw support from its own decisions relating to a cartel is consistent with the principles of fair proceedings and equality of arms as referred to in Article 6 ECHR. Both questions are answered in the affirmative by the Advocate-General. The Advocate-General had the following to say about *Masterfoods* (emphasis added):

46. In the *Masterfoods* judgment the Court of Justice had the opportunity to define the scope of the decisions given by the Commission pursuant to Article 81(1) EC. The content of that judgment was then taken over into Article 16 of Regulation No. 1/2003 on the implementation of the rules on competition. Very briefly that judgment and this provision impose on all national authorities, including the judge, *the obligation not to take decisions that conflict with a decision of the Commission* that is established pursuant to Article 81 EC. *The decisions given by the Commission pursuant to these provisions are in other words binding on the national judge.*

47. In the *Masterfoods* judgment no answer was in fact given to the important questions that could considerably help in determining the extent to which the decisions of the Commission are binding in competition cases. It is not at all clear whether these consequences apply for the operative part of the decision or for its whole content, including the actual assessments. In the hearing, after a question from the Court of Justice the Commission commented that not all the parts of its decisions are binding on government entities, but it did not specify which parts this concerned. *Be*

[4] ibid, Opinion of Advocate-General Cosmas dated 16 May 2000 (emphasis added).

[5] Opinion of Advocate-General Cruz Villalon from 26 June 2012 in Case C-199/11 *Europese Gemeenschap v Otis NV and Others*. See also: Judgment of Grand Chamber of 5 November 2012.

that as it may – where important in this case – it seems beyond dispute that the finding of unlawful conduct reached in the decision is in any case binding for the national judge. This finding forms the basis for liability claims for damages due to unlawful conduct existing in the national legal systems, for which reason among other things it is required that there are damages due to unlawful conduct.

48. . . .

49. *Firstly the national judge is not competent to declare the decision of the Commission inapplicable or to assess its validity,* not only because this was declared in the *Masterfoods* judgment, but also because established case law since the *Foto-Frost* case prohibits the national authorities from assessing the validity of the acts of the Union. It would affect the monopoly on the validity assessment that belongs to the Union judge, and only this judge, should a national judge in an action to obtain compensation call into question unlawful conduct previously established in the European Commission's decision. In this case the legal system of the Union grants the national judge the competence to refer to the Court of Justice a validity question for a preliminary ruling, so that the independence of the national judge as well as the unity and the coherence of the source of law system of the Union are safeguarded.

50. Furthermore the parties involved in the decision, in this case defendants in the main action, have always had the opportunity to bring an appeal for nullification to the General Court and in the last instance the Court of Justice. . .

51. After specifying these things it can therefore be commented that the national judge has various options when faced with a decision of the Commission within a civil claim for compensation.

52. *First of all* the national judge may, as already commented at point 47 of this opinion, refer a question on the validity of the action of the Commission for a preliminary ruling *if he doubts its legitimacy. In addition, if the decision has a specified addressee, that party must have disputed its validity* before the General Court. *In that case* the national judge can suspend the hearing of the case in anticipation of a final decision from the Union judge, as happened in this case. This is suggested in Article 16(1) of Regulation No. 1/2003, which provides that it is for the national judicial bodies to 'consider whether it is necessary to suspend their proceedings' if they can take 'decisions . . . that would conflict with a decision contemplated by the Commission in proceedings it has initiated'.[6] *Therefore when the court doubts the validity of the decision and in addition finds that this decision is the subject of proceedings before the Union judge, by suspending the hearing of the national case they can avoid the Union judge and the [national] judge making conflicting judgments.*[7]

53. This conclusion is not only offered because of the principle of legal certainty, but also because of the principle of loyal cooperation. In the *Masterfoods* judgment the Court of Justice has declared that '[w]hen the settlement of the dispute depends for the national judge on the validity of the decision of the Commission, . . . the obligation of loyal cooperation [means], that the national court, *so as not to take a decision that runs counter to the decision of the Commission,* stays the hearing of the case until a final decision of the Community judicial bodies on the appeal for nullification, unless he is of the opinion that in the given circumstances the Court of Justice is

[6] The Regulation in Art 16(1) seems to offer the national court the opportunity to stay proceedings where the European Commission is contemplating a decision. It makes sense for a national court to stay its own ruling until the European Commission has taken its decision, in order to avoid conflicting decisions. Because it is not clear from the wording that it would also justify a stay in the event that the decision has been taken, the Advocate-General uses the term 'suggested'.

[7] That would after all happen if the national court decided in accordance with the decision, and the European judge then invalidated the decision. If the national court has no doubt about the validity of the decision, there is theoretically of course always a possibility that in due course the European Court will annul the decision, but the mere existence of this possibility does not constitute a reason for staying the proceedings. The national court must itself doubt the validity of the decision, otherwise the requirements for staying proceedings under *Masterfoods* are not met.

> justified in referring a question on the validity of the decision of the Commission for a preliminary ruling . . .
>
> 54. In short, *the Court is bound by the finding of unlawful conduct in the decision of the Commission,* but this in no way means that the judicial review is limited and that parties have no access to a 'court'. On the contrary, the court must in this case establish and quantify the damage suffered by the Union, after having established the causal relationship. This requires a thorough and complicated assessment of a judicial nature.
>
> *If the court doubts the validity of the Commission's decision, it may* not call into question its content because the Union court has the review monopoly, but in circumstances like those of this case *shall always stay the hearing of the case* until the General Court or the Court of Justice confirms the validity of the decision.[8]

The Advocate-General makes it clear that a national court, precisely because it is bound by the decision, may only suspend proceedings if two cumulative conditions are met. First, the party addressed in the decision must have lodged a legal remedy against the decision with a European Court. Second, the national court must itself have doubts about the validity of the decision. There is no place for a stay if both conditions are not met. It may also be added that where these doubts by definition can only take root in response to an examination of the decision and of what the parties state about it in the debate between them, staying the proceedings even before the court has been able to examine the decision and even before the discussion between the parties in the principal action has started, is extremely premature. A further comment can be made that a mere summary of the grounds for appeal raised in European proceedings obviously is insufficient to raise such doubts, since these grounds themselves offer no indication of their chance of success. The fact that an annulment of a European Commission decision is claimed says nothing about the nature and scope, let alone the soundness, of the objections on which it is based. It is also possible for an appellant to claim an annulment on the basis of unsubstantiated grounds for appeal. A national court that follows *Masterfoods* cannot have doubts about the validity of the decision from the mere fact that a defendant party is claiming in an appeal the annulment of a decision of the European Commission.

III. BEYOND *MASTERFOODS*

A national court may also misunderstand in another way the binding force of a decision of the European Commission, and its significance for civil proceedings in those cases in which the court does not doubt the validity of the decision. It could do so by holding that a decision of the European Commission that is being contested before a European Court is by that token not yet final and conclusive. It could take the view that a discussion before a national court as to the grounds, pending the European appeal, would therefore in fact mean an exchange of suppositions and expectations of parties about the result of the proceedings before the European Court. It could find that in view of due-process requirements, defendants should not be required to conduct the debate in such a way. Such a misunderstanding would go beyond the limited meaning of *Masterfoods. Masterfoods* itself allows no misunderstanding about the binding force of the decision. At point 47 the

[8] *Otis NV* (n 5). Opinion of Advocate-General Cruz Villalon, 26 June 2012 (emphasis added)

European Court of Justice points out that the decisions of the Commission 'produce[s] direct effects in relations between individuals'. And at paragraph 53, the European Court of Justice added: 'Acts of the Community institutions are in principle presumed to be lawful until such time as they are annulled or withdrawn.' According to the European Court of Justice this is even the case if the enforcement of such decisions is (provisionally) suspended in the Community proceedings against such decisions. The fact that a national court would note that a European Commission decision 'is not yet final and conclusive' would illustrate that the national court had misunderstood these fundamental notions of European Union law. A European decision after all does not involve a sort of legal concept that only acquires binding legal force when it becomes final and conclusive. A European decision is a different type of legal concept, ie a legal act performed by a European institution that, based on rules and principles of European Union law is granted binding force *ab initio*, and until this is reversed in a European proceeding (by annulment or withdrawal). This view, based on Article 288 of the Treaty on the Functioning of the EU, is endorsed in legal literature: decisions which are addressed to an individual party, including the decisions of the European Commission directed at undertakings which infringe the European antitrust rules, may be submitted to a national court, which has an unqualified obligation to apply these as they contain European Union law with direct effect. Their application is not dependent on treaty infringement proceedings, and need not be postponed until these are finalised.[9] If this is not done, the most important aim of direct effect – ie safeguarding judicial protection of individuals' own claims – degenerates to an empty shell. The court would have lost sight of this aspect in a staying order, because such a ruling would have as a result that the defendants as members of a cartel, by bringing an appeal against a decision of the European Commission, would de facto be made immune for the duration of that appeal from having to answer for themselves in civil proceedings at a national level. It is not difficult to imagine such a (far-reaching) consequence of bringing the appeal as not being compatible with a system of effective remedies for injured parties against infringements of cartel law, which the Court of Justice also brings to the fore in many judgments (see eg *Courage v Crehan*[10] and *Manfredi*[11]).[12] A national court should not misunderstand all this under the pretext of a European Commission decision being 'not final and conclusive' by actually attributing such decision only a sort of 'provisional status'. It would ignore the fact that the binding force granted to that decision is in fact granted from the start and that it forms a sufficient basis for a continuation of the litigation. And as Advocate-General Cruz-Villalon commented in this respect in paragraph 47:

> Be that as it may – where important in this case – it seems beyond dispute that the conclusion reached in the finding of unlawful conduct is in any case binding for the national court. This finding forms the basis for the liability claims existing in the national legal systems for damages due to unlawful conduct.

[9] See in this sense M Verhoeven, 'De rechtstreekse werking van de communautaire beschikking' ('The direct effect of the Community decision'), *Ars Aequi*, 2008, 214–16; and JH Jans and M de Jong with their commentary on Court of Appeal of The Hague, judgment of 2 August 2001, *M&R* 2001, 95.

[10] Case C-453/99, *Courage Ltd v Crehan* [2001] ECR I-6297.

[11] Joined Cases C-295/04–C-298/04 *Manfredi v Lloyd Adriaticco* [2006] 5 CMLR 17.

[12] See also the usual press releases of the European Commission upon taking cartel decisions exhorting those harmed by cartels to initiate proceedings before national courts to demand compensation. Interestingly, the European Commission always insists that it follows from the case law of the European Court of Justice, as well as from Regulation 1/2003 that its decisions can be used as binding evidence in national courts.

Should a national court consider that the debate between litigants at that stage would in fact come down to an exchange of suppositions and expectations of parties about the result of the European proceedings, that surely would be incorrect. Defendants in a principal follow-on action are asked to answer the substantiated civil claim, which in particular rests on a binding decision of the European Commission. Only if that discussion between parties and examination of the decision would lead to the national court doubting the validity of the decision (i.e. that it would become convinced that the European Commission is wrong and that the decision will probably not survive the appeal brought against it) could there be a reason to stay the proceedings. This doubt may not be based on the mere fact that an appeal is pending; according to the opinion of Advocate-General Cruz-Villalon and *Masterfoods* itself, this must after all be a situation in which the national court takes a different view than the European Commission in its decision, but is not allowed to express it because of its loyalty, and therefore must stay the proceedings. A national court may also misunderstand the binding force of a decision of the European Commission and its significance for the civil proceedings, notwithstanding the appeal brought against it. It might reason along the following lines: the plaintiff wishes to enforce a damages claim as an injured party based on a decision of the European Commission; it asks in the first place for a declaratory ruling that the defendants have acted unlawfully by participating in the cartel and are to be held liable for the resulting damages (at a later stage in the litigation it will ask the court to quantify damages and order the defendant to compensate the plaintiff); the unlawfulness allegedly lies in the fact that the cartel has agreed prices by which the plaintiff as an injured party has paid too much for the products or services purchased over a number of years; the defendant asserts without being contradicted that it is applying for the complete annulment of that decision by a European Court; the plaintiff has not submitted any specific details from which it can be concluded that its claim as an injured party has nothing to do with the grounds of appeal of the defendant before the European Court; in view of the state of affairs at this juncture it must be considered that the ruling of a European Court on the specific nature, duration and scope of the defendant's participation in the cartel (and the soundness of the reasons given by the European Commission on these points) may be important in answering the question whether the defendant has acted unlawfully vis-à-vis the plaintiff as an injured party by participating in the cartel; after all, in answering this question it is not only important whether in a general sense the defendant has acted unlawfully towards injured parties by participating in the cartel, but also and above all what the defendant has done specifically in what periods, in what places and in what way relating to which services or goods and what possible consequences this may have had for the plaintiff as an injured party; the plaintiff on the other hand has insufficiently explained with respect to the contentions of the defendant that the ruling of the European Court on the appeal brought by the defendant is not important for the assessment of these points. Insofar as a national court faces a case like this and wants to say that a ruling of a European Court must be awaited and that the underlying European Commission's decision cannot serve as a starting point for continuing the debate between the parties, such an opinion is not correct, in view of the immediate binding legal force of the decision as discussed above. If a national court were to decide that only a final ruling by a European Court can offer a solid basis for continuing proceedings, it would ignore the fact that the decision itself constitutes in accordance with European Union law – according to the Court of Justice in *Masterfoods* – a solid basis and allows the national court to decide in accordance with the decision even if appeal proceedings are already underway before a

European Court. A national court's thinking that it is for a plaintiff to explain that the opinion of a European Court is not important for the assessment of the points made in the damages claim, and that a plaintiff may have failed to do so, is based on the same incorrect assumption regarding the binding force of a decision of the European Commission. A plaintiff cannot be expected to demonstrate that a decision will be upheld upon appeal. It would also be misplaced and legally incorrect to expect a plaintiff to reduce the importance of the ruling of a European Court on a cartel to zero in order to make a national court continue the matter on the basis of the decision. The essential point is that the binding force of a decision serves as a starting point, notwithstanding the appeal. A national court should recognise that, however much wisdom may be expected from the General Court and the European Court of Justice, appeal proceedings against a decision do not justify a stay even if there is a possibility that the decision might be invalidated on appeal. Since *Masterfoods* decided that there is no objection for a national court to follow a decision of the European Commission in its own ruling, notwithstanding an appeal against the decision, continuing the proceedings should therefore be appropriate. Neither in *Masterfoods*, nor in any other ruling, has the European Court of Justice held that continuing the proceedings before a national court on the basis of a decision against which an appeal is underway before a European Court, would deny the valuable role of the European judiciary. On the contrary, with a stay a national court would frustrate the very safeguards that are obtained from the binding nature of a decision under European Union law. A national court must assume the binding force of a European Commission decision and may not therefore make any ruling in conflict with that decision. Only if the national court has doubts about the validity of that decision, and therefore expects that that decision will not survive the appeal proceedings brought against it, may the national court stay its ruling in order to wait for the result of that appeal. The court will by definition only have such a doubt after examining the decision and after a debate between the parties relating to that decision. A defendant identified in a decision as a cartel member and having brought an appeal against that decision before the European Court, may ask a national court to stay its ruling under *Masterfoods*, but for this purpose will have to demonstrate specific reasons why the contested decision is invalid. A motion to stay proceedings is therefore consistent with a principal defence that that decision as evidence in the civil case – in view of the probability that the decision will be annulled upon appeal – would not deserve to be taken as a basis for its ruling by the national court. The motion to stay the proceedings based on *Masterfoods* is thus a principal defence against a European Commission decision as evidence in civil litigation, and can only be assessed by a national court in the context of a debate on the merits of the case. A principal defence cannot be raised by way of a motion in incidental proceedings, let alone in incidental proceedings before the defence on the merits.

IV. DESSERT: SOME HUMAN RIGHTS

The sole fact that an appeal is pending cannot prejudice the binding force of a decision of the European Commission and its significance for civil proceedings. A defendant also does not have the privilege of postponing a substantive defence in civil proceedings for years until the General Court and possibly the Court of Justice have formed an opinion on the contested decision and through this about parts of its defence. That is no different if the claim in a civil action (largely) depends on the validity of that decision. In weighing the due-process interests of litigants, a national court should recognise that considerable weight is given to the right safeguarded by Article 6(1) of the European Convention on Human Rights to the hearing of cases within a reasonable period of time. This fundamental right normally also forms part of the national rules of civil procedure requiring that a national court exercises restraint in permitting a stay of proceedings. Restraint is possible if a workable alternative to a stay of proceedings exists, ie a conditional judgment, which at the same time respects the interests of defendants in civil litigation. A national court should understand that a defendant is perfectly able in its defences to comment on what a plaintiff has alleged in its claim and on the documents supporting that claim. A defendant can very well give an account of what it has done in the cartel period identified by the European Commission. A defendant in a principal action does not need the help of the European Courts to know its own conduct and to account for it. It is free to bring its defence as it sees fit. It can in addition also indicate which facts that are considered in the contested decision are in its opinion correct or incorrect. It may submit the decision itself to the national court and remove everything that it believes is confidential and should not be part of a non-confidential version. It may also submit to the national court all the information that it has available. It may in addition indicate on what grounds it challenges the European Commission's decision before the European Court and what relevance this has for the civil litigation. The only risk it has is that contentions it would make in its defence in the civil case are refuted in a ruling of a European Court. That is an appraisal the defendant has to make bearing in mind its obligation under most national rules of civil procedure in Europe to be truthful and complete when stating facts.

15

Some Procedural Aspects and How They Could/Should be Reformed

KPE LASOK QC

I. INTRODUCTION

From the perspectives of the effective enforcement of EU competition law, ensuring respect for private rights, and (more parochially) determining the jurisdiction within which a claim is to be brought, the applicable procedural rules are of paramount, but not sole, importance. Other important factors are the reliability of the national court that may hear the case (that is, the confidence that litigants have in the ability of the national court to grasp the issues, and deal properly with them) and the time taken to reach finality in the proceedings (which is a matter not only of the time required to bring the case from the commencement of proceedings to the delivery of judgment, but also the time that may be taken up by consequential appeals). In relation to that last factor – time – most claimants wish the time to be as short as possible, whereas many (but not all) defendants wish the time to be as long as possible.[1]

One topic that tends to come up when discussing the procedural aspects of cross-border EU competition law claims – alluded to in the reference to 'reform', in the title to this chapter – is the harmonisation of national procedural rules, about which it may be useful to say a word at the outset.

The national procedural rules that have developed in the different Member States tend to reflect a range of influences. The most important reflect the prevailing legal culture in the Member State in question, and policy decisions regarding the different trade-offs that have to be made when litigation procedure is devised and developed. By way of example, litigation can be conducted with a view to arriving at as near perfect a solution to the litigation as is humanly possible; but that would result in increased costs for the litigants, and increased burdens for the national courts. The very advantages of such a regime can generate disadvantages that make the regime less effective (deterring litigation; court delays and so forth). On the other hand, if corners are cut (to a greater or lesser degree of seriousness), justice becomes much more approximate and, in some cases, may not be achieved.

[1] Business litigants (whether claimants or defendants) are generally interested in achieving certainty as soon as possible. For example, the need for a defendant to mention a large but unresolved potential liability in its accounts is often a commercial disadvantage that acts as an incentive to achieving resolution of the exposure at the earliest opportunity. However, for tactical reasons, a defendant may, in a particular case, prefer to play a long game, in the hope of exhausting the claimant or forcing the latter to the negotiating table.

On the whole, there are few features of competition actions that justify treating them as so special that they should be immune from the particular trade-offs adopted for the generality of litigation in a particular national legal system. For example, competition cases are not the only forms of litigation in which a national court may be called upon to evaluate expert evidence in a highly technical domain (if anything, competition cases tend to generate expert evidence that is, in many respects, more approachable than the kind of expert evidence brought forward in, say, a medical negligence case or a patent dispute).

Further, in the particular context of competition actions, there appears to be a sound basis in principle for letting the different national systems of the Member States compete with one another. An imposed, harmonised, solution will simply reflect one way of doing things; and not necessarily the best way in any or any given legal culture in the Member States. In contrast, if one particular legal system develops a particularly effective (or ineffective) way of dealing with competition actions, or certain procedural aspects of a competition action, other legal systems may learn from that experience.

Proposals for the reform of procedural rules should therefore be advanced – and evaluated – with a certain degree of caution. Procedural reforms are usually proposed to deal with one particular problem, but inevitably run the risk of creating or worsening a different problem, or of unbalancing some of the trade-offs that feature in the national litigation regime.

II. GENERAL OBSERVATIONS

When considering procedural aspects of EU law competition claims, a technical question of classification arises: what is and what is not a procedural matter? For present purposes, substantive matters are taken to include limitation periods and questions concerning causation and the recoverable heads of loss. They are not dealt with here. In addition, collective redress and questions concerning jurisdiction and applicable law are dealt with elsewhere and are not, for that reason, considered here.

The main issues concerning procedural matters orient themselves around two particular aspects of competition actions: the difference between so-called 'follow-on' and 'stand-alone' actions; and the differences between actions brought by one claimant and so-called 'class' actions and the like.[2]

In principle, few procedural issues should arise in jurisdictions in which a follow-on action may be brought; the problem posed by procedural rules is most acute in the context of stand-alone actions.

So far as the difference between single and multiple claimants is concerned, in general terms, a situation in which the defendant(s) is/are exposed to claims that may be brought, separately and independently, by more than one person (perhaps, by a relatively large number of persons) is quite distinct from that where the only claimants are (small) consumers who may not, individually, be able to mount a claim.

In the first situation, the claimants can bring their claims effectively and the essential question is how to manage a multiplicity of similar claims without swamping the courts with what is essentially duplicate litigation. The simple solution is to take a test, or repre-

[2] Various terms may be used to describe actions brought by a multiplicity of persons; and different procedural techniques may be used to deal with them.

sentative, case. The primary objective is to manage court resources fairly having regard to the interests of all litigants (not just those involved in the competition cases in question); but there is also an interest in protecting the defendant from being swamped by the need to fend off a large number of duplicate claims simultaneously.

In the second situation, the problem to be addressed arises from the fact that the right(s) infringed and the consequential claims that can be made lie in the hands of persons who, individually, cannot in practice be expected to be able, or be likely, to mount a claim, perhaps because of a lack of resources or because the loss suffered by them individually is not great enough to justify a claim made by each claimant individually. Unless the view is taken that all claimants, however, great or small, lie under the same litigation discipline, special procedural rules are required in order to enable competition litigation initiated by small claimants.

The problems associated with multiple litigation, noted above, do not arise in all competition cases.

III. FOLLOW-ON ACTIONS

Follow-on actions generate few conceptual problems of a procedural nature. Typically, the question of liability (that is, the existence of an infringement of the competition rules) has been determined. Normally, the remedy sought is damages because, ordinarily, the decision of the competition authority on which the action is based ('the infringement decision') will require the defendant to cease and desist from the impugned conduct. Accordingly, in principle at least, the remaining questions concern causation and quantification of the recoverable loss.

However, there are some quirks connected with follow-on actions. First, the infringement decision will normally have been made for the purposes of the exercise by the relevant competition authority of its powers and not, expressly, for the purpose of providing the basis of a follow-on (damages) action. The decision may not, therefore, provide a complete basis for pursuing such an action. It may even be the case that material aspects of the liability finding are insufficient to provide the basis for asserting that any, or any discernible, loss has been caused by the impugned conduct. Secondly, there is a question about the definitive or final nature of findings made by the competition authority that are peripheral to the infringement finding, as well as of findings integral to the infringement finding that are, in addition, relevant to the questions of causation and loss to be considered by the national court in the follow on action. Thirdly, without wishing to be perceived as unfairly critical of competition authorities, infringement decisions made by an essentially administrative body are often couched in ways that are not attractive to a court and may, for policy reasons peculiar to the exigencies under which the competition authority operates, be phrased in a manner that is not especially helpful in the context of a follow-on action.[3]

[3] *Enron* [2011] EWCA Civ 2 is an example of a follow-on action in which the defendant's opportunity, to re-run before a court evidence considered by the competition authority, undermined the court's confidence in the relevance and/or strength of passages in the competition authority's decision. A rather different problem arises where, in the infringement decision, the competition authority is using the facts found by it to drive a particular theory, which may cause difficulties in a follow-on action if it becomes necessary to link the infringement to the facts of the case and, more particularly, the facts relating to causation and loss.

Arguably, those matters are not procedural but substantive, and therefore fall outside the scope of this chapter. The second point mentioned above certainly raises an aspect of procedure, even though it crosses over into matters of substance: the extent to which findings made in the infringement decision are binding on the court when the latter is considering matters of causation and loss (but not reconsidering the infringement finding).[4] On that question, it is possible to take up an intellectually respectable position in defence of each of the potential answers to the question, depending upon the view that one takes of the underlying policy to be pursued.

IV. STAND-ALONE ACTIONS

As stand-alone actions are not based upon an infringement decision made by a competition authority that provides a short-cut through part, at least, of the thicket of issues in a competition action, the procedural issues in a stand-alone action start at the outset of the proceedings and run through to the very end.

A. The Pleading of the Claim and Amendments

In cartel cases, the claimant usually has extremely limited information about the parties, nature and extent of the anti-competitive arrangement at the outset of the proceedings. Commonly, waiting until, in the fullness of time, sufficient information becomes available is problematic because of the applicable limitation periods and because, unless there is an infringement decision in some jurisdiction somewhere,[5] only the litigation may offer the means of obtaining the evidence needed to mount the claim. In those circumstances, a less restrictive approach to the pleading of a competition claim, and a more flexible approach to the amendment of pleadings, may be taken,[6] either alone or in combination with the adoption of a limitation period that responds to the problem.[7]

Where sufficient information is available at the outset of the proceedings, however, it does not follow that there are no difficulties in pleading a competition claim. Some aspects of competition claims are technical and, ultimately, will require expert economic evidence; and those aspects typically create the opportunity for pleading rules to be used by the defendant against the claimant. It is not unusual to see a narrow view being taken of pleading requirements in such circumstances, to the disadvantage of the claimant, even where there is no perceptible justification for doing so. A large part of the difficulties for the parties that arise from pleading requirements can ultimately be traced to one of two situations:

[4] See the discussion in *Enron* (above).

[5] If the infringement decision is that of a competition authority in the EU, a follow-on action could be brought. However, that decision might be directed at a different infringement (but, conceivably, throw up relevant evidence of a different infringement or one that the competition authority has not pursued in the exercise of its administrative discretion). A follow-on EU competition law action could not (at present) be based on an infringement decision made by a third country competition authority applying the law of that third country.

[6] See the discussion in *Nokia v AU Optronics and others* [2012] EWHC 731 (Ch).

[7] Such as a limitation period that starts to run at the point at which the information reasonably necessary for making the claim and bringing the action was known or could with reasonable diligence have been known.

an error made by the party submitting the pleading; or the court's limited understanding of competition law.

Normally, pleading rules do not work to the disadvantage of the defendant.

B. Interim Relief

Where a competition action is brought in connection with an ongoing infringement, the possibility of obtaining interim relief may well be of crucial importance for the protection or, indeed, the survival of the claimant. In England and Wales, the procedural rule that is often regarded as the principal barrier to obtaining interim relief is the usual obligation, imposed on the claimant as the price for obtaining interim relief, of providing a cross-undertaking in damages.[8] However, that obligation is part of the achievement of a balance of justice (or injustice) as between the parties at a point in the litigation at which it is not known which of them is right and which of them is wrong. The removal of the obligation to provide a cross-undertaking is also capable of resulting in an injustice. The balance achieved by common law procedures is not perfect; but then the imperfections are not noticeably greater in competition actions than in any other action.

C. Disclosure and the Obtaining of Evidence

The procedural opportunities for obtaining relevant evidence, usually from the defendant(s), are particularly important in cartel cases. Here, the procedural aspect is complicated by the style of judicial proceedings: are they accusatorial or inquisitorial? As a general observation, most legal systems operate mixed accusatorial/inquisitorial regimes for civil actions, with the preponderant influence being one or the other, depending upon the prevailing legal culture. In systems where the bias is towards the inquisitorial mode, the efficiency of the system depends on the energy and competence of the court.

As a general proposition, the common law disclosure regimes are more appropriate in competition actions. The expense that they entail is, these days, significant, but less so than in former times.

Disclosure rules can be properly assessed only in the light of the rules relating to burden and standard of proof and the operation of presumptions (here, collectively referred to as rules concerning the assessment of evidence).

D. Assessment of Evidence

In principle, the intellectual exercise required to weigh evidence is the same, whichever the legal system, subject to possible variations in the burden or standard of proof.

[8] That is, an obligation to compensate the defendant for the loss suffered by it as a result of the grant of interim relief should the claimant ultimately be unsuccessful in the action. There are, of course, other procedural barriers to the grant of interim relief, such as the absence of a case for it.

Competition cases are not atypical so far as concerns the principles concerning the burden and standard of proof, the drawing of inferences, and evidential presumptions. There is no particular reason why competition cases should attract any special rules in relation to those matters – apart from the problem caused by the fact that illegal anti-competitive arrangements are often deliberately hidden. That factor is not unique to competition cases: civil frauds are, likewise, typically hidden from view.

However, problems concerning the acquisition of the evidence needed to commence proceedings and bring them successfully to trial have raised the question of reversing the burden of proof or the use of presumptions that the defendant must rebut.

In two respects, some lowering of the evidential burden in advancing a case under EU competition law already exists as a matter of substantive law.

Thus, on one view, the difference between 'object' and 'effect' infringements of Article 101 of the TFEU is derived from the distinction drawn in US law between 'per se' and 'rule of reason' infringements of US anti-trust law; and the rule of reason in US anti-trust law is a judicial technique that was developed in order to enable the policy choice made by the US legislator in the Sherman Act to be kept as closely as possible in tune with economic and commercial reality while at the same time managing, in as effective a way as possible, the realities of anti-trust litigation.[9]

The concept of an 'object' infringement (which is a matter of substance, not of procedure) enables the evidential burden on the claimant in an Article 101 case to be alleviated to some extent; but that advantage seems to be of little real value in a case in which the claim is for damages because, even if an 'object' infringement can be established, it is still necessary to prove causation and loss.

The second illustration of the alleviation of the evidential burden lying on a claimant is to be found in the principle that, in order to prove participation in a cartel, it is sufficient to show that the defendant participated in a meeting at which anti-competitive arrangements were concluded, without manifestly opposing them. It is then for the defendant to advance exculpatory evidence to rebut that inference.[10] However, that is nothing more than a reflection of the fact that, in any case, the factual evidence on which a party relies may be such as to require the opposing party to produce an explanation or justification, failing which the burden of proof falling on the former party will be discharged.[11] It is not, in formal terms at least, a reversal of the burden of proof or a lowering of the standard of proof.

In relation to the assessment of evidence generally, a useful indication of one approach adopted in the UK is to be found in *JJB Sports plc v OFT*.[12] Ultimately, the matter boils down to the application of common sense to the evidence relied on by the parties, rather than the application of procedural rules.

[9] *cf* KPE Lasok QC, 'Recent Developments in the Rule of Reason in EU Antitrust Law' (2008) 7 *Competition Law Journal* 226.

[10] eg Cases C-204/00P and others *Aalborg Portland A/S and others v Commission* [2004] ECR I-123 [81].

[11] ibid [79].

[12] *JJB Sports plc v OFT* [2004] CAT 17 [286]–[294].

E. Treatment of Evidence (Examination and Cross-Examination of Witnesses and Experts)

Different legal systems have different ways of handling evidence; in particular, taking evidence from witnesses and experts and evaluating the relative importance of documentary evidence and live witness evidence seeking to explain a document.

The (apparently) cursory treatment of sources of evidence in some legal traditions and the (apparent) obsession with evidence exhibited by others seem to stem in large part from culture and tradition, but are undoubtedly influenced to a material extent by the need to ration court resources. Thus, restrictions applied by courts in England and Wales on the extent of the cross-examination of witnesses appear to be motivated in most instances by the need to limit the court time devoted to the proceedings in question and to protect the interests of other court users who are deprived of the court resources taken up by the case while it is going on.

Competition cases are not always fact-intensive cases. However, complex cartel cases generally are. Experience tends to suggest that one disadvantage with the administrative processes used for finding the existence of an infringement is that, because of the heavy reliance on documentary evidence and the absence of proper examination of witnesses, the full evidential picture is not always brought to light. The same can occur if courts act in the same way as competition authorities. That, however, is usually a consequence of judicial practice, rather than a procedural rule.

The comment just made should not be regarded as an implicit claim that cross-examination of witnesses is the only effective way of investigating a suspected infringement. In many cases, the contemporary documentary evidence is sufficient. Further, national courts are well-used to extracting evidence from a witness in non-competition cases. Extensive cross-examination in the common law style can prove to be a complete waste of time. On the other hand, it can also prove to be an extremely effective way of establishing the accuracy and credibility of witness evidence. Like many procedural matters, the existence and extent of cross-examination form part of the trade-offs involved in establishing the rules governing litigation and in applying those rules.

V. COSTS

The costs of litigation and the regime for determining who is liable to pay those costs can be important incentives or disincentives to engaging in litigation. The policy reasons for adopting any particular costs regime are not unique to competition cases; and there is no obvious reason why such cases should be treated any differently from any other case.

VI. CONCLUSION

Litigation is not a perfect instrument for securing respect for individual rights or compliance with the law. Procedures for litigating disputes are also imperfect instruments, usually (as noted above) because they reflect a trade-off, or series of trade-offs, between competing considerations that arise in the context of litigation. Competition actions possess all the features that lead to the need to achieve some kind of a balance between those competing considerations: achieving at least an approximation of perfect justice in a stand-alone competition action is possible only by devising an expensive and time-consuming procedural regime. Follow-on actions are much easier to deal with; but here the attention switches to the efficiency of the relevant competition authority in producing, in good time, a properly reasoned and expressed decision that contains reliable, relevant, findings.

A further point that should be made is that devising a procedural rule is one thing; its application in practice is another. The end result in any piece of litigation is usually informed, in a procedural sense, by a combination of the applicable procedural rules, the way in which they are exploited by the parties, and the way in which they are applied, and their use is controlled, by the court itself. It is perfectly possible to have an efficient system of procedural rules and yet to have a completely inefficient system of dispensing justice in a case where the rules are not properly observed and applied.

16

Observations on the Implications of *Pfleiderer* for Leniency Programmes

JAMES WEBBER*

I. INTRODUCTION

On 14 June 2011, the European Court of Justice (ECJ) handed down a judgment with the potential for serious repercussions for cartel enforcement in the EU. The decision in *Pfleiderer AG v Bundeskartellamt*[1] confirmed that, under EU law, documents relating to a leniency procedure[2] are potentially disclosable in civil damages claims. In cases where disclosure of leniency documents is requested, it is 'for the courts and tribunals of the Member States, on the basis of their national law, to determine the conditions under which such access must be permitted or refused by weighing the interests protected by European Union law'.[3] This section discusses the early application of this weighing exercise and the potential implications for leniency programmes.

The EU leniency regime is widely recognised as the most effective 'tool' for detecting secret cartels available to the authorities.[4] Underpinning any leniency regime is an overt trade-off between letting a wrongdoer go unpunished, and obtaining sufficient information to successfully investigate infringing behaviour. The system depends on creating an incentive strong enough for putative cartelists to come forward. The EU leniency regime has traditionally awarded complete immunity from all fines to the first leniency applicant to provide sufficient evidence to enable targeted inspections or to find an infringement of Article 101 TFEU. Immunity is the key concept. The policy choice is to make a promise that the successful immunity applicant will go unpunished for turning in his co-conspirators.

In formal legal terms this promise of immunity has always been incomplete. The ECJ confirmed in *Manfredi*[5] that a victim of a breach of Article 101 has a legal right to an effective civil damages claim before the national courts; a right that is not removed by a leniency application. The Commission's 2002 and 2006 leniency notices both also acknowledge this point.[6]

* I am particularly grateful to Mark Steenson, Associate at Shearman & Sterling, for his help in researching and preparing this section. Any errors are my own.

[1] C–360/09 *Pfleiderer AG v Bundeskartellamt* [2011] 5 CMLR 7.

[2] ibid [32].

[3] ibid [32].

[4] See eg the Resolution of the Head of the European Competition Authorities of 23 May 2012: 'These [leniency] programmes are among the most effective tools for the detection, investigation and punishment of cartels as well as for providing effective deterrence against cartelisation.'

[5] Joined Cases C-295/04–C-298/04 *Manfredi v Lloyd Adriaticco* [2006] 5 CMLR 17.

[6] 2002 Notice [2002] OJ C45/3 para 31; 2006 Notice, [2006] OJ C298/17 para 39.

The ECJ's decision in *Pfleiderer* does not alter this substantive position or introduce a new legal liability for leniency applicants. However, it does mean that competition authorities can no longer promise that evidence provided by a leniency applicant in support of their leniency application will not be provided to claimants in subsequent damages actions. To the extent that this increases the likelihood that a leniency applicant will face claims for significant subsequent civil damages, the incentive to apply for leniency – particularly but not exclusively for the immunity applicant – can be expected to diminish.

II. *PFLEIDERER* AND SUBSEQUENT CASE LAW

The ECJ in *Pfleiderer* stated that, in the absence of firm EU rules on the disclosure of leniency documents in civil actions, national courts must decide, on a case-by-case basis, what information provided by a leniency applicant to a competition authority should be disclosed.[7]

To do this the courts must weigh the claimant's interest in disclosure against the importance of preserving the effectiveness and integrity of the leniency programme; further, this balancing act must comply with the general principles of equivalence and effectiveness.[8] The ECJ did not give any guidance as to the factors (or weighting of factors) that ought to be taken into account in this weighing of interests and so it has been left to the national courts to establish a set of criteria upon which to base their '*Pfleiderer* balancing'.

At the time of writing there are a small number of cases where the *Pfleiderer* balancing has been considered both at national level and at the General Court. The first case to apply the *Pfleiderer* balancing in England was *NGET v ABB and others.*[9] This was a follow-on damages action brought by National Grid against a number of producers of gas-insulated switchgear (GIS). These companies were fined €750 million by the Commission in 2007 for operating a global bid-rigging, price-fixing and market allocation cartel for supply of GIS. National Grid had been a customer of the undertakings involved in this cartel and was seeking damages for the alleged overcharge that it believed it had suffered as a result. In seeking evidence to support its case, National Grid applied for disclosure of documents that some of the defendants had provided to the Commission as part of their leniency submissions. In considering that application, Mr Justice Roth first confirmed that the ECJ's determination in *Pfleiderer* applied to the leniency programme of the Commission; dismissing arguments (although not from the Commission itself[10]) that *Pfleiderer* only applied to national leniency programmes.[11] Taking the views of the Commission into account, Roth J then decided that there were three relevant factors to consider in the application of the *Pfleiderer* balancing. The test was to be whether disclosure of the material would: (i) serve to prejudice the current leniency applicants;[12] (ii) deter future leniency applicants;[13] and (iii) be proportionate.[14]

[7] The case did not extend to the European Commission's leniency programme, although similar logic applied. The Commission chose not to oppose the application of *Pfleiderer* to its leniency regime during its amicus submissions in the National Grid case (see below).

[8] *Pfleiderer* (n 1) [30].

[9] *NGET v ABB and others* [2012] EWHC 869 (Ch).

[10] The Commission had filed written observations on the case which are available at: http://ec.europa.eu/competition/court/amicus_curiae_2011_national_grid_en.pdf.

[11] *NGET* (n 9) [25].

[12] ibid [35].

[13] ibid [37].

[14] ibid [39].

Roth J then examined each document that National Grid had requested disclosure of. These documents were essentially the extracts from the corporate statements made by the leniency applicants and included by the Commission in the confidential version of its decision, the reply to SO by one of the defendants (ABB), and the replies to requests for information by Areva (another defendant)[15] and ABB which repeated or referred to leniency information.

The information at issue was not the pre-existing evidential material (memos, emails, notes of meetings etc) that had been supplied by the leniency applicants in support of their applications and was on the Commission's file to which access had been granted during the Commission's administrative procedure. It was common ground that this pre-existing evidence fell to be considered as normal evidence under the English procedural rules.

As to the first factor (prejudice to current leniency applicants), Roth J determined that there was no prejudice to the defendant/leniency applicants, as they had all been sued by National Grid together. There was therefore no risk that the leniency evidence would be used against the immunity applicant as a single anchor defendant and leave that company to recover contributions from the other cartelists.

As to the second factor (deterrence of future leniency applicants), Roth J considered that the deterrent effect had to be measured against the amount of the fine avoided. The fine that ABB (as the successful immunity applicant) avoided was particularly high, as it had been involved in a previous cartel and so would have been liable for a 50 per cent uplift for recidivism. Roth J said:

> it is significant that a decision not to go to the Commission would not have given ABB any guarantee of protection from civil liability since if any of the other participants had informed the Commission of the cartel it would have been exposed. Then ABB would similarly have been liable to civil claims but in addition would have faced a very substantial fine. . . . This would have been a very high risk gamble for ABB to take.[16]

As to the third factor (proportionality), Roth J divided his assessment of proportionality into two: i) whether the information is available elsewhere; and ii) the relevance of the material. Roth J did not consider that witnesses of fact (the principal alternative source available to National Grid) would be 'an adequate substitute for the comprehensive overview of the cartel obtained by the Commission from the participating undertakings'.[17] As to relevance, Roth J took a paragraph-by-paragraph review of relevance – although on a narrower basis than whether the documents were within standard disclosure.

Such an approach has its difficulties. For any given follow-on case, leniency applicants will either be co-defendants with other cartel members, or not. Prejudice to current leniency applicants (Factor 1) therefore is effectively fixed for the case before the national judge – indeed a future claimant might be wise to ensure that, so far as possible, all the leniency applicants are included in the claim so as to avoid this problem. Likewise if future deterrence (Factor 2) is measured by the severity of the original cartel, then this too is fixed for any given follow-on case – the severity of the infringement having been established in the Commission's infringement decision.

Proportionality (Factor 3) is therefore the only variable factor assessed at the level of the documents themselves. The key to this analysis in Roth J's approach is the importance of

[15] The author acts for Areva SA in respect of this litigation.
[16] *NGET* (n 9) [37].
[17] ibid [43].

the document to the claimant measured by relevance and how easy or difficult it is to obtain such evidence elsewhere. In effect therefore, for any given follow-on case, leniency applicants can expect that the more harmful the information is to their defence the more likely it is to be disclosed.

Notwithstanding this, in practice the disclosure made by Roth J was in fact significantly narrower than requested by National Grid. This resulted directly from Roth J's assessment of relevance (the second limb of the proportionality assessment in the approach above). The judge clearly took a conservative view of relevance in this context resulting in disclosure being limited to specific information in paragraphs, footnotes and tables contained in the confidential version of the Commission's Decision, the Commission's requests for information and defendants' responses to these requests. The practical application of the test therefore fell far short of a wholesale disclosure of the corporate statements made by the relevant defendants.

III. *AMTSGERICHT BONN*

The other major decision taken by a national court to date was by the *Amtsgericht Bonn*, the national court that had made the preliminary reference in the *Pfleiderer* case itself. Following the ECJ's judgment on the preliminary reference, the *Amtsgericht Bonn* undertook its weighing exercise and upheld the decision of the *Bundeskartellamt* refusing Pfleiderer access to the leniency case file – including pre-existing documents annexed to the leniency submissions. In doing so, the court gave significant weight to the BKartA's submissions about the deterrent effect disclosure would create for future leniency applications, particularly in the most serious cases. This analysis is almost the opposite of that of Roth J in *NGET*:

> The higher the amount of compensation potentially claimed and the higher the likelihood of a potential applicant bringing a claim, the more likely a potential leniency applicant/whistleblower will be deterred from applying for leniency. . . . This particularly applies to so-called hard-core cartels.

The General Court has also now had the opportunity to apply *Pfleiderer*, albeit in a different context as follow on damages claims cannot be brought directly before the General Court. The issue arose in the cases of *CDC Hydrogene Peroxide v Commission*[18] and *Energie Baden-Württemberg v Commission.*[19] In both cases the claimants were proceeding directly against the Commission to obtain evidence to support claims (or potential claims) in Germany. Claimants in Germany do not benefit to the same extent as their counterparts from England from the disclosure rules that facilitate disclosure of the pre-existing evidential material submitted in support of a leniency application.[20]

In *CDC* the General Court permitted the claimant to see the index of the Commission's file which allows CDC to better particularise requests for specific documents. This did not involve disclosure of leniency material as such and the Commission, although resisting disclosure at the General Court, opted not to appeal the General Court's judgment.

[18] Case T-437/08 *CDC Hydrogene Peroxide v Commission* [2012] 4 CMLR 23.

[19] Case T-344/08 *Energie Baden-Württemberg v Commission* [2012] 5 CMLR 4.

[20] See fn 1 of the ECN Resolution 'Protection of leniency material in the context of civil damages actions', 23 May 2012, where the differing national approaches to what is covered by 'leniency material' are acknowledged.

EnBW v Commission involved a German claimant, also suing members of the GIS cartel (the same cartel at issue in the *NGET* case). EnBW applied for disclosure of information contained in the Commission's case file under Regulation 1049/2001 regarding public access to documents of the European institutions.[21]

Before the General Court's judgment in May 2012, the Commission had agreed to provide some of these documents (namely the responses of the Statement of Objections of French defendants, Alstom and Areva[22]) to the English High Court in the *NGET* case following a request pursuant to Article 15 of Regulation 1/2003; here, however the Commission was refusing to disclose such information under Regulation 1049/2001 on the basis that to do so would undermine leniency and it was excessively onerous to review all the documents and allow partial access. The General Court did not accept this, and following *Pfleiderer,* ordered the Commission to review the documents individually and reconsider its decision as to whether information can be disclosed in light of this review – much in the same way that national courts are required to following *Pfleiderer.* The Commission subsequently appealed this judgment to the ECJ.

These early practical applications of the *Pfleiderer* balancing have been relatively cautious. There have been no instances of full corporate statements being disclosed and even the more liberal approach of Roth J resulted in only limited disclosure of extracts of leniency material. Whether this will be the case in future is less clear. Indeed for this reason, the *Pfleiderer* judgment may have increased the Commission's motivation to propose legislation to clarify the status of leniency information in damages claims:

> We are committed to protecting our leniency policy following last year's Pfleiderer judgment.
>
> This is a matter of common concern for Europe's public enforcers. Just a few weeks ago, the heads of the agencies associated in the European Competition Network adopted a joint resolution on the protection of leniency material in the context of damage actions.
>
> But we are seeking a more general solution. I intend to propose legislation later this year that will strike the right balance between the protection of leniency programmes and the victims' rights to obtain compensation.[23]

Ahead of such a 'general solution' it is interesting to consider at this stage what the impact *Pfleiderer* might have on incentives to make leniency applications in future.

IV. RISK TO THE LENIENCY REGIME

The ECJ, in *Pfleiderer* itself recognised that potential leniency applicants may be deterred from using the programme should leniency materials be disclosed.[24] The resolution from the European Competition Network from May 2012 referred to above makes the same point. Leniency programmes rely heavily on potential applicants having faith in the process. If the authorities are not seen to be upholding their end of the bargain, this could

[21] *EnBW v Commission* [2001] OJ L145/43.

[22] Alstom and Areva could not provide these documents directly to National Grid, due to impediments under French law. Both Areva and Alstom subsequently appealed the Commission's decision, although Areva later withdrew after the Commission agreed to adjust the text of the document it intended to disclose.

[23] Speech by Joaquín Almunia Vice President of the European Commission responsible for Competition Policy, *Antitrust Enforcement: Challenges Old and New,* 19th International Competition Law Forum, St Gallen, Switzerland, 8 June 2012.

[24] *Pfleiderer* (n 1) [26].

quickly lead to a loss of confidence in the system – something which might happen without the authorities even realising – given that cartels are secret and authorities cannot know how many go undetected. And while it may be true that private damages actions act as a deterrent to undertakings forming a cartel, thereby promoting the effective application of Articles 101 and 102 TFEU, it is undeniable that the discovery and punishment of existing cartels has historically very much relied on the effectiveness of leniency programmes.

Leniency requires an admission of liability for involvement in a cartel. It is therefore effectively an invitation for follow-on damages claims. Leniency does not and cannot provide any protection from the level of damages claimed by direct and indirect customers in Europe or elsewhere. Such damages and the costs involved in handling such claims might well ultimately be larger than the administrative fines imposed by the authorities. This is already a serious concern for potential leniency applicants as the ECN resolution notes:

> The experience of the CAs [European competition authorities] shows that when deciding whether or not to cooperate with CAs under a leniency programme, potential leniency applicants consider as an important factor the impact of such cooperation on their position in civil proceedings as compared with the situation where they decide not to cooperate.

Follow-on civil damages claims will always therefore serve to hinder the detection of existing cartels to a certain degree – ie there is a trade-off. The ECN resolution captures this well:

> if the incentives to cooperate under the leniency programmes are not preserved, the victims of currently hidden and future cartels are unlikely to learn about those cartels in the first place and would be deprived of exercising their rights to an effective remedy [through damages actions].

V. PROBATIVE VALUE OF LENIENCY MATERIAL

Given the acknowledged risk to public enforcement, a relevant question therefore is whether leniency documents really are as useful to the claimant in a civil damages claim as is commonly assumed.

Claimants clearly consider that leniency material is valuable to them as they invest effort in seeking disclosure of such documents. The perceived usefulness of any leniency materials to claimants in civil damages actions is also something to which leniency applicants also attach a great deal of importance. Yet there are reasons to believe that the role of leniency material may in fact be overstated – at least for some types of cartel infringement.

When the Commission opens a cartel investigation, as a result of a leniency application or otherwise, its chief objective is to gather proof as to the existence of the cartel, when it may then impose fines. A cartel is, of course, an infringement by object not effect. Therefore, evidence prepared and submitted for a leniency application need only concern the liability of the cartel members. In particular, when investigating secretive cartels, which by their nature rarely leave a paper trail capable of establishing liability, the Commission is primarily interested in the 'story' of the cartel. Information as to who the participants were, the type of cartel they operated, for how long. Documents supporting the story such as diary entries of meetings, notes if any of phone calls all serve to help this purpose. The Commission is not interested in evidence relating to the *effect* of the cartel as such, and need make no findings as to effect in its decision.

When a claimant comes to bring a follow on damages claim, the liability of the undertakings for the infringement will, by definition already have been established. The difficulty that remains for the claimant is to prove in the claimant's specific case that the cartel caused them loss. The file of evidence held by the Commission (including the leniency material) was not compiled for this purpose and may therefore be of limited value. This is particularly the case where the cartel did not operate by fixing prices. In a price-fixing cartel the evidence of effect (eg by how much the price was uplifted) may well be integral to the evidence proving the existence of the infringement and therefore overlap with the evidence held by the Commission from leniency applicants. Conversely, for cartels that operated by way of market sharing or bid rigging, the evidence of the existence of the cartel is far less likely to overlap with evidence of effects. Evidence showing that a market was reserved to a particular firm might help prove an infringement but does not help in showing the amount by which the resulting price was above a competitive level. The relatively limited disclosure ordered by Roth J of the High Court in *NGET*, having done a detailed review of relevance, is consistent with the leniency material in that case being of limited use in proving causation and loss – the GIS cartel predominately operated by market allocation.

It is at best unclear therefore that claimants will obtain significant benefits from having access to leniency material and likely that such benefits will be tangential to the reason why the evidence was compiled and highly fact-dependent.

VI. POTENTIAL IMPACT OF *PFLEIDERER* ON LENIENCY INCENTIVES

Disclosure of leniency materials was not anticipated when the current leniency rules were drafted. The Commission Notice on Immunity from fines and reduction of fines in cartel cases[25] (the '2006 Leniency Notice') states that the Commission 'considers that normally public disclosure of documents and written or recorded statements received in the context of this notice would undermine certain public or private interests . . . even after the decision has been taken'.[26] The protection from disclosure of leniency materials was apparently intended – at the time of drafting the 2006 Notice at least – to be indefinite. Although Roth J found that this did not create any formal legitimate expectation on the part of the leniency applicant that the documents would be invulnerable from disclosure in a follow on damages action – indeed the Commission did not argue this in its *amicus* brief to the High Court either – leniency is ultimately based on trust. Undertakings are placing very significant trust in the authorities when making a leniency application and exposing themselves to liability against an uncertain promise of relief from fines. The more predictable and reliable the agencies, the more effective the leniency regime is likely to be.

The risk of disclosure of leniency material in subsequent damages actions is a material uncertainty and must now be added to the list of factors to be considered in deciding whether to make a leniency application. A list of some common factors illustrates that the decision to apply for leniency may be a finely balanced one:

(i) whether another participant will be 'first-in' or the authorities will already be investigating the cartel. Even if an undertaking submits an application for leniency prior to a

[25] 2006 Leniency Notice, OJ 2006, C298/17

[26] ibid [40].

raid or information request, there is no guarantee that they will be granted immunity from fines. If they are not the first participant to apply, or fail to provide additional useful information, then they will receive no reduction in fines while facing the same risk of being sued in a civil damages action;

(ii) the potential exposure of individuals to criminal prosecution in certain jurisdictions;

(iii) the level of fines that would be imposed by the Commission, including a potential increase in such fines if the participant is a recidivist;

(iv) any potential limitation periods left to run – particularly if it has been a number of years since the unlawful behaviour occurred – correlated to this the judgment as to whether other participants have detected the infringement or are likely to do so;

(v) the nature of the potentially infringing conduct. Some cartel infringements are clear-cut, others are less so. For instance where the evidence points to information exchange but no concrete agreement or concerted practice; and

(vi) legal and reputation costs of admitting to cartel behaviour and defending subsequent damages actions – potentially around the world.

The fact that claimants may get access to materials submitted in a leniency application complicates this analysis further. To what extent will the party applying for leniency be providing information that may assist a future claimant? What will be the eventual approach of a national court in conducting a *Pfleiderer* balancing? What is the likelihood that the leniency material will be disclosed in courts outside the EU, particularly those with punitive damages regimes such as in the United States, now that the EU courts themselves are making such disclosures? Some of these factors may well deter a leniency submission that would otherwise have been made.

Yet, despite this, powerful incentives remain. A successful immunity applicant avoids fines which have got significantly more severe. This benefit is relatively certain and timely compared to the more distant and uncertain prospect of damages claims. Moreover, leniency applicants know and have known for a long time, they will be liable to follow-on claims which could lead to significant sums in damages being awarded. Leniency applicants may also be in a position, albeit an imperfect one, to estimate the quantum of such claims.

As noted above, the probative value of any leniency material provided may in any event be limited in the hands of a damages claimant – ie it may not be very useful in establishing causation and loss. This last factor suggests that leniency applicants may now give more thought to what they disclose in their applications, particularly if it is possible to limit that information to that sufficient to prove the existence rather than the effects of the infringement. As noted above, in practice this is likely to be easier for some types of infringement than others.

17

Collective Redress Proceedings: Specific Issues Regarding Jurisdiction and Choice of Law

DIMITRIOS-PANAGIOTIS L TZAKAS

I. INTRODUCTION

The private enforcement of EU competition rules – encompassing civil actions for damages and declaratory or injunctive relief – has long been seen as a 'problem child'[1] or as 'largely alien to European competition law experience'.[2] Despite the early call of the European Parliament for the adoption of a uniform, pan-European rule relating to actions for damages in cases of infringements of Articles 101 and 102 TFEU,[3] the absence of any specific provision on this matter has led the CJEU to the conclusion that it is for the domestic legal system of each Member State to designate the courts and tribunals having jurisdiction and to lay down the detailed procedural rules governing actions for safeguarding rights which individuals derive from the direct effect of primary EU law and, in particular, of Articles 101 and 102 TFEU[4] (the so-called 'dualistic approach'). The reform of the European procedural framework after enactment of Regulation 1/2003[5] as well as the landmark CJEU rulings in *Courage v Crehan*[6] and *Manfredi*[7] made clear the need for strengthening private actions in order to 'put some extra wind in the sails of [the] enforcement boat', as ex-Commissioner *N Kroes* stated.[8] Although the policy rationale of safeguarding

[1] J Fitchen, 'Allocating Jurisdiction in Private Competition Law Claims within the EU' (2006) 13 *Maastricht Journal of European and Comparative Law* (MJ) 381, 382.

[2] TMJ Möllers and A Heinemann, *The Enforcement of Competition Law in Europe* (Cambridge, Cambridge University Press, 2007) 452. See also Commission, 'Staff Working Document, Accompanying document to the White Paper on Damages actions for breach of the EC antitrust rules, Impact Assessment' SEC (2008) 405, 2 April 2008 [33]–[39].

[3] See the German version of the Resolution 'Entschließung in Beantwortung der vom Ministerrat der EWG zu dem Vorschlag einer ersten Durchführungsverordnung zu den Artikeln 85 und 86 des EWG-Vertrages vom Parlament erbetenen Konsultation' [1961] OJ 73/1409 [11]. *cf* furthermore European Council, 'Resolution of 29 June 1995 on the effective uniform application of Community law and on the penalties applicable for breaches of Community law in the internal market' [1995] OJ C188/1.

[4] Joined cases C-430/93 and C-431/93 *Jeroen van Schijndel and Johannes Nicolaas Cornelis van Veen v Stichting Pensioenfonds voor Fysiotherapeuten*, [1995] ECR I-4705 [17]; Case C-242/95, *GT-Link A/S v De Danske Statsbaner (DSB)* [1997] ECR I-4449 [24]; Case T-24/90 *Automec Srl v Commission* [1992] ECR II-2223 [50]. See furthermore Commission, 'Answer to Written Question No 519/72' [1973] OJ C67/54.

[5] Council Regulation (EC) No 1/2003 of 16 December 2002 on the implementation of the rules on competition laid down in Articles 81 and 82 of the Treaty [2003] OJ L 1/1.

[6] Case C-453/99 *Courage Ltd v Bernard Crehan* [2001] ECR I-6297.

[7] Joined Cases C-295/04 to C-298/04 *Vincenzo Manfredi and others v Lloyd Adriatico Assicurazioni SpA and others* [2006] ECR I-6619.

[8] 'Enhancing Actions for Damages for Breach of Competition Rules in Europe' SPEECH/05/533.

the *acquis communautaire*[9] and, in particular, individual rights in cases of antitrust violations cannot be seriously doubted, the task of optimising the national statutory rules as to tort liability has in fact[10] been undertaken by the Member States,[11] since the existing legislative proposals at EU level remain far from being finalised.

Furthermore, a current trend as to the interpretation of the EU competition rules has evolved especially in the European Commission practice,[12] which is known as the 'more economic approach'[13] and which focuses on the standard of consumer welfare.[14] Accordingly, attention is to be shifted to advantages in terms of efficiency gains which also benefit the consumer and may counterbalance or outweigh the disadvantageous effects of specific business practices on competition.[15] Despite the controversially discussed policy underpinnings of such an approach,[16] the imperative of elaborating an effective redress mechanism at either the EU or the national level has to be held as indisputable, at least in terms of maximising consumer welfare. From this perspective, consumer redress should be considered as a cornerstone of the competition enforcement policy given the unequivocal wording used by the CJEU in both *Courage/Crehan*[17] and

[9] See R Becker, 'Schadensersatzklagen bei Verstoß gegen das Kartell- und Missbrauchsverbot: Europäische Vorgaben und Vorhaben' in S Augenhofer (ed), *Die Europäisierung des Kartell- und Lauterkeitsrechts* (Tübingen, Mohr Siebeck, 2009) 15, 19–22; AP Komninos, *EC Private Antitrust Enforcement, Decentralised Application of EC Competition Law by National Courts* (Oxford, Hart Publishing, 2008) 232–35.

[10] *cf* also the attempts to ascertain an autonomous EU law remedy that can be traced back to the opinion rendered by the Advocate General Walter Van Gerven in Case C-128/92 *H J Banks & Co Ltd v British Coal Corporation* [1994] ECR I-1209. See further G Mäsch, 'Private Ansprüche bei Verstößen gegen das europäische Kartellverbot – "*Courage*" und die Folgen' (2003) 38 *Europarecht* (EuR) 825, 841 et seq; C Nowak, 'Note' (2001) 12 *Europäische Zeitschrift für Wirtschaftsrecht* (EuZW) 718.

[11] See, eg, in England the Enterprise Act 2002 and in Germany the Seventh Amendment of the Act against Restrictions of Competition (*Gesetz gegen Wettbewerbsbeschränkungen* – GWB). See also the interview data collected by the UK-based (pp 8–9, 34) and the Germany-based research teams (pp 1–2) illustrating an increase in competition-related litigation.

[12] See, eg, Communication from the Commission, 'Notice – Guidelines on the Application of Article 81(3) of the Treaty' [2004] OJ C101/971; Commission Regulation (EU) No 330/2010 of 20 April 2010 on the application of Article 101(3) of the Treaty on the Functioning of the European Union to categories of vertical agreements and concerted practices [2010] OJ L102/1; Commission, 'Guidelines on Vertical Restraints' [2010] OJ C130/1; Communication from the Commission, 'Guidance on the Commission's enforcement priorities in applying Article 82 of the EC Treaty to abusive exclusionary conduct by dominant undertakings' [2009] OJ L45/7; Commission, 'Guidelines on the assessment of non-horizontal mergers under the Council Regulation on the control of concentrations between undertakings' [2008] OJ C265/6.

[13] See C Esteva Mosso, 'The More Economic Approach Paradigm – An Effects-based Approach to EU Competition Policy' in J Basedow and W Wurmnest (eds) *Structure and Effects in EU Competition Law Studies on Exclusionary Conduct and State Aid* (Alphen aan den Rijn, Kluwer Law International, 2011) 11; K Fountoukakos and S Ryan, 'A New Substantive Test for EU Merger Control' (2005) 26 *ECLR* 277.

[14] On the standard of consumer welfare see J Madill and A Mexis, 'Consumers at the Heart of EU Competition Policy' (1/2009) *Competition Policy Newsletter* 27; KJ Cseres, 'The Controversies of the Consumer Welfare Standard' (2006) 3(2) *Competition Law Review* 121.

[15] See, eg, C-95/04 P *British Airways Plc v Commission and others* [2007] ECR I-2331 [86]; Case C-52/09 *Konkurrensverket v TeliaSonera Sverige AB and Tele2 Sverige AB* [76]; Case C-209/10 *Post Danmark A/S v Konkurrencerådet and Forbruger-Kontakt a-s* [41]–[44].

[16] See D Zimmer, 'Protection of Competition v. Maximizing (Consumer) Welfare' in J Basedow and W Wurmnest (eds) *Structure and Effects in EU Competition Law Studies on Exclusionary Conduct and State Aid* (Alphen aan den Rijn, Kluwer Law International, 2011) 23.

[17] *Courage* (n 6) [26]. See on this topic J Drexl, 'Zur Schadensersatzberechtigung unmittelbarer und mittelbarer Abnehmer im europäisierten Kartelldeliktsrecht' in A Heldrich et al (eds), *Festschrift für C. Canaris*, vol I (CH Beck, 2007) 1342–43, 1346–51; J Keßler, 'Private Enforcement – Zur deliktsrechtlichen Aktualisierung des deutschen und europäischen Kartellrechts im Lichte des Verbraucherschutzes' (2006) 52 *Wettbewerb in Recht und Praxis* (WRP) 1061, 1066–70; W Wurmnest, 'Private Durchsetzung des EG-Kartellrechts nach der Reform der VO Nr 17' in P Behrens, E Braun and C Nowak (eds), *Europäisches Wettbewerbsrecht im Umbruch* (Baden-Baden, Nomos, 2004) 213, 217 et seq.

Manfredi,[18] where the eligibility of any individual ('toute personne', 'jedermann') to seek compensation for the harm caused to him by anti-competitive practices has been underscored.

However, the implementation and effectiveness of any private antitrust enforcement system has to give proper consideration to the fact that damages sustained by consumers are usually – due to their low value – non-viable as a basis for litigation unless aggregated. In this context, the need for an adequate procedural framework ensuring access to justice for all consumers and effectively safeguarding the protection of the 'weak party' has been outlined by the ECtHR,[19] which ruled with regard to representative actions that 'in modern-day societies, when citizens are confronted with particularly complex administrative decisions, recourse to collective bodies such as associations is one of the accessible means, sometimes the only means, available to them whereby they can defend their particular interests effectively.'

The present chapter focuses on the peculiarities of consumer redress and discusses the operability of different collective redress schemes in the international context. Emphasis will be given to the constitutive elements of an effective collective redress mechanism and its implications for cross-border litigation.[20] From that perspective, identifying the main problems arising in such proceedings constitutes the first step in order to assess the existing propositions of the European Commission and suggest adequate solutions which meet the two aims of guaranteeing procedural efficiency and avoiding unmeritorious claims.[21]

II. ADDRESSING THE MAIN PROBLEMS OF CROSS-BORDER LITIGATION

A. Requirements Emanating from Articles 101 and 102 TFEU

Although the eligibility of end-consumers as private plaintiffs – even when they do not constitute the direct purchasers of the tortfeasors[22] – seems to be beyond reasonable doubt

[18] The so-called 'each individual-requirement' has been repeated five times in *Manfredi* (n 7) [60], [61], [63], [90], [95].

[19] *Gorraiz Lizarraga and others v Spain* (App No 62543/00) ECHR 2004-III [38].

[20] For a comparative analysis of the existing instruments in the Member State laws see the national reports available at http://ec.europa.eu/competition/antitrust/actionsdamages/study.html. In the field of consumer protection law, see Katholieke Universiteit Leuven, 'An Analysis and Evaluation of Alternative Means of Consumer Collective Redress other than Redress through Ordinary Judicial Proceedings, Final Report', available at http://ec.europa.eu/consumers/redress/reports_studies/comparative_report_en.pdf. As to the existing collective litigation forms, see D Fairgrieve and G Howells, 'Collective Redress Procedure: European Debates' (2009) 58 ICLQ 379; R Mulheron, 'The Case for an Opt-Out Class Action for European Member States: A Legal and Empirical Analysis' (2009) 15 *Columbia Journal of European Law* 409, 415–27. On the collective redress instruments provided by the laws of the Nordic countries, see H Lindblom, 'Group Litigation in Scandinavia' (2008) 13 *Zeitschrift für Zivilprozeß International* (ZZPInt) 85; K Viitanen, 'Nordic Experiences on Group Actions for Compensation' in M Casper and others (eds), *Auf dem Weg zu einer europäischen Sammelklage?* (Munich, Sellier, 2009) 219. See furthermore Commission, 'Staff Working Document Public Consultation: Towards a Coherent European Approach to Collective Redress' SEC (2011) 173 final, 4 February 2011 [9].

[21] See also A Halfmeier and P Wimalasena, 'Rechtsstaatliche Anforderungen an Opt-out-Sammelverfahren: Anerkennung ausländischer Titel und rechtspolitischer Gestaltungsspielraum' (2012) 67 *JuristenZeitung* (JZ) 649, 651–52, 657–58.

[22] See the recent ruling of the German Supreme Court BGH, Decision of 28.6.2011, case No KZR 75/10 (ORWI) (2012) 55 *Neue Juristische Wochenschrift* (NJW) 928 as well as the opinion of the German Monopolies Commission (*Monopolkommission*), *Sondergutachten 41: Das allgemeine Wettbewerbsrecht in der Siebten GWB-Novelle*

in light of the aforementioned CJEU rulings in *Courage/Crehan* and in *Manfredi*, a significant number of procedural and substantive law impediments will often discourage the initiation of individual stand-alone actions. Even where the European Commission or an NCA has already found an infringement of Articles 101 or 102 TFEU and imposed a fine, end-consumers will be dissuaded from initiating proceedings. As the main obstacles, one can name litigation costs and risks, the difficulties in assessing and quantifying damages, the low value of the sustained damages, procedural inefficiencies, etc.[23] In the case of long-term price fixing practices relating to mass products, it is more than probable that an end consumer will not even be able to assess the extent of the detriment he suffered.[24] Assuming that the cartel overcharges paid by a consumer are already known,[25] it is quite debatable whether consumers will be able to estimate or even prove the units of the product they bought in the period during which the price fixing lasted.

In the light of these findings, it can be viably argued that in most cases consumer claims cannot and will not be brought before court unless aggregated.[26] Therefore, the lack of collective rights of action may be held as contravening the right to an effective remedy in the fields covered by Union law pursuant to Article 19(1)(b) TEU and Article 47(1) Charter of Fundamental Rights of the EU.[27] Referring to collective redress, Advocate General Francis Jacobs stated that 'collective rights of action are an equally common feature of modern judicial systems.'[28] The first question arising in this context refers to the requirements emanating from Articles 101 and 102 TFEU and, in particular, as to whether an autonomous EU collective redress mechanism may be ascertained. Notwithstanding the controversial discussion of the CJEU rulings in *Courage v Crehan* and *Manfredi* concerning the EU law basis of civil antitrust liability, it is far from clear whether and to what extent the EU courts

(Baden-Baden, Nomos, 2004) 41–42. See furthermore J Basedow, 'Perspektiven des Kartelldeliktsrechts' (2006) *Zeitschrift für Wettbewerbsrecht* 294, 304; Wurmnest (n 17) 243–44; Komninos (n 9) 202–206. But see OLG Karlsruhe, Decision of 11 June 2010, case no 6 U 118/05 *(Kart); A Jones and D Beard, 'Co-contractors, Damages and Artikel 81: The ECJ finally speaks' (2002) 23 ECLR* 246, 253–55; H Köhler, 'Kartellverbot und Schadensersatz' (2004) 106 *Gewerblicher Rechtsschutz und Urheberrecht* (GRUR) 99, 100–103; N Reich, 'The "Courage" Doctrine: Encouraging or Discouraging Compensation for Antitrust Injuries?' (2005) 42 *CML Rev* 35, 42–48.

[23] See Conseil de la Concurrence, 'Avis du 21 septembre 2006 relatif à l'introduction de l'action de groupe en matière de pratiques anticoncurrentielles', available at www.autoritedelaconcurrence.fr/doc/classactions.pdf, [26]–[27], [35]–[36]; Office of Fair Trading (OFT), 'Private actions in competition law: effective redress for consumers and businesses, Discussion Paper' (April 2007) available at www.oft.gov.uk/shared_oft/reports/comp_policy/oft916.pdf, [4.2]. See furthermore J Bernhard, *Kartellrechtlicher Individualschutz durch Sammelklagen* (Tübingen, Mohr Siebeck, 2009) 35–37.

[24] See also European Parliament, 'Resolution of 26 March on the White Paper on damages actions for breach of the EC antitrust rules' (2008/2154(INI)) PA_TA(2009)0187 [4]; European Economic and Social Committee (EESC), 'Opinion on the collective actions system and its role in the context of Community consumer law (Own-initiative opinion)'[2008] OJ C162/1 [4.4]–[4.5]. *cf* furthermore Commission, 'Green Paper on Consumer Collective Redress' COM (2008) 794 final, 27 November 2008, [8]–[9].

[25] See, eg, *Manfredi* (n 7) [14] where investigation carried out by the Italian Competition Authority revealed that the average price of civil liability auto insurance premiums was 20% higher than would have been the case if the competitive conduct of the insurance companies had not been distorted by the concerted practice.

[26] Commission Staff Working Document (n 20) [4]–[6]; Commission, 'Damages Actions for Breach of the EC antitrust rules' (White Paper) COM (2008) 165 final, 2 April 2008, 4; Commission, 'Staff Working Paper Accompanying the White Paper on Damages actions for breach of the EC antitrust rules' SEC (2008) 404, 2 April 2008, [24]–[25], [39]–[40].

[27] *cf* also EESC Opinion on the collective actions system (n 24) [1.3].

[28] Opinion in Case C-195/98 *Österreichischer Gewerkschaftsbund, Gewerkschaft öffentlicher Dienst v Republik Österreich* [2000] ECR I-10497 [47]. *cf* also *Gorraiz Lizarraga and others v Spain* (App No 62543/00) ECHR 2004-III [38]. See furthermore Case C-199/08 *Erhard Eschig v UNIQA Sachversicherung AG* [2009] ECR I-8295 [61]–[64].

may consider collective litigation mechanisms as a non-procedural issue that Member States laws are bound to enable.

John Temple Lang[29] considers it likely that Article 10 EC (now as amended Article 4(3) TEU) imposes on national courts a duty 'to enable groups of consumers or other individuals to join together to claim compensation in accordance with the principles stated in *Crehan*'. Furthermore, in light of the CJEU decision in *Océano Grupo*,[30] he advocates 'a special duty on national courts to ensure that citizens get rights under Community law that in practice they may not otherwise be able to obtain'.[31] However, it seems debatable to what extent the CJEU is willing to examine the various forms of collective litigation in light of the principles of equivalence and effectiveness. For instance, in *Manfredi*[32] the Court refrained from a detailed scrutiny of the Italian rules on the competence of domestic courts and merely obliged the Italian judges to undertake this task pursuant to the aforementioned principles.

From the perspective of collective redress, an in-depth analysis of the existing forms of litigation, encompassing representative actions, collective actions and test cases, is needed. Pursuant to the wording used by the European Commission, the term 'representative action' describes actions brought by a natural or legal person on behalf of two or more individuals who are not themselves party to the action, and which are aimed at obtaining either injunctive relief or damages for the individual harm caused to the interests of all those represented (and not to the representative entity).[33] 'Collective or group actions' characterise claims of individuals or businesses which are combined into one single action.[34] In a test case procedure a single individual case is submitted to the judge in order to enable him to make an assessment of the problem, so that the judgment can provide a basis for deciding the common facts and legal issues of similar legal actions and serve as an example for the other cases.[35]

Such scrutiny is inextricably linked to an assessment of the effectiveness of the opt-in in comparison to the opt-out model. In opt-in proceedings the individual harmed has to make deliberate representations in order to be a party to the procedure, whereas under the opt-out system the initiation of the action automatically involves the participation of all (or at least a large number of) persons having suffered damages in the procedure without it being necessary that they make themselves known.[36] Although opt-out proceedings are

[29] J Temple Lang, 'Developments, Issues, and New Remedies: The Duties of National Authorities and Courts under Article 10 of the EC Treaty' (2004) 27 *Fordham International Law Journal* 1904, 1917.

[30] Joined Cases C-240/98 to C-244/98 *Océano Grupo Editorial SA v Rocío Murciano Quintero* [2000] ECR I-4941. See also Case C-372/99 *Commission of the European Communities v Italian Republic* [2002] ECR I-819 [14]–[16].

[31] J Temple Lang, 'European Community Competition Policy: How Far Does it Benefit Consumers?' (2004) 18 *Boletín Latinoamericano de Competencia*, available at http://ec.europa.eu/competition/publications/blc/boletin_18_3.pdf, 128, 133. *cf* also F Cafaggi and HW Micklitz, 'Introduction' in F Cafaggi and HW Micklitz (eds), *New Frontiers of Consumer Protection* (Antwerp, Intersentia, 2009) 1, 19.

[32] *Manfredi* (n 7) [70]–[72]. *cf* also Case C-432/05 *Unibet (London) Ltd and Unibet (International) Ltd v Justitiekanslern* [2007] ECR I-2271 [40]–[44], [62], [64]–[65].

[33] Commission Staff Working Paper, Accompanying the White Paper (n 26) [49]. *cf* also Commission, 'Staff Working Paper, Annex to the Green Paper, Damages actions for breach of the EC antitrust rules' SEC (2005) 1732, 19 December 2005 [192]; EESC Opinion on the collective actions system (n 24) [5.2].

[34] Commission Staff Working Paper, Accompanying the White Paper (n 26) [57]. *cf* also Commission Staff Working Paper, Annex to the Green Paper (n 33) [237]. See also EESC Opinion on the collective actions system (n 24) [5.4] characterising collective actions as 'a collective procedural application of individual rights'.

[35] EESC Opinion on the collective actions system (n 24) [7.2.1.1].

[36] See Commission Staff Working Paper, Accompanying the White Paper (n 26) [57]–[58]; EESC Opinion on the collective actions system (n 24) [7.2].

more apt to safeguard the full effectiveness of the EU competition rules – since the right to obtain compensation for the sustained damages is guaranteed for all putative claimants and especially end consumers – it remains rather questionable if the CJEU may undertake such a broad interference with the Member States' procedural autonomy[37] under the present state of law.[38] Such a far-reaching view of the *acquis communautaire* and of the effectiveness of the EU competition rules could amount to an *obligation de résultat*[39] of the national courts and laws to offer effective judicial protection by means of collective actions. However, this approach is linked to providing concrete standards to a whole set of specific procedural requirements such that national peculiarities could potentially be overlooked.[40]

B. Substantive Law Issues

The ambiguous nature of the requirements imposed by the primary EU law as to the national instruments of collective proceedings should not be deemed to hinder the adoption of either opt-in or opt-out mechanisms depending upon the person of the putative claimants as well as the procedural peculiarities of each legislating Member State. In fact, the CJEU ruling in *Eschig*[41] does not dismiss opt-out instruments as long as sufficient opportunities are ensured which allow harmed individuals to seek their exclusion from group proceedings. However, in view of the substantial potential for unmeritorious claims in such proceedings, specific safeguards have to be put in place.

Of importance, in this context, are the specific requirements relating to the eligibility of the representative entity (or the representative of the class claimants) entitled to initiate proceedings. Indeed, the variety of the approaches adopted by the Member States' laws reflects inevitably the choice-of-law underpinnings of cross-border consumer redress. In this regard, it has to be noted that the admissibility of any type of collective redress mechanism (representative actions, collective actions or test cases) will be considered as a procedural issue governed by the law of the forum state (*lex fori*) pursuant to the generally acknowledged principle: *forum regit processum*.[42] From this aspect, it seems quite unlikely

[37] As to the so-called second generation EU legislative acts directly interfering with the Member States procedural autonomy see D Saam, *Kollektive Rechtsbehelfe zur Durchsetzung von Schadensersatzansprüche im europäischen Wettbewerbs- und Verbraucherrecht* (Baden-Baden, Nomos, 2011) 162–67. As to the Member States' procedural autonomy, see Bernhard (n 23) 73–77.

[38] See also Bernhard (n 23) 41–42; V Milutinovic, 'Private Enforcement: Upcoming Issues' in G Amato and CD Ehlermann (eds), *EC Competition Law, A Critical Assessment* (Oxford, Hart Publishing, 2007) 725, 753. But see WH Roth, 'Sammelklagen im Bereich des Kartellrechts' in M Casper and others (eds), *Auf dem Weg zu einer europäischen Sammelklage?* (Munich, Sellier, 2009) 109, 121.

[39] See on this term AP Komninos, 'New Prospects for Private Enforcement of EC Competition Law: *Courage v Crehan* and the Community Right to Damages' (2002) 39 *CML Rev* 447, 480.

[40] DP Tzakas, 'International Litigation and Competition Law: The Case of Collective Redress' in J Basedow and S Francq and L Idot (eds), *International Antitrust Litigation Conflict of Laws and Coordination* (Oxford, Hart Publishing, 2012) 161, 163–64. *cf* also N Reich, 'Legal Protection of Individual and Collective Consumer Interests' in HW Micklitz et al (eds), *Understanding EU Consumer Law* (Antwerp, Intersentia, 2009) 317, 351.

[41] '[E]ven supposing that new situations, at Member State level, were to lead to an increase in the number of actions seeking to protect the collective interests of members of a group of persons, such situations cannot, as Community law currently stands, restrict the freedom of persons with legal expenses insurance to either participate or not in such an action and to choose, where appropriate, a legal representative.' *Eschig* (n 28) [64].

[42] D Bureau and H Muir Watt, *Droit International Privé*, vol I, Partie Générale (Paris, Presses Universitaires de France (PUF), 2007) 189; M Fallon, 'An Essay on the Mutual Recognition of Group Actions (Governmental, Organizational or Class Actions) in Cross-Border Consumer Conflicts within the European Community' in

that in the absence of a specific EU rule a Member State court would be willing to permit proceedings based on a right or remedy which is not also prescribed for domestic entities.[43]

For instance, under German law, section 34a of the Act against Restrictions of Competition (*Gesetz gegen Wettbewerbsbeschränkungen* – GWB) entitles specific associations promoting the commercial or independent professional interests of their members to require the wrongdoer to surrender to the federal budget the economic benefit obtained at the expense of multiple purchasers or suppliers to the extent that the cartel authority has not ordered the skimming-off of the economic benefit by the imposition of a fine.[44] English law, pursuant to section 47B Competition Act 1998 (as inserted by section 19 Enterprise Act 2002) allows only 'specified bodies' to initiate proceedings before the Competition Appeal Tribunal (CAT).[45] A similar policy rationale can be identified in the joint representative action (*action en représentation conjointe*) of Article L422-1 of the French Consumer Code[46] which is prescribed for any approved association recognised as being representative on the national level. Furthermore, trade or professional associations are entitled under Article L470-7 of the French Commercial Code to commence actions for damages or injunctive relief with regard to facts directly or indirectly harming fair competition or the collective interests of the profession or sector they represent.[47] These findings are illustrative of the need for a uniform rule at EU level which could set at least minimum requirements as to the eligible representatives.[48]

A further substantial aspect relates to the prerequisites for claims aggregation. In this respect, US courts require for class members that they or, at least, the claims represented can 'be adequately defined and clearly ascertain[ed]'.[49] The significance of these aspects is

T Bourgoignie (ed), *Group Actions and Consumer Protection, L'Action Collective et la Défense des Consommateurs* (Brussels, Kluwer, 1992) 245, 254–55; A Halfmeier, *Popularklagen im Privatrecht, Zugleich ein Beitrag zur Theorie der Verbandsklage* (Tübingen, Mohr Siebeck, 2006) 283; WF Lindacher, 'Die internationale Verbandsklage in Wettbewerbssachen' in H Prütting and H Rüssmann (eds), *Festschrift G Lüke* (Munich, CH Beck, 1997) 377, 384–85; P Rott, 'Cross-Border Collective Damage Actions in the EU' in F Cafaggi and HW Micklitz (eds), *New Frontiers of Consumer Protection* (Antwerp, Intersentia, 2009) 379, 385–86. *cf* also H Koch, 'Internationaler kollektiver Rechtsschutz' in C Meller-Hannich (ed), *Kollektiver Rechtsschutz im Zivilprozess* (Baden-Baden, Nomos, 2008) 53, 60–61.

[43] See especially Fallon (n 42) 252. See also C Kessedjian, 'L'action en justice des associations de consommateurs et d'autres organisations représentatives *d'intérêts* collectifs en Europe' (1997) 33 *Rivista di Diritto Internazionale Privato e Processuale* 292–93; A Morin, 'Group Action and the Settlement of Cross-Border Consumer Disputes: A French Perspective' in HW Micklitz and N Reich (eds) *Public Interest Litigation before European Courts* (Baden-Baden, Nomos, 1996) 419, 424. *cf* also Rott (n 42) 386.

[44] See on this provision C Alexander, 'Marktsteuerung durch Abschöpfungsansprüche' (2006) 61 JZ 890; A Stadler, 'Der Gewinnabschöpfungsanspruch: eine Variante des private enforcement?' in S Augenhofer (ed), *Die Europäisierung des Kartell- und Lauterkeitsrechts* (Tübingen, Mohr Siebeck, 2009) 117.

[45] See O Dayagi-Epstein, 'Representation of Consumer Interest by Consumer Associations: Salvation for the Masses?' (2007) 3 *Competition Law Review* 209, 218–21; B Rodger, 'Private Enforcement and the Enterprise Act: An Exemplary System of Awarding Damages' (2003) 24 *ECLR* 103, 108.

[46] See H Beuchler, 'Länderbericht Frankreich' in HW Micklitz and A Stadler (eds), *Das Verbandsklagerecht in der Informations- und Dienstleistungsgesellschaft* (Münster, Landwirtschaftsverlag, 2005) 57, 125–41; J Calais-Auloy and F Steinmetz, *Droit de la consommation*, 7th edn (Paris, Dalloz, 2006) 650–51; R Martin, 'L'action en représentation conjointe des consommateurs' (1994) 68 *Juris-Classeur Périodique La Semaine Juridique* I-3756.

[47] See Cour de Cassation (Ch comm), Decision of 24 November 2009, No 08-13052; L Usunier, 'Collective Redress and Class Actions in France' in M Casper and others (eds), *Auf dem Weg zu einer europäischen Sammelklage?* (Munich, Sellier, 2009) 293, 301–302.

[48] See also EESC Opinion on the collective actions system (n 24) [1.3], [3.5]–[3.6], [4.4].

[49] *DeBremaecker v Short*, 433 F 2d 733, 734 (5th Cir 1970). See also *Lewis v National Football League*, 146 FRD 5, 8 (DDC 1992); *Robertson v National Basketball Association*, 389 F Supp 867, 897 (DCNY 1975) according to which the class is to be 'neither amorphous, nor imprecise'. See furthermore *Coleman v Watt*, 40 F 3d 255, 259 (8th Cir 1994); *Harris v General Development Corp*, 127 FRD 655, 659 (ND Ill 1989).

common to both opt-in and opt-out mechanisms, and they have to be considered by the person launching the proceedings. In the first case, concrete criteria have to be set in order to make it possible for consumers having suffered harm as a result of anti-competitive practices to assess whether their claims are eligible to be included in the action.[50] In opt-out cases, the requirements for claims aggregation[51] have to give proper consideration to the cross-border implications of consumer redress. In particular, commonality as to several specific aspects – such as the nationality (or domicile) of the consumers, the anticompetitive effects producing consumer detriment, the place where the aggregated damages occurred as well as the market level of the plaintiffs (direct or indirect purchasers)[52] – has a bearing on several questions such as ascertaining standing, assessing the *lis pendens* doctrine, granting effective notification to absentee claimants and specifying the binding effect of the anticipated ruling.[53] From the defendant's perspective, an unambiguous definition as to the size either of the group claimants or of the aggregated claims influences his ability to estimate the extent of his liability for damages.[54] A judicial review as to the requirements set by the representative entity for claims aggregation seems necessary in order to ensure procedural efficiency.

Of core importance for a European-wide framework governing collective proceedings is the elaboration of specific standards as to the notification mechanisms for group litigants, and especially absentee claimants. In that respect, a US court[55] accurately pointed out that '[the] right to be heard has little reality or worth unless one is informed that the matter is pending and can choose for himself whether to appear or default, acquiesce or contest'. From an EU perspective, proper consideration has to be given to the traditions of the Member States, the legal fundamentals of the right to a fair trial pursuant to Article 6(1) of the ECHR and Article 47(2) of the Charter of Fundamental Rights of the EU.[56] In this context, a notification to the party adversely affected by a Commission or court decision (as long as his identity is known) has been held by the CJEU[57] to be a substantial aspect of the right to be heard. A similar line of reasoning was followed by the Higher Regional Court of Düsseldorf, finding that service by publication is at variance with German procedural public policy, unless a party seeking to justify service by publication sets out and proves that it

[50] See furthermore Bernhard (n 23) 227–28.

[51] See DP Tzakas, 'Effective Collective Redress in Antitrust and Consumer Protection Matters: A Panacea or a Chimera?' (2011) 48 *CML Rev* 1125, 1141–43.

[52] *cf Emerald Supplies Ltd v British Airways Plc* [2009] EWHC 741 (Ch).

[53] Becker (n 9) 30. See furthermore in the US *Simer v Rios*, 661 F 2d 655, 670 (7th Cir 1981) cert denied, 456 US 917 (1982).

[54] *cf* also EESC Opinion on the collective actions system (n 24) [7.2.2.3.2]; H Koch and J Zekoll, 'Europäisierung der Sammelklage mit Hindernissen' (2010) 18 *Zeitschrift für Europäisches Privatrecht (ZEuP)* 107, 117. See furthermore V Magnier, 'Class Actions, Group Litigation and Other Forms of Collective Litigation, Protocol for National Reporters', http://globalclassactions.stanford.edu/sites/default/files/documents/France_National_Report.pdf 18 arguing that a US class action could be held as infringing the French principle 'dispute over a right' to the extent that absentee French claimants have not appeared in court and have not been heard by the judges. This situation impedes the defendant from properly developing his strategy since he has to encounter unknown French victims. *cf* also R Schütze, 'Die Zustellung US-amerikanischer Class Actions und die Anerkennung und Vollstreckbarkeitserklärung US-amerikanischer Class Action-Urteile und -Vergleiche' in National and Kapodistrian University of Athens, Faculty of Law (ed), *Essays in Honour of K Kerameus* (Athens, Ant N Sakkoulas Publishers, 2009) 1245, 1248–49, 1252–53.

[55] *Mullane v Central Hanover Bank & Trust Co*, 339 US 306, 314 (1950).

[56] See also OFT (n 23) [4.24]. See furthermore Halfmeier and Wimalasena (n 21) 652–56.

[57] Case 32/95 P *Commission v Lisrestal and others* [1996] ECR I-5373 [35]–[44]; Case 49/84 *Leon Emile Gaston Carlos Debaecker and Berthe Plouvier v Cornelis Gerrit Bouwman* [1985] ECR 1779 [10-3], [19-22]. *cf* also Case T-450/93, *Lisrestal and others v Commission* [1994] ECR II-1177 [50-1].

has done everything necessary and possible to determine the unknown whereabouts of the other party.[58] In the case of an opt-out settlement under Dutch law,[59] the *Gerechtshof* Amsterdam[60] underlined that the victims of the infringement in question have to be made reasonably aware of the existence of the agreement and the content thereof, as well as its binding effect and the possibility to opt out. In view of the aforementioned findings, the need for effective notification directed to absentee claimants can hardly be contested, such that attention has therefore to be shifted to the means enabled especially when the putative plaintiffs are localised in the territory of a different Member State than the forum state.

The diversity of Member State laws as to collective proceedings initiated on behalf of consumers is also illuminated by the divergent rules governing the use of unclaimed funds. Such problems will rarely arise in opt-in proceedings since damage funds are requested on behalf of specific persons having to plead and substantiate that the damage occurred to them. In contrast, opt-out instruments entail the risk of acquiring funds which cannot be fully distributed to the consumers harmed by an anticompetitive practice since their identity is unknown, a declaration on their part is not necessary for initiating proceedings and, furthermore, consumers are often unable to prove or even assess the amount of damage they suffered (especially in situations where the violation relates to mass consumer goods). The divergent approaches prevailing in the Member State laws as to this matter are illustrative of the need for legislative action at the EU level.

For example,[61] German law explicitly provides in §34a GWB as well as in §10 of the Unfair Competition Act (*Gesetz gegen den unlauteren Wettbewerb* – UWG) that certain entities are entitled to sue the wrongdoer for the economic benefit obtained at the expense of multiple purchasers or suppliers. However, the disgorged funds have to be surrendered to the federal budget, thus endorsing a government escheat model.[62] A different approach underlies French law, pursuant to which the obtained damage funds remain with the claiming professional association, in the case of proceedings pursuant to Article L470-7 of the Commercial Code.[63] The same applies for civil actions under Article L421-1 of the Consumer Code (*action civile*),[64] whereas the mechanism of the joint representative action of Article L422-1 of the Consumer Code (*action en représentation conjointe*) is based on the distribution of the obtained sums to the persons who provided the suing consumer

[58] OLG Düsseldorf, Decision of 29 November 1999, (2002) 13 *International Litigation Procedure* (ILPr) 71. See also BVerfG, Order of 26 October 1987, (1988) 41 NJW 2361. *cf* also Cour de Cassation, Decision of 30 June 2004, (2005) 16 ILPr 266.

[59] Thereafter, a court can confer binding effect on a settlement concluded between a foundation or association which represents the interests of harmed persons and parties who have committed themselves by this agreement to pay compensation for the damage caused by an event or similar events. See on Dutch law WH van Boom, 'Collective Settlements of Mass Claims in The Netherlands' in M Casper and others (eds), *Auf dem Weg zu einer europäischen Sammelklage?* (Munich, Sellier, 2009) 171.

[60] Gerechtshof Amsterdam, 1783/05, 25 January 2007, LJN: AZ7033. See also M Fallon and DP Tzakas, '*Res Judicata* Effects of Foreign Class Action Rulings in the EU' in Boele-Woelki et al (eds), *Convergence and Divergence in Private International Law: Liber Amicorum Kurt Siehr* (Eleven International Publishing, 2010), 653, 666–69; Mulheron (n 20) 426.

[61] As to the regime governing the distribution of compensation funds obtained after a collective settlement has been reached pursuant to the Dutch law, see van Boom (n 59) 186–88.

[62] Alexander (n 44) 890; Stadler (n 44) 117. But see the criticism expressed and the alternatives proposed by G Wagner, 'Kollektiver Rechtsschutz – Regelungsbedarf bei Massen- und Streuschäden' in M Casper and others (eds), *Auf dem Weg zu einer europäischen Sammelklage?* (Munich, Sellier, 2009) 41, 78–79.

[63] Usunier (n 47) 301–302.

[64] Calais-Auloy and Steinmetz (n 46) 642–45.

association a personally signed authorisation.[65] In contrast, pursuant to Greek law,[66] prescribing in Article 10(16)(b) of the Act on Consumer Protection (No 2251/1994) the right of qualified consumer associations to sue for moral prejudice relating to the general consumer interests harmed by an infringement, only 30 per cent of the obtained sum is disbursed to the state budget, the rest going to consumer associations (35 per cent to the claiming consumer association and 35 per cent being disbursed to consumer associations of second degree) for the purposes of informing, educating and generally protecting consumers (Article 10(22) Act on Consumer Protection). Portuguese law does not establish any system for distributing compensation funds obtained by an opt-out 'popular action', and, therefore, it has been suggested that the parties to such a dispute should resort 'exclusively to arbitration, setting up a highly specialized court or arbitration committee alongside the court in question which processes the payment of all the indemnities.'[67]

C. Jurisdictional Issues

From a jurisdictional perspective, it has to be noted that cross-border collective proceedings brought on behalf or in the interest of consumers are not excluded – at least *de lege lata* – from the scope of application of the Brussels I Regulation.[68] It has been argued[69] that the Brussels I Regulation is not suited to the needs of collective proceedings since it is premised upon the concept of two-party-proceedings. However, in *Henkel*[70] the CJEU rejected the arguments of the UK Government and held that an action brought by a consumer association in order to obtain an injunction preventing traders from the use of certain unfair terms in their contracts with consumers constitutes a civil and commercial matter falling within the scope of the Brussels I Regulation. In view of the scrutiny undertaken by the Court as to the applicability of specific jurisdictional bases on such an action, the aforementioned arguments have to be considered as policy proposals.[71]

The Green Paper on the Review of the Brussels I Regulation gives consideration to the ongoing initiatives at the EU level on collective redress and poses the question whether

[65] Calais-Auloy and Steinmetz (n 46) 650–51. *cf* also L Cadiet and E Jeuland, *Droit judiciaire privé*, 5th edn (Paris, LexisNexis, 2006), 239.

[66] See on Greek law A Mikroulea, 'Verbandsklage auf Schadensersatz im griechischen Verbraucherschutzgesetz' in KJ Hopt and D Tzouganatos (eds), *Europäisierung des Wirtschaftsrechts* (Tübingen, Mohr Siebeck, 2006) 309.

[67] See H Sousa Antunes, 'Class Actions, Group Litigation and Other Forms of Collective Litigation (Portuguese Report)', http://globalclassactions.stanford.edu/sites/default/files/documents/Portugal_National_Report.pdf 27.

[68] Council Regulation 44/2001 of 22 December 2000 on jurisdiction and the recognition and enforcement of judgments in civil and commercial matters [2001] OJ L12/1.

[69] European Consumer Consultative Group, 'Opinion on private damages actions' (2010), http://ec.europa.eu/consumers/empowerment/docs/ECCG_opinion_on_actions_for_damages_18112010.pdf, 4–5. *cf* also Consultation paper presenting the first working analysis of the impact of the options in the light of the replies to the Green Paper on consumer collective redress, http://ec.europa.eu/consumers/redress_cons/docs/consultation_paper2009.pdf [31]–[32], pointing out the lack of specific provisions. See furthermore C Kessedjian and others, 'Response to the Commission Green Paper on Consumer Collective Redress', http://ec.europa.eu/consumers/redress_cons/responses/pract_Coll_Europeen_Paris_fr.pdf, 13–14; B Hess, 'Cross-border Collective Litigation and the Regulation Brussels I' (2010) 30 *Praxis des Internationalen Privat- und Verfahrensrechts* (IPRax) 116; H Muir Watt, 'Brussels I and Aggregate Litigation or the case for Redesigning the Common Judicial Area in Order to Respond to Changing, Functions and Structures in Contemporary Adjudication and Litigation' (2010) 30 IPRax 111, 112.

[70] Case C-167/00, *Verein für Konsumenteninformation v Karl Heinz Henkel* [2002] ECR I-8111 [25]–[31]. See M Danov, 'The Brussels I Regulation: Cross-Border Collective Redress Proceedings and Judgments' (2010) 6(2) JPIL 359, 376.

[71] See also Green Paper on Consumer Collective Redress (n 24) [58].

specific jurisdiction rules are necessary for collective redress.[72] The subsequent Commission Proposal identifies the divergent approaches of Member States as to collective proceedings and, therefore, acknowledges a deficit as to the required level of trust. For that reason, the most important precondition for a potential abolition of *exequatur* is not met such that recognition and enforcement of collective redress rulings rendered by Member State courts will continue to be governed by the present regime.[73] In alignment with this policy reasoning, the Commission Consultation Paper identifies the absence of specific jurisdictional rules relating to collective litigation mechanisms and raises the question whether the current rules of the Brussels I Regulation can sufficiently achieve the objective of the efficient functioning of collective redress instruments.[74]

Notwithstanding the need to clarify the existing rules, the creation of a separate jurisdictional framework tailored only for these cases seems – at least in competition-related litigation – rather debatable.[75] Three arguments are of importance in this regard. First, the aggregation of claims on the plaintiff-side cannot, *ab initio*, be considered as establishing an inferior position on the part of the wrongdoer,[76] provided that the represented consumers are appropriately identified and designated.[77] This finding is supported by the restrictive understanding of the CJEU as to the rules on special jurisdiction which are entailed in the Brussels I Regulation.[78] Secondly, it has to be borne in mind that a specific jurisdictional framework tailored exclusively for the needs of collective proceedings may hamper jurisdictional predictability and uniformity where the aggregated claims are viable.[79] The adoption of a distinct set of rules would open a right of choice for the harmed individuals as to the Member State courts that can be seised, depending upon the initiation of individual or collective proceedings. A last argument in this context relates to the substantial regulatory and factual impediments when proceedings have to be concentrated before a single Member State court. This is the case when different laws are applicable to the aggregated claims or when the degree of passing-on differs due to the price elasticity of demand

[72] Commission, 'Green Paper on the Review of Council Regulation (EC) No 44/2001 on Jurisdiction and the Recognition and Enforcement of Judgments in Civil and Commercial Matters' COM (2009) 175 final, 21 April 2009, 11. See also Commission, 'Report to the European Parliament, the Council and the European Economic and Social Committee on the application of Council Regulation (EC) No 44/2001 on jurisdiction and the recognition and enforcement of judgments in civil and commercial matters' COM(2009) 174 final, 21 April 2009, 7–8, 10; European Economic and Social Committee (EESC), 'Opinion on Green Paper on the review of Council Regulation (EC) No 44/2001 on jurisdiction and the recognition and enforcement of judgments in civil and commercial matters'[2008] OJ C162/1 [1.6], [4.12.4]–[4.12.5].

[73] See Commission, 'Proposal for a Regulation of the European Parliament and of the Council on jurisdiction and the recognition and enforcement of judgments in civil and commercial matters' COM(2010) 748 final, 14 December 2010, 5–7, 18.

[74] Commission Staff Working Document (n 20) [28]. also EESC Opinion on the collective actions system (n 24) [4.5] stipulating the beneficial effect of a European collective action in order to make set out precise definitions of the rules governing jurisdiction.

[75] See Green Paper on Consumer Collective Redress (n 24) [58]. See furthermore Tzakas (n 51) 1153–58.

[76] *cf* however Kessedjian (n 43) 287–90.

[77] *cf* however from a French perspective Magnier (n 54) 16–18, arguing that the principle of the equality of arms may be at stake if the defendant is not aware of all its opponents.

[78] See generally on Arts 5 and 6 Brussels I Regulation Case 189/87 *Athanasios Kalfelis v Bankhaus Schröder and others* [1988] ECR 5565[19]. See on Art 5(1) Case C-533/07 *Falco Privatstiftung and Thomas Rabitsch v Gisela Weller-Lindhorst* [2009] ECR I-3327 [37]. See on Art 5(3) Case C-364/93 *Antonio Marinari v Lloyds Bank plc and Zubaidi Trading Co* [1995] ECR I-2719 [13]–[15]; Case C-168/02 *Rudolf Kronhofer v Marianne Maier and others* [2004] ECR I-6009 [14]; Case C-189/08 *Zuid-Chemie BV v Philippo's Mineralenfabriek NV-SA* [2009] ECR I-6917 [22].

[79] *cf* also Commission Staff Working Paper, Accompanying the White Paper (n 26) [61].

in each national market,[80] such that the need to build various sub-groups of claimants amounts to hampering jurisdictional efficiency.

As to the individual jurisdictional bases of the Brussels I Regulation, no specific problems in case of cross-border collective actions on behalf of consumers are posed by Articles 2 (domicile/seat of the defendant),[81] 5(5) (establishment of the defendant)[82] and 6(1) (domicile/seat of one of the multiple defendants).[83]

In contrast to actions for nullity of contracts infringing Articles 101 and 102 TFEU, the large majority of tort claims for damages, cessation or injunctive relief are to be deemed as non-contractual, thus falling under Article 5(3) of the Brussels I Regulation. The enactment of a specific rule in Article 6 of the Rome II Regulation[84] designating the law applicable to non-contractual obligations arising out of a restriction of competition argues in favour of this approach.[85] Specific aspects regarding the interpretation of Article 5(3) of the Brussels I Regulation are not to be considered as posing peculiarities in case of collective redress instruments. This applies to matters such as the applicability of the so-called *Shevill* doctrine[86] and the construction of the connecting factor of the 'place where the harmful event occurred',[87] which encompasses both the place of the event giving rise to the claimed damage as well as the place where the damage occurred.[88]

[80] See Commission, 'Draft Guidance Paper, Quantifying harm in actions for damages based on breaches of Article 101 or 102 of the Treaty on the Functioning of the European Union, Public consultation' (2011), http://ec.europa.eu/competition/consultations/2011_actions_damages/draft_guidance_paper_en.pdf [142]–[151]; Oxera and a multi-jurisdictional team of lawyers led by Dr A Komninos, 'Quantifying antitrust damages, Towards non-binding guidance for courts, Study prepared for the European Commission' (2009), http://ec.europa.eu/competition/antitrust/actionsdamages/quantification_study.pdf, 36, 117, 139, 141. See furthermore FW Bulst, *Schadensersatzansprüche der Marktgegenseite im Kartellrecht* (Baden-Baden, CH Beck/Nomos, 2006) 281–86.

[81] See Danov (n 70) 365–67; Rott (n 42) 383.

[82] See Danov (n 70) 368–71; DP Tzakas, *Die Haftung für Kartellrechtsverstöße im internationalen Rechtsverkehr* (Baden-Baden, CH Beck/Nomos, 2011) 122–26; Kessedjian (n 43) 291.

[83] Danov (n 70) 371–72; Rott (n 42) 384–85; Tzakas (n 82) 126–30; M Wilderspin, 'Jurisdictional Issues: Brussels I Regulation Articles 6(1), 23, 27 and 28 in Antitrust Litigation' in J Basedow and S Francq and L Idot (eds), *International Antitrust Litigation Conflict of Laws and Coordination* (Oxford, Hart Publishing, 2012) 41. *cf* also C Kessedjian, R Garnett and G Verhoosel, 'Transnational Group Actions' in International Law Association, *Report of the Seventy-Third Conference* (London, International Law Association, 2008) 534, 552–53.

[84] European Parliament and Council Regulation 864/2007 of 11 July 2007 on the law applicable to non-contractual obligations (Rome II) [2007] OJ L199/40.

[85] On the delineation between contractual and non-contractual obligations arising out of infringements of antitrust legislation see S Poillot-Peruzzetto and D Lawnicka, 'Relevance of the Distinction between the Contractual and Non-Contractual Spheres (Jurisdiction and Applicable Law)' in J Basedow and S Francq and L Idot (eds), *International Antitrust Litigation Conflict of Laws and Coordination* (Oxford, Hart Publishing, 2012) 131.

[86] Case C-68/93 *Fiona Shevill and others v Presse Alliance SA* [1995] ECR I-415, where the CJEU ruled that the victim of a libel by a newspaper article distributed in several Member States may bring an action for damages against the publisher before the courts of each Member State in which the publication was distributed and where the victim claims to have suffered injury to his reputation, which have jurisdiction to rule solely in respect of the harm caused in the state of the court seised.

[87] See the leading Case 21/76 *Handelskwekerij G. J. Bier BV v Mines de potasse d'Alsace SA* [1976] ECR 1735. See furthermore Case C-220/88 *Dumez France SA and Tracoba SARL v Hessische Landesbank and others* [1990] ECR I-49 [10]; Case C-51/97, *Réunion européenne SA and others v Spliethoff's Bevrachtingskantoor BV* [1998] ECR I-6511 [28].

[88] See on this issue J Basedow, 'International Cartels and the Place of Acting under Article 5(3) of the Brussels I Regulation' in J Basedow and S Francq and L Idot (eds), *International Antitrust Litigation Conflict of Laws and Coordination* (Oxford, Hart Publishing, 2012) 31; FW Bulst, 'Internationale Zuständigkeit, anwendbares Recht und Schadensberechnung im Kartelldeliktsrecht', (2004) 15 *Europäisches Wirtschafts- und Steuerrecht* (EWS) 403; G Mäsch, 'Vitamine für Kartellopfer – Forum shopping im europäischen Kartelldeliktsrecht' (2005) 25 IPRax 509; L Radicati di Brozolo, 'Antitrust Claims: Why exclude them from the Hague Jurisdiction and Judgments Convention?' (2004) 25 *ECLR* 780, 787–88; Tzakas (n 82) 100 et seq.

D. Conflict-of-Laws Issues

The enactment of the Rome II Regulation and its inclusion in Article 6 of a specific rule for the law applicable to non-contractual obligations arising out of a restraint of competition ensures, to a certain extent, legal certainty and a level playing field within the EU as far as concerns the choice-of-law implications of civil antitrust liability. However, the peculiarities of collective redress have not been properly taken into account such that concrete issues of private international law impeding cross-border collective proceedings still remain unresolved.[89]

(i) Recognition of Representative Entities

Both Article 1(2)(d) of the Rome II Regulation and Article 1(2)(f) of the Rome I Regulation[90] exclude matters of creation, recognition and legal capacity of companies and other bodies corporate or unincorporated from their field of application. The absence of a uniform EU rule amounts to diverging approaches as to the appropriate connecting factors used in order to recognise foreign legal persons and designate the law applicable to them. Of note are the 'real seat theory', postulating the applicability of the laws of the country where the central administration of a foreign legal person is situated, and, in contrast, the 'incorporation theory', which shifts attention exclusively to the law under which a legal person has been incorporated.[91] It is quite debatable whether the CJEU cases *Überseering*[92] and *Inspire Art*[93] mitigate the existing discrepancies,[94] since consumer associations and other representative entities seem not to fall under the scope of application of the freedom of establishment pursuant to Article 54 TFEU.[95] Thereafter, the *ratione personae* applicability of the EU right is confined to 'companies or firms constituted under civil or commercial law, including cooperative societies, and other legal persons governed by public or private law, save for those which are non-profit-making'. Assuming that in the case of consumer associations and other representative entities the incorporation will more often than not coincide with the real seat, this aspect seems to be of limited importance.

(ii) Questions of Standing

The usual distinction drawn in continental legal systems between the standing of representative entities (*Verbandsklagebefugnis*, *qualité pour agir en justice*) and the existence of a right to sue (*Aktivlegitimation*, *intérêt à agir*)[96] is linked to diverging approaches as to their

[89] *cf* also EESC Opinion on the collective actions system (n 24) [4.5].

[90] European Parliament and Council Regulation 593/2008 of 17 June 2008 on the law applicable to contractual obligations (Rome I) [2008] OJ L177/6.

[91] See P Kindler, 'Internationales Handels- und Gesellschaftsrecht' in HJ Sonnenberger (ed) *Münchener Kommentar zum Bürgerlichen Gesetzbuch*, vol 11, 4th edn (Munich, CH Beck, 2006) 130 et seq.

[92] Case C-208/00 *Überseering BV v Nordic Construction Company Baumanagement GmbH* [2002] ECR I-9919.

[93] Case C-167/01 *Kamer van Koophandel en Fabrieken voor Amsterdam v Inspire Art Ltd* [2003] ECR I-10155.

[94] See also EM Kieninger, 'The Law Applicable to Corporations in the EC' (2009) 73 *Rabels Zeitschrift für ausländisches und internationales Privatrecht* 607.

[95] See also P Jung, 'Artikel 48 EGV' in J Schwarze (ed), *EU-Kommentar*, 2nd edn (Baden-Baden, Nomos, 2009) 686 [7].

[96] On the German law see K Maurer, *Grenzüberschreitende Unterlassungsklagen von Verbraucherschutzverbänden* (Münster, LIT Verlag, 2001) 56; HW Micklitz, 'Efficacité internationale de l'action en suppression des clauses

classification in the context of choice of law.[97] On the one hand, the sole application of the *lex fori* may amount to broad forum shopping in the EU since representative entities will seek to initiate proceedings before the courts of a Member State providing the most far-reaching remedies and possibilities for compensation. On the other hand, it could be argued that both standing and the right to sue are governed by the law applicable on the merits pursuant to Article 15(a) and (f) of the Rome II Regulation. This approach seems functional only in those cases to which the mosaic principle (*Mosaikprinzip*) entailed by Article 6(3)(a) of the Rome II Regulation[98] applies. For example, a German trade association representing enterprises having suffered harmed by an anti-competitive practice implemented in Germany would, thereafter, be entitled to seek injunctive relief under section 33(2) GWB before the courts of another Member State.

The case stands, however, differently if the concentration rules entailed by Article 6(3)(b) of the Rome II Regulation come into play. A literal application of the rule[99] would amount to allowing a German consumer association certified under the German consumer protection law and representing exclusively German consumers who have suffered damages because of an anti-competitive practice affecting the markets in more than one country to initiate proceedings before the English courts under section 47B of the Competition Act 1998. One cannot overlook the significant potential for far-reaching forum shopping that would effectively allow specific entities more rights of action than under the law of their incorporation or the law applicable under the basic rule of Article 6(3)(a) of the Rome II Regulation.[100]

(iii) Interchangeability of Representative Entities

One of the main obstacles impeding cross-border litigation by means of representative actions is the fact that most of the procedural instruments prescribed in the Member State laws are usually drafted for domestic entities or, at least, require a domestic act of certifica-

abusives: Le point de vue allemand' (2000) 52 *Revue Internationale de Droit Comparé* 867, 871; S Tsantinis, *Aktivlegitimationen und Prozeßführungsbefugnisse von Individuen und Organisationen im UWG-Prozeßrecht* (Frankfurt am Main, Peter Lang, 1995) 17–23, 28–31. On the French law, see H Croze, C Morel and O Fradin, *Procédure civile* (Paris, Éditions du Juris-Classeur, 2003) 125 et seq; G Cornu and J Foyer, *Procédure Civile*, 3rd edn (Paris, PUF, 1996) 334 et seq; S Amrani Mekki, 'Inciter les actions en dommages et intérêts en droit de la concurrence: Le point de vue d'un processualiste' (2009) *Concurrences*, édition spéciale, L Idot (ed), *Actes du colloque sur le livre blanc sur les actions en dommages et intérêts pour infraction aux règles communautaires sur les ententes et les abus de position dominante* 11, 14–16.

[97] For a comparison of the classification of standing and the right to sue under German and French law see Tzakas (n 40) 172–73.

[98] As to the mosaic principle see S Francq and W Wurmnest, 'International Antitrust Claims under the Rome II Regulation' in J Basedow and S Francq and L Idot (eds), *International Antitrust Litigation Conflict of Laws and Coordination* (Oxford, Hart Publishing, 2012) 91, 124, 127; J Fitchen, 'Choice of Law in International Claims Based on Restrictions of Competition: Article 6(3) of the Rome II Regulation' (2009) 5 JPIL 337, 355–58; P Mankowski, 'Das neue Internationale Kartellrecht des Art 6 Abs 3 der Rom II-Verordnung' (2008) 54 *Recht der Internationalen Wirtschaft* 177, 188–89; U Scholz and G Rixen, 'Die neue europäische Kollisionsnorm für außervertragliche Schuldverhältnisse aus wettbewerbsbeschränkendem Verhalten' (2009) 20 *Europäische Zeitschrift für Wirtschaftsrecht* 327, 330. See furthermore from a comparative perspective DP Tzakas, 'Civil Antitrust Liability in the International Context: From *Empagran* to the Rome II Regulation' (2012) *Deutsch-Amerikanische Juristen-Vereinigung Newsletter* (DAJV-NL) 19, 23–25.

[99] For the applicability of the concentration rules entailed in Art 6(3)(b) Rome II Regulation only in case the cross-border infringement in question causes damages to the claimant in the territories of different Member States such that more than one Member State's laws are deemed to apply under the basic rule of Art 6(3)(a), see Francq and Wurmnest (n 98) 127; Tzakas (n 82) 572–74.

[100] See on this matter Tzakas (n 40) 174–75.

tion. This is, for instance, the case in the UK, where the remedy of section 47B of the Competition Act 1998 is prescribed only for entities 'specified' in an order made by the Secretary of State,[101] or in France, where the joint representative action (*action en représentation conjointe*) under Article L422-1 of the Consumer Code is allowed only for approved associations recognised as being representative at the national level.[102] This means that the initiation of proceedings under Article L422-1 of the Consumer Code by a specified body pursuant to section 47B(9) of the Competition Act 1998 requires, at a first stage, the recognition of the order made by the UK Secretary of State and, further, the acknowledgement that this order is equivalent to certification (*agrément*) under Articles R411-1–R411-6 of the Consumer Code. In that respect, each Member State court is required to provide an answer 'whether the institutions representing the same aspect of the case correspond to each other to such an extent as to be interchangeable'.[103]

A further issue relates to the allowance of such remedies in favour of foreign entities whose law of incorporation either does not provide for a similar certification or does not require an equivalent act for the initiation of domestic proceedings. A mutual recognition of such entities would be consistent with both the principle of effectiveness of EU competition law and the need to abolish any discrimination at the expense of such entities.[104] Nevertheless, it remains rather debatable whether the national legislator or the national judge can be forced to afford certain persons more powers than they possess under the law of their origin.[105]

(iv) Representation of Foreign Claimants

The need for allowing cross-border litigation in case of infringements of Articles 101 and 102 TFEU by means of collective redress instruments is inextricably linked to the adoption of a specific rule governing the requirements for bringing claims of foreign (especially absentee) plaintiffs. Indeed, the aim of creating an EU Internal Market without internal frontiers in which free movement of goods, persons, services and capital is ensured pursuant to Article 26(2) TFEU (formerly Art 14(2) EC) argues against the exclusion of such possibilities. In opt-in proceedings, the deliberate representations made by a foreign claimant in order to become a party to the procedure are, therefore, not to be prohibited, at least to the extent that his claims are eligible for inclusion pursuant to the criteria for claims aggregation set out at the time when the action was initiated. The same takes on considerable significance in the case of opt-out mechanisms where the representative entity has to substantiate the persons – potentially comprising foreigners – whose claims will be included. In the case of a representative action brought before the German courts by a

[101] See, eg, the Specified Body (Consumer Claims) Order 2005, SI 2005/2365.

[102] See also Beuchler (n 46) 142–47; Calais-Auloy and Steinmetz (n 46) 650–51; D Hoffmann, 'Directive 'Actions en cessation en matière de protection des intérêts des consommateurs' (Dir 98/27/CE du 19/5/98)' (2000) 8 *European Review of Private Law* 147, 149.

[103] K Lipstein, *Principles of the Conflict of Laws, National and International* (The Hague, Martinus Nijhoff Publishers, 1981) 103. See also Bureau and Muir Watt (n 42) 474–78; J Kropholler, *Internationales Privatrecht*, 6th edn (Tübingen, Mohr Siebeck, 2006) 231–34.

[104] *cf* E Kapnopoulou, *Das Recht der mißbräuchlichen Klauseln in der Europäischen Union* (Tübingen, Mohr Siebeck, 1997) 250; P Lakkis, *Der kollektive Rechtsschutz der Verbraucher in der Europäischer Union* (Bielefeld, Verlag Ernst und Werner Gieseking, 1997) 152–54; Micklitz (n 96) 876.

[105] B Audit, *Droit International Privé*, 8th edn (Paris, Economica, 2008) 370 fn 3. *cf* also Fallon (n 42) 258; A Morin, 'Les Actions Collectives Transfrontalières: Rapport Français' in B Stauder (ed), *Les Actions Collectives Transfrontalières des Organisations de Consommateurs* (Zurich, Schulthess, 1997) 69, 76–77.

German consumer association, the German Federal Court of Justice[106] relied on the fact that the business practice in question constituted an act of unfair competition producing effects only in the French market, such that only French law was to apply on the merits. The court's decision did not turn on the issue of a domestic consumer association's standing where only the interests of foreign EU consumers are at stake; rather, the court rejected the association's right to sue under German law, since the matter was being decided under the law applicable on the merits, French law, to which the plaintiff had not referred. In the same case, the Higher Regional Court of Köln[107] devised an interesting standard as to the representation of claimants domiciled outside the forum state. The court undertook a scrutiny of the statutes of the claiming association and focused on the reach of its responsibilities considered from a personal, operational and territorial perspective, empowering the claiming association with the protection of the interests of foreign consumers.

Furthermore, it has to be noted that the Rome II Regulation creates a significant amount of legal uncertainty as to the choice of law rule governing the issue. Indeed, the representation of foreign plaintiffs could be regarded as a matter related to the internal organisation of the entity and, consequently, excluded from the reach of the Rome II Regulation pursuant to Article 1(d). The opposite approach is advocated by Article 15(f), prescribing that the law applicable under the Rome II Regulation shall, inter alia, govern the matter of the persons entitled to compensation for damage sustained personally. In the latter case, the mosaic principle under the basic rule of Article 6(3)(a) of the Rome II Regulation amounts to the distributive application of several national laws providing different instruments and standards for representation of foreign absentee claimants. Jurisdictional inefficiencies of this kind might be countered with recourse to the concentration rules of Article 6(3)(b) of the Rome II Regulation.[108] With regard, however, to the concerns about forum shopping, many scholars distinguish the issue of representation and, therefore, allege that the representative authorisation is properly governed by the law applicable to the collective entity.[109]

(v) Distribution of the Obtained Damage Funds

The aforementioned variety of the national collective redress mechanisms as to the use of the obtained damage funds reflects the choice-of-law implications of cross-border litigation. On the one hand, a procedural classification of the issue – such that the *lex fori* will be deemed to apply (see Article 1(3) of the Rome II Regulation) – creates a significant amount of possibilities for forum shopping and promotes 'cherry picking' tactics on the part of the representative entities. On the other hand, the application of the *lex causae* to this matter could pursuant to the rules of Article 15(c) and (e) of the Rome II Regulation be considered as designating the reach of the law applicable on the merits. Indeed, the application of the mosaic principle enshrined in Article 6(3)(a) of the Rome II Regulation may lead to

[106] BGH, Decision of 26 November 1997, (1998) 13 *Verbraucher und Recht* (VuR) 171, 172–74 note N Reich. *cf* also BGH, Decision of 15 November 1991, (1991) 44 NJW 1054, 1055. See furthermore Rott (n 42) 388.

[107] OLG Köln, Decision of 12 May 1995, (1995) 10 VuR 289, 292–93.

[108] Becker (n 9) 22.

[109] JY Carlier, 'Les Actions Collectives Transfrontalières: Rapport Belge' in B Stauder (ed), *Les Actions Collectives Transfrontalières des Organisations de Consommateurs* (Zurich, Schulthess, 1997) 45, 58–61; Fallon (n 42) 253–54, 261. See also H Koch, 'Internationale Verbandsklage?' (1996) 11 *Verbraucher und Recht* 67, 68; Maurer (n 96) 98–99.

proper consideration of the law governing the claims that the representative entity brings before court. However, the case assumes a different posture when the concentration rules entailed in Article 6(3)(b) Rome II Regulation are deemed to govern the use of obtained and – especially – undistributed damage funds. For instance, a German trade association would be interested in skimming off the profits of a cartel member under section 34a of the German GWB without being obliged to surrender the obtained benefits to the federal budget.[110]

III. ASSESSING THE LEGISLATIVE PROPOSALS

A. The European Commission's Initiatives

In the Green Paper on 'Damages actions for breach of the EC antitrust rules',[111] the European Commission gives specific consideration to the policy rationale of defending consumer interests by enabling appropriate redress mechanisms. In view of this objective, enabling a cause of action for consumer associations or other qualified entities which does not prevent individual consumers from bringing an action is discussed. Of importance, in this regard, are issues of standing, the adoption of an opt-in mechanism consisting of a possible registration or authorisation system, as well as the distribution and quantification of damages. Furthermore, the Green Paper also discusses the introduction of a special provision for collective action by groups of purchasers other than final consumers.

The subsequent White Paper on 'Damages actions for breach of the EC antitrust rules'[112] departs from the need for mechanisms allowing the aggregation of individual claims and therefore suggests the adoption of two complementary mechanisms of collective redress, namely a representative action and an opt-in collective action. The representative action can be initiated by qualified entities, such as consumer associations, state bodies or trade associations, which are either officially designated in advance or certified on an ad hoc basis by a Member State. The proceedings are brought on behalf of some or all of their members. In case of collective actions, the victims have to expressly decide to combine into one single action their individual claims for the harm that they suffered. The underlying policy rationale is formed by the need to complement the victims' individual rights of

[110] See on this matter Tzakas (n 40) 180–81.

[111] Commission, 'Damages actions for breach of the EC antitrust rules' (Green Paper) COM (2005) 672 final, 19 December 2005, 8–9. See also Commission, 'Staff Working Paper, Annex to the Green Paper, Damages actions for breach of the EC antitrust rules' (Staff Working Paper) SEC (2005) 1732, 19 December 2005 [31], [188]–[201]; European Economic and Social Committee, 'Opinion on the Green Paper – Damages Actions for breach of the EC antitrust rules' [2006] OJ L324/1.

[112] Commission, 'Damages actions for breach of the EC antitrust rules' (White Paper) COM (2008) 165 final, 2 April 2008, 4. See also Commission, 'Staff Working Paper Accompanying the White Paper on Damages actions for breach of the EC antitrust rules' SEC (2008) 404, 2 April 2008 [24]–[64]; Commission, 'Staff Working Paper Accompanying the White Paper; Commission Staff Working Document, Accompanying document to the White Paper on Damages actions for breach of the EC antitrust rules, Impact Assessment' SEC (2008) 405, 2 April 2008 [39]–[56]. See furthermore European Parliament, 'Resolution of 26 March on the White Paper on damages actions for breach of the EC antitrust rules' (2008/2154(INI)) PA TA(2009)0187; European Economic and Social Committee (EESC), 'Opinion on the White Paper on damages actions for breach of the EC antitrust rules' [2009] OJ C228/40.

action and guarantee procedural efficiency, while at the same time multiple recoveries for the same harm have to be avoided.[113]

The unofficial pre-draft Directive recognises the need to guarantee the full effectiveness of Articles 101 and 102 TFEU and, therefore, considers that the exercise of the EU right to compensation must be effectively ensured in all Member States through a set of common standards. Following the approach of the White Paper, the enactment of a combination of two complementary mechanisms, namely group and representative actions, is suggested such that injured parties are in a position to launch the collective redress instrument that is most appropriate to the circumstances of each case (Recital 7). Pursuant to Article 4 of the pre-draft Directive, group actions have to be treated by national courts as one single action and are jointly brought by two or more individuals. The defendant is not to be prevented from raising defences that might be relevant to one or several of the plaintiffs. As far as representative actions are concerned, Article 5(1) of the pre-draft Directive obliges the Member States to ensure that qualified entities can bring an action for damages on behalf of injured parties having suffered harm caused by the same violation. Qualified entities constitute pursuant to Article 6(1) of the pre-draft Directive either entities representing legitimate interests and which are designated by a Member State as entities generally entitled to bring representative actions on behalf of injured parties, or bodies representing legitimate interests of their members and are authorised by a Member State in relation to a specific infringement of Articles 101 or 102 TFEU. Recital 8 stipulates that only consumer organisations, trade associations and state bodies fall within the scope of the rule.

The Joint information note by Vice-President Viviane Reding, Vice-President Joaquín Almunia and Commissioner John Dalli entitled 'Towards a Coherent European Approach to Collective Redress: Next Steps',[114] identified a first set of core principles which could form part of a European framework for collective redress. Furthermore, the note highlighted the objective of avoiding unmeritorious claims and announced a public consultation in order to elaborate a coherent European approach. In 2011, the Commission launched a horizontal public consultation in order to identify the common legal principles underpinning the Member States' legal traditions on collective redress and underscore the added value of such mechanisms for improving the enforcement of EU legislation and protecting the victims' rights.[115] The consultation focuses on the relationship between different forms of collective redress instruments and enforcement of EU law by public authorities and the compliance of such initiatives with the principles of EU law. Specific consideration is given to the main features of collective redress systems as well as to the safeguards needed in order to avoid abuses or lengthy and costly litigation. As to representative actions, attention is shifted to the standing of the eligible entity and the notification requirements, especially in the international context. Further issues discussed in the public consultation are the alternative dispute resolution systems, the safeguards protecting against unmeritorious claims and issues of financing collective redress. Specific reference

[113] Commission White Paper (n 112) 4; Commission Staff Working Paper, Accompanying the White Paper (n 112) [43], [60]–[61]; European Parliament Resolution (n 112) [8]; Opinion on the White Paper (n 112) [4.4.4]. *cf* also Commission Staff Working Document (n 20) [21]. *cf* also EESC Opinion on the collective actions system (n 24) [7.1.2]. *cf* furthermore the parallel initiative in the fields of consumer protection law: Green Paper on Consumer Collective Redress (n 24) [18], [52], [55].

[114] SEC (2010) 1192. *cf* also Commission Staff Working Paper, Accompanying the White Paper (n 112) [62]–[64].

[115] Commission, 'Staff Working Document Public Consultation: Towards a Coherent European Approach to Collective Redress' SEC (2011) 173 final, 4 February 2011. See also European Parliament Resolution (n 112) [5]–[6]; EESC Opinion on the White Paper (n 112) [4.2.1].

is, furthermore, made to the cross-border aspects of collective redress encompassing both jurisdictional and conflict-of-law issues.

B. The Principle of Mutual Recognition

As to the entities entitled to launch representative actions, the Commission Staff Working Paper accompanying the White Paper names consumer associations defending consumers' interests, or trade associations defending the interests of their members active in a given industry.[116] Furthermore, the Paper distinguishes between entities representing legitimate and defined interests, which are officially designated in advance by their Member State, and ad hoc certified entities. The latter are eligible to initiate actions only in relation to a particular infringement and on an ad hoc basis according to the procedures laid down in the national law of their Member State such that sufficient assurance is given that abusive litigation will be avoided.[117] The same reasoning is followed in Recital 8 and Article 6(1) of the pre-draft Directive.

In view of this finding, the mutual recognition of both kinds of representative entities is foreseen in the White Paper such that entities having standing in one Member State should automatically be granted standing in all other Member States without having to be certified in the latter.[118] The same approach is endorsed in Article 6(5) of the pre-draft Directive providing that both kinds of entities prescribed in Article 6(1) are to have the right to bring representative actions in all other Member States according to the procedural rules applicable in these Member States without any additional requirements. This effective implementation of the principle of mutual recognition following the model of Directive 98/27[119] facilitates cross-border actions and serves to alleviate problems emanating from the diverging classification of standing and right to sue in the laws of the EU Member States.[120] Thereafter, entities designated in advance or certified ad hoc by a Member State acquire a pan-European 'pass' such that they will be held as interchangeable with the entities eligible to commence proceedings under the domestic laws of every Member State. This approach provides an effective means to strengthen the European Area of Justice where individuals and especially cartel victims are prevented or dissuaded from exercising their rights beyond the national borders of their home country.

C. Notification Mechanisms

Regarding the notification requirements, the Commission Staff Working Paper accompanying the White Paper acknowledges the mandatory nature of providing for effective mechanisms in order to inform the victims of the initiation of the proceedings and the

[116] Commission Staff Working Paper, Accompanying the White Paper (n 112) [49]–[50], [52]–[53], [60]; European Parliament Resolution (n 112) [9]; EESC Opinion on the White Paper (n 112) [4.4.4].

[117] Commission Staff Working Paper, Accompanying the White Paper (n 112) [52]–[53].

[118] ibid [55]. *cf* also Green Paper on Consumer Collective Redress (n 24) [24].

[119] Council Directive 98/27 of 19 May 1998 on injunctions for the protection of consumers' interests [1998] OJ L166/51.

[120] See also European Parliament Resolution (n 112) [9]; EESC Opinion on the Green Paper (n 111) [5.4.3.1].

inclusion of their claims.[121] The same policy rationale is followed by Recital 9 to the pre-draft Directive stipulating the obligation of qualified entities to implement effective mechanisms for informing the individuals represented in the proceedings. A more elaborated rule is entailed by Article 6(3) of the pre-draft Directive, providing that:

> The qualified entity shall take the appropriate means to make the representative action known to all those who may have claims for damages within the scope of the representative action. It shall inform the court of the means by which it has done so or intends to do so. The court shall either approve such means, if it is satisfied that they are suited to the particular circumstances of the case and provide those concerned with a reasonable opportunity to learn of the existence of the representative action, or request appropriate amendments.

Although the rule introduces a well-balanced standard, further guidance as to the specific means of notification and to their hierarchy should be provided for national judges such that legal certainty and harmonisation of the diverging national standards can be ensured.[122]

D. Operability of the Opt-Out Requirement

Although reservations may be expressed as to the adoption of the opt-out model in view of the inefficiencies of the US class actions and the Member State approaches relating to the principle of party disposition,[123] it must be recalled that national legislators maintain a significant margin of appreciation when designating the eligible representative entities. Besides the duty of monitoring such bodies, it has to be borne in mind that the obligation of safeguarding the full effectiveness of any future EU legislative act is inextricably linked to the designation of certain legal persons which, pursuant to the peculiarities of each national law, can be relied upon to undertake such actions and eliminate the risk of unmeritorious litigation.[124] Of note, in this context, are the US 'parens patriae suits',[125] empowering a state to sue for damages in its quasi-sovereign capacity on behalf of its citizens. In this regard, the Commission Staff Working Paper accompanying the Green Paper on Damages actions for breach of the EU antitrust rules shifts attention to public group actions that may be instituted by an authority held as suitable to represent the members of the group and entrusted by the government to institute such actions.[126]

Of interest should be the conditions under which opt-out based litigation may be established. In this regard, one controversial idea is the adoption of an autonomous EU 'superiority standard' making opt-out mechanisms available only when they constitute a superior

[121] Commission Staff Working Paper, Accompanying the White Paper (n 112) [49]. *cf* also Green Paper on Consumer Collective Redress (n 24) [56]. See on this requirement Tzakas (n 51) 1143–47.

[122] See on this matter OFT (n 23) [4.30]. See furthermore Bernhard (n 23) 271–72; Danov (n 70) 378–80; Fairgrieve and Howells, 'Collective Redress Procedure: European Debates' (n 20) 407; Halfmeier and Wimalasena (n 21) 652–56; Tzakas (n 51) 1146–47.

[123] Bernhard (n 23) 230–32, 325–29. But see R Gaudet, 'Turning a Blind Eye: The Commission's Rejection of Opt-Out Class Actions Overlooks Swedish, Norwegian, Danish and Dutch Experience' (2009) 30 *ECLR* 107; Halfmeier and Wimalasena (n 21) 656–57.

[124] See also Green Paper on Consumer Collective Redress (n 24) [52] arguing that 'Certification of the representative entity acts as a gatekeeper'.

[125] See on the US law S Calkins, 'An Enforcement Official's Reflections on Antitrust Class Actions' (1987) 39 *Arizona Law Review* 413, 433–37.

[126] Commission Staff Working Paper, Annex to the Green Paper (n 111) [196].

means for litigating claims in comparison to other mechanisms, such as the opt-in proceedings or test cases, especially when the aggregated claims are not expected to be furthered in individual proceedings because of their small amount.[127] This approach, following the example of Danish[128] and Norwegian law,[129] may guarantee procedural efficiency and alleviate the risk of abusive litigation. However, one cannot overlook the need to effectively construe any 'low amount' requirement in relation to the value of the claims raised at the EU level. The adoption of the standard entailed in Article 2(1) of the Small Claims Regulation[130] (claims not exceeding EUR 2000) has met with significant reservations[131] which are illustrative of the diverging approaches in the Member States.

Another core aspect influencing the operability of opt-out instruments relates to the proper identification of absentee claimants, as already highlighted. The Green Paper on consumer collective redress entails no specific criteria since only alternative litigation models are discussed therein without proposing a concrete regulatory framework. The Commission Staff Working Paper accompanying the White Paper on damages actions for breach of the EU antitrust rules[132] enunciates alternative means for defining the group of victims: strictly (eg by naming the victims and strictly identifying the harm) or more loosely (especially by specifying the similarity of the harm). Recital 8 to the pre-draft Directive regards the adoption of the opt-out model as a precondition of the effectiveness of representative actions. Thereafter, qualified entities should not be required to individually identify all the injured parties belonging to the group. Article 6(2) of the pre-draft Directive entails an obligation of the representative entity merely to provide the court with an identification of the group without needing to take recourse to an individual identification of all absentee claimants. However, the Consultation Paper does not expressly address this aspect and merely refers to the role of 'associations representing victims' interests'.[133]

In this context, it has to be remembered that opt-out mechanisms necessitate an amplification of the notion of a 'party to a proceeding', since absentee plaintiffs will be deemed to have

[127] See ibid [196]; ECCG Opinion (n 69) 4; EESC Opinion on the collective actions system (n 24) [7.2.3.1], [7.2.3.3]; OFT, 'Response to the EU Green Paper on Consumer Collective Redress' (March 2009) www.oft.gov.uk/shared_oft/reports/oft_response_to_consultations/oft1063.pdf, [4.16]. See furthermore Koch and Zekoll (n 54) 128; Tzakas (n 51) 1139–41. See also from the perspective of Italian law R Caponi, 'The Collective Redress Action in the Italian Legal System' (2008) 13 ZZPInt 15–6. *cf* also from the perspective of US class actions *Kern v Siemens Corp*, 393 F 3d 120, 129 Fn 8 (2nd Cir 2004).

[128] Under the Danish Administration of Justice Act, opt-out proceedings are allowed upon a court decision if it is expected that the aggregated claims will not be pursued (especially due to their small size) in individual actions. See Danish Ministry of Justice, Department of Law, 'New rules on class actions under Danish law' (June 2007) available at www.justitsministeriet.dk/fileadmin/downloads/rules.pdf, 5–6; T Bogelund, 'Introduction of class actions in Denmark' (2007 September) 23 *Young Lawyers Committee Newsletter* 24; E Werlauff, 'Class actions in Denmark – from 2008', http://globalclassactions.stanford.edu/sites/default/files/documents/Demark_National Report.pdf 5.

[129] As to the similar provision of section 35-7 of the Norwegian Dispute Act 2005 see its English translation available at www.law.stanford.edu/display/images/dynamic/events_media/Norway_Legislation.pdf. See furthermore Gaudet (n 123) 112–13; C Bernt-Hamre, 'Class Actions, Group Litigation and Other Forms of Collective Litigation in the Norwegian Courts', http://globalclassactions.stanford.edu/sites/default/files/documents/Norway_National_Report.pdf, 14–15.

[130] Regulation (EC) No 861/2007 of the European Parliament and of the Council of 11 July 2007 establishing a European Small Claims Procedure, [2007] OJ L199/1.

[131] More restrictive S Augenhofer, 'Private enforcement: Anforderungen an die österreichische und deutsche Rechtsordnung' in S Augenhofer (ed) *Die Europäisierung des Kartell- und Lauterkeitsrechts* (Tübingen, Mohr Siebeck, 2009) 39, 53 fn 79. See also Bernhard (n 23) 32–34. *cf* furthermore the reservations expressed by the EESC Opinion on the collective actions system (n 24) [7.2.3.1]–[7.2.3.3].

[132] Commission Staff Working Paper, Accompanying the White Paper (n 112) [46]; Opinion on the White Paper (n 112) [4.4.2].

[133] Commission Staff Working Document (n 20) [18].

'formally appeared as a party in the proceedings' as the CJEU already ruled.[134] In order to guarantee procedural efficiency and an EU-wide level playing field in cross-border antitrust litigation, both the level in the distribution chain where the damages occurred (eg direct or indirect purchasers)[135] as well as the localisation of anti-competitive effects giving rise to the damages claimed within the market of the same Member State[136] have to be substantiated. An unambiguous definition of the represented consumers may alleviate concerns that opt-out mechanisms could amount to multiple recoveries for overlapping claims. Indeed, the initiation of proceedings encompassing all consumers domiciled in a Member State hinders the initiation of subsequent proceedings for the same claimants, since Article 27 of the Brussels I Regulation will apply. Parallel proceedings are conceivable only on the part or on behalf of the consumers that have already opted-out, such that for the admissibility of all subsequent proceedings a previous opt-out declaration on the part of the claimants is required.

Furthermore, it has to be observed that opt-out proceedings are more apt to overcome both damage-quantification problems and rational apathy on the part of cartel victims.[137] For instance, in the case of a price-fixing conspiracy regarding mass products, it is much more reasonable to quantify the sustained consumer detriment by reference to the volume of the said goods sold in a specific country (which can be easily estimated by accessing the accounting records of the cartelists), as opposed to requiring consumers to estimate, plead and prove the damage they sustained when opting-in to the collective proceedings.[138] The *Replica Football Shirts* case[139] is illustrative of this finding. Not coincidentally, the French Competition Authority[140] has already endorsed the adoption of collective actions complementing the public enforcement of competition rules, whereas the criticism expressed by the German Federal Competition Authority[141] seems to rely mainly on the potential for abuses resulting from the opt-out requirement of US class actions. In contrast, the Office of Fair Trading[142] and the BIS[143] are also discussing a far-reaching approach such as adopting opt-out representative actions.

[134] *cf* Case C-167/08 *Draka NK Cables Ltd and others v Omnipol Ltd* [2009] ECR I-3477 [31]. *cf* also Art 6(4)(b) of the pre-draft Directive stipulating that any decision by the court on the merits will be binding for all injured parties represented by the qualified entity at the time when such decision is issued. See furthermore Danov (n 70) 387.

[135] *cf* also R Hempel, *Privater Rechtsschutz im Kartellrecht* (Baden-Baden, Nomos, 2002) 316–17.

[136] This approach can guarantee the applicability of the same Member State law under Art 6(3)(a) of the Rome II Regulation to all tort claims, especially when they are brought before a court having jurisdiction under Art 5(3) of the Brussels I Regulation.

[137] OFT (n 23) [4.28].

[138] ECCG Opinion (n 69) 4. *cf* also Commission Green Paper (n 111) 9; Commission Staff Working Paper, Annex to the Green Paper (n 111) [19]; Commission Staff Working Paper, Accompanying the White Paper (n 112) [58]; Opinion on the White Paper (n 112) [4.4.1]; EESC Opinion on the collective actions system (n 24) [7.2.3.3]–[7.2.1.3.5]; Green Paper on Consumer Collective Redress (n 24) [55].

[139] Case no 1078/7/9/07 *Consumers Association v JJB Sports Plc*, registered 5 March 2007, CAT. See on this proceeding G Howells, 'Collective Consumer Redress Reform – Will it be a Paper Tiger?' in F Cafaggi and HW Micklitz (eds), *New Frontiers of Consumer Protection* (Antwerp, Intersentia, 2009) 329, 332–33. See furthermore the empirical data presented by Mulheron (n 20) 432–34.

[140] Conseil de la Concurrence (n 23).

[141] Bundeskartellamt, 'Private Kartellrechtsdurchsetzung, Stand, Probleme, Perspektiven, Diskussionspapier vom 26.9.2005', www.bundeskartellamt.de/wDeutsch/download/pdf/Diskussionsbeitraege/05_Proftag.pdf, 30–31.

[142] OFT (n 23) [4.1] et seq. *cf* also in consumer protection matters OFT (n 127); OFT, 'Response to the EU Discussion Paper on Consumer Collective Redress' (July 2009), www.oft.gov.uk/shared_oft/reports/oft_response_to_consultations/oft1100.pdf.

[143] See the thorough analysis of the BIS – Department for Business Innovation and Skills, Private 'Actions in Competition Law: A Consultation on Options for Reform' (April 2012), www.bis.gov.uk/assets/biscore/consumer-issues/docs/p/12–742-private-actions-in-competition-law-consultation.pdf and 'Actions in Competition Law: A Consultation on Options for Reform – Impact Assessment' (April 2012), www.bis.gov.uk/assets/biscore/consumer-issues/docs/p/12–743-private-actions-in-competition-law-impact-assessment.pdf.

E. A Need for Concentrating Proceedings?

Neither the Green or White Papers on Damages actions for breach of the EU antitrust rules, nor the unofficial pre-Draft Directive, stress or recommend any proposal or provision regarding the concentration of collective redress actions before a single Member State court in the EU. As to this issue, the Consultation Paper[144] merely refers to the need and feasibility of additional specific rules on the applicable law and jurisdiction in the field of collective redress. The Consultation Paper, presenting the first working analysis of the impact of the options in the light of the replies to the Green Paper on consumer collective redress, suggests an adaptation of the Brussels I Regulation in order to facilitate the handling of the case. Thereafter, the competent court should be the court of the Member State where the defendant is domiciled, or the court of the Member State where the market is most affected by the illegal practice for the test case, and the court of the Member State where the consumer is domiciled for the follow-up procedure.[145]

At the national level, the need for a concentrated proceeding is readily established, given the need to ensure a uniform assessment of the peculiarities of a Member State market especially with regard to economic parameters such as market elasticity and passing-on.[146] This policy rationale can also apply in the event that the cartelised goods have been imported from abroad such that the entity representing indirect purchasers is eligible to take part in the actions brought by the direct purchaser(s). In cross-border antitrust litigation, these findings weigh in favour of the applicability of the rule of Article 28(3) of the Brussels I Regulation such that representative actions on the part of consumers or indirect purchasers can be deemed to be related to the claims brought by the first purchaser(s), since they are so closely connected that it is expedient to hear and determine them together to avoid the risk of irreconcilable judgments resulting from separate proceedings.[147] In this regard, a concentrated proceeding taking place before the courts of one Member State may guarantee a uniform assessment of the extent of the damages suffered by consumers or purchasers downstream from the direct purchaser. This is definitely the case when allocating the cartel overcharges to the different market levels, but it has no bearing on the entitlement to compensation of other harm suffered, such as the loss of profit.[148]

However, this approach cannot be held as adequate for application in all cases of cross-border infringements of Articles 101 and 102 TFEU, especially when various commercial channels have been enabled. Indeed, the implementation of anti-competitive practices requires a conspiracy on the part of multiple market actors and/or their subsidiaries which can be held as jointly liable. In relation to the imposition of fines, the CJEU in *Akzo*[149] imputed the conduct of a subsidiary to the parent company where, although having a separate legal personality, the subsidiary did not decide independently upon its own conduct on the market, but instead carried out, in all material respects, the instructions given to it by the parent company. In the specific case where a parent company has a 100 per cent

[144] Commission Staff Working Document (n 115) [28].

[145] *cf* also Consultation paper presenting the first working analysis (n 69) [62].

[146] See also Bernhard (n 23) 286–88.

[147] See M Danov, 'EU Competition Law Enforcement: Is Brussels I Suited to Dealing with all the Challenges?' (2012) 61 ICLQ 27, 41–45; Wilderspin, 'Jurisdictional Issues' (n 83) 58–59.

[148] See Commission Staff Working Paper, Accompanying the White Paper (n 112) [202]; Recital 17 and Art 1(2) pre-Draft Directive. *cf* also European Parliament Resolution (n 112) [16].

[149] Case C-97/08 P *Akzo Nobel NV and others v Commission* [2009] ECR I-8237.

shareholding in a subsidiary the Court construed a rebuttable presumption that the parent company does in fact exercise a decisive influence over the conduct of its subsidiary. This approach has also been followed in *Química*, where the CJEU held a holding company to be 'jointly and severally liable for the infringements of EU competition law committed by a subsidiary of its group whose capital it did not hold directly, in so far as that holding company exercised decisive influence over that subsidiary, even indirectly via an interposed company.'[150] A similar line of reasoning has also been followed by the UK courts with regard to civil antitrust liability.[151]

Notwithstanding the need to provide for a limitation of the liability of leniency applicants,[152] it seems rather difficult to elaborate a rule concentrating liability in a single legal person and, thus, jurisdiction before the courts of one Member State. The idea of a single court being competent to hear all actions brought on behalf of consumers within the EU may also have detrimental effects in respect of both deterrence and procedural efficiency, since it is hardly possible to stay proceedings or decline jurisdiction when follow-up representative actions on behalf of different groups of end consumers are simultaneously brought before the courts of different Member States where the seats of different cartel members are located.[153] In fact, the rule entailed in Article 11 of the pre-Draft Directive has to be interpreted with regard to these findings. Pursuant to this rule, Member States are to enable national courts that are seised with an action for damages to give due consideration to any parallel or preceding action for damages concerning the same antitrust violation provided that proceedings are brought by a claimant from another level of the same supply chain. The same restrictive understanding applies also to Recital 19 to the pre-Draft Directive, which considers actions brought by direct and indirect purchasers as falling within the scope of Article 28 of the Brussels I Regulation. A different understanding of the rule neglects the fact that both market elasticity and pass-on vary within the EU such that a separate scrutiny as to the factual situation relating to the implementation of a price-fixing conspiracy in every Member State seems unavoidable. In light of these findings, the need and feasibility of concentrated proceedings seems of limited importance.

F. Unanswered Issues

Although the Commission adopts in the White Paper and the pre-Draft Directive a well balanced approach, it cannot be overlooked that specific aspects of collective redress have to be dealt with by much more elaborated rules. Of note are the following issues.

[150] Case C-90/09 P *General Química SA and others v Commission* [2011] ECR I-1 [86].

[151] See furthermore Commercial Court, *Provimi Ltd v Roche Products Ltd* [2003] 2 All ER (Comm) 683 [25]–[34], [38]; Commercial Court, *Cooper Tire & Rubber Co v Shell Chemicals UK Ltd* [2009] EWHC 2609 [33] et seq. See furthermore FW Bulst, 'The Provimi Decision of the High Court: Beginnings of Private Antitrust Litigation in Europe' (2003) 4 *European Business Organization Law Review* (EBOR) 623, 636–38.

[152] See on this issue Commission White Paper (n 112) 10; Commission Staff Working Paper, Accompanying the White Paper (n 112) [303]–[306]; Commission Green Paper (n 111) 9–10; Commission Staff Working Paper, Annex to the Green Paper (n 111) [224]–[236].

[153] *cf* also Commission Staff Working Paper, Accompanying the White Paper (n 112) [60]. But see Bernhard (n 23) 286–88, 294–97.

(i) Minimum Harmonisation of Collective Redress Instruments

Neither the Green nor White Papers on Damages actions for breach of the EU antitrust rules discuss the reach of the anticipated EU legislation as full or maximum harmonisation rules. Recitals 4 and 5 to the pre-Draft Directive refer to this matter and regard national provisions on damage actions as unaffected to the extent that they meet the future Directive standards, do not hamper its objectives and are not at variance with the EU principles of effectiveness and equivalence. In this regard, Article 3(3) of the pre-Draft Directive stipulates that Member States are not to be prevented from maintaining or introducing other forms of actions for damages. From the perspective of collective redress, this approach might open the possibility for national legislators to introduce alternative instruments (such as test cases), maintain existing remedies (such as the Dutch scheme of conferring binding effect on a settlement reached between the tortfeasor(s) and a foundation or association representing the victims' interests by means of a court order) or amplify the scope and requirements for group and representative actions (such as opt-out group actions, under Portuguese law, or representative actions brought by non-qualified entities). Although it remains far from certain whether and to what extent Member State laws may provide for the afore-mentioned mechanisms, it seems arguable that in such cases the illustrated problems of recognition and standing will remain present. From this perspective, it has to be discussed whether a future legislative act should be restricted to setting minimum standards as opposed to safeguarding a level playing field by enacting uniform remedies within the whole EU internal market.[154]

(ii) Representation of Foreign Claimants

The Commission Staff Working Paper accompanying the White Paper[155] acknowledges that infringements of the EU antitrust rules may affect consumers and businesses in several Member States, such that 'the court competent to hear a damage claim may be located in a Member State different from the one where the qualified entity willing to bring an action is located'. However, neither the White Paper nor the pre-Draft Directive discusses the possibility of and requirements for representing foreign claimants. The Consultation Paper 2011[156] provides as a matter of ensuring the efficiency of collective redress that representative entities should be able to represent in their home Member State victims of other Member States without, however, referring to the specific requirements that eventually have to be put in place.

Assuming that this matter is inextricably linked to the certification requirements such that sufficient safeguards are to be enabled in order to avoid abusive litigation, a brief depiction thereof is needed. Indeed, under Recital 8 to the pre-Draft Directive eligibility shall be subjected to regular monitoring aimed, inter alia, at establishing that representative actions are brought in the victims' best interests. This policy reasoning is further specified in Article 6(2) of the pre-Draft Directive, obliging Member States to set eligibility conditions ensuring that the entity has the capacity to effectively bring a representative

[154] Bernhard (n 23) 245–48. *cf* also in consumer protection matters OFT (n 127) [1.6], [2.7], [3.4], [3.12]; OFT (n 142) [3.7].

[155] Commission Staff Working Paper, Accompanying the White Paper (n 112) [55].

[156] Commission Staff Working Document (n 115) [18]. *cf* also Green Paper on Consumer Collective Redress (n 24) [24].

action and that it acts, or can be expected to act, in the best interests of those it represents. In view of this requirement, Member States are required to take effective measures under Article 6(3) of the pre-Draft Directive in order to enable an effective monitoring as to the continued eligibility of the qualified entities designated pursuant to their laws. Designation on a general or ad hoc basis may be withdrawn pursuant to procedures that Member States have to devise in advance. Withdrawal depends upon providing evidence that the entity in question is abusing the right to bring representative actions or is not acting in the best interest of those it represents.

Returning to the issue of representing foreign claimants, two aspects have to be illuminated. First, it can arguably be said that allowing a foreign entity to represent either claims governed by another Member State's law or victims domiciled in another Member State amounts to circumventing the designation requirement and monitoring mechanisms enabled by the national legislation of the latter state. However, such deficits should be ascribed to the lack of rules as to the jurisdiction to grant a general or an ad hoc certification. Secondly, it has to be borne in mind that a Member State court or authority having to certify a representative entity will hardly undertake any scrutiny as to whether the eligibility requirements provided by its domestic laws are fulfilled with regard to the foreign claimants. Furthermore, it seems quite debatable whether public authorities of a Member State might be able or even interested in monitoring the foreign activities of a consumer organisation or trade association. From that perspective, allowing the inclusion of foreign claimants may be desirable since this approach fosters the EU internal market; however, it may result in enforcement loopholes as to the requirements laid down in Article 6(2) and (3) of the pre-Draft Directive. Furthermore, it is quite uncertain whether consumers may avail themselves of the procedures for the withdrawal of the certification granted to the foreign entity given that such proceedings have to be initiated abroad. In view of these concerns, the proposed rules of the pre-Draft Directive have to be further elaborated.

(iii) Jurisdiction to Certify Ad Hoc Entities

As already analysed, while both the White Paper and the pre-Draft Directive endorse a general entitlement of entities designated in advance to bring representative actions before the domestic and foreign Member State courts, ad hoc certified entities are eligible to initiate proceedings only after certification in relation to a particular infringement is granted pursuant 'to the procedures laid down in the national law of their Member State'.[157] The White Paper and the pre-Draft Directive provide for a mutual recognition of both kinds of entities; however, they provide no guidance as to the courts and authorities that are empowered to grant a prior or an ad hoc certification. This finding is of particular importance, since certification either in advance or on an ad hoc basis presupposes that concrete safeguards are put in place by the domestic laws of the country of certification so as to avoid abusive litigation.[158] Since national legislators have a certain margin of appreciation regarding the specification of the aforementioned requirements, the elaboration of certain rules as to the designation of the competent Member State courts or authorities seems necessary in order to avoid a regulatory race to the bottom.[159] As to this particular aspect, the Consultation Paper 2011 refers to the Member States laws implementing the Aarhus

[157] Commission Staff Working Paper, Accompanying the White Paper (n 112) [49]–[50].
[158] ibid [52]–[53].
[159] See Tzakas (n 40) 178, 180.

Convention which sets specific requirements for NGOs, such as a certain period of existence, a geographical scope of activity, a certain number of members, the aim of promoting the public interest, etc.[160]

It could be argued that the drafters of the aforementioned documents held as competent the courts or authorities of the Member State where the incorporation seat – perhaps also the real seat[161] – of the representative entity is located. Such criteria may be effective in case of generally certified entities since it could be expected that Member States will provide for a scrutiny of their statutes including an effective supervision as to the exercise of the task of representing legitimate and defined interests from a personal, operational and territorial perspective. The situation is quite different when ad hoc certified entities are merely established under the most favourable Member State law in order to acquire certification and, thus, empowerment to initiate proceedings in the whole EU. From this perspective, it has to be recalled that according to Article 6(3) of the pre-Draft Directive, the Member State that granted certification is also entrusted with the monitoring of the activities of the qualified entities certified under its laws. In view of these concerns, a specific rule has to be put in place in order to avoid any kind of forum shopping or regulatory competition and, furthermore, set uniform certification standards for such entities.

(iv) Distribution of the Obtained Damage Funds

As to the distribution of the obtained damage funds, both the White Paper[162] as well as the pre-Draft Directive set as a principal policy rationale their use to directly compensate the harm suffered by all those represented in the action. Nevertheless, the use of a portion of the awarded damages to cover litigation expenses is not banned. However, in view of the high probability that, especially in opt-out proceedings, a significant amount of damage funds may remain undistributed, alternative means of funds distribution and, in particular, the introduction of some form of the US *cy près* doctrine (also called 'fluid recoveries system'[163]) has been discussed.[164] In this context, the European Commission considers a loose definition of the group claimants as posing problems in actually distributing the damages awards to the victims. Article 5(5) of the pre-Draft Directive articulates the obligation to distribute the awarded damage funds, to the largest possible extent, to the represented injured parties. Expenses reasonably incurred by the qualified entity may be covered only by a portion of the damages award.

The reluctance of the European Commission should be understood not only by reference to the multitude of mechanisms used to implement the *cy près* doctrine in the US,[165] but also with regard to formulating a choice-of-law rule governing the matter of the use of

[160] Commission Staff Working Document (n 115) [25].

[161] *cf* on this matter Case C-210/06 *Cartesio Oktató és Szolgáltató bt* [2008] ECR I-9641.

[162] Commission Staff Working Paper, Accompanying the White Paper (n 112) [47], [56]. See furthermore European Parliament Resolution (n 112) [10]; Consultation paper presenting the first working analysis (n 69) [62]. See generally on the issue R Mulheron, '*Cy-Près* Damages Distribution in England: A New Era for Consumer Redress' (2009) 20 *European Business Law Review* 307.

[163] See on this matter JR McCall and others, 'Greater Representation for California Consumers: Fluid Recovery, Consumer Trust Funds, and Representative Actions' (1995) 46 *The Hastings Law Journal* 797, 808.

[164] OFT (n 23) [4.37]. See also in consumer protection cases, Green Paper on Consumer Collective Redress (n 24) [56]–[57] where, inter alia, the distribution of compensation funds by the court is discussed. *cf* furthermore EESC Opinion on the collective actions system (n 24) [7.1.1.3]; Bernhard (n 23) 343–45.

[165] See on that issue NA DeJarlais, 'The Consumer Trust Fund: A Cy Pres Solution to Undistributed Funds in Consumer Class Actions' (1987) 38 *Hastings Law Journal* 729, 738–48.

undistributed damage funds. Even if the government escheat scheme – as the Commission Staff Working Paper accompanying the White Paper implies by the reference to surrendering the undistributed funds to a public interest foundation[166] – is adopted at the EU level, this approach results in significant problems when having to designate the entitled state or the foundation in case of foreign claimants claims or actions brought by foreign representative entities. The potential for regulatory competition among Member States in order to establish a favourable (in respect of foreign plaintiffs) collective redress forum is immanent and cannot be overlooked by merely invoking the Member States' procedural autonomy.

IV. ENCOUNTERING ENFORCEMENT LOOPHOLES

A. Strengthening Mutual Trust as a Leading Policy Rationale

Before addressing potential solutions for encountering enforcement loopholes, as described above, it has to be borne in mind that the cornerstone for elaborating an effective EU framework on collective redress is the principle of mutual trust. Indeed, a handful of EU acts relating to choice-of-law or procedural issues, such as the Brussels I Regulation, the Rome I and Rome II Regulations or the Regulation on insolvency proceedings, rely on mutual trust in the administration of justice as an effective means of attaining the objective of free movement of judgments in the internal market.[167] This leading policy rationale underpins the mutual recognition of representative entities and advocates for prescribing a pan-European 'pass' that empowers them with both standing and the right to sue before the courts of every Member State. A similar system in order to facilitate cooperation and enhance mutual assistance between public authorities responsible for enforcement of the laws protecting consumers' interests is provided in Regulation 2006/2004.[168] In this respect, specific means for coordinated action are prescribed such as exchange of information, requests for enforcement measures, coordinated market surveillance and enforcement activities.[169] Not coincidentally, the Green Paper on Consumer Collective Redress[170] suggests that the work of a future cooperation network among representative entities could be facilitated by the European Consumer Centres Network (ECC Net).

Although both the Commission White Paper and the pre-Draft Directive endorse the policy rationale of enhancing mutual trust by creating a pan-European 'pass' for entities entitled to bring representative actions, this proposition falls – as already shown – short of

[166] Commission Staff Working Paper, Accompanying the White Paper (n 112) [47].

[167] See, eg, Recitals 6 and 16 Brussels I Regulation; Recital 6 Rome I Regulation; Recital 6 Rome II Regulation; Recital 22 Council Regulation 1346/2000 of 29 May 2000 on insolvency proceedings [2000] OJ L160/1; Recital 18 European Parliament and Council Regulation (EC) 805/2004 of 21 April 2004 creating a European Enforcement Order for uncontested claims [2004] OJ L143/15; Recital 21 Council Regulation (EC) No 2201/2003 of 27 November 2003 concerning jurisdiction and the recognition and enforcement of judgments in matrimonial matters and the matters of parental responsibility, repealing Regulation (EC) No 1347/2000 [2003] OJ L338/1.

[168] European Parliament and Council Regulation 2006/2004 of 27 October 2004 on cooperation between national authorities responsible for the enforcement of consumer protection laws (the Regulation on consumer protection cooperation) [2004] OJ L364/1.

[169] See on this aspect Green Paper on Consumer Collective Redress (n 24) [43]–[44]; Consultation paper presenting the first working analysis (n 69) [40].

[170] Green Paper on Consumer Collective Redress (n 24) [29]. See also OFT, 'Response to the EU Green Paper on Consumer Collective Redress' (n 127) [4.4]–[5].

enabling effective monitoring with regard to claims governed by the laws of a Member State different than the one that granted a general or an ad hoc certification. It seems quite uncertain that a future EU legislative act will also provide for a public international law authorisation allowing the competent authorities of a Member State to expand their monitoring mechanisms outside the home territory. This loophole has to be addressed at two levels: Initially, a further specification of the eligibility conditions under Article 6(2) of the pre-Draft Directive has to take place such that regulatory competition among Member States and the potential for forum shopping is alleviated.[171] General criteria – such as the capability to effectively bring a representative action or acting in the best interests of the represented claimants – seem quite vague, leave a vast margin of appreciation and can hardly be scrutinised as to their accordance with the aims of a future EU legislative act.

At a second level, the territorial scope as to the assessment of the afore-mentioned eligibility conditions and the effective monitoring under Article 6(2) of the pre-Draft Directive has to be counterbalanced by elaborating a cooperation system between the authorities vested with these tasks. Indeed, the notion of an EU internal market ensuring the free movement of goods, persons, services and capital presumes the possibility that a competent national entity also represents consumers from other Member States.[172] Therefore, the territorial scope of the surveillance mechanisms has to be counterbalanced by an enhanced cooperation among the national authorities, while the European Commission must undertake a coordinating role which is not solely restricted to the public availability of a list of the authorised national entities under Article 6(4) of the pre-Draft Directive. In this regard, the Green Paper on Consumer Collective Redress[173] includes interesting policy proposals, such as establishing a cooperation network bringing together the entities that have the power to launch a collective redress action in those Member States having such mechanisms.

B. Promoting Coordination

Another point of interest is related to the coordination of collective redress mechanisms in light of the nature of antitrust violations and the unavoidable regulatory peculiarities of Member States laws. The first issue that has to be clarified in this regard deals with making the concentration rules enshrined in Article 6(3)(b) of the Rome II Regulation available to the specific aspects of representative actions such as prerequisites for certification, notification requirements and the distribution of the awarded damage funds. Given the mandatory nature of the national rules (especially the constitutional underpinnings of the right to be heard) as well as the policy rationale of establishing a coherent EU framework, it seems arguable to take recourse to the law applicable on the merits under the basic rule of Article 6(3)(a) of the Rome II Regulation. Still, the concentration rules rely on the effective exercise of a claimant's right and, therefore, hardly correspond to the need for legal certainty since a handful of different Member State laws may come into play pursuant to the factual situation of the case. By contrast, the distributive application of different Member State laws under the mosaic principle gives proper consideration to the diverging national laws

[171] *cf* also Koch and Zekoll (n 54) 122–23; Tzakas (n 51) 1147–50.
[172] *cf* also Green Paper on Consumer Collective Redress (n 24) [24].
[173] ibid [25].

regulating on a mandatory basis the issues of granting certification, effective notice and distributing the obtained damage funds.

The distributive application of different Member State laws has to be counterbalanced by effective means for safeguarding procedural efficiency. In fact, providing for the mandatory cooperation of the entity initiating proceedings with other entities located in the Member States whose laws come into distributive application seems appropriate in regard to the need for enhanced coordination.[174] Indeed, the Green Paper on Consumer Collective Redress[175] discusses measures promoting an enhanced procedural coordination, such that bodies located in the territory of the forum Member State may either bring a representative action on behalf of consumers from other Member States upon request of their counterpart entities in these Member States, or assist these counterpart entities to take direct action. Requiring an authorisation from an entity having its real seat in the Member State in the market of which the victims of an antitrust violation suffered damages seems an adequate requirement for initiating any representative action on behalf of these foreign plaintiffs.[176] The mandatory involvement of such entities should not be deemed to overburden proceedings. In contrast, a body located in the Member State whose laws apply under Article 6(3)(a) of the Rome II Regulation to the aggregated claims may effectively undertake a handful of tasks and, especially, effectively notifying absentee claimants[177] on their right to opt out, and advising them as to the course of the proceedings. Furthermore, the use of the obtained damage funds in order to directly compensate the harm suffered by the foreign claimants seems, thus, better ensured.

V. CONCLUDING REMARKS

Although the European Commission accurately notes in the Consultation Paper 2011 that '[r]ights which cannot be enforced in practice are worthless',[178] the progress achieved as to the elaboration of uniform EU collective redress mechanisms or of even the regulatory framework relating to civil antitrust liability leaves little room for optimism. The conflicting policy interests as well as the diverging approaches among Member States' laws arise as impediments to the enactment of a legislative act in the near future. Especially in the fields on collective redress, Aristotle's observation that 'there is nothing more unequal than the equal treatment of unequal people' is illustrative of the need for enacting collective redress mechanisms by means of Union law such that the EU may safeguard effective compensation, substantive justice for all its citizens and the deterrent effect of competition law rules.[179] In contrast, tolerating the victims' rational apathy due to existing procedural impediments and the small amount of their claims seems rather problematic both for EU competition policy and the future perspectives of the internal market.[180]

[174] *cf* furthermore the proposition of Danov (n 70) 391–93.

[175] See Green Paper on Consumer Collective Redress (n 24) [26].

[176] See Tzakas (n 40) 180.

[177] See Bernhard (n 23) 273.

[178] Commission Staff Working Document (n 115) [1].

[179] See the interview data collected by the Germany-based research team where one respondent stated 'consumers are really the losers in the current system' (p 18). See also the interview data collected by the UK-based research team, p 25.

[180] OFT (n 23) [2.12]; Bernhard (n 23) 126–29. *cf* also Conseil de la Concurrence (n 23) [26], referring eloquently to the 'asymétrie entre la capacité d'agir'.

18

Collective Redress Antitrust Proceedings: How to Close the Enforcement Gap and Provide Redress for Consumers*

MIHAIL DANOV, DUNCAN FAIRGRIEVE AND GERAINT HOWELLS

I. INTRODUCTION

The Ashurst Report on the conditions of claims for EU competition law damages addressed, inter alia, the need for class actions in Europe.[1] In the Green Paper on antitrust damages actions, the European Commission noted that consideration should therefore be given to ways in which consumers and purchasers with small claims would be encouraged to bring actions for damages for breach of antitrust law through collective actions.[2] Better enforcement and redress, including collective redress, feature among the priorities of the EU Consumer Policy Strategy 2007–2013.[3] It is well established that an important issue to be addressed by any institutional framework concerns:

> the difficulty of creating incentives to bring private damages actions in situations in which the victims of an antitrust violation are so numerous that the individual injury is too small to make suing attractive although the aggregate injury may be great. The class is the law's standard answer to the problem of aggregating a multitude of small claims, but it has serious drawbacks. First, class members typically lack an incentive . . . or the ability . . . to monitor their lawyers, who may negotiate for weak settlements involving large attorneys' fees. Second, the aggregation of claims that is central to the class action permits class action lawyers to make plausible though not necessarily valid arguments for damages so immense that even though the probability that a court would award anywhere near the amount sought is very slight, the expected cost of the suit . . . may be sufficient to induce a settlement.[4]

The specific difficulties to be addressed in the European context were highlighted in the report 'Making Antitrust Damages Actions More Effective in the EU: Welfare Impact and

* Mihail Danov presented an earlier version of sections V, VI, VII and VIII of this chapter at Workshop 1 of the Jean Monnet Series of Workshops on 'Cross-Border Litigation in Europe', held in the University of Aberdeen on Friday 5 October 2012.

[1] D Waelbroeck, D Slater and G Even-Shoshan, *Study on the Conditions of Claims for Damages in Case of Infringement of EC Competition Rules (Ashurst Report)* http://ec.europa.eu/competition/antitrust/actionsdamages/comparative_report_clean_en.pdf.

[2] Green Paper on damages actions for breach of the EC antitrust rules COM(2005) 672 final [2.5]. See also: White Paper on damages actions for breach of the EC antitrust rules COM(2008) 165 [2.1].

[3] EU Consumer Policy Strategy 2007–2013 COM(2007) 99 final 10–11.

[4] RA Posner, *Antitrust Law*, 2nd edn (Chicago, University of Chicago Press, 2001) 274–75.

Potential Scenarios' which was produced for the European Commission.[5] The authors of that report noted the high costs of harmonising the Member States' laws with a view to adopting a harmonised collective redress mechanism at EU level,[6] and went on to conclude that:

> The vast majority of Member States, however, so far only allow opt-in collective actions or joinder procedures. Due to constitutional and other restrictions in the legal systems of Member States, introducing opt-out collective actions would require substantially larger changes than other forms of group litigation in many legal systems. Under opt-out, members of the group who never were aware of the proceeding may be bound by the outcome. Such a possibility creates conflicts with constitutional rights (for example in Germany) and seems to be a major reason why opt-out collective actions are generally rejected in the Member States.[7]

When the European Commission became interested in collective redress for competition law infringements,[8] the directorate that then was responsible for unfair competition law (DG Sanco) also became interested in promoting collective redress proceedings in respect of multiple consumer claims.[9] As one official commented, if such collective actions are possible in the competition field where there are complex issues of assessing damages (which we shall come to below), then how much more appropriate they must be in the unfair competition field where the loss from say a misleading advertisement is more readily assessed. The same would be true of losses resulting from unfair terms. However, DG Sanco has subsequently backpeddled, as is indicated by one former Commissioner[10] who expressed the view that there would be no 'class action' on her watch, and though there has been a general consultation on collective redress,[11] the most we have are some possible benchmarks on collective redress of doubtful status. Therefore it looks as if the competition field may be the standard bearer for consumer collective redress reform at the European level.

Why should collective redress antitrust proceedings be encouraged in Europe? As already noted,[12] 'the standard economic rationale for making a cartel illegal is . . . that it restricts output causing a deadweight or efficiency loss . . . – a loss to consumers without an offsetting gain to producers.'[13] Research[14] clearly shows that there is an enforcement gap at the moment, as there is no redress for consumers. This deduction has been recently confirmed by research undertaken by the UK Government[15] which states that 'currently it is rare for

[5] Report for the European Commission, Contract DG COMP/2006/A3/012, *Making Antitrust Damages Actions More Effective in the EU: Welfare Impact and Potential Scenarios* http://ec.europa.eu/competition/antitrust/actionsdamages/files_white_paper/impact_study.pdf.

[6] ibid 310–11 and 316–17.

[7] ibid 316–17.

[8] White Paper (n 2).

[9] Green Paper on Consumer Collective Redress COM(2008) 794 final.

[10] An opinion expressed by Commissioner Kuneva quoted by D Fairgrieve and G Howells, 'Collective Redress Procedures: European Debates' in D Fairgrieve and E Lein (eds), *Extraterritoriality and Collective Redress* (Oxford, OUP, 2012) 15, 18.

[11] Green Paper (n 9).

[12] See Ch 1.

[13] WM Landes, 'Optimal Sanctions for Antitrust Violations' (1983) 50 *University of Chicago Law Review* 652, 675. See more: Ch 23.

[14] See Chs 2, 3, 4 and 5.

[15] Department for Business Innovation & Skills, *Private Actions in Competition Law: A Consultation on Options for Reform,* 24 April 2012, www.bis.gov.uk/assets/biscore/consumer-issues/docs/p/12-742-private-actions-in-competition-law-consultation.pdf. The BIS's proposed options for reform were discussed at a BIICL seminar, 'Rapid-Response Seminar: Private Actions in UK competition law: BIS's proposed options for reform', British Institute of International and Comparative Law, London, 9 May 2012.

consumers and SMEs to obtain redress from those who have breached competition law, and it can be difficult and expensive for them to go to court to halt anti-competitive behaviour.'[16] Similarly, a very recent research on collective redress actions across Europe[17] demonstrates that 'the number of actions related to antitrust infringements is still very limited.'[18] The authors of the report have made the following recommendation:

> Besides being more in line with European legal tradition, the opt-in model has the important advantage of limiting the risk of unmeritorious claims, and it appears overall preferable to the opt-out model. However, it might be useful to also consider **hybrid solutions** that, while retaining opt-in as the general rule, permit adopting an opt-out model in some clear and limited circumstances, such as for instance when injured consumers have suffered a damage of small value and are therefore unlikely to opt in [to] a collective action. Courts may be granted discretion as to whether the opt-out model is necessary to guarantee that a significant proportion of injured parties are compensated for the damages suffered.[19]

Does the opt-in model really have advantages given the current low level of such actions in Europe? Is it possible to achieve harmonisation in Europe[20] and agree upon a workable solution? What are the specific issues arising in the context of antitrust enforcement in the European context? How is it possible to close the enforcement gap and provide redress for consumers across Europe? The aim of this chapter is to provide some answers to those complex questions and propose some solutions. In this context, we will consider the cross-border implications of the EU competition law infringements which in most cases would affect businesses and consumers in a number of Member States. The chapter will open with a brief review of some interesting national developments in the area of collective redress. Then, we will explain why an opt-out mechanism is important in consumer collective redress actions, and raise also the connected question of whether there should be any gatekeeper. The United Kingdom experience is reviewed in this context. We then note the specific features of the collective redress antitrust damages actions by examining two litigation patterns which are displayed in *Emerald Supplies v British Airways*[21] and in *Re International Air Transportation Surcharge Antitrust Litigation.*[22] Although that latter case was brought before the US District Court for the Northern District of California, it relates to an infringement of Chapter I of the Competition Act 1998 and/or Article 101 TFEU.[23] Finally, we will put forward some proposals for reform, which take account of the specific features of collective redress proceedings in antitrust as well as of the distinctive attributes of the European juridical system and of the way the current regime shapes the litigants' strategies.[24]

[16] *A Consultation on Options for Reform* (n 15) [3.12].

[17] P Buccirossi, M Carpagnano, L Ciari and others, *Collective Redress in Antitrust* www.europarl.europa.eu/document/activities/cont/201206/20120613ATT46782/20120613ATT46782EN.pdf.

[18] ibid 11 and 37.

[19] *Collective Redress in Antitrust* (n 17) 89.

[20] *Making Antitrust Damages Actions More Effective in the EU* (n 5) 310–11 and 316–17.

[21] *Emerald Supplies v British Airways* [2009] EWHC 741 (Ch), aff'd *Emerald Supplies v British Airways* [2010] EWCA Civ 1284.

[22] Case No M:06-cv-01793-CRB, *Re International Air Transportation Surcharge Antitrust Litigation* MDL No 1793 (United States District Court for the Northern District of California, San Francisco Division). See www.airpassengerrefund.co.uk/Documents.aspx. See also: R Mulheron, 'The Recognition, and *Res Judicata* Effect, of a United States Class Actions Judgment in England: A Rebuttal of *Vivendi*' (2012) *Modern Law Review* 180.

[23] Office of Fair Trading **Case reference:** CE/7691-06, *Investigation into alleged price fixing of airline passenger fuel surcharges for long-haul passenger flights* – closed 19 April 2012 www.oft.gov.uk/OFTwork/competition-act-and-cartels/civil-cartels-complete/fuel-surcharges.

[24] See Chs 2, 3, 4, 5, 11 and 12.

II. AN OVERVIEW OF NATIONAL DEVELOPMENTS

Whilst the enthusiasm at an EU level for substantive reform in this area has seemingly faltered, one perceptible side-effect has been a renewed interest in this topic in Member States. Over the past few years, a number of national initiatives have occurred in this area. In this section, we will briefly review these developments, and consider lessons that might be drawn about collective redress in general.

The first point to make is that most legal systems in the EU provide for a mechanism within civil procedure which allows for the possibility of joining together similar claims by means of a simple joinder procedure, or something similar.[25] Packaging claims together in such a way can hardly, however, be described as an enhanced collective redress procedure, and such a technique suffers from the inefficiencies traditionally associated with what is essentially an aggregate of individual lawsuits.[26]

In some countries, the inadequacies of the traditional approach were recognised at an early stage and addressed by law reform efforts. The case of Portugal is an example of such a phenomenon. The 'popular action' introduced in the 1990s[27] by legislation established that a group of persons may collectively bring actions related to public health, environment, consumer protection, cultural heritage and public property.[28] The procedural model contained in the legislation is potentially very broad. The procedure is based on an 'opt-out' model, as the relevant legislation provides that the courts' decisions thereunder have an effect *erga omnes*, except as regards those who exercise the right to exclude themselves. In that sense, this is potentially the most liberal collective redress procedure in Europe. However, it is also probably the most under-used: very few claims have ever been brought in practice,[29] which has been variously explained by reference to flaws in the procedure, the limited resources of the Portuguese Association for Consumer Protection[30] or by financial disincentives given that costs can be awarded against the class.[31]

In Europe generally, most civil justice reforms in collective redress are of more recent vintage. Scandinavia has been in the vanguard in facilitating collective redress, with the reform effort first launched by Per Hendrik Lindblom in Sweden, giving rise to legislation in 2003. This has been followed by a number of countries across Scandinavia.[32] Of some

[25] See for instance s 147 ZPO, German Code of Civil Procedure. See also the ameliorated version of such a procedure in France known as the joint representative action *(action en représentation conjointe)* whereby a joint representative action can be taken by an accredited association where 'several identified individuals have suffered individual harm, caused by the same professional person or body and which have a common origin'. The utility of this action has been strictly circumscribed by the need to receive individual written instructions from the claimants for all procedural steps. See generally Article L 422-1 of French Consumer Code.

[26] See eg W Micklitz and A Stadler, 'The Development of Collective Legal Actions in Europe, especially in German Civil Procedure' (2006) 17 *European Business Law Review* 1473.

[27] By Law 83/1995 of 31 August 1995.

[28] Law 83/1995. Subsequent legislation has been adopted, with only limited impact on this earlier law (eg the Law on Defence of the Consumer of 31 July 1996, 24/96). See also Portuguese Constitution, Art 52 para 3.

[29] For details of the three actions undertaken, see R Mulheron, *Reform of Collective Redress in England and Wales: A Perspective of Need* (a research paper for the Civil Justice Council, February 2008) 100.

[30] ibid.

[31] Capped at a level of between 10% and 50% of normal costs.

[32] In Denmark, new rules governing group actions were introduced on 1 January 2008 (by virtue of Act No 181 of 28 February 2007). Class action procedures were introduced into Norwegian law in 2005 (by virtue of the Dispute Act 2005). In Finland, the Act on Class Actions was approved by Parliament in February 2007 and came into force on 1 October 2007 (Act on Class Actions, *Ryhmäkannelaki*, 444/2007.)

import is the fact that certain of the Scandinavian jurisdictions allow for an opt-out approach to be adopted, albeit only in restricted circumstances.[33]

Other reforms have occurred recently. In Italy, the Consumer Code was modified in 2008 – somewhat precipitately – to allow for the introduction of new group procedures.[34] The end result is not a model of the utmost simplicity, including as it does a complex multi-phase procedure, and creating much scope for delay, but a number of claims have been filed since the new legislation entered into force, and the first claim was declared admissible by the Court of Milan in December 2010, which related to misleading information in respect of a test for swine and avian flu.

Another further category of countries are those that have been toying with reform ideas for a while. Both the United Kingdom and France fall into this category, with – on a number of occasions – reform efforts proceeding as far even as legislative Bills, only to be withdrawn at the last minute.[35] The current financial climate has strengthened the hand of those that would prefer the status quo rather than the introduction of an additional litigation tool for aggregate claims for corporate wrongdoing.

Two exceptions to this rule should be mentioned. In the United Kingdom, the Department for Business, Innovation and Skills recently launched a consultation on Private Actions in Competition Law,[36] which explicitly proposes that an opt-out collective action procedure should be introduced in the competition law sphere. In France,[37] the history of reform in this area has been a checkered one. Presidents Chirac and Sarkozy announced during their presidencies that legislation on group action procedures would be enacted,[38] but both subsequently changed their minds, and ultimately abandoned reform efforts. In June 2012 the new Socialist government announced its intention to legislate in this area, but it remains to be seen whether this comes to fruition or not.

A final category, and one that has traditionally been overlooked, is that of collective settlements. Whilst this is a well-known complement to the civil justice armoury on the other side of the Atlantic, it was unknown in Europe until collective settlement legislation was introduced into Dutch law in 2005.[39] The Dutch WCAM[40] legislation provides for the court approval of collective settlements whereby claimants (organised together in the form of a non-profit organisation or 'representative entity') and one or more infringing parties can

[33] In Denmark, the legislation does allow for an opt-out approach to be adopted in restricted circumstances, essentially where the court accepts that claims cannot be expected to be brought through individual actions due to their limited size (below DKK 2,000) and thus that the opt-in group action approach is deemed to be inappropriate. In Norway, whilst the procedure is primarily based upon an 'opt-in' model, there is also provision for an opt-out version. If the action concerns claims or obligations which are of such a minor value individually that a separate legal action would not be viable, then the court may approve the action as an opt-out class action, provided that the individual claims making up the class are not likely to give rise to specific, non-generic, questions.

[34] Art 140-*bis* of the Italian Consumer Code.

[35] In the UK, a proposal was made in 2010 to enact an opt-out class actions regime within the Financial Services Bill, though this feature was not ultimately included in the Financial Services Act 2010.

[36] *A Consultation on Options for Reform* (n 15).

[37] Two current collective mechanisms in France should be noted: collective interest actions *(action d'intérêt collectif)* and joint representative actions *(action en représentation conjointe)*, which are however of limited application.

[38] In a New Year address on 4 January 2005, President Jacques Chirac surprised commentators by announcing an initiative to introduce into French law collective actions for damages claims. Presdient Sarkozy instructed his Minister of Finance, Christine Lagarde on 11 July 2007, to, 'create a group action *à la française*', but this initiative ultimately stalled and was abandoned.

[39] The Collective Settlement of Mass Damage Act was incorporated in Arts 7:907–7:910 of Book 7 of the Dutch Civil Code.

[40] *Wet collectieve afwikkeling massachade* 2005.

apply to court to declare the settlement fair and binding even on non-parties to the agreement, therefore on an opt-out basis.[41] The collective settlement procedure is premised on an opt-out method. The settlement is widely publicised and those who wish to opt out must elect to do so within a judicially decided period of time,[42] otherwise they will be deemed bound by the settlement. Six collective settlements have been approved by the Amsterdam Court of Appeal in the cases of *DES*, *Dexia*, *Vie d'Or*, *Shell*, *Vedior* and *Converium*, and several other cases are said to be ongoing.

The success of the Dutch model shows that there is a demand for a collective settlement mechanism in a European context. Whilst the initial Dutch cases focused on domestic issues, the more recent cases have increasingly had an international focus.[43] This is a product of a number of issues, but clearly the Dutch mechanism is increasingly viewed as the forum of choice for non-US class action settlements. This has occurred within a context where case law developments in the US have meant that the opportunities for foreign claimants to make use of US procedures (such as in the case of *Morrison v NBA*[44] in respect of securities claims) are much reduced.

As yet, the Dutch mechanism is still the sole example in a European forum of a collective settlement model. In the aforementioned consultation in the UK,[45] the Government considered whether it would be beneficial to introduce an opt-out collective settlement mechanism, over and above the proposed implementation of a collective action for breaches of competition laws. In the Consultation, a number of benefits of a collective settlement procedure were identified, as follows:

> A legally certified collective settlement has the advantage for the infringer in that it creates certainty, ensuring that it is able to draw a line under its losses without fear of future court action. There may also be strong reputational advantages to voluntarily providing redress to those that have suffered loss. For consumers, clearly, something that encourages an infringer to make redress will mean that they are more likely to be compensated for their loss.[46]

The UK Government ultimately declined to recommend the introduction of a collective settlement procedure on the basis that the existence of a proposed opt-out model of collective actions 'would obviate the need for a separate provision for collective settlement in the field of competition law.'[47] This was in some ways a surprising conclusion. It is not at all certain that the mere introduction of an opt-out model of collective action obviates the need for a complementary provision for collective settlement in the field of competition law. Indeed, there are many reasons why a separate mechanism would be advantageous, not least the desire to further Government policy of encouraging and facilitating alterna-

[41] Parties who do not wish to be bound by the settlement agreement can so declare within a term to be determined by the court.

[42] A number of claimants chose to opt out of the Dexia settlement (relating to missold retail investment products) and pursued individual claims.

[43] Some foreign parties were involved in the *Dexia*, *Vie d'Or* and *Vedior* settlements, but it was not until the *Shell* settlement of 2009, and the more recent *Converium* settlement (binding as of 17 January 2012 – *Converium*, Court of Appeal of Amsterdam of 17 January 2012, LJN: BV1026), that cross-border implications have taken centre-stage.

[44] *Robert Morrison et al v National Australia Bank Ltd et al*, 130 S Ct 2869 (2010). See L Silberman, *Morrison v National Australia Bank: Implications For Global Securities Class Actions* (2010) 12 *Yearbook of Private International Law* 123.

[45] *A Consultation on Options for Reform* (n 15).

[46] ibid [6.21].

[47] ibid [6.25].

tive means of dispute resolution. It would therefore be advantageous to allow for a choice of different mechanisms for the resolution of disputes in this area of the law. Moreover, on the present proposals, it would be a somewhat unattractive requirement for parties who had already reached a settlement to proceed by means of a collective action procedure, rather than a bespoke judicially certified settlement procedure. This is particularly true, given that experience shows that there is a demand for a collective settlement mechanism in Europe.

As will have been gathered from the foregoing, the procedural mechanisms' models in Europe are still very diverse. Whilst it is certainly not possible to talk of a European model, one can nonetheless identify some commonality in the considerations which European reforms have taken into account. Setting aside the opt in/opt out debate – which we will cover in the next section – a series of issues should be mentioned. First, law reformers in Europe have often looked to a form of gatekeeper, by means of an accredited consumer organisation, and ombudsman or public body, as a guarantor of the legitimacy and coherence of the civil justice process. We will also explore this further in the next section.

Second, reforms have often provided for a filter mechanism to occur at an early stage of procedure so as to allow for weaker claims to be weeded out. Whilst the gatekeeper process can play a role in this respect, other jurisdictions have adopted multi-stage civil procedures, allowing for an early consideration of merits by a judicial authority through some form of admissibility hurdle. Third, there has been a recognition that collective redress reforms need to be viewed in a broader perspective, taking into account issues such as access to justice considerations, costs, and funding of claims – all of which ultimately impact upon the pattern of litigation in group cases. Moreover, the broader context of dispute resolution in Europe needs also to be borne in mind. When mass damage has been caused in Europe, the criminal justice system has often been given a predominant role in continental Europe.[48]

III. OPT-OUTS AND GATEKEEPERS

We have already noted that there is a recognition that in some circumstances there may be a need for an opt-out solution if collective redress is to play any role. Consumer competition claims are one example where the opt-out solution may be appropriate. If enterprises collude and as a result manipulate the market so that the price of consumer goods is a few percentage points higher most consumers will have no incentive to litigate.[49] Even for large products, the value to consumers is not likely to be worth litigating, except for those consumers consumed by 'super-spite',[50] whereas for everyday products even the most tenacious consumer would be unwilling to litigate for what might individually amount to a few pence of damage.[51]

[48] See in France, J Calais-Auloy and F Steinmetz, *Droit de la consommation*, 7th edn (Paris, 2006) para 18: 'Numerous obligations imposed on traders for consumer protection purposes are accompanied by criminal sanctions.'

[49] M Olsen, *The Logic of Collective Action: Public Goods and the Theory of Groups*, revd edn (Harvard University Press, 1971).

[50] A Leff 'Ignorance, Injury and Spite' (1970) 80 *Yale Law Journal* 1.

[51] See more: section V below.

One response to this is to suggest that if those suffering harm have so little interest in litigating it must be overkill to provide a collective right of private redress.[52] Any harm it is argued can be addressed through public regulation. Allowing a private right of redress on top of what can be substantial fines could even be over deterrence. In any event, the passing-on defence[53] would have to be taken into account if indirect purchasers are allowed standing. In the US such indirect consumers are not allowed standing under the Supreme Court decision of *Illinois Brick Co v Illinios*[54] (although several states have passed legislation allowing indirect purchasers to sue), but this is balanced by there being no passing on defence that would prevent claimants suing for costs they had passed on to ultimate consumers.[55] In the EU it is unlikely that consumers will be denied standing and this then calls into question whether the passing on defence can be denied or else the defendant may be exposed to duplicitous claims.[56] Given that consumer claims will most likely be dogged by causation and remoteness issues it might be thought good policy to keep a strong claim by the direct purchaser and not dilute this by introducing the passing on defence. This is, however, unlikely to be politically acceptable, for whilst it might disgorge profits it does not provide restorative justice to consumers and this seems to be a major driver for collective redress at both the EU and UK levels. Indeed there may be cases where the competition infringement takes place at the retail level and consumers are directly harmed.[57]

Thus in Europe it looks like consumers will be given a direct claim. There are always issues of finding the right balance between public fines and private damages,[58] but these arise in all competition law claims and not just consumer claims. The development of such claims gives rise to two diametrically opposed fears. One is that the new right will be a paper tiger, as consumers will not actually use it.[59] The other is that it will become a bounty hunter's charter. Fears of the latter kind are inflamed by the sight of US law firms locating in Europe to take advantage of prospective opportunities.

One solution to reduce fears is to have a gatekeeper. Whilst individuals should not be denied the right to claim for the damages they have suffered, when collective procedures are introduced it may be legitimate to introduce filters to control who can take advantage of these more flexible procedures. It is quite common for court-based procedures to have a certification stage which allows the judiciary control over the cases allowed into the collective redress procedures.

Another type of gatekeeping role is performed by entrusting the power to represent the collective consumer interest to a body that is seen as having the general consumer interest at heart. In some states this is a public institution. Particularly in the Nordic states, the Ombudsman is seen as having a crucial role. In other states it is the consumer organisa-

[52] D-PL Tzakas, 'Effective Collective Redress in Antitrust and Consumer Protection Matters: A Panacea or a Chimera?' (2011) 48 *CML Rev* 1125. See also: C Hodges, *The Reform of Class and Representative Actions in European Legal Systems: A New Framework for Collective Redress in Europe* (Oxford, Hart Publishing, 2008); A Layton, 'Collective Redress: Policy Objectives and Practical Problems' in Fairgrieve and Lein (n 10) 93, 93–94.

[53] eg *Emerald Supplies* (n 21) (HC) [36]; *Devenish Nutrition v Sanofi-Aventis* [2008] EWCA Civ 1086. See more: Ch 11, above; section V below. See also: RA Posner, *Economic Analysis of Law*, 8th edn (Wolters Kluwer, 2010) 419–20.

[54] 431 US 730 (1977).

[55] *Hanover Shoe Co v Union Shoe Machinery Corporation* 392 US 481 (1968).

[56] A succinct review is provided by G Olsen, 'Compensation and Deterrence? The passing on Defence and the Future Direction of UK Private Proceedings' *Competition Law Insight* 10 May 2005.

[57] See more: section V below.

[58] Ch 23.

[59] G Howells, 'Collective Consumer Redress – Will it be a Paper Tiger?' in F Cafaggi and H Micklitz (eds) *New Frontiers of Consumer Protection – The Interplay of Private and Public Enforcement* (Antwerp, Intersentia, 2009).

tions that play this role. Consumer organisations differ throughout the EU. In some states, like the UK or Netherlands, there is one main consumer organisation that is privately financed by membership subscription. In Germany the consumer organisations are subsidised by the state. In others, like Italy and Greece, there are some large organisations, but others which are very small and in order to fulfil this gatekeeping function they probably will have to pass additional tests to demonstrate they represent the broader consumer interest.

A gatekeeper can be a major help in organising consumers. Particularly in the competition field – where another agency has normally done the spade work and established a breach of competition law and all that is needed is a follow-on damages action – this might seem an appealing prospect. However, there remains the risk that these gatekeepers will not see such claims as a priority. Government agencies may see prevention and deterrence through public law enforcement as more of a priority than restorative justice actions. They are likely to have scarce resources. Consumer associations are likely to have even scarcer resources; in some parts of Europe they are very much surviving on a shoestring. Although a few, like the Austrian associations, are familiar and comfortable working with private sector lawyers who work for a percentage of any damages recovered, this is not the usual case. Consumer associations may invest in the occasional collective action out of goodwill and a desire to promote their profile, but unless there is some underlying incentive they cannot be relied upon to bring such actions consistently.

Of the two gatekeepers – state body or consumer organisation – the choice may very often vary between European states, depending upon tradition and context. State bodies may be viewed as more conservative in bringing actions, which may reassure business but concern consumers. Certainly it is less obvious what they have to gain by seeking private redress, given that they or another state body can normally take public law enforcement in any event. This might lead one to favour consumer organisations, but the problem there is to provide them with procedures they can practically use, together with the incentives to use them. As our case study of the UK Football Shirts action demonstrates, an opt-out action seems to be a prerequisite to effective consumer collective redress action in the field of competition law. However, this probably has to be aligned with a *cy-près* doctrine whereby funds not claimed by individuals can be diverted to serve purposes in the general consumer interest.[60]

IV. UK EXPERIENCE[61]

The United Kingdom is unique in Europe in having a collective redress procedure for breaches of competition law, found in section 47B Competition Act 1998.[62] This provides for a follow-on action for consumers once an infringement of competition law has been established by the regulatory authorities or the courts. Such actions can only be brought by consumer organisations recognised by the Secretary of State as meeting set criteria. As noted in

[60] R Mulheron, *The Modern Cy-près Doctrine: Applications and Implications* (Abingdon, Taylor & Francis, 2006).

[61] See generally Mulheron (n 29); J Peynser, and A Nurse, 'Representative Actions and Restorative Justice' (University of Lincoln, 2008); Hodges (n 52).

[62] See O Dayagi-Epstein, 'Representation of Consumer Interest by Consumer Associations – Salvation for the Masses?' (2007) 3 *Competition Law Review* 209.

the competition law field, the availability of an opt-out procedure can be particularly significant if the procedures are actually to be used in practice. This is a weakness of the UK procedure, as damages are in principle awarded to named individuals.[63] It is true that the Tribunal may, with the consent of the specified body and the individual, order that the sum awarded must be paid to the specified body (acting on behalf of the individual). However, this is unlikely to happen frequently. Few individuals will be motivated to sign up to participate in this action and then sign away their rights to individual compensation.

There has been one case brought using this procedure to date. The consumer organisation *Which?* sued JJB Sports over price-fixing of football shirts. This was a follow-on action after the OFT[64] had imposed fines totalling £18.6m against the firms and subsequent appeals to the CAT[65] and the Court of Appeal[66] on the competition law breaches had been unsuccessful. Despite an estimated two million consumers being affected, it proved to be very hard to persuade many consumers to make the effort necessary to recover modest amounts of compensation.[67] Only a few hundred signed up. Reasons for the low sign-up rate probably included the time since the purchase of the shirts and the small amounts involved. Many people probably just put it down to experience. JJB Sports also made its own offer to customers to give them a free replica England shirt and a mug if they could prove by receipt or bringing in a relevant shirt that they had been affected. This highlights that if market regulation, deterrence and profit skimming are motivations for such laws then opt-out solutions are necessary.[68] *Which?* had originally sought exemplary damages, indicating that if organisations are to bring such cases they need an inducement to do so: if it is not to be exemplary damages it might be some type of *cy-près* scheme.[69] Another interesting aspect of the case was that it had proved impossible to obtain after-the-event insurance. The final settlement provided for members of the claim to be compensated £20 and all others £10 on presentation of proof of purchase. Although this can be presented as a good outcome, the legal resources expended (that were in the event paid for by the defendant as part of the settlement) were no doubt a multiple of the actual compensation awarded. *Which?* used Clyde and Co, a major City law firm. It is perhaps telling that no subsequent actions have been brought and this experience has doubtless left many in the consumer and legal world wondering just how effective a system can be that is not based on an opt-out regime.

V. SPECIFIC FEATURES OF EU COMPETITION LAW COLLECTIVE REDRESS PROCEEDINGS

In view of the foregoing, it is hardly surprising that a reform of the UK collective redress regime has again appeared on the agenda, this time in respect of competition claims

[63] s 47B(6) Competition Act 1998.

[64] Office of Fair Trading, PN 107/03, 'Large fines for replica football kit price-fixers', 1 August 2003 www.oft.gov.uk/news-and-updates/press/2003/pn_107–03# .

[65] Cases Nos 1021 and 1022/1/1/03 *JJB Sports PLC v The Office of Fair Trading* [2004] CAT 17; Cases Nos 1019, 1020, 1021 and 1022/1/1/03 *JJB Sports PLC v The Office of Fair Trading* [2005] CAT 22.

[66] *JJB Sports PLC v The Office of Fair Trading* [20061 EWCA Civ 1318.

[67] Case No 1087/7/9/07 *The Consumer Association v JJB Sports PLC* [2009] CAT 2.

[68] Mulheron (n 29) 38–46.

[69] See generally R Mulheron, *Modern Cy-près Doctrine: Applications and Implications* (London, Cavendish UCL Press, 2006).

specifically.[70] A case for adopting an opt-out regime in England has been made by Mulheron.[71] As a part of her empirical study, Mulheron has demonstrated that:

> Both opt-out and opt-in regimes can have quite low participation rates. However, on the basis of the statistics gathered to date, participation rates are skewed very much in favor of the opt-out. Under opt-out regimes, the vast majority of the class members do *not* opt-out, and this necessarily entails a high level of 'participation' in the litigation (albeit that, for most purposes until the common issues are resolved, the class members are non-parties). Where the eventual take-up rate in an opt-out action is less than 100%, either the defendant will 'benefit' in that it will retain the unclaimed portion of damages, or some alternative solution for the unclaimed sum (such as a *cy-près* distribution, or an escheat to the Treasury, or a *pro rata* distribution among the class members who did claim their individual compensation) may be permitted by the relevant opt-out regime.[72]

The debate in England on whether to maintain an opt-in regime,[73] to introduce an opt-out regime or instead to have them both,[74] is in line with the current discussions in Europe which were fuelled by the recent comparative report on *Collective Redress in Antitrust.*[75] In other words, a reform appears to be on the agenda in the UK[76] as well as in Europe, where 'an EU framework for collective redress' features in the Commission Work Programme 2012.[77] Although it remains to be seen whether the reforms at an EU level will come to fruition at all, and if they do, whether an initiative at EU level would be legislative and/or non-legislative, the lack of redress for consumers[78] and the level of variation, when it comes to EU competition law enforcement across Europe,[79] appear to indicate that an appropriately designed collective redress system, which incorporates an opt-out regime,[80] may be needed to close the enforcement gap and provide redress for consumers. It has been submitted that 'The key is to know how to design strategies that help consumers to successfully activate competition and what competition law tools are needed in order to keep the market structure competitive.'[81] However, as already noted in earlier sections of this chapter, the diverse nature of collective redress models in Europe suggests that the Union legislator would think very carefully before making any attempt to undertake any reform in the area. The question, which must be considered in this regard, is: how to design an adequate collective redress mechanism in the European context?

[70] *A Consultation on Options for Reform* (n 15).

[71] R Mulheron, 'The case for an opt-out class actions for European Member States: A legal and empirical analysis' (2008–2009) 15 *Columbia Journal of European Law* 409.

[72] ibid 434.

[73] See CPR 19.6 Representative Parties with Same Interest; CPR 19.11 – Group Litigation Order; section 47B of the Consumer Act 1998.

[74] White Paper (n 2) [2.1]; Office of Fair Trading, 'Private Actions in Competition Law: Effective Redress for Consumers and Business – Recommendations from the Office of Fair Trading', OFT916 resp; Civil Justice Council, 'Improving Access to Justice Through Collective Actions – Developing a More Effective and Efficient Procedure for Collective Actions', Final Report; Mulheron (n 29).

[75] *Collective Redress in Antitrust* (n 17) 89.

[76] *A Consultation on Options for Reform* (n 15). See more: section II above.

[77] Commission Work Programme 2012 http://ec.europa.eu/atwork/pdf/cwp2012_annex_en.pdf .

[78] See Chs 3, 4 and 5. See also: *Collective Redress in Antitrust* (n 17).

[79] See Chs 3, 4 and 5. See also: *Ashurst Report* (n 1).

[80] See more on the advantages of an opt-out regime in Mulheron, 'The case for an opt-out class actions for European Member States' (n 71).

[81] KJ Cseres, 'The Impact of Consumer Protection on Competition And Competition Law: The Case of Deregulated Markets', Amsterdam Center for Law & Economics, Working Paper No 2006–05 http://papers.ssrn.com/sol3/papers.cfm?abstract_id=903284, 2–3.

It seems to us that any reform which is intended to promote collective redress proceedings and encourage an opt-out regime in Europe must take account of the specific features of collective redress proceedings in antitrust as well as of the distinctive attributes of the European juridical system and of the way the current regime shapes the litigants' strategies. Accordingly, in this part of the paper, the peculiar aspects of collective redress EU competition law proceedings will be briefly introduced with a view to proposing such proceedings could be promoted in Europe in order to provide adequate redress for those who have suffered damages as a result of EU competition law infringements. In other words, before putting forward the proposed solutions, the distinctive features of the EU competition law infringements will be briefly presented in order to identify the specific problems which will need to be addressed by the national and EU legislators.

The specific features of the collective redress antitrust damages actions can be best illustrated by making reference to the two litigation patterns displayed in *Emerald Supplies v British Airways*[82] and *Re International Air Transportation Surcharge Antitrust Litigation*.[83] In *Emerald*, the claimants imported cut flowers using the air freight services provided by the defendant, British Airways. As a result, the claimants sought damages for breach of Article 101 TFEU which was established by a decision of the European Commission in Case COMP 39.258.

Although *Transportation Surcharge Antitrust Litigation* was brought before the US District Court for the Northern District of California, it relates to an infringement of Chapter I of the Competition Act 1998 and/or Article 101 TFEU, and, as a result, its analysis would allow us to better illustrate distinctive features of the antitrust litigation and litigants' strategies. Moreover, given that the settlement required the companies to refund up to £73,531,076 to members of the UK Settlement Classes who submit valid claim forms, the case may be regarded as a good example as to how a non-EU court could award compensatory damages to UK consumers for damages they have suffered as a result of a competition law infringement in Europe. In particular, in *Transportation Surcharge Antitrust Litigation*, a class action was brought on behalf of persons who purchased long-haul passenger air transportation between the UK and the US (or a third country) during a specified period of time from Virgin Atlantic and British Airways as well as some other airlines. 'Long-haul' flights included most flights of British Airways between the UK and non-EU destinations, as well as all Virgin Atlantic flights. The action was preceded by investigation of the US Department of Justice and the UK Office of Fair Trading.

A. Cross-Border Aspects of EU Competition Law Infringements – A Distinctive Feature

As already noted,[84] a distinctive feature of most EU competition law infringements is that they would be cross-border in nature in so far as they may involve legal entities from different countries and affect the market/s, businesses and consumers in several countries. The cross-border implications of collective redress proceedings were put forward by Lord Justice Mummery sitting at the Court of Appeal, who made the following observation:

[82] *Emerald Supplies* (n 21) (HC).
[83] *Re International Air Transportation Surcharge Antitrust Litigation* (n 22). See also: Mulheron (n 22).
[84] Ch 1.

> The claims are for global infringements of competition law by illegal price-fixing cartels operating in the area of air freight charges. The aim of the litigation is to obtain collective redress for consumers of the services. They are a very extensive group, numerically and geographically. It is asserted that forms of collective redress are now widely regarded as essential for breaches of competition law. Without them there are difficulties in ensuring effective compensation for law-abiding businesses and consumers on whom huge costs are imposed by illegal price-fixing.[85]

The deduction that most competition law proceedings would be cross-border in nature can be further strengthened by the *Transportation Surcharge Antitrust Litigation* case, where claims of both US and UK victims arising from a global price-fixing conspiracy were settled. In view of that, one could go a step further and say that any collective redress regime, which does not take account of the fact that there would be numerous victims of EU competition law infringements across Europe, would not effectively close the enforcement gap. In this context, an important policy issue, which might need to be addressed at EU level, is whether the court in a Member State where the opt-out regime is in force would have jurisdiction over the class members who are domiciled abroad and have not opted out from the collective redress action.[86]

On the one hand, if the regime is only opt-out for locally domiciled victims of an infringement, and the victims from other Member States were to participate in collective redress proceedings only if they were to opt in, then the enforcement gap would remain unchanged and it may even widen in the countries where the legal systems have less experience in dealing with EU competition law actions.[87] In other words, the inconsistent enforcement of EU competition law would continue to be a significant issue, and consumers in these countries would be denied access to justice and redress. Moreover, if the opt-in regime remains in force for victims from other Member States, this will inevitably lead to parallel collective redress proceedings, pending before different Member State courts, in respect of the same infringement raising similar issues of fact and law. Indeed, such a regime would not take account of the cross-border nature of the business, nor of the fact that groups of companies are active and engage in anti-competitive conduct through their subsidiaries in a number of Member States. Given the cross-border nature of the EU competition law infringements, an opt-in regime would significantly increase the defendants' exposure to parallel suits and, as a result, their incentives to settle and achieve finality with a large number of businesses and consumers would be reduced, so that they might be tempted to employ delaying strategies.

On the other hand, if a pan-European opt-out regime was adopted, then opt-out collective redress proceedings brought in one country might also bind victims from abroad who wished to sue the defendant in their home state. It has been submitted[88] that a fundamental issue that needs to be determined in this context is how the victim's right to a 'fair trial and hearing', as embodied in Article 6(1) of the ECHR, would be safeguarded by the Member States' courts. As noted elsewhere,[89] the jurisdictional rules contained in the Brussels I Regulation contain no requirement for an adequate notice to be served to all the victims of an EU competition law infringement, so that one may argue that this would not arise as an

[85] *Emerald* (n 21) (CA) [2].

[86] M Danov, 'The Brussels I Regulation: Cross-border collective redress proceedings and judgments' (2010) 6 *Journal of Private International Law* 359, 378–79.

[87] See Chs 3, 4 and 5. See also: *Collective Redress in Antitrust* (n 17).

[88] ibid.

[89] Danov (n 86). See also: M Danov, *Jurisdiction and Judgments in Relation to EU Competition Law Claims* (Oxford, Hart Publishing, 2010).

issue at the jurisdictional stage. The preclusive effect of the judgment/settlement as an issue, however, would be bound to arise at the recognition and enforcement stage.[90] Accordingly, if the legislator aimed at introducing an opt-out regime aimed at rendering a judgment that is binding on all members of the claimant's class and enforceable in the other Member States, an important issue would be how to make this notice consistent with the claimant's class right to a 'fair trial and hearing' as embodied in Article 6(1) of the ECHR. The Service Regulation[91] is meant to be used in deciding the adequacy of a notice in the European context. However, what is specific to an opt-out regime regarding EU competition law case is that there would be a group of victims whose members (eg large purchasers) are identified, and another group of victims (eg thousands of consumers) whose members may only be identifiable, but not identified. The Regulation would be relevant when determining the adequacy of notices served to identified parties, but not when deciding on the adequacy of public notices made to identifiable parties. A liberal interpretation of the requirement for adequacy of a public notice may be justified by the principle of mutual trust that appears to be prevalent in Europe. However, it is well established that 'the granting of access to the courts in one State leads to denial of access in another State because of mechanical rules on *lis pendens* and related actions'.[92] Thus, the victims of an EU competition law infringement, who are based in Germany, might well prefer to bring their collective redress action before the German courts, being the courts located in their home state.[93]

The above analysis suggests that cross-border context of most EU competition law infringements is a specific issue which needs to be carefully considered by the legislator. How should the EU legislator strike the balance, and ensure that some victims are not denied access to justice? In this context, the difficulties in assessing small consumer damages, which is yet another distinctive feature of EU competition law infringements, must be considered.

B. Antirust Damage Caused to Victims of EU Competition Law Infringements – Another Distinctive Feature

As already demonstrated, antitrust damage may be caused to a number of businesses and consumers. But, how easy is it to ascertain the damage suffered by the individual victims (and consumers in particular), in order to distribute it to them?

On the one hand, *Transportation Surcharge Antitrust Litigation* shows that such damage may well be identifiable in some cases. As already noted, the claim was brought on behalf of consumers from the US and UK before the US District Court for the Northern District of California. The settlement resolved the claims of the victims of antitrust infringements, and provided for settlement class members submitting valid claims to receive refunds of 33.3 per cent of the fuel surcharges they paid on qualifying flights,[94] plus 90 days of interest

[90] See Danov (n 86) 378–80; D Fairgrieve, 'The Impact of the Brussels I Enforcement and Recognition Rules on Collective Actions' in Fairgrieve and Lein (n 10) 171. See more: Part V, below.

[91] Regulation (EC) No 1393/2007 on the service in the Member States of judicial and extrajudicial documents in civil or commercial matters (service of documents), and repealing Council Regulation 1348/2000.

[92] J Fawcett, 'The Impact of Article 6(1) of the ECHR on Private International Law' (2007) 56 *ICLQ* 1, 7.

[93] Danov (n 86) 378–79.

[94] See the List of Qualifying Long-Haul British Airways Flights www.airpassengerrefund.co.uk/Documents/British%20Airways%20Plc%20Long-Haul%20Flights.pdf.

on such payments. Although there were numerous victims, the damage was relatively straightforward to ascertain and distribute to claimants who completed and returned claim forms,[95] providing the required passenger and/or flight information by 31 December 2012. In this context, it has been noted that 'the English (foreign) class was treated on an *opt-in* basis, and not as an opt-out class.'[96]

On the other hand, there would be occasions where antitrust damages caused to individual consumers may be far from straightforward to ascertain, and their distribution may be even more difficult to materialise.[97] It has been noted that 'where the plaintiffs are consumers, distribution of damage awards becomes more problematic, not only because of the size of the class, but also because of the difficulty and expense in verifying relatively small consumers claims.'[98] The difficulties can be easily demonstrated by making reference to *Emerald*, in which the Chancellor of the High Court noted:

> damage is a necessary element in the cause of action of individual members of the class. Whether or not an individual member of the class can establish that necessary ingredient will depend on where in the chain of distribution he came and who if anyone in that chain had absorbed or passed on the alleged inflated price. Given the nature of the cause of action and the market in which the relevant transactions took place there is an inevitable conflict between the claims of different members of the class.[99]

The problems in establishing that there is harm may be particularly serious in cases where (as in *Emerald*) the claim is being brought by companies further up the chain of distribution. It may be argued by a defendant that such a claimant has passed the cartel-induced overcharge on to his purchasers, and, as a result, the claimant has suffered no loss. The issues regarding the passing-on defence, which were put forward above,[100] were noted by Lord Justice Longmore and Lord Justice Tuckey in *Devenish Nutrition v Sanofi-Aventis*:[101]

> if . . . the claimant has in fact passed the excessive price on to its purchasers and not absorbed the excess price itself, there is no very obvious reason why the profit made by the defendants (albeit undeserved and wrongful) should be transferred to the claimant without the claimant being obliged to transfer it down the line to those who have actually suffered the loss.[102]

Thus, there may well be difficulties in many EU competition law cases. On the one hand, a claimant, who is further up the chain of distribution, may have passed on the whole of the cartel-induced overcharge to his customers,[103] so possibly the whole damage will be absorbed by the end consumers of a cartelised product. On the other hand, the damage suffered by an individual consumer may be very difficult to ascertain as its amount may indeed be negligible in some cases.[104] For example, this appears to be the case in *Emerald*. If one assumes that the claimants, who were importers of cut flowers, had passed the overcharge down to the

[95] See the Claim Form www.airpassengerrefund.co.uk/Documents/UK%20Claim%20Form.pdf .

[96] R Mulheron, 'In Defence of the Requirement For Foreign Class Members to opt in to an English Class Action' in Fairgrieve and Lein (n 10) 245, 263.

[97] LA Sullivan and WS Grimes, *The Law of Antitrust: An Integrated Handbook*, 2nd edn (Thomson West, 2006) 997.

[98] ibid 997.

[99] *Emerald Supplies* (n 21) (HC) [36].

[100] See section III, above.

[101] *Devenish*, (n 53) (CA).

[102] ibid [147] (Longmore LJ).

[103] ibid [151] (Tuckey LJ).

[104] M Handler, 'The Shift From Substantive To Procedural Innovations In Antitrust Suits – The Twenty-Third Annual Antitrust Review' (1971) 71 *Columbia Law Review* 1, 9.

end buyer of a bouquet of cut flowers, then it would be far from easy to ascertain how much of the price of the bouquet was increased as a result of the overcharge, in order for it to be claimed back by the individual consumers. Another case which may be used to illustrate the difficulties is *Devenish*. If one assumes that the cartel-induced overcharge in selling a unit of vitamins to Devenish Nutrition was £40,[105] and the cartelised product was purchased by them to manufacture speciality products for the intensive livestock sector, then how much of the cartel-induced overcharge contributes to the raised price which is ultimately paid by the end consumer?[106] It is beyond doubt that if a claim is brought by the end consumer, then 'the non-assessable cost of responding to discovery and the like will substantially erode, if not exceed, any recovery.'[107]

Hence, an important issue to be considered is what damage remedies may be best used to compensate consumers, and achieve collective redress in Europe. Before providing the answer to this question, it would be useful to consider who is bringing the competition law actions at the moment.

C. Who is Suing? Where are the Actions being Brought?

Emerald reaffirms that, as already noted,[108] companies[109] generally (encompassing large businesses and SMEs) are more active than consumers in bringing competition law damages actions at present. The qualitative interviewing data from Germany and England appear to suggest that Germany, England, the Netherlands and possibly Spain are attracting more such actions in comparison with the other Member States.[110] Some of the EU competition law actions involve groups of companies on the claimants' side as well as on the defendants' side.[111] However, there have at the moment been only a few actions brought by consumers, and/or on behalf of the consumers in Europe. As already noted,[112] the authors of the 'Collective Redress in Antitrust' have concluded that:

> collective actions on antitrust have been brought only in six countries (Austria, France, Germany, Italy, Spain and UK), but in none of them were there more than five of these actions over the last five years . . . Moreover, only in Austria, Spain, France and the UK some collective actions have been admitted by courts and have reached the trial stage. To date collective actions resulting in damages awarded to the victims have been observed only in Austria and in the UK.[113]

[105] See the example given by Tuckey LJ in *Devenish* (n 53) (CA) [151].

[106] These difficulties were noted by an interview respondent.

[107] Handler (n 104) 9.

[108] See Ch 5.

[109] eg *Enron Coal Services Ltd (In Liquidation) v English Welsh & Scottish Ltd* [2011] EWCA Civ 2; *Roche Products Ltd, Roche Vitamine Europe AG (Switzerland), F Hoffmann-La Roche AG (Switzerland) v Provimi Ltd* [2003] EWHC 961 (Comm); *Cooper Tire & Rubber Company Europe Ltd & Others* [2010] EWCA Civ 864; *Toshiba Carrier UK Ltd and Other v KME Yorkshire Ltd & Others* [2012] EWCA Civ 1190; Case No 1077/5/7/07 *Emerson Electric* [2008] CAT 8, 28 April 2008. See also: Ch 11.

[110] Chs 2, 3, 4 and 5.

[111] *Cooper Tire* (n 109).

[112] See Ch 5.

[113] *Collective Redress in Antitrust* (n 17) 39. Regarding the UK, it should be noted that the authors are referring to the *JJB* case which settled, and is far from being an example of effective redress for consumers due to the small numbers of consumers receiving compensation. See more: *Which?*, 'JJB Sports: a case study in collective action', www.which.co.uk/documents/pdf/collective-redress-case-study-which-briefing-258401.pdf.

Therefore, the data indicates that it is primarily corporates who are suing for EU competition law damages, and those actions are being predominantly brought in a few Member States. How does one encourage claims by consumers? *Transportation Surcharge Antitrust Litigation*, in which a foreign court could award compensatory damages to consumers in the UK, may be regarded as proof that 'procedural innovations'[114] should be considered by the legislators, if they want to close the existing enforcement gap by providing for collective redress in antitrust. It is worrying that England, which is regarded as one of the leading jurisdictions attracting competition litigation in Europe, has so far witnessed only one consumer action.[115]

There are several main reasons why so few actions are brought by consumers. The low number of claims brought by consumers may find its explanation in the high costs incurred in competition law claims.[116] Indeed, the high level of litigation costs, which could be fuelled by the high level of uncertainty with regard to cross-border EU competition law claims,[117] can be a significant deterrent for claims brought by consumers because, as already noted, the amount of damages suffered by the consumer may be negligible in some cases.[118] There may be even more evidential hurdles in claims brought by consumers, as many of them may not keep their sale receipts, for example. Even in claims brought by corporates, the 'evidential difficulties (in the sense that it may be difficult to prove to the satisfaction of the court the facts that do exist, or would have existed in the "no cartel" world)' have been put forward before the High Court by counsel for the claimants in *Devenish.*[119] Hence, the difficulties in proving the damage suffered by individual consumers and the negligible amount of such damage as well as the high litigation costs may explain why there are only a few consumer actions at the moment.

Therefore, should the legislator wish to design an effective collective redress system, there are three important issues which need to be carefully considered. First, one of the important features of EU competition law actions is that there would be multiple victims in various countries. Secondly, the multiple victims may have suffered different levels of damages, and, as a result, they may have different interests in so far as those affected by an EU competition law infringement may be up or down in the chain of distribution (ie passing on or absorbing the inflated price). Thirdly, consumers would be reluctant to bring such actions due to the negligible amount of damages suffered by them in comparison with the high litigation costs.

VI. PROPOSED SOLUTIONS: PROCEDURAL AND SUBSTANTIVE LAW INNOVATIONS

The foregoing analysis appears to suggest that the difficulties in proving the damage suffered by individual consumers and the negligible amount of such damage as well as the high litigation costs are the main issues which need to be addressed by the legislator. The analyses of *Transportation Surcharge Antitrust Litigation* and *Emerald* (as well as *Devenish*)

[114] Handler (n 104).

[115] Case No 1087/7/9/07 *The Consumer Association v JJB Sports PLC* [2009] CAT 2. See more: Section IV, above.

[116] Case No 1178/5/7/11 *2 Travel Group PLC (In Liquidation) v Cardiff City Transport Services Ltd* [2011] CAT 30 [17]. See also: *Yeheshkel Arkin v Borchard Lines and Others* [2005] EWCA Civ 655.

[117] Ch 3.

[118] Handler (n 104) 9.

[119] *Devenish Nutrition v Sanofi-Aventis* [2007] EWHC [23]–[32].

suggest that an important criterion, which is to be used when the policy-makers are selecting and identifying gatekeepers,[120] relates to the question whether the end consumers, on whose behalf the action is brought, are direct or indirect purchasers. If the consumers in question are direct purchasers (as they were in *Transportation Surcharge Antitrust Litigation*), then consumer associations would be best placed to bring representative actions aggregating numerous small damages claims on behalf of the consumers.[121] However, the UK experience[122] clearly shows that an opt-in regime is far from efficient in competition cases, and indicates that an opt-out regime[123] is indeed required to address the existing enforcement gap.

Nonetheless, even if an opt-out regime were introduced, the consumer associations may not be well placed to bring EU competition law damage claims in cases where 'consumers do not buy directly from manufacturers but instead from middlemen'.[124] In such cases, the consumer associations would hardly have any necessary information regarding the purchased/sold quantities of a cartelised product and must rely entirely on the data provided by the consumers. This would make them less efficient gatekeepers, as the data provided by consumers would often be incomplete due to the fact that the numerous consumers, who have suffered negligible amounts of damage, would be remote from the infringing undertakings. How can those difficulties, which are so important with regard to EU competition law actions, be best dealt with? Posner has submitted:

> There have long been techniques for aggregating a number of small claims into one large enough to justify the costs of suit – or, stated otherwise, for realizing economies of scale in litigation. A department store performs this function with respect to the claims of its customers against the manufacturers whose products the store sells.[125]

Bearing in mind that it is the large companies that generally appear to be bringing EU competition law damages actions, it seems to us that one way of closing the enforcement gap in Europe would be to allow large purchasers, for example, to aggregate claims on behalf of purchasers down the chain of distribution (including end consumers). This would allow large companies to aggregate claims on behalf of consumers of a cartelised product and/or consumers who are paying a monopoly price. Indeed, companies appear to be better placed to bring the actions as they may have the means to meet the high litigation costs as well as the necessary information regarding the purchased/sold quantities of a cartelised product over a number of years. In such cases, a gatekeeping role will be performed by the judges who would exercise judicial control over the cases at the certification stage when 'judges must clarify with great accuracy the requirements of commonality between the parties and the adequacy of representation.'[126] The volume of sales of the large purchasers, who have opted in to the collective redress proceedings, can be an objective criterion in assessing their adequacy to act as representatives of the end consumers who would be involved on an opt-out basis. The courts would, inter alia, ensure that the class is well informed.

[120] See section III, above.
[121] See s 47B of the Competition Act 1998.
[122] See section IV, above
[123] See section III, above. See further Fairgrieve and Howells (n 10) 39–40.
[124] Posner (n 53) 419–20.
[125] Posner (n 53) 785.
[126] D Corapi, 'Class actions and collective actions' in Fairgrieve and Lein (n 10) 3, 7.

Therefore, a proposed gatekeeper test may be: are the consumers, on whose behalf an EU competition law action is brought, direct purchasers? If the answer is affirmative, then a consumer association would be better placed to bring such an action as they 'may see it as part of their mission to bring such actions to serve their members or highlight issues'.[127] If the answer is negative, then companies would be better placed to bring the action (and aggregate small consumer claims on behalf of the end consumers), as they may have the means to meet the high litigation costs as well as the necessary information regarding the purchased/sold quantities of a cartelised product over a number of years, so that, in this scenario, the gatekeeping role will be performed by the courts at the certification stage. If one applies the proposed gatekeeper test, then the question whether a claim by a consumer association would have a priority over a claim by a large purchaser, for example, would not arise as the consumer associations would act as gatekeepers only if the consumers, on whose behalf an EU competition law action is brought, are direct purchasers.

Moreover, a solution, which allows large companies to aggregate claims on behalf of consumers, could potentially address the specific problems[128] associated with proving the small amount of damages suffered by consumers as well as the passing-on defence[129] which may be raised in claims brought by large purchasers. In this context, it has been very recently submitted:

> Given that it is normally the large companies that tend to bring competition law actions, one should say that if the pass on defence were denied such direct purchaser may gain significant advantages by recovering damages for loss they would have passed down the distribution chain. On the other hand, if the pass through were available, then the *infringer* would not compensate the victims of the EU competition law infringement and would receive a windfall as not all indirect purchasers of the cartelised product would be seeking damages. The latter deduction is supported by research which shows that there is an enforcement gap at the moment.[130] The foregoing concerns would be addressed if the direct purchasers were allowed to bring opt-out competition law actions as representatives for all the indirect purchasers down the chain unless the concrete entities down the chain have explicitly opted out from such an action. Indeed, such direct purchasers would normally be large companies which will have the funds to bring the actions, and they would also have more information to prove that there was infringement/damage. Moreover, by being direct purchasers, such larger companies would be in a position to distribute the unclaimed damages by making discounts which could easily be passed down the chain (i.e. they would increase their sales etc). However, any move towards an opt-out system would depend crucially on safeguards to ensure that the class is well informed, and compensation appropriately distributed. Additionally, if the direct purchaser made no move to bring the claim, or distribute the proceeds of any settlement, it would be important to preserve the ability of another party in the distribution chain to bring the consolidated claim on behalf of the class of claimants, possibly after consultation with the direct purchaser.[131]

In other words, an appropriate collective redress mechanism may be set up by allowing some purchasers to aggregate claims on behalf of other purchasers down the chain of distribution (including end consumers). Such a mechanism would work on an opt-in basis for purchasers up the chain of distribution, and on an opt-out basis for the other victims of

[127] Fairgrieve and Howells (n 10) 39.
[128] See above.
[129] See section III, above.
[130] Ch 3.
[131] M Danov and S Dnes, 'Private actions in competition law: a consultation on options for reform. Response form' submitted to the UK Government, Department for Business, Innovation and Skills on 24 July 2012.

an EU competition law infringement. The opt-out regime for purchasers down the chain of distribution and consumers in particular may be justified by the fact that the amount of damage suffered by an individual consumer is significantly smaller in comparison with the litigation costs, which would make any litigation of small individual claims unsustainable.

The large purchasers, who bring the claims on an opt-in basis, should ensure that distribution happens and that it does so in a fair and transparent way. The court would scrutinise and approve the system which will be implemented in this context. Given the difficulties in distributing the damage relief to many consumers with small claims,[132] the unclaimed damages may be passed on through discounts[133] by the large purchasers down the chain to the end consumer of a cartelised product and/or to the end consumers who are paying a monopoly price.[134] Indeed, some substantive law innovations with regard to damage remedies as discounts may be best used to provide redress for consumers who 'stop buying the product when the price rises from the competitive to the monopoly level'[135] rectifying inter alia the deadweight lost by encouraging the consumers to buy the product in question at a reduced price. The incentives for firms to bring actions on behalf of purchasers down the chain of distribution (including end consumers) would be significant. In EU competition law cases, there would be large sums of money to be distributed down the chain of distribution because the assumption is that most corporates would pass on the cartel induced overcharge to the end consumers. Hence, providing discounts is regarded as 'a sound marketing device beneficial to the participants'[136] and the opt-in corporate claimants in particular. In other words, the proposed remedies may also rectify the loss, which the large purchasers would have suffered by encountering fewer sales than would have materialised if no EU competition law infringement had occurred.

One might question the adoption of such an opt-out mechanism as it may potentially increase the defendant's exposure to damages actions and compel them to settle.[137] However, it has been noted that an effective opt-out regime will also serve defendants' interests in so far as such a regime may be used to determine, once and for all, the defendants' liability with respect to multiple individual damages claims, so that they can get on with their business.[138] Moreover, it has been pointed out that:

> companies that commit billion-dollar torts [should face billion dollar losses at trial]. A civil justice system in proper working order should therefore always cause a person with an enormous legal obligation to fear losing an enormous sum at trial. When such a person settles instead of going to trial, a persuasive case of wrongful coercion cannot be made.[139]

[132] Sullivan and Grimes (n 97) 997.

[133] *cf. Re Domestic Air Transportation Antitrust Litigation* 148 FRD L 297, 306, 315 (ND Ga 1993) discussed in Sullivan and Grimes (n 97) 997.

[134] The issue of damages remedies for consumers was raised by Dr Deborah Prince at the 'Cross-border EU competition law actions' which took place in Brunel University on 12 November 2010.

[135] Posner (n 53) 419. See also: S Bishop and M Walker, *The Economics of EC Competition Law: Concepts, Application and Measurement* (London, Sweet & Maxwell, 2010) 27–28.

[136] Sullivan and Grimes (n 97) 997.

[137] Handler (n 104) 9. See European Parliament, Report on 'Towards a Coherent European Approach to Collective Redress' (2011/2089(INI)), 12 January 2012, 15–16. See also: ZS Tang, 'Consumer Collective Redress in European Private International Law' (2011) 7 *Journal of Private International Law* 101, 112; E Lein, 'Cross-border collective and jurisdiction under Brussels I: A mismatch' in Fairgrieve and Lein (n 10) 129, 142.

[138] Layton (n 52) 94.

[139] C Silver, '"We're scared to death": Class certification and blackmail' (2003) 78 *New York University Law Review* 1357, 1367.

Indeed, the data from England[140] indicates that a settlement may be difficult to achieve if the claim is weak. Nonetheless, the high number of settlements[141] under the current regime appears to suggest that a mechanism allowing for collective settlements,[142] and their finality should be considered in a cross-border context.[143] Therefore, any proposed solution must inter alia address the question whether there should be more harmonisation or whether the EU legislator should rather promote inter-jurisdictional regulatory competition in order to close the enforcement gap in Europe.

VII. HARMONISATION OR REGULATORY COMPETITION

An effective collective redress mechanism may be needed if the Union wants to significantly increase the efficiency of the enforcement system.[144] But, should such a mechanism be harmonised at EU level? As already noted, some commentators favour harmonisation[145] (which presupposes more centralisation), while others favour regulatory competition[146] (which presupposes more decentralisation) when it comes to EU competition law actions. In the context of this debate, it should be noted that Snell[147] has made the following analysis:

> 'Centralisation may sometimes be beneficial. A centralised system can be politically stable, which also brings benefits of economic stability and predictability. Centralisation reduces transaction costs of private operators, who only have to familiarise themselves with one set of regulations. A centrally run system can also cope with distortions caused by market failure, such as negative externalities.
>
> However, the economics of federalism teaches us that it is better to have multiple legislators than just a single one. The best approach is to allocate regulatory competence to the lowest appropriate level, which corresponds to the principle of subsidiarity. Most importantly, the existence of different jurisdictions may allow competition between legal orders with all ensuing static and dynamic efficiencies.'[148]

Although the authors of the *Ashurst Report*[149] and of the Report on *Collective Redress in Antitrust*[150] appear to favour harmonisation, the qualitative data[151] appear to suggest that a

[140] Ch 3.
[141] Ch 3.
[142] See section II, above. See also: I Tzankova and H van Lith, 'Class Actions and Class Settlements Going Global: the Netherlands' in Fairgrieve and Lein (n 10) 67.
[143] See more: Ch 27.
[144] KW Dam, 'Class Actions: Efficiency, Compensation, Deterrence, and Conflict of Interest' (1975) 4 *Journal of Legal Studies* 47, 73.
[145] W van Gerven, 'Harmonisation of Private Law: Do we need it?' (2004) 41 *CML Rev* 505, 524; G Betlem, 'Torts, a European *Ius Commune* and the private enforcement of Community law' (2005) 64 *Cambridge Law Journal* 126, 142. See also: M Dougan, *National Remedies Before the Court of Justice* (Oxford, Hart Publishing, 2004) 65.
[146] S Weatherill, 'Why harmonise?' in T Tridimas and P Nebbia, *European Union Law for the Twenty-First Century: Rethinking the New Legal Order*, Vol 2 (Oxford, Hart Publishing, 2004) 11; F Marcos and AS Graells, 'Damages for breach of the EC antitrust rules: harmonising Tort Law through the back door' (2008) *InDret* 1–18, www.indret.com/code/getPdf.php?id=1088&pdf=518_en.pdf .
[147] J Snell, *Goods and Services in EC Law: A Study of the Relationship between the Freedoms* (Oxford, OUP, 2002).
[148] ibid 35.
[149] *Ashurst Report* (n 1).
[150] *Collective Redress in Antitrust* (n 17).
[151] Chs 2, 3, 4 and 5.

better way forward for the EU legislator is to promote inter-jurisdictional regulatory competition in the area of EU antitrust law dispute resolution. A harmonised and efficient pan-European collective redress mechanism may be very difficult to achieve at EU level. Indeed, devising such a mechanism presupposes a level of harmonisation with respect to procedural issues which are to be addressed at EU level, and then applied by national legal orders sharing different legal traditions and heritages. The procedural rules and the experience of the Member States' judiciary would be key. Some of the judges of the new Member States may find it difficult to apply the newly devised mechanism as well as to deal with complicated EU competition laws. The problems are rooted in the fact that antitrust laws in some of those countries were adopted only in the 1990s. Although, those laws mirrored the western model, they ignored the specific features of the socialist heritage and lack the decades of experience in applying those laws.[152]

Moreover, the Commission has outlined the risk that some of the new Member States may be unable to correctly apply EU law unless they achieve irreversible progress on their judicial reforms.[153] Procedural aspects may be a problem in some of the old Member States. As already noted, the English Court of Appeal stated: 'the fact that it may take different periods of time for similar proceedings to come to a conclusion in different jurisdictions [and Italy in particular on this occasion], for whatever reasons, is not a criticism; it is merely a fact of life to which a judge cannot be expected to close his eyes.'[154] In other words, the legislators in the various Member States and their judiciaries may be faced with different challenges, and they may be best placed to deal with them. It is highly unlikely for the EU legislator to be able to resolve the specific problems facing the diverse body of Member States. Any such attempt is bound to be inefficient, expensive and inflexible.[155] Indeed, as already noted,[156] one might question the effectiveness of more centralisation in the area of private antitrust enforcement by devising another legislative instrument which is a result of a compromise reached at EU level. This would also fly in the face of the White Paper on Modernisation of the Rules Implementing Articles 101 and 102 TFEU which intended inter alia to promote decentralised enforcement of EU competition law.[157] In view of that, the best way forward may be for the specific procedural issues to be best addressed at national level as the EU legislator's intervention in these matters may bring fresh uncertainty. The Union should rather devise an adequate institutional framework to promote regulatory competition between Member States to attract claimants, so that the EU competition law enforcement system can produce efficient results.

Strong arguments for promoting regulatory competition have been recently put forward by the editorial board of *Legal Issues of Economic Integration*:

> National laboratories . . . produce different rules that allow for different experiences and can improve the understanding of alternative legal solutions. These advantages are relevant both to

[152] T Varady, 'The Emergence of Competition Law in (Former) Socialist Countries' (1999) 47 *American Journal of Comparative Law* 229, 261.

[153] eg Commission (EC), 'Bulgaria's progress on accompanying measures following Accession' (Report) COM (2007) 377 final; Commission (EC), 'Romania's progress on accompanying measures following Accession' (Report) COM (2007) 378 final.

[154] *Cooper Tire* (n 109) [54]–[55].

[155] W Kerber, 'Interjurisdictional competition within the European Union' (1999–2000) 23 *Fordham International Law Journal* S217, S229.

[156] Ch 2.

[157] White Paper on Modernisation of the Rules Implementing Articles 85 and 86 of the EC Treaty, Commission Programme No 99/027 [58]–[61].

> the formulation of substantive rules and to law enforcement. Moreover, legal diversity and competition do not necessarily exclude harmonization. In fact, dynamic competition between legal rules can lead to voluntary convergence, which in turn can be more effective and successful than forced coordination of legislation.[158]

However, the qualitative interviewing data[159] show that there is a lack of mobility amongst the consumers and SMEs who have suffered damages as a result of an EU competition law infringement. In view of that, it is a relatively safe prediction that the inter-jurisdictional regulatory competition market would fail to address the current enforcement gap unless the private international law framework is designed to promote regulatory competition. Is the current private international law framework capable of promoting regulatory competition? How should the private international law framework be reformed?

VIII. A NEED FOR A NEW PRIVATE INTERNATIONAL LAW REGIME PROMOTING REGULATORY COMPETITION

It has been demonstrated that private international law rules have a vital role to play with respect to cross-border collective proceedings arising in the European context.[160] This would be particularly so in EU competition law cases, which would often be cross-border in nature. As already noted,[161] there are no specific provisions to allocate jurisdiction in relation to collective redress EU competition law proceedings, and the question whether a national court has jurisdiction to deal with Articles 101 and 102 TFEU is to be determined by the Brussels I Regulation.[162] As a result, a Member State court should consider whether it has personal jurisdiction over such a collective redress action under the Brussels I Regulation. This is a problem as there are specific issues which would arise with regard to cross-border collective redress proceedings in antitrust. In addition to the jurisdictional problems identified in the English case law[163] and discussed in Chapters 11 and 13, there would be even more problems with regard to collective redress proceedings, as some Member States have adopted the opt-in regime and others have taken up the opt-out regime.

There is a strong case that the EU jurisdictional rules may need some amendments in order to deal with the cross-border collective redress actions.[164] In a very recent report by the European Parliament, it has been noted that 'with regard to jurisdiction, a special clause in the horizontal instrument should provide that the courts for the place where the defendant is domiciled should have jurisdiction.'[165] However, such a solution would have a chilling effect on cross-border collective redress proceedings. As already noted,[166]

[158] From the Board, 'Two steps forward and one step back: harmonizing the unharmonizable', (2011) 38 *Legal Issues of Economic Integration* 207, 211.

[159] Chs 2, 3, 4 and 5.

[160] Danov (n 86); Tang (n 137); Tzakas (n 52); Fairgrieve and Lein (n 10).

[161] Ch 13.

[162] Danov (n 86). See also: Tang (n 137).

[163] eg *Provimi* (n 109); *SanDisk Corporation v Koninklijke Philips Electronics and others* [2007] EWHC 332 (Ch), [2007] Bus LR 705; *Cooper Tire* (n 109); *Toshiba Carrier* (n 109).

[164] Danov (n 86). See also: Lein (n 137); JN Stefanelli, 'Parallel litigation and cross-border collective actions under the Brussels I framework: Lessons from abroad' in Fairgrieve and Lein (n 10) 143.

[165] 'Towards a Coherent European Approach to Collective Redress' (n 137) 16.

[166] See Ch 13. See also: Ch 11.

the ongoing litigation in *Emerson v Carbone* before the English Court of Appeal appears to suggest that even big multinational companies would aim to avoid bringing their damages claim in France (the Member State in which Carbone is domiciled).[167] It has been very recently submitted by Hess:[168]

> one might be tempted to propose the simple solution of introducing an exclusive head of jurisdiction for opt-out collective redress. Such a provision would concentrate all lawsuits as the seat of the corporate defendant.[169] Parallel litigation would be impossible, the recognition of a respective judgment would not be barred by Article 34(3) Brussels Regulation. Yet, this solution comes at its price: first of all, it would favour the (corporate) defendant who could profit from a so-called 'home bias'. Furthermore, litigation against several defendants (for the same infringement) under Article 6(1) would be excluded.[170]

In addition to the outlined drawbacks of the exclusive head of jurisdiction proposal, one should add that even parallel litigation would not be avoided with regard to EU antitrust law infringements. As already noted,[171] groups of companies would often engage in anti-competitive conduct by setting up subsidiaries across Europe, the subsidiaries of the various groups of companies may implement in the various Member States the same cartel agreement that is entered into by their parents. Parallel proceedings would be bound to arise across Europe as claimants from the various Member States may not be able to sue more than one group of companies at a time.

Therefore, it seems to us that if the private international law framework does not provide the claimants with a choice where to bring their actions, then the inter-jurisdictional regulatory competition would lead to economic externalities – giving rise to welfare losses and market distortions[172] across Europe. However, in the new Proposal for a Regulation on Jurisdiction and the Recognition and Enforcement of Judgments[173] there is no indication that special rules for dealing with the challenges of collective redress EU competition law proceedings in the successor to Regulation 44/2001 are on anyone's agenda.[174] Thus, there is a case for a reform which would involve an amendment of Regulation 1/2003 to address the issues of jurisdiction in cross-border EU competition law cases and promote regulatory competition.

In this context, it should be noted that the low mobility of individual consumers in Europe (which is easily explained by the high costs of cross-border EU competition litigation[175]), on

[167] *Emerson Electric Co v Morgan Crucible Company PLC and Ors* – still pending before the Court of Appeal – Case Reference C3/2011/1658. See also: J Basedow, 'International cartels and the place of acting under Article 5(3) of the Brussels I Regulation' in J Basedow, S Francq and L Idot (eds), *International Antitrust Litigation: Conflict of Laws and Coordination* (Oxford, Hart Publishing, 2012) 31, 35.

[168] B Hess, 'A coherent approach to European Collective Redress' in Fairgrieve and Lein (n 10) 107.

[169] 'Such a provision should be inserted into Art 22 Brussels Regulation and read as follows: "The following courts shall have exclusive jurisdiction, regardless of domicile . . . in proceedings under Articles 4(2), 6 and 7 of Directive (EC) xxx, the courts of the Member State at the domicile of the defendant"', quoted by Hess (n 168) 117.

[170] ibid.

[171] See Ch 13.

[172] DC Esty and D Geradin, 'Regulatory Co-Operation' in DC Esty and D Geradin (eds), *Regulatory Competition and Economic Integration* (Oxford, OUP, 2001) 30, 34.

[173] COM(2010) 748 final.

[174] Although the Commission recast proposal did recommend the abolition of the exequatur procedure with the exception of judgments given in collective compensatory proceedings, the original proposal was subsequently modified. See Arts 37(3) and 48 of the Commission Proposal for a Brussels I Regulation COM (2010) 748 final. *cf.* Art 37 of the amended text of the Commission recast proposal – 10609/12 ADD 1 of 1 June 2012. See more: Ch 26.

[175] Chs 2, 3, 4 and 5.

the one hand, and the high mobility of corporates,[176] on the other hand, suggest that there is a need for jurisdiction rules which allow a claimant to centralise litigation against a group of the same companies before the courts at his preferred jurisdiction. Where, for example, there is a corporate group with numerous subsidiaries (all of whom form a single infringing undertaking), then it should be open for a claimant to centralise litigation against the whole group of companies (as well as against the other group/s of companies who were party to the same anti-competitive agreement) by establishing jurisdiction against one of the subsidiaries. Since EU competition law infringements would often directly and substantially affect the markets in several countries and/or regions, such a rule may be used to promote regulatory competition with regard to enforcement across Europe. Such a rule would allow consumer associations (acting as gatekeepers) or purchasers up the chain of distribution to bring collective redress proceedings against legal entities in their preferred jurisdiction. It will also allow them to aggregate claims on behalf of end consumers, potentially on an opt-out basis for the other victims of an EU competition law infringement, provided that a Member State decides to launch such a mechanism. Indeed, given the diverse nature of the EU, regulatory competition with regard to cross-border damages claims may happen if claimants can directly choose between damages regimes of different jurisdictions and bring their claims there by benefitting from procedural and substantive laws[177] of the jurisdiction where the claim is brought, provided that they can rely on the law of the forum (*lex fori*).

There are very good reasons to defend 'the requirement for foreign class members to opt in to an English class action'.[178] One may however balance against this consideration the distinctive features of the cross-border antitrust actions which might suggest that such a requirement should be set aside with regard to EU competition law collective redress proceedings brought in the European context. As there is low mobility of consumers across Europe, it might thus be argued that an amendment of Regulation 1/2003 would promote regulatory competition only if it allows for an opt-out regime, implemented by a particular Member State, to operate for consumers from across Europe. It is well established that 'no rational defendant . . . will want to settle if [the settlement] could be reopened years later, instead of settling, defendants will litigate and add to the burden of our already overburdened courts.'[179] Given that the majority of EU competition law infringements could cause damage to businesses and consumers in several countries,[180] it would seem necessary that the questions related to the preclusive effects of collective judgment/settlements are carefully considered at EU level.[181]

A final consideration in the antitrust context is that if the regime is only *opt-out* for locally domiciled victims of an infringement, and the victims from other Member States were to participate in collective redress proceedings only if they opt in, then it might be argued that the enforcement gap in Europe would remain unchanged and it may even

[176] Chs 2, 3, 4 and 5.

[177] See Chs 21 and 22.

[178] Mulheron (n 96) 245. See also: Danov (n 86).

[179] DA Dana, 'Using the Veil of Ignorance to Ensure Distributive Justice in Class Actions: A Rawlsian Approach to "adequacy of representation" after Stephenson' (2005) *Northwestern University School of Law Public Law and Legal Theory Papers*, Paper 5, p 51.

[180] See Chs 2, 3, 4 and 5. See also: *Collective Redress in Antitrust* (n 17).

[181] A similar view was expressed by Mr Jon Lawrence at the 'Cross-Border EU Competition Law Actions' Conference which was held at the London School of Economics on Friday, 20 April 2012. See also: B Hess, 'The Brussels I Regulation: Recent case law of the Court of Justice and the Commission's proposed recast' (2012) 49 *Common Market Law Review* 1075, 1091–92.

widen in the countries where the legal systems have less experience in dealing with EU competition law actions. The cross-border nature of most EU competition law infringements and the fact that Articles 101 and 102 TFEU form part of each Member State's legal order appear to suggest that there is a case for the EU legislator to 'ensure that consumers throughout the EU are able to use the collective redress mechanisms that are available in different Member States'.[182]

If such a broad solution was considered appropriate by policy-makers, then a specific issue that would need to be addressed at EU level in this context is that of the identity of the parties to the parallel collective redress actions brought under opt-out regimes in several Member States. For example, if England were to adopt an opt-out regime and if collective redress opt-out actions, involving the same cause of action in respect of the same infringement by the same defendant, were brought in England and, for example, in Portugal, it would not be clear which of the identifiable parties to the parallel opt-out proceedings would be bound by the English and Portuguese actions, respectively, unless the class members had opted in to one of the class actions.[183]

This is of course one of the problems associated with the broader solution of cross-border opt-out regimes. It might thus militate in favour of a regime whereby out of jurisdiction claimants have to opt-in to an action. Alternatively, if a broader solution was adopted with a view to closing the enforcement gap and providing 'an effective remedy'[184] for consumers across Europe, then the courts could perhaps deal with the problem if an amended version of Regulation 1/2003 directs the Member States courts to have an appropriately devised certification regime. To this end, the Regulation could impose a requirement for a national judge to identify the countries where the businesses (or the consumer associations), which have opted in to the action, operate (and/or direct their activities to). The countries in question should be clearly identified by the judge with a view to certifying that the businesses (or the consumer associations) could adequately represent the consumers from these countries. For example, if the action was brought by a large purchaser, then the courts may certify that the opt-in direct purchasers are suitable representatives of the claimants from several Member States by identifying the volume of their sales (or the sales of their subsidiaries) in the countries in question. In other words, the volume of sales of the businesses, which have opted into the collective redress proceedings, can be an objective criterion in assessing their adequacy to act as representatives of the end consumers from the Member States in which, for example, a cartelised product has been sold.

As already noted,[185] in order to allow the parties to avoid parallel EU competition law proceedings, and centralise litigation before the court that is clearly appropriate to deal with the case, avoiding the problem of irreconcilable or inconsistent judgments, Regulation 1/2003 could go a step further and allow the court first seised to stay its proceedings, in cases where another court is better placed to deal with the case. Although such a rule could work well in theory, the proposed solution in practice may bring even more uncertainty unless the architecture of the European judiciary is reconsidered by the EU legislator. Indeed, a discretionary power without devising an appropriate civil justice institutional architecture could bring fresh uncertainty. This would be particularly so in cross-border

[182] Green Paper (n 9) [23].

[183] Danov (n 86).

[184] Section 47(1) of the Charter of Fundamental Rights of the European Union [2000] OJ C364/1. The importance of the Charter with regard to collective redress is discussed inter alia by Tzakas in Ch 17.

[185] Ch 13.

EU competition law actions. However, as already noted,[186] this is not a competition law specific issue, and may need to be addressed by the EU legislator in a wider context.

The fact that many EU competition law disputes would settle suggests that the question of whether an opt-out collective settlement would be enforceable should be carefully addressed by the legislator.[187] Since there would be multiple victims of EU competition law infringements, defendants would not settle unless the preclusive effect of collective settlements is properly addressed at EU level. Given the public interest in the enforcement of EU competition law, it would be appropriate if a settlement is approved by a judgment recording the consent of the parties,[188] and providing safeguards to ensure that the class is well informed.[189] It has been argued that the issue of recognition and enforcement of judgments rendered in an opt-out regime needs to be addressed by the European legislature.[190]

The inherent problems concern the binding effect of such judgments and the question of which group members are actually bound by such judgments as a 'fair trial and hearing' defence may be raised by the absent members of the claimant's class.[191] This gives rise to the question of whether there would be a breach of Article 6 ECHR in cases where the foreign court has issued a class judgment that is binding to absent/unrepresented members of the plaintiff's class who had not opted out from the foreign collective redress proceedings.[192] The right to a 'fair trial and hearing' is embodied in the ECHR. A breach of Article 6(1) of the ECHR could trigger the public policy exception contained in Article 34(1) of the Brussels I Regulation[193] or the natural justice defence contained in Article 34(2), which covers the right to a fair trial.[194] It has been submitted that 'using the [public policy] defence, the courts automatically should hold that enforcement would be against public policy where there has been a breach of Article 6 standards in the judgment granting state'.[195]

The fact that the Commission originally proposed a special regime for the recognition and enforcement of collective redress judgments might appear to underline that the public policy defence is an important issue to be considered in this context.[196] Indeed, the distinctive features of cross-border collective redress EU competition law proceedings suggest that the issue of recognition and enforcement of judgments in relation to such actions should be considered in Regulation 1/2003 with a view to promote regulatory competition

[186] Ch 13.

[187] See more: Ch 27.

[188] *cf.* the so-called 'judgment by consent'. See CPR 40.6. See more, N Andrews, *English Civil Procedure – Fundamentals of New Civil Justice System* (Oxford, OUP, 2003) 551.

[189] The English Court of Appeal held that 'if a party agrees to a judgment being entered by conceding the issues, the judgment is . . . within Article [32 of Brussels I]'. See *Landhurst Leasing Marcq* [1998] ILPr 822 [37].

[190] Danov (n 86).

[191] See T Eisenberg and G Miller, 'The Role of Opt-Outs and Objectors in Class Action Litigation: Theoretical and Empirical Issues' (2004) 57 *Vanderbilt Law Review* 1529; Hodges (n 52) 120–26. As for the unique status occupied by the absent class members under an opt-out regime, see R Mulheron, *The Class Action in Common Law Legal Systems: A Comparative Perspective* (Oxford, Hart Publishing, 2004) 36.

[192] Danov (n 86). See also: Fairgrieve (n 90) 178–86.

[193] Case 7/98 *Krombach v Bamberski* [2000] ECR I-1935. See also *Pordea v Times Newspaper* [2000] ILPr 763 (French Cour de Cassation). See Fawcett (n 92) 24–29.

[194] *Maronier v Larmer* [2002] EWCA Civ 774, [2003] QB [27].

[195] Fawcett (n 92) 44. See also the opinion of AG Kokott in Case C-394/07 *Marco Gambazzi v Daimler Chrysler Canada Inc* [2009] ECR I-2563, [2009] ILPr 38. See also P Beaumont and E Johnston, 'Can *Exequatur* Be Abolished in Brussels I Whilst Retaining a Public Policy Defence?' (2010) 6 *Journal of Private International Law* 249.

[196] See Arts 37(3) and 48 of the Commission Proposal for a Brussels I Regulation COM (2010) 748 final. cf: Art 37 of the amended text of the Commission recast proposal – 10609/12 ADD 1 of 1 June 2012.

in Europe. An appropriate solution[197] would be to hold that the recognising court should apply a presumption that the opt-out collective EU competition law redress regimes of other Member States are compliant with Article 6(1) of the Human Rights Convention as well as with section 47(2) of the Charter of Fundamental Rights of the European Union.[198] Indeed, such an approach might find support in section 47(1) of the Charter of Fundamental Rights of the European Union, which states that 'Everyone whose rights and freedoms guaranteed by the law of the Union are violated has the right to an effective remedy'. Hence, the European Commission's efforts to close the enforcement gap, which are important for Europe to be able to sustain economic growth, as well as the policy-makers' impetus to provide redress for those, who have suffered damages as a result of an EU competition law infringement, by encouraging collective redress antitrust proceedings in Europe might be strong arguments favouring the proposed approach.

IX. CONCLUSION

It has been canvassed above that in some circumstances there may be a need for an opt-out solution if collective redress is to play a role with regard to collective redress proceedings in antitrust. Consumer competition claims are one example where the opt-out solution may be appropriate. Should the legislator wish to design an effective collective redress system, there are three important issues which need to be carefully considered. First, one of the important features of these actions is that there would be multiple victims in various countries. Secondly, the multiple victims may have suffered different levels of damages, and, as a result, they may have different interests in so far as those affected by an EU competition law infringement may be up or down in the chain of distribution (ie passing on or absorbing the inflated price). Thirdly, consumers would be reluctant to bring such actions due to the negligible amount of damages suffered by them in comparison with the high litigation costs.

Given the negligible amount of antitrust damages suffered by the numerous individual consumers across Europe, a gatekeeper can be a major help in organising consumers. If the consumers in question are direct purchasers, then consumer associations would be best placed to organise consumers and bring representative actions aggregating numerous small damages claims on behalf of the consumers on an opt-out basis. However, the consumer associations may not be well placed to bring EU competition law damages claims in cases where consumers are indirect purchasers of a cartelised product. In such cases, the consumer associations would hardly have any necessary information regarding the purchased/sold quantities of a cartelised product and must rely entirely on the data provided by the consumers. This would make them less efficient gatekeepers as the data provided by consumers would often be incomplete due to the numerous consumers, who have suffered negligible amounts of damages, being too remote from the infringing undertakings.

[197] A less appropriate solution would be to adopt the opt-in regime in respect of claimant's class domiciled in another Member State. The latter approach would not solve all problems due to the low mobility of consumers across Europe, and the low number of collective redress proceedings in the overwhleming majority of the Member States.

[198] *cf. Maronier* (n 194) [25]. Criticised by Fawcett (n 92).

Bearing in mind that it is the large companies that generally appear to be bringing EU competition law damages actions, it seems to us that one way of closing the enforcement gap in Europe would be to allow large purchasers, for example, to aggregate claims on behalf of purchasers down the chain of distribution (including end consumers). This would allow large companies to aggregate claims on behalf of consumers of a cartelised product and/or consumers who are paying a monopoly price. In such cases, a gatekeeping role will be performed by the judges who would exercise judicial control over the cases at the certification stage. The volume of sales of the large purchasers, who have opted into the collective redress proceedings, can be an objective criterion in assessing their adequacy to act as representatives of the end consumers who would be involved on an opt-out basis.

Therefore, an appropriate collective redress mechanism may be set up by allowing some purchasers to aggregate claims on behalf of other purchasers down the chain of distribution (including end consumers). Such a mechanism would work on an opt-in basis for purchasers up the chain of distribution, and on opt-out basis for the other victims of an EU competition law infringement, subject to deciding whether the opt-out regime should also be applicable to out of jurisdiction claimants. The opt-out regime for purchasers down the chain of distribution and consumers in particular may be justified by the fact that the amount of damage suffered by an individual consumer is significantly smaller in comparison with the litigation costs, and makes any litigation of small individual claims unsustainable. Given the difficulties in distributing the damage relief to many consumers with small claims,[199] the unclaimed damages may be passed on through discounts[200] by the large purchasers down the chain of distribution to the end consumer of a cartelised product and/or to the end consumers who are paying a monopoly price. Indeed, some substantive law innovations with regard to damage remedies as discounts may be best used to provide redress for consumers who 'stop buying the product when the price rises from the competitive to the monopoly level',[201] rectifying, inter alia, the deadweight lost by encouraging the consumers to buy the product in question at a reduced price.

However, a distinctive feature of most EU competition law infringements is that they are cross-border in nature in so far as they involve legal entities from different countries and affect the market(s), businesses and consumers in more than one country. The diverse nature of the European Union leaves no doubt that the legislators in the various Member States and their judiciaries may be faced with different challenges, and they may be best placed to deal with them. Therefore, there is a strong case that the EU legislator should aim to promote inter-jurisdictional regulatory competition. Indeed, there is a case for reforming the current private international law framework with a view to promoting regulatory competition. There are specific issues which would arise with regard to cross-border collective redress proceedings in antitrust. In addition to the jurisdictional problems identified in the English case law[202] and discussed in Chapter 13, there would be even more problems with regard to collective redress proceedings as some Member States have adopted the opt-in regime and others have taken up the opt-out regime. In this context, it might be argued that the cross-border nature of most EU competition law infringements as well as the public interest to close the enforcement gap and provide redress across Europe

[199] Sullivan and Grimes (n 97) 997.

[200] *Re Domestic Air Transportation Antitrust Litigation* 148 FRD L 297, 306, 315 (ND Ga 1993) discussed in Sullivan and Grimes (n 97) 997.

[201] Posner (n 53) 419. See also: Bishop and Walker (n 135) 27–28.

[202] eg *Provimi* (n 109); *SanDisk* (n 163); *Cooper Tire* (n 109); *Toshiba Carrier* (n 109).

could suggest that the low mobility of consumers might be an important factor to be considered when deciding whether an opt-out regime, implemented by a particular Member State, would operate for consumers from other Member States. One might suggest that an opt-out regime applicable to out of jurisdiction claimants might be necessary to provide an 'effective remedy' within the meaning of Article 47(1) of the Charter of Fundamental Rights for consumers from across Europe. Also, a broad solution might create incentives for defendants to settle and achieve finality with a large number of businesses and consumers. It might thus be argued that such a regime could take account of the cross-border nature of EU competition law infringements, and the fact that groups of companies engage in anti-competitive conduct through their subsidiaries in a number of Member States. To this end, it would be essential to have an appropriately devised certification regime which may be implemented through an amendment to Regulation 1/2003. To this end, the Regulation could impose a requirement for a national judge to identify the countries where the businesses (or the consumer associations), which have opted in to the action, operate (and/or direct their activities to). The countries in question should be clearly identified by the judge with a view to certifying that the businesses (or the consumer associations) can adequately represent the consumers from these countries.

However, the new Proposal for a Regulation on Jurisdiction and the Recognition and Enforcement of Judgments[203] does not suggest that special rules facilitating collective redress EU competition law proceedings in the successor to Regulation 44/2001 are on anyone's agenda. In view of that, a way forward may be an amendment of Regulation 1/2003 to address the specific issues of jurisdiction in collective redress in antitrust proceedings and promote regulatory competition.

[203] COM(2010) 748 final.

19

Conclusion: Proposing Specific Solutions to Promote Regulatory Competition and Address the Enforcement Gap

MIHAIL DANOV AND FLORIAN BECKER

The foregoing analysis clearly shows that litigants' strategies are shaped by the specific features of EU competition law infringements and the current enforcement structure. It is beyond doubt that the two-task EU competition law enforcement structure results in predominantly follow-on damages actions being brought. The importance of the role of Member States' laws, which would determine whether a claimant would be entitled to recover the pleaded loss, suggests that the high level of uncertainty due to the cross-border implications of these cases is best reflected in litigants' tactics. This part of the book clearly shows that the enforcement gap would be closed if policy-makers addressed the specific issues associated with the cross-border nature of EU competition law claims as well as the issues surrounding the two-task enforcement structure of EU competition law.

I. CROSS-BORDER NATURE OF EU COMPETITION LAW INFRINGEMENTS: SPECIFIC ISSUES REQUIRING SPECIFIC SOLUTIONS

Lawrence and Morfey observe that cartel claims by direct purchasers have been brought based on European Commission decisions as well as on the decision by national competition authorities. Although none of the claims to date has come to trial, and, as a result, there is no damages award in a cartel case, there is increasingly frequent settlement of claims, with substantial compensation payments being made.[1] The high level of uncertainty in the area may be best illustrated by Lawrence and Morfey's review of the issues which are proving to be battle-grounds between claimants and defendants in cartel damages litigation. The analysis made by Lawrence and Morfey is indicative as to which issues need to be considered by the policy-makers as well as to how the issues in question should be reformed with a view to closing the current enforcement gap in Europe. In particular, the predominant litigants' strategies, which are thoroughly presented by Lawrence and Morfey, indicate that the issues of jurisdiction, limitation periods, overcharge and pass-on

[1] Ch 11. See also: Part I.

as well as costs are to be carefully considered by policy-makers, if they want to provide for more legal certainty in the area.[2]

Reher's chapter[3] reaffirms the conclusion that the limited private litigation is heavily dependent on a regulator's decision establishing an infringement. He goes further to elaborate on the issues which the claimants consider when bringing cross-border follow-on damages claims in Germany. His analysis identifies the issues which the policy-makers across Europe may wish to consider with a view to attracting more cross-border EU competition law actions, provided the EU legislators decides to promote inter-jurisdictional regulatory competition. In this context, it seems clear that the important aspects, which Member States might wish to consider, are: the possibility to aggregate individual claims via the assignment model; joint and several liability; limitation periods; and lower or higher standard of proof. In particular, Reher shows that a claimant would consider the following aspects of the law before deciding where to bring his EU competition law claim: the mechanisms for aggregation of individual claims and collective actions; the applicable procedural laws; and the applicable substantive laws.[4]

Given the importance of the mechanisms for aggregation of individual claims, Tzakas[5] argues that consumers would not get redress unless there are adequate mechanisms for collective redress. He goes on to state that the lack of collective rights of action may be held as contravening the right to an effective remedy in the fields covered by EU law pursuant to Article 19(1) second subparagraph TEU and Article 47(1) Charter of Fundamental Rights of the EU.[6] In view of the cross-border nature of many EU competition law infringements, Tzakas takes account of the jurisdictional and choice-of-law aspects surrounding cross-border collective proceedings brought on behalf or in the interest of consumers, he makes several observations. In spite of the fact that such proceedings are within the scope of application of the Brussels I Regulation, he first notes that 'it has been argued[7] that the Brussels I Regulation is not suited to the needs of collective proceedings since it is premised upon the concept of two-party proceedings.'[8] Secondly, Tzakas appears to believe that 'Notwithstanding the need for clarifying the existing rules, the creation of a separate jurisdictional framework tailored only for these cases seems – at least in competition-related

[2] Ch 11.

[3] Ch 12.

[4] Ch 12.

[5] Ch 17.

[6] Ch 17. See also: European Economic and Social Committee (EESC), 'Opinion on the collective actions system and its role in the context of Community consumer law (Own-initiative opinion)' [2008] OJ C162/1 para 1.3.

[7] European Consumer Consultative Group, 'Opinion on private damages actions' (2010) available at http://ec.europa.eu/consumers/empowerment/docs/ECCG_opinion_on_actions_for_damages_18112010.pdf, 4–5. *cf* also Consultation paper presenting the first working analysis of the impact of the options in the light of the replies to the Green Paper on consumer collective redress, available at http://ec.europa.eu/consumers/redress_cons/docs/consultation_paper2009.pdf, paras 31–32 pointing out the lack of specific provisions. See furthermore C Kessedjian and others, 'Response to the Commission Green Paper on Consumer Collective Redress', http://ec.europa.eu/consumers/redress_cons/responses/pract_Coll_Europeen_Paris_fr.pdf, 13–14; B Hess, 'Cross-border Collective Litigation and the Regulation Brussels I' (2010) 30 *Praxis des Internationalen Privat- und Verfahrensrechts* 116; H Muir Watt, 'Brussels I and Aggregate Litigation or the case for Redesigning the Common Judicial Area in Order to Respond to Changing Functions and Structures in Contemporary Adjudication and Litigation' (2010) 30 *Praxis des Internationalen Privat- und Verfahrensrechts* 111, 112.

[8] See Ch 17.

litigation – rather debatable.'[9, 10] In his subsequent analysis, he inter alia identifies some choice-of-law issues which have not been properly taken into account in the context of collective redress. These issues are: recognition of representative entities; questions of standing; interchangeability of representative entities; representation of foreign claimants; and distribution of the obtained damage funds. After considering the European initiatives in the field, he goes on to conclude that 'the progress achieved as to the elaboration of uniform EU collective redress mechanisms or of even the regulatory framework relating to civil antitrust liability leaves little room for optimism.'[11] But, should there be a uniform EU collective redress mechanism in Europe? Is it possible to harmonise procedural rules?

Dr Lasok QC elaborates on the appropriate way forward in view of the importance of the procedural rules. He unequivocally demonstrates that the national procedural rules developed in the different Member States tend to reflect their prevailing legal culture.[12] Given the diverse nature of the European Union, the unification of procedural rules may be not only difficult to achieve, but also undesirable. In this context, Dr Lasok QC concludes:

> The end result in any piece of litigation is usually informed, in a procedural sense, by a combination of the applicable procedural rules, the way in which they are exploited by the parties, and the way in which they are applied, and their use is controlled, by the court itself. It is perfectly possible to have an efficient system of procedural rules and yet to have a completely inefficient system of dispensing justice in a case where the rules are not properly observed and applied.[13]

Thus, one might argue that the harmonisation of procedural rules may not result in uniformity unless the harmonised rules are applied by judges who share a 'common legal culture'.[14]

Hence, in the field of collective redress, Danov, Fairgrieve and Howells propose a solution which takes account of the specific features of collective redress proceedings in antitrust as well as of the distinctive attributes of the European juridical system and of the way the current regime shapes the litigants' strategies.[15] Bearing in mind that it is the large companies that generally appear to be bringing EU competition law damages actions, it seems to us that one way of closing the enforcement gap in Europe would be to allow large purchasers, for example, to aggregate claims on behalf of purchasers down the chain of distribution (including end consumers). This would allow large companies to aggregate claims on behalf of consumers of a cartelised product and/or consumers who are paying a monopoly price. In such cases, a gatekeeping role will be performed by the judges who would exercise judicial control over the cases at the certification stage. The volume of sales of the large purchasers, who have opted into the collective redress proceedings, can be an objective criterion in assessing their adequacy to act as representatives of the end consumers who would be involved on an opt-out basis.

[9] See Commission, 'Green Paper on Consumer Collective Redress' COM (2008) 794 final, 27 November 2008 para 58. See furthermore DP Tzakas, 'Effective Collective Redress in Antitrust and Consumer Protection Matters: A Panacea or a Chimera?' (2011) 48 *CML Rev* 1125, 1153–58.

[10] Ch 17.

[11] Ch 17.

[12] Ch 15.

[13] Ch 15.

[14] T Andersson, 'Approximation of procedural law in Europe' in M Storme (ed), *Procedural Laws in Europe* (Antwerp, Maklu, 2003) 55, 64–65.

[15] Ch 18.

Therefore, an appropriate collective redress mechanism may be set up through an amendment of Regulation 1/2003 by allowing some purchasers to aggregate claims on behalf of other purchasers down the chain of distribution (including end consumers). Such a mechanism would work on an opt-in basis for purchasers up the chain of distribution, and on an opt-out basis for the other victims of an EU competition law infringement, subject to deciding whether the opt-out regime should also be applicable to out of jurisdiction claimants. The opt-out regime for purchasers down the chain of distribution and consumers in particular may be justified by the fact that the amount of damages suffered by an individual consumer is significantly smaller in comparison with the litigation costs, and makes any litigation of small individual claims unsustainable. Given the difficulties in distributing the damages relief to many consumers with small claims,[16] the unclaimed damages may be passed on through discounts[17] by the large purchasers down to the chain of distribution to the end consumer of a cartelised product and/or to the end consumers who are paying a monopoly price. Indeed, some substantive law innovations with regard to damage remedies as discounts may be best used to provide redress for consumers who 'stop buying the product when the price rises from the competitive to the monopoly level'[18] rectifying the deadweight lost by encouraging consumers to buy the product in question at a reduced price.[19]

The Report on Collective Redress in Antitrust unequivocally suggests that only a few Member States appear to be attracting such actions at the moment. As there is low mobility of consumers across Europe, it might thus be argued that the proposed solution would close the enforcement gap only if it allows for an opt-out regime, implemented by a particular Member State, to operate for consumers from across Europe. Indeed, a distinctive feature of most EU competition law infringements is that they would be cross-border in nature, in so far as they may involve legal entities from different countries and affect the market(s), businesses and consumers in several countries. The diverse nature of the European Union leaves no doubt that the legislators in the various Member States and their judiciaries may be faced with the different challenges, and they may be best placed to deal with them. Therefore, there is a strong case that the EU legislator should rather aim to promote inter-jurisdictional regulatory competition. Indeed, there is a case for reforming the current private international law framework with a view to promoting regulatory competition.[20]

Regulatory competition may be best promoted, if Regulation 1/2003 was amended to address the issues of jurisdiction in cross-border EU competition law cases as well as the problem of parallel EU competition law proceedings in order to avoid irreconcilable or inconsistent decisions in the European context. Although it would be difficult to elaborate a special basis for jurisdiction which requires a substantial connection between the breach of Articles 101 and 102 TFEU and effects of the anti-competitive agreement or conduct

[16] LA Sullivan and WS Grimes, *The Law of Antitrust: An Integrated Handbook,* 2nd edn (Thomson West, 2006) 997.

[17] *Re Domestic Air Transportation Antitrust Litigation* 148 FRD L 297, 306, 315 (ND Ga 1993), discussed in A Sullivan and WS Grimes, *The Law of Antitrust: An Integrated Handbook,* 2nd edn (Thomson West, 2006) 997.

[18] RA Posner, *Economic Analysis of Law,* 8th edn (Wolters Kluwer, 2010) 419. See also: S Bishop and M Walker, *The Economics of EC Competition Law: Concepts, Application and Measurement* (London, Sweet & Maxwell, 2010) 27–28.

[19] See Ch 18. See also: Ch 23.

[20] See Chs 13 and 18.

within the territory of the Member State where the action is brought and in respect of which the EU antitrust law claim is brought,[21] there is a need for a jurisdiction rule which allows a claimant to centralise litigation against a group of the same companies before the courts at his preferred jurisdiction. Where, for example, there is a corporate group with numerous subsidiaries (all of whom form a single infringing undertaking), then it should be open for a claimant by establishing jurisdiction against one of the subsidiaries to centralise litigation against the whole group of companies as well as against the other group(s) of companies who were party to the same anti-competitive agreement. This could be justified by the fact that EU competition law infringements would often directly and substantially affect the markets in several countries and/or regions. Such a regime would address some of the legal uncertainty surrounding the issues regarding jurisdiction and procedure at the moment.[22]

However, in order to allow the parties to avoid parallel EU competition law proceedings, and centralise litigation before the court that is clearly appropriate to deal with the case, avoiding the problem of irreconcilable or inconsistent judgments, Regulation 1/2003 should go a step further and allow the court (or NCA) first seised to stay their proceedings, in cases where the agreement or practice has no substantial direct effects (whether actual or foreseeable) on competition within the Member State and where another court is better placed to deal with the case.[23] Such an approach would be better suited to deal with the difficulties that could arise in parallel court proceedings, as well as with the problems arising in proceedings before an NCA located in one Member State and private proceedings related to the same infringement of Article 101 and/or Article 102 before another Member State court.[24] Although such a rule could work well in theory, the proposed solution in practice may bring even more uncertainty unless the architecture of the European judiciary is reconsidered by the EU legislator.

Indeed, a discretionary power without devising an appropriate institutional architecture would bring fresh uncertainty. This would be particularly so in cross-border EU competition law actions. It may be difficult to identify an appropriate court in Europe unless there are clear and objective criteria as to how the discretion could be best exercised. The specific issues arising with regard to EU competition law actions in the European context may need to be addressed by the EU legislator in a revised version of Regulation 1/2003. The institutional architecture for civil justice, however, is not a competition-specific concern, and needs to be examined in a wider cross-border context in Europe.[25]

Moreover, the success of regulatory competition would depend on the choice of law rules in force as well as on the recognition and enforcement regime, which will be

[21] M Danov, *Jurisdiction and Judgments in relation to EU Competition Law Claims* (Oxford, Hart Publishing, 2010).

[22] See Ch 13.

[23] Compare the European approach in respect of allocation of cases between the NCAs. See the Commission Notice on Cooperation within the Network of Competition Authorities [2004] OJ C101/43 [8]. See further Danov (n 21) 281–83.

[24] J Basedow (ed), *Private Enforcement of EC Competition Law* (Kluwer, 2007) 1–2; A Komninos, *EC Private Antitrust Enforcement: Decentralised Application of EC Competition Law by National Courts* (Oxford, Hart Publishing, 2008) 7–8. See more: M. Danov, 'EU Competition Law Enforcement: Is Brussels I suited to dealing with all the challenges?' (2012) 61 *ICLQ* 27.

[25] The issue was discussed as a part of the First Workshop from a Jean Monnet Series of Workshops on 'Cross-Border EU Competition Law Actions' held in the University of Aberdeen on 5 October 2012. See B Hess, 'The Brussels I Regulation: Recent case law of the Court of Justice and the Commission's proposed recast' (2012) 49 *CML Rev* 1075, 1112.

examined in Parts IV and V of this book. However, the proposed solution would not address the difficulties surrounding the two-task enforcement structure of EU competition law.

II. THE TWO-TASK ENFORCEMENT STRUCTURE OF EU COMPETITION LAW: ISSUES TO BE CONSIDERED

Bos and Möhlmann[26] as well as Webber[27] in their respective chapters go a step further to analyse some specific problems which, in view of the two-task enforcement structure, could influence litigants' behaviour as well as the outcome of the private EU competition law proceedings and the enforcement of claimants' rights. The first set of difficulties is analysed by Bos and Möhlmann[28] who clearly demonstrate that if a national court stays its proceedings until the decision of the European Commission (or a ruling given on it by a European Court) has become final and binding, then that national court would delay the adjudication on such a case for several years. It has been submitted that a national court should aim to safeguard the rights of the litigants to have the case determined within a reasonable period of time in compliance with Article 6(1) of the European Convention on Human Rights.

The second set of practical issues, which relate to the two-task structure of EU competition law enforcement, is thoroughly presented by Webber. His analysis of *Pfleiderer*[29] and *National Grid*[30] shows that an inherent difficulty for a claimant in a follow-on action is to prove that the cartel caused him loss. Although claimants appear to believe that leniency material would be valuable to them, Webber shows that 'the file of evidence held by the Commission (including the leniency material) was not compiled for this purpose and may therefore be of limited value'.[31] Webber's chapter appears to further strengthen the case for procedural inefficiencies of the current two-step adjudication (ie before the regulator with a view to establish an infringement, and before the courts to seek damages) under the current enforcement regime.[32] Before looking at the question of whether there is a case for consolidating the two sets of proceeding, one should consider whether the two-task enforcement structure gives rise to specific difficulties in so far as the assessment of damages and choice of law rules are concerned in a cross-border context.

26 Ch 14.
27 Ch 16.
28 Ch 14.
29 Case C-360/09 *Pfleiderer AG v Bundeskartellamt* [2011] 5 CMLR 219.
30 See *National Grid Electricity Transmission PLC v ABB Ltd & Others* [2012] EWHC 869 (Ch) [56]–[60].
31 Ch 16.
32 Ch 5.

Part IV

Applicable Law: Cross-Border EU Competition Law Actions

20

Introduction: The Importance of Damages in a Cross-Border Context

MIHAIL DANOV AND FLORIAN BECKER

I. INTRODUCTION

In a private EU competition law damages claim, 'the claimant must prove not only that the relevant [provision] has been broken, but also that the breach in question has caused him a relevant loss.'[1] Which law would determine liability, causation and quantum in a private antitrust damages claim with an international element? It is well established that Articles 101 and 102 TFEU do not define the 'damage' for the purposes of a private EU competition law claim. In *Manfredi*, the Court of Justice held that a person who is injured by anti-competitive practice or conduct, must be able to seek compensation for actual loss and loss of profit plus interest.[2]

However, it has been submitted that 'The principle of national procedural autonomy means that in considering the issues of causation and quantum, it is appropriate first to apply the ordinary domestic rules applicable to claims of breach of statutory duty.'[3] Hence, depending on the applicable law, different amounts of damages could be awarded as, for example, different countries may have different rules with regard to remoteness of damage or availability of exemplary or punitive antitrust damages. A recent study has presented the various methods and models which can be used in quantifying the antitrust damage.[4] In the absence of unified practice throughout the EU, different Member States could employ different methodologies as to quantification of antitrust damages. Which law is to be applied when a Member State court is assessing damages for that breach? The answers to these questions matter, as the applicable law would indicate the scope of the defendant's liability, and what a plaintiff would be entitled to recover in a private antitrust damages claim.[5]

[1] *Devenish Nutrition Ltd v Sanofi-Aventis SA* [2007] EWHC 2394, [2008] 2 WLR 637 (Ch) [18]; aff'd *Devenish Nutrition Ltd v Sanofi-Aventis SA* [2008] EWCA Civ 1086, [2009] 3 WLR 198, CA.

[2] Joined Cases C-295/04–C-298/04 *Manfredi v Lloyd Adriaticco* [2006] 5 CMLR 17 [26].

[3] D Beard, 'Damages in Competition Law Litigation' in T Ward and K Smith (eds), *Competition Litigation in the UK* (London, Sweet & Maxwell, 2005) 257, 270.

[4] Oxera and multi-jurisdictional team of lawyers led by Dr A Komninos, 'Quantifying Antitrust Damages: Towards Non-Binding Guidance for Courts – Study Prepared for the European Commission' http://ec.europa.eu/competition/antitrust/actionsdamages/quantification_study.pdf.

[5] M Danov, 'Awarding Exemplary (or Punitive) Antitrust Damages in EC Competition Cases with an International Element – the Rome II Regulation and the Commission's White Paper on damages' (2008) 29 ECL Rev 430. See more: M Danov, *Jurisdiction and Judgments in Relation to EU Competition Law Claims* (Oxford, Hart Publishing, 2010).

II. FOLLOW-ON ACTIONS AND EXEMPLARY DAMAGES: ISSUES TO BE CONSIDERED

In addition to the compensatory damages,[6] exemplary antitrust damages as a remedy may be available in some Member States. It is generally accepted by the Court of Justice that it is possible for a Member State court to award exemplary or punitive damages.[7] Visscher has submitted that:

> Victims who claim damages in essence serve the social goal of deterrence. However, starting a lawsuit entails costs, which are privately borne. This might lead to too few lawsuits being brought. Increasing the expected damages of victims by awarding punitive damages may solve this problem.[8]

However, exemplary damages by definition are 'additional to an award which fully compensates the claimant for his loss, and which are intended to punish and deter'.[9] As a result, exemplary damages may not be available as a remedy in a Member State which does not recognise a claimant's right to be punitive (ie the civil aspect of punitive damages) and regards such damages as merely punishing and deterring the defendant's conduct (ie involving a criminal law aspect only).[10]

The availability of punitive damages in England was first tested in *Devenish* – a very important judgment which looked at the question of the interrelation between fines imposed by the regulator and damages awarded by the courts.[11] In this case, the claimants brought a follow-on action, which was preceded by a decision of the European Commission establishing that certain vitamin manufacturers had engaged in anti-competitive activities by entering into worldwide cartels in respect of various vitamins in breach of Article 101 TFEU. Although the fine imposed on one of the defendants, Aventis, was commuted because of its activities as 'whistleblower', the European Commission imposed significant fines on the other companies.[12] One of the questions before the English courts was whether the claimants would be entitled to exemplary damages. In this context, it was noted that the infringements of Article 101 were 'deliberate', and carried out 'with full knowledge of the illegality of their actions'[13] which, according to Mr Justice Lewison, was the same as a finding that the tort was carried out 'in the knowledge of and in wilful disregard of the Claimant's rights'.[14]

Before looking at the question whether punitive damages are available in a follow-on damages action, the judge stated that the '"*non bis in idem*" . . . principle is a reflection of the common principle that a person is not to be punished twice for the same wrong.'[15] Mr Justice Lewison went on to conclude that 'the imposition of fines and an award of exemplary damages serve the same aim: namely to punish and deter anti-competitive

[6] *Manfredi* (n 2) [26].
[7] ibid [93] and [99].
[8] LT Visscher, 'Economic Analysis of Punitive Damages' in H Koziol and V Wilcox (eds), *Punitive Damages: Common Law and Civil Law Perspectives* (Vienna/New York, Springer, 2009) 220, 224–25.
[9] *Devenish* (n 1) (HC) [14].
[10] BC Zipursky, 'A Theory of Punitive Damages' (2005–2006) 84 *Texas Law Review* 105, 106–107.
[11] *Devenish* (n 1) (HC). See also: Ch 22, below.
[12] ibid [2]–[3].
[13] ibid [44].
[14] ibid [44].
[15] ibid [40].

behaviour'[16] as well as to make a distinction between fines and compensatory damages which do pursue different goals.[17] Hence, the court considered the implications of the two-task enforcement structure by focusing on the interplay between the Leniency programme and a subsequent follow-on damages action with regard to heads of damages available to the claimant, and held:

> 51. Mr Layton also argued that in the case of the Aventis companies the fines had been commuted to zero as a result of the application of the Leniency Notice. Thus he said that these companies, at least, had not been sanctioned for the unlawful conduct at all. I do not accept this submission. The Commission decided in principle that fines should be imposed on the Aventis companies. It is true that by the application of the Leniency Notice, those fines were commuted to zero as a result of Aventis' conduct as whistleblower; but the starting point for the application of the Leniency Notice was the finding of unlawful conduct coupled with the imposition, in principle, of a fine. The application of the Leniency Notice serves the important policy aim that it is of even more importance to encourage whistleblowers than to punish participants in a cartel. In my judgment the national court should not undermine that policy by an award of exemplary damages against a person who has had his fine commuted as a result of the application of the Leniency Notice. If Mr Layton's submission were correct, then a more guilty wrongdoer would escape liability for exemplary damages, while a less guilty wrongdoer, whose fines had been commuted would not. This seems to me to be wrong in principle.
>
> 52. In my judgment, therefore, the principle of *non bis in idem* precludes the award of exemplary damages in a case in which the defendants have already been fined (or had fines imposed and then reduced or commuted) by the European Commission.[18]

The question whether a claimant is entitled to recover exemplary damages in a follow-on action was very recently considered by the Competition Appeal Tribunal in *Cardiff City Transport.*[19] In this case, a follow-on damages claim was brought pursuant to section 47A of the Competition Act 1998. The claim was preceded by a decision of the OFT[20] in which it was found that Cardiff Bus committed an infringement of the Chapter II prohibition contained in section 18 of the 1998 Act. The claimant inter alia sought exemplary damages. The CAT held that 'exemplary damages can in theory be awarded where there is an intentional breach of the law i.e. the defendant acts knowing that what he does constitutes an infringement of competition law and intending that infringement',[21] and went on to consider the interrelationship between public and private enforcement:

> Whilst we accept that in the general scheme of competition enforcement, punishment and deterrence are matters for the public authorities, this does not preclude an award of exemplary damages under section 47A in an appropriate case. Clearly, the 1998 Act has a policy of conferring a limited immunity from penalties on small undertakings. However, this policy operates in a context where the OFT is not considering, as this Tribunal is, the specific harm caused by infringing conduct to a specific claimant. No-one would suggest that – where a small undertaking has caused loss or damage to such a claimant – an award of damages should not follow. The proposition only has to be stated, to be rejected. Equally, if such a small undertaking were to have behaved in so

[16] ibid [48].

[17] ibid [49]–[50].

[18] ibid [51]–[52].

[19] Case Number: 1178/5/7/11, *2 Travel Group Plc (In Liquidation) v Cardiff City Transport Services Ltd* [2012] CAT 19.

[20] OFT decision number CA98/01/2008, *Abuse of a dominant position by Cardiff Bus*, dated 18 November 2008 (Case CE/5281/04).

[21] ibid 485.

outrageous a manner as to trigger an award of exemplary damages, we fail to see why (as a matter of policy) such an undertaking should be immune. Section 47A of the 1998 Act applies to 'any claim for damages' or 'any other claim for a sum of money' which 'a person who has suffered loss or damage as a result of the infringement of a relevant provision may make in civil proceedings brought in any part of the United Kingdom': section 47A(1). Section 47A does not specify the rules by which the Tribunal is to determine what loss or damage has been sustained by a claimant, but it is obvious that, in a claim made in England and Wales, that claim is governed by the law of England and Wales. That law allows for the recovery of exemplary damages in the limited cases we have described. If a claimant advances a well-founded claim to exemplary damages, then we consider that such a claim cannot be rejected simply because (in an altogether different sphere) the defendant would have had an immunity from a penalty because it was a small undertaking. If the limits on the OFT's ability to fine were intended by Parliament to have been read across to section 47A, then we consider that that section would have been very differently worded.[22]

Thus, the court made a distinction between a case in which the fine is commuted to zero, following a leniency application, on the one hand, and a case where a defendant would have immunity from penalty under the 1998 Act, on the other. The court stated:

we hold that there are no reasons of policy why exemplary damages may not be awarded in this case. Cardiff Bus urged us to measure any award of exemplary damages by reference to the sort of penalty that the OFT has jurisdiction to impose for breaches of the Chapter II prohibition. We decline to assess the level of exemplary damages in this way: the OFT has a statutory jurisdiction to punish and deter in this way, and although exemplary damages also have as their object punishment and deterrence (see paragraph 448 above), our jurisdiction derives from section 47A of the 1998 Act and the line of cases beginning with *Rookes v Barnard*. We are also very conscious that – contrary to fines imposed by the OFT – exemplary damages are paid to the claimant. We consider that:

(1) Whilst exemplary damages do have to punish and deter, we consider that they also have to bear some relation to the compensatory damages being awarded, which in this case are low.
(2) In assessing the amount of exemplary damages, it is important to have regard to the economic size of the defendant. In some cases, a defendant may be so economically powerful that exemplary damages will have to be of an order of magnitude sufficient to make that defendant take notice. Here, we do bear in mind that Cardiff Bus is a relatively small company.
(3) As an entity with an association with a local authority, Cardiff Bus will no doubt take very full account of the Judgment, even if exemplary damages are (in numerical terms) quite low. In these circumstances, we consider that the punishment and deterrence effect of exemplary damages can be obtained by an award of exemplary damages at a level that is relatively low.[23]

Therefore, the review of the case law clearly suggests that there are two issues which should be considered by the policy-makers when designing an effective enforcement system which promotes regulatory competition across Europe. First, in England, there are instances in which the plaintiff can recover not only the compensatory loss, which will put the injured party in the same position he would have been in had he not sustained the wrong,[24] but also exemplary damages.[25] Indeed, it is now established that exemplary damages are available in England if the infringements of EU competition law were deliberate

[22] ibid 496.
[23] ibid 596.
[24] *Livingston v Rawyards Coal Co* (1880) 5 App Cas 25, 39.
[25] *Rookes v Barnard* [1964] AC 1129; *Devenish* (n 1) (HC) [44]. See also V Wilcox, 'Punitive Damages in England' in Koziol and Wilcox (n 8) 7.

and carried out with the full knowledge of the illegality of the actions leading to an important distortion of competition, which is of exclusive benefit to the infringers.[26] If *Devenish* is to be believed, punitive damages are also known in Cyprus and in Ireland. However, punitive (or exemplary) damages are not only unknown in some Member States (eg France[27], Hungary[28] and Spain[29]), but they may also be contrary to public policy of the forum in some Member States (eg Germany[30] and Italy[31]). This is reflected in Recital 32 of the Rome II Regulation, which states that non-compensatory or punitive damages of an excessive nature may be regarded as being contrary to the public policy of the forum.[32] This seems to suggest that the *lex fori* may still be important in antitrust damage actions brought in the European context. Indeed, as a result of not dealing with the available remedies for breach of Articles at EU level, a plaintiff should carefully choose the EU jurisdiction, in which to bring private proceedings to enforce competition law as the *lex fori* may have a role to play in this regard.[33]

Secondly, the interplay between fines and damages is an important issue which needs to be carefully considered in view of the current two-task structure of antitrust enforcement. In this context, it should be noted that the whether the extent to which a company has made redress should be taken into account by the competition authorities when determining what level of fine to impose is being considered by the UK legislator.[34] The issue was also noted in a recent Report by the European Parliament,[35] which stated:

> specific criteria need to be developed which allow for fines or other public sanctions to be deducted after damages have been awarded in order not to put disproportionate financial burdens on the defendant. In the field of antitrust law, Council Regulation (EC) No 1/2003 of 16 December 2002 on the implementation of the rules on competition laid down in Articles 81 and 82 of the Treaty would need to be amended accordingly.[36]

Therefore, these issues will be addressed inter alia in this Part.

III. THE STRUCTURE OF THIS PART

Part IV examines the issue of the applicable law and the problems associated with defining it. Dr Jonathan Fitchen addresses the question of applicable law in cross-border competition law actions by highlighting the important role of Article 6(3) of Rome II. Hugh Mercer

[26] *Devenish* (n 1) (HC) [44].

[27] JS Borghetti, 'Punitive Damages in France' in Koziol and Wilcox (n 8) 55.

[28] A Menyhard, 'Punitive Damages in Hungary' in Koziol and Wilcox (n 8) 87, 91.

[29] P del Olmo, 'Punitive Damages in Spain' in Koziol and Wilcox (n 8) 137.

[30] Punitive damages may be incompatible with fundamental principles of German law. See N Jansen and L Rademacher, 'Punitive Damages in Germany' in Koziol and Wilcox (n 8) 75, 76. See also *Devenish* (n 1) (HC) [33].

[31] AP Scarso, 'Punitive Damages in Italy' in Koziol and Wilcox (n 8) 103, 108.

[32] Danov (n 5). See also MR Isidro, 'Punitive Damages from a Private International Law Perspective' in Koziol and Wilcox (n 8) 237.

[33] Danov (n 5).

[34] Department for Business Innovation & Skills, *Private Actions in Competition Law: A Consultation on Options for Reform,* 24 April 2012, www.bis.gov.uk/assets/biscore/consumer-issues/docs/p/12-742-private-actions-in-competition-law-consultation.pdf.

[35] European Parliament, 'Towards a Coherent European Approach to Collective Redress'(2011/2089(INI)), 12 January 2012.

[36] ibid 15.

QC examines the issue of forum shopping in the context of the assessment of antitrust damages. He discusses amongst other things the mandatory character of competition laws as well as the public policy exception under the Rome II regime. Stephen Dnes considers the issue of remedies in private damages claims from an economic perspective. In particular, his chapter addresses the friction between different damages' regimes and the imposition of fines by the regulator. He convincingly demonstrates that it would be difficult to separate the deterrent and compensatory aims of antitrust enforcement, and argues that the overlap should be embraced.

21

The Applicable Law in Cross-Border Competition Law Actions and Article 6(3) of Regulation 864/2007

JONATHAN FITCHEN

This chapter deals with various issues arising from the selection of the applicable law for cross-border tort/delict claims concerning breach of competition laws; it concerns the private international law rules which determine which substantive law or laws will eventually govern those parts of such a claim and are not already independently determined by the public law/administrative law operation of competition law at either the European Union level or the national level.[1] Within EU legal systems other than Denmark the applicable law for non-contractual competition law claims, in relation to events giving rise to damage occurring after 11 January 2009,[2] is intended to be determined by applying Article 6(3) of the Rome II Regulation.[3] The law or laws indicated by Article 6(3) will, subject to the latitude accorded by the Regulation to mandatory rules[4] and public policy,[5] then govern the wide range of legal issues which Article 15 of Rome II indicates comprise the applicable law.[6] Thus Rome II is intended to reveal the identity of each substantive law which will then separately be applied by the litigation court to determine matters such as, inter alia, the basis and extent of legal liability (including who may be deemed wholly or partially liable for another's actions); the existence, nature and assessment of the damage and also of the remedies claimed; the transferability of the right to claim damages or other remedies; and the rules concerning limitation periods, prescription, and the extinction of the relevant non-contractual obligation.[7]

Rome II is intended not only to assist EU courts with cross-border competition claims, but also to assist the claimant and defendant by enhancing legal certainty and predictability by applying common rules to the identity of the applicable law or laws.[8] Accordingly, as well

[1] Thus while the applicability of either Arts 101 or 102 TFEU (or a national equivalent) is not at issue, the law according to which the consequences of an infringement appear in private law, eg the rules concerning the private law damages flowing from an infringement, are at issue. See M Illmer in P Huber (ed) *Rome II Regulation, Pocket Commentary* (Munich, Sellier, 2011) (hereafter: Illmer), para 65 p 179.

[2] The temporal scope of the Rome II Regulation is discussed below in section IIA.

[3] Regulation (EC) 864/2007 of the European Parliament and Council of 11 July 2007 on the law applicable to non-contractual obligations. OJ L199/40 (hereafter: Rome II).

[4] Art 16 of Rome II.

[5] Art 26 of Rome II.

[6] See Ch 22.

[7] See Art 15 of Rome II.

[8] See Rome II Recitals 6, 13, 14, and 16.

as considering how Member State courts will potentially respond to the novelties and challenges posed by Article 6(3) and the Rome II Regulation, it is, given the specific purpose of this book, more than usually important to also consider how actual and potential parties will understand the choice of law processes provided for cross-border competition law claims. This is not merely because it is these parties who will, given the potential risks of establishing the applicable law(s) and the potential rewards indicated by Article 15, make the decisions involved in commencing a claim, litigating and or settling it: it is also because though expressly forbidding choice of law agreements in the context of competition law claims,[9] Rome II paradoxically allows the claimant to avoid the complexities of establishing the applicable law or laws via Article 6(3)(a) by instead opting for the *lex fori* in the defendant's domicile as a single applicable law covering all Rome II issues should the claim fall within Article 6(3)(b). In these situations it is the claimant rather than the court who appears to determine the identity of the applicable law, ie the *lex fori,* by instituting the required proceedings in that court and informing it of his election that Article 6(3)(b) shall apply.[10]

Ideally this chapter would be based upon the responses of the interviewees to the legal and practical issues arising from Article 6(3) of the Regulation; unfortunately the interviewees in the study addressed by this book did not overtly refer to the potential application of the Rome II Regulation.[11] The absence of direct comment upon Article 6(3) is a consequence of the temporal scope of the Regulation,[12] the relatively long lead-in times which typically afflict private non-contractual claims based on competition law infringements, and the current tendency for claims to settle once issues of jurisdiction have been resolved.

Once Article 6(3) claims do start to materialise, the determination of the applicable law will be of comparable importance to the determination of jurisdiction at present: the applicable law will indicate the likely costs and potential benefits of conducting any given claim. It is accordingly a matter of regret that in the type of complex tort claims which naturally may be expected in connection with cross-border competition claims, Article 6(3)(a) exhibits a tendency towards complexity and unpredictability in its practical operation. This bleak assessment is a consequence of the complexities potentially arising from Article 6(3)(a) when presented with the type of actively contested complex commercial torts involved in cross-border competition law claims and also from the basic uncertainties which continue to bedevil the development of private law competition law claims within the legal systems of the European Union.

[9] Concerning Art 6(4) of Rome II, see P Mankowski, 'Das neue Internationale Kartellrecht des Art.6 Abs. 3 der Rom II-Verordnung', (2008) *Recht der Internationalen Wirtschaft* 177, 192 (hereafter Mankowski RIW); A Dickinson, *The Rome II Regulation: The Law Applicable To Non-Contractual Obligations* (Oxford, OUP, 2008) (hereafter Dickinson mainwork) paras 6.74–6.75; A Dickinson, *The Rome II Regulation: The Law Applicable To Non-Contractual Obligations,* first updating supplement (Oxford, OUP, 2010) (hereafter Dickinson supplement) paras 6.74–6.75; for a strong critique see Th M de Boer, 'Party Autonomy and its Limitations in the Rome II Regulation', (2007) 9 *Yearbook of Private International Law* 19, 22; also J Fitchen, 'Choice of Law in International Claims Based on Restrictions of Competition: Art 6(3) of the Rome II Regulation', (2009) 5 J Priv Int L 337, 344–46 (hereafter Fitchen); for milder observations tending in the same direction see J von Hein, 'Something Old and Something Borrowed, but Nothing New? Rome II and the European Choice of Law Evolution' (2008) 82 *Tulane Law Review* 1663, 1701 (hereafter von Hein *Tulane*); P Beaumont and P McEleavy, *Private International Law,* 3rd edn (SULI/W Green, 2011) 669 (hereafter Beaumont and McEleavy).

[10] Assuming that the other conditions for the application of Art 6(3)(b) are made out and that Art 6(3)(b) is applicable to the relevant issues, see section IIF, below.

[11] The interviewees (see Part I) did however repeatedly refer to legal issues which will *eventually* fall within the scope of the applicable law set out by Art 15 of Rome II. See Ch 22.

[12] See section IIA, below.

In the absence of legal practice applying Article 6(3), this chapter works from policy, the Regulation text and the reasoned extrapolation of existing competition law practice. The policy considerations are challenging, not merely because competition law famously lacks a single theory explaining its regulatory function,[13] but because to consider such policy in the context of the Rome II Regulation it is necessary to appreciate the interaction of policies concerning private international law with enforcement policies concerning *sui generis* European competition law rights and also national competition laws. Such a concatenation of private international law and substantive law is ostensibly alien to private international lawyers trained in the orderly and neutral application of European and national private international law to well-defined categories and private law concepts. That said, a willingness to depart from such nationally rooted conceptual orthodoxy is advisable when what is at issue is a supranational European private international law instrument such as Rome II possessing direct applicability and, at least in the context of Article 6(3), relating to the private enforcement of horizontally directly effective European competition law treaty provisions.[14] It is suggested at various points below that Article 6(3) would have benefitted from a greater display of such willingness in the drafting process.

I. THE DRAFTING PROCESS

It is useful to briefly notice the timeframe within which the specific rules concerning competition law claims appeared in the developing text of Rome II. The proposal document for the Rome II Regulation was published in July 2003 by the Commission's Directorate General for Justice Freedom and Security.[15] Competition law claims were deliberately excluded from this 2003 proposal because another Directorate General of the European Commission, Directorate General Competition, was then engaged in consultations which would lead to the publication of its Green Paper on Damages Actions for Breach of EC

[13] Competition law lacks a generally agreed theory which describes its regulatory purpose: economics does not occupy this regulatory no-man's-land, but economists have put forward various schools of thought to attempt to address the regulatory gap. For example, the Chicago School, the Post-Chicago (or New Industrial Economics) School, and within the EU, the Ordoliberal School. For further discussion see D Gerber, *Law And Competition In Twentieth Century Europe* (Oxford, Clarendon Press, 1998) Chs VI–XI; R Whish and D Bailey, *Competition Law*, 7th edn (Oxford, OUP 2012) (hereafter Whish and Bailey) ch 1; D Geradin, A Layne-Farrar and N Petit, *EU Competition Law and Economics* (Oxford, OUP, 2012) paras 1.43–1.47, 1.61–1.72, 2.35–2.54 (hereafter Geradin et al); and J Basedow, 'Competition (Internal Market)' in J Basedow, K J Hopt, R Zimmermann and A Stier (eds), *The Max Planck Encyclopedia of European Private Law* (Oxford, OUP, 2012).

[14] It follows from the decision of the Court of Justice of the European Union (CJEU) in C-435/99 *Courage v Crehan* [2001] ECR I-6297 that any national procedural impediment which entirely prevents the assertion of directly effective treaty rights may be incompatible with those rights such that it can no longer be automatically applied. The Rome II Regulation and given domestic methods of applying it are not excluded from the application of this basic principle.

[15] Proposal for a Regulation of the European Parliament and the Council on the law applicable to non-contractual obligations (Rome II) COM (2003) 427 final 10. See S Francq and W Wurmnest, 'International Antitrust Claims under the Rome II Regulation', in J Basedow, S Francq and L Idot (eds) *International Antitrust Litigation Conflict of Laws and Coordination* (Oxford, Hart, 2012) 91, 93 (hereafter Francq and Wurmnest); A Halfmeier and N Sonder 'Rome Regulations', in G-P Calliess (ed) *Commentary On The European Rules Of The Conflict Of Laws* (Amsterdam, Kluwer, 2011) 396 (hereafter Halfmeier and Sonder in Calliess); Mankowski RIW (n 9) 178–79. Unfair competition claims were included but competition law claims were deliberately excluded at this point.

Antitrust Rules:[16] equally DGCOMP had its own ideas as to what was required for a choice of law rule concerning an infringement of Article 101 or 102 TFEU.[17]

Although by the end of 2004 the Directorate General Justice, Freedom and Security had 'publically' accepted[18] that the choice of law rule in Article 4(1) would pose problems for competition law claims, it was not until September 2006 that a draft version of what would become Article 6(3)(a) was officially introduced as the special choice of law rule for claims arising from 'restrictions of competition'.[19] The new provision was included in the Council Common Position and accompanied by three new Recitals which would eventually be modified to form present Recitals 21, 22 and 23. As a consequence of controversy over the affected market connecting factor[20] and also because of contemporaneous attempts by DGCOMP to address the under-developed nature of the substantive claims based on the infringement of European competition law, Article 6(3)(a) came late in the legislative process: this necessarily curtailed the time available for discussion and also meant that the competition law rule encountered other draft provisions which, by late 2006, were already firmly established, at least in the Council's text, and were therefore relatively non-negotiable.[21]

Article 6(3)(b) was introduced even later, during the Conciliation Stage of the legislative process in May 2007, seemingly as a consequence of 'horse-trading' between the Council, the Commission and the European Parliament which resulted in the Council dropping its principled objection to the potential for forum-shopping inherent in this Commission proposal and Parliament led amendment.[22] If viewed in the narrow context of Article 6(3), Article 6(3)(b) is paradoxical; it reflects a different and less artfully neutral ethos than Article 6(3)(a). As well as legal differences, the rushed drafting process created textual differences between Article 6(3)(a) and Article 6(3)(b) which introduce a series of interpre-

[16] COM (2005) 672 final 19 December 2005. The Green Paper was preceded by the so-called Ashurst Report, D Waelbroeck, D Slater and G Even-Shoshan, *Study on the Conditions of Claims for Damages in Case of Infringement of EC Competition Rules*, http://ec.europa.eu/comm/competition/cartels/studies/comparative_report_clean_en.pdf, and then followed by White Paper On Damages Actions For Breach Of The EC Antitrust Rules, COM (2008) 165, 2.4.2008 (hereafter White Paper) which eventually led to a draft Directive that was abandoned after the draft and critical comments from various Member States were then leaked, see JS Kortmann and CRA Swaak, 'The EC White Paper on antitrust damage actions: why the Member States are (right to be) less than enthusiastic' (2009) ECLR 30(7), 340–51. The issue remains on the Commission's agenda, see Interview with Mr Joaquin Almunia, 34 (2011) *World Competition* 1–2.

[17] Hellner mentions an otherwise unreferenced note from DGCOMP requesting that the *lex fori* should be the applicable law in all cases involving an infringement of Arts 81 or 82 EC (though not requesting the *lex fori* for infringements of national competition laws). See M Hellner, 'Unfair Competition And Acts Restricting Free Competition. A Commentary On Article 6 Of The Rome II Regulation', (2007) 9 *Yearbook of Private International Law* 49 (hereafter Hellner) fn 67 p 66. Art 6(3)(b) is arguably an echo of this early request.

[18] Commission Document COMP/A/1AS/jw of 16 December 2004, discussed in Francq and Wurmnest (n 15) 94. It is not suggested that the prior absence of a specific competition law provision in the Rome II proposal was attributable to a belief that what is now Art 4 could suffice, nor to any confusion between unfair competition and competition law claims.

[19] Common Position 22/2006 of 25 September 2006 adopted by the Council, acting in accordance with the procedure referred to in Art 251 of the Treaty establishing the European Community, with a view to adopting the Regulation of the European Parliament and the Council on the law applicable to non-contractual obligations (Rome II) [2006] OJ C 289E/68. See Francq and Wurmnest (n 15) 95 and Buchner in Calliess (n 15) 452 discussing Art 6(3). Mankowski notes that what became Art 6(3)(a) first appeared for discussion from the end of Febraury 2006, see Mankowski RIW (n 9) 178–79; referring to document 6623/06 JUSTCIV 33 CODEC 172, p 3, available from http://euzpr.eu/eudocs/03kollisionsr/20romiivo/romiivo-151-rat_6623-06.pdf.

[20] The intensity of the earlier debate in the Council on the draft Art 6(3) is noted by Illmer (n 1) p 178 para 63.

[21] Mankowski notes that much of the discussion concerned whether or not there should be a competition law provision and that the fine detail of such claims was never really on the agenda, see Mankowski RIW (n 9) 179.

[22] Report on the joint text approved by the Conciliation Committee for a regulation of the European Parliament and the Council on the law applicable to non-contractual obligations (Rome II) A6-0257/2007, p 7.

tive complications into the application of either as it is not necessarily immediately clear what significance to place upon differences in the terminology of the different provisions in Article 6(3)(a) and (b).

II. PRIVATE INTERNATIONAL LAW ISSUES ARISING FROM ARTICLE 6(3) OF THE ROME II REGULATION

Throughout this discussion it is important to keep in mind that European private international law reflects a more general problem of the under-development of private competition claims based on European law. This wide-ranging problem cannot be confined by European private international law, nor by its scholars, to matters of substantive law falling outwith the traditional scope of private international law conceptualised in national form. European competition law rights are derived directly from the European Treaty[23] and thus not only prevail over Member State private laws but also prevail over European secondary legislation, such as Rome II, should the two conflict: private international law is not immune to the influence of such treaty-based rights.

The private international law issues arising from Article 6(3) are now addressed in the following order: a) the temporal application of Rome II in the context of Article 6(3); b) matters of proof and procedure; c) characterisation within Rome II and within Article 6; d) claims falling under Article 6(3); e) determining the applicable law via Article 6(3)(a); f) determining the applicable law via Article 6(3)(b).

A. The Temporal Application of Rome II in the Context of Article 6(3)

The question of the temporal application of the Rome II Regulation occasions considerable critical comment given the absence of a clear date in the final Regulation text which made plain the point from which the national courts should use Rome II instead of earlier private international law.[24] Article 31 of Rome II tells us that the Regulation applies to events which occur after its entry into force but does not tell us when this entry into force occurs. Article 32 does not use the phrase 'entry into force', but tells us that the 'Regulation shall apply from 11 January 2009, except for Article 29, which shall apply from 11 July 2008'. As in the final text Articles 31 and 32 are distinct[25] and use different terminology, it was

[23] See *BRT v SABM* [1974] ECR 51; cases C-46/93, C-48/93 *Brasserie du Pecheur SA v Germany* and *R v SoS for Transport, ex parte Factortame Ltd* [1996] 1 CMLR 889; C-344/98 *Masterfoods Ltd v HB Ice Cream Ltd* [2001] 4 CMLR 449; C-435/99 *Courage v Crehan* [2001] ECR I-6297; C-295/04 and 298/04 *Manfredi v Lloyd Adriatico Assicurazioni SpA, Cannito v Fondiaria Sai SpA, Tricarico and Murgolo v Assitalia SpA* (joined cases) [2006] All ER (D).

[24] See critical discussion by G Légier, 'Le règelment "Rome II" sur la loi applicable aux obligations non contractuelles' *La semaine Juridique*, Edition générale 2007 No 47, para 8; Dickinson mainwork (n 9) paras 3.315–3.324 and Dickinson supplement (n 9) paras 3.318–3.324B; Wilderspin, 'The Rome II Regulation: Some policy observations' [2008] NIPR 411; R Plender and M Wilderspin, *The European Private International Law of Obligations*, 3rd edn (London, Sweet & Maxwell, 2009) paras 17.015–17.020; Halfmeier and Sonder in Calliess (n 15) paras 1–13 p 651; Illmer (n 1) Art 32, pp 457–66; Beaumont and McEleavy (n 9) p 712 comment on the difficulty of resolving the issues via a conciliation committee.

[25] Though earlier in the drafting process the text of the two Articles had been contained in a single Article, see Dickinson para 3.318 p 287.

initially suggested that the latter could not provide the date missing from the former and thus, by default, Article 254(1) EC[26] would bring the Regulation into force 20 days after its publication in the Official Journal, ie on 20 August 2007.[27]

Unsurprisingly, the first response to a reference from a national court by the CJEU concerned the question of the temporal application of the Rome II Regulation. In *Homawoo* the national court faced the problem of whether or not Rome II affected a damages calculation concerning an overseas traffic accident.[28] The Court of Justice advised that the national court should only apply the Regulation to events giving rise to damage occurring after 11 January 2009.[29] *Homawoo* thus supplies a datum point. If 'the events giving rise to damage' occurred before 12 January 2009, the Rome II Regulation has no temporal application (as a matter of EU law) before Member State courts; in such circumstances the national court must determine the applicable law with reference to whatever choice of law rules are available to it in default of Rome II. If 'the events giving rise to damage' occurred on or after 12 January 2009, the Rome II Regulation is applicable in temporal terms.

What though is meant by the phrase 'events giving rise to damage', as used in Article 31? This question was recently raised en passent in the English case of *Alliance Bank JSC v Aquanta Corporation (and others)* [2011], where Burton J commented that the answer in *Homawoo* did not identify whether the date of the 'events giving rise to damage' referred to the date 'when the damage is caused or whether it is the date of the event which subsequently, possibly years later, caused the damage'.[30] Burton J suggested that of the two options, the date when the damage is caused, rather than the date of the events which gave rise to the damage, should be preferred. He reasoned that as Article 4(1) of the Regulation bases the applicable law upon the location of direct damage, and that Article 4(2) also refers to the time of the occurrence of this damage, it is more appropriate to use the date of the occurrence of the damage to assess whether the Regulation is applicable in a temporal sense.[31] In tentatively preferring this conclusion, Burton J seems to have sought to mitigate the complexities of determining an applicable law in those situations in which the damage occurs many years after the act constituting the tort.[32]

Though the aim of Burton J is not without attraction, his preferred construction of 'events giving rise to damage' is not supported by a direct reading of Article 31 (pre- or post-*Homawoo*), by academic comment, or by the jurisprudence of the German Bundesgerichtshof (BGH).[33] When in July 2009, prior to the judgment of the CJEU in *Homawoo*, the BGH was faced with a reference concerning, inter alia, which choice of law rules were applicable to an

[26] Now Art 297(1) TFEU.

[27] For discussion of the problems see Plender and Wilderspin (n 24) paras 17–018 to 17–020.

[28] Case C-412/10 *Deo Antoine Homawoo v GMF Assurances SA* (Fourth Chamber, 17 November 2011) nyr ECR [2011] 00000.

[29] ibid para 37. Halfmeier and Sonder in Calliess (n 15) argued convincingly for this conclusion to *Homawoo* prior to the decision of the case, see para 9, p 653.

[30] See *Alliance Bank JSC v Aquanta Corporation (and others)* [2011] EWHC 3281 (Comm) 14/12/2011 para 36.

[31] ibid paras 37–38.

[32] ibid para 38.

[33] See Halfmeier and Sonder in Calliess (n 15) paras 3, 6–9 pp 651–53, considering non-contractual obligation in general and citing supporting academic authorities such as Schaub, 'Rom II Art 32' in Prütting, Wegen and Weinrich (eds), *Kommentar zum Bürgerlichen Gesetzbuch*, 3rd edn (2008) para 1; G Wagner, 'Der neue Rom-II Verordnung', IPrax (2008) 17; X Kramer, 'The Rome II Regulation', NIPR (2008) 414, 417; von Hein, 'Europäisches Internationales Deliktsrecht nach der RomII-Verordnung', ZEup (2009) 6, 11. Additional explicit support for the event based construction is provided by, inter alios, FJ Garcimartin Alférez, 'The Rome II Regulation: On the way towards a European Private International Law Code', (2007) *The European Legal Forum* 77, 81 para 22 and Dickinson mainwork (n 9) [4.33].

application for an injunction prospectively restraining a Latvian airline from using a given term in its standard terms and conditions directed towards German consumers, the court clarified the meaning of Article 31 and found the Rome II Regulation to be temporally applicable to determine the applicable law concerning the injunction. This clarification made it absolutely clear that the BGH regarded the Regulation's temporal application as concerning 'damage causing events which have occurred after its coming into force on 11 January 2009'.[34] Unfortunately this BGH decision does not appear to have been cited to Burton J in the course of the *Alliance Bank* case.

It is suggested that the approach of the BGH to the temporal applicability of the Rome II Regulation is probably correct and should be preferred over the tentative suggestion of Burton J. Thus in the context of competition law claims, the temporal applicability of the Rome II Regulation will depend upon being able to successfully demonstrate to a Member State court that damage causing events falling within Article 6(3)(a) or (b) occurred on or after 12 January 2009; without this demonstration Rome II cannot be regarded as temporally applicable. Though consistent with the Regulation text, this conclusion poses general and particular problems for the selection of the applicable law in the context of private competition claims.

General problems arise should damage-causing events occur on either side of the 11 January 2009 datum point. Assuming (what may well be unlikely, in view of the costs and likely complexities) that a claimant wishes to bring a single claim in such a circumstance, it will presumably be necessary for the court to first employ whatever may be the pre-Rome II choice of law rules to the parts of the claim up to and including 11 January 2009, and thereafter to employ the Rome II rules for the damage causing events subsequent to the Rome II datum point.[35] As there is presently no mechanism included in the Rome II Regulation to address this sort of 'transitional issue' the differences between the nature and consequences of the choice of law rules contained in Rome II and whatever may be the default choice of law rules of the forum may be considerable. For example, in the context of traditional English private international law the quantum of damages in tort is still deemed to be a matter of procedure and thus is calculated according to the lex fori, whereas under Article 15(c) of Rome II damages are prima facie subject to the indicated *lex causae*: the potential for serious asymmetries in the damages on offer either side of the Rome II datum point are obvious.[36] It may be equally important that two different choice of law processes are capable of indicating different applicable laws in respect of the same matter, depending on which side of the datum point the matter falls.[37]

[34] Author's own translation of part of the second sentence of para 17 of the BGH Decision of 9 July 2009 (case Xa ZR 19/08) which reads, 'Diese Verordnung ist auf schadensbegründende Ereignisse, die nach ihrem Inkrafttreten am 11. Januar 2009 eingetreten sind (Art. 1, 31 und 32 Rom-II- VO) und damit ab diesem Zeitpunkt wegen der in die Zukunft gerichteten Wirkung des geltend gemachten Unterlassungsanspruchs auf das Streitverhältnis anzuwenden'. Here the BGH clearly does more than merely re-state the German text of Art 31 ('Diese Verordnung wird auf schadensbegründende Ereignisse angewandt, die nach ihrem Inkrafttreten eintreten'). See discussion of this case by Dickinson supplement (n 9) para 3.319A referring to a post by V Gaertner (in English) of 17 January 2010 available from http://conflictoflaws.net/2010/german-judgment-on-rome-ii/.

[35] In the UK the pre-Rome II rules will be found in the Private International Law (Miscellaneous Provisions) Act 1995.

[36] For the reassertion of the traditional UK position see *Harding v Wealands* [2007] 2 AC 1, see also Art 15(c) of Rome II discussed in Ch 22.

[37] Given the possibility of a *Mosaikbetrachtung* (discussed below) under Art 6(3)(a) of Rome II, there is not even a guarantee that the number of applicable laws would only be two.

More specific problems concerning the temporal applicability of Rome II arise from the typical competition law infringements upon which the private claims will probably be based. Anti-competitive behaviour is unlawful and may attract severe civil and criminal sanctions; it is thus conducted in conditions of utmost secrecy.[38] Consequently it may be many years before the potential claimant learns of the competition law infringement and the economic damage it has inflicted. Such information is most likely to come to light as a consequence of an investigation by a competition law agency.[39] However unless it can be shown that the damage-causing events of the claim occurred on or after 12 January 2009, Rome II cannot apply, meaning that default choice of law rules will apply instead: accordingly, for many years to come it may be that the applicable law in cross-border competition law claims brought after 11 January 2009 will still be wholly or partially governed by pre-Rome II methods of determining the applicable law.

As such an outcome does not appear to accord with the general policy of increasing legal certainty in the context of cross-border claims, it is worth considering whether, in the circumstance that an infringement of competition law is alleged to be ongoing both before and after the temporal datum point of Rome II, it is wrong to split the ascertainment of the applicable law.[40] Possibly the fact that the damage causing events of the competition law tort continue past the Rome II datum point should cause the alleged tort to be regarded as occurring continuously and to therefore legitimate the application of the Rome II Regulation to determine the applicable law for the entire claim?[41] Though increasing legal certainty and simplifying the choice of law process for cross-border competition law claims, this suggestion has to contend with the principled objection that it would be an unfair departure from the general stance of Rome II of neutrality between claimant and defendant.[42] This objection is possibly less convincing in the specific context of follow-on competition law claims as here the existence of an anti-competitive act is already established: in these cases such neutrality may be argued to perversely favour the wrongdoer. Considerations of principle aside, the most formidable obstacle to any suggestion that competition claims which straddle the temporal datum point should benefit from a single method of applicable law selection is Rome II itself: the text currently lacks any provision supporting retrospective temporal applicability whether immediate or deferred in time.[43]

It is suggested that a case based upon increasing legal certainty can be made for a legislative amendment to address the problem of an absence of transitional provisions concerning the temporal applicability in Rome II for follow-on competition claims either by allowing a deferred form of retrospective temporal applicability after the effluxion of a certain period of time from 11 January 2009, or, by providing follow-on competition claims with a new specific regime which includes private international law measures more appropriate to this specific type of competition claim.

[38] For an indication of the lengths to which the anti-competitive will go, see Whish and Bailey (n 13) 513–14; also the Commission Decisions cited below.

[39] The investigation itself will be triggered by a complaint, a leniency application, or a sectoral enquiry.

[40] The point is considered concerning torts in general, rather than in the specific context of competition law torts, by Dickinson supplement (n 9) para 3.324B, and also in a similarly general sense by Halfmeier and Sonder in Calliess (n 15) paras 10–11 pp 653–54.

[41] Dickinson supplement (n 9) para 3.324B briefly mentions an alternative possibility of not applying Rome II at all in such a continuing tort situation. Though this is as much a solution as to apply Rome II with retrospective temporal effect, it is difficult to see how Dickinson's alternative suggestion could avoid the Rome II Regulation.

[42] See Halfmeier and Sonder in Calliess (n 15) para 11 p 654.

[43] This conclusion is also supported by Halfmeier and Sonder in Calliess (n 15) para 11 p 654.

B. Matters of Procedure and Proof

Article 1(3) of Rome II explicitly allows the rules concerning the evidence and civil procedure concerning the claim to be determined in accordance with the procedural rules of the forum. Subject to the clarifications contained in Articles 15, 21 and 22, as to what actually falls within the *lex causae*, Rome II continues the general competence-driven trend of EU private international law to 'allow' Member States to retain domestic control over their own procedural laws.[44] That said, though the forum remains notionally free to determine the nature and content of its procedural rules, this freedom is subject to the overriding principle of European law that national procedures may not prevent the exercise of directly effective rights, eg those derived from Articles 101 and 102 TFEU which the claimant would litigate via Article 6(3)(a) or (b) of Rome II.[45]

The domestic control of rules of procedure extends to the important issue of the means by which a foreign law is proven or otherwise determined by a Member State legal system. The diversity within the Member States concerning such methods of proof (or determination) of foreign law has assumed considerable importance within EU choice of law provisions, as they may seriously affect the uniformity of application of Rome II. The greatest effect may come in the UK's three legal systems which each regard foreign law as a matter of fact which must be pleaded by the parties. If the parties mutually decline to plead a foreign law under Rome II, or should only plead a small portion of it, the court will 'fill-in-the-blanks' with its domestic law: the court is seemingly not required to apply the foreign law in an *ex officio,* manner despite the applicability of Rome II.[46]

If both parties to a claim litigated before a UK court agree to conduct their litigation without pleading any foreign law, the fact that domestic control continues over procedure and proof of law will lead to the entire circumvention of Rome II. Although Article 6(4) of Rome II expressly forbids derogation by choice of law agreements from the applicable law indicated by Article 6, this prohibition cannot affect domestically permissible procedural coordination by the parties concerning pleadings which disclose no need to determine any applicable law whether under Rome II or otherwise.[47] One reason for such mutual circumvention could be that the parties could thereby avoid the difficulties and expenses of applying Article 6(3)(a) of Rome II to a complex claim: another might be escaping the Article 6(4) prohibition on choice of law clauses.[48]

Though there are undoubtedly loopholes and associated peculiarities in the legal systems of the Member States arising from the domestic control of matters of procedure and proof,

[44] An autonomous conception of procedure and evidence has been suggested by Illmer to narrow the nature of the exception; M Illmer, 'Some Thoughts About The Rome Regulations And The So-Called Dichotomy Of Substance And Procedure In European Private International Law', (2009) *Civil Justice Quarterly* 237, 243 ff.

[45] See Case C-435/99 *Courage Ltd v Crehan* [2001] ECR I-6297.

[46] Art 30(1)(i) of Rome II only required the Commission to produce a report on the proof of foreign laws amongst Member States and the application of foreign law under Rome II; currently little more has transpired. See I Bach, 'Rome II Regulation' in P Huber (ed) *Pocket Commentary* (Munich, Sellier, 2011) 57 for further details (hereafter *Bach*).

[47] See Art 1(3) Rome II, discussed by Halfmeier and Sonder in Calliess (n 15) 390; also Bach (n 46) 56; and Beaumont and McEleavy (n 9) 623–24 .

[48] Art 6(4) was introduced at the request of the Commission because – astonishingly – it feared that otherwise, undertakings might succeed in 'contracting-out' of EU competition law. It strains credulity to believe that such an obvious evasion of law would succeed before a court in the EU. For comment upon and criticism concerning the ban, see the references in n 9 above.

it is important not to overstate their potential to subvert the Rome II Regulation.[49] A UK court will apply Rome II (assuming it to be technically applicable) if either party to the litigation so pleads. There may be very strong reasons for a claimant to plead Rome II, eg Article 6(3)(b) or Article 15, and equally strong reasons for the defendant to prefer to plead Article 6(3)(a). Though the simplest way to address national procedural loopholes is to increase the attractiveness of using Rome II or other European choice of law provisions to determine the applicable law, it is possible that some harmonisation of the means of ascertaining foreign law may take place in the future.[50]

C. Characterisation within Rome II and within Article 6

A claim which concerns 'civil and commercial matters',[51] and falls within the temporal scope of European private international law, next presents the issue of the characterisation of the cause of action. This characterisation allows the relevant Regulation to allocate the legal claim to the correct autonomous private international law category which then indicates the applicable law. In Rome II matters are complicated by the presence of specific types of non-contractual claims within that Regulation. Given significant differences between Member State legal systems concerning non-contractual obligations, European private international law requires that characterisation be carried out via the autonomous concepts employed in the Regulation to describe and express its concepts and available claims.[52] Domestic legal concepts are still relevant at certain points in the characterisation process but they are necessarily subservient to autonomous European concepts and must not prevent European private international law from functioning.

In the EU context, the most important characterisation concerning choice of law is whether the competition claim involves a contractual or a non-contractual obligation. The answer to this question determines whether it will be the Rome I or Rome II Regulation which will determine the applicable law(s) of the claim.[53] As the Regulations avoid specific definition of their obligations, it is necessary to look elsewhere to find the meaning of these concepts. The jurisprudence of the CJEU concerning the difference between contractual and non-contractual obligations within the Brussels I regime currently offers the best method of such differentiation.[54] Though a transfer of the Brussels I jurisprudence to the

[49] See Bach (n 46) 57, who notes the equally odd or natural fact (depending upon what one is used to) that § 293 ZPO allows the German court to seek external non-judicial assistance to determine the applicable law.

[50] ibid fn 112.

[51] The recurring phrase 'civil and commercial matters' signifies and demarcates the boundary between matters which are within and matters which are without the material scope of given European private international law regulations. In the particular context of Rome II, it is also a useful means of distinguishing competition claims of a 'public law' nature, which are outwith the material scope of Rome II, from those of a 'private law' nature for which Rome II may identify an applicable law.

[52] See Recital 11 to Rome II. See A Rushworth and A Scott, 'Rome II: choice of law for non-contractual obligations' (2008) LMCLQ 274, 296–304; Fitchen (n 9) 346; A Scott, 'The Scope of "Non-Contractual Obligations"', in J Ahern and W Binchy (eds) *The Rome II Regulation on the Law Applicable to Non-Contractual Obligations: A New International Litigation Regime*, (Leiden, Nijhoff, 2009) 57 (hereafter Ahern and Binchy).

[53] The Regulations are designed so as to avoid the possibility of the dual application of Rome I and II to the same obligation at the same time in a single claim.

[54] Council Regulation 44/2001 22 December 2000 on Jurisdiction and the Recognition and Enforcement of Judgments in Civil and Commercial Matters [2001] OJ L12/1 and the Brussels Convention on Jurisdiction and the Enforcement of Judgments in Civil and Commercial Matters of 27 September 1968 (consolidated version of amended text) [1998] OJ C27/1.

context of applicable law selection under Rome I or Rome II requires sensitivity, interpretative consistency between the provisions of the different Regulations is adverted to by their redactors and thus may cautiously be used to fill the temporary gaps.[55]

In 2002 the CJEU advised, in the context of a reference concerning whether Article 5(1) or 5(3) of the Brussels Convention was applicable to a matter of pre-contractual liability, that, 'the expression matters relating to a contract within the meaning of Article 5(1) of the Brussels Convention is not to be understood as covering a situation in which there is no obligation freely assumed by one party towards another'.[56] In the context of applicable law it seems reasonable to suppose from this statement that a claim will only fall within Rome I if it is based on an obligation which has been 'freely assumed by one party towards the other'. Thus Rome I (or the earlier Rome Convention of 1980) will apply to claims based upon the validity or performance of a freely assumed obligation which is later impugned, or even asserted, with reference to primary or secondary competition law provisions.[57] That said, it must not be forgotten that if Article 101(2) TFEU is applied to decide that a given contract or a contract term is invalid, this decision is directly binding upon Member State courts regardless of any private legal action by the creditor or debtor: consequently regulatory decisions by competition law authorities may significantly reduce the circumstances in which private international law will be called upon to make a choice of law concerning claims alleging contractual invalidity.[58]

The remainder of this chapter concerns applicable law selection under Rome II. Thus only competition claims which are based on private law obligations arising from the alleged breach by one party of the competition law rights of the other are considered. These claims are technically independent of any surrounding contractual relationship that may also exist between the parties.

Having determined that the claim falls within Rome II's basic category of 'non-contractual obligation', the court is then confronted by different subcategories concerning non-contractual obligations. The applicable law concerning obligations arising by reason of Rome II torts is covered by six Articles in Chapter II. The applicable law concerning non-contractual obligations arising from unjust enrichment, *negotiorum gestio* or *culpa in contrahendo* are each provided with a separate Article located in Chapter III. While it seems reasonable to expect that the majority of private competition claims will fall within Chapter II, the possibility of needing to decide between Chapters II and III should not be entirely discounted: Article 10 of Rome II might offer either a less complex route to the selection of a given applicable law or offer a tactically preferable alternative applicable law.[59]

[55] See Rome I Recital 7, Rome II Recital 7. See also: Francq and Wurmnest (n 15) 91, 96; note the caution advised by the CJEU with regard to transferring its jurisprudence between private international law regulations in Case C-435/06 C [2007] ECR I-10141 [40]–[53].

[56] Case C-334/00 *Fonderie Officine Meccaniche Tacconi SpA v Heinrich Wagner Sinto Maschinenfabrik GmbH* [2002] ECR I-7357 [23]–[26], keeping to the principle expressed earlier in Case C-261/91 *Jakob Handte v TMCS* [1992] ECR I-3967.

[57] Reasons of space prevent coverage of contractual choice of law claims under Rome I; for further details see M Fallon and S Francq, 'Private Enforcement of Antitrust Provisions and the Rome I Regulation', in *International Antitrust Litigation Conflict of Laws and Coordination* (Oxford, Hart, 2012) 63–90.

[58] Halfmeier appears to suggest that a contract which is forced (ie concluded under circumstances of pressure which act to defeat the voluntary aspect of the assumption of the obligation) should still be regarded as a contractual obligation and hence as subject to the Rome I rather than the Rome II Regulation; see Halfmeier in Calliess (n 15), p 381 fn 30. It is respectfully suggested that considering the obligation which forms the basis of the claim may prove to be more enlightening in determining whether the matter falls within Rome I or II.

[59] Though for reasons of space this chapter will only examine parts of Chapter II in detail, it should not be forgotten that cross-border competition claims could involve unjust enrichment and thereby necessitate the

i. *The Tort Categories in Rome II*

During the legislative process the Council and the Parliament clashed fundamentally over the nature of the choice of law rules for torts which Rome II should feature.[60] For better or worse, the modified Savignyian system preferred by the Council and the Commission prevailed over the modified interest-balancing approach advocated by the European Parliament.[61] Accordingly Article 4 provides a so-called general rule, followed by Articles 5–9 which contain various specific choice of law rules for different categories of torts. For Rome II to operate as intended, the national court must be able to decide where the claim belongs within these autonomously conceptualised provisions.[62] How though is a court, which does not know in advance that the claim fits into a given category, to correctly determine the appropriate category? If each party argues for the application of a different Rome II category, which given the range of issues the applicable law will thereafter govern will be increasingly probable, the court must grapple with the categories of Rome II to decide the matter. Unfortunately the drafting and organisation of Rome II offer scant assistance in this regard as, save for Recitals of varying degrees of usefulness, the text is silent upon the meaning and precise scope of the specific categories in Articles 5–9.[63] The difficulties escalate if the tort categories at issue are unfamiliar to the legal system of the forum; even domestically familiar categories may be rendered unfamiliar by the need for an autonomous interpretation.

Of all the tort categories in Rome II, those contained in Article 6 are arguably the least clear, and potentially the most troublesome. From the perspective of a UK court the choice of law rules in Article 6(1) and (2) concern an unknown category of torts which, if present at all in another Member State, will be organised according to legal policies with no immediate UK equivalent.[64] The choice of law rule in Article 6(3)(a) not only concerns an alien category of tortious liability which the common law, and to a lesser extent statute law, has arguably traditionally been at pains to resist, but also concerns an uncertain and yet irresistible form of tortious liability which is slowly developing as a consequence of the UK's membership of the EU.[65] For UK courts the characterisation of torts within Article 6 of Rome II may require multiple references to the European Court of Justice seeking clarification of these uncertain categories.[66]

application of Art 10 of Rome II. See Francq and Wurmnest (n 15), 99 briefly discussing an oral suggestion by M Hellner. For a detailed consideration of Art 10 see Dickinson mainwork, and Dickinson supplement (n 9) ch 10; Plender and Wilderspin (n 24) ch 24 and B Schinkels in Calliess (n 15) 498–512.

[60] See D Wallis, 'Rome II – A Parliamentary Tale', in Ahern and Binchy (n 52) 1, 2; Halfmeier in Calliess (n 15) paras 3–5 pp 372–73; Illmer (n 1) para 5 pp 27–28.

[61] See von Hein Tulane (n 9) 1668–75; Halfmeier in Calliess (n 15) 373 para 5.

[62] The possibility of overlap, eg between Arts 6 and 8, probably should not arise but the text does not make this entirely plain. See the criticisms of the clear distinction which the legislation assumes to exist between torts concerning intellectual property and those concerning unfair competition law by C Wadlow, 'Trade Secrets And The Rome II Regulation On The Law Applicable To Non-Contractual Obligations' [2006] *European Intellectual Property Review* 309; C Wadlow, 'The New Private International Law of Unfair Competition and the "Rome II" Regulation', (2009) 4 *Journal Of Intellectual Property Law and Practice* 789, 792.

[63] Recitals 21, 22 and 23 are dedicated to Art 6.

[64] Concerning Art 6(1) and (2) see Hellner (n 17) 67; Beaumont and McEleavy (n 9) 661–64. The existence of a tort category of unfair competition in English law was rejected by the Court of Appeal in *L'Oreal SA v Bellure NV* [2007] EWCA Civ 968 [161] (Jacobs LJ). Concerning classification in Art 6 for the English courts, see Fitchen (n 9) 348–52.

[65] See *Crehan v Inntrepreneur* [2006] UKHL 38; *Garden Cottage Foods v MMB* [1984] 1 AC 140, overruling *Garden Cottage Foods v MMB* [1982] QB 1114.

[66] Post-Lisbon, such references may now be made by any court, Art 267 TFEU.

D. Article 6(3) Claims

For reasons of space the following discussion assumes that the domestic court has concluded that the claim before it concerns 'acts restricting free competition' and therefore that the applicable law falls to be determined in accordance with either Article 6(3)(a) or (b) of Rome II. Before addressing the question of which sub-paragraph of Article 6(3) should be applied, it is advisable to consider the likely effects of Article 4 – the so-called 'General Rule' – upon the interpretation of the special rules contained in Article 6(3).

i. The Lingering Interpretative Relevance of Article 4

As Chapter II of Rome II initially presents the court with Article 4 which is headed 'General Rule', this may be expected to mark the starting point for dutiful judicial expeditions in search of the law or laws applicable to tort claims. Considered rather loosely, the entire Article could be regarded as 'general' in the sense that Article 2 of the Brussels I Regulation is said to be 'general'; which is to say that it should be applied if the circumstances envisaged in the following Articles do not prevent its application. Though the contents of Article 4 Rome II are indeed variously referred back to, partially derogated from or wholly disapplied by the later provisions of Chapter II,[67] this cannot affect the conclusion indicated by reading Recitals 18 and 21 together with the Regulation text that, despite unfortunate drafting which causes the Regulation text to seem to suggest that 'the' general rule comprises two different choice of law rules plus an escape clause, in reality only Article 4(1) contains the general rule that the *lex loci damni* indicates the applicable law. [68]

It has been perceptively observed by von Hein that if the interpretive precedent established under the Brussels I regime should be followed in Rome II, the presence of a general rule in Article 4(1) will probably induce the CJEU to adopt a restrictive approach towards the interpretation of the 'derogations' from that general rule.[69] Should von Hein's conjecture be correct, it would follow that everything in Chapter II which is not Article 4(1) or directly related thereunto by the text or the Recitals[70] will probably be interpreted more restrictively to retain the generality of the *lex loci damni* as an indicator of the applicable law.

The obverse of this suggestion is that matters which do fall within Article 4(1) may presumably benefit from a less restrictive approach to interpretation. Where then does Article 6(3) belong, is it an exception to Article 4(1) or is it within this general rule? The answer seems likely to depend upon the interpretation of Recital 21 which declares in its first sentence that, 'The special rule in Article 6 is not an exception to the general rule in Article 4(1) but rather a clarification of it.' The unfortunate use of the singular 'rule' and the fact that the Recital thereafter only discusses 'matters of unfair competition' in its remaining two sentences do not make it clear that all of the choice of law rules in Article 6 should be

[67] Art 4 is also disapplied by a valid choice of law agreement (see Art 14). Art 6(4) of Rome II forbids private choices of law in connection with the applicable law selected by Art 6, see n 9 above.

[68] See J von Hein in Calliess (n 15) paras 1 – 2 pp 400–401. Contrary to the title in Chapter II of Rome II, Recital 18 only deems the *lex loci damni* of Art 4(1) to be the general rule, describing Arts 4(2) and (3) respectively as an exception to the *lex loci damni* and an escape clause. Recital 21, below, is consistent with this narrow identification of the general rule.

[69] ibid para 4 p 401.

[70] eg Recital 21 concerning Art 6 and Art 6(2) itself insofar as it refers the court back to the first sub-para of Art 4.

understood to be within Article 4(1)'s general rule.[71] An examination of the legislative history of Recital 21 can be argued to suggest that a connection between Article 4(1) and the choice of law rule in Article 6(3)(a) may have been intended:[72] concerning Article 6(3)(b) less information is available. It remains to be seen whether either Article 6(3)(a) or Article 6(3)(b) can or will be treated as part of the general rule for interpretative purposes: it cannot be doubted that Article 4(1) will not necessarily indicate the same applicable law as Article 6(3)(a) or Article 6(3)(b), further clarification of this issue would be advantageous.[73]

E. Determining the Applicable Law (or laws) via Article 6(3)(a)

Having determined that Article 6(3) is applicable, the question of whether Article 6(3)(a) or Article 6(3)(b) should be used to select the applicable law necessarily arises. At present, unhappy drafting in Article 6(3)(a) juxtaposed against the last-minute addition of Article 6(3)(b) can obscure this essential information, and clarification is thus required.

At first glance the drafting could be understood to indicate that Article 6(3)(a) is restricted to cases in which the damage arising from the restriction of competition is located in a single country and that Article 6(3)(b) applies whenever it is necessary to determine the applicable law for cases featuring damage or defendants located in multiple countries. No mention of claims concerning damage or defendants located in multiple legal systems is made in Article 6(3)(a). This contrasts with the text of Article 6(3)(b) which *only* deals with damage located in multiple legal systems or multiple defendant cases where the defendants are located in different legal systems.

Though the Regulation text is unnecessarily and unfortunately Delphic on this point, logic dictates that the true relationship between the choice of law rules in Article 6(3) must be that of a basic rule, contained in Article 6(3)(a), supplemented by a limited exception represented by Article 6(3)(b). This conclusion follows from a consideration of the legislative background concerning Article 6(3); from considering the wide range of claims from inside and outside the EU which Article 3 and Recital 22 respectively allow and indeed contemplate (and which only Article 6(3)(a) could accommodate); and also from the logical impossibility of treating Article 6(3)(b) other than as an exception without creating significant gaps in the scheme of Rome II concerning even intra-EU cases involving restrictions of competition which Article 6(3)(b) cannot in its present form accommodate.[74]

[71] It is uncontroversial that Recital 21 connects Art 4(1) with Art 6(1) and also that Art 6(2) explicitly refers the court back to Art 4. If Art 6(2) leads to resolution under Art 4(1), this remains within the general rule.

[72] What is now Recital 21 was introduced as Recital 19 in the Council's Common Position 22/2006 (9751/7/2006–C6-0317/2006) OJ C 289E/68, at the same time as what are now amended Recitals 22 and 23, it thus accompanied the introduction of Art 6(3), albeit in its simpler one paragraph form, and it can therefore be suggested that the first sentence of Recital 21 probably does also apply to the choice of law rule contained in Art 6(3)(a). This view differs from that originally advanced by the present author concerning the ambit of Recital 21 see Fitchen (n 9) 369 but, on further reflection, can be argued to be better supported by the evidence: it may be suggestive that the response by the Parliament to the Council's Common Position A6-9999/2006 dated 22 December 2006 (reproduced in Ahern and Binchy (n 52), 417) deleting Art 6 and draft Recital 19, was justified not only with reference to the aptness of the general rule to deal with matters of unfair competition, but also with reference to the alleged encroachment of the Council and its Recital into the realm of choice of law concerning competition law.

[73] See Francq and Wurmnest (n 15) 98.

[74] See Fitchen (n 9) 355; M Danov, *Jurisdiction and Judgments in Relation to EU Competition Law Claims* (Oxford, Hart Publishing, 2011) 163 (hereafter Danov).

A further and systemic point which argues in favour of regarding Article 6(3)(b) as exceptional is that it *always* clashes with the general rule laid down in Article 4(1): despite the presence of factors which would usually signify the applicability of multiple laws Article 6(3)(b) can only select the law of the litigation court as the applicable law. It follows that Article 6(3)(a) must be regarded as the default applicable law rule concerning a Rome II restriction of competition, hence Article 6(3)(a) cannot be regarded as restricted to cases in which the damage or defendants are located in a single country.

i. The Recitals and the Regulation Text

Before exploring the difficulties with the text, it is useful to briefly consider the guidance and information concerning Article 6(3) currently provided by Recitals 22 and 23.[75] Recital 22 explains: 'The non-contractual obligations arising out of restrictions of competition in Article 6(3) should cover infringements of both national and Community competition law'.[76] This clarifies the intended width of the application of Rome II, which Article 3[77] later confirms: infringements of EU competition law, infringements of Member State competition law and even infringements of third State competition laws all generate non-contractual obligations concerning which the applicable law is determined by Article 6(3).[78] The Recital confirms that the applicable law should be determined by identifying the law of the country where the market is (or is likely to be) affected, before concluding with a reference to the possibility of the claimant consolidating claims to the law of the court seised, should the market be affected in multiple countries.[79]

Recital 23 attempts to illustrate, in what, given the width of the Regulation text and of Recital 22, is here suggested to be a non-exhaustive fashion,[80] the meaning of the autonomous concept of a 'restriction of competition'. Two reference points are provided: the first concerns acts which would potentially infringe Article 101 TFEU or Member State anti-cartel laws; the second concerns acts which would potentially infringe Article 102 TFEU or Member State anti-abuse of dominance laws. Both reference points are explicitly located either within the (European) Internal Market or an EU Member State; there is no reference to violations of third-state competition laws. Illmer, correctly, explains the apparent departure from Recital 22 by distinguishing Recital 23's purpose, which he submits is the furtherance of the interpretation of the autonomous concept of 'a restriction of competition', from

[75] For an assessment of the possible relevance of Recital 21 see section IID above.

[76] See Hellner (n 17) 69; Plender and Wilderspin (n 24) para 20-039 p 613; and Illmer (n 1) p 182 para 73-4 all support the suggestion that the use of the undifferentiated term 'competition law' in this context suggests that Art 6(3) may also be used to determine the applicable law for matters falling outside Arts 101–102 TFEU but within Title VII Chapter 1 TFEU such as private claims arising from infringements of state aid rules or the Merger Regulation; see discussion on this point by Beaumont and McEleavy (n 9) 665–66, who note that if Art 6(3) is not so construed, the torts in question would fall under Art 4.

[77] See W-H Roth, ‚Internationales Kartelldeliktsrecht in der Rom II-Verordnung', in D Baetge, J von Hein and M von Hinden (eds) *Die richtige Ordnung, Festschrift für Jan Kropholler zum 70.Geburtstag* (Tübingen, Mohr Siebeck Verlag, 2008), 637 and 644 (hereafter Roth); Illmer (n 1) 184 para 77; Beaumont and McEleavy (n 9) 624.

[78] Despite Art 3, Art 6(3)(b) is comparatively restricted in this respect, see discussion below. Concerning the potential difficulties of the application of non-Member-State law within Member State courts, see the detailed evaluation offered by Francq and Wurmnest (n 15) 107–19.

[79] See discussion of Art 6(3)(b) in section IIF below.

[80] Concurring with this assessment see Illmer (n 1) 182; Roth (n 77) 643 et seq; T Rosenkranz and E Rohde, 'The Law Applicable To Non-Contractual Obligations Arising Out Of Acts Of Unfair Competition And Acts Restricting Free Competition Under Article 6 Rome II Regulation', (2008) 4 *Nederlands Internationaal Privaatrecht* 435, 436.

the different question of the territorial scope of Article 6(3) which he, again convincingly, asserts to be a matter that Recital 23 does not attempt to address.[81]

The text of Article 6(3)(a) provides: 'The law applicable to a non-contractual obligation arising out of a restriction of competition shall be the law of the country where the market is, or is likely to be, affected.' Subject to the availability of Article 6(3)(b), or sufficient latitude within the procedural law of the forum to allow the parties to either 'plead around' or otherwise reach a tacit procedural 'agreement' to effectively circumvent it, Article 6(3)(a) is a rigid rule which offers no exception nor any other means of escape from the law or laws it selects as applicable. As Article 6(4) also forbids choice of law agreements between the parties, the choice of law rule in Article 6(3)(a) must be applied in the above-mentioned circumstance to decide the applicable law: there is no other option. It is desirable that if a rule be rigid, it should also be both clear in its meaning and simple to apply: unfortunately, as presently drafted, the rule in Article 6(3)(a) is neither clear nor simple.

For Article 6(3)(a) to function requires determination of 'the country where the market is, or is likely to be, affected'. The widely acknowledged difficulty of making this determination is a consequence of several unfortunate decisions by the redactors of Rome II concerning the atypical cross-border torts with which Article 6(3) is concerned. These unfortunate decisions are necessarily manifested in the current drafting of Article 6(3) and its associated provisions; sometimes positively, by the use of undefined and ambiguous words such as 'market' or 'affected', sometimes accidentally, eg the interpretative dissonances consequent upon the juxtaposition of Article 6(3)(a) and Article 6(3)(b), and sometimes negatively, when an important matter, eg the potential for the applicable law concerning a single claim to become applicable laws to reflect the fact that damage has occurred in different countries, is not explicit in the text and must be deduced. These difficulties will now be addressed.

ii. Missing Methodology in Article 6(3)(a): the Potential for Mosaikbetrachtung

Though the lack of clarity concerning the relative scope of Article 6(3)(a) and Article 6(3)(b) has already been noted, and 'resolved' by the application of logical propositions to seemingly establish that the second paragraph of Article 6(3) must be understood to be a narrow exception to the first, the difficulty which arises from this conclusion has not yet been addressed. Should Article 6(3)(b) not be available to allow the consolidation of the applicable law when the damage is scattered across different legal systems what is the court then to do? The redactors of Rome II had already adopted a default solution for cases where the actionable tort damage was scattered across different legal systems long before competition claims were incorporated into the draft text.

The court which would determine the applicable 'law' in such circumstances must engage in a *Mosaikbetrachtung*[82] exercise to split and distribute the applicable law accord-

[81] Illmer's conclusion is convincing, as otherwise Recital 23 would clash with Art 3; see Illmer (n 1) 184 para 77. Beaumont and McEleavy (n 9) 665 speculate to similar effect while noting the potential of the CJEU to render an autonomous interpretation.

[82] For details concerning ubiquity, see von Hein *Tulane* (n 9) 1682; concerning *Mosaikbetrachtung* see D Ashton and C Vollrath, 'Choice of Court and Applicable Law in Tortious Actions for Breach of Community Competition Law', (2006) ZWeR 1, 24–26 (hereafter Ashton and Vollrath); von Hein in Calliess (n 15) para 15, p 407; Dickinson mainwork (n 9) paras 3.298–3.301 pp 277–78; Fitchen (n 9) 355; A Mills, 'The application of Multiple Laws Under The Rome II Regulation', in Ahern and Binchy (n 52) 133 et seq (hereafter Mills); Beaumont and McEleavy (n 9) 640–41; for a different assessment of *Mosaikbetrachtung* see Danov (n 74) 166–67.

ing to the different laws in the locations of the actionable damage disclosed by the claim. It is accordingly an astonishing defect in drafting that Rome II does not state anywhere in its text that a *Mosaikbetrachtung* may be required:[83] the best clues are however found associated with Article 6(3) in the final sentence of Recital 22, which may be read to imply that a Mosaikbetrachtung would be required were consolidation not an option, and in Article 6(3)(b) which when inapplicable to scattered damage can only leave recourse to Article 6(3)(a).

The theoretical aim of *Mosaikbetrachtung* is to maintain neutrality in the operation of private international law rules by avoiding the impression of bias towards the claimant which would otherwise be created should a legal system require its courts to treat alleged conduct by the defendant occurring in state 'A' and also in state 'B' as entirely subject to the law of only one such state as effectively 'chosen' by the claimant when he decides where to bring his case. The special jurisdiction allocation under Article 5(3) of Brussels I is a variation of the *Mosaik* approach and reflects its ethos of *inter partes* neutrality by striking a balance between allowing jurisdiction in the places in which the consequences of the 'tort' occurred and the losses which a claimant, bringing a legal action other than in the domicile of the defendant, may recover if he opts to so sue outside that domicile. That said, it must be noted that a *Mosaik* approach to the question of jurisdiction is much less onerous for the court than a *Mosaik* approach to the question of choice of law: a court which is restricted as to what it can hear is less burdened than a court which must identify and then hear a case subject to different applicable laws each of which possesses its own Article 15 scope.

Though the aim of neutrality between the parties concerning private international law rules is generally laudable, the extent to which the defendants in tort-based competition law claims have tended to suffer from an unfair bias towards the claimants in cross-border cases heard according to Member State private international laws is, to say the least, unclear. In the absence of earlier evidence of unreasonable claimant bias in the context of what are now Article 6(3)(a) cases, it seems most likely that *Mosaikbetrachtung* is included in this specific context as a consequence of national theoretical concerns as to the methodology of private international law. The validity of such concerns is most obviously open to question in follow-on claims based upon infringements of EU competition law given that Articles 101 and 102 TFEU are common to the laws of all Member States and also that such cases are rarely confined to a single legal system.[84] It may even plausibly be suggested that the redactors of Rome II must have doubted the utility of *Mosaikbetrachtung* in the circumstance of applicable law selection concerning intra-EU cross-border competition claims: what else can explain the presence of Article 6(3)(b) in the Regulation?[85]

Be this as it may, once an Article 6(3)(a) *Mosaikbetrachtung* exercise has indicated that different laws should be applicable to different parts of the claim, the proof of such aspects of the said laws as fall within Article 15 must then be attempted by whomsoever has this responsibility under the forum's civil procedure rules. In the event that the proof of law falls to the parties, the *Mosaikbetrachtung* will either lead to a significant increase in the duration and hence the costs of the litigation or, should the prospects of such costs be too

[83] This trivial omission may lead to a wholly unnecessary reference to the CJEU to clarify the matter. See Fitchen (n 9) 358.

[84] There being both a need for an effect on interstate trade built into Arts 101 and 102 TFEU and a tendency on the part of the Commission to focus on the bigger more important infringements.

[85] For Art 6(3)(b) see section IIF below.

daunting for the claimant, to a decision to only proceed with the parts of the claim which can be proven most 'cheaply'. In the event that the court is charged with the responsibility of discovering the foreign law it, or its agents, will presumably take longer to do so if multiple laws must be considered and established; again the costs of conducting the claim will rise.[86]

It is difficult to convincingly reconcile either outcome, or for that matter the existence of Article 6(3)(b), with the goal of neutrality in the determination of the applicable law:[87] indeed the *Mosaikbetrachtung* potentially required by Article 6(3)(a) may advantage the defendant insofar as it obstructs the claimant. The extent of this advantage to the defendant may be concealed by the tempting option of circumventing Article 6(3)(a) and its potential *Mosaikbetrachtung* by proceeding instead via Article 6(3)(b). The as yet unresolved question is whether, assuming the suggestion that the status of Article 6(3)(b) is as a limited exception to the general rule of Article 6(3)(a) is correct, it is possible to ignore Article 6(3)(a) and to proceed directly to apply the Article 6(3)(b) exception? This question will be particularly acute for those legal systems which require the litigants to prove the law; argument upon whether Article 6(3)(a) or (b) are applicable may certainly be expected to prolong the choice of law stage.[88]

iii. Ambiguous Terminology in Article 6(3)(a): What 'Affects', and What is Meant by the 'Market'?

As Article 6(3)(a) provides that the applicable law concerning torts based on restrictions of competition is 'the law of the country where the market is, or is likely to be, affected', it is necessary for the court to understand both what is meant by 'the market' and also what will suffice to produce the necessary effects upon that market to then allow the intended operation of Article 6(3)(a). Unless and until this affected market can be identified and located within a country the applicable law for the tort remains undetermined. Though it is clear that the reference to 'the market', and to that by which it may be 'affected', are intended to allow Article 6(3) to point to the applicable law of a given country (or countries), questionable drafting coupled with a novel approach to the operation of the connecting factor, mean that it is not presently clear that this provision will function optimally in practice.

[86] See Mills (n 82) 151; Dickinson mainwork (n 9) para 6.64 p 422; Mankowski RIW (n 9) sets out both the pros and the cons of the *Mosaik* approach but concedes that it brings a rise in costs, resources and time for the parties (especially the claimant) and also for the court, p 188.

[87] A slightly different question explored by Beaumont and McEleavy (n 9) 667 is whether a form of practical neutrality can be said to have been achieved in relation to the combined impact of European jurisdictional and applicable law rules. Thus, though the claimant may enjoy the *lex fori* advantage of Art 6(3)(b), he does so at the 'cost' of having to sue the defendant (or anchor defendant) via Art 2 of Brussels I; if the claimant chooses to forgo Art 2 for an alternative jurisdiction, via Art 5(3) of Brussels I, he must bear the 'cost' of proving any applicable foreign laws which arise via Art 6(3)(a) of Rome II. While the reckoning of the costs and benefits of Brussels I and Rome II *could* indicate a trade-off suggestive of such practical (rather than theoretical neutrality), there is no need for it to do so. Problematic asymmetries may arise concerning the relative costs of determining jurisdiction and determining/employing the applicable law(s), particularly as there is a requirement for direct and substantial effects to arise from the infringement; the claimant cannot compel the court to apply the *lex fori* via Art 6(3)(b), absent the necessary effects. Lastly, as Beaumont and McEleavy (p 668) concede, even practical neutrality is difficult to maintain in connection with those who are sued under Art 6(1) of Brussels I, other than as anchor defendant, as they may be sued outside their domicile and subjected to a *lex fori* chosen by the claimant.

[88] See Fitchen (n 9) 358; Mankowski RIW (n 9) 188.

iv. Problems with the Article 6(3)(a) Connecting Factor

The choice of the connecting factor by which Article 6(3)(a) selects the applicable law or laws, ie the affected market, is partly responsible for a lack of clarity. This connecting factor is based upon the so-called 'Effects Doctrine'[89] as favoured and followed in unilateral form by, inter alios, the European Commission, if arguably not the CJEU, in its regulation of European competition law.[90] Briefly summarised, this doctrine has previously been used in competition law to legitimise the assumption by competition law regulators of what might otherwise seem to be unjustifiable extra-territorial prescriptive jurisdiction over 'foreign' anti-competitive acts. This legitimation is conditional on the demonstrable presence of what are usually required to be the direct, substantial and potentially even foreseeable effects/consequences of such 'foreign' acts within one's territorial jurisdiction.[91] Though the effects doctrine is thus useful to legitimise the application of European or US competition laws, despite the 'foreign' location of either the target undertaking or the act from which the damaging effects flow, it is not in this sense used to select a *foreign* applicable law; on the contrary it justifies the application of the domestic regulator's law to acts by 'foreigners' which are deemed to have sufficiently affected the regulator's legal system.[92]

In the context of Article 6(3)(a) the effects doctrine seems to offer a more abstract reflected form of such legitimisation by transferring the doctrine into the methodology of determining the application of *foreign* competition laws: whenever such a law is violated and actionable 'effects' are thereby produced, it is these effects which determine the applicable law or laws. Because the connecting factor is based on such *effects*, rather than on the implementation of the anti-competitive acts, the more familiar private international law connections such as the place(s) of acting or the seat of the undertaking are notionally irrelevant in the determination of the applicable law or laws under Article 6(3)(a).[93] Were it otherwise, the argument runs, the 'correct' applicable law or laws might be evaded and also the goal of neutrality in law

[89] Though now somewhat dated, see I Schwartz and J Basedow, 'Restrictions on Competition', *International Encyclopedia Of Comparative Law*, Vol III Private International Law (Tübingen, JCB Mohr, 1995) ch 35, (hereafter Schwartz and Basedow), concerning the effects doctrine. For a more recent account see J Adolphsen, 'The Conflict Of Laws In Cartel Matters In A Globalised World: Alternatives To The Effects Doctrine', (2005) JPIL 151 (hereafter, Adolphsen).

[90] See Adolphsen (n 89) 158; Plender and Wilderspin (n 24) para 20-058 p 621 who note at fn 124 that the doctrine is also used by Germany, Australia, New Zealand, France, Italy, Denmark, Poland, Sweden and Switzerland. The CJEU has preferred to consider the implementation rather than the effects of anti-competitive acts, see *Wood Pulp No1*, Cases 89, 104, 114, 116–17, 125–29/85 *Ahlström v Commission* [1988] ECR 5193 [16]. Schwartz and Basedow suggest that by normally confirming Commission Decisions the CJEU has de facto adopted the effects doctrine (§56) and, while noting the utility of the court developing the single economic entity doctrine (§57) and the implementation doctrine (§58), also suggest that the ostensible delicacy of the CJEU on explicitly approving the effects doctrine is a compromise to accommodate the public international law concerns of some CJEU judges: see Schwartz and Basedow (n 89) 58–60. Earlier (p 48) the same authors suggest that the compromise seeks to accommodate the differences between the continental Member States (which favoured the effects doctrine) and the UK (which favoured territorial connections). It is suggested by Geradin, Layne-Farrar and Petit that the CJEU has accepted a qualified version of the effects doctrine in Case C-306/96 *Javico v Yves Saint Laurent Parfums* [1998] ECR I-1983 [12], see Geradin et al (n 13) 52 fn 261. The CJEU has, thus far, still not explicitly accepted the effects doctrine.

[91] See Francq and Wurmnest (n 15) 122 with references; Illmer (n 3) para 94 p 190; Mankowski RIW (n 9) 184–87.

[92] See Adolphsen (n 89) 169; see also Schwartz and Basedow (n 89) paras 10–13, 34–35, 51–59 (though with care, as much in the legal systems addressed in 1995 has changed).

[93] See Roth (n 77) 640, Illmer (n 1) paras 90 and 94 pp 189 and 190, Francq and Wurmnest (n 15) 122. Of course the traditional connectors may still coincide with the affected market.

selection between the litigating parties would be compromised.[94] Though there is logic in the proposition that an undertaking which breaches competition law, thereby producing actionable 'effects', should be subject to that law to the extent of those effects regardless of where (within the EU) the claim is litigated, the application of the effects doctrine on a multilateral basis rather than on the more traditional unilateral basis immediately suggests problems of differentiation which will fall to be identified by a *Mosaikbetrachtung* exercise.[95] This however is not the only practical difficulty which raises questions concerning the aptness of the version of the effects doctrine presently contained in Article 6(3)(a).

The most obvious issue concerning the use of the effects doctrine to indicate the applicable law for cross-border competition claims within the EU is that, in what may confidently be predicted will be the majority of such claims, the claim will concern an infringement of EU competition law: such law is already necessarily common and directly applicable throughout the legal systems of the EU as a consequence of the Treaty on the Functioning of the European Union and its predecessors.[96] Though it is clear that the law governing the legal issues arising in competition law claims which cannot presently be directly derived from the TFEU or from the jurisprudence of the CJEU must still be determined by private international law, it may be wondered whether the current effects focus of Article 6(3)(a) is really needed as a matter of practice as opposed to theory? Though the riposte that the doctrine still may be of use in the context of the national competition laws of the Member States may eventually prove telling; the limitations upon national laws consequent upon the existence of European competition law and its implementing legislation, arguably diminish this point.[97] Even considered in the context of third state competition law, the practical application of Article 6(3)(a) promises to be problematic: inconsistency of drafting between the two paragraphs of Article 6(3) and the unexplained alteration of the operation of the effects doctrine during the drafting process have each generated enduring uncertainties concerning the nature of the effects required to trigger Article 6(3)(a).

v. What Effect Suffices to 'Affect' a Market under Article 6(3)(a)?

Though Article 6(3)(a) is based upon the effects doctrine, it is a novel and to some extent even a controversial adaptation of this doctrine, both because of its multilateral aspect and also because there is no obvious limitation upon the 'effects' upon 'the market' which will compel a choice of law.[98] Does this mean that a court must conclude that *any* effect,

[94] See Plender and Wilderspin (n 24) para 20-059 p 623 where these justifications are briefly noted. Though it strains credulity to believe in a serious prospect of successfully evading competition laws within the EU, still less before Member State courts, it seems that evasion of law was a live issue for DGCOMP during the drafting of Rome II.

[95] For an abstract discussion of the problems of *Mosaikbetrachtung* in the context of the effects docrine, see Ashton and Vollrath (n 82) 24–26. Other problems and controversies connected with the effects doctrine are discussed by Adolphsen (n 89) 160–62 and for Rome II Art 6 specifically see Hellner (n 17) 61 and also Mankowski RIW (n 9) 184–87.

[96] Member State competition laws are compelled not to contradict the lead of EU law, see Art 3 of Regulation 1/2003 [2003] OJ L1/1.

[97] See Plender and Wilderspin (n 24) paras 20-081–20-085, pp 632–34.

[98] As under Art 6(3)(a) the applicable law will not simply be that of the regulatory forum, and as there is no explicit threshold for the effects which compel a choice of law, Art 6(3)(a) could select foreign third state competition laws which would not be domestically applicable for lack of compliance with their own threshold requirements. Thus a Member State court could deem the competition law of state 'A' applicable, even though a court in state 'A' itself would not do so. The matter and the academic reactions thereunto are discussed at length by Francq and Wurmnest (n 15), who conclude that a wholly satisfying resolution of the different opinions is not yet possible, ibid 111–19. See also Illmer (n 1) paras 102–103, 193–94, discussed below.

whether positive or negative, upon 'the market' compels the application of Article 6(3)(a) to select a competition law or, more probably, a range of competition laws by which the substantive law aspects of the litigation will thereafter be governed?

Previously it has been usual, for obvious reasons of public international law, to require that the use of the effects doctrine be conditional upon the effect in question passing some sort of threshold to indicate that it is of a sufficiently serious nature within the regulatory area in question to justify the extension of prescriptive jurisdiction.[99] Thus the demonstration of 'direct effects', 'substantial effects', or even 'foreseeable effects' and combinations thereof are typical threshold requirements for the application of the effects doctrine concerning competition law.[100] Though Article 6(3)(a) now ostensibly eschews any such useful and necessary thresholds, it was not ever thus: a Recital in the Council's common position of September 2006 recorded agreement that the effects on the market of a state must be 'direct and substantial', but this was later deleted from the final text of what became Recital 22 for reasons which remain unclear.[101]

Matters are further complicated by the unavoidable fact that Article 6(3)(b),[102] an exception to Article 6(3)(a)'s method of determining the applicable law, explicitly requires the market in the relevant defendant's domiciliary Member State court to be directly and substantially affected before it will allow the claimant to select the *lex fori* of that court as the applicable law concerning the entire claim. As Article 6(3)(a), as a general rule, does not feature any threshold criteria concerning the effects doctrine while Article 6(3)(b), as the exception, does so, it is difficult to avoid the obvious *a contrario* arguments and conclusions.[103]

Given this opaque legislative background and the difficulties and uncertainties which arguably flow from the atypical use of the effects doctrine by Article 6(3)(a),[104] some academics have been tempted to anticipate the inevitable references to the CJEU by attempting to propose means by which the seeming defect in the final Regulation might be remedied. Such remedial work often amounts to finding a way of re-introducing either or both of the 'direct' and 'substantial' thresholds dropped between the September 2006 Council common position and the final Rome II text.[105] Of the two threshold criteria, the simplest to initially argue for is an implicit requirement of directness in Rome II based upon the above-mentioned connection between Article 4(1) and Article 6(3)(a) as general rule and clarification thereof.[106] As only 'direct' damage is relevant for Article 4(1) it could

[99] See Hellner (n 17) 61–64; Plender and Wilderspin (n 24) para 20-060 p 623.

[100] Hellner (n 17) 61 notes that Swiss law requires 'direct effects', German law requires 'direct and substantial' effects, and US law requires 'direct, substantial and reasonably foreseeable effect'.

[101] The second sentence of old Recital 20 from the 2006 Council common position of 25 September 2006, above, read, 'The law applicable to such non-contractual obligations should be the law of the country on whose market the restriction has, or is likely to have, effect, *provided that the effect is direct and substantial*' (my emphasis). Hellner (who was part of the Swedish delegation involved in the drafting of Rome II) is frank concerning his mystification concerning the deletion, see Hellner (n 17) 61. Dickinson provides a little more information but the mystery remains, see Dickinson mainwork (n 9) para 6.65, p 423.

[102] See section IIF below.

[103] See Hellner (n 17) 61–62; Dickinson mainwork (n 9) para 6.65 p 423; Fitchen (n 9) 365–66; Plender and Wilderspin (n 24) para 20-064 p 625; Illmer (n 1) para 112 p.197; Francq and Wurmnest (n 15) 122–23; W-H Roth, convincingly rejects any *a contrario* implication that Art 6(3)(a) cannot benefit from a *de minimis* threshold concerning the required effects simply because only Art 6(3)(b) features explicit thresholds, see Roth (n 77) 641, discussed below n 111.To similar effect see also Mankowski RIW (n 9) 186.

[104] Francq and Wurmnest (n 15) deprecate the academic overemphasis of this issue, see ibid 123.

[105] See Beaumont and McEleavy (n 9) 668, fn 275 who note the textual difficulties of 're-introduction' but also the potential for guidance from the CJEU.

[106] See discussion of this relationship in section IID above, also Beaumont and McEleavy (n 9) 668, fn 275.

be argued that therefore only 'direct' effects are sufficient to allow the application of Article 6(3)(a).[107] The attractiveness of this seemingly logical suggestion may though depend upon the presumably autonomous meaning which is to be given to the 'directness' in this implicit threshold. If the transfer of principles concerning direct damage from Article 4(1) is such that the jurisprudence concerning direct and indirect economic losses under Article 5(3) Brussels I is also copied over,[108] this has a potential to prove awkward for those who may regularly be injured 'indirectly'.[109] Though an additional interpretative hurdle is provided by Article 6(3)(b)'s exceptions, which explicitly require that the market be affected 'directly and substantially'; it is suggested that under Article 6(3)(a) 'directness' of effect should be confirmed as an implicit requirement and then receive an interpretation which better reflects the reality of economic losses in relation to infringements of competition law.[110] Roth, who also discusses the quantification of the required effect, sensibly suggests that the court could usefully adopt an independent *de minimis* standard concerning the necessary effect under Article 6(3)(a).[111]

Concerning any 'substantial' effect threshold, Hellner rightly rejects any role for the European Commission's so-called *de minimis* Notice[112] and advances a more sophisticated two level argument for deducing a substantial effect threshold for Article 6(3)(a) so as to better explain the alignment of Rome II with public international law and also with the various state legal systems which also require that the effect must be substantial to justify the application of the effects doctrine.[113] Hellner suggests that the public international law concept of substantive effect operates in Rome II where it is '"embedded" in Article 6 itself', and also at the level of national law where it is, 'entrenched in Article 15 on the scope of the applicable law, in particular lit. a.'.[114] In the course of his arguments for a substantial effect threshold, Hellner twice makes the point that it is senseless to seek to apply a law if that law is not applicable to a claim according to its own scope of application.[115] Illmer, who with most others, disagrees with the utility of this substantial effect threshold in Rome II's private international law, suggests otherwise: he regards the issue as most properly resolved by

[107] See Art 4(1) of and Recital 17 to Rome II and comment by Illmer (n 1) paras 99–101; Plender and Wilderspin (n 24) para 20-064 p 624; Beaumont and McEleavy (n 9) 668 fn 275.

[108] In particular in Cases C-220/88 *Dumez France SA v Hessiche Landesbank* [1990] ECR I-49; C-364/93 *Marinari v Lloyd's Bank Plc* [1995] ECR I-2719; C-168/02 *Kronhofer v Maier* [2004] ECR I-6009: see discussion of these cases and this issue in the context of Art 4(1) by Beaumont and McEleavy (n 9) 638 et seq.

[109] For further consideration of 'direct, indirect and consequential damage' in the context of Art 6(3) including the problematic position of consumers, see Plender and Wilderspin (n 24) paras 20-060–20-067 pp 623–26. Reasons of space prevent consideration of the difficult questions which arise concerning the potential substantive and procedural interactions of the pass-on/passing-on defence with the principle that the damage determining the applicable law(s) must be 'direct': see Fitchen (n 9) 368; criticised by Danov (n 74) 169; Illmer (n 1) paras 100–101, pp 192–93 and fn183 comments upon the difficulties and the example provided by Plender and Wilderspin (n 24) para 20-066, above.

[110] Concerning Art 6(3)(b) see the discussion in section IIF below.

[111] Roth (n 77) 641, is not referring to the European Commission's *de minimis* Notice (which Hellner dismisses, below), but rather to an independent concept particular to the procedural operation of private international law.

[112] Commission Notice on agreements of minor importance which do not appreciably restrict competition under Art 81(1) of the Treaty establishing the European Community (*de minimis*), OJ C368 22/12/2001 at 13. Even without Hellner's critique, see Hellner (n 17) 63, three excellent reasons to reject any such attempt to use the de minimis notice itself are: a) that it does not apply to Art 102 TFEU, b) that it does not precisely set liability or appreciability thresholds for Art 101 TFEU for EU or for national courts, and, c) that the 'safe harbour' does not apply to hardcore restrictions of competition; see Whish and Bailey (n 13) 140–44.

[113] See Hellner (n 17) 63–64. See also Plender and Wilderspin (n 24) para 20-065 p 624.

[114] See Hellner (n 17) 63–64.

[115] ibid 62 and 64.

the substantive law.[116] Illmer's basic point is that it is futile to consider the substantial effect issue in private international law as, even if established for private international law purposes, this cannot decide the issue at the substantive stage: thus if the substantive competition law of state 'A' should require a substantial effects threshold to be reached before its competition law can be substantively applied, any failure to reach this threshold under the substantive law merely indicates that there is no viable claim under that substantive competition law.[117] Though logically disposing of Hellner's point, this detached argument may undervalue the unnecessary additional complexities and costs which the current drafting of Article 6(3)(a) can provoke as a consequence of the interaction of its novel version of the effects doctrine with the potential for *Mosaikbetrachtung* inspired fragmentation of the claims to which it is applied. While private international law certainly should not attempt to remedy a claim which is fatally compromised at the substantive level, there are good reasons for it to avoid unnecessary misalignments between its internal rules and legal rules generally. Whether this be achieved by creative interpretation of the abovementioned implied directness threshold or by redrafting, the need for a clarification of that which will and will not 'affect' the market seems clear.[118]

vi. What is Meant by 'the Market' in Article 6(3)(a)?

Concerning the basic question of what precisely is meant by 'the market' as that term is used in Article 6(3)(a), the Regulation is unhelpfully silent.[119] As referring to the discipline of economics will tend to lead a court into what for it will be unhelpful abstractions arising from the absence of national borders in economic concepts,[120] it will probably be to European competition law that the court will instinctively turn, to try and understand what is meant by 'the market' and how it is to achieve the necessary geographic connection of that concept with a legal system.[121] The nature of the task which the court then faces will vary, depending upon whether it is presented with a stand-alone or a follow-on claim.

If the court faces a stand-alone action, there will be no pre-existing Decision or market definition by a competition law regulator. Assuming that domestic procedures cannot be exploited to provide an alternative route to the selection of an applicable law, and that Article 6(3)(b) is not available, the court will presumably have to undertake some attenuated form of 'market definition' to allow the operation of Article 6(3)(a).[122] Though any

[116] See Illmer (n 1) para 102, p 193, drawing support from observations favouring a literal interpretation of 'affected' in Art 6(3)(a) by E Rodriguez Pineau, 'Conflict Of Laws Comes To The Rescue of Competition Law: The New Rome II Regulation', (2009) 5 *Journal of Private International Law*, 311, 322 (hereafter Rodriguez Pineau). The shift of the issue from the private international law to the substantive law is supported by Francq and Wurmnest (n 15) 123.

[117] ibid.

[118] Francq and Wurmnest (n 15) disagree and suggest that there is no need for legislation as courts and commentators can better shape the reach of the effects doctrine, ibid 124. It may be optimistic to assume that the courts and commentators will often be afforded such opportunities: uncertainty in relation to the private enforcement of EU competition law is not attributable to a lack of potential cases and nor is it entirely accidental, it is a direct result of the manipulation of the private and procedural laws of Member State legal systems by well-resourced defendants who have every incentive to avoid a 'fair fight' in front of a court. With respect, if the drafting of Art 6(3) can be improved it should be improved.

[119] See Beaumont and McEleavy (n 9) 666.

[120] See Fitchen (n 9) 358–62.

[121] As EU competition law is supreme in Member States' legal systems it remains influential in terms of concepts even if the matter concerns a Member State's domestic competition law. Even third state competition laws tend to share such basic concepts as market definition.

[122] See Francq and Wurmnest (n 15) 120–21.

such exercise will only be conducted on the basis of such evidence as the court can be said to possess at the choice of law stage, it may still present considerable difficulties because as yet all concerned parties are unfamiliar with the niceties of defining 'the market' in the novel context of Article 6(3)(a).

A court which attempts to define 'the market' by referring to the market definition process used in European competition law will be confronted by the irksome fact that for its substantive purposes European competition law does not engage in this activity to select an applicable law (other than EU law) and so does not geographically conceptualise 'the market' in the sense in which Article 6(3)(a) intends the concept to be employed.[123] Market definition in substantive EU competition law describes the process by which a regulator attempts to establish the characteristics of a given market to better appreciate its actual operation and competitive conditions so as to inform the regulatory assessment concerning the lawfulness or otherwise of the actions of the defendant.[124] Thus the European Commission[125] begins by fragmenting the general economic market concept into a product market and a geographic market before attempting to assess the demand side and the supply side substitutability of each of these markets to identify, '. . . alternative sources of supply for the customers of the undertakings involved, in terms both of products/services and of geographic location of suppliers'.[126] By doing so it hopes to allow the regulator to reach a 'reasoned hypothesis' as to the likelihood of the conduct of the undertakings at issue being susceptible of a lawful explanation.[127]

In the light of the above, it is doubtful that attempting to imitate the Commission's approach to either the product market[128] or the geographic market will assist the national court in defining 'the market' for the purpose of applying Article 6(3)(a) in a stand-alone action.[129] The Commission's concept is too different to be simply transplanted into 'the market' referred to in Article 6(3)(a) which is surely intended to be the location of the actionable effects rather than a more abstract and non-conclusive indicator of the area of

[123] See Fitchen (n 9) 363, noting the different methodologies of geographical market definition contemplated by the Commission's Notice on the definition of relevant market for the purposes of Community competition law [1997] OJ C 372/5; Danov (n 74) 164, comments, 'it should be noted that the connecting factor for choice-of-law purposes – "the country where the market is affected" – is different from the concept of "relevant geographic market" for substantive law purposes'.

[124] The Commission has published a notice in which it seeks to explain the various methods by which it seeks to answer these and other associated questions necessary to define the market for the purposes of enforcing EU competition law. See Relevant Market Notice of 9/12/1997 OJ 1997 C372/5.

[125] See ibid p 5 and P Roth & V Rose (eds), *Bellamy & Child: European Community Law Of Competition Law*, 6th edn (Oxford, OUP, 2008) and Second Cumulative Supplement (2012) ch 4.

[126] Commission's Market Definition Notice (n 124) para 13.

[127] There are a number of conditionals present in this exercise the most basic of which is that market definition exercises are based upon assumptions as to what should/would usually be expected to occur in a market in given situations: a market definition exercise cannot work if the conditions are too 'abnormal'. Ironically, anti-competitive activity is one factor which might 'pervert' the market conditions to the point at which normal assumptions cease to apply and standard market definition techniques break down.

[128] Reasons of space prevent full discussion of the potential relevance of the product market to the determination of the applicable law: there is a rather revealing tendency on the part of certain private international law commentators to downplay the product market and to concentrate on the geographic market: for serious drawbacks with such an approach, see Fitchen (n 9) 363.

[129] For further evidence of what is suggested to be incompatibility between the probable methodologies of the Commission and of Member State courts, consider the Commission's Market Definition Notice (n 124) paras 28–30, 33–35 and particularly 44–52. The guidance of the UK's Competition Appeals Tribunal upon market definition runs to 16 paragraphs (over 1,880 words) and is just as obviously impractical at the choice of law stage, see *Aberdeen Journals Ltd v Director General of Fair Trading (Aberdeen Independent Ltd intervening)* [2002] All ER (D) 291 (Mar) [88]–[104] (inclusive).

potential supply and demand.[130] Should the matter first arise in a stand-alone case it seems inevitable that there will be a reference to the CJEU.

What is more probable is that the issue of the meaning of 'the market' will first arise in a follow-on action. Here the national court will arguably be assisted not only by a pre-existing market definition but also by a binding legal Decision reached by the competition law regulator. The regulator most likely to produce Decisions relevant to cross-border follow-on claims within the EU is the European Commission.[131] Unless successfully challenged before a European court, such a Commission Decision is binding upon its addressees and is also admissible as binding evidence within Member State courts upon those matters which it formally decides in connection with those addressees.[132] This fact has understandably led commentators to treat Commission Decision based follow-on actions as the most plausible basis for cross-border litigation involving Article 6(3)(a). To what extent, though, will a follow-on action supported by a Commission Decision differ from a stand-alone action in relation to the necessary identification of 'the market' required to apply Article 6(3)(a)?

Though it is still important to remember that the market definition exercise carried out by the Commission, or national regulator, has a different purpose to the definition of 'the market' required for the purpose of applying Article 6(3)(a) of Rome II, it might be supposed that in the post-Rome II legal environment the presence of a Decision reached by competition lawyers who belong to a regulatory body which has repeatedly stated the need for increased private enforcement, must therefore assist the determination of 'the market' when attempting to apply Article 6(3)(a). Though in many other respects a Commission Decision will obviously affect and assist a claim, it is not yet clear that this assistance will necessarily extend to the identification of 'the market'. This observation is based, in the absence of reported cases, upon a modest examination of some of the most recent publicly available Commission Decisions concerning cartel infringements delivered in the period after the publication of Rome II. The examination sought to establish the extent to which these Decisions might theoretically assist a national court by providing useful guidance upon the geographical location of 'the market' affected by the actionable damage resulting from the cartel activities which they concern.[133]

In the Decisions concerning *Refrigeration Compressors*, *CRT Glass*, *Power Transformers* and *Calcium Carbide/Magnesium*, the geographic extent of the infringement was actually scaled up from the EU to cover the European Economic Area when each cartel was described as 'an

[130] *Illmer* (n 1) 190–91 while noting the great width of the effects concept attempts to offer a methodology by which it may be narrowed to eventually function.

[131] For reasons of space it is not possible to also address the possibility that the regulator will be a national competition authority whether or not from within the EU.

[132] See Regulation 1/2003 (n 96) Art 16 which prevents a Member State court from contradicting a Commission Decision, but see also *Crehan v Inntrepreneur* [2006] UKHL 38 in which the House of Lords made the point that a Decision which is addressed to 'A' does not therefore also affect 'B'. It remains to be seen how a Decision addressed to a parent company will affect the liability of a subsidiary (or vice versa); either Art 15(a) or (g) appear to direct such matters to be determined by the applicable law or laws thus potentially leading to further fragmentation of the claim, see Bach (n 46) 344 and 350.

[133] See Case COMP/39600 *Refrigeration Compressors*, 7/12/2011; Case COMP/39605 *CRT Glass*, 19/10/2011; Case COMP/39579 *Consumer Detergents*, 13/4/2011; Case COMP/39482 *Exotic Fruit (Bananas)*, 12/10/2011; Case COMP/38866 *Animal Feed Phosphates*, 20/7/2010; Case COMP/39129 *Power Transformers*, 7/10/2009; Case COMP/39396 *Calcium Carbide and Magnesium Based Reagents for the Steel and Gas Industries*, 22/7/2009 all available from http://ec.europa.eu/competition/cartels/cases/cases.html.

EEA-wide cartel'.[134] In the other three Decisions the geographic extent of the cartels was most narrowly described in *Exotic Fruit (Bananas)*, where it was said that 'The infringement which is the subject of this Decision relates to the supply of bananas to Greece, Italy and Portugal'.[135] In *Consumer Detergents* the market was wider: 'these proceedings concern a single and continuous infringement operated at European level and covering Belgium, France, Germany, Greece, Italy, Portugal, Spain and the Netherlands'.[136] In the complex and long lasting cartel concerning *Animal Feed Phosphates* it was first said that, 'The overall infringement covered most of the Union and subsequently a great part of the EEA territory' and then by paragraph 54, 'the agricultural years 1968/69 and 1969/70 indicate that the agreement initially included: Austria, Belgium, Denmark, Finland, France, Western Germany, DDR, Italy, Netherlands, Norway, Poland, Sweden, and the United Kingdom . . . other European countries were also covered by the agreement, counted into the total for Europe and . . . (initially Spain, Ireland, Portugal, Czechoslovakia and Hungary)'.[137]

This cursory examination of a small number of Decisions concerning infringements admittedly falling outside the temporal scope of Rome II did not suggest that the availability of a Commission Decision will necessarily act as a panacea for the above-mentioned difficulties of defining 'the market' to apply Article 6(3)(a): indeed, further problems concerning the identification of 'the market' using a Commission Decision were arguably revealed as the geographic market definition considered often expanded beyond the borders of the EU, and did so in respect of multiple participants involved at different times in different aspects of the illicit cartel activity.[138]

A fundamental point concerning the oft-stated utility of Commission Decisions in the private enforcement of cross-border competition claims is that such Decisions are on a wholly different scale to the individual claims of those who seek to privately 'enforce' competition law seeking compensation for their individual losses. Commission Decisions concern specific addressees who are increasingly parent companies held responsible in law for the defalcations of some of their constituents concerning the biggest and most complex examples of multi-party competition law infringements inside and outside the EU. The point is made to question the wisdom of adopting a vaguely formulated connecting factor for Article 6(3)(a) which is not more obviously congruent with the information concerning the breaches of the law actually or potentially contained in public enforcement Decisions.[139] If Article 6(3)(a) referred instead to the law of the country in which the restriction of competition, affected *trade*, the geographic location choice of law process would be simpler for the courts to use.

[134] *Refrigeration Compressors*, §§ 25, 33, 50; *CRT Glass*, §§ 1, 20, 30; *Power Transformers*, § 2, 'single and continuous infringement . . . covering the entire EEA' and also Japan, §§ 139, 140; and *Calcium Carbide/Magnesium*, § 1 'single and continuous infringement . . . on a substantial part of the EEA market', §§ 44–46 then detail four relevant subdivisions of the geographic areas, § 201, 'the cartel arrangements related to customers within the EEA, except Spain, Portugal, Ireland and the UK'.

[135] *Exotic Fruit (Bananas)* (n 133) § 73; see also § 212.

[136] *Consumer Detergents* (n 133) § 27; see also § 35.

[137] *Animal Feed Phosphates* (n 133) § 3 and See also § 71 for more detail and § 123. The square brackets indicate that information has been deleted by the Commission from the public version of its Decision.

[138] In *Calcium Carbide/Magnesium* (n 134) § 177 'The Commission acknowledges that the events which are the subject of this Decision took place on what may be considered to be two different markets and cover three products'. The likely impact of such a Decision noting cartel activity in different states upon the potential for a *Mosaikbetrachtung* may also be relevant.

[139] It seems significant that the competition law specialists in DGCOMP wished for the *lex fori* as applicable law in all EU competition law based cases, see n 17 above.

As matters presently stand, a court facing Article 6(3)(a) in either a stand-alone or a follow-on claim may either refer a question seeking the attenuation of neutralisation of the abstraction inherent in 'the market' to the CJEU or may itself attempt to resolve the abstraction. As noted above, merely adopting the method of geographic market definition used by the European Commission or other regulators for the different purposes of substantively applying competition law is unlikely to suffice.[140] The court could however attempt to 'cancel-out' the abstraction of 'the market' by notionally allocating a different market to each legal system so as to ease the task of localising the effects connected with the restriction of competition during the choice of law stage of litigation.[141]

The critical coverage of the drafting and likely operation of Article 6(3)(a) thus far attempted has proceeded on the basis that Article 6(3)(b) is not available to the claimant and thus has highlighted the uncertainties which flow from Article 6(3)(a) which either bold judicial interpretation or redrafting will be required to address and correct. Article 6(3)(b) will now be addressed.

F. Determining the Applicable Law (or Laws) via Article 6(3)(b)

The most eloquent and convincing demonstration of the range and scope of the impracticalities present in Article 6(3)(a) of Rome II is provided by the presence and likely operation of Article 6(3)(b) within the same Regulation.[142] Article 6(3)(b) provides two exceptions to Article 6(3)(a) which allow the claimant, in circumstances discussed below, to elect to apply the law of the court seised to the entire claim if either, a) the market is affected in more than one country and the claimant sues in the court of the defendant's domicile, or b) should multiple defendants be jointly sued (eg under a provision such as Article 6(1) of Brussels I) in the domiciliary Member State court of one of them as long as the restriction of competition alleged against each defendant so sued directly and substantially affects the market in the Member State of that court.

A restricted, but claimant-driven, option to choose venue and law while escaping the vagaries of Article 6(3)(a), including its seemingly threshold-free affected market and potential for fragmentation and expense via *Mosaikbetrachtung*, all make Article 6(3)(b) preferable for the claimant who wishes to conduct follow-on litigation based upon a Commission Decision concerning a multi-state or a multi-party infringement of EU competition law: it is generally agreed that this was the outcome intended by the Commission when it made the suggestion and also of the redactors of Rome II who then, however grudgingly, adopted and then applied it to both stand-alone and follow-on claims.[143] If Article 6(3)(b) can be used it will contain the uncertainties threatened by Article 6(3)(a) by allowing the claimant to determine a single applicable law and dedicated legal procedure

[140] See Fitchen (n 9) 382–83. Interestingly, Hellner (n 17) 60 states that he was preparing to investigate the potential utility of the geographic market in this matter.

[141] For more detail see Fitchen (n 9) 363–64; Danov (n 74) 165; Ashton and Vollrath (n 82) 25, while discussing the effects doctrine in connection with an earlier draft version of Rome II commented, 'It will be necessary to link a certain damage – such as an overcharge paid by a purchaser – to a certain territory of a certain state'.

[142] The late appearance and lack of preparatory materials concerning the proposal from the Commission which via the Parliament became Art 6(3)(b) has been noted above, see also Plender and Wilderspin (n 24) para 20-070 p 627, Illmer (n 1) para 63 p 178; Mankowski RIW (n 9) 178.

[143] Hellner (n 17) 64; Plender and Wilderspin (n 24) para 20-072 Rodriguez Pineau (n 116) 323; Illmer (n 1) para 110 p 196. Beaumont and McEleavy (n 9) 667–69.

with which the domestic court and lawyers will be familiar. Not only litigation but also settlement will be simpler as the reduction in the imponderables will allow a better cost-benefit analysis and the formulation of more realistic settlement/litigation strategies.

Though nothing in the preceding paragraph is technically impossible in connection with the operation of Article 6(3)(b); to avoid forming an unduly rose-tinted view of the possibilities it offers, it is important to consider the indicated requirements for its operation and also to notice that as an exception it will probably be narrowly interpreted. The requirements for the application of Article 6(3)(b) will be treated first. Thereafter other issues and drafting problems will be considered.

i. The Requirements for the Application of Article 6(3)(b)

The first Article 6(3)(b) exception will apply the *lex fori* of a Member State court to the entire multi-state claim when the market is, or is likely to be, affected in more than one country, if the claimant: a) opts for the application of this exception, b) sues the defendant in a Member State court located in the defendant's domicile, and c) the market in the Member State where the litigation is to be conducted is, '*amongst those* directly and substantially affected by the restriction of competition'.[144] The second Article 6(3)(b) exception will apply the *lex fori* of the Member State court to the entire claim when multiple defendants are sued, if the claimant: a) opts for the application of this exception, b) sues one of the defendants before a Member State court located in that defendant's domicile while, 'in accordance with the applicable rules on jurisdiction' joining the other defendant's to that claim, or c) the restriction on competition forming the basis of the claim against each defendant also 'directly and substantially affects' the market in the Member State of the said court.

a. First Requirement: The Claimant Must So Elect

The most general requirement for the application of either exception contained in Article 6(3)(b) is that the claimant, and only the claimant, must so elect. The Regulation gives no further information on this point, thus the details concerning the operation of this election are, subject to the overriding need not to improperly obstruct a claimant in the exercise of his right to claim deriving from Articles 101 and 102 TFEU, left to the civil procedure laws of the Member States. Such 'details' may include when in the course of litigation the election may or must be made, whether and when the claimant may later withdraw or reinstate an election and the different cost implications attending each decision. Though Article 6(3)(b) does not address the eventuality of multiple claimants, domestic civil procedure may take the view that, subject to the abovementioned caveats, it is proper to do so.

The durability of the choice of law under Article 6(3)(b) is also worth briefly considering. The claimant who elects to use Article 6(3)(b) must presumably ensure that he does not change the circumstances which allow its application during the course of the litigation, eg because of reaching a settlement with the anchor defendant. Such a settlement would presumably reopen the choice of law question but this time under Article 6(3)(a).

[144] Art 6(3)(b) my emphasis. Buchner in Calliess (n 15) concurs with Mankowski RIW (n 9) 189 when he notes that there is no need for the market in the venue Member State to be 'the one primarily affected', para 42 p 460. This clarification applies to both of the Art 6(3)(b) exceptions.

To avoid this eventuality the claimant may be presented with an awkward choice between the costs and delays of reopening choice of law questions under Article 6(3)(a) and the costs consequences of refusing a reasonable offer to settle. Defendants are unlikely to be slow to notice the tactical possibility offered by the exceptional nature of Article 6(3)(b).

b. Second Requirement: Claim must be Brought in the Defendant's Domicile

The second of the above-mentioned requirements for the application of Article 6(3)(b) turns upon the claimant's decision to locate the litigation in the domicile of the relevant defendant. Each Article 6(3)(b) exception requires that the litigation be conducted before a Member State court located in the domicile of the defendant. The second exception additionally requires that the other defendants are sued 'in accordance with the applicable rules on jurisdiction'[145] and joined to the claim brought against the 'anchor defendant'[146] in that domicile. 'Domicile' means domicile within the meaning of the Brussels I Regulation; the consolidation possible under Article 6(3)(b) is connected with the idea of suing the relevant defendant in his domicile via Article 2 of Brussels I.[147] As Article 60 of Brussels I allows the domicile of the company or legal person at issue to be located wherever it has its statutory seat,[148] or central administration, or principal place of business, the claimant is likely, given the type of litigation at issue, to be presented with a range of differently located Brussels I domiciles from which it may, subject to the third requirement, freely choose the one most advantageous for its claim.

One factor in the choice of venue, for a case involving the second Article 6(3)(b) exception, is deciding which of the available Member States offers the best 'anchorage' to allow the joinder of other defendants sued, 'in accordance with the applicable rules on jurisdiction'. Though 'the applicable rules on jurisdiction' certainly includes Article 6(1) of Brussels I, there is no indication in the Rome II text that only the Brussels I Regulation rules so qualify;[149] accordingly, residual Member State rules on joinder are also available and should be considered when deciding between available anchor defendants in the event that the claim could also include defendants domiciled outside the EU.

c. Third Requirement: Directly and Substantially affecting the Market in the Lex Fori

It is in the context of the third requirement for the application of the Article 6(3)(b) exceptions that the most difficult interpretative issues arise. Article 6(3)(b) potentially allows the claimant to engage in a limited but blatant form of forum shopping. Though competition lawyers may be predisposed to favour such 'competition' between legal systems, for the redactors of Article 6(3)(a) the exception of Article 6(3)(b) represented a

[145] If brought under the Brussels I Regulation this would indicate jurisdiction assumed via Art 6(1) but not via Art 5(3), see Hellner (n 17) 65, who is mildly critical of the omission. Illmer (n 1) paras 115–16 pp 199–200 sets out the possible interactions of jurisdiction under Brussels I with choice of law options under Art 6(3).

[146] The anchor defendant is the defendant to whom the other defendants are joined as a consequence of the operation of either Art 6(1) Brussels I or a domestic equivalent thereof.

[147] See Illmer (n 1) para 115 p 199.

[148] For common law countries, which lack a statutory seat concept, Art 60(2) Brussels I allows that concept to be replaced by the location of the registered office or, if none, by the place of incorporation, or if no such incorporation, by the place under the law of which the formation took place.

[149] Concurring, Hellner (n 17) 64–65; Dickinson mainwork (n 9) para 6.70 p 424; Rodriguez Pineau (n 116) 326; Plender and Wilderspin (n 24) para 20–069 p 627 fn 139; see also Beaumont and McEleavy (n 9) 668 fn 276.

significant departure from principle.[150] Consequentially, given its status as an exception and given the injury which it arguably inflicts upon the theoretical framework of Rome II, the third requirement for the applicability of Article 6(3)(b) attempts to impose a brake upon untrammelled forum shopping by requiring that the market in the Member State selected by the claimant as his venue must be directly and substantially affected by an alleged restriction of competition by each defendant so sued.

Though the nature of the direct and substantial effects required differs slightly between the first (multi-state-damage) exception[151] and the second (multi-party) exception[152] both were clearly intended to reduce forum shopping within the EU by adding threshold criteria to the ostensibly threshold free Article 6(3)(a).[153] As noted above, when considering Article 6(3)(a), uncertainty as to the 'effect' which suffices for that provision has a knock-on effect upon Article 6(3)(b): it is thus unclear what differentiates a direct and substantial effect[154] under Article 6(3)(b) from either an 'effect' or even from an 'effect reflecting the requirement of directness' as suggested above to be implicit in Article 6(3)(a). At present all that can meaningfully be done by academe is to emphasise that clarification of what currently appear to be oddly juxtaposed examples of drafting in Article 6(3)(a) and (b) would assist the concretisation of the connecting factors. Buchner reveals the current difficulty of establishing a useful meaning for Article 6(3)(b)'s 'direct and substantial' threshold when commenting that 'the restriction must have a certain impact in the forum: it must be noticeable'.[155]

The market concept employed in the multi-state and multi-party context of Article 6(3)(b) is no less abstract than that provided for in Article 6(3)(a) and addressed above.[156] The redactors continue to appear to assume that for choice of law purposes it does not matter whether 'the market' is an undefined melange of interdisciplinary concepts, a geographical indicator of the territory of a legal system or an extemporised hybrid of the two. That said, given that the decision as to whether or not Article 6(3)(b) and the *lex fori* applies will be made by national courts, it may be that the natural tendency towards the application of the

[150] Ashton and Vollrath (n 82), writing long before the final version of the Rome II text was agreed, referred disapprovingly to both the suggestion that the law of the forum should always be applicable (see ibid 24), as this would depart from established EU private international law principles, and also to the suggestion that a claimant should be allowed to opt to avoid the application of several applicable laws attributable to a *Mosaikbetrachtung*, both for reasons of 'policy shopping' and because the claimant might actually be the tortfeasor seeking a negative declaration, see ibid p 25 and fn 94 referring to Question K, Option 34 contained in the Commission's Green Paper (unpublished of 18 January 2001) which mooted the possibility of the claimant having the right to avoid the application of several laws by choosing one governing law. Mankowski discusses the 'dangers' of forum shopping but is quite refreshingly sanguine as to the lot of the cartellists who may regret their association in light of the second exception in Art 6(3)(b), 'Wie man sich bettet so leigt man eben', see Mankowski RIW (n 9) 191.

[151] For the first (multi-state-damage) exception Art 6(3)(b) requires of the defendant's domicile as selected by the claimant that 'the market in that country is amongst those directly and substantially affected by the restriction of competition'.

[152] For the second (multi-party) exception Art 6(3)(b) requires that if the claimant chooses a defendant's domicile in which to anchor his suit against multiple defendants the joined claim 'against each of these defendants . . ., directly and substantially affects also the market in the Member State of that court'.

[153] According to Art 6(3)(a) 'the market' must merely be 'affected', see section IIE above. Beaumont and McEleavy (n 9) 668 fn 575 note: 'the pursuer does face an additional hurdle in art 6(3)(b)'.

[154] An unadopted draft Recital suggested by the Commission attempted to clarify how direct and substantial effects upon a market might be assessed and suggested examining 'prices, output, innovation or the variety of products on that market', while paying due regard to 'the position and the importance of the undertakings involved on the market for the products concerned'. See Commission Document SPI (2007) 42[3.5.2007], 9, partially reproduced in Dickinson mainwork (n 9) para 6.71, p 425. It has been suggested that the 'substantial' requirement should be removed when Rome II is revised, see Beaumont and McEleavy (n 9) 668–69.

[155] See Buchner in Calliess (n 15) , supra, para 42.

[156] See section IIE above.

lex fori will see practice defeat abstraction even without the assistance of answers to references provided by the CJEU.[157]

d. The Scope of Article 6(3)(b)

Assuming Article 6(3)(b) is to be applied by the court of the relevant domiciled defendant, the question of its scope then arises. As Article 6(3)(b) always applies the *lex fori* of a Member State court, but is not drafted so as to only cover claims based on the infringement of EU competition law, there is a possibility that the competition law liability of a third state undertaking, joined to the claimant's litigation by 'applicable rules on jurisdiction' could also be determined by the application of the same Member State *lex fori* as the intra-EU claims despite the potential absence of direct and substantial effects within the EU.[158] The difficulty for the third state undertaking would be acute in the event that its actions were lawful under the law of the third state but unlawful by the *lex fori* of the EU venue.[159] Plender and Wilderspin point to poor drafting concerning Article 6(3)(b) and suggest that Article 17 of Rome II might, for the present, serve to avoid the improper application of intra-EU law to the preliminary question of liability concerning a third state undertaking.[160]

Others, who have also noticed the possibility of Article 6(3)(b) determining the question of infringement concerning third State competition laws via intra-EU competition laws without due reference to intra-EU effects, have instead proposed that, despite the current Regulation text and the claimant's election, Article 6(3)(a) rather than Article 6(3)(b) should be understood to cover the single question of the determination of the fact of a competition law infringement in those circumstances where this matter is at issue.[161] Illmer notes that this solution would leave the determination of the other issues to Article 6(3)(b) and the *lex fori* selected by the claimant: while this is true, convincing the national court of such a suggested scope for Article 6(3)(a) and (b) may be difficult and, at best, will probably provoke a reference to the CJEU. At present, Plender and Wilderspin's Article 17 suggestion appears the preferable solution to this drafting difficulty in Article 6(3)(b). Yet again a legislative amendment or a reference to the CJEU seems to be required.

III. CONCLUSION

Rome II was predominantly designed and drafted by European private international lawyers. It was intended to function across the entire range of non-contractual obligations and to do so by determining the applicable law for such obligations as it comprises in a neutral

[157] Ironically, such an outcome would accord with the initial view of DGCOMP that for private claims concerning Arts 101 or 102 (but not for breaches of national competition laws) the applicable law should be the *lex fori*, see Hellner (n 17) 66 referring to a note from DG Competition dated 16 December 2004.

[158] The eventuality is discussed with a three-state example featuring French, German and Swiss undertakings by Plender and Wilderspin (n 24) para 20-072 p 628.

[159] ibid.

[160] ibid, and at fn 142 noting the inapt nature of the word 'country' in the first line of Art 6(3)(b). For the implications of this usage for Member States composed of multiple legal systems, see Beaumont and McEleavy (n 9) 668.

[161] Illmer argues in favour of the adjustment but does not otherwise address the textual issue, Illmer (n 1) para 110 p 197 with references. The Art 6(3)(b) aspects of this problem are also more generally discussed by Francq and Wurmnest (n 15) 125–26 who,, ibid 128, suggest legislative clarification by the insertion of a new Recital.

manner. Unhappily, as the foregoing has suggested, Article 6(3) of Rome II appears to contain a disproportionate number of difficulties and examples of questionable drafting: even allowing for haste in drafting and for novelty in connection with the type of underdeveloped non-contractual obligations at issue, this is puzzling. Why should there be so many difficulties in Article 6(3)?

One reason might be that the drafting of Article 6(3) saw a 'conflict' between the differing outlooks of private international law and competition law enforcement. A compelling argument for some such conflict can be advanced merely by noting the two radically different approaches to the determination of the applicable law provided by Article 6(3)(a) and Article 6(3)(b) of the Regulation: taken together, they represent the proverbial compromise which is famously a solution which manages to please nobody at all.

It has been suggested at various points above that Article 6(3)(a) and (b) are presently less than optimally drafted and designed. The relevance of these observations is connected to the fact that the provisions of Article 6(3) will, eventually, be required to operate in the highly complex and contentious commercial arena of cross-border competition law claims. In such an environment even clear and well-drafted provisions will be thoroughly tested. While the fate of Article 6(3)(a) and (b) as presently drafted is as yet unclear, it is difficult to be optimistic that either provision will operate smoothly across the legal systems of the EU in the context of the vigorously contested commercial disputes within which they will be required to function.

In light of such a conclusion it remains to consider the two questions which lie at the heart of this study: namely, 'Should the private international law framework be used to implement the post-2003 policy of the European Union favouring private enforcement of EU competition law?', and, 'Should there be a special Regulation dealing with private EU competition law actions?'

The answer to the first question, as it concerns the determination of the applicable law in cross-border competition law claims, is strongly affirmative. It is however important to note that such a policy has already been imperfectly brought to bear upon the drafting of Article 6(3) – in particular concerning Article 6(3)(b) – care must be taken to improve rather than complicate the existing situation by remedying the abovementioned drafting defects and also, where possible, by clarifying current legal uncertainties. The method of achieving such clarifications remains to be established but at the point of its periodic review there will potentially be an opportunity to improve the Rome II Regulation concerning these issues.

The existence of a possibility of periodic review in Rome II does not necessarily dismiss the possibility raised by the second question as to whether there should be a new legislative instrument concerning the private enforcement of European competition law. In the event that the choice of law rules currently located in Article 6(3) of Rome II can either be detached from that general provision and included, in amended form, in a special provision, or, clarified by such a special provision, there would potentially be a considerable gain for legal certainty, and also a consequent saving in terms of litigation costs.

22

Applicable Law in Cross-Border EU Competition Law Actions – Forum Shopping, Mandatory Rules and Public Policy

HUGH MERCER QC

I. INTRODUCTION

For the applicable law, as for most other issues in competition damages actions, the fundamental issue for private claimants is to minimise uncertainty. As we learn from the other chapters which form part of this study, defendants' tactics in such actions are essentially to exploit uncertainty, so as to wear down the will of the claimants, or at least their financial resources. Examples of such tactics are: challenges to the jurisdiction; claims by defendants that the law applicable is the law of the state where each of them is established; challenging the particularity of the pleading; challenging the scope of the regulatory decision in follow-on actions. Each tactic involves exploiting a lack of a track record in competition law damages claims proceeding to trial. On the other hand, claimants are becoming more subtle in some respects. Thus for example jurisdictional challenges can be reduced by claimants suing only one[1] or perhaps a small number of cartel members. But issues such as the applicable law depend on the courts both applying rules and developing rules where there are gaps. It is the development of rules which is both risky and expensive for private claimants.

Already inherent in the system introduced by EU Regulation 864/2007 ('Rome II') is a major change to the dividing line between the law of the forum and the applicable law. Article 15 on the scope of the applicable law purports to sweep away existing lines of demarcation between procedure and substance, as operated by the English courts.[2] The reality is that the line has simply been moved to expand the scope of the applicable law but necessarily leaving certain issues for the law of the forum. Thus the 'existence, the nature and the assessment of damage or remedy claimed' is for the applicable law. It seems doubtful that the intent of such a provision would permit cross-border claims to continue as usual with claims being treated as a national claim with the added cost of a foreign law expert. The claim will now have to be constructed and pleaded applying the methodology and objectives of foreign law. It is possible that specialist fields might even require the quantum experts to be imported from the relevant country.

[1] eg BA alone is being sued in the air cargo cartel private damages litigation in the English courts, and BA has joined other members of the cartel.

[2] *Harding v Wealands* [2007] 2 AC 1 (cap on damages under Australian law held to be couched in terms which are in the nature of 'instructions to the courts of NSW' and therefore procedural).

But what about evidence, organisation of the court, means of proof, disclosure, inferences, abuse of process etc? To what degree can an expert speak to the ultimate issue? What if foreign law requires a jury trial? Those examples appear more on the internal procedural rules side of the line but the absence of a definitive response to each point provides further examples of uncertainties to be exploited by defendants.

Proof of foreign law is a further such issue. Some courts (Germany for example) would generally use their own resources (eg the Max Planck Institute) to prove foreign law; others (France) would appoint a single expert witness to give evidence whereas in the English courts each party would use a legal practitioner or other professional[3] to explain the law to the court. What if one of the parties contends that a feature of the foreign law is insufficiently proven? Would this lead to the claim failing for lack of proof or could a court apply a presumption (such as that applied in English law where evidence of foreign law is not before the court) that foreign law is assumed to be the same as the law of the forum?

The critical point in resolving such issues is to apply Rome II as an integral part of EU law. Thus, unless expressly modified in some way by applicable EU law, national procedural rules are a matter for Member States, provided that they are 'not less favourable than those governing similar domestic action nor render virtually impossible or excessively difficult the exercise of rights conferred by Community law'.[4] Moreover, a combination of the principle of effectiveness, which prohibits national law from restricting the application of the rules on applicable law laid down in Rome II,[5] and the principle of loyal cooperation in Article 4(3) TEU provides further limitations on the freedom of action of Member States.

It is plain from the above introduction that the ability of claimants to choose the law of the forum as the applicable law where the conditions of Article 6(3)(b) are applicable (as considered in more detail by others) is fundamental to the certainty and therefore viability of a competition damages action.

II. FORUM SHOPPING

Traditionally, choice of forum is considered to be a relatively binary decision – does forum A or forum B provide the most advantageous result, in terms of damages? Legislators have previously been concerned by how rules of jurisdiction and applicable law can prevent or limit such choice being exercised. An increase in cross-border litigation and the rise of private litigation in relation to competition law and other regulatory infringements (eg securities) shows that the decision on how to exercise the choice is more complex.

A recent commentator[6] identified five types of factor affecting the claimant's choice of forum: cultural, economic, press/political, contractual and legal factors.

Into the cultural box can be placed the litigation culture; whether there is a reliable efficient court system with good judges; sufficient scrutiny of each case by the courts; critical mass of competent lawyers; lawyers prepared to work in cross-border teams; experience of managing claimant groups in such a way as to avoid local law problems (eg champerty and other restrictions on assignment); whether pre-judgment settlements are encouraged.

[3] eg ambassador, embassy official, vice consul, merchant, bank manager or police officer.

[4] Case C-312/93 *Peterbroeck* [1995] ECR I-4599 [12].

[5] Applying by analogy Case 365/88 *Kongress Agentur v Zeehaghe* [1988] ECR I-1845 [20].

[6] PL Krauskopf and A Tkacikova, 'Competition Law Violations and Private Enforcement: Forum Shopping Strategies' (2011) 4 *Global Competition Litigation Review* 26.

Economic issues include the cost of litigation and the funding methods available. Are conditional or contingency fees available, and how are expenses to be funded during the litigation? What are the public policy risks of a contingency funding model being used in one country to finance litigation in another? To what degree are legal and other costs recoverable in the event of a successful claim? To what degree are experienced funders and after-the-event insurers available in the posited forum? What time and energy is necessary in order to bring a claim to trial?

Press and political factors are perhaps a little surprising as a class, but are nonetheless real. Press coverage of a private competition law damages claim can constitute a form of collateral damage for the cartel members. The general press may well not have picked up the original regulatory decision finding an infringement, but large national court litigation coupled with a cartel member joining as third parties fellow members of the cartel in open public litigation can start to have a negative impact on the brand image of the members of the cartel.

Contractual matters are a minor factor in relation to private claims for competition law damages.

Several of the cultural and economic factors also have a legal angle to them, but there are also purely legal factors. Differing private international law rules still matter, as the applicability of the Rome II Regulation depends on whether the event giving rise to the damage occurred after 11 January 2009.[7] For anti-competitive acts prior to that date, claimants are faced with a complex network of conflicts rules, and of course the anti-competitive activity may well bridge that date for some time to come. Limitation periods would generally follow the substantive law applicable[8] and, given the range of periods (as short as one year and as long as 30 years), may well present an incentive to adopt a particular substantive law.

Procedural law can be critical for getting to the bottom of a case. Examples of relevant rules include: differing rules on disclosure of documents or on preparation of witness evidence; whether witnesses are heard; the availability (or not) of cross-examination, whether oral pleading is permitted, or whether this is a simple formality with all argument being contained in written briefs. The availability or not of follow-on claims also has procedural aspects, in so far as such cases would normally be removed from the general courts to be heard by a more specialist tribunal, though there are also substantive ramifications as such claims would normally benefit from a fresh limitation period for the conduct which is the subject of the regulatory decision. Whether or not there is a system for dealing with group litigation or class actions is also a relevant consideration in many competition law claims, as is the availability of special procedures to settle such multi-party litigation. Finally, the level of damages and the degree to which the relevant forum investigates and analyses the quantum of damage is plainly an important factor for claimants.

The result is therefore a complex matrix of issues, of which the level of damages is important but far from determinative. More critical is the range of tools available and the degree of practical experience available in the forum in applying such tools.

Moreover the solution adopted in the Rome II Regulation for cross-border competition law claims is expressly to provide a choice between, on the one hand, the law of the country where the market is, or is likely to be, affected, and on the other hand the law of the court seised, provided that the claimant is suing in the domicile of the defendant. Accordingly, if

[7] C-412/10, *Homawoo v GMF Assurances SA*, 17 November 2011.
[8] Foreign Limitation Periods Act 1984.

the cartel members are from different countries, an astute choice of defendant and of jurisdiction can provide a free choice of available laws. The position as regards forum shopping is therefore atypical for claims based on cross-border torts in that the cross-border nature of a cartel authorises forum shopping by the claimant.

Furthermore the status of the claimants as victims of cartels may suggest that the term 'forum shopping' should not be used in a pejorative sense. Where a tort committed by a group of defendants based in various EU Member States has effects in many jurisdictions, the number of jurisdictions in which the effects of the tort are felt, combined with the variety of jurisdictions in which the defendants are based, create a de facto choice both of forum and of applicable law.

Had Rome II simply applied the general rule in Article 4 (law of place where damage occurs) to claims arising from restrictions of competition, the result would be likely to have been an atomisation of the applicable law. Defendants would have exploited this by seeking to allocate the loss to each country in which damage occurred and requiring proof of local law for each such country. The result would have been vast expense and complexity, with any choice effectively being exercised by the defendants. Article 6(3) seeks to grant any choice to the claimant, and Article 6(3)(b) is important for claimants seeking certainty and simplicity. This is because it permits the centralisation of the applicable law on the law of the forum, provided that it is amongst the markets directly and substantially affected.

Such centralisation is particularly important, given the theories circulating with regard to the simultaneous application of the laws of all countries where markets are affected to be 'applied to the claim on some other distributive basis such as market shares of sales by country and producer'.[9] Though one might expect a judge in applying Article 6(3) to take a pragmatic view on whether the market of country X is among those markets directly and substantially affected, the mere existence of a debate over the possible meaning of the provision gives rise to litigation risk for potential claimants.

Accordingly the special provision for non-contractual claims arising out of restrictions of competition is a positive development despite the fact that this derogation from the general rule in Article 4 means that the accumulated experience of the operation of Rome II for other non-contractual obligations will be of limited assistance.

III. PUBLIC POLICY AND MANDATORY RULES

In principle, public policy has both a negative and a positive sense; negative, in that it can avoid the application of foreign law that is objectionable on grounds of public policy, and positive in the sense that it can give rise to the application of rules of the forum. A single unified concept of public policy is reflected in Recital (32) of the Regulation, but effect is given to that recital by two articles. Article 16 deals with the positive expression of public policy in which overriding mandatory provisions of the forum are to be applied irrespective of the law otherwise applicable to the non-contractual obligation. Article 26 deals with restricting the application of a foreign applicable law if it is manifestly incompatible with the public policy of the forum.

[9] See R Plender and M Wilderspin, *The European Private International Law of Obligations,* 3rd edn (London, Sweet & Maxwell, 2009) paras 20-051, 20-057, discussing the views expressed by A Dickinson, *The Rome II Regulation: The Law Applicable to Non-contractual Obligations* (Oxford, OUP, 2008).

A. Mandatory Rules

These are rules which are so drafted in the laws of Member States as to apply to a situation whatever the applicable law. Such rules must therefore be international in nature and not simply the expression of national public policy as it is to be hoped that every legislative provision is based on public policy. The issue is to identify what there is about the relevant rules which requires reference to them in all circumstances.

In *Arblade*,[10] the Court of Justice effectively provided an initial definition of overriding mandatory rules as

> national provisions compliance with which has been deemed to be so crucial for the protection of the political, social or economic order in the Member State concerned as to require compliance therewith by all persons present on the national territory of that Member State and all legal relationships within that State.

A similar approach was adopted in the text of Article 9(1) of the Rome I Regulation, but not in the text of Rome II. It is, as yet, unclear whether the desire to treat the Rome I and Rome II as a single harmonious regime would lead to a similarly strict approach to mandatory rules under Rome II as is evident under Rome I.

However the approach of the Court of Justice in *Ingmar v Eaton*[11] appears less exacting. The EU rules on commercial agents were found to be mandatory in nature on the basis of the text itself (the restriction on derogating from the rules) and because their purpose was to protect freedom of establishment and operation of undistorted competition in the internal market. That provides an indication of which rules derived from EU law are to be considered mandatory. The Court of Justice in *Arblade* also underlined that the mandatory rules of a forum must be compatible with the fundamental freedoms of the internal market.

The concept of mandatory rule is to be distinguished from the special provision in Article 6(3)(b) for determining the law applicable to restrictions of competition. That provision can however have a similar effect in cases where, for example, the law generally applicable to a restriction of competition would not consider the conduct to be unlawful but the conduct is unlawful by the law of the forum.

Article 16 only permits reference to the law of the forum. Article 7(1) of the Rome Convention had permitted reference to mandatory rules of foreign countries. The omission of a similar provision in Rome II suggests that internationally mandatory rules of foreign law are not to be given effect. Some argue[12] that ignoring overriding mandatory provisions of other countries would tend to create unenforceable judgments in that enforcing states would simply invoke public policy arguing a failure to apply mandatory rules. Comity is also relied upon. But the *travaux préparatoires* suggest the contrary in that discretionary application of mandatory rules of another country was proposed but not adopted.

[10] Case C-369 & 376/96 *Arblade* [1999] ECR I-8453 [30].

[11] Case C-381/98 *Ingmar v Eaton* [2000] ECR I-9305.

[12] G-P Calliess, *The Rome Regulations: Commentary on the EC Regulations on Conflict of Laws* (The Hague, Kluwer Law International, 2011) 567, relying on a German Supreme Court case which characterised violations of foreign embargo laws as offending substantive German public policy: Bundesgerichtshof VI ZR 6/90.

In the field of restrictions of competition, each EU Member State law includes Articles 101 and 102 in addition to relevant national competition law provisions, thereby providing the courts of all Member States with a means of applying competition law as a mandatory rule of the law of the forum,[13] whether or not the applicable law omits or restricts the ambit of competition law.

B. Public Policy

Article 26 caters for the fact that Rome II can give rise to the applicable law being that of any state. It provides a safety valve as regards rules which are repugnant to the values of the forum. The European Parliament sought to include in Rome II an indicative list of circumstances in which public policy could justifiably be invoked: a breach of fundamental rights, of national constitutional provisions or of international humanitarian law. Though not adopted, these examples are indicative of the grounds of public policy which may block the application of a rule of the applicable law.

It is of course the application of the rule as opposed to the content of the rule itself which offends against public policy. The result therefore is not to replace the offending law with the law of the forum, but to continue to give effect to the provisions of the applicable law which are unobjectionable.

Actually applying a foreign applicable law with objectionable elements appears more likely to give rise to issues of public policy than enforcing judgments. That said, the best indication of the content of the public policy rule is provided by the case law of the Court of Justice on refusals to enforce judgments on grounds of public policy.

In that regard, while underlining the exceptional nature of the public policy clause, the Court of Justice has recognised on the one hand that Member States remain free to determine according to their own conceptions what public policy requires but on the other hand that the limits of the concept are a matter for interpretation. Accordingly the content of public policy is for Member States whilst the Court is required to review the limits within which Member States may have recourse to the concept.[14] The exceptional nature of public policy was underlined a short time later by the Court which said that recourse to public policy would be permissible only where recognition:

> would be at variance to an unacceptable degree with the legal order of the State in which enforcement is sought inasmuch as it infringes a fundamental principle.[15]

Thus, for example, the House of Lords held that the seizure of Kuwaiti aircraft by Iraq upon the invasion of Kuwait was a 'gross violation of established rules of international law of fundamental importance' such that, as a matter of public policy, an English court ought to decline to recognise the Iraqi resolution which purported to divest Kuwait Airways of its title to the aircraft. The comments of Lord Steyn, though under pre-Rome II law, appear germane to the discussion of *manifestly* contrary to public policy under Rome II:

[13] Protection of competition is a 'fundamental provision which is essential for the accomplishment of the tasks entrusted to the Community': Case C-126/97 *Benetton* [1999] ECR I-3055.

[14] Case C-7/98 *Krombach v Bamberski* [2000] ECR I-1935 [21]–[23] (enforcement of a French judgment in Germany where French procedural rule prevented German defendant from being represented in his absence – public policy raised was failure to observe the right to a fair hearing).

[15] Case C-38/98 *Renault v Maxicar* [2000] ECR I-2973.

> The conception of public policy is, and should be, narrower and more limited in private international law than in internal law . . . Local values ought not lightly to be elevated into public policy on the transnational level . . . The public policy condemning Iraq's flagrant breaches of public international law is yet another illustration of such a truly international public policy in action.[16]

Recital 32 provides an express indication of matters which may be regarded as contrary to public policy:

> In particular, the application of a provision of the law designated by this Regulation which would have the effect of causing non-compensatory exemplary or punitive damages of an excessive nature to be awarded may, depending on the circumstances of the case and the legal order of the Member State of the court seised, be regarded as being contrary to the public policy (ordre public) of the forum.

It is deeply engrained in many systems that damages are intended to be compensatory. Thus German law[17] excludes enforcement of claims subject to the law of another state if they either reach substantially beyond that which is necessary to provide reasonable compensation or manifestly serve other purposes than providing reasonable compensation. Recent English authority considered whether damages should be assessed under English law or under the principles applied by German law when English law permitted a substantial degree of double recovery whereas the substantive right under German law was limited to the net loss. German law therefore provided a ready method for assessing the loss, whereas English law was the law applicable to assess the damages but had no method, given that the scope of the substantive right under English law was substantially different from that under German law. The conclusion was that the principles applied by German law provided 'a perfectly coherent, logical and fair financial award, indeed more so than the award of damages under [English law]'[18] so that, though it was open to English law to develop its own rules from scratch, 'as a matter of expediency, however, it seems obvious to start by examining the way another jurisdiction carries out such an assessment'. In effect, though English law governed the issue of assessment, a framework for assessment developed by German law would be used.

Indeed, even where national law permits an award of damages to go beyond what is compensatory, case law suggests a reluctance to accede to such claims. Thus even though the European Court of Justice has held that exemplary damages are not excluded by EU law[19] and accordingly the English court must, applying the principle of equivalence, make available in principle exemplary damages for breach of competition law, it has been held that an award of exemplary damages for breach of competition law is precluded by the EU principle of *non bis in idem*.[20] This prohibits the same person from being sanctioned more than once for the same wrong where there is an identity of facts, unity of offender and unity of legal interest. The court further considered that an award of exemplary damages by a national court would run counter to the decision of the European Commission and effectively determine that the decision was insufficient to punish and deter. In any event, as a matter of English law, the court would not exercise its jurisdiction to award exemplary damages in the light of the cumulative effect of double jeopardy, claimants members of a class not all of which before the court, the scale of fines imposed by the Commission and the effectiveness of compensatory damages. A

[16] *Kuwait Airways v Iraqi Airways (Nos 4 and 5)* [2002] 2 AC 883 [114]–[116].

[17] Art 40(3) of the German EGBGB.

[18] *Cox v Ergo* [2012] EWCA 812 (in the context of damages under the Fatal Accidents Act).

[19] Case C-295/04 *Manfredi v Lloyd Adriatico Assicurazioni SpA* [2007] ECR I-6619.

[20] *Devenish Nutrition v Sanofi-Aventis SA* [2008] 2 WLR 637 (this aspect was not appealed).

feature of the reasoning was that 'the court should be wary of granting a remedy which is potentially unavailable in most Member States'.[21]

The main issue if faced with a claim for damages which appears to exceed reasonable compensation for the loss is one of classification which involves identifying the objective pursued by the remedy under the applicable law. Damages which merely go beyond what a national court considers to be appropriate compensation (such as the first limb of the German rule) are unlikely to reach the standard necessary to invoke public policy. An award of exemplary damages as part of an applicable law could also scarcely be objectionable to a system (such as the English) where exemplary damages are in principle available.

That leaves multiple damages awards and punitive damages. Multiple damages awards are not enforceable in the United Kingdom as a matter of express statutory provision.[22] Similarly to Recital (32) to Rome II, this provides an argument that English public policy should not apply a foreign applicable law providing for multiple awards though it has been held that unexceptionable parts of a foreign judgment which can be readily distinguished, separated and quantified.[23] Such an approach to limiting the applicable law would be consistent with the focus in Article 26 on the effects of applying the foreign rule, not the content of the rule itself. A second category of objectionable rules would be rules giving rise to manifestly excessive compensation on the basis of infringement of fundamental rights.[24] Thirdly the nature and objective of the foreign law rules requires close scrutiny to ensure that the English courts are not being asked to enforce penal or public law of a foreign state.[25] Though it would be too wide to exclude reliance in the English courts on foreign antitrust legislation it may be arguable that certain features of damages rules would enforce foreign public law and therefore result in the extension of the sovereign power of the foreign state.[26]

IV. CONCLUSION

The conclusion for the purposes of this study is that the current rules on the applicable law for competition damages actions are new, make express provision for competition law claims in a way which is positive for claimants and which needs repeated judicial consideration in order to eliminate the type of uncertainties which give rise to risks for claimants. Of much greater practical utility therefore than new dedicated private international law rules for competition damages claims would be an online database of national court case law applying Rome II. Such a database is maintained on the European Court's website for national court decisions on Regulation 44/2001,[27] but it is of equal importance for Rome II.

[21] ibid [68].

[22] Protection Trading Interests Act 1980 s 5.

[23] *Lewis v Eliades* [2004] 1 WLR 692 (damages award included a sum allocated in respect of a US racketeering statute).

[24] *Miloslavsky v UK* (1995) 20 EHRR 442 (excessive damages infringing right to freedom of expression) but *cf* Supreme Court of Canada in *Beals v Saldanha* [2003] 3 SCR 416 (enforcing Florida judgment for excessive damages).

[25] L Collins and others (eds) *Dicey, Morris and Collins on the Conflict of Laws,* 15th edn (London, Sweet & Maxwell, 2012) para 5R-019.

[26] *cf* Canadian and Australian authorities which accept civil claims based on US public law discussed in *Dicey, Morris and Collins* (n 25) para 5-038.

[27] http://curia.europa.eu/common/recdoc/convention/en/artidx/01r44-artidx.htm.

23

An Economic Approach to Remedies in Private Competition Claims

STEPHEN DNES

An increased role for private damages claims in competition law implies an increasingly important role for the remedies they apply. Until relatively recently, the fines and conditions imposed by public enforcers have all but overshadowed the relatively limited role for the remedies applied in private actions. As this balance changes, defining the appropriate remedy in private damages claims will become more pressing, and may need to be addressed in the context of jurisdictional reforms.

This chapter will analyse the issue of remedies in private damages claims from an economic perspective, in line with the increasingly economic approach that is taken to competition law, and in the context of relatively limited guidance under EU law on the policy that national courts should apply at the remedial stage. This analysis strongly suggests that the deterrent objective found in current fining policy, especially that of the European Commission, should be carried over to private damages claims. In fact, it reveals a tension between deterrent and compensatory aims, which current policy statements may overlook or, at least, understate. As such, a failure to accommodate the deterrent aspects inherent to private damages claims may lead to undesirable conflicts between litigation and administrative sanctions. The chapter concludes that a greater focus on deterrence rather than on compensation could overcome this issue, and could profitably be pursued through rules designed to account for the strength of the theory of harm at the remedial stage.

I. LEGAL AND POLICY CONTEXT

A. European Union Case Law

This section will analyse the guidance provided by EU courts on the objectives to be pursued through private litigation. Specifically, it will consider whether any concrete guidance exists as to whether the actions are to be primarily compensatory or deterrent in nature.

The EU courts have allowed national courts considerable latitude in choosing which remedies to apply to competition law claims. In fact, they have provided little guidance beyond general effectiveness and equivalence requirements. For example, the rule on quantum in *Courage v Crehan* leaves ample scope for national courts to adopt a variety of approaches:

> As regards the possibility of seeking compensation for loss caused by a contract or by conduct liable to restrict or distort competition, it should be remembered from the outset that, in accordance with settled case-law, the national courts whose task it is to apply the provisions of Community law in areas within their jurisdiction must ensure that those rules take full effect and must protect the rights which they confer on individuals . . .
>
> However, in the absence of Community rules governing the matter, it is for the domestic legal system of each Member State to designate the courts and tribunals having jurisdiction and to lay down the detailed procedural rules governing actions for safeguarding rights which individuals derive directly from Community law, provided that such rules are not less favourable than those governing similar domestic actions (principle of equivalence) and that they do not render practically impossible or excessively difficult the exercise of rights conferred by Community law (principle of effectiveness) (see Case C-261/95 *Palmisani* [1997] ECR I-4025, paragraph 27).[1]

This provides little guidance as to the appropriate remedy, beyond the requirements that a claim based on EU law must not be disadvantaged compared with comparable domestic claims, in line with the equivalence principle, and that it must be possible to exercise the rights conferred, in line with the effectiveness principle. The Court noted the policy context, and suggested that private damages claims might potentially further deterrence aims.[2] Beyond this, however, it declined to articulate a rule on remedies, regarding the issue as part of procedural rules still defined at the national level.

The Court took a similarly deferential approach in *Manfredi*.[3] This time, the Court was asked specifically whether the effective enforcement of Article 101 requires an award of punitive damages. As in *Courage*, it upheld broad national procedural autonomy, subject to equivalence and effectiveness principles:

> As to the award of damages and the possibility of an award of punitive damages, in the absence of Community rules governing the matter, it is for the domestic legal system of each Member State to set the criteria for determining the extent of the damages, provided that the principles of equivalence and effectiveness are observed.[4]

Although the Court noted that 'actions for damages before the national courts can make a significant contribution to the maintenance of effective competition in the Community',[5] it provided little guidance on the approach national courts are supposed to take beyond restating the effectiveness and equivalence principles, noting that actions for unjust enrichment might be available,[6] and insisting that damages to account for loss of profit must be available in addition to recovery of loss suffered.[7] Under *Manfredi*, the position therefore appears to be that national courts must apply whatever punitive or compensatory damages are available in equivalent domestic litigation, subject to equivalence and effectiveness requirements, which are specifically defined to include a requirement not to exclude damages for lost profit.

[1] Case C-453/99 *Courage v Crehan* [2001] ECR I-6297 [25]–[29].

[2] ibid [27].

[3] Joined Cases C-295/04 to C-298/04 *Vincenzo Manfredi v Lloyd Adriatico Assicurazioni SpA* [2006] 5 CMLR 17.

[4] ibid [93].

[5] ibid [91].

[6] ibid [94].

[7] ibid [95]. The focus of the Court on unjust enrichment and analysis of lost profit in terms of *damnum emergens* and *lucrum cessans* may show a preponderance of thought on compensatory approaches.

B. European Union Policy Statements

By contrast, the executive arm of the European Union, the European Commission, has suggested that 'full compensation' is the 'overriding objective' of its attempts to encourage private competition litigation.[8] Indeed, the White Paper on private competition claims noted at the outset that full compensation would be a 'guiding principle' throughout:

> This White Paper considers and puts forward proposals for policy choices and specific measures that would ensure, more than is the case today, that **all victims** of infringements of EC competition law **have access to effective redress mechanisms so that they can be fully compensated** for the harm they suffered . . .
>
> **Full compensation is, therefore, the first and foremost guiding principle.**[9]

On the specific question of damages, the White Paper proposes a specific legislative instrument to address at least the quantum aspect of competition litigation remedies.[10] In doing so, it picks up on the compensatory focus on the Court of Justice jurisprudence and suggests that this will be the foundation of legislative action:

> The Commission welcomes the confirmation by the Court of Justice of the **types of harm** for which victims of antitrust infringements should be able to obtain compensation. The Court emphasised that victims must, as a minimum, receive **full compensation** of the **real value of the loss suffered.** The entitlement to full compensation therefore extends not only to the **actual loss** due to an anti-competitive price increase, but also to the **loss of profit** as a result of any reduction in sales and encompasses a **right to interest.**[11]

This focus on a compensatory approach certainly accords with the focus in the rest of the White Paper on decreasing barriers to litigation, which would seem to be based on a premise that compensatory claims by those harmed by infringements are to be encouraged.[12] Overwhelmingly, the Commission seems primarily focused on encouraging compensation through litigation.

The Commission's reading of the case law and its incorporation into the legislative agenda does, however, raise some questions. First, it is clear that the Court was looking only to restate the minimum level of common practice to be found between Member States, in line with the principle of national procedural autonomy. It was not looking to set a legislative agenda, or to probe the vexed question of the optimal rule to apply in these cases. In fact, to the extent that it departed from a conservative approach of merely restating common practice, it seemed to align itself, to a certain extent, with deterrence of cartels as a public policy goal. Although it did not go so far as to require any punitive damages to be awarded, the Court did stress:

[8] White Paper on Damages Actions for Breach of the EC Antitrust Rules, COM (2008) 165, 2 April 2008.

[9] ibid [1.2]

[10] ibid [2.5]: 'To **facilitate** the **calculation of damages**, the Commission therefore intends to draw up a framework with pragmatic, non-binding guidance for **quantification** of damages in antitrust cases, e.g. by means of **approximate methods of calculation** or **simplified rules on estimating** the loss.'

[11] ibid [2.5]. Footnote omitted.

[12] Sections on standing, access to evidence, and the use of NCA and Commission decisions in follow on litigation in particular build on the 'guiding principle' of 'full compensation'.

> The existence of such a right strengthens the working of the Community competition rules and discourages agreements or practices, frequently covert, which are liable to restrict or distort competition.[13]

The Court therefore appears to have identified an additional purpose to the litigation, beyond compensation, although it did not go so far as to require this in the absence of common practice between the Member States. For its part, however, the White Paper appears to read this backwards, taking on board the points on compensation, while not responding to the suggestion that deterrence might be served by competition litigation. Not only does this miss the important policy role for deterrence identified by the Court, but it also allows the minimum harmonisation identified by the Court to drive the legislative agenda. This approach is particularly questionable given the purposive approach to interpretation that is required under EU law.[14]

This strong focus on compensation to the exclusion of other aims is echoed more powerfully in Commission speeches and policy statements. Joaquin Almunia, Commissioner for Competition, stated recently:

> Our legislative action must make possible that every victim of the companies that breach competition law should exercise their right to be compensated for damages regardless of where they are in the EU and regardless of whether they bring individual or collective actions.[15]

The orthodox position therefore appears, at least at the Commission, to be that increased private litigation is to serve those harmed by infringements, rather than broader policy objectives such as deterring cartels. This is echoed in the approach the Commission takes to fines, which is the flip side of the same formal separation between compensation and deterrence aims.

Although the fining guidelines leave some scope for the Commission to take account of compensation paid in setting a fine, there are very few cases in which this has been invoked, and the reduction in these rare cases has been only a very small percentage of the fine imposed.

The Commission's Fining Guidelines contemplate a reduction in fines 'where the undertaking concerned has effectively cooperated with the Commission outside the scope of the Leniency Notice and beyond its legal obligation to do so.'[16] Indeed, there is a fairly long history of granting such reductions, running back to an early decision in *General Motors*.[17] Despite its long history, the provision has only been invoked very rarely, and the reductions involved have been very small. For example, in the leading case, *Nintendo*, the Commission granted a €300,000 reduction on the basis that Nintendo had voluntarily paid compensation.[18] This amounted to a 0.2% discount on a fine of €149,128,000. Likewise, in

[13] *Manfredi* (n 3) [91].

[14] Case C-17/10 *Toshiba Corp v Ú ad Pro Ochranu Hospodá ské Sout že* [2012] 4 CMLR 22 [73]: 'In interpreting a provision of EU law, it is necessary to consider not only its wording, but also the context in which it occurs and the objectives pursued by the rules of which it is part (see, in particular, Case 292/82 *Merck* [1983] ECR 3781 [12]; Case C-162/09 *Secretary of State for Work and Pensions v Lassal* [2011] 1 CMLR 31, [49]).'

[15] Joaquin Almunia, 'Public Enforcement and Private Damages Actions in Antitrust,' Speech to the Economic Committee of the European Parliament, Brussels, 22 September 2011.

[16] 'Guidelines on the method of setting fines imposed pursuant to Article 23(2)(a) of Regulation 1/2003' [2006] OJ C210 [29]. See also the Leniency Notice, 'Commission Notice on Immunity from fines and reduction of fines in cartel cases' [2006] OJ C298/17.

[17] Case IV/28.851 *General Motors Continental* [1975] OJ L29 [18].

[18] Cases COMP/35.587, COMP/35.706, COMP/36.321 *Nintendo* [2003] OJ L255 [440].

Pre-Insulated Pipes, the Commission granted a 5 million ECU reduction, to arrive at a final fine of 100 million ECU because of the payment of 'substantial compensation'.[19]

Not only are the reductions in fines small, but they are also far smaller than the discounts given for cooperation with the investigation. For example, John Menzies, a distributor in *Nintendo*, received a 40 per cent reduction for cooperation with the investigation. Thus compensation seems to be taken into account rarely, and even then is clearly not given the same weight as policy objectives relating to deterrence in the form of the leniency policy.

The availability of private remedies to compensate claimants may affect the Commission's calculus in deciding whether to pursue a complaint in the first place: 'the fact that a complainant can secure the protection of his rights by an action before a national court', for example, is a factor considered by the relevant Commission notice.[20] Once a complaint is taken up, however, the remedial question seems to pay very little regard to compensation paid as a factor in setting the fine, let alone the prospect that compensation might be available to suitably motivated litigants, or might pass to them through settlements agreed in the shadow of the Commission's decision.

There may be practical difficulties in aligning compensation claims with the fine applied by the Commission, which are beyond the scope of this chapter.[21] Nonetheless, the rigid focus of the Commission on litigation as a vehicle for compensation, rather than other goals, is remarkable. Throughout its policy proposals and implementation of its fining policy, the Commission maintains an almost watertight separation between compensation, to be achieved via litigation, and deterrence, to be achieved through fines.

C. Private Enforcement in the Member States

By contrast, there has been greater scope for a variety of policy objectives to come into play in private litigation at the member state level. Although private competition litigation is still in its infancy in Europe, it is certainly picking up.[22] Indeed, it has become commonplace to bring a follow-on damages claim in the wake of a cartel decision, especially in those member states that seem particularly disposed to allowing them, notably Germany, the Netherlands, and England and Wales. As such, the litigation tends to focus almost exclusively on questions of causation and standing, with almost no analysis of the underlying theory of harm put forward in the case. Instead, the infringement in the administrative decision is credited, and a remedy awarded if the relevant national procedural rules are fulfilled.

In the case of England and Wales, on which this chapter will focus, courts have shown a willingness to award both injunctions and damages to claimants.[23] Moreover, and perhaps more remarkably, they recently awarded exemplary damages for the first time.[24] In contrast

[19] Case IV/35.691 *Pre-Insulated Pipes* [1999] OJ L24 [172].

[20] Commission Notice on the handling of complaints by the Commission under Articles 81 and 82 of the EC Treaty [2004] OJ C101/65 [17].

[21] Notably, it is unclear when the Commission would take account of compensation which might emerge after the fine is decided.

[22] See Ch 3.

[23] *Purple Parking Ltd v Heathrow Airport Limited* [2011] EWHC 987 (Ch).

[24] *2 Travel Group PLC (in liquidation) v Cardiff City Transport Services Limited* [2012] CAT 1 '*Cardiff Bus*'. See also: Ch 20.

to the Commission's focus on compensatory damages awards, a broader range of remedies therefore appears to be available to claimants in litigation in England and Wales. This wider range of remedies must implicitly be based, to some extent, on a blurring of compensatory and public policy objectives, in contrast to the approach of the Commission.

Seeking compensatory damages in business-to-business follow-on litigation has become fairly commonplace in English litigation. For the purposes of this chapter, however, that litigation took a decisive and interesting step in July 2012 when the Competition Appeal Tribunal awarded exemplary damages for the first time. In its *Cardiff Bus* decision, the Office of Fair Trading ('OFT') found an abuse of dominance by the incumbent public transport operator in Cardiff, Wales. The OFT found that the launch of a competing 'no frills' service was predatory and exclusionary in intent, and therefore contrary to the prohibition on the abuse of a dominant position. 2 Travel subsequently brought a follow-on action in the Competition Appeal Tribunal, a specialist body for competition law disputes.

In the follow-on action, certain key findings of facts were directed by the CAT on the basis of the OFT's decision, including the relevant market, the allegedly abusive conduct, the duration of the infringement, and its effect on trade.[25] The sole remaining question for the CAT was therefore causation. However, causation posed significant complexities in the case. Although the OFT decision had found an abuse of a dominant position, it was far from clear that had caused the liquidation of 2 Travel. In fact, there was considerable evidence that 2 Travel was on a path to serious difficulties regardless of the alleged predation: notably, 2 Travel tended to use very expensive sources of capital, and received numerous complaints of poor service from a number of key customers. So it was far from clear that the allegedly predatory activity had caused the company to fail.

Attempting to get around this causation issue, 2 Travel therefore argued for a more permissive test of causation than the usual 'but for' test, under which it would have sufficed that the alleged abuse had been a 'substantial cause' of the loss. This would have encompassed not only a loss of traffic, but also resulting cash flow issues and knock-on effects on its working capital requirement. It therefore claimed that further losses were caused by the predation, including a claim for up to £3,848,121 in future profits forgone, the loss of a capital asset worth £6.8 million, a £10 million loss from not purchasing real estate, and £152,635 in lost staff time.

The CAT gave these claims short shrift, and applied the conventional 'but for' test, under which the cause must be a *sine qua non* of the damage. As it did not consider that the liquidation was caused by the abuse, it rejected all claims for compensation except for a loss of £33,818.79, plus interest, in lost sales. All of the more speculative claims were therefore rejected, with one notable exception.

In addition to its claim for actual losses, 2 Travel requested exemplary (punitive) damages on the basis of the intentional nature of Cardiff Bus's activities. Perhaps surprisingly, the CAT agreed and awarded £60,000 in exemplary damages on the basis of the 'cynical disregard' of 2 Travel's rights:

> We find that Cardiff Bus's behaviour is only consistent with that of an organisation that had deliberately decided to disregard the law, and that this conduct was done in cynical disregard of 2 Travel's rights.[26]

[25] para 36 of the CAT decision in *Cardiff Bus* (n 24).
[26] para 593 of the CAT decision in *Cardiff Bus* (n 24).

The result is very surprising, not least because exemplary damages awards are only rarely awarded in English litigation.[27] It is also a marked contrast with the approach of the European Commission: by rejecting all but one compensatory claim, and awarding exemplary damages, the CAT took the exact opposite of the position articulated by the Commission above.

Not only that, but the CAT did so in the face of precedent that, although not binding on the issue, seemed strongly to favour a compensatory approach. We already saw above that the EU case law only requires compensation as a bare minimum, unless equivalence principles come into play. Beyond this, it had widely been thought that exemplary damages were seldom available in follow-on litigation under a precedent which seemed substantially to limit their availability. In *Devenish Nutrition v Sanofi-Aventis*, the Court of Appeal held that the punitive element in competition law is satisfied by regulatory fines, and that an exemplary award in follow-on litigation would therefore result in double punishment and unjust enrichment.[28] In principle, the decision in *Devenish* therefore bars exemplary damages awards where a fine has been imposed, unless there are special circumstances, in line with the approach of the European Commission.

The CAT distinguished the case on the basis that no fine was, in fact, applied in *Cardiff Bus*, on the basis of a de minimis exception contained in the applicable legislation.[29] The broader impact of *Cardiff Bus* therefore remains to be seen, and its interplay with the *Devenish* decision is likely to be subtle and complex. There may be scope for future courts to distinguish *Cardiff Bus*, and it may be that *Devenish* remains good law for some time to come. However, there is considerable significance in the approach taken by the CAT, which took a practical approach to conflate deterrent and compensatory aims, in contrast with the approach taken by the Commission.

This suggests that national courts may be more flexible and open to a deterrent element in their analysis in future litigation. For example, it is now quite foreseeable that exemplary damages might become available where the follow-on litigation encompasses a novel aspect, such as new parties not considered in the original decision, or where the fine appears insufficient.

This flexible approach suggests that national courts will be more flexible than the Commission, and may look to blend compensatory and deterrent aspects of private competition litigation.

The remarkable result is almost the polar opposite of the approach taken by the Commission. All of the compensatory damages claims were excluded, but punitive damages were awarded – perhaps the result of stricter rules at the national level. It seems to be only the Commission that is maintaining a strict division between compensatory litigation and deterrent administrative fines.

[27] *Rookes v Barnard* [1964] UKHL 1 sets out a stringent test under which damages awards may only have a punitive element (i) where they are expressly authorised by statute, (ii) where the wrongdoer intentionally and 'calculatingly' wishes to profit from the action, or (iii) where public servants perform deliberately oppressive acts.

[28] *Devenish Nutrition Ltd v Sanofi-Aventis and others* [2008] EWCA (Civ) 1086. The decision has already been criticised by two leading commentators: See O Odudu and G Virgo, 'Inadequacy of Compensatory Damages', 17 *Restitution Law Review* 117 (2009).

[29] s 40(3) of the Competition Act 1998. See also Ch 20.

II. ECONOMIC CONTEXT

The case law and practice surrounding private competition litigation demonstrates a blending of compensatory and deterrent aims at the national level, in contrast to a distinction made between the two at Commission level. This section will analyse the latter approach, which regards compensation through litigation and deterrence through fines as separate, complementary objectives, on an economic approach.

A. Welfare Effects of a Cartel

A helpful starting point for an economic analysis of remedies for competition law claims is to revisit the standard economic analysis of a cartel. In the simplified diagrams below, a monopolist decreases output and decreases price.[30] This results in two important welfare effects: (a) a transfer of wealth from the purchaser to the monopolist, and (b) a deadweight loss of the output forgone from the restriction in output.

The diagrams show the familiar relationship between supply and demand, in which market demand falls as price rises. In a competitive market, the seller is a price taker and cannot sell above the market clearing price, Pc, where market supply meets market demand, or the seller risks being undercut by another seller who can provide the goods more cheaply:

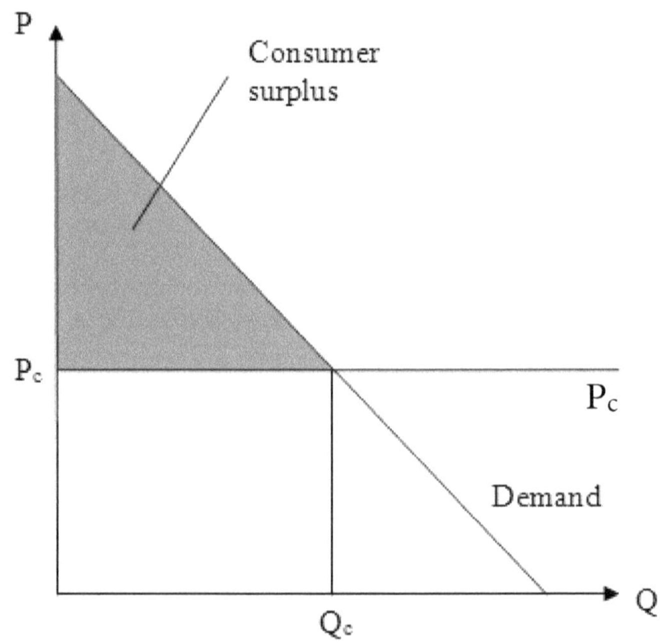

Figure 1: Competitive Equilibrium

[30] The diagrams below are simplified and assume constant costs. This does not significantly alter the analysis and aids with exposition. For more detailed diagrams, please see K Viscusi, J Harrington and J Vernon, *Economics of Regulation and Antitrust*, 4th edn (London, MIT Press, 2005) ch 4.

This results in a competitive price, Pc, and a competitive quantity of the good produced, Qc. 'Early' consumers who value the good more than the market price will enjoy consumer surplus from the purchase, indicated by the green area. The producer does not generate any producer surplus, as surplus would attract a new entrant in a competitive market.[31] The producer will not therefore make a profit beyond the normal profit necessary to compensate for the opportunity cost of capital, or the return that the capital would have generated had it been employed elsewhere.

Assume the monopolist increases price per unit to PM as in Figure 2.[32] This results in a decrease in output to QM. However, the monopolist generates profits from the price increase – unlike in the competitive market in Figure 1, where the producer generates no surplus.[33] Sellers in rivalrous markets, as in Figure 1, cannot do this without risking being undercut by a price between the increased price, PM, and the competitive price, PC. This creation of artificial scarcity under monopoly, which cannot occur in a competitive market, is the key economic concern about cartels.

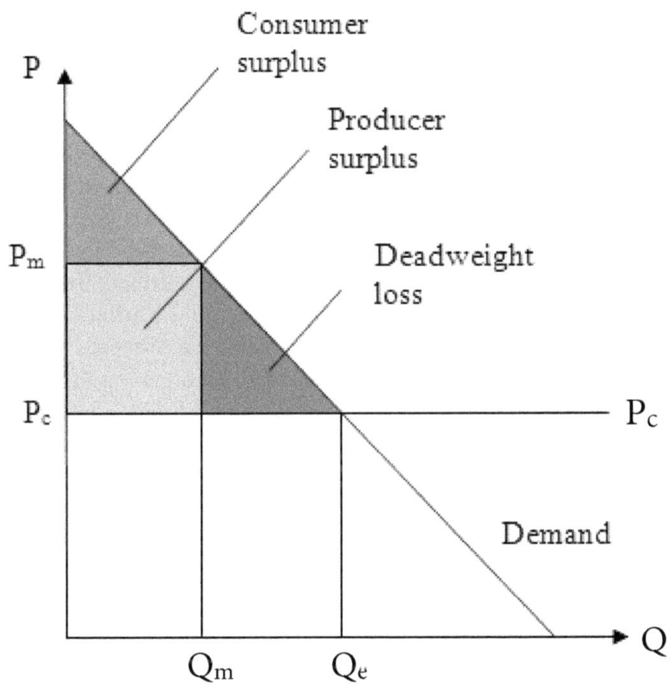

Figure 2: Monopoly

[31] The market need not be perfectly competitive for this to occur. In fact, a 'contestable' market in which entry and exit are easy may demonstrate the same features as a perfectly competitive one, despite a relatively low number of market players. *See* W Baumol, 'Contestable Markets: An Uprising in the Theory of Industry Structure,' (1982) 72 *American Economic Review* 1–15.

[32] Technically the monopolist will produce until marginal cost is equal to marginal revenue. *See* Viscusi et al, (n 30).

[33] In the sense that no extra profits are made beyond those needed to compensate for the opportunity cost of employing capital, the so-called 'normal'profit.

The restriction in output affects the welfare of market participants in two key ways:

(a) It creates a deadweight loss of welfare, shaded red in Figure 2. This is the increase in value that would have been created had output been at the competitive level, but that is forgone with the reduction in output from the monopolist.
(b) A transfer of welfare from consumers to producers: the yellow producer surplus area has increased at the expense of the green consumer surplus area. The producer is somewhat enriched at the expense of the consumer.

An economic approach to competition law suggests that the deadweight loss (a) is a much more significant problem than the transfer from consumer to producer. It represents a loss of output that will never be recovered and should be distinguished from (b). Although both result from the same restriction of output, and will therefore share some causal similarities, differences between (a) and (b) suggest a nuanced approach that takes their different characteristics into account.

By contrast, the transfer (b) from consumer to producer may be a more limited concern. Although distributional effects are, of course, important, there are reasons to suggest that they are not as serious a concern as the deadweight loss. Whereas the deadweight welfare lost will never be recovered, the enrichment of the producer at the expense of the consumer is merely a transfer: it simply moves some wealth around, rather than destroying it.

There is no reason in principle why consumers would not still benefit from the wealth transferred to the producer. It may be reinvested in new production or new research that generates jobs and innovative, cheaper goods and services. Although a consumer in the instant case appears to have lost, there is no reason to assume that they will be *systematically* disadvantaged across the entire economy: in some transactions, they may lose some surplus to producers. In others, they may gain from being on the other side of the transaction (eg through the purchase of products developed with the proceeds of the transfer, or employment generated by investments by corporations). Intervening to redistribute in an isolated case carries a cost, and may ignore this larger picture that is likely to balance out effect (b).

Stated more formally, 'pecuniary' and 'technological' externalities from (a) and (b) should be distinguished.[34] A pecuniary externality occurs when a transfer does not have any welfare significance overall: it simply transfers from one party to another. Transfer (b), from consumer to producer, is one such pecuniary externality. By contrast, a technological externality involves a loss of overall welfare, as in the deadweight loss (a). A technological externality is a much higher order of concern and should receive significantly more weight than the pecuniary externality, including in the case of private enforcement.[35]

Indeed, the difference between the two is already reflected in common law rules on pure economic loss. At common law, a claim for purely economic loss cannot normally be recovered for reasons not unrelated to the analysis outlined above.[36] The cost of bringing the case may be high, and where one party is merely enriched at the expense of another, only a 'pecuniary' externality occurs. The reasons driving the rule on pure economic loss

[34] R Holcombe and R Sobel, 'Public Policy Toward Pecuniary Externalities,' (2001) 29 *Public Finance Review* 304-325.

[35] The objection that the deadweight loss should be addressed solely through public enforcement understates the limited resources public enforcers face. If there are marginal returns from increased private enforcement, it is unclear why private enforcement should not also aim to minimise technological rather than pecuniary externalities.

[36] *Spartan Steel and Alloys Ltd v Martin & Co* [1972] EWCA Civ 3.

are beyond the scope of the present analysis, but the parallel here is striking. In effect, the cartel victim is allowed to claim for being made marginally worse off by virtue of a claim based on breach of statutory duty that would not be allowed for a wide range of domestic tort claims, and that would normally require a contractual basis.[37]

It is therefore unclear why the damages rules should be expanded in the case of cartels unless there is a distinctive aspect to justify this. From an economic perspective, the diffuse effects described above are one distinctive feature that may not be present in a normal pure economic loss case – and in the case of a cartel the level of diffusion may be particularly high. An additional feature is that cartels are by their nature covert. The rate of detection is therefore likely to be less than perfect, unlike other cases of pure economic loss. This means that even if compensation passes when the losses are detected by the legal system, a significant incentive may remain for the monopolist to increase prices – and thereby to cause a deadweight loss. Damages aimed solely at compensation may not therefore adequately address the most significant issue, the deadweight loss.

Of course, if the monopolist could be perfectly disgorged of the transfer (b), there would remain no incentive to increase prices and cause deadweight loss (a). This might suggest that an exception to the rule against recovery for pure economic loss could be justified to the extent that compensating for the transfer removes the incentive to cause the deadweight loss. However, if damages are fully to address the deadweight loss issue, and therefore justify a departure from the usual rule, they should be designed with this aim in mind. This suggests that private damages for cartel fines should take account of the distinctive features justifying the departure from the rule against recovery of purely economic loss. In other words, they should address diffuse damage and imperfect detection. Thus an uplift in damages to address these factors may be in order, rather than an exclusive focus on compensation on equity grounds.

Indeed, the rule against recovery of pure economic loss, and its correlation to economic literature on pecuniary and technological externalities, suggests that pursuing compensation *as an independent aim* should be regarded with skepticism. Unless there are distinctive factors to justify different treatment, it is unclear why recovery should be allowed for its own sake. If an exception is made, it should surely reflect these distinctive features of cartels, namely a particularly high level of diffusion of damage and their covert nature. This approach to the damages question notably suggests that the overlap between public and private enforcement is foundational, as it appears that both public and private enforcement need to address similar aspects of the cartel.

Damages should therefore address, or at least take some account of, the more pressing issue from an economic perspective, the deadweight loss. This loss is likely to persist unless public enforcement perfectly catches all cartels – which has certainly not been the experience to date. In the absence of perfect detection in either public or private enforcement, there is therefore a strong case to ensure that any increase in private enforcement takes account of the effect of the deadweight loss, rather than simply focusing on the transfer of wealth from consumers to producers. Otherwise it would seem to be simply a special rule applied to cartels without distinctive justification.

It should be noted that the above analysis takes a wealth-maximising approach, that is, the concept that legal rules should seek to maximise wealth. This has proven a controversial claim in some settings, and is subject to debate, even though it should be distinguished from

[37] *Garden Cottage Foods Ltd v Milk Marketing Board* [1984] 1 AC 130, [1983] 2 All ER 770, HL.

straightforward utilitarianism.[38] However, it has come to be uncontroversial that competition law should generally be used to enhance efficiency, rather than pursue distributional concerns.[39] As such, it should be uncontroversial to apply law and economics analysis that seeks to distinguish cases in which legal rules enhance efficiency from those that merely redistribute, which is no longer commonly considered to be a key aim of competition law, however appropriate it may be in other contexts.

B. Welfare Effects of the Pursuit of Compensation as an Independent Aim

Beyond the static analysis of the welfare effects of (a) and (b), there may be an important sense in which compensation of the transfer (b) could expand the deadweight loss (a), if pursued for its own sake. Assume for a moment that the damages awarded in litigation only compensate, and do not deter. Assume also that the monopolist has market power and can pass on the price increase. The result of litigation may be to increase costs and shift supply in still further than had the monopolist.

The cost of compensation becomes a cost borne by the industry, increasing costs as in Figure 3. If the monopolist continues to hold market power, it is very likely that this cost will be passed on to consumers. As a result, the price increases and quantity decreases as happened in Figure 2. In order to pursue compensation as an independent aim, a very similar effect to that in Figure 2, monopoly, takes place:

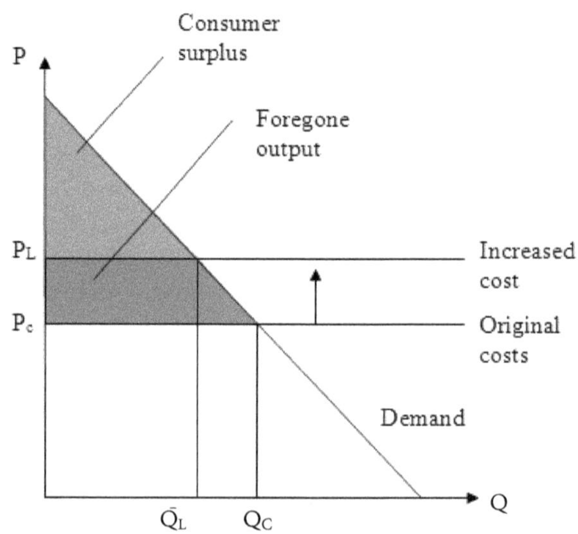

Figure 3: Response to Litigation

[38] See in particular the famous debate between Ronald Dworkin and Judge Posner: R Posner, 'Utilitarianism, Economics, and Legal Theory', (1979) 8 *Journal of Legal Studies* 103; R Dworkin, 'Is Wealth A Value?' (1980) 9 *Journal of Legal Studies* 191.

[39] The classic works leading to the acceptance of efficiency as the primary focus of competition law were written by two federal court judges in the United States: R Bork, *The Antitrust Paradox* (New York, Free Press, 1978) and R Posner, *Antitrust Law,* 2nd edn (Chicago, Univ of Chicago Press, 2000). For a survey of recent developments in this approach, see in particular, Kwoka and White (eds), *The Antitrust Revolution,* 8th edn (Oxford, OUP, 2008). The approach is also well-established in Europe: see R Van den Bergh and P Camasaca, *European Competition Law and Economics: A Comparative Perspective* (London, Sweet & Maxwell, 2006).

The remarkable outcome is that the monopoly problem has been exacerbated for the sake of compensating someone who had consumer surplus to begin with: someone who bought regardless of the price increase. The ranks of those who did not buy, and did not gain any surplus at all, swell in order to compensate parties with consumer surplus who have only been made marginally worse off.

It should be stressed that the above analysis is a simplification and an abstraction. In the real world, the prospect of litigation is likely to be a strong deterrent, and therefore is likely to prevent the inward shift in supply in the first place. As a matter of fact, it is likely to decrease the size of the deadweight loss (a). Damages awards could well be justified in this way: litigants are awarded damages to serve wider public policy goals in deterring cartels.

The purpose of Figure 3 is rather to show that it is difficult to support attempting to rectify transfer (b), without justifying this through in terms of a consequential decrease in deadweight loss (a). It is only this consequential deterrent effect that justifies the damages. It is therefore difficult to see why compensation should be regarded as an autonomous aim, and if so, why deterrent aims should not be taken into account. This suggests that careful attention should be paid to the *overall* level of sanctions applied to deter the cartel throughout all enforcement, public and private, rather than pursuing compensation as an independent aim.

C. Optimality of Sanctions

The above analysis highlights two key issues with competition damages awards from an economic perspective: first, the compensation award may focus excessively on a transfer of wealth, and insufficiently on the destruction of wealth involved in a deadweight loss. Secondly, at least when analysed in isolation, it may increase the deadweight loss for the sake of compensating parties who already have surplus, if it results in an inward shift in supply.

The significance of these issues will depend to a certain extent on the wider context in which litigation occurs. A key teaching in the economic literature on cartels concerns the concept of optimal sanctions.[40] In general, a sanction should be set with careful regard to the probability of detection. The expected value of sanction – the sanction multiplied by the probability of detection – should be set to the estimated social cost of the activity.[41] Sanctions should not depart from this optimal level: if they are too low, they will not deter harmful activity. If they are too high, they will deter lawful activity and may attract resources in enforcement and compliance that would have been better spent elsewhere.[42] Sanctions at the correct level could potentially provide incentives leading to decreases, or even the elimination, of the deadweight loss.

This is not the place for a lengthy analysis of the policy of the European Commission to apply very large fines in several recent competition cases.[43] It could well be that this represents

[40] See in particular the seminal article, W Landes, 'Optimal Sanctions for Antitrust Violations', (1983) 50 *Journal of Law and Economics* 652–78. The approach has also been followed in a European context: see, eg W Wils, 'Is Criminalization of EU Competition Law the Answer?' Paper presented at the Amsterdam Center for Law and Economics Conference, 'Remedies and Sanctions in Competition Policy', Amsterdam, 17–18 February 2005.

[41] This approach to modelling incentives surrounding sanctions can be traced to G Becker, 'Crime and Punishment: An Economic Approach', (1968) 76 *Journal of Political Economy*, 169–217.

[42] This is a variant on the 'greener grass' fallacy described in H Demsetz, 'Information and Efficiency: Another Viewpoint', 12 *Journal of Law and Economics* 1 (1969).

[43] Between 2006 and 2012, the Commission applied fines of over €2 billion in Article 102 cases alone. Source: Commission press releases available at http://europa.eu/rapid/searchAction.do.

the optimal level, taking account of the probability of detection; it might be below the optimal level, suggesting that there is room for further sanctions; it could amount to harmful over-deterrence, chilling innovative business practices through penalties applied against successful competitors who, having been urged to compete, are 'turned upon when they win'.[44] It is not possible to say in the abstract which category practice falls into. However, the implications of the various possibilities for the above analysis can be considered.

If the current level of sanctions is suboptimal, the above issues may not pose practical problems: damages in litigation simply act to increase the penalty closer to the optimal level, decreasing the deadweight loss. In this case, damages awards appear to have a clear role to enhance sanctions that are currently below the optimal level. The oddity of increasing the deadweight loss in order to award a remedy to a party that already has consumer surplus does not arise, as this windfall can be justified in wider policy terms: the litigant is simply being rewarded for a socially beneficial lawsuit.

If, however, the current level of sanctions is above the optimal level, an effect similar to that in Figure 3 is likely. Litigation adds to the total sanction for the cartel activity. Increasing sanctions above the optimal level may increase costs to the industry, decreasing supply, as in Figure 3. Where there are barriers to entry, as is likely where there is a cartel, the effect is likely to be passed on to the consumer in the form of higher prices and decreased output. In this case, there would seem to be little role for litigation – unless, that is, it is to be encouraged in order to compensate *despite* these issues.

The potential impact of litigation on the total sanction will affect the overall level of penalty for a cartel. As such, there is no getting away from the interplay between administrative fines and damages from litigation. In fact, there may be a tension between pursuing compensation as an independent aim, and optimal deterrence, under the circumstances analysed above. This interplay may be understated in current discussions of litigation, where more of a focus on overall optimality of sanction may therefore be in order.

It may be that the intention is to compensate *despite* the issues identified above with compensation as an independent aim. It is hoped that this is not the case. Encouraging litigation *purely* for the sake of rectifying transfer (b) is likely to be expensive and in some circumstances may conflict with the correction of deadweight loss (a). In fact, as this redistribution uses resources without generating any output, it can be identified as a rent-seeking claim.[45] As such, it should be strongly discouraged, especially in the antitrust field where the law is supposed to promote efficiency, rather than redistribution for its own sake.[46] Instead, litigation should focus squarely on the promotion of optimal deterrence of the deadweight loss, and coherence between this shared aim of litigation and administrative enforcement should be promoted.

[44] *US v Aluminum Company of America*, 148 F 2d 416, 430 (2d Cir 1945).

[45] For more on the concept of rent-seeking, see eg KM Murphy, A Shleifer, and RW Vishny, 'Why is Rent-Seeking So Costly to Growth?', (1993) 83(2) *American Economic Review* 409–14.

[46] See especially W Landes, 'Optimal Sanctions for Antitrust Violations', (1983) 50 *U Chi L Rev* 652; W Baumol and J Ordover, 'Use of Antitrust to Subvert Competition', (1985) 28(2) *Journal of Law and Economics* 247.

III. ECONOMIC ANALYSIS OF CURRENT PRACTICE

This section will compare the issues identified in the above analysis with current administrative practice by the European Commission and judicial practice of the EU and national courts.

A. European Commission Practice

The above tensions are not therefore insurmountable, and potentially admit a considerable role for litigation, provided that due regard is had to the overall level of sanctions in a case. However, the issues cannot be so easily dispelled on the approach that the European Commission has taken to date. As noted above, the Commission has sought to distinguish the role of compensation and fines. It foresees a strict separation between deterrent administrative fines, on the one hand, and compensatory damages awards to those harmed by the practices.

The above analysis poses some tricky questions for this approach. If fines and damages are to serve distinct ends, then we should presumably understand that the Commission regards its current fining policy as an expression of the optimal fine that should be applied.[47] If so, then the additional sanction applied in order to compensate by implication has the unintended consequences described above: the fine having accounted for the deterrent aspect, the damages must logically amount to over deterrence. As such, the litigation will increase the deadweight loss for the sake of compensating a party who already has consumer surplus.

If, however, the underlying thought is that sanctions are presently too low, the separation between deterrent fines and compensatory damages in Commission thinking is equally puzzling. This, surely, would be a case for increasing the level of the fines still further, rather than encouraging litigation to account for an (arbitrary) percentage of the total deterrence the Commission wishes to seek. Indeed, if this were the intention, one would expect more of a focus on the interplay between fines and damages claims in the Commission practice to date.[48]

Either way, the strong focus the Commission has placed on compensation as an independent aim, rather than picking up on suggestions in the caselaw for a more mixed set of objectives, sits uneasily with the tensions identified above. The Commission may thereby be able to avoid having to engage directly with difficulties involved with the interplay of administrative fines and damages awards, but it risks taking insufficient account of the potential for litigation and fines to cut across each other, with some of the adverse effects described above. Instead of an artificial distinction between the roles of public and private enforcement, more attention might be paid to their interplay and their shared potential to deter cartels.

[47] 'Guidelines on the method of setting fines imposed pursuant to Article 23(2)(a) of Regulation 1/2003,' [2006] OJ C210.

[48] See discussion of *Nintendo* (n 18).

B. Judicial Analysis

The case law provides ample scope to depart from the Commission's compensation-centric stance. In places, the Court in *Manfredi* seems to be in step with the Commission's approach, notably in its reference to potential unjust enrichment claims, which are closer to a compensatory than to a deterrent approach.[49] Nonetheless, it kept these statements to the level of observations, and left the door open to alternative approaches, including punitive damages on a deterrent approach if appropriate.

It is therefore notable that the Competition Appeal Tribunal appears to have departed from the Commission orthodoxy in *Cardiff Bus.* Rather than following a rigid focus on compensation, the CAT took a more flexible approach in which wider policy factors, such as deterrence, can play their important role. To the extent that the impact of litigation on the level of deterrence in a case is unavoidable, this stance is to be welcomed. In fact, the CAT seemed to arrive at exactly the result the above analysis suggests, by awarding exemplary damages to fill a potential shortfall in the sanction (no fine having been applied in the case), and stopping short of awarding some of the more speculative claims, the latter being dangerously close to rent-seeking claims aimed more at redistribution than efficiency.

It should be noted, however, that the CAT did not approach the question in these more economic terms. Instead, it took an almost fiercely orthodox approach to applying the legal tests from the applicable precedents. The reasons behind this are perfectly understandable in the context of follow-on litigation, where the assumption appears to be that the administrative decision takes account of all such issues, but this may understate the important competition policy aspects at play in all stages of the decision. The underlying theory of harm in the case is relevant throughout, especially because it will impact the size of the deadweight loss involved. As such, it may be desirable to keep the economic context of the practices in mind throughout the litigation, and not to assume that the relevance of these issues was exhausted at the point that an infringement was found.

Nonetheless, the result in *Cardiff Bus* suggests that national courts may provide the necessary flexibility to account for the concerns with the Commission approach identified above. Even so, care will be needed on the part of administrative enforcers to take account of increased awards of the type in *Cardiff Bus.* It may be that fines will need to decrease with time if this litigation comes to be more common, requiring a revision to administrative practices in setting fines.

IV. CONCLUSION

As the above analysis shows, it is not possible cleanly to separate the deterrent and compensatory functions of litigation. Certainly, the interplay between the two is complicated, and merits significant analysis possibly even reform, and this is proving to be a fertile area of research.[50] However, merely ignoring the interplay that economic analysis suggests liti-

[49] *Manfredi* (n 3) [94].

[50] See eg C Hodges, 'European Competition Enforcement Policy: Integrating Restitution and Behaviour Control', (2011) 34 *World Competition* 382.

gation and administrative fines are likely to have is unlikely to provide a solid foundation for policy moving forward.

Litigation that awards compensatory damages to parties who purchased goods anyway, and therefore have consumer surplus, makes little sense. A static and somewhat myopic focus on a transfer from consumer to producer ignores the much more serious problem of the wealth destroyed through forgone output. There are even times when the latter problem can be exacerbated by well-intentioned efforts to redress the former. At its worst, this approach can provide compensation to those who continued to buy the cartelised goods anyway, at the expense of those who did not, even though the second group may be the greater concern.

It is only in the wider context of furthering a public policy of deterrence that this litigation appears sensible. In terms of its effects on incentives, sanctions applied in litigation mirror administrative fines. As such, they are both relevant to ensuring that the optimal level of sanctions, or at least a workable approximation of it, is maintained. Sanctions applied in litigation *displace* sanctions that might have been applied through an administrative fine, and the implications of this interplay should be addressed head-on.

In place of the current approach by the Commission to distinguish litigation and fines, this chapter respectfully submits that their overlap should be embraced. Given the theoretical and practical difficulties inherent in using competition damages claims as compensatory devices, it seems sensible to regard both as devices to further optimal deterrence of genuinely anticompetitive behaviour. The debate could profitably address in more detail the question of optimal sanctions and their relationship with litigation, and focus less on the pursuit of compensation as an independent aim. If, as this analysis suggests, technological and pecuniary externalities from a cartel cannot easily be distinguished, both public and private damages claims should squarely acknowledge that they *both* serve deterrent aims.

If litigants are therefore regarded as 'private attorneys general', bringing cases in the general interest, the issues surrounding compensation of those with surplus go away. Likewise, due regard to optimality of total sanctions in a case removes the prospect of excessive litigation harming the very parties competition law is supposed to help. Instead of analysing litigation in isolation, the debate could profitably shift its focus more onto how litigation can be accommodated into the existing framework and its interaction with existing sanctions.

Moreover, such a focus has the potential to take considerable heat out of the debates surrounding damages claims. If commentators broadly accept, in principle, that public fines are needed to deter illegal activity, there can be little objection to litigation with the same aim – unless, that is, there is some institutional objection to an increased role for courts rather than administrative bodies on principle.[51] The role of litigation to deter genuinely anticompetitive conduct should be embraced, allowing the integration of litigation into the proper focus of modern competition law: the deterrence of inefficient restrictive practices.

[51] See more: D Crane, *The Institutional Structure of Antitrust Enforcement* (Oxford, OUP, 2011).

V. A PRACTICAL SUGGESTION

One pitfall of some economic analysis of law is sometimes alleged to be a degree of abstraction from concrete legal questions faced by regulators and practitioners. This chapter will therefore conclude with a simple suggestion that could be adopted in the context of ongoing reforms to take account of the issues identified above.

As they stand, the EU competition rules make no distinction at the remedial stage regarding the theory of harm put forward by the claimant, even though the Commission certainly has capacity to do so.[52] There is no analogue to the 'antitrust standing' rule[53] used in other jurisdictions or the heightened pleading requirements designed to keep unmeritorious cases out of the courts.[54] The rule is simply that full damages must be paid to all proven claims, in line with *Manfredi* and *Courage*.

This one-size-fits-all approach sits oddly in an age when competition law analysis takes an increasingly economic approach, as it does not reflect significant differences between theories of harm advanced in various claims. From an economic perspective, there is a world of difference between a tenuous claim of predatory pricing, subject as it is to trenchant criticism in both the economic literature and a variety of leading antitrust jurisdictions,[55] and a clear-cut, hardcore cartel. Yet the EU position on damages claims appears to be to treat these, in principle, as identical theories for the purposes of quantification. If there is to be a distinction, it appears to be on the basis of the loss suffered by a competitor, rather than the deadweight loss experienced by society.

Not only is this the exact opposite of what the economic approach suggests is appropriate, but it is also remarkable from a legal perspective: the Commission's fining guidelines make clear that graver infringements are subject to graver sanction, and the few member states imposing criminal sanctions only do so in the clearest-cut, hardcore cases.[56]

Some reflection of the strength of the theory of harm at the remedial stage may therefore be called for.[57] Awarding more damages where the strength of the theory is strongest, possibly even a multiple of the loss suffered, would be a practical step to allow litigation to play a significant role in deterring the worst competition law violations. By contrast, awarding ordinary damages subject to deductions for passing on, or failure to mitigate, in cases where the theory is weak would decrease the scope for rent-seeking claims. At a stroke, such a rule would bring litigation much closer into line with the economic theory justifying it, and would also encourage convergence between litigation remedies and fining policy.

In a sense, this would only mirror recent moves by the Court of Justice, in another context, to adopt a 'sliding scale' that is responsive to the theory of harm put forward. In *Tomra*, the Court noted that the concept of a dominant position is not subject to variation

[52] Consider the invitation to do so in *Manfredi* (n 3) discussed above.

[53] *Brunswick Corp v Pueblo Bowl-O-Mat, Inc* 429 US 477 (1977).

[54] *Bell Atlantic Corp v Twombly* 127 S Ct 1955 (2007); *Ashcroft v Iqbal* 556 US 662, 129 S Ct 1937 (2009).

[55] See eg Frankin M Fisher, *Matsushita: Myth v Analysis in the Economics of Predation*, 64 Chi-Kent L Rev 969 (1988) (predation as 'one of the most persistent antitrust fairy tales'). The scepticism towards predation theories in the US case law is well-known: see eg *Brooke Group Ltd v Brown & Williamson* 509 US 209 (1993). The European Commission's 'Guidance on its enforcement priorities in applying Article 82 of the EC Treaty to abusive exclusionary conduct by dominant undertakings', OJ C45/7–20, likewise adopts an effects-based approach which is sensitive to the strength of the economic theory underlying the alleged harm.

[56] See esp s 188 of the Enterprise Act 2002 in the UK, which criminalises cartels.

[57] See more, F Easterbrook, 'Detrebling Antitrust Damages', (1985) 28(2) *Journal of Law and Economics* 445.

'in form or degree,' but nonetheless went on to analyse the finding of the requisite 'form' of dominance in terms of the market effects of the conduct.[58] In similar vein, a sliding scale of damages awarding more damages in the worst hardcore cartels, and less in more speculative claims, could be a useful element in future jurisdictional reforms. Private litigation to deter the very worst hardcore cartels should not be controversial; much of the controversy over it might be avoided if rules on quantum reflect this.

[58] 'Article 102 TFEU does not envisage any variation in form or degree in the concept of a dominant position. Where an undertaking has an economic strength such as that required by Article 102 TFEU to establish that it holds a dominant position in a particular market, its conduct must be assessed in the light of that provision. *None the less, the degree of market strength is, as a general rule, significant in relation to the extent of the effects of the conduct of the undertaking concerned rather than in relation to the question of whether the abuse as such exists.*' Case C-549/10 *Tomra* [39] (emphasis added).

24

Conclusion: EU Competition Law Damages in a Cross-Border Context

MIHAIL DANOV AND FLORIAN BECKER

The foregoing analysis clearly shows that the current private international law framework would have an important role to play with a view to identifying the national laws which should be used to assess damages in a cross-border context. This clearly would be so with regard to issues on which EU competition law is silent. Indeed, the European definition of the quantum of damages from *Manfredi* and the principle of national procedural autonomy leave considerable scope for national deviations, and, as a result, depending on the applicable law, there could be different amount of damages awarded as, for example, different countries may have different rules with regard to remoteness of damages. Given that most EU competition law infringements would potentially affect businesses and consumers in several Member States, a private antitrust claimant in Europe should carefully select where to bring his EU competition law claim. Indeed, there could be different outcomes if exemplary or punitive antitrust damages are pleaded, as they may be available in one Member State, but not in another.

Although one could say that it may be unfair that different amounts of damages may be awarded for the same breach of the very same rule, a different level of redress would come as no surprise in view of the fact that the EU has opted for a private international law solution. Indeed, the purpose of Rome II is the unification of choice-of-law, not the harmonisation of the Member States' remedies in tortious actions based on EU competition law. Should the Union's legislator continue to rely on Rome II? Or should there be a uniform approach to damages? On the one hand, Fitchen has noted that the private international law framework in so far as it concerns the determination of the applicable law in cross-border competition law claims may be used to implement the post-2003 policy of the European Union favouring private antitrust enforcement.[1] On the other hand, Dnes has submitted that the question of optimal sanctions and in particular the relationship between fines and damages should be at the top of the legislator's agenda in so far as the EU position on damages claims may need to be reviewed.[2]

[1] See Ch 21.
[2] Ch 23.

II. *LEX FORI* – CERTAINTY AND REGULATORY COMPETITION

Fitchen[3] not only identifies the hurdles in applying Article 6(3) with regard to EU competition law infringements, but also finds the main cause for them by looking at the legislative history of the roots of the problems.

In the latter context, Fitchen[4] explains that Rome II was predominantly designed and drafted by European private international lawyers. This may well be justified by the fact that the Regulation was intended to ascertain the applicable law for the entire range of non-contractual obligations. As a result, the challenge for the Union legislator may have been how to strike the balance between the differing outlooks of private international law and private enforcement of EU competition law. According to him, the legislator's impetus to strike the balance between the different viewpoints of private international lawyers and EU competition lawyers may explain why Rome II incorporates the two radically different approaches reflected in paragraph 6(3)(a) and paragraph 6(3)(b) of the Regulation. In the latter context, he notes that Article 6(3)(b) was a last minute addition to Rome II.[5]

Fitchen's thoughtful analysis[6] shows that Article 6(3)(a), which is intended to be a rigid rule that offers no exception nor any other means of escape from the law or laws it selects as applicable, is very unclear and difficult to apply in practice. He goes on to demonstrate that the use of ambiguous words such as 'market' or 'affected' in Article 6(3)(a) inevitably results in uncertainty for the litigants.[7] In this context, Mercer[8] states that the ability for claimants to choose the law of the forum as the applicable law where the conditions of Article 6(3)(b) are applicable is fundamental to the certainty and therefore viability of a competition damages action. Mercer[9] also indicates that defendants' tactics may exploit uncertainty so as to wear down the will of the claimants, or at least their financial resources, with a view to driving them into a settlement on terms which they would not otherwise accept. Accordingly, challenges by defendants that the law applicable is the law of the state where each of them is established could be a strategy which would explore the uncertainty surrounding Rome II.[10]

Bearing this in mind, Fitchen[11] and Mercer[12] appear to share the view that Article 6(3)(b) may provide for certainty by allowing the claimant to determine a single applicable law and dedicated legal procedure with which the domestic court and lawyers will be familiar. However, Fitchen[13] states that Article 6(3)(b) will contain the uncertainties threatened by Article 6(3)(a). In this context, he holds that 'Article 6(3) of Rome II appears to contain a disproportionate number of difficulties and examples of questionable drafting: even allowing for haste in drafting and also for novelty in connection with the type of under-developed non-contractual obligations at issue, this is puzzling. Why should there be so many difficulties in Article 6(3)?'[14]

[3] Ch 21.
[4] ibid.
[5] ibid.
[6] ibid.
[7] ibid.
[8] Ch 22.
[9] ibid.
[10] ibid.
[11] Ch 21.
[12] Ch 22.
[13] Ch 21.
[14] ibid.

There is certainly a case for reform, which may be strengthened by putting forward that the level of uncertainty may even rise if one considers the availability of the exemplary damage awards in some Member States. *Manfredi* states that 'in accordance with the principle of equivalence, it must be possible to award particular damages, such as exemplary or punitive damages, pursuant to actions founded on the Community competition rules, if such damages may be awarded pursuant to similar actions founded on domestic law.'[15] Given that the English Competition Appeal Tribunal recently awarded exemplary damages in a domestic competition case, *Cardiff City Transport*,[16] it seems clear that exemplary damages may be awarded under English law in an appropriate EU competition law case. Will a German court award exemplary damages when applying English law under Rome II?

Mercer[17] notes that 'German law[18] excludes enforcement of claims subject to the law of another state if they either reach substantially beyond that which is necessary to provide reasonable compensation or manifestly serve other purposes than providing reasonable compensation'.[19] He goes on to state that the main issue is to identify the objective pursued by the remedy under the applicable law noting that damages which merely go beyond what a national court considers to be appropriate compensation are unlikely to reach the standard necessary to invoke public policy. However, it has been submitted elsewhere[20] that given the fact that the exemplary damages by definition are 'additional to an award which fully compensates the claimant for his loss, and which are intended to punish and deter',[21] it is difficult to see how in practice a national court that regarded an award of exemplary or punitive damages as being contrary to public policy would not categorise such damages as excessive for the purposes of the Rome II Regulation. Professor Hay has noted that 'Recital 32 . . . acknowledges the aversion of many states against punitive damages and expressly authorizes the refusal to award them under the law otherwise applicable under the Regulation.'[22] Therefore, it has been argued that Recital 32 could be used to reduce the effect of the applicable law, entitling a Member State court not to give effect to *lex causae*, if the awarded damage would be non-compensatory and excessive under the *lex fori*.[23]

Nonetheless, categorising exemplary damages as excessive within the meaning of Recital 32 presupposes an analysis of what is the optimal level of damages for an EU competition law infringement. Refusal to award exemplary damages without an appropriate analysis of the effectiveness[24] of a Member State's remedy would fly in the face of Article 47(1) of the Charter of Fundamental Rights which appears to suggest that 'effective remedy' could

[15] Joined Cases C-295/04–C-298/04 *Manfredi v Lloyd Adriaticco* [2006] 5 CMLR 17 [93].

[16] Case Number: 1178/5/7/11, *2 Travel Group Plc (In Liquidation) v Cardiff City Transport Services Ltd* [2012] CAT 19.

[17] Ch 22.

[18] Art 40(3) of the German EGBGB.

[19] Ch 22.

[20] M Danov, *Jurisdiction and Judgments in Relation to EU Competition Law Claims* (Oxford, Hart Publishing, 2010).

[21] *Devenish Nutrition Ltd v Sanofi-Aventis SA* [2007] EWHC 2394; [2008] 2 WLR 637 (Ch) [14].

[22] P Hay, 'The Development of the Public Policy Barrier to Judgment Recognition within the European Community' (2007) *European Legal Forum* 289, 293.

[23] See more: M Danov, 'Awarding Exemplary (or Punitive) Antitrust Damages in EC Competition Cases with an International Element – the Rome II Regulation and the Commission's White Paper on Damages' (2008) 29 *ECLR* 430, 432–33.

[24] *Manfredi* (n 15) [62]. For the principle of effectiveness, which could be used to limit Member States' procedural autonomy, see more: F Becker, 'Application of Community law by Member States' Public Authorities: Between Autonomy and Effectiveness' (2007) 44 *CML Rev* 1035.

not be denied. Indeed, exemplary damages may well be justifiable from an economic perspective.[25]

Dnes[26] shows that an efficiency-based approach to antitrust damages suggests that the focus should be on deterrence rather than compensation, and efficiency rather than transfers. He suggests that there may even be a direct conflict between efficiency and compensatory aims. He goes on to argue that from an economic perspective, a debate on the optimal level of damages may be more fruitful than one on the evils of punitive damages or sham litigation.[27]

Therefore, the above analysis clearly shows that there is a level of uncertainty under Rome II which should be clarified with a view to reduce the risks for litigants.

III. WAYS FORWARD: ISSUES TO BE CONSIDERED

Fitchen[28] and Mercer[29] clearly demonstrate that allowing a private antitrust claimant to base his claim on the *lex fori* in cases where the markets in several countries have been affected would be key if the EU legislator wants to address the existing level of uncertainty. Indeed, Fitchen's analysis unambiguously suggests that the Union can achieve this 'by allowing the claimant to determine a single applicable law and dedicated legal procedure with which the domestic court and lawyers will be familiar. Not only litigation but also settlement will be simpler as the reduction in the imponderables will allow a better cost-benefit analysis and the formulation of more realistic settlement/litigation strategies.'[30]

A number of options for reform, which may address the current level of uncertainty, may be considered. Mercer is of the opinion that 'Of much greater practical utility therefore than new dedicated private international law rules for competition damages claims would be an online database of national court case law applying Rome II.'[31] The proposed tool could be useful in view of Fitchen's suggestion[32] that clarification of the uncertainties may be achieved through a periodic review of Rome II. However, Fitchen's proposal does not necessarily exclude a special Regulation dealing with private EU competition law actions. Indeed, the EU legislator has adopted a special Regulation 1/2003, which is meant to ensure that Articles 101 and 102 TFEU are applied effectively and uniformly across Europe.[33]

An amendment of Regulation 1/2003 to deal with the difficulties may be preferable in view of Tzakas's analysis in Chapter 17. Tzakas[34] convincingly raises some important choice-of-law issues which have not been properly taken into account in the context of collective redress. These issues are: recognition of representative entities; questions of

[25] Ch 23.
[26] ibid.
[27] ibid.
[28] Ch 21.
[29] Ch 22.
[30] Ch 21.
[31] Ch 22.
[32] Ch 21.
[33] See Recitals 1-8 of Council Regulation No 1/2003 on the implementation of the rules on competition laid down in Arts 101 and 102 TFEU.
[34] Ch 17.

standing; interchangeability of representative entities; representation of foreign claimants; and distribution of the obtained damages funds. This issue may be best addressed in a consistent way through an amendment of Regulation1/2003.

Indeed, an amendment of the Regulation may be justified if the Union legislator wishes to address the interplay between fines and damages which could be an issue under the current two-task structure of antitrust enforcement. As already noted,[35] this issue was considered by the UK legislator.[36] In their response to the Department for Business Innovation & Skills, Danov and Dnes have noted:

> The fine is meant to punish and deter the infringer. The redress is meant to compensate the victims of the competition law infringement. To date, these have been altogether different goals of the enforcement policy. However, the total level of the damages and fines paid would determine the incentives faced by infringing parties. If competition policy is to encourage growth by optimal deterrence of the most harmful infringements, it is important that these incentives are maintained close to an optimal level (neither too high nor too low). If damages claims became larger, fines may need to be adjusted. Although with the current state of competition law enforcement, this point may be some way off, it should be noted there is no scope for offsetting fines and damages in the current system. A public enforcement action would normally precede a damages action. The level of damages would be far from certain at the stage when an authority decides on the level of fines. Similarly, in a follow-on action, the court is supposed to award damages which would compensate the victim/s irrespective of the fine imposed by the competition authority. This shows once again that it is inefficient to have one set of proceedings before the OFT in order to establish a breach of competition law, and another set of proceedings before the CAT in order for a claimant to prove that damage has been caused to him. In other words, there is limited scope for consolidation of the fines and the damages in the current system, and consolidating both procedures before the CAT might be a good way to achieve this.[37]

There may be a case for addressing the issue at EU level as the recent Report by the European Parliament[38] suggests that Regulation 1/2003 may need to be amended with a view to addressing the interplay between fines and damages.[39] Dnes has convincingly demonstrated that 'the role of litigation to deter genuinely anticompetitive conduct should be embraced, allowing the integration of litigation into the proper focus of modern competition law: the deterrence of inefficient restrictive practices.'[40] The case for a reform may be strengthened if the Union legislator aims to promote free circulation of decisions in relation to EU competition law further safeguarding the defendant's right to a fair trial, as well as upholding the independence of Member State courts vis-à-vis NCAs.[41] These difficulties will be discussed in the following Part of this book.

[35] Ch 20.

[36] Department for Business Innovation & Skills, *Private Actions in Competition Law: A Consultation on Options for Reform*,24April2012,www.bis.gov.uk/assets/biscore/consumer-issues/docs/p/12-742-private-actions-in-competition-law-consultation.pdf .

[37] M Danov and S Dnes, 'Private actions in competition law: a consultation on options for reform. Response form' submitted to the UK Government, Department for Business, Innovation and Skills on 24 July 2012.

[38] European Parliament, Report on 'Towards a Coherent European Approach to Collective Redress' (2011/2089 (INI)), 12 January 2012.

[39] ibid p 15.

[40] Ch 23.

[41] M Danov, 'EU Competition Law Enforcement: Is Brussels I suited to dealing with all the challenges?' (2012) 61 *ICLQ* 27.

Part V

Recognition and Enforcement of Foreign Judgments

25

Introduction: Preclusive Effects of Foreign Judgments/Settlements across Europe

MIHAIL DANOV AND FLORIAN BECKER

I. INTRODUCTION

The fact that the majority of EU competition law infringements cause damage to businesses and consumers in several countries[1] clearly demonstrates that the preclusive effects of any judgment/settlement is an important consideration for litigants who would like to make sure that the issues would not be reopened in other jurisdictions. It is well established that foreign judgments have a *res judicata* effect in England only after they have been duly recognised,[2] which suggests that the recognising court should be entitled to determine whether a foreign judgment is in conflict with its public policy, and EU competition law in particular. No foreign judgment can be enforced in England until it has been recognised.[3] Enforcement will not always follow, though. Recognition alone is sufficient, for example, where a foreign court's decision is merely declaring that a contract is contrary to Articles 101 and 102 TFEU and thus void. It is well established that an English court will have jurisdiction to hear and determine a claim for enforcement of a judgment of a foreign court.[4] Is the Brussels I Regulation suited to dealing with all the challenges arising with regard to EU competition law enforcement across Europe?

The Brussels regime is based on mutual trust in the legal systems within the EU.[5] Article 33 of the Brussels I Regulation clearly stipulates that 'a judgment given in a Member State shall be recognised in the other Member States without any special procedure being required'. Judgments of the Member States' courts are eligible for registration for enforcement in England.[6] Such registration serves as a decision that the judgment is recognised for the purposes of the Brussels I Regulation.[7] Article 36 of the Regulation holds that under no circumstances may a foreign judgment be reviewed as to its substance. In other words, the accuracy of findings of law or fact made by the adjudicating court cannot be reviewed by

[1] See Chs 2, 3, 4, 5, 13 and 18.

[2] For the position under English common law, see P Barnett, *Res Judicata, Estoppel and Foreign Judgments: The preclusive effects of foreign judgments in private international law* (Oxford, OUP, 2001) 31 and 41. For the position under the Brussels I Regulation, see Case 42/76 *Josef de Wolf v Harry Cox* [1977] ECR 1759 [3] (judgment), 1772 (AG Mayras).

[3] CPR 74.9(2)(a).

[4] CPR PD 6B, para 3.1(10).

[5] Recital 16 of the Brussels Regulation. See also: Case C-172/91 *Sonntag v Waidmann* [1993] ECR I-1963 [70].

[6] See CPR 74.3.

[7] See CPR 74.10.

the recognising court.[8] Reopening on the merits an EU competition law claim, which has been tried in a Member State's court, would run directly against the Regulation's aim for rapid recognition and enforcement of foreign judgments. As a result, a judgment given in a Member State would be easily recognised in England. Such '[r]ecognition gives the foreign judgment the force of *res judicata*'.[9] But, does this mean that under the Brussels I Regulation a foreign judgment in relation to an EU competition law claim would automatically be given the same effects in the recognising state as it has in the state in which it was rendered?[10]

II. THE PUBLIC POLICY EXCEPTION AND SOME SPECIFIC ISSUES

Article 34(1) lays down an important exception to the duty of an English court to recognise a foreign judgment.[11] It provides that a judgment given by the court of a Member State shall not be recognised 'if such recognition is manifestly contrary to public policy in the state in which recognition is sought.'[12] Although Articles 101 and 102 TFEU regulate relationships between private undertakings, EU competition law provisions may often be enforced in the public interest. The importance of competition policy for achieving the objectives of the EU could suggest that the public policy defence would be often pleaded where foreign judgments in relation to EU competition claims are at issue.[13] Does a non-application or a wrong application of Articles 101 and 102 TFEU entitle the English court to refuse recognition of a foreign judgment in relation to an EU competition law claim? What are the specific issues arising with regard to EU competition law actions?

A. Complex Issues: Two-task Enforcement Structure – Interplay between Public and Private Enforcement

The fact that the National Competition Authorities (NCAs) and national courts have the powers to apply Articles 101 and 102 TFEU in individual cases suggest that there could be specific issues.

First, one may raise the question of whether proceedings before a national competition authority seeking to establish an EU competition law infringement fall within the scope of Brussels I.[14] It is well established that the question as to whether there is an EU competition law infringement should be determined as a matter of EU substantive law by an NCA (which is an administrative public authority) as well as by any Member State court.

[8] Case C-7/98 *Krombach v Bamberski* [2000] ECR I-1935 [36]. See also Jenard Report [1979] OJ C59/1, 46.
[9] *Josef de Wolf* (n 2) 48 (AG Mayras) and [3] (Court of Justice decision). See also Barnett (n 2) 273.
[10] Compare: Case 145/86 *Hoffmann v Krieg* [1988] ECR 645 [11].
[11] *Josef de Wolf* (n 2) [3].
[12] It should be specified that the meaning of that provision is that the question is not whether a judgment is itself contrary to public policy, but whether its recognition or an order for its enforcement would have that effect. See *Hoffmann* (n 10) [17] (AG Darmon).
[13] See Case C-126/97 *Eco Swiss China Time v Benetton International ('Eco Swiss')* [1999] ECR I-3055 [38]; Case C-38/98 *Renault v Maxicar* [2000] ECR I-2973. See more: Ch 26.
[14] M Danov, 'EU Competition Law Enforcement: Is Brussels I suited to dealing with all the challenges?' (2012) 61 *ICLQ* 27.

However, there would be an important difference as far as the procedure is concerned. While a national court would apply civil procedure rules that presuppose respect of due process, an NCA would apply administrative procedure rules that could potentially raise concerns as to the undertaking's right to a fair trial and hearing.[15] Should Article 32 of the Brussels I Regulation be interpreted broadly to cover decisions of a national competition authority? Can NCAs' decisions be recognised and enforced under Brussels I? Are decisions of NCAs within the scope of the Brussels I Regulation?

Secondly, the interplay between fines and damages is an important issue, which needs to be carefully considered, in this Part as well. Professor Kessedjian has argued:

> if in the same case, the same company is ordered to pay fines and is also ordered to pay damages for private enforcement, the requested judge should probably take into consideration the overall amount of penalties paid before it accepts the recognition and enforcement of the damages ordered by the judge of origin.[16]

The proposal is very innovative and original, but controversial in view of the fact that the UK government is considering whether the extent to which a company has made redress should be taken into account by the competition authorities when determining what level of fine to impose.[17] However, it raises questions: should a recognising judge be entitled to reduce a compensatory damage award by taking into account fines imposed in entirely different proceedings (between a regulator and an infringing legal entity) which the judgment creditor was not a party to? Should a recognising judge be entitled to take account of the high fines imposed by a regulator in order to reduce an award which compensates the claimant for his loss? May a judge assess the excessiveness of the compensatory damages at the recognition and enforcement stage without reviewing the merits of the foreign judgment? The two-task enforcement structure of competition law and the interplay between fines and damages raise important and complex issues, which need to be carefully considered.

B. Recognition and Enforcement of Foreign Judgments in Relation to Collective Redress Antitrust Proceedings

Given the cross-border nature of most EU competition law infringement, it seems clear that the questions related to the preclusive effects of collective judgment/settlements need to be carefully considered at EU level.[18] There are three main issues that need to be considered in

[15] IS Forrester, 'Due Process in EC Competition Cases: A Distinguished Institution with Flawed Procedures' (2009) 34 EL Rev 817; J Killick and P Berghe, 'This is Not the Time to Be Tinkering with Regulation 1/2003 – It is Time for Fundamental Reform – Europe Should Have Change We Can Believe in' (2010) *Competition Law Review* 259. See Art 6(1) TEU. See also Art 6(1) ECHR and Art 47(2) of the Charter of Fundamental Rights of the European Union [2000] OJ C364/1. See further, J Kuhling, 'Fundamental Rights' in A von Bogdandy and J Bast (eds), *Principles of European Constitutional Law*, 2nd edn (Oxford, Hart Publishing, 2010) 479–514; P Craig, *The Lisbon Treaty: Law, Politics and Treaty Reform* (Oxford, OUP, 2010) 193–245.

[16] C Kessedjian, 'Recognition and Enforcement of Foreign Judgments', in J Basedow, S Francq and L Idot (eds), *International Antitrust Litigation: Conflict of Laws and Coordination* (Oxford. Hart Publishing, 2012) 245, 255.

[17] Department for Business Innovation & Skills, *Private Actions in Competition Law: A Consultation on Options for Reform*,24April2012www.bis.gov.uk/assets/biscore/consumer-issues/docs/p/12-742-private-actions-in-competition-law-consultation.pdf.

[18] B Hess, 'The Brussels I Regulation: Recent case law of the Court of Justice and the Commission's proposed recast' (2012) 49 *Common Market Law Review* 1075, 1091–92.

the context of recognition and enforcement of foreign class judgments in the European context. As already noted,[19] no rational defendant will want to settle unless the questions related to the preclusive effects of collective settlements are addressed at EU level. What are the preclusive effects of collective settlements? Will the requirement for a 'fair trial and hearing' trigger the public policy defence in relation to a class judgment issued against absent plaintiffs under the opt-out regime?

C. Recognition and Enforcement of Foreign Judgments Awarding Exemplary Damages[20]

The fact that the CAT has very recently awarded exemplary damages in a competition law case suggests that the English courts would normally enforce a Member State's court judgment awarding punitive damages in EU antitrust claims. However, Recital 32 indicates that on the basis of Article 34(1) of the Brussels I Regulation, other Member State courts can deny recognition and enforcement of the part of a judgment awarding excessive punitive antitrust damages, as being contrary to their public policy to recognise and enforce it.[21]

One may argue that a court charged with the recognition of a foreign judgment under the Brussels I Regulation is not at liberty to consult Rome II's Recitals to determine public policy for the purposes of Article 34 of Brussels I. This may be strengthened by noting that to refer to Rome II at this stage seems very like reopening the merits of the earlier case to question the application of the law of the original court. However, it should be recalled that Recital 32 is meant to acknowledge that punitive damages awards may be against the public policy of some Member States.[22] If this were so for choice of law purposes, it is difficult to see why the concept of public policy should be different for recognition and enforcement purposes.[23] Is a Member State entitled to refuse recognition of part of the judgment, the exemplary antitrust damages as being contrary to its public policy in view of *Manfredi*? Is there a case for reform?

D. *Res Judicata*: Joint Tortfeasors – Parties and their Privies

A claimant may often wish to pursue an EU competition law claim against two defendants who are joint tortfeasors as, for example, being parties to a cartel agreement in breach of EU competition law. In *Cooper Tire*,[24] Mr Justice Teare stated in a different context that

[19] See Ch 18.

[20] See M Danov, *Jurisdiction and Judgments in Relation to EU Competition Law Claims* (Oxford, Hart Publishing, 2010). See also: M Danov, 'Awarding Exemplary (or Punitive) Antitrust Damages in EC Competition Cases with an International Element – the Rome II Regulation and the Commission's White Paper on damages' (2008) 29 ECLR 430, 434–35.

[21] Danov (2010) (n 20) 174 - 178. See also: P Hay, 'The Development of the Public Policy Barrier to Judgment Recognition within the European Community' (2007) *The European Legal Forum* 289, 293–94; MR Isidro, 'Punitive Damages from a Private International Law Perspective' in H Koziol and V Wilcox (eds), *Punitive Damages: Common Law and Civil Law Perspectives* (Vienna/New York, Springer, 2009) 237, 250.

[22] Hay (n 21) 293. See also: Commission (EC) 'The common position of the Council on the adoption of a Regulation of the European Parliament and of the Council on the law applicable to non-contractual obligations ("Rome II")' (Communication) COM (2006) 566 final; Isidro (n 21) 250; R Plender and M Wilderspin, *The European Private International Law of Obligations* 3rd edn (London, Sweet & Maxwell, 2009) 751–52.

[23] Hay (n 21) 293–94.

[24] *Cooper Tire & Rubber Company v Shell Chemicals UK Ltd* [2009] EWHC 2609 (Comm).

'[w]hether joint tortfeasors have a sufficient privity of interest that might lead to the application of *res judicata* is not the subject of clear authority'.[25] In this context, it is well established that:

> A *res judicata* is a decision pronounced by a judicial or other tribunal with jurisdiction over the cause of action and the parties, which disposes once and for all of the fundamental matters decided, so that, except on appeal, they cannot be re-litigated between persons bound by the judgment. A judgment *in personam* binds the parties and their privies.[26]

There are specific issues arising with regard to EU competition law infringements involving joint tortfeasors in a European context because at the moment, national 'rules as to parties and privies apply to foreign decisions *in personam*'.[27] Section 6 of the Law Reform (Married Women and Tortfeasors) Act 1935 and sections 3 and 4 of the Civil Liability (Contribution) Act 1978 would be the relevant rules in England. Might *res judicata* apply as between joint tortfeasors (eg parties to the same cartel agreement; or parent and subsidiary)? Do joint tortfeasors have a sufficient privity of interest that might lead to the application of *res judicata*? Mr Justice Teare held that whether or not *res judicata* applied to joint tortfeasors on the grounds of privity of interest depended upon the facts of each case. Is there a need for these issues to be addressed by the EU legislator in the context of cross-border EU competition law actions? Or should they be dealt with by the individual Member State's legal orders?

III. THE STRUCTURE OF THIS PART

Part V addresses questions regarding the recognition and enforcement of foreign judgments in relation to EU competition law actions. In this context, Professor Beaumont focuses on the specific difficulties arising in this context. Inter alia, he presents the Commission proposal for the recast of Brussels I, which was made in December 2010,[28] and its subsequent evolution following the Justice and Home Affairs Council of the EU meeting on 13 and 14 December 2011 on which political guidelines were adopted on the abolition of *exequatur* in the recast of Brussels I.[29] Professor Bariatti writes on the recognition and enforcement of foreign class action judgments, focusing on the specific issues which arise in the context of the US and Dutch class judgments and settlements. Finally, some conclusions are drawn.

[25] ibid [80].
[26] KR Handley, *Spence, Bower and Handley, Res Judicata*, 4th edn (London, LexisNexis, 2009) 1.
[27] ibid 127. See also: *Carl-Zeiss (No 2)* [1967] 1 AC 853.
[28] COM (2010) 748 final.
[29] See more: Ch 26.

26

Abolition of *Exequatur* under the Brussels I Regulation as it Affects EU Competition Law

PAUL BEAUMONT

I. INTRODUCTION

The Commission's proposal for the recast of Brussels I was made in December 2010.[1] The complete abolition of *exequatur* (the declaration of enforceability) was proposed for all subjects except for cases of defamation and other non-contractual obligations relating to privacy and personality rights, and for certain types of collective redress claims.[2] In the areas where *exequatur* was to be abolished, the Commission proposed deletion of the public policy defence currently found in Article 34(1) of Brussels I. The Commission proposed replacing the public policy defence with a narrower defence in the country of enforcement, based on the 'fundamental principles underlying the right to a fair trial'. The Commission proposed retention in Article 43 of the recast of the defences relating to irreconcilable judgments that are currently in Article 34(3) and (4) of Brussels I. The Commission also proposed deletion of the special defence in Article 34(2) of Brussels I where a judgment was given in default of appearance and the courts of enforcement can judge whether service on the defender was done in such a way that he could not arrange for his defence and where he was unable to challenge the judgment in the country of origin. The Commission proposed that this ground should cease to exist in the country of enforcement and be replaced by a new review mechanism in the country of origin that would have the same content as Article 34(2) of Brussels I.[3]

At the Justice and Home Affairs Council of the EU meeting on 13 and 14 December 2011 political guidelines were adopted on the abolition of *exequatur* in the recast of Brussels I.[4]

[1] COM (2010) 748 final (referred to as the 'Commission recast' in this paper).

[2] See Art 37(3) of the Commission recast.

[3] See Art 45 of the Commission recast. One additional ground for review was added by the Commission: where the defender 'was prevented from contesting the claim by reason of force majeure or due to extraordinary circumstances without any fault on his part'. It is wise to assume that this additional ground will be covered in the final version of Brussels I by the public policy defence in the country of enforcement because the Member States in the Council wanted a wider basis for review than that offered by the Commission, and wanted it to be concentrated in the country of enforcement to save the costs and time involved for a defender in having to initiate a review in the country of origin and raise defences in the country of enforcement.

[4] See www.consilium.europa.eu/uedocs/cms_data/docs/pressdata/en/jha/126932.pdf.

See p 22 of the press release. Unfortunately neither the press release nor the background note that is referred to in the press release give the reader any information about the nature and content of the political guidelines.

As anticipated earlier,[5] the Council has fulfilled the mandate set for it by the European Council of abolishing *exequatur* by seeing that as the abolition of a stage in the process, rather than as a requirement to abolish the 'grounds for refusal of enforcement'.[6] By doing so it has been able to agree to abolish the *exequatur* in all cases covered by Brussels I, including those relating to privacy and personality rights and collective redress. No longer will there be a declaration of enforceability stage of proceedings at which only the Brussels I grounds for non-enforcement can be invoked, but instead all grounds for non-enforcement (the ones in Brussels I and the national ones) will be heard together. This will have the effect of reversing the outcome of the recent decision of the Court of Justice of the European Union in *Prism Investments*.[7] In that case the defender alleged that he had already paid the debt that he owed, but the Court of Justice decided that this was not a defence under Brussels I and therefore could not be raised at the declaration of enforceability stage, but only later at the actual enforcement stage. This seems to be a very impractical and unwise decision by the Court of Justice. In a case where the defender is arguing full or partial payment of the debt but has an alternative EU ground for non-enforcement that he might wish to argue (public policy, irreconcilable judgments or unable to defend himself properly in a default judgment case), the defender currently has to make a tactical decision whether to invoke the EU grounds at the declaration of enforceability stage (possibly losing the argument and the costs associated with it), or only contest the judgment at the actual enforcement stage relying on the prior payment of the debt and losing the EU defences. Dealing with all the relevant defences in one procedure is surely more economical in terms of time and costs for both parties, and removes the need for difficult tactical decisions by the defender.[8] This will be one of the improvements achieved by the revised Brussels I.

In the final version of the recast of Brussels I agreed by the Council in December 2012 it is clear that all of the grounds for refusal of enforcement contained in Article 34 of Brussels I are retained in Regulation 1215/2012 (OJ 2012 L351/1). In particular, substantive, as well as procedural, public policy is retained as a defence. This is very important in the context of EU competition law because of earlier case law of the Court of Justice of the European Union indicating that certain aspects of EU competition law are part of the public policy of each of the laws of the Member States.

II. COURT OF JUSTICE OF THE EUROPEAN UNION CASE LAW ON EU COMPETITION LAW BEING PART OF EU PUBLIC POLICY

A. *Eco Swiss*

The leading case is that of *Eco Swiss*.[9] This Full Court judgment concerns a Dutch court's decision whether to recognise and enforce an arbitration award rendered in Amsterdam.

[5] See P Beaumont and E Johnston, 'Can Exequatur Be Abolished in Brussels I whilst Retaining a Public Policy Defence?' (2010) 6 *Journal of Private International Law* 249.

[6] ibid 249–50.

[7] Case C-139/10 *Prism Investments BV v Jaap Anne van der Meer*, judgment of 13 October 2011, [2012] I.L.Pr. 13.

[8] The German Government specifically asked the Court of Justice to allow for such procedural economy by dealing with the EU grounds and the national grounds for non-enforcement at the same time, ibid para 41, but this was rejected by the Court at paras 42–43.

[9] Case C-126/97 *Eco Swiss China Time Ltd v Benetton International NV* [1999] ECR I-3055.

The arbitration award of damages was based on an illegal contract under EU competition law. Despite the illegality of the agreement not being pled before the tribunal, the judgment debtors objected to enforcement of the award on the basis that, under national law, such an award based on a void contract is an affront to national public policy. The Netherlands Supreme Court requested a preliminary ruling from the CJEU on a number of questions. The key question for our purposes was the second one, which was as follows:

> (2) If the court considers that an arbitration award is in fact contrary to Article 85 of the EC Treaty [now Article 101 TFEU], must it, on that ground and notwithstanding the rules of Netherlands procedural law set out in paragraphs 4.2 and 4.4 above [according to which a party may claim annulment of an arbitration award only on a limited number of grounds, one ground being that an award is contrary to public policy, which generally does not cover the mere fact that through the terms or enforcement of an arbitration award no effect is given to a prohibition laid down by competition law], allow a claim for annulment of that award if the claim otherwise complies with statutory requirements?

Advocate General Saggio noted that the proper functioning of the competition rules is a fundamental objective of the Community. He quoted the ECJ in *Hoechst*,[10] where it was observed that 'the function of the rules on competition in the common market is to prevent competition being distorted to the detriment of the public interest, individual undertakings and consumers'.[11] He concluded that the Court of Justice should tell the Dutch court that:

> the Community rules on competition and in particular the prohibition on agreements contained in Article 85 [now Article 101 TFEU] [should be regarded] as matters of 'public policy' and to extend the ambit of the Netherlands rule on judicial review of arbitration awards to include matters of 'public Community policy' . . . This view that the rules on competition are part of the 'public economic policy of the Community' finds wide support in the legal literature and in the case-law of many Member States.[12]

The Court of Justice (sitting as a plenary of 13 judges) found that the review of arbitration awards should be limited in scope. Refusal to recognise an arbitration award should only be in exceptional circumstances.[13] In a few short paragraphs the full Court set out its reasoning why this was one of those exceptional circumstances:

> 36. However, according to Article 3(g) of the EC Treaty (now, after amendment, Article 3(1)(g) EC), Article 81 EC (ex Article 85) constitutes a fundamental provision which is essential for the accomplishment of the tasks entrusted to the Community and, in particular, for the functioning of the internal market. The importance of such a provision led the framers of the Treaty to provide expressly, in Article 81(2) EC (ex Article 85(2)), that any agreements or decisions prohibited pursuant to that article are to be automatically void.
>
> 37. It follows that where its domestic rules of procedure require a national court to grant an application for annulment of an arbitration award where such an application is founded on failure to observe national rules of public policy, it must also grant such an application where it is founded on failure to comply with the prohibition laid down in Article 81(1) EC (ex Article 85(1)).

[10] Joined Cases 46/87 and 227/88 *Hoechst AG v Commission of the European Communities* [1989] ECR 2859 [25].
[11] Case C-126/97 (n 9), para 36 of his Opinion.
[12] ibid para 38.
[13] ibid para 35 of the judgment.

38. That conclusion is not affected by the fact that the New York Convention of 10 June 1958 on the Recognition and Enforcement of Foreign Arbitral Awards, which has been ratified by all the Member States, provides that recognition and enforcement of an arbitration award may be refused only on certain specific grounds, namely where the award does not fall within the terms of the submission to arbitration or goes beyond its scope, where the award is not binding on the parties or where recognition or enforcement of the award would be contrary to the public policy of the country where such recognition and enforcement are sought (Article V(1)(c) and (e) and II(b) of the New York Convention).

39. For the reasons stated in paragraph 36 above, the provisions of Article 81 EC (ex Article 85) may be regarded as a matter of public policy within the meaning of the New York Convention.

40. Lastly, it should be recalled that, as explained in paragraph 34 above, arbitrators, unlike national courts and tribunals, are not in a position to request this Court to give a preliminary ruling on questions of interpretation of Community law. However, it is manifestly in the interest of the Community legal order that, in order to forestall differences of interpretation, every Community provision should be given a uniform interpretation, irrespective of the circumstances in which it is to be applied (Case C-88/91 *Federconsorzi* [1992] ECR I-4035, paragraph 7). It follows that, in the circumstances of the present case, unlike *Van Schijndel and Van Veen*, Community law requires that questions concerning the interpretation of the prohibition laid down in Article 81(1) EC (ex Article 85(1)) should be open to examination by national courts when asked to determine the validity of an arbitration award and that it should be possible for those questions to be referred, if necessary, to the Court of Justice for a preliminary ruling.

41. The answer to be given to the second question must therefore be that a national court to which application is made for annulment of an arbitration award must grant that application if it considers that the award in question is in fact contrary to Article 81 EC (ex Article 85), where its domestic rules of procedure require it to grant an application for annulment founded on failure to observe national rules of public policy.

It is only paragraph 36 of the Court's judgment which explains why what is now Article 101 TFEU is a rule of Community/Union public policy. The Court's reasoning is very short and seems to contain only two elements: reliance on Articles 3(1)(g) and 81(2) EC.

The Court relied on Article 3(1)(g) of the European Community Treaty as authority for the proposition that Article 81 EC (now Article 101 TFEU) is a 'fundamental provision'; it seems relevant to ask whether the Court's view that Article 101 TFEU is an aspect of EU public policy would be altered by the fact that the Lisbon Treaty did not directly replace Article 3(1)(g) EC?

It seems highly unlikely that this Treaty change would alter the Court's view on Article 101 TFEU being a matter of EU public policy. The loss of Article 3(1)(g) EC – which only provided that 'a system ensuring that competition in the internal market is not distorted' is one of the activities of the European Community – is surely adequately compensated for by Article 3(1)(b) TFEU providing that 'the establishing of the competition rules necessary for the functioning of the internal market' is an area falling within the exclusive competence of the Union. While the latter loses the sense that the Treaty articles on competition are themselves part of the activity of the EC in securing a good internal market, they establish how core the whole of the EU's competition rules, impliedly including the Treaty articles which are at the pinnacle of those rules, are to the Union by including them within the small band of issues that the Union has a priori exclusive competence to regulate.[14]

[14] Further arguments can be made based on Art 119 TFEU which refers to the activities of the Member States and the Union set out in Art 3 TEU being 'conducted in accordance with the principle of an open market economy

Article 101(2) TFEU retains the terms of Article 81(2) EC that any agreement or decision prohibited by the Article 'shall be automatically void'.

The next part of the Court's reasoning is rather surprising, at two levels:

(1) The New York Convention is not part of EU law and therefore the Court of Justice had no jurisdiction in a preliminary ruling to give an interpretation of its provisions. What is now Article 267 TFEU gives the Court jurisdiction to give preliminary rulings on the interpretation of the EU Treaties and on the validity and interpretation of acts of the institutions of the Union. Thus it was perfectly competent for the CJEU to rule on whether Article 101 TFEU is a provision of EU public policy, and even to say that by definition that makes it a rule of public policy of each of the laws of the Member States of the EU, but not to rule on the scope of application of the public policy exception to recognition and enforcement of arbitral awards under the New York Convention. It should have left it to the national court to make the very simple deduction that if a breach of a particular provision of Union law is contrary to Union public policy, and therefore contrary to its national public policy, it should, where it has competence to do so, apply the public policy exception to refuse to recognise an arbitral award that is contrary to that provision of Union law.
(2) The reference for a preliminary ruling did not concern a case under the New York Convention, and the issue of its interpretation was not referred to the Court of Justice by the Dutch court.[15]

The Court stated that the New York Convention provides that recognition and enforcement of an arbitration award may be refused where the award is contrary to the public policy of the country where recognition and enforcement is sought. Nevertheless, here, an arbitration award is to be annulled even though it is in conformity with domestic rules of public policy, as it fails to comply with EU Competition law provisions. Thus, the ECJ was suggesting that the competition law provisions are of such importance that they should be regarded as aspects of national public policy in the future. The Court went further, and for some unknown reason, added that the EU Competition rules must be considered part of the national public policy exception in the New York Convention. If this is the case under the New York Convention, there is little reason to doubt that the same must be true for the public policy clause under Article 34(1) of the Brussels I Regulation.

This authority suggests that an illegal competitive agreement under EU law, at least one falling under the prohibition in Article 101 TFEU, could be caught by the public policy defence under Brussels I and therefore prevent the recognition and enforcement of a judgment upholding such an agreement.

In paragraph 40 of its ruling the Court is treading on the dangerous ground of whether national courts have any kind of EU law obligation to review arbitration awards to ensure that the content of those awards is compatible with EU law. This could be read as pointing

with free competition'. The Protocol on the Internal Market and Competition Annexed to the TEU also states that the 'internal market as set out in Article 3 of the Treaty on European Union includes a system ensuring that competition is not distorted'.

[15] Not only did the Dutch court not refer any issues on the interpretation of the New York Convention, but the matter is not discussed at all in the Advocate General's Opinion. Komninos points out that: 'the New York Convention was not applicable to the case at issue, because the award had been rendered domestically and was subject to a setting aside and not to an *exequatur* procedure in a foreign country.' see A Komninos, 'Arbitration and EU Competition Law', in J Basedow, S Francq and L Idot (eds) *International Antitrust Litigation* (Oxford, Hart, 2012) 191, 218.

out an implication of the Court's own desire for the uniform interpretation of EU law throughout the Union (something it infers from the obligation of the highest courts in the EU to refer cases on the interpretation of EU law to the CJEU). This implication is that although arbitral tribunals cannot refer questions to the CJEU for a preliminary ruling, national legal systems must provide a mechanism for review of arbitral awards by their courts so that those national courts can, and ultimately the highest court competent to entertain such a review must, refer such cases to the CJEU, or follow established decisions of the CJEU, on any question of interpretation of EU law that might impinge on the validity of the arbitral award. Of course the Court cannot and did not explicitly require such a structure of review in each legal system of the EU in a case that was referred by one national court seeking instruction on whether it could extend the national public policy review of arbitral awards made in that country to an EU public policy review. The case before the CJEU was decided just by saying that Article 101 TFEU is a rule of EU public policy, and if the national court can review an arbitral award because it is contrary to national public policy, then it can review it as being contrary to Article 101 TFEU, as it is part of national public policy (this is the ratio of the Court's decision seen in paragraph 41). It is a pity that the CJEU did not confine itself to saying so, because it is not a matter for the CJEU or for EU law to determine the nature of the relationship between arbitral awards and their review by national courts. This is something that was explored in the review of Brussels I and it reinforced the exclusion of arbitration from the scope of Brussels I. Brussels I clearly does not apply to 'any action or judgment concerning the annulment, review, appeal, or recognition and enforcement of an arbitral award'.[16] One of the reasons why the CJEU should not be laying down obligations on national courts to review arbitral awards for compliance with Union law (even parts of Union law that constitute Union public policy) is that there is no consensus on which national courts have the responsibility to review arbitral awards. The Commission proposal for a recast of Brussels I sought to clarify that it is only the national courts of the seat of the arbitration that would have competence to rule on the validity of the arbitration agreement when it is contested. However, this was not agreed by the Council and even the Commission proposal shied away from regulating which courts in the EU have jurisdiction to rule on the validity of an arbitral award. Therefore paragraph 40 of the Court's judgment in *Eco Swiss* should be read narrowly as applying only to the situation that presented itself to the Dutch courts in that particular case of review of a Dutch arbitral award, consistent with the Court's own careful use of 'in the circumstances of the present case' in that paragraph.

[16] See Reg 1215/2012 Recital 12. In any case this is the current law as noted by Advocate General Kokott in her opinion in Case C-185/07 *Allianz SpA v West Tankers* [2009] ECR I-663:

> '47. The New York Convention lays down rules which must be respected not by the arbitrators themselves but by the courts of the States in question, for example, rules relating to agreements whereby parties refer a dispute to arbitration or on the recognition and enforcement of arbitral awards by the courts of a Contracting State. As the wording also suggests, the parties to the Brussels Convention thus wished to exclude arbitration in its entirety, over and above the actual arbitration proceedings, including proceedings brought before the national courts which are related to arbitration.
>
> 48. In the Schlosser Report the following cases are given as examples: the appointment or dismissal of arbitrators, the fixing of the place of arbitration or the extension of the time-limit for making awards. In the same way a judgment determining whether an arbitration agreement is valid or not, or because it is invalid, ordering the parties not to continue the arbitration proceedings, is not covered by the Brussels Convention. Nor does the Brussels Convention cover proceedings and decisions concerning applications for the revocation, amendment, recognition and enforcement of arbitral awards.'

The national court case law following *Eco Swiss* has largely given a narrow construction to the power of national courts to strike down an arbitral award as being contrary to public policy on the basis that the award violates EU competition law.[17] Only the Dutch courts have given a relatively broad construction to this power.[18] Komninos therefore advocates a minimalist approach[19] to the exercise of the power by national courts to strike down arbitral awards on grounds of public policy on the basis that they are in breach of EU competition law. He believes that arbitral awards should be 'accorded the same degree of deference'[20] under the New York Convention as court judgments are under Brussels I. Thus review of the merits must be avoided when deciding on the review of arbitral awards[21] or when seeking recognition and enforcement of a judgment under the Brussels I Regulation.[22] Komninos proposes that:

> a public policy violation and a corresponding duty of national courts to set aside or refuse to enforce an arbitral award should only arise when the competition law issue has been totally neglected by the arbitrators with the manifest aim to evade the competition rules or in the case of a prima facie illegality or conflict with such rules.[23]

He further argues that:

> The competition law violation must be very serious, in order for an arbitral award to be refused recognition or enforcement on public policy grounds. A restriction of competition in a horizontal agreement is likely to be more detrimental for competition than a restriction in a vertical agreement. A cartel would certainly qualify as a repugnant infringement of the competition rules. Another similar distinction can be made between per se rules of prohibition and rule of reason competition law violations. It should be only per se violations that should attract attention by State courts when reviewing an arbitral award.[24]

B. *Renault*

The *Renault* case[25] was decided by the Fifth Chamber of the CJEU after the decision of the Full Court of the CJEU in *Eco Swiss*. A French company sought enforcement of a French judgment concerning free circulation of goods and freedom of competition against an Italian undertaking in Italy. The Italian company appealed the decision to recognise and enforce the judgment in Italy. The Court of Appeal in Turin referred questions on the interpretation of the Treaty provisions on free movement of goods and abuse of a dominant position and on the interpretation of the public policy provision under the Brussels Convention to see whether it could deny recognition and enforcement to the French judgment under Article 27 of the Brussels Convention (the predecessor of Article 34 of the Brussels I Regulation).

[17] See the cases in Belgium, France, Germany, Greece and Italy discussed by A Komninos, 'Arbitration and EU Competition Law' in J Basedow, S Francq and L Idot (eds) *International Antitrust Litigation* (Oxford, Hart, 2012) 191, 213–18.

[18] ibid 217.

[19] ibid 218.

[20] ibid 220.

[21] ibid 221.

[22] Art 36.

[23] Komninos (n 17) 220.

[24] ibid.

[25] Case C-38/98 *Renault v Maxicar* [2000] ECR I-2973.

Advocate General Alber gave his opinion on 22 June 1999 just 21 days after the Full Court decision in *Eco Swiss*. Unfortunately it is clear that he had written his opinion before the judgment in *Eco Swiss*, because that case is not referred to at all in his opinion.[26] The Advocate General correctly emphasised the exceptional nature of the public policy defence and noted that the Convention prevented the foreign court from substantially reviewing the decision.[27] Therefore a mere error in the application of EU competition law by the court of origin is not enough to justify the refusal of recognition of that judgment in another Member State on the basis of public policy.[28] The error would have to be a 'clear violation of fundamental principles' of EU law.[29] In this case Advocate General Alber gave a clear opinion that there was no breach of EU competition law. He did this by analysing what is now Article 102 TFEU and applying what had already been decided by the CJEU in an earlier case between the same parties. That earlier decision had clarified that Article 102 TFEU did not apply to the simple acquisition of rights in respect of ornamental designs for bodywork components for automobiles. Such an abuse could occur if there were to be an arbitrary refusal to deliver spare parts to independent repairers, if prices were fixed for spare parts at an unfair level or if a decision were taken no longer to produce spare parts for particular models even though many cars of that model were still in circulation, provided that such conduct would be liable to affect trade between Member States.[30] Advocate General Alber concluded that there was no breach of Article 102 TFEU because 'Such conduct is not apparent in the present case.'[31]

The key part of the judgment of the Fifth Chamber of the Court of Justice of the EU is as follows:

> 30. Recourse to the clause on public policy in Article 27, point 1, of the [Brussels] Convention can be envisaged only where recognition or enforcement of the judgment delivered in another Contracting State would be at variance to an unacceptable degree with the legal order of the State in which enforcement is sought inasmuch as it infringes a fundamental principle. In order for the prohibition of any review of the foreign judgment as to its substance to be observed, the infringement would have to constitute a manifest breach of a rule of law regarded as essential in the legal

[26] Therefore he was able to say that 'In the present case it is even questionable whether freedom of competition . . . constitute such fundamental principles' as to fall within public policy (ibid 2993) without pointing out that freedom of competition is a matter of public policy, in the context of a clear violation of what is now Art 101 TFEU as had been decided in *Eco Swiss*.

[27] ibid 2991.

[28] ibid 2992.

[29] ibid 2993.

[30] ibid 3004, referring to Case 53/87 *Cicra and another v Renault* [1988] ECR 6039.

[31] ibid 3004. It is worth noting that Advocate General Alber also considered the argument made by the defendants that the French judgment violated Italian, rather than EU, competition law in so far as the claimants (Renault) abused their dominant position by granting exclusive protective rights in respect to spare parts that had no independent aesthetic value. At that time the establishment of requirements for conferring protective rights in respect of designs and models was a matter for the laws of Member States rather than EU law, and therefore in principle such an issue could fall within Italian public policy. However, in this case the Advocate General strayed into the interpretation of national law by ruling that any such principle under Italian law could not be sufficiently 'fundamental' to justify the use of the public policy defence to deny the recognition of a judgment from another EU Member State under the Brussels Convention. His main reason seems to be that in the 1980s, when the Italian courts referred the *Cicra* case to the CJEU, Italian law did allow for the protection of designs and models on automobile parts and therefore the prohibition of such protection in Italian law introduced in the 1990s could not be such a 'fundamental principle' of Italian law as to fall within the type of national public policy that can be used to block recognition and enforcement of a foreign judgment. See ibid, 2993. With all due respect to Advocate General Alber, he should not decide that a national rule is not a fundamental principle of national law simply because it was introduced recently. A state must have the capacity to decide that a change in its law is so fundamental that the new law constitutes a fundamental principle that must be respected even in the face of a foreign judgment.

order of the State in which enforcement is sought or of a right recognised as being fundamental within that legal order (*Krombach*, paragraph 37).

31. In this case, what has led the court of the State in which enforcement was sought to question the compatibility of the foreign judgment with public policy in its own State is the possibility that the court of the State of origin erred in applying certain rules of Community law. The court of the State in which enforcement was sought is in doubt as to the compatibility with the principles of free movement of goods and freedom of competition of recognition by the court of the State of origin of the existence of an intellectual property right in body parts for cars enabling the holder to prohibit traders in another Contracting State from manufacturing, selling, transporting, importing or exporting such body parts in that Contracting State.

32. The fact that the alleged error concerns rules of Community law does not alter the conditions for being able to rely on the clause on public policy. It is for the national court to ensure with equal diligence the protection of rights established in national law and rights conferred by Community law.

33. The court of the State in which enforcement is sought cannot, without undermining the aim of the Convention, refuse recognition of a decision emanating from another Contracting State solely on the ground that it considers that national or Community law was misapplied in that decision. On the contrary, it must be considered whether, in such cases, the system of legal remedies in each Contracting State, together with the preliminary ruling procedure provided for in Article 177 of the Treaty [now Article 267 TFEU], affords a sufficient guarantee to individuals.

34. Since an error of law such as that alleged in the main proceedings does not constitute a manifest breach of a rule of law regarded as essential in the legal order of the State in which enforcement is sought, the reply to the third question must be that Article 27, point 1, of the Convention must be interpreted as meaning that a judgment of a court or tribunal of a Contracting State recognising the existence of an intellectual property right in body parts for cars, and conferring on the holder of that right protection by enabling him to prevent third parties trading in another Contracting State from manufacturing, selling, transporting, importing or exporting in that Contracting State such body parts, cannot be considered to be contrary to public policy.

The CJEU stated that recognition could only be refused on the ground of public policy where the judgment would be at variance to such an unacceptable degree with the legal order of the state of enforcement that it infringes a fundamental principle of that legal order. The public policy clause must be interpreted strictly and thus, a mere misapplication of EU law, even if it concerns competition rules, is not enough to defend against recognition in the state of enforcement. In *Renault*, any breach of EU competition law was not 'manifest' and so the public policy clause could not be relied on to defend against recognition and enforcement.

An interesting difference between *Renault* and *Eco Swiss* is that the breach of competition law in *Renault* is unproven at best, and probably non-existent, whereas in *Eco Swiss* it was clear. The judgment of the Full Court in *Eco Swiss* could not have been overturned by the Fifth Chamber in *Renault* and therefore we have to try to distinguish the decision in *Renault* from that in *Eco Swiss*. The basis for distinguishing is not clear because the Fifth Chamber only asserts a conclusion in paragraph 34 of its judgment without explaining on what basis that conclusion is arrived at. Why does the 'error of law' by the French court, alleged in the main proceedings for recognition of the French judgment in Italy, not constitute a 'manifest breach' of a fundamental principle of the Italian legal order?

Professor Francq in her analysis of Article 34 of Brussels I distinguishes the two cases as follows:

> As a result, the established misapplication of Article 81 (now Art 101 TFEU) is contrary to public policy in one context, but the alleged misapplication of Article 82 (now Art 102 TFEU) cannot be considered as infringing public policy in another context. The explanation of this apparent contradiction must therefore have something to do with the context. And maybe with the provisions at stake. Art 34(1) opposes the recognition of judgments rendered in Member States which present two advantages in comparison with arbitral awards. Firstly, they enjoy a presumption of regularity which could explain that the test of public policy should be even lighter in their case. Secondly, they can be submitted to the system of legal remedies organized by the Treaty, especially the preliminary ruling. Such a possibility is not offered in the framework of arbitration and this consideration seems to have puzzled the ECJ in the *Eco Swiss* Case. From the comparison between Art 81 and 82 of the EC Treaty,it comes out that agreements concluded in contradiction with the first one are automatically void, a specification not provided by the latter one. Would this explain why the infringement of Art 81 would amount to a manifest breach of a fundamental principle, when the same is not true for Art 82 EC? The mutual trust accorded to judgments rendered in Member States and the system of legal remedies offered to the parties in order to raise their claims seems a more convincing explanation.[32]

It seems highly unlikely that the difference between what is now Article 101 TFEU and Article 102 TFEU is the reason why *Renault* appears to distinguish *Eco Swiss* because the Court of Justice of the European Union has subsequently clarified that both Articles 101 and 102 TFEU form part of EU 'public policy'.[33] Professor Francq may be right that the explanation lies in the different context of the two cases rather than the provisions at stake.[34] However, it seems more likely that the distinguishing should be done on the basis of the different fact/law matrix in the two cases and where that does not give a complete answer to accept that *Eco Swiss* is the higher authority (being a Full Court of 13 rather than a Chamber of five) and follow it.

The Court had the opportunity in *Renault* to explore the issue of when a breach of competition law is enough to trigger the national public policy defence. Unfortunately, the CJEU failed to discuss why any possible breach of competition law on the facts in *Renault* would not be enough to trigger the public policy defence under what is now Article 34(1) of Brussels I. In doing so the Court declined to clarify when the public policy exception should be upheld to prevent recognition of judgments in violation of fundamental EU competition rules and which provisions of EU competition law are so fundamental as to constitute EU public policy. We can infer from the Advocate General's Opinion that there was no breach of EU competition law in this case, but the Court of Justice does not confirm or deny that conclusion. The Court could have clarified that a breach of what is now Article 102 TFEU could be sufficiently manifest that it would justify invoking the public policy

[32] U Magnus and P Mankowski (eds), *Brussels I Regulation,* 2nd edn (Munich, Sellier, 2012) section on Art 34 by S Francq 644–97, 664.

[33] Joined Cases C-295/04 to C-298/04 *Manfredi and Others v Lloyd Adriatico Assicurazioni Spa and others* [2006] ECR I-6619 [31]. See M Fallon and S Francq, 'Private Enforcement of Antitrust Provisions and the Rome I Regulation' in J Basedow, S Francq and L Idot (eds) *International Antitrust Litigation* (Oxford, Hart, 2012) 63, 74. It is a little ironic that Professor Francq refers to *Manfredi* as indicating that Art 102 TFEU is part of EU public policy in her chapter with Professor Fallon, but does not allude to this point in her own analysis of a possible distinction in public policy terms between Arts 101 and 102 TFEU in her commentary on *Eco Swiss* and *Renault* in her section on Art 34 in the Magnus and Mankowski book on Brussels I, ibid. For detailed arguments as to why both Arts 101 and 102 TFEU should be treated as part of EU public policy, see M Danov, *Jurisdiction and Judgments in Relation to EU Competition Law Claims* (Oxford, Hart, 2011) 189–92.

[34] Danov, ibid 191, whilst arguing that EU public policy is the same whether the context is the public policy exception to recognition of arbitral awards under the New York Convention or the public policy exception to recognition of court judgments in Brussels I, acknowledges that the 'powers of the national courts to deny enforcement of a judgment will be more limited in comparison to their powers to refuse enforcement of arbitral awards'.

exception, but that on any conceivable interpretation of the facts presented in this case no such manifest breach of Article 102 TFEU took place even if the Advocate General was wrong in concluding that no breach of Article 102 took place. So, on the EU competition law point, the best assumption is that the Chamber in *Renault* accepted in principle that Article 102 TFEU is a matter of EU public policy (and we know now from *Manfredi* that it is), but that on the facts of the case before them there was either no breach of Article 102 TFEU (the view of the Advocate General, and highly likely as it was based on an earlier decision of the Court involving the same parties), or even if there was one, it could not be sufficiently manifest or serious to justify denial of recognition of the French judgment on the basis of EU public policy. In any case the most that the Fifth Chamber should have done was to rule that on the facts it was presented with in the preliminary reference there was no evidence to suggest any breach of Article 102 TFEU.

In relation to the alleged breach of Italian public policy based on national competition law the Fifth Chamber by its sweeping words in paragraph 34 and in its ruling seems to be deciding that any such breach in this case could not be sufficiently fundamental to justify the application of the public policy exception. However, it makes that decision without any analysis of Italian law to see whether its prohibition of exclusive rights being granted to car body parts that have no independent aesthetic value could be so fundamental to the Italian legal order as to justify its invocation of public policy. In relation to Italian competition law the Fifth Chamber's only role is to interpret the outer limits of the 'public policy' exception and in doing so it should simply assert that the Italian court can only apply the public policy exception when the breach of the Italian law is manifest/serious and where that aspect of Italian law is fundamental to the Italian legal order even in international cases. It is not within the jurisdiction of the CJEU to determine whether on the facts of the particular case (which of course are not proven to the Court in a preliminary ruling) the breach of the Italian legal principle is a sufficiently serious or manifest one nor to determine whether the Italian legal principle at stake is sufficiently fundamental to the Italian legal order to form the basis of a public policy exception. Both of these assessments should be left to the national courts under the distribution of competences between the Union and its Member States under the Union Treaties and in particular under Article 267 TFEU.

III. OTHER ISSUES

A. Punitive damages

If a national court in the EU were to award punitive damages to a claimant as a result of a violation of competition law by a defendant, the non-compensatory element of the damages award might be struck down on the basis of public policy when the judgment is being enforced in another EU Member State under Brussels I.[35] It would be appropriate for at least the compensatory element of the award to be enforced.

[35] See C Kessedjian, 'Recognition and Enforcement of Foreign Judgments', in J Basedow, S Francq and L Idot (eds) *International Antitrust Litigation* (Oxford, Hart, 2012) 245, 252–54. See also M Danov, *Jurisdiction and Judgments in Relation to EU Competition Law Claims* (Oxford, Hart, 2011) 210–11. *cf* J Basedow, 'Recognition of Foreign Decisions within the European Competition Network' in J Basedow, JP Terhechte and L Tichy (eds) *Private Enforcement of Competition Law* (Baden-Baden, Nomos, 2011) 169, 175.

B. Administrative Penalties

It is a particular feature of competition law that persons face a risk of a kind of double jeopardy[36] in that they may be liable to pay large administrative fines imposed by the national or EU competition authorities and then also be required to pay damages to the persons who have been damaged by their anti-competitive behaviour. Crudely speaking, the former addresses the public interest harm done to the market in general and the latter addresses the private interests of those who can prove they have been harmed by that same behaviour. Professor Kessedjian has argued that a specific rule could be added to Brussels I to allow a judge in the country of enforcement to 'lower the amount of damages if the judgment debtor has also been fined by competition authorities'.[37] However, it seems appropriate to treat these cases in the same way as one would treat a foreign judgment that has awarded punitive damages. The principle should be that the party who has suffered damage should be able to enforce in full, at least, the compensatory element of the foreign judgment.[38] This should happen even if the administrative fine may have taken account of potential damages to market actors in calculating how much the fine should be. The reality is that exposure to large fines and compensatory damages awards could have the beneficial effect of deterring companies from engaging in what can otherwise be highly profitable anti-competitive activities.

C. Collective Actions

Professor Kessedjian rightly argues that if a judgment were to be awarded in favour of a group of collective redress claimants operating under an opt-out scheme in any EU Member State, an absent claimant should be able to get a ruling from a court in any other Member State that the judgment should not be recognised as binding on him if he had not been duly informed of his rights to opt out.[39] In the absence of law reform on this point (and none took place in the recast of Brussels I), it will be for the absent claimant to argue that any such recognition would be contrary to public policy as a violation of his due process rights.

D. Local Public Interest of National Competition Authorities

Professor Basedow has suggested that recognition of a court judgment in a Member State of the EU that Article 101 or 102 TFEU has been violated may be refused on public policy grounds by a national competition authority in another Member State if it believes that recognition of that judgment would undermine the public good in that state.[40]

[36] Kessedjian ibid, 254–55.

[37] ibid 256.

[38] This principle is supported by Professor Kessedjian, ibid 254–55, and she expressly says that this power to lower the foreign damages award should not 'deprive the injured private persons of legitimate damages.' (ibid 255).

[39] ibid 255–56. See also in much more detail M Danov, *Jurisdiction and Judgments in Relation to EU Competition Law Claims* (Oxford, Hart, 2011) 207–10, who believes the matter should be addressed by the EU legislature.

[40] See Basedow (n 35) 176. It would have been interesting if Basedow had given an example of when such non-recognition on grounds of public policy would be justified.

IV. CONCLUSION

Danov argues that the concept of EU public policy includes Articles 101 and 102 TFEU, but that a mere error in the application of those Articles in a judgment in one country of the EU is not enough to permit the non-recognition of that judgment in other EU countries on the ground of public policy under Brussels I. He argues however that where previously unavailable evidence on the illegality of an agreement comes to light after the case has been decided in the court of origin, then the judgment debtor should be able to use this as the basis for invoking public policy to deny recognition of the judgment.[41] This approach of Danov is appropriate. However, it could be argued, along the lines of Komninos in relation to arbitration awards, that even a minimalist approach to a public policy exception must allow for the enforcing court to deny recognition to a foreign judgment from another EU court if it has clearly violated EU competition law (either by ignoring it or patently getting it wrong) and the defendant did all that he could to raise the competition law issues at all levels in the foreign courts, even if no new evidence has come to light since the judgment in the court of origin. In the end of the day this can be defended as being part of the essence of retaining a substantive public policy defence in the recast of Brussels I. In such a scenario, enforcing courts must be careful not to act as appeal courts against the decisions of courts of origin on EU competition law by normally requiring the defendant to have exhausted his domestic remedies on the competition law issue in the country of origin. As a counter argument it can be pointed out that EU law provides at least a theoretical solution in the country of origin to cases where there has been a manifest breach of EU law (including competition law) by the courts in that country. If the defendant had contested the EU competition law issue in the courts dealing with the merits of his case all the way to the court against whose decision there was no judicial remedy then that court would have a duty to refer the case to the Court of Justice of the EU for a preliminary ruling unless the point of law was already decided by an earlier case of the CJEU that the national court was following or the correct answer was so obvious as to cause no reasonable doubt. If that highest national court erroneously failed to refer the case to the Court of Justice and applied the clearly wrong law then the remedy for the defendant would be an action for damages against the state because of the manifest violation of EU law by the highest national court.[42]

[41] M Danov, *Jurisdiction and Judgments in Relation to EU Competition Law Claims* (Oxford, Hart, 2011) 195–200.

[42] See Case C-224/01 *Köbler v Austria* [2003] ECR I-10239.

27

The Recognition and Enforcement in the EU of Foreign Judgments in Antitrust Matters: The Case of US and Dutch Judgments and Settlements Rendered upon Class Actions

STEFANIA BARIATTI

I. INTRODUCTORY REMARKS

The issue of the recognition and enforcement in the Member States of the European Union of judgments rendered upon class actions has been studied extensively in recent times, mainly with regard to US decisions, due to the impressive numbers of class actions commenced in the United States against European companies, primarily aimed at recovering damages arising from alleged breaches of US antitrust and securities laws. The intra-EU aspects have recently been addressed as well, after some EU Member States adopted specific rules and procedures for collective redress, and the European Commission has started to study the possibility of introducing specific, harmonised rules in Europe, in particular with regard to consumer and competition law, including the private international law aspects.[1] The recognition and enforcement of judgments rendered upon class actions has been specifically addressed also within the framework of the review of Regulation (EC) 44/2001 on jurisdiction, recognition and the enforcement of judgments in civil and commercial matters (Brussels I Regulation).

This chapter will first offer a brief overview of US class actions and the general problems that the recognition and enforcement of US judgments and settlements encounter in Europe (section 2), and will then address the issues raised by the circulation within the EU of judgments rendered in the Netherlands under the Law for the Collective Settlement of Mass Claims (WCAM), involving a number of challenges to the system of the Brussels I Regulation (section 3).

[1] The relevant documents and studies can be found at the Commission's website, http://ec.europa.eu/dgs/health_consumer/dgs_consultations/ca/collective_redress_consultation_en.htm and http://ec.europa.eu/competition/antitrust/actionsdamages/index.html.

II. THE RECOGNITION AND ENFORCEMENT OF US JUDGMENTS AND SETTLEMENTS RENDERED UPON CLASS ACTIONS IN EUROPE

The recognition and enforcement of US judgments and settlements does not fall within the scope of the Brussels I Regulation, but is governed by the domestic law of the EU Member States.[2] The issues that arise in this field have been thoroughly examined, discussed, and criticised in the last few years, mainly with regard to cases concerning the infringement of US securities laws.[3]

While many non-US plaintiffs have made recourse to the US class action system against non-US defendants, the recognition and enforcement in the EU of judgments rendered and settlements reached in this country may find several obstacles. Indeed, the main difficulties relate to the assessment of the indirect competence of US courts, the amount of damages that may be awarded to plaintiffs, and the mechanism of the class action itself, ie the fact that the judgment or settlement reached in court binds all hypothetical class members, even where they have not declared their intention to participate in the proceedings (opt-out system). Under Federal Rule of Civil Procedure 23(c)(2)(B), this system prevents all class members from commencing an individual claim based upon the same conduct of the defendant.

A. Opt-Out System, Preclusion and Procedural Public Policy

Indeed, under US Federal Rule of Civil Procedure 23, one or more individuals may bring an action on behalf of all persons with similar claims, to be certified as a class by the court. The respective adversary positions of the plaintiffs and defendant in the proceedings are clear and well-defined from the outset. The court will then direct notice to the unnamed class members of the existence of the lawsuit and will give them an opportunity to opt out in order to exclude themselves from the class. Only those class members who have properly requested exclusion will no longer be considered to be members of the class and will not be bound by any judgment or settlement reached in the case. On the contrary, class members who do not opt out

[2] Nor was this topic addressed in the Commission's proposal for a recast Brussels I Regulation (COM (2010) 748 of 14 December 2010). A draft set of articles was adopted by GEDIP at its Copenhagen meeting in 2010 (www.gedip-egpil.eu/reunionstravail/gedip-reunions-20-fr.htm).

[3] Among the most recent studies see in particular (also for further references) Danov, *The Brussels I Regulation: Cross-Border Collective Redress Proceedings and Judgments*, 6 *JPIL* (2010) 359, and *Jurisdiction and Judgments in Relation to EU Competition Claims* (Oxford, Hart Publishing, 2011) 182 et seq; Fallon and Tzakas, '*Res Judicata* Effects of Foreign Class action Rulings in the EU', in Boele-Woelki, Einhorn, Girsberger, Symeonides (eds), *Convergence and Divergence in Private International Law, Liber Amicorum Kurt Siehr*, (The Hague, Eleven International Publishing, 2011) 653 et seq; Stiggelbout, 'The Recognition in England and Wales of United States Judgments in Class Actions', 52 *Harvard International Law Journal* (2011) 433; Monestier, 'Transnational Class Actions and the Illusory Search for *Res Judicata*', 86 *Tulane Law Review* (2011) 1; Tzakas, 'Effective Collective Redress in Antitrust and Consumer Protection Matters: A Panacea or a Chimera?', 48 *CML Rev* (2011) 1125, and 'International Litigation and Competition Law: The Case of Collective Redress', in Basedow, Francq, Idot (eds), *International Antitrust Litigation. Conflicts of Laws and Coordination* (Oxford, Hart Publishing, 2012) 161–89, 185 et seq; Kessedjian, 'Recognition and Enforcement of Foreign Judgments', ibid 245–56; Bariatti, 'Recognition and Enforcement in the EU of Judicial Decisions Rendered upon Class Actions: The Case of US and Dutch Judgments and Settlements', in I Viarengo, F Pocar, F Villata (eds), *Recasting Brussels I, Proceedings of the Conference Held at the University of Milan on November 25–26, 2011* (Padua, Cedam, 2012) 319–39.

will be considered to be part of the class and will be bound by any judgment or settlement, even if they have not entered an appearance in the case through counsel and even if they were not in any way individually identified in the action and in the judgment, but only described as part of the class of persons who were directed to receive notice by the court.

Thus, under the doctrines of issue preclusion and claim preclusion, a valid and final judgment on the merits rendered in a class action will preclude any member of the class – other than those who have affirmatively chosen to be excluded according to the terms of the court order – from re-litigating in a US court any of the issues or claims raised in the course of the proceedings. Preclusion is crucial in the system insofar as it aims at meeting the needs and interests of the defendant to prevent any individual claims after the settlement is reached.

If one looks at preclusion from a different angle and calls it *res judicata* effect, the focus shifts from certification for purposes of establishing jurisdiction to the recognition of the judgment abroad. In this respect many commentators – mainly in Europe – have expressed serious doubts as to the possibility to recognise such judgments, which seem to violate procedural public policy. Indeed, in the US proceedings on the merits, the correct development of adversary proceedings appears to be hindered and thus the rights of the defence to be restricted. Said rights and the adversary process principle apply equally to plaintiffs and defendants, and guarantee that all litigants enjoy the same rights with respect to prosecuting and defending actions for the protection of their own interests.

Moreover, the recognition of such US decisions would also infringe the *res judicata* principle, since a judgment normally binds only the parties that have taken part in the judicial proceedings. To preclude unnamed class members, who did not participate in the proceedings, from bringing suit in their home country – provided that its courts have jurisdiction – would deny those persons their inviolable right to sue in court to protect their own rights and interests, that is granted by many national constitutions, as well as in the European Convention of Human Rights and in the Charter of Fundamental Rights of the EU. In fact, as mentioned above, opt-out systems prevent the unnamed class members from lodging an individual claim for the same facts or conduct.

B. Punitive Damages and Public Policy

Another obstacle to the recognition and enforcement of US judgments in Europe is raised where punitive damages are awarded to plaintiffs. While these damages are not an issue that arises only in class actions, it is worth mentioning them here since Regulation (EC) 864/2007 on the law applicable to non-contractual obligations (Rome II Regulation) and some judgments of the CJEU concerning damages arising out of antitrust violations have addressed the issue. Indeed, Recital 32 of the Rome II Regulation provides that the application of a provision of the law designated by it which would have the effect of causing non-compensatory exemplary or punitive damages of an excessive nature to be awarded may, depending on the circumstances of the case and the legal order of the Member State of the court seised, be regarded as being contrary to the public policy (***ordre public***) of the forum.

In this respect, it should be noted that in EU Member States, civil liability is compensatory only,[4] while in many sectors where class actions usually apply, public authorities have

[4] *cf* Magnus, 'Why is US Tort Law so Different?', (2010) 1 *Journal of European Tort Law* 102.

powers to create deterrent effects (antitrust violations, market manipulations, unfair commercial practices). The practice of the EU Member States with regard to the recognition of US judgments awarding punitive damages is not uniform. While in some countries punitive damages have been considered disproportionate and have not been recognised, in other countries recognition has been granted and the amount of the damages has been reduced in order to bring it into line with the domestic legal order.[5]

In the field of antitrust violations the CJEU has tackled this issue in *Manfredi*,[6] a well-known case concerning a claim for damages arising out of a cartel. The Court has stated that, lacking any EU rules governing the matter, each Member State is empowered to set the criteria for determining the extent of damages, provided that the principles of equivalence and effectiveness are observed. The equivalence principle requires that 'it must be possible to award particular damages, such as exemplary or punitive damages, pursuant to actions founded on the Community competition rules, if such damages may be awarded pursuant to similar actions founded on domestic law', but national courts may take such steps as are necessary 'to ensure that the protection of the rights guaranteed by Community law does not entail the unjust enrichment of those who enjoy them'. Compensation may be sought for both actual loss and for loss of profit, plus interest.

A recent judgment of the Competition Appeal Tribunal,[7] following *Rookes v Barnard*,[8] has awarded exemplary damages in an abuse of dominance case (exclusionary practice). The Tribunal considered that exemplary damages might be awarded 'where compensation is inadequate to punish the defendant for his outrageous conduct'. It rejected, however, the claimant's suggestion that the amount of the damages should be measured 'by reference to the sort of penalty that the OFT has jurisdiction to impose for breaches of the Chapter II prohibition' since the OFT's jurisdiction to fine derives from the law, and since exemplary damages are paid to the claimant. It rather considered that exemplary damages have to bear some relation to the compensatory damages being awarded, and that due regard should be had to the economic size of the defendant. Finally, the Tribunal did not award any interest on this sum, since 'an award of interest is intended to compensate a claimant from being kept out of his money, and is obviously appropriate in the case of compensatory damages, and not exemplary damages'.

C. Assessment of the Indirect Competence of the US Courts

Among the many conditions for the recognition of US judgments rendered upon class actions, the control of the indirect competence of the US court would be specifically relevant. Indeed, lacking an international (multilateral or bilateral) convention on recognition and enforcement of judgments between the requesting state and the requested state, most

[5] For the state of the art in the EU Member States, see Janke, Licari, 'Enforcing Punitive Damage Awards in France after *Fountaine Pajot*', http://ssrn.com/abstract=1985578; Danov, *Jurisdiction and Judgments* (n 3) 210 et seq; Kessedjian (n 3) 251 et seq.

[6] Case C-295/04 to C-298/04 *Manfredi v Lloyd Adriatico Assicurazioni SpA* [2006] 5 CMLR 17, paras 92 et seq. See also Case C-453/99 *Courage v Crehan* [2001] ECR I-6297, paras 29 et seq.

[7] Case Number: 1178/5/7/11, *2 Travel Group Plc (in Liquidation) v Cardiff City Transport Services Ltd* [2012] CAT 19.

[8] *Rookes v Barnard* [1964] 1 AC 1129.

national laws make the recognition and enforcement of a foreign judgment conditional upon compliance with the general principles or rules on jurisdiction of the requested state. Indirect jurisdiction depends upon the subject matter of the dispute. Much has been written on the well-known cases where the US courts have established jurisdiction in foreign cubed class actions over foreign defendants in securities litigation on the basis of the purported extraterritorial application of certain provisions of the Securities Exchange Act. Many commentators and *amici curiae* briefs submitted to the Supreme Court in the *Morrison* case have concluded that the US judgments would be denied recognition in the EU, since the link between the US and the case was too loose and thus they would not meet the indirect jurisdiction condition.[9] Obviously, in other fields such as antitrust claims, the outcome may be different.

D. US Settlements are not Enforceable

Last but not least, problems may arise where the US proceedings are closed with a settlement reached before a court and/or enshrined in a judgment. A settlement is a legally enforceable agreement in which a claimant agrees not to seek recovery outside of the agreement for specified injuries or claims from some or all of the persons who might be liable for those injuries or claims. Under rule 23, there are three required steps to settle class action lawsuits: (i) a court must preliminarily approve the proposed settlement; (ii) class members must then be given notice of the proposed settlement; and (iii) a hearing must be held to determine whether the proposed settlement is fair, reasonable, and adequate.

The recognition of the US settlement may be excluded where the requested state lacks any specific rules in this respect and no international convention applies. A settlement cannot be considered as a judgment, because it is essentially a contractual agreement between the parties to the dispute.[10] In approving class action settlement agreements, US courts do not adjudicate any disputed issues between the parties; rather, they only evaluate whether the parties' agreement is fair, adequate, and reasonable. Thus, a settlement in a US class action might not be enforceable in the EU where it does not qualify as a judgment under the domestic law of the requested state and there are no provisions on the recognition of foreign settlements.

But even if a court in an EU Member State found that a court-approved settlement agreement in a US class action could equate to a judgment under their domestic law, the settlement agreement would not be enforceable against unnamed class members for all of the reasons described above regarding the enforceability of a US class action judgment, in particular for lack of consent. The failure to opt out or object cannot be considered an acceptable alternative to express consent, as silence and inaction do not constitute consent.

[9] The Supreme Court has now substantially reduced recourse both to f-cubed and to f-squared class actions in the field of securities law: see Silberman, '*Morrison v. National Australia Bank*: Implications for Global Securities Class Actions' (2010) 12 *Yearbook of Private International Law* 123; Bariatti, 'Riflessioni sull'applicazione extraterritoriale delle norme relative ai servizi finanziari: dal caso *Morrison* al *Dodd-Frank Act* e oltre', (2012) *Diritto del commercio internazionale* 417.

[10] See Case C-414/92 *Solo Kleinmotoren GmbH v Emilio Boch* [1994] ECR I-2237 [17]–[18].

III. THE RECOGNITION OF DUTCH COLLECTIVE SETTLEMENTS RENDERED UNDER WCAM WITHIN THE BRUSSELS SYSTEM

A. The Application of the Brussels I Regulation to Collective Redress Proceedings and Judgments

While the issue of the recognition of a judgment given in proceedings commenced by a class action (or 'collective redress') under the 1968 Brussels Convention or the Brussels I Regulation has never been raised in a national court or before the CJEU, there is wide consensus among commentators that such an action and the conclusive judgment rendered in an EU Member State would fall under this system. This conclusion is supported also by the fact that the Commission's proposal for a recast of the Brussels I Regulation provided for an exception to the new regime of recognition and enforcement for certain judgments rendered upon a collective action.[11] Yet, several difficulties in applying these rules to collective actions have been analysed and cannot be overlooked.

As concerns opt-in systems, the main difficulties derive from the fact that the provisions of the Brussels I Regulation do not take into account the peculiarities of collective actions that have been examined at length, mainly in respect to the establishment of jurisdiction.[12] Apart from the case of a plurality of defendants, the serious difficulties arise on the side of plaintiffs. These difficulties are found in consumer class actions and in all cases where the court seised is not the court of the defendant, but the court of the domicile of one or more plaintiffs, since the Regulation and the Lugano Convention do not allow rejoinder of plaintiffs. Once the judgment is rendered, though, the Brussels system of recognition and enforcement fully applies.

The Commission's proposal for the recast of the Brussels I Regulation did not provide any new rules on jurisdiction specifically designed for collective actions, and it excluded from the new 'abolition of *exequatur*' regime judgments given

> in proceedings which concern the compensation of harm caused by unlawful business practices to a multitude of injured parties and which are brought by (i) a state body, (ii) a non-profit making organisation whose main purpose and activity is to represent and defend the interests of groups of natural or legal persons, other than by, on a commercial basis, providing them with legal advice or representing them in court, or (iii) a group of more than twelve claimants.[13]

This raised a few doubts and left the main questions open,[14] and – as anticipated – was not endorsed by the Council.

[11] This exception has not been endorsed by the Council: see doc 10609/12 ADD 1 of 1 June 2012 and the Political Guidelines for future work of 16 December 2011, doc 17402/11 ADD 1.

[12] Danov, *Jurisdiction and Judgments in Relation to EU Competition Law Claims* (Oxford, Hart, 2011); Bariatti, 'Violazione di norme antitrust e diritto internazionale privato: il giudice italiano e i cartelli' (2008) *Rivista di diritto internazionale privato e processuale* 349–62, and 'Le azioni collettive dell'art. 140-bis del Codice del consumo: aspetti di diritto internazionale privato e processuale', (2011) *Rivista di diritto internazionale privato e processuale* 19–54; Tzakas, 'International Litigation and Competition Law' (n 3) 183 f.

[13] Art 37(3)b of the Proposal for a Regulation on Jurisdiction and the Recognition and Enforcement of Judgments in Civil and Commercial Matters COM(2010) 748 final (Brussels I Proposal).

[14] In particular, it has been observed that the choice to qualify as a collective action any action brought by a group of more than 12 people prevailed over any different qualification provided by the domestic law of the Member States, which are not harmonised so far. Second, it was hard to understand why the exception to the new 'abolition of *exequatur*' regime applied only to collective actions concerning damages arising out of unlawful busi-

B. The General Features of WCAM and the Brussels I Regulation

Among the various national mechanisms adopted by the EU Member States, the Dutch system introduced by the *Wet collectieve afwikkeling massaschade* (WCAM) in 2005 raises interesting and controversial issues with regard to the application of the Brussels I Regulation that will be examined here even if it has not been applied to any antitrust infringement cases so far. The mechanism is very similar to the US system, since it provides for a settlement certified by the Amsterdam Court of Appeal, which binds all the class members who have not explicitly declared that they do not wish to take part in the settlement within a specific period of time established by the Court.[15]

Having a domestic opt-out system, the Dutch courts were the first courts in Europe to recognise a US judgment rendered in a foreign cubed class action in securities laws matters against a Dutch company listed in the Netherlands, that had also issued ADRs listed in New York. The Amsterdam Court of Appeal has declared that the interests of the damaged parties had been taken into proper account in the US proceedings, the class members had received the necessary information in due time and through efficient means of communication concerning the pending of the proceedings and the possibility to declare their will not to take part in it, and that the US court had jurisdiction since it was the court of the tort/damaging event/infringement. However, the Amsterdam Court has left open the possibility to refuse recognition vis-à-vis individuals who could prove that their rights had not been respected in the foreign proceedings.[16] The similarities between the US and the Dutch proceedings have also allowed parties to reach settlements in the Netherlands concerning the foreign class members in foreign cubed class actions pending in the US, in particular in the *Royal Dutch Shell* and the *Converium* cases.[17]

The issues raised by the circulation of Dutch settlements within the EU differ from those described above with reference to US judgments, since common rules are in force in Europe that allow the requested court to control the jurisdiction of the requesting state only in exceptional cases, providing for the automatic recognition of the foreign judgment in the other Member States, and offering a simplified mechanism for its enforcement.

According to Dutch commentators and the Amsterdam Court of Appeal, the opt-out mechanism created by WCAM is compatible with the rules on jurisdiction and recognition of judgments of the Brussels system. Thus the Dutch decision authorising the settlement

ness practices. The reasons given at Recital 23 were not convincing and the report accompanying the proposal offered only a generic comment. Third, since the proposal confirmed that the jurisdiction provisions of the Brussels system apply to collective claims, specific provisions concerning at least the rejoinder of plaintiffs would have been welcome.

[15] WCAM's provisions have been inserted into the Dutch Civil Code at Arts 907 et seq and in the Dutch Civil Procedure Code at Arts 1013 et seq. An extended analysis of WCAM and of the related private international issues has been carried out by van Lith, *The Dutch Collective Settlements Act and Private International Law* (Antwerp, Maklu-Uitgevers, 2011). *See also* Arons, van Boom, 'Beyond Tulips and Cheese: Exporting Mass Securities Claim Settlements from The Netherlands' (2010) *Eur Bus Law Rev* 857 et seq; Polak, Hermans, 'International Class Actions Settlements in the Netherlands After the *Morrison* and *Ahold* Decisions', in *Class & Group Actions 2011* (London, 2010) 6 et seq.

[16] Amsterdam Court of Appeal, 23 June 2010, *Royal Ahold*, *Jurisprudentie Ondernemingsrecht*, 2010, 225 et seq, with a comment by Tzankova.

[17] The decision in *Royal Dutch Shell* can be found at http://zoeken.rechtspraak.nl/resultpage.aspx?snelzoeken=true&searchtype=ljn&ljn=BI5744. See also the dedicated websites www.royaldutchshellsettlement.com, www.shellsettlement.com, www.shellcompensation.com, www.shellvergoeding.nl, www.veb.net, www.shell.com, www.abp.nl, www.apg.nl, e www.pfzw.nl. The *Converium* decision on jurisdiction can be found at http://jure.nl/bo3908.

can freely circulate within the EU (and the countries party to the Lugano Convention of 2007). In particular, the Amsterdam Court of Appeal has stated that these disputes fall within the notion of 'civil and commercial matters', since WCAM applies to most claims for damages. While this statement is undisputed, the Dutch system raises some difficulties in cross border cases that should not be overlooked and are difficult to solve.

Some concerns arise in particular with respect to jurisdiction and the preclusive effect of the certified settlement vis-à-vis parties that have neither opted in nor opted out. In this respect the WCAM is biased – if one may say so – by its origin, which was fully domestically oriented. In fact, WCAM aimed at meeting the concerns and expectations of the first undertaking which was subject to it, a Dutch company that was sued for damages caused by its products in the Netherlands and had accepted to settle only if the legislator adopted a law that would preclude any individual claims. The application of WCAM to cross-border cases came into the picture later and in the last three years has covered cases that have very tenuous links with the Netherlands. The legislature is well aware that the structure of the mechanism and the reasoning followed by the Amsterdam Court contain some inconsistencies when applied to international cases and have carried out consultations also with foreign experts on cross-border litigation in order to explore possible amendments.

C. Does a Settlement under WCAM Qualify as a Court Settlement under Brussels I?

The first question is whether the settlement reached according to WCAM qualifies as a court settlement under Article 58 of the Brussels I Regulation.

In this respect it appears that the settlement is reached between the parties to the dispute – ie the defendant and one or more trusts or foundations under which veil the class members are organised and which represent their interests – *prior to the commencement of proceedings* before the Amsterdam Court of Appeal, to which they apply for approval. The binding effect on persons to whom the damage was caused is awarded by the Court and not by the will of the parties, thus this settlement cannot be assimilated to a contract.

Whilst the Brussels I Regulation does not define the notion of 'settlement', that should then be interpreted as an autonomous notion in order to avoid discrimination and inequalities in the enjoyment of the rights granted by its rules in all the Member States, Article 58 applies to a settlement 'which has been approved by a court *in the course of proceedings* and is enforceable in the Member State in which it was concluded'. Such settlement 'shall be enforceable in the State addressed under the same conditions as authentic instruments' (ie upon an application pursuant to Articles 38 et seq), and subject to appeal as per Articles 43 or 44). The only ground for refusing recognition is that the enforcement is manifestly contrary to public policy. At the request of any interested party, the court or competent authority of a Member State where a court settlement is approved issues a certificate using the standard form in Annex V to the Regulation.

The English text of Article 58, however, does not correspond to the text in the other languages. While the English text seems to require the approval of the court, the French, German, and Italian texts only require that the settlement is reached *in the presence of the judge in the course of the proceedings.*[18] Thus, Article 58 provides that in order to enjoy the

[18] 'Les transactions conclues devant un juge au cours d'un procès'; 'Vergleiche, die vor einem Gericht im Verlauf des Verfahrens geschlossen werden'; 'Le transazioni concluse davanti al giudice nel corso di un processo'.

simplified recognition and enforcement proceedings of the Regulation, the settlement must be reached in the course of proceedings that are pending at the time when it is reached and – impliedly – that were commenced according to the jurisdiction criteria provided by the Regulation. We will return to this latter condition, that concerns the jurisdiction of the Amsterdam Court, but with regard to the pendency condition, if the Dutch settlement is reached prior to instituting the judicial proceedings, it appears to fall outside the provision of Article 58.

The situation will be solved by the recast of the Brussels I Regulation, where Article 2(d) of the English version defines a court settlement 'as a settlement which has been approved by a court *or* concluded before a court in the course of proceedings'. Thus the future Regulation will accommodate the divergences in the various languages and align it with Articles 3(1)(a) and 24(1) of Regulation No 805/04 on the European Enforcement Order. Such amendment had been suggested by the Heidelberg Report, which explained that it would 'include out-of-court settlements which are concluded in out-of-court proceedings (i.e. mediation), but at a later stage formally approved by a competent court'.[19]

D. Is the Amsterdam Court of Appeal the Competent Court under the Brussels I Regulation?

While the settlement reached according to WCAM is entered into by the parties prior to seising the court, one would expect that it would not be difficult to differentiate the respective position of the parties bound by it with regard to the object of the dispute. The actual applicants, the foundations established under Dutch or under foreign law representing the class members, would play the role of the plaintiff acting against one or more undertakings, from which damages are claimed based upon a conduct carried out by the latter. Indeed, setting aside for a moment a clause conferring jurisdiction to the Amsterdam Court of Appeal, in the first cases the claims were directed against Dutch companies and the Court could derive its jurisdiction directly from Article 2 of the Brussels I Regulation.

The last two cases, however, involved companies domiciled outside the Netherlands. The *Royal Dutch Shell* case concerned both a Dutch company and a company registered in England, and *Converium* involved a Swiss company. Thus, in the former case, Article 6 of the Regulation could apply in order to join the claims against the two companies, but in the latter case Article 2 would not suffice. Moreover, the Amsterdam Court had to assert its jurisdiction on the absent class members as well, in order to extend the preclusive effect to them, who had neither joined the application nor opted out, and could be domiciled anywhere in the world.

The Amsterdam Court of Appeal has carefully examined the issue of its jurisdiction and has asserted it on the basis of the domicile of some of the potential class members in the Netherlands, which were qualified as defendants pursuant to Article 2 of the Brussels I Regulation. The Court considered that the members of the class are bound by the settlement like the undertaking involved and that they receive the notice that an application has been filed with the court in order to get the certification of the settlement, to which they can object. However, the Court did not look at the underlying claim, the object of the dispute

[19] Hess, in Hess, Pfeiffer, Schlosser, *The Brussels I-Regulation (EC) No 44/2001, The Heidelberg Report on the Application of Regulation Brussels I in 25 Member States* (Munich, Beck, 2008) 161.

that was settled. The analysis of the Amsterdam Court is mostly confused in *Converium*, where it took into account also Article 5(1) of the Regulation, and indicated the obligation to pay compensation as the relevant obligation. The Court then extended its jurisdiction over the class members domiciled in the other EU Member States and Lugano Contracting Parties pursuant to Article 6(1) of the Regulation, and finally it applied a domestic rule of the Code of Civil Procedure in order to further assert jurisdiction to the class members domiciled in other countries.[20]

Thus the Amsterdam Court has treated the proceedings for certifying the settlement as adversary proceedings in order to apply the Brussels I Regulation, but it is doubtful that this solution is correct. The members of the class seem more like plaintiffs than defendants, and they actually were the plaintiffs in the US cases that originated the two Dutch settlements concerning non-US claimants in *Royal Dutch Shell* and *Converium.*

With respect to opting-in class members, the issue of jurisdiction may be solved through Article 23, which empowers the parties to choose the competent forum. Such choice may indeed be expressed in the text of the settlement itself.[21] Article 24 may also apply to opting-in class members, as indicated by the CJEU in *ČCP*:[22] 'since the rules on jurisdiction set out in Sections 3 [and 4] of Chapter II of Regulation No 44/2001 are not rules on exclusive jurisdiction, the court seised, where those rules are not complied with, must declare itself to have jurisdiction where the defendant enters an appearance and does not contest that court's jurisdiction'. For this purpose, however, the class members should qualify as defendants.[23]

E. Due Process

The provisions described above, however, may apply only to class members who have consented to the settlement, thus prorogating the jurisdiction of the Amsterdam Court, either explicitly or tacitly, through the foundation or simply claiming the compensation after the approval of the settlement.[24] Such consent, however, cannot be presumed. Even if the Amsterdam Court's approach is followed and the absent class members are qualified as defendants in order to establish jurisdiction over a non-appearing defendant, Article 26 of the Regulation would still oblige the Court to establish that the defendant 'has been able to receive the documents instituting the proceedings or an equivalent document in sufficient time to enable him to arrange for his defence'.

[20] See van Lith (n 15) 36 et seq.

[21] In the case of insurance and consumer contracts, however, it should be carefully verified whether such choice complies with the stringent conditions set forth at Arts 13 and 17, in particular that they allow the weaker party to bring proceedings in a court other than those listed at the relevant articles. This seems to imply, however, as far as Arts 13(2) and 17(2) are concerned, that the weak party qualifies as a plaintiff and not as a defendant, contrary to what the Amsterdam Court has done. It should also be underlined that the lack of jurisdiction of the court of origin in these matters prevents the recognition and enforcement of the judgment in the other Member States pursuant to Art 35(1).

[22] Case C-111/09 *Česká podnikatelská pojišťovna as, Vienna Insurance Group v Michal Bilas* [2010] ECR I-4545 [26].

[23] In this respect, a new para 2 has been inserted into Art 24 of the proposed recast of the Brussels I Regulation, stating that in matters concerning insurance, consumers and employment contracts, before asserting jurisdiction the court must check that the document instituting proceedings informed the defendant that he/she had the right to contest jurisdiction and of the consequences of entering an appearance.

[24] Under Art 907(6) of the Dutch Civil Code, a person entitled to compensation may claim the compensation within a period of one year from the date when he or she became aware of the right to demand payment.

The respect of the principle of due process and the rights of the defence is crucial regarding absent class members pursuant to Article 6 of the ECHR and Article 47 of the Charter of Fundamental Rights. Many of the criticisms of the US opt-out system that have been discussed above apply to Dutch settlements as well, mainly with reference to the preclusive effect of the settlement over all class members.

According to the Amsterdam Court of Appeal, the respect for the rights of the defence – which were given much attention in the process of approving WCAM – is assured by the wide publicity that is given to the negotiations and later to the pending proceedings and the modalities for opting out in all the countries where interested parties may be located. Also the decision authorising the settlement is communicated through the media in order to allow again the potential class member to opt out within a period of time that is established by the Court. In *Royal Dutch Shell*, for example, more than 100,000 communications were served (out of around 500,000 investors) and notices were published in 44 newspapers and periodicals around the world.

It is doubtful that this procedure for informing the potential class members fully complies with the procedural public policy of the Member States and the standards developed under the ECHR and the EU Charter for absent class members, especially when it is difficult to identify them, as may happen in claims based upon violations of competition law. The *amicus* briefs submitted by many EU Member States and states party to the Lugano Convention prove that an opt-out system goes counter their procedural public policy. The Amsterdam Court, however, stated that WCAM does not prevent an absent class member from contesting the settlement, and thus to commence new proceedings against the same undertaking, in individual cases when he/she proves that his/her procedural rights have been violated.[25] This solution, which is very pragmatic, reduces concerns in this respect within the Brussels system, without fully overcoming them.

F. Does a Dutch Settlement under WCAM Enjoy Preclusive Effect?

Should one reach the conclusion that the mechanism established by WCAM complies with the principles on due process, some concerns still exist with regard to the preclusive effect of a settlement in respect to individual claims in cross border cases under the Brussels I Regulation. Upon a preliminary analysis the following situations may be envisaged.

The Dutch settlement may come into consideration in another Member State where, for example, an absent class member, who has not been aware of the Dutch proceedings and has not opted out from them, brings proceedings claiming damages from an undertaking that has settled the dispute in the Netherlands and thus is bound by and relies upon the Amsterdam Court's authorisation. The preclusive effect of the Dutch settlement will be assessed by a court of another Member State, that will have to decide whether the proceedings that led to

[25] *Royal Ahold*; *cf* van Lith (n 15) 99 ss, spec 102 ss. According to Art 1015 of the Dutch Civil Procedure Code, all pending individual claims against the party from whom compensation is sought under WCAM are suspended and can be resumed – inter alia – if the individual plaintiff entitled to compensation has opted out from the collective proceedings. It might be worth recalling that under Art 40 of Regulation (EC) 1346/2000 on insolvency proceedings, the court having jurisdiction or the liquidator has the duty to inform *known creditors* located in other Member States of the opening of the proceedings. The publication in another Member State of a judgment opening insolvency proceedings is not mandatory, however, unless the Member State where the debtor has an establishment so imposes (Art 21).

the Dutch authorisation have respected the rights of the defence under Article 34(2) of the Regulation (if such court believes that the class members qualify as defendants in the proceedings in the Netherlands) or whether the settlement complies with the forum's procedural public policy according to Article 57(1), that applies to settlements as per Article 58. The court will thus have to check, as indicated by the Amsterdam Court of Appeal, whether there are any specific circumstances that have prevented the plaintiff/consumer from being aware of the Dutch proceedings. The Dutch settlement will be recognised and thus preclude individual claims in the other Member States only if that court is satisfied with this assessment and if it shares the view of the Dutch legislator that the lack of explicit opting out equates to consent[26]. In the affirmative, the claim will be rejected and the plaintiff will be able to collect damages in the Netherlands, provided however that the time period established by WCAM has not elapsed. If the court of the forum Member State is not satisfied with the above assessment, however, it will decide the case and it may order the undertaking to pay compensation for damages for the same type of events and/or conducts for which a Dutch settlement has been authorised.

A second difficulty may arise in the Netherlands where the request for enforcing such a judgment over the assets of the undertaking may be filed. As indicated by the CJEU, settlements are not treated as domestic judgments when recognition of a foreign judgment is at stake. The CJEU has stated that an enforceable settlement reached before a court of the state in which recognition of a foreign judgment is sought in order to settle legal proceedings which are in progress does not constitute a judgment for the purposes of Article 34(3), and thus may not preclude the recognition of that foreign judgment.[27] Thus, it may not be taken for granted that a Dutch settlement would be the basis for resisting a request for enforcement of a judgment rendered in another Member State granting to an absent class member a compensation for damages from the same undertaking and for the same conduct.

The Amsterdam Court will probably apply the same test that applies to individual claims brought in the Netherlands – ie that the absent class member could not have been aware of the prior pending of the settlement proceedings – and in this case it would probably grant recognition. One would then expect that the claimant would not be entitled to compensation under the Dutch settlement. In other words, bringing the claim in another Member State would qualify as an opting out under WCAM, even if it does not respect the formal conditions set forth by its provisions. In any case, the judgment given in the other Member State would have preclusive effect on a claim to receive compensation under the Dutch settlement since it would be contrary to common sense and all principles of law that the injured parties could avail themselves of both mechanisms. Should the party requesting the enforcement of the foreign judgment fail to satisfy the Amsterdam Court of Appeal in this respect, the refusal of recognition of the foreign judgment due to the existence of the Dutch settlement might amount to a violation of the Regulation as interpreted by the CJEU in *Solo Kleinmotoren*.

Another possibility is that a collective action is brought under an opt-in system in another Member State. While the Dutch settlement purports to accommodate the claims of all possible class members wherever they are located, the conflict should be solved at the

[26] An open issue is whether a settlement enjoys recognition, since the wording of Art 58 equates settlements with authentic instruments and the latter do not enjoy recognition.

[27] Case C-414/92 *Solo Kleinmotoren* [1994] ECR I-2237.

level of *lis pendens*, for example by carving out of the Dutch proceedings the claims of those injured parties who opt in to the collective action brought in the other Member State, as happened with respect to the claims of non-US plaintiffs in the US class actions proceedings, that later gathered in the Netherlands. However, if the class action is brought in another Member State after the Dutch settlement is approved and if a judgment is given in that Member State, its recognition and enforcement in the Netherlands (for example, in order to attach assets of the undertaking concerned) would raise the same issues examined above with respect to the relationship between a foreign judgment and a Dutch settlement. The judgment obtained abroad upon the opt-in class action should bar a claim to receive compensation under the Dutch settlement.

The conflict of a Dutch settlement and a court judgment rendered in another Member State may also arise in a third Member State where the enforcement of the judgment is requested over local assets of the undertaking concerned. What shall the requested court in the third Member State do when the undertaking invokes the Dutch settlement, under which the plaintiff can get the appropriate compensation pursuant to WCAM? It appears that under *Solo Kleinmotoren* the judgment would take precedence over the Dutch settlement, but certainly the requested court would have to carry out a careful and thorough analysis of the competing settlement and judgment, which may prove to be a very difficult task at the actual enforcement stage under the simplified mechanism of the Brussels I Regulation.

No cases are reported so far on the effects of Dutch settlements abroad, which may mean that WCAM has worked well in the two cross-border cases that have been settled and that the potential class members have received all the necessary information concerning the existence of the proceedings and are satisfied with the damages awarded. The Dutch Government, though, has started consultations with foreign experts in order to assess whether amendments of the WCAM are necessary or advisable in order to exclude any possible objection to their circulation within the EU.

28

Conclusion: Some Specific Problems: A Case for Reform

MIHAIL DANOV AND FLORIAN BECKER

The cross-border nature of most EU competition law infringements indicates that the preclusive effects of any judgment/settlement would be an important consideration for litigants who would like to make sure that the issues would not be reopened in other jurisdictions. However, Professor Beaumont's analysis[1] of *Eco Swiss* and *Renault*, along with the Commission proposal for the recast of Brussels I, shows that public policy will be retained as a defence in EU competition law cases, and, as a result, may be pleaded in cases concerned with Member States' judgments in relation to such claims.

The long-term objective of the European Union to abolish the *exequatur* for all judgments in civil and commercial matters[2] was taken forward in the Commission proposal for the recast of Brussels I which was made in December 2010.[3] In this context, Professor Beaumont[4] notes that the complete abolition of *exequatur* (the declaration of enforceability) was proposed for all judgments in civil and commercial matters except for cases of defamation and other non-contractual obligations relating to privacy and personality rights, and for certain types of collective redress claims.[5] In this context, Professor Beaumont[6] notes that the Tampere objective of abolishing *exequatur* has been pursued by seeing it as the abolition of a stage in the process, rather than as a requirement to abolish the 'grounds for refusal of enforcement'.[7] By doing so it has been possible to agree to abolish the *exequatur* in all cases covered by Brussels I, including those relating to privacy and personality rights and collective redress. In this context, Professor Beaumont[8] clarifies that no longer will there be a declaration of enforceability stage of proceedings at which only the Brussels I grounds for non-enforcement can be invoked, but instead all grounds for non-enforcement (the ones in Brussels I and the national ones) will be heard together. As a

[1] Ch 26.

[2] See Tampere European Council 15/16 October 1999: Conclusions of the Presidency www.europarl.europa.eu/summits/tam_en.htm [34]; Commission (EC), 'Review of Council Regulation (EC) No 44/2001 on Jurisdiction and the Recognition and Enforcement of Judgments in Civil and Commercial Matters' (Green Paper) COM (2009) 175 final.

[3] COM (2010) 748 final.

[4] Ch 26.

[5] See Art 37(3) of the Commission Recast. *cf*: Art 37 of the amended text of the Commission recast proposal – 10609/12 ADD 1 of 1 June 2012.

[6] Ch 26.

[7] See P Beaumont and E Johnston, 'Can Exequatur Be Abolished in Brussels I whilst Retaining a Public Policy Defence?' (2010) 6 *Journal of Private International Law* 249, 250.

[8] Ch 26.

result, all of the grounds for refusal of enforcement contained in Article 34 of Brussels I will be retained in the revised Brussels I. This will give rise to specific issues which need to be addressed in a cross-border context as well as in view of the two-task enforcement structure of the EU competition law.

I. CROSS-BORDER NATURE OF EU COMPETITION LAW INFRINGEMENTS: A CASE FOR REFORM

Professor Beaumont's argument[9] that substantive, as well as procedural, public policy is retained as a defence[10] means that there are specific issues to be addressed. First, the public policy character of Articles 101 and 102 TFEU means that it is for the court addressed to verify whether recognition is contrary to EU competition law.[11] Secondly, the issue of recognition and enforcement of judgments in relation to cross-border collective redress EU competition law proceedings may give rise to specific difficulties which may need to be addressed in Regulation 1/2003. Thirdly, the issues regarding the recognition and enforcement of foreign judgments awarding exemplary damages need to be carefully considered.

A. Misapplication of EU Competition Law as a Public Policy Defence

Professor Beaumont demonstrated that the distinction between *Eco Swiss* and *Renault* should be done on the basis of the different fact/law matrix in the two cases, and where that does not give a complete answer, to accept that *Eco Swiss* is the higher authority (being a Full Court of 13 rather than a Chamber of five) and follow it. In his analysis, he goes on to clarify that the Chamber in *Renault* accepted in principle that Article 102 TFEU is a matter of EU public policy (and we know now from *Manfredi* that it is) but that on the facts of the case before them there was either no breach of Article 102 TFEU (the view of the Advocate General and highly likely as it was based on an earlier decision of the Court involving the same parties), or even if there was one it could not be sufficiently manifest or serious to justify denial of recognition of the French judgment on the basis of EU public policy. In this context, Professor Beaumont states:

> It is not within the jurisdiction of the CJEU to determine whether on the facts of the particular case (which of course are not proven to the Court in a preliminary ruling) the breach of the Italian legal principle is a sufficiently serious or manifest one nor to determine whether the Italian legal principle at stake is sufficiently fundamental to the Italian legal order to form the basis of a public policy exception. Both of these assessments should be left to the national courts under the distribution of competences between the Union and its Member States under the Union Treaties and in particular under Article 267 TFEU.[12]

[9] ibid.
[10] ibid.
[11] See Jenard Report OJ [1979] C59/1, 44. See also: Joined Cases C-430/93 and C-432/93 *Jeroen Van Schijndel v Stichting Pensioenfonds* [1995] ECR I-4705; Joined Cases C-295/04–C-298/04 *Manfredi v Lloyd Adriaticco* [2006] 5 CMLR 17 [31].
[12] Ch 26.

The concept of EU public policy includes Articles 101 and 102 TFEU, but a mere error in the application of those Articles in a judgment in one country of the EU is not enough to permit the non-recognition of that judgment in other EU countries on the ground of public policy under Brussels I. He notes that where previously unavailable evidence on the illegality of an agreement comes to light after the case has been decided in the court of origin, then the judgment debtor should be able to use this as the basis for invoking public policy to deny recognition of the judgment. He goes on to state that 'a minimalist approach to a public policy exception must allow for the enforcing court to deny recognition to a foreign judgment from another EU court if it has clearly violated EU competition law and the defendant did all that he could to raise the competition law issues at all levels in the foreign courts, even if no new evidence has come to light since the judgment in the court of origin'.[13] Strong arguments for this can be found in the Union legislator retaining a substantive public policy defence in the recast of Brussels I. In such a scenario, enforcing courts must be careful not to act as appeal courts against the decisions of courts of origin on EU competition law by normally requiring the defendant to have exhausted his domestic remedies on the competition law issue in the country of origin.[14]

B. Recognition and Enforcement of Collective Judgments/Settlements

The fact that the Commission originally proposed a special regime for the recognition and enforcement of collective redress judgments might appear to underline that the public policy defence is an important issue to be considered in this context.[15]

Professor Bariatti[16] puts forward very strong arguments demonstrating that the opt-out mechanism created by the Dutch WCAM is incompatible with the rules on jurisdiction and recognition of judgments of the Brussels system. Thus the Dutch decision authorising the settlement can freely circulate within the EU (and the countries party to the Lugano Convention of 2007). In this context, Professor Bariatti[17] notes that respect for the principle of due process and the rights of the defence is crucial regarding absent class members pursuant to Article 6 of the ECHR and Article 47 of the Charter of Fundamental Rights. Should one reach the conclusion that the mechanism established by WCAM complies with the principles on due process, Professor Bariatti[18] goes on to show that some concerns still exist with regard to the preclusive effect of a settlement in respect of individual claims in cross border cases under the Brussels I Regulation. Professor Bariatti's arguments suggest that there is a level of uncertainty at the moment.[19]

The distinctive features of cross-border collective redress for EU competition law proceedings suggest that the issue of recognition and enforcement of judgments/settlements in

[13] ibid.
[14] ibid.
[15] See Art 37(3) and Art 48 of the Commission Proposal for a Brussels I Regulation COM (2010) 748 final. *cf.* Art 37 of the amended text of the Commission recast proposal – 10609/12 ADD 1 of 1 June 2012.
[16] Ch 27.
[17] ibid
[18] ibid.
[19] ibid.

relation to such actions should be considered in Regulation 1/2003 with a view to promoting regulatory competition in Europe.[20] An appropriate solution,[21] would be to hold that the recognising court should apply a presumption that an opt-out collective EU competition law redress regime of other Member States are compliant with Article 6(1) of the Human Rights Convention as well as with Article 47(2) of the Charter of Fundamental Rights of the European Union.[22] Indeed, such an approach might find support in Article 47(1) of the Charter of Fundamental Rights of the European Union, which states that 'Everyone whose rights and freedoms guaranteed by the law of the Union are violated has the right to an effective remedy'. Hence, the European Commission's efforts to close the enforcement gap, which would be so important for Europe to achieve sustainable economic growth, as well as the policy-makers' impetus to provide redress for those who have suffered damages as a result of an EU competition law infringement, by encouraging collective redress antitrust proceedings in Europe are strong arguments favouring the proposed approach.[23]

C. Recognition and Enforcement of Judgments Awarding Exemplary Damages

Professors Beaumont[24] and Bariatti[25] reaffirm that the issue of the recognition and enforcement of judgments awarding exemplary damages is important in an EU context. As noted elsewhere,[26] the fact that courts in England award exemplary (or punitive) damages in certain cases suggests that the English courts would normally enforce a Member State's court's judgment awarding punitive damages in EU antitrust claims. However, Recital 32 indicates that on the basis of Article 34(1) of the Brussels I Regulation, other Member State courts can deny recognition and enforcement of the part of a judgment awarding excessive punitive antitrust damages, as being contrary to their public policy to recognise and enforce it.[27] In this context, the recognising court would not review the Member State's court's judgment with regard to its merits, but would simply refuse recognition of part of the judgment, so far as the exemplary antitrust damages being contrary to its public policy was concerned. It is the effect of the part of the judgment awarding punitive antitrust damages that would affect the essential values of the legal system which regards such damage awards as being in conflict with its pub-

[20] Ch 18.

[21] A less appropriate solution would be to adopt the opt-in regime in respect of a claimant's class domiciled in another Member State. The latter approach would not solve all problems, due to the low mobility of consumers across Europe, and the low number of collective redress proceedings in the overwhelming majority of the Member States.

[22] *cf. Maronier v Larmer* [2002] EWCA Civ 774, [2003] QB [25]. Criticised by J Fawcett, 'The Impact of Article 6(1) of the ECHR on Private International Law' (2007) 56 *ICLQ* 1.

[23] Ch 18.

[24] Ch 26.

[25] Ch 27.

[26] See M Danov, *Jurisdiction and Judgments in Relation to EU Competition Law Claims* (Oxford, Hart Publishing, 2010).

[27] M Danov, 'Awarding Exemplary (Or Punitive) Antitrust Damages in EC Competition Cases with an International Element – the Rome II Regulation and the Commission's White Paper on damages' (2008) 29 ECLR 430. See also: P Hay, 'The Development Of The Public Policy Barrier To Judgment Recognition within the European Community' (2007) *European Legal Forum* 289, 293–94; MR Isidro, 'Punitive Damages from a Private International Law Perspective' in H Koziol and V Wilcox (eds), *Punitive Damages: Common Law and Civil Law Perspectives* (Vienna/New York, Springer, 2009) 237, 250.

lic policy, so that no reopening of the merits would occur at the stage where a recognising court is denying recognition of an award of punitive damages.[28]

However, this could be a problem, and would fly in the face of any framework which is intended to promote regulatory competition. The public policy nature of Articles 101 and 102 TFEU as well as the need to provide 'an effective remedy' within the meaning of Article 47(1) of the Charter of Fundamental Rights strongly suggest that the issue must be addressed in light of *Manfredi*, which appears to suggest that punitive damages may be an appropriate remedy with regard to antitrust infringements in Europe.[29]

A reform of Regulation 1/2003 may well address the above issues along with the specific issues surrounding the recognition and enforcement of judgments against two defendants who are joint tortfeasors as, for example, being parties to a cartel agreement in breach of EU competition law. There are important issues to be considered in this context. Might *res judicata* apply as between joint tortfeasors (eg parties to the same cartel agreement; or parent and subsidiary)? Do joint tortfeasors have a sufficient privity of interest that might lead to the application of *res judicata*? These are very important issues which may need to be addressed by the EU legislator in the context of cross-border EU competition law actions with a view to address the existing uncertainties in the area.

II. TWO-TASK ENFORCEMENT STRUCTURE: A CASE FOR CONSOLIDATION

In addition, the two-task enforcement structure gives rise to specific difficulties which may need to be considered by the EU legislator when revising Regulation 1/2003. Judge Pelikánová's proposal[30] to confer to the European Commission exclusively the powers to investigate and prosecute by initiating proceedings before the court which would have decision-making powers may need to be considered in the context of NCAs' proceedings as well. Indeed, the fact that the National Competition Authorities (NCAs) and national courts have the powers to apply Articles 101 and 102 TFEU in individual cases suggest that there could be specific issues to be addressed. Although decisions of NCAs are given in the context of administrative public proceedings in which NCAs enjoy extensive investigative and decision-making powers,[31] decisions of NCAs do enjoy finality.[32] The White Paper on damages seems to indicate that Member State courts should avoid taking decisions running counter to a final decision of an NCA finding an infringement of Articles 101 and 102 TFEU.[33] Would such a decision be within the scope of the Brussels I Regulation? Would there be any specific problem? Should the issue be dealt with by Regulation 1/2003?

[28] Hay (n 27) 294. See also: Commission (EC) 'The Common Position of the Council on the Adoption of a Regulation of the European Parliament and of the Council on the Law Applicable to Non-Contractual Obligations ("Rome II")' (Communication) COM (2006) 566 final; Isidro (n 27) 250; R Plender and M Wilderspin, *The European Private International Law of Obligations*, 3rd edn (London, Sweet & Maxwell, 2009) 751–52.

[29] See also: Ch 23.

[30] Ch 7.

[31] A Komninos, *EC Private Antitrust Enforcement: Decentralised Application of EC Competition Law by National Courts* (Oxford, Hart Publishing, 2008) 119.

[32] X Groussot and T Minssen, '*Res Judicata* in the Court of Justice Case-law: Balancing Legal Certainty with Legality?' (2007) 3 *European Constitutional Law Review* 385.

[33] Commission (EC), *Damages Actions for Breach of the EC Antitrust Rules* (White Paper) COM(2008) 165 final [2.3].

There are good arguments indicating that an appropriate solution would be to hold that a decision of an NCA would be within the scope of the Brussels I Regulation as long as it is related to a civil or commercial matter.[34] However, such a broader interpretation would suggest that the recognition of an NCA decision (or part of a decision) would often have to overcome a public policy defence that could be based on the breach of the undertaking's right to fair trial and hearing in administrative proceedings.[35] The recognition would be particularly difficult in cases where the decision was taken by an NCA that is an administrative body, combining the function of a party to competition law proceedings and a judge.[36] Such NCA proceedings could undermine the right to a fair trial and hearing and the rendered NCA decision could raise 'due process' concerns. A general principle of EU law is that everyone is entitled to a fair trial and hearing,[37] which is indeed a fundamental human right.[38] It is well established that a manifest breach of a fundamental human right would trigger the public policy defence under Brussels I.[39] In determining whether an NCA's proceedings safeguard the infringing undertaking's right to a fair trial and hearing, the recognising court should be guided by the case law of the European Court of Human Rights (ECtHR). As already submitted, the ECtHR requires that, in the determination of civil rights and obligations, decisions taken by administrative authorities should be subject to a judicial body that has full jurisdiction.[40] In other words, if a decision taken by an NCA were not reviewed by a court with full jurisdiction, then it could be argued that the right to fair trial of an infringing undertaking would be undermined[41] and hence that recourse to the public policy defence under Brussels I would be possible.[42] Although the European Commission has proposed the abolition of *exequatur*,[43] it seems that there will be safeguards that may be triggered if the right to fair trial of the defendant is undermined.[44] In spite of the fact that a broader interpretation of Article 32 of Brussels I would further uphold the independence of Member State courts, which would be entitled to deny the recognition of a decision taken by a foreign NCA whose proceedings did not respect the right to a fair trial and hearing of the defendant, this would create difficulties and a high level of uncertainty which would need to be carefully considered by policy-makers.[45]

Hence, there is a strong case for the EU legislator to consider an amendment to Regulation 1/2003 that would promote free circulation of decisions in relation to EU competition law further safeguarding the defendant's right to a fair trial, as well as upholding the independence of Member State courts vis-à-vis NCAs.[46] This would be important with a view to ensuring that the whole enforcement system is compliant with the ECHR and

[34] M Danov, 'EU Competition Law Enforcement: Is Brussels I suited to dealing with all the challenges?' (2012) 61 *ICLQ* 27.

[35] Art 34(1) and (2) of Brussels I. See also Case C-7/98 *Krombach v Bamberski* [2000] ECR I-1395 [43]; Fawcett (n 22) 25; Beaumont and Johnston (n 7) 253–54.

[36] WPJ Wils, *Principles of European Antitrust Enforcement* (Oxford, Hart Publishing, 2005) 88.

[37] *Krombach* (n 35) [26].

[38] See Art 47(2) of the Charter of Fundamental Rights; Art 6(1) ECHR.

[39] *Krombach* (n 35) [39]–[45].

[40] *Le Compte v Belgium* (1982) 4 EHRR 1. See also: Wils (n 36) 46–47; IS Forrester, 'Due Process in EC Competition Cases: A Distinguished Institution with Flawed Procedures' (2009) 34 *EL Rev* 817, 821.

[41] Wils (n 36) 89.

[42] *Krombach* (n 34) 42.

[43] Art 38 of the Proposal for a Regulation on Jurisdiction and the Recognition and Enforcement of Judgments in Civil and Commercial Matters COM (2010) 748/3 (Brussels I Proposal). See more: Ch 26.

[44] Beaumont and Johnston (n 7) 253.

[45] Danov (n 34).

[46] ibid.

Charter of Fundamental Rights. Centralising proceedings before the national courts might be a good way to achieve this, by conferring the powers to investigate and prosecute to the competition authorities, and leave decision-making powers to the courts which would be able to hear and determine related damages actions as well.

The case for consolidation of proceedings before the national courts may be strengthened if the EU legislator wants to make sure that the extent to which a company has made redress is taken into account by the competent authorities when determining what level of fine to impose.[47] There is no scope for offsetting fines and damages in the current system,[48] and this may be rectified by an amendment of Regulation 1/2003. The proposal of Professor Kessedjian to add a specific rule to Brussels I with a view to allow a judge in the country of enforcement to 'lower the amount of damages if the judgment debtor has also been fined by competition authorities'[49] seems unsustainable. Professor Beaumont[50] has noted that it seems appropriate to treat these cases in the same way as one would treat a foreign judgment that has awarded punitive damages. He goes on to state that the principle should be that the party who has suffered damage should be able to enforce in full, at least, the compensatory element of the foreign judgment.[51] This should happen even if the administrative fine may have taken account of potential damage to market actors in calculating how much the fine should be.[52]

[47] See more: Ch 23. See also: question 30 of the BIS consultations – Department for Business Innovation & Skills, *Private Actions in Competition Law: A Consultation on Options for Reform*, 24 April 2012 www.bis.gov.uk/assets/biscore/consumer-issues/docs/p/12-742-private-actions-in-competition-law-consultation.pdf.

[48] M Danov and S Dnes, 'Private Actions In Competition Law: A Consultation On Options For Reform. Response Form' submitted to the UK Government, Department for Business, Innovation and Skills on 24 July 2012.

[49] C Kessedjian, 'Recognition and Enforcement of Foreign Judgments' in J Basedow, S Francq and L Idot (eds), *International Antitrust Litigation: Conflict of Laws and Coordination* (Oxford, Hart Publishing, 2012) 245, 256.

[50] Ch 26.

[51] This principle is supported by Professor Kessedjian (n 49) 254–55, and she expressly says that this power to lower the foreign damages award should not 'deprive the injured private persons of legitimate damages' (ibid 255).

[52] Ch 26.

29

The Way Forward: A Strong Case for Reform at EU Level

MIHAIL DANOV AND FLORIAN BECKER

The foregoing analyses suggest strongly that there is an enforcement gap at present. The following specific features of the EU competition law enforcement structure need to be considered by the Union legislator with a view to closing the existing enforcement gap.

First, due to the cross-border nature of many EU competition law infringements, some Member States are attracting less competition law actions than others. This may be an indication that some Member States' courts may have less experience than others when it comes to dealing with complex cross-border EU competition law cases. Also, the effectiveness and consistency with which EU competition law provisions are enforced across Europe may be questioned, as there seems to be an enforcement gap in some Member States where there may be less redress for businesses and consumers who have suffered harm as a result of EU competition law infringements.

Secondly, it is beyond any doubt that an enforcement pattern in which the private litigation is normally seen as a follow-on action based on a public enforcement action will leave an enforcement gap. The public enforcers across Europe are unlikely to have the resources to investigate all the complaints they receive. In other words, there is a strong case that it will not be possible for the public enforcers to investigate and detect all the infringements. Indeed, even in cases where EU competition law infringements have been established by a regulator's decisions, a significant number of victims of those infringements will remain uncompensated, as it would normally be only the large purchasers bringing the actions. Even jurisdictions like England and Germany, which are among the leading competition law jurisdictions at the moment, appear to be attracting primarily follow-on actions brought by large purchasers. Hence, there appears to be a wide enforcement gap in so far as there is no redress for consumers at the present. This may be explained by the fact that the damage suffered by an individual consumer may be very difficult to ascertain, as its amount may indeed be negligible in some cases. It is beyond doubt that if a claim is brought by an end consumer, then 'the non-assessable cost of responding to discovery and the like will substantially erode, if not exceed, any recovery.'[1] Therefore, there is certainly a case for reform in order to close the enforcement gap and provide redress for consumers.

It has been demonstrated that should the legislator wish to design an effective collective redress system, there are three important issues which need to be carefully considered.

[1] M Handler, 'The Shift from Substantive to Procedural Innovations in Antitrust Suits – The Twenty-Third Annual Antitrust Review' (1971) 71 *Columbia Law Review* 1, 9. See more: Ch 18.

First, one of the important features of EU competition law actions is that there would be multiple victims in various countries. Secondly, the multiple victims may have suffered different levels of damages, and, as a result, they may have different interests in so far as those affected by an EU competition law infringement may be further up or down in the chain of distribution (ie passing on or absorbing the inflated price). Thirdly, consumers would be reluctant to bring such actions due to the negligible amount of damages suffered by them in comparison with the high litigation costs.[2] However, answers to questions as to who should undertake the reform, and what reform should be carried out in Europe, could not be given without taking account of the distinctive features of the European judiciary.

I. EUROPEAN JUDICIAL ARCHITECTURE: A CASE TO PROMOTE INTER-JURISDICTIONAL REGULATORY COMPETITION

Before discussing the proposed solutions, the specific features of the EU civil justice system must be considered. The EU relies on the individual Member States' legal orders and national courts to enforce the rights of the individuals derived from the TFEU, and provide redress for those who have suffered as a result of an EU competition law infringement. The EU legislator has adopted special Regulation 1/2003 which is meant to ensure that Articles 101 and 102 TFEU are applied effectively and uniformly across Europe.[3] It has been clearly stated that 'in order to ensure compliance with the principles of legal certainty and the uniform application of the [Union] competition rules in a system of parallel powers, conflicting decisions must be avoided.'[4] The cause of action for EU competition law damages is a mixture of EU law and Member States' laws. The possibility for different Member States' laws to apply to matters of procedure and substance in claims, based on the very same directly applicable Treaty provisions, may lead to a situation where some Member States' courts are enforcing EU competition law more efficiently than others. Harmonisation at EU level may be an obvious solution.

The fact that EU competition law provisions are to be applied by the European Commission and national competition authorities as well as by the courts of 27 Member States (28 as from 2013) clearly suggests that these specific characteristics, which are shaping the litigants' tactics, would need to be carefully considered by the policy-maker. The chapters by Lawrence and Morfey[5] as well as by Reher[6] very clearly summarise the aspects which shape the litigants' decisions to sue and/or settle at present. Lawrence and Morfey[7] indicate that the issues of jurisdiction, limitation periods, overcharge and pass-on as well as costs are key. Reher shows that a claimant would consider the following aspects of the law before deciding where to bring his EU competition law claim: the mechanisms for aggregation of individual claims and collective actions, the applicable procedural law, and the applicable substantive law.[8] Should the legislator want to promote litigation with a view to

[2] Ch 18.

[3] See Recitals 1–8 of Council Regulation No 1/2003 on the implementation of the rules on competition laid down in Arts 101 and 102 TFEU.

[4] Recital 22 of Regulation 1/2003.

[5] Ch 11.

[6] Ch 12.

[7] Ch 11.

[8] Ch 12.

closing the enforcement gap, the issues identified by Reher,[9] Lawrence and Morfey[10] inter alia must be carefully considered.

However, it seems that, even if one makes a case for harmonisation of substantive and procedural laws in Europe, the current European juridical structure would not be capable of promoting uniform application of the adopted harmonised instrument. Indeed, a new instrument harmonising substantive and procedural laws may bring fresh uncertainty, and it thus may increase the workload of the European Courts, which may result in further delay resulting in a wider enforcement gap. It seems clear that it is not feasible to have a 'single scheme of jurisdiction'[11] with regard to private EU competition law actions. Although a possibility for private parties to make an appeal on a point of EU competition law before any of the European Courts (eg the General Court) could be potentially considered in theory (and perhaps in the long run), such a solution would be very difficult to be achieved in practice. Andreangeli demonstrates that ensuring coherence, speed and finality in EU competition litigation is a concern for the overall EU competition law enforcement structure which might justify legislative intervention at EU level.[12] However, she unambiguously demonstrates that allowing private parties to make an appeal on a point of EU competition law before the European courts would fly in the face of the current institutional architecture of the Union.[13]

A solution including increased involvement of the General Court, by granting to it an appellate function in matters of EU competition law, which could provide for greater uniformity and more certainty, was also rejected in England and Germany on the basis of concerns about increased delay as well as on the basis that EU competition law issues are not special in comparison with other EU law actions. Other commentators have also noted that allowing for an appeal to be made on a point of EU competition law before the European Union courts would have drawbacks.[14] The major drawbacks are that a system of appeals would have affected the autonomy of the Member States' Supreme Courts in matters of EU competition law as well as parties' willingness to raise EU competition law issues due to the increased costs and delay.[15]

Judge Pelikánová proposes another very original solution, which might potentially result in a single jurisdiction over EU competition law damages actions. In particular, her proposal is to confer on 'the General Court competence to decide, as a court of first instance, in actions for damages in competition cases decided by the European Commission'.[16] However, she herself acknowledges the difficult political reality in the Union, and admits that amending the Treaty to add a new competence of the General Court to hear damages actions will not be received well by the Member States. Moreover, Judge Pelikánová[17] goes further to demonstrate how inefficient the current juridical architecture is as well as to question the effect of the proposed increase of the number of judges in the General Court. There are indeed

[9] ibid.

[10] Ch 11.

[11] P Eleftheriadis, 'Federalism and Jurisdiction' in E Cloots, G de Baere and S Sottiaux (eds), *Federalism in the European Union* (Oxford, Hart Publishing, 2012) 45, 54.

[12] See Ch 8.

[13] See Ch 8.

[14] DWK Anderson and M Demetriou, *References to the European Court* (London, Sweet & Maxwell, 2002) 5.

[15] Anderson and Demetriou (n 14) [1-012].

[16] See Ch 7.

[17] ibid.

persuasive arguments that an increase in the number of judges may adversely affect the quality and standards of work, because it would bring about a rotation of judges.[18]

The political reality in the Union and the inefficient European legal system clearly suggest that a new mode of governance which might produce efficient enforcement results in the area may be based on an effective private international law instrument to promote regulatory competition across Europe. Indeed, the overwhelming majority of respondents from England[19] and Germany[20] favoured allowing the system to evolve in its current form. Thus, the respondents appear to favour inter-jurisdictional regulatory competition in the area of EU antitrust law dispute resolution to attract claimants and produce efficient enforcement results.

In this way, strong jurisdictions for bringing cross-border EU competition law actions might emerge. In this context, it should be noted that the UK Government has very recently launched public consultations seeking to reform the UK regime for private actions in competition law.[21] The contemplated reform is meant to 'allow consumers and businesses to obtain compensation for losses they have suffered as a result of anticompetitive behaviour',[22] which would address the current enforcement gap at national level.

Indeed, the relative importance of the procedural rules might suggest that a national legislator could be best placed to address the problems. The national legislator may be best placed to 'devise an institutional architecture of competition law enforcement [at national level] which encourages the claims, where there is really harm to the market and the process of competition, and creates safeguards against claims where companies might be using the system for a variety of purposes not necessarily beneficial to the market and the process of competition.'[23] Encouraging reforms at national level could even allow for regulatory competition as a claimant could bring its action in the 'jurisdiction judged most hospitable',[24] provided that the jurisdictional rules were appropriate.[25]

Whilst a reform at national level must address these issues in a German or British context, the cross-border nature of most European competition law infringements, in which damages would often be suffered by businesses and consumers in a number of jurisdictions, could complicate the picture unless there is a legislative intervention by the EU legislator. An increased number of claims might be seen in some Member States, if they undertake an appropriate reform at national level. However, given that the collected data suggest that there is no redress for consumers and SMEs who are not particularly active in bringing competition law actions at the moment, one may argue that there would be Member States in which the enforcement gap would remain or even widen unless there

[18] See more: Ch 7.

[19] See more: Ch 3.

[20] See more: Ch 4.

[21] Department for Business Innovation & Skills, *Private Actions in Competition Law: A Consultation on Options for Reform,* 24 April 2012 www.bis.gov.uk/assets/biscore/consumer-issues/docs/p/12–742-private-actions-in-competition-law-consultation.pdf. The BIS's proposed options for reform were discussed at a BIICL seminar, 'Rapid-Response Seminar: Private Actions in UK competition law: BIS's proposed options for reform', British Institute of International and Comparative Law, London, 9 May 2012.

[22] ibid p 3.

[23] M Danov and S Dnes, 'Private Actions In Competition Law: A Consultation On Options For Reform. Response Form' submitted to the UK Government, Department for Business, Innovation and Skills on 24 July 2012.

[24] S Weatherill, 'Why Harmonise?' in T Tridimas and P Nebbia, *European Union Law for the Twenty-First Century: Rethinking the New Legal Order,* Vol 2 (Oxford, Hart Publishing, 2004) 11, 14.

[25] See Ch 13. See also: M Danov, *Jurisdiction and Judgments in Relation to EU Competition Law Claims* (Oxford, Hart Publishing, 2010).

is a reform at EU level to address this. Externalities, which may give rise to welfare losses and market distortions,[26] could be one cause for market failure when it comes to inter-jurisdictional regulatory competition in the area of EU antitrust law dispute resolution in the European context.

Furthermore, the success of the regulatory competition model would be subject to the claimant being able and being prepared to pay the cross-border litigation costs[27] which could, of course, be offset against a potential damages award. The qualitative data clearly shows that costs and damages would be other important factors to be considered by the claimants. Thus, the lack of mobility of the SMEs and consumers, who prefer to bring their EU competition law claims in their home states, may be the other cause of the regulatory market failure.[28]

Therefore, given the cross-border nature of many EU competition law actions, EU intervention may be required as the cross-border implications would make any national legislation less than effective in the EU context.[29] Article 81 TFEU clearly states that the EU has competence in all private international law matters with a cross-border element even when such legislative measures are not necessary for the proper functioning of the internal market.[30] Indeed, a special private international framework should be drafted with a view to ensuring that the regulatory competition would not be adversely affected by any market failures driven by externalities or lack of mobility of market participants.[31] The case for reforming the private international law framework at EU level could be further strengthened, if one takes account of the high litigation costs which would adversely affect the mobility of the 'cross-border litigant [who would], as a practical matter, require two lawyers, one in his Home State to give preliminary advice, and one in the Host State to conduct the litigation.'[32]

In view of the foregoing, there is a strong case for the Union to build upon its success[33] with the Brussels I Regulation and design an instrument on jurisdiction and judgments in relation to EU competition law claims. Given the fact that in the new Proposal for a Regulation on Jurisdiction and the Recognition and Enforcement of Judgments[34] there is no indication that special rules for parallel EU competition law proceedings in the successor to Regulation 44/2001 are on anyone's agenda, an appropriate way forward with a view to addressing the specific issues arising in a cross-border context, might be amending Regulation 1/2003 to address the issues of jurisdiction as well as the problem of proceedings in order to avoid irreconcilable or inconsistent decisions in the European context.

However, one may question the ability of a private international law instrument to address all the problems and the two-task enforcement structure of EU competition law in

[26] DC Esty and D Geradin, 'Regulatory Co Operation' in DC Esty and D Geradin (eds), *Regulatory Competition and Economic Integration* (Oxford, OUP, 2001) 30, 34.

[27] Green Paper from the Commission, *Legal Aid in Civil Matters: The Problems Confronting the Cross-border Litigant* COM(2000) 51 final p 9.

[28] Esty and Geradin (n 26) 34.

[29] HM Watt, 'Integration and Diversity: The Conflict of Laws as a Regulatory Tool' in F Cafaggi (ed), *The Institutional Framework of European Private Law* (Oxford, OUP, 2006) (n 1) 107.

[30] P Beaumont and P McEleavy, *Private International Law, Anton* (Edinburgh, SULI/W Green, 2011) 16–17. See also: P Craig, 'The Lisbon Treaty: Law, Politics and Treaty Reform (Oxford, OUP, 2010) 343.

[31] Esty and Geradin (n 27) 32–40.

[32] Green Paper from the Commission, *Legal Aid in Civil Matters: The Problems Confronting the Cross-border Litigant* COM(2000) 51 final p 9.

[33] R Garnett, *Substance and Procedure in Private International Law* (Oxford, OUP, 2012) 67–68. See also: The American Law Institute/UNIDROIT Principles of Transnational Civil Procedure (2004) www.unidroit.org/english/principles/civilprocedure/ali-unidroitprinciples-e.pdf.

[34] COM(2010) 748 final.

particular. As already noted,[35] the real concern is that the pattern which is developing in Europe and England in particular appears to indicate that the limited private litigation which occurs normally proceeds as a follow-on action based on a public enforcement action. In view of that, one may argue that '[t]he current ineffectiveness of antitrust damages actions'[36] is best to be addressed by an amendment of Regulation 1/2003 with a view to address the specific issues of jurisdiction and judgments in relation to EU competition law claims as well as the issues due to the ineffective two-task structure. In the course of such a reform, private international law techniques may be used to promote regulatory competition.

II. REGULATING CROSS-BORDER EU COMPETITION LAW PROCEEDINGS AT EU LEVEL: HOW TO PROMOTE REGULATORY COMPETITION

There are several main issues which need to be considered in order to address the lack of mobility of claimants with a view to closing the enforcement gap and avoiding parallel proceedings.

i. *A Key Issue: How to Close the Enforcement Gap?*

The analyses in Chapter 18 show that a gatekeeper can be a major help in organising consumers due to the negligible amount of antitrust damages suffered by the numerous individual consumers across Europe. If the consumers in question are direct purchasers, then consumer associations would be best placed to organise consumers and bring representative actions aggregating numerous small damage claims on behalf of the consumers on an opt-out basis. However, the consumer associations may not be well placed to bring EU competition law damages claims in cases where consumers are indirect purchasers of a cartelised product. Nonetheless, even if an opt-out regime were introduced, the consumer associations may not be well placed to bring EU competition law damages claims in cases where 'consumers do not buy directly from manufacturers but instead from middlemen'.[37]

Bearing in mind that it is the large companies that generally appear to be bringing EU competition law damages actions, it seems to us that one way of closing the enforcement gap in Europe would be to allow large purchasers, for example, to aggregate claims on behalf of purchasers down the chain of distribution (including end consumers).[38] This would allow large companies to aggregate claims on behalf of consumers of a cartelised product and/or consumers who are paying a monopoly price. In such cases, a gatekeeping role will be performed by the judges who would exercise judicial control over the cases at the certification stage. The volume of sales of the large purchasers, who have opted into the collective redress proceedings, can be an objective criterion in assessing their adequacy to act as representatives of the end consumers who would be involved on an opt-out basis. Such a proposal inter alia would address the passing-on defence.[39]

[35] See Chs 3 and 5.

[36] Commission (EC), 'White Paper on Damages actions for the breach of the EC antitrust rules', COM (2008) 165 [1.1].

[37] RA Posner, *Economic Analysis of Law,* 8th edn (Wolters Kluwer, 2010) 419–20.

[38] Ch 18. See also: Danov and Dnes (n 23).

[39] See more: Ch 18. See also: Ch 3; Danov and Dnes (n 23).

The low mobility of consumers might be an important factor to be considered when deciding whether an opt-out regime, implemented by a particular Member State, would operate for consumers from other Member States. Indeed, an opt-out regime applicable to out-of-jurisdiction claimants might be necessary to provide an 'effective remedy' within the meaning of Article 47(1) of the Charter of Fundamental Rights for consumers from across Europe. Also, such a solution might create incentives for defendants to settle and achieve finality with a large number of businesses and consumers. In other words, such a regime could take account of the cross-border nature of EU competition law infringements, and the fact that groups of companies engage in anti-competitive conduct through their subsidiaries in a number of Member States. To this end, it would be essential to have an appropriately devised certification regime which requires a judge to identify the Member States where the businesses (or the consumer associations) that have opted in to the action operate and direct their activities to. For example, if the action was brought by a large purchaser, then the courts may certify that the opt-in direct purchasers are suitable representatives of the claimants from several Member States by identifying the volume of their sales (or the sales of their subsidiaries) in the countries in question. In other words, the volume of sales of the businesses, which have opted into the collective redress proceedings, can be an objective criterion in assessing their adequacy to act as representatives of the end consumers from the Member States in which, for example, a cartelised product has been sold.[40]

ii. How to Promote Mobility of Large Purchasers (and Consumer Organisations), so that they can Aggregate Consumer Claims before an Appropriate Court?

Although it would be difficult to elaborate a special basis for jurisdiction which requires a substantial connection between the breach of Articles 101 and 102 TFEU and the effects of the anti-competitive agreement or conduct within the territory of the Member State where the action is brought and in respect of which the EU antitrust law claim is brought,[41] there is a need for a jurisdiction rule which allows a claimant to centralise litigation against a group of the same companies before the courts at his preferred jurisdiction. Where, for example, there is a corporate group with numerous subsidiaries (all of which form a single infringing undertaking), then it should be open for a claimant by establishing jurisdiction against one of the subsidiaries to centralise litigation against the whole group of companies as well as against the other group(s) of companies who were party to the same anti-competitive agreement. This could be justified by the fact that EU competition law infringements would often directly and substantially affect the markets in several countries and/or regions.[42]

iii. Centralising Litigation

In order to allow the parties to avoid parallel EU competition law proceedings, and centralise litigation before the court that is clearly appropriate to deal with the case, avoiding the problem of irreconcilable or inconsistent judgments, Regulation 1/2003 should go a step further and allow the court (or NCA) first seised to stay their proceedings, in cases where

[40] Ch 18.

[41] M Danov, *Jurisdiction and Judgments in Relation to EU Competition Law Claims* (Oxford, Hart Publishing, 2010).

[42] See more: Chs 13 and 18.

the agreement or practice has no substantial direct effects (whether actual or foreseeable) on competition within the Member State and where another court is better placed to deal with the case.[43] Such an approach would be better suited to deal with the difficulties that could arise in parallel court proceedings as well as with the problems arising in proceedings before an NCA located in one Member State and private proceedings related to the same infringement of Article 101 and/or Article 102 before another Member State court.[44] Although such a rule could work well in theory, the proposed solution in practice may bring even more uncertainty unless there are clear criteria for the courts on the basis of which they can exercise their discretion. If the Union legislator decides to promote regulatory competition, then procedural laws, experience of judges, potential delays as well as heads of damages and remedies could perhaps be considered as relevant criteria with a view to closing the enforcement gap in Europe.

iv. Applicable Laws

Fitchen[45] and Mercer[46] clearly demonstrate that allowing a private antitrust claimant to base his claim on the *lex fori* in cases where the markets in several countries have been affected would be key, if the EU legislator wants to address the existing level of uncertainty. Indeed, such an approach would also promote inter-jurisdictional regulatory competition across Europe.

Fitchen in Chapter 21 makes a strong case for legislative intervention with a view to addressing the uncertainties under Article 6(3) of Rome II.[47] Tzakas's analysis in Chapter 17 may be used to strengthen the case for a reform. Indeed, Tzakas convincingly raises some important choice-of-law issues which have not been properly taken into account in the context of collective redress. These issues are: recognition of representative entities, questions of standing, interchangeability of representative entities, representation of foreign claimants, and distribution of the obtained damages funds.[48] These issues may be best addressed in a consistent way through an amendment of Regulation1/2003, which may be a golden opportunity for the policy-maker to promote inter-jurisdictional regulatory competition across Europe.

v. Preclusive Effect of Judgments/Settlements – Ensuring Finality

Ensuring finality presupposes an appropriately designed mechanism which allows the parties to avoid parallel EU competition law proceedings, and centralise litigation before the court that is clearly appropriate to deal with the case, avoiding the problem of irreconcilable or inconsistent judgments.

[43] Compare the European approach in respect of allocation of cases between the NCAs. See the Commission Notice on Cooperation within the Network of Competition Authorities [2004] OJ C101/43 [8]. See further Danov (n 41) 281–83.

[44] J Basedow (ed), *Private Enforcement of EC Competition Law* (Kluwer 2007) 1–2; A. Komninos, *EC Private Antitrust Enforcement: Decentralised Application of EC Competition Law by National Courts* (Hart Publishing, Oxford 2008) pp 7–8. See more: M. Danov, 'EU Competition Law Enforcement: Is Brussels I suited to dealing with all the challenges?' (2012) 61 *ICLQ* 27.

[45] Ch 21 – Fitchen.

[46] Ch 22 – Mercer.

[47] Ch 21 – Fitchen.

[48] Ch 17 – Tzakas.

Another specific issue, which needs to be addressed by the EU legislator, concerns the preclusive effects of opt-out collective redress judgments/settlements. The fact that the Commission originally proposed a special regime for the recognition and enforcement of collective redress judgments might appear to underline that the public policy defence is an important issue to be considered in this context.[49] Professor Bariatti puts forward very strong arguments demonstrating that the opt-out mechanism created by the Dutch WCAM is incompatible with the rules on jurisdiction and recognition of judgments of the Brussels system. Thus the Dutch decision authorising the settlement can freely circulate within the EU (and the countries party to the Lugano Convention of 2007). In this context, Professor Bariatti notes that the respect of the principle of due process and the rights of the defence is crucial regarding absent class members pursuant to Article 6 of the ECHR and Article 47 of the Charter of Fundamental Rights. Should one reach the conclusion that the mechanism established by WCAM complies with the principles on due process, Professor Bariatti[50] goes on to show that some concerns still exist with regard to the preclusive effects of a settlement in respect to individual claims in cross border cases under the Brussels I Regulation.[51] Professor Bariatti's arguments suggest that there is a level of uncertainty at the moment.

The distinctive features of cross-border collective redress of EU competition law proceedings suggest that the issue of recognition and enforcement of judgments/settlements in relation to such actions should be considered in Regulation 1/2003 with a view to promoting regulatory competition in Europe.[52] An appropriate solution,[53] would be to hold that the recognising court should apply a presumption that the opt-out collective EU competition law redress regimes of other Member States are compliant with Article 6(1) of the Human Rights Convention as well as with Article 47(2) of the Charter of Fundamental Rights of the European Union.[54] Indeed, such an approach might find support in Article 47(1) of the Charter of Fundamental Rights of the European Union, which states that 'Everyone whose rights and freedoms guaranteed by the law of the Union are violated has the right to an effective remedy'.[55] Hence, the European Commission's efforts to close the enforcement gap, which would be important for Europe to achieve sustainable economic growth, as well as the policy-makers' impetus to provide redress for those, who have suffered damages as a result of an EU competition law infringement, by encouraging collective redress antitrust proceedings in Europe might be strong arguments favouring the proposed approach.[56]

[49] See Arts 37(3) and 48 of the Commission Proposal for a Brussels I Regulation COM (2010) 748 final. *cf.* Art 37 of the amended text of the Commission recast proposal – 10609/12 ADD 1 of 1 June 2012.

[50] Ch 27.

[51] ibid.

[52] Ch 18.

[53] A less appropriate solution would be to adopt the opt-in regime in respect of the claimant's class domiciled in another Member State. The latter approach would not solve all problems due to the low mobility of consumers across Europe, and the low number of collective redress proceedings in the overwhelming majority of the Member States.

[54] cf: *Maronier v Larmer* [2002] EWCA Civ 774, [2003] QB [25]. Criticised by J Fawcett, 'The Impact of Article 6(1) of the ECHR on Private International Law' (2007) 56 *International and Comparative Law Quarterly* 1.

[55] Regarding the implications of Art 47(1) of the Charter of Fundamental Right, see Ch 17.

[56] Ch 18.

III. REVISING THE INSTITUTIONAL ARCHITECTURE OF EU COMPETITION LAW ENFORCEMENT

Furthermore, the institutional architecture of antitrust enforcement may need to be revamped, in order for the EU legislator to close the enforcement gap, which appears to exist at the moment, and to provide for consistent and efficient enforcement of EU competition law provisions across Europe.

Regulation 1/2003 provides for mechanisms to ensure that 'competition authorities of the Member States shall apply the [EU] competition laws in close co-operation'.[57] Articles 15 and 16 of Regulation 1/2003 are meant to guarantee uniform and consistent application of EU competition law in proceedings before the Commission and in cross-border EU competition law before Member State courts. However, Regulation 1/2003 does not deal with the problem of coherent and uniform application of EU competition law in proceedings before an NCA located in one Member State and private EU antitrust law proceedings related to the same breaches of Article 101 TFEU and/or Article 102 TFEU before a court in another Member State. Problems are bound to arise in such cases as potentially irreconcilable decisions on the same (or a related) EU competition law issue by an English court and a foreign competition authority should be avoided.[58] Indeed, it may be far from efficient to have one set of proceedings before an NCA in order to establish a breach of competition law, and another set of proceedings before Member State courts in order for a claimant to prove that damage has been caused to him. Judge Pelikánová also addresses the problems which are related to the two-task EU competition law enforcement by suggesting that the legislator should 'leave to the European Commission solely the inquiry, with the duty to introduce a criminal or civil action before the Court. The system would better fulfil the requirements of the ECHR.'[59]

The first set of difficulties is analysed by Bos and Möhlmann,[60] who clearly demonstrate that if a national court stays its proceedings until the decision of the European Commission (or a ruling given on it by a European Court) has become final and binding, then that national court would delay the adjudication on such a case for several years. It has been submitted that a national court should aim to safeguard the rights of the litigants to have the case determined within a reasonable period of time in compliance with Article 6(1) of the European Convention on Human Rights.

Secondly, a case for procedural inefficiencies of the current two-task enforcement structure may be made if one looks at the problems before the courts in follow-on actions brought against defendants, who, despite being a part of an infringing undertaking, are not named in the operative part of the Commission's infringement decision (ie *dispositif*).[61] The issue was considered by the CAT in *Emerson*. In this case, the claimants brought a cross-border EU competition law action against Carbone GB and several other defendants including Carbone SA. The claim was preceded by a decision of the European Commission

[57] Arts 11–14 of Council Regulation 1/2003. See also: Commission Notice on Cooperation within the Network of Competition Authorities [2004] OJ C101/43. See further, S Brammer, *Co-operation Between National Competition Agencies in the Enforcement of EC Competition Law* (Oxford, Hart Publishing, 2009) 153–61.

[58] M Danov, 'EU Competition Law Enforcement: Is Brussels I suited to dealing with all the challenges?' (2012) 61 *ICLQ* 27.

[59] ibid.

[60] Ch 14.

[61] See *Emerson Electric Co v Morgan Crucible Company PLC and Ors* [2011] CAT 4 [38].

establishing a single and continuous infringement of Article 101(1) TFEU.[62] As a result, the Commission imposed fines on a number of legal entities, including Carbone SA. However, Carbone GB was not mentioned at all in the operative part of the Commission decision, which raised the question whether the finding that the parent company, Carbone SA, has infringed EU competition law is binding on the subsidiary, Carbone GB, so that it can be imputed with liability.[63] The concerns reappeared in *Toshiba Carrier and others v KME Yorkshire and others*[64] as the issue reappeared before the High Court. In this case, the claimants sought damages against the defendants, who were involved in a complex of anti-competitive agreements and concerted practices consisting of price-fixing and market-sharing in the industrial tubes sector. The infringement was detected and established by a decision of the European Commission which preceded the damages actions. Those named as undertakings and as legal entities in the Commission decision included KM Europa Metal AG, Trefimetaux SA and Europa Metalli SpA (ie companies in the KME group), Wieland-Werke AG (a company in the Wieland-Werke group) and Outokumpu Oyj (a company in the Outokumpu group). None of the named companies were domiciled in England. The claimants, however, decided to bring their actions in England against UK-domiciled anchor defendants, KME Yorkshire (a company in the KME group) as well as against Nemco and WW (UK) (companies in the Wieland-Werke group). This led to delay and heated debated while the court decided if it had jurisdiction to hear and determine the action.

Thirdly, further issues for the claimant may relate to the fact that, even in a follow-on action, a claimant would face numerous evidential hurdles.[65] As the Court noted, 'since a finding of infringement [by a regulator] does not require proof that damage has in fact been caused to a rival undertaking, the fact that an infringement has been established [by a regulator] does not show, as a necessary implication, that such damage has been caused.'[66] Indeed, specific issues, which relate to the two-task structure of EU competition law enforcement, are presented by Webber.[67] His analysis of *Pfleiderer*[68] and *National Grid*[69] shows that an inherent difficulty for a claimant in a follow-on action is to prove that the cartel caused him loss. Although claimants appear to believe that leniency material would be valuable to them, Webber shows that 'the file of evidence held by the Commission (including the leniency material) was not compiled for this purpose and may therefore be of limited value.'[70] Similarly, Lasok has noted that a 'problem arises where, in the infringement decision, the competition authority is using the facts found by it to drive a particular theory, which may cause difficulties in a follow-on action if it becomes necessary to link the infringement to the facts of the case and, more particularly, the facts relating to causation and loss.'[71] There is a strong case that an infringement decision made by a regulator may not be especially helpful in the context of a follow-on action before national courts.[72]

[62] Case No C.38.359, *Electrical and Mechanical Carbone and Graphite Products* (2004) OJ L125/45. See also: *Emerson* (n 61) [47].
[63] See the transcript of the hearing before the CAT, pp 2–3 and 41.
[64] *Toshiba Carrier UK Ltd and Other v KME Yorkshire Ltd & Others* [2011] EWHC 2665 (Ch).
[65] *Enron Coal Services Ltd (In Liquidation) v English Welsh & Scottish Ltd* [2011] EWCA Civ 2.
[66] ibid [130].
[67] Ch 16.
[68] Case C-360/09 *Pfleiderer AG v Bundeskartellamt* [2011] 5 CMLR 219.
[69] See *National Grid Electricity Transmission PLC v ABB Ltd & Others* [2012] EWHC 869 (Ch) [56]–[60].
[70] Ch 16.
[71] Ch 15.
[72] Ch 15.

Moreover, given that a reference to the Court of Justice, which could potentially result in a further delay, may also be required in some EU competition law cases,[73] it appears that the current two-step adjudication (ie before the regulator with a view to establish an infringement, and before the courts to seek damages) may be regarded as inefficient.[74]

The consolidation of proceedings before the national courts may be necessary if the EU legislator wants to make sure that the extent to which a company has made redress is taken into account by the competent authorities when determining what level of fine to impose.[75] There is no scope for offsetting fines and damages in the current system.[76] A public enforcement action would normally precede a damages action. The level of damages would be far from certain at the stage when an authority decides on the level of fines. Similarly, in a follow-on action, the court is supposed to award damages which would compensate the victim/s irrespective of the fine imposed by the competition authority. This clearly shows that there is limited scope for consolidation of the fines and the damages in the current system, and consolidating both procedures before the national courts might be a good way to achieve this.[77]

Furthermore, due to the two-task enforcement structure, difficulties might arise from the fact that while a national court would apply civil procedure rules that presuppose respect for due process, an NCA would apply administrative procedure rules that could potentially raise concerns as to the undertaking's right to a fair trial and hearing.[78] As already noted, Nazzini has very recently argued that 'the current EU competition enforcement regime, which is characterized by an administrative decision-maker with no guarantees of independence and impartiality and deferential judicial review, is unconstitutional.'[79] In view of that, mechanisms allowing for some form of consolidation of the two sets of proceedings before national courts[80] might be desirable as the national courts would be best placed to be a major venue for competition law actions, if adequately supported by the NCAs and the European Commission.

Finally, the case for consolidation may be necessary if the EU legislator aims to provide an 'effective remedy'[81] for those who have suffered harm as a result of an EU competition law infringement. As already noted,[82] it may be far from efficient to have one set of proceedings before an NCA in order to establish a breach of competition law, and another set of proceedings before Member State courts in order for a claimant to prove that damage

[73] eg *Pfleiderer* (n 70). See also: C-453/99, *Courage v Crehan* [2001] ECR I-6297; Joined Cases C-295/04–298/04 *Manfredi v Lloyd Adriatico Assicurazioni SpA* [2006] 5 CMLR 17.

[74] Ch 5.

[75] Ch 23. See also: question 30 of the BIS consultations (n 21).

[76] Danov and Dnes (n 23).

[77] ibid.

[78] IS Forrester, 'Due Process in EC Competition Cases: A Distinguished Institution with Flawed Procedures' (2009) 34 EL Rev 817; J Killick and P Berghe, 'This is Not the Time to Be Tinkering with Regulation 1/2003 – It is Time for Fundamental Reform – Europe Should Have Change We Can Believe in' (2010) *Competition Law Review* 259. See Art 6(1) TEU. See also Art 6(1) ECHR and Art 47(2) of the Charter of Fundamental Rights of the European Union [2000] OJ C364/1. See further, J Kuhling, 'Fundamental Rights' in A von Bogdandy and J Bast (eds), *Principles of European Constitutional Law,* 2nd edn (Oxford, Hart Publishing, 2010) 479–514; P Craig, *The Lisbon Treaty: Law, Politics and Treaty Reform* (Oxford, OUP, 2010) 193–245.

[79] R Nazzini, 'Administrative Enforcement: Judicial Review and Fundamental Rights in EU Competition Law: A Comparative Contextual-Functionalist Perspective' (2012) 49 *CML Rev* 971, 1005.

[80] *cf.* BIS Consultations (n 21) [241]–[243].

[81] See Art 47(1) of the Charter of Fundamental Rights.

[82] See Ch 3.

has been caused to him.[83] The procedural inefficiencies of the current two-step adjudication (ie before the regulator, and before the courts) increases uncertainty, which can fuel litigation costs, and could fly in the face of Article 47(1) of the Charter of Fundamental Rights.

A revised version of Regulation 1/2003 may also address the issue of taking evidence by a foreign NCA in support of private proceedings in a Member State. Indeed, the question of whether a Member State court could request evidence from another Member State's competition authority in support of private proceedings in the former would have to be addressed by the Union legislator.

IV. REVISING THE CIVIL JUSTICE FRAMEWORK IN EUROPE: A NEED FOR FURTHER RESEARCH

Whilst Regulation 1/2003 could address the specific competition law problems, employing a private international law instrument in the context of cross-border EU competition law enforcement would suggest that an institutional reform, which might consider the role of the EU courts, would need to be considered in a wider context. The need for such a reform was first signalled by a Report by the Working Party on the Future of the European Communities' Court System.[84] The report clearly stated that 'the Working Party considers that preliminary questions concerning judicial cooperation should be withdrawn from the Court of Justice and assigned to a Community court with members drawn from specialist private international lawyers.'[85] Similarly, Hill has submitted that: 'The suggestion that, within the ECJ, there should be established a specialist chamber (of PIL experts) to deal with references under the Brussels I Regulation (and other PIL instruments) has been knocking around for well over 30 years. Such reform is seriously overdue.'[86] The current institutional architecture might need to be reviewed if the EU legislator decided to employ private international law when allocating jurisdiction and identifying the applicable law in cross-border private EU competition law actions, which seem to pose particularly acute problems under the current system. However, the ability of the Court of Justice to deal appropriately with the private international law issues may be questioned. Sometimes it takes too long for the Court of Justice to deliver a judgment.[87]

Indeed, the increased importance of private international law for disputes in civil and commercial matters, which may affect businesses and consumers, raises concerns as to the costs of cross-border litigation as well as to the uniform application of the various private international law instruments across the Member States within the EU. This could potentially

[83] See Ch 5. See also: KW Dam, 'Class Actions: Efficiency, Compensation, Deterrence, and Conflict of Interest' (1975) 4 *Journal of Legal Studies* 47, 48.

[84] Report by the Working Party on the Future of the European Communities' Court System' (Working Party for the European Commission, January 2000), 34–35, http://ec.europa.eu/dgs/legal_service/pdf/due_en.pdf.

[85] ibid 33.

[86] J Hill, 'Comments on the Review of the Brussels I Regulation', http://conflictoflaws.net/2009/brussels-i-review-jonathan-hill/.

[87] The Court must be given credit for bringing down the average length of preliminary rulings from 19.8 months in 2006 to 16.1 months in 2010. It has also dealt well with sensitive private international law cases concerning child abduction which have been referred to it under the urgent preliminary ruling procedure, that takes on average only 2.1 to 2.5 months. See Court of Justice Annual Report 2010: Statistics concerning the judicial activity of the Court of Justice http://curia.europa.eu/jcms/upload/docs/application/pdf/2011-05/ra2010_stat_cour_final_en.pdf.

undermine the rule of law, because the high costs and the high level of uncertainty could adversely affect cross-border claimants' litigiousness as a number of potential litigants may believe that the risks of litigation outweigh the benefits.[88] Such an outcome would fly in the face of the Stockholm Programme, which aims to create 'a Europe of law and justice'.[89] An important hypothesis, which needs to be investigated by a cross-border research consortium, is that the increased reliance on harmonised private international law instruments in the EU indicates that the preliminary references seeking their interpretation should go to a special European Court or a specialised chamber of the Court of Justice.[90]

[88] See Chs 3 and 5. See also: the economic literature: JA Ordover, 'Costly Litigation in the Model of Single Activity Accidents' 7 (1978) *Journal of Legal Studies* 243; See S Shavel, 'Suit, Settlement and Trial: A theoretic analysis under alternative methods for the allocation of legal cost' (1982) 11 *Journal of Legal Studies* 55; S Shavel, 'The Social Versus the Private Incentives to Bring Suit in a Costly Legal System' (1982) 11 *Journal of Legal Studies* 333; HSE Graville, 'The Efficiency Implications of Cost Shifting Rules' (1993) 13 *International Review of Law and Economics* 3; CF Beckner III and A Katz, 'The Incentive Effects of Litigation Fee Shifting When Legal Standards Are Uncertain' (1995) 15 *International Review of Law and Economics* 205.

[89] The Stockholm Programme – *An Open and Secure Europe Serving and Protecting The Citizens,* p 21.

[90] A debate on these issues has been initiated by a research network led by Professor Beaumont from the University of Aberdeen Centre for Private International Law. The issues will be discussed as part of a Jean Monnet Series of Workshops on 'Cross-Border Litigation in Europe', funded by the European Commission.

Index

www.ingramcontent.com/pod-product-compliance
Ingram Content Group UK Ltd.
Pitfield, Milton Keynes, MK11 3LW, UK
UKHW021911150926
475560UK00003B/315

9 781849 463744